Pre-Registration Segment

THE RESIDENTIAL
REAL ESTATE TRANSACTION

The Residential Real Estate Transaction
© 2016 Real Estate Council of Ontario

DISCLAIMERS

This Course Has Been Approved By The Registrar Under The *Real Estate And Business Brokers Act, 2002.*

Real Estate Council of Ontario
3300 Bloor Street West
Suite 1200, West Tower
Toronto, ON M8X 2X2

International Standard Book Number: 978-0-9780344-4-3
Content Development: Ontario Real Estate Association and Acronamic Learning Systems Inc.
Design and Graphics: Automation Plus Ltd.

Printing and Binding: MediaLinx Printing Group   Reprint: April, 2016

ROLE OF THE REGISTRAR UNDER REBBA 2002 IN EDUCATION

The Registrar under the *Real Estate and Business Brokers Act, 2002* (REBBA 2002) is responsible for setting the educational requirements for individuals who wish to obtain and maintain registration as a real estate broker or salesperson. In order to trade in real estate in Ontario, real estate brokerages, brokers and salespersons must be registered with the Real Estate Council of Ontario (RECO) under REBBA 2002. Before beginning a career as a real estate salesperson, individuals are required to complete the required pre-registration courses.

The Registrar, through an Educational Services Agreement, had designated the Ontario Real Estate Association as the organization authorized to provide the pre-registration, articling and broker educational program. All registration-related courses of study, including associated course content, must be approved by the Registrar prior to being offered to students.

DESIGNATE

The Ontario Real Estate Association, through its OREA Real Estate College, takes great pleasure in delivering this program on behalf of the Registrar pursuant to an Educational Services Agreement between the Real Estate Council of Ontario and the Ontario Real Estate Association.

The course curriculum supports the Real Estate Council of Ontario's mandate to protect the public interest through the development of skilled and educated real estate professionals by providing students with timely, comprehensive, accurate and up-to-date education that will allow them to succeed in the real estate marketplace. The OREA Real Estate College fulfills many of its responsibilities to the Registrar, the public of Ontario and the real estate profession by providing learning opportunities so that individuals, either contemplating registration or currently holding registration, can receive appropriate and timely training.

The real estate profession makes a valuable contribution to the economy of Canada and the welfare of its people. Congratulations on taking the first step towards real estate registration in Ontario. The Real Estate Council of Ontario and the Ontario Real Estate Association hope that the successful completion of *The Residential Real Estate Transaction* course will inspire and motivate you to pursue advanced educational offerings throughout your new career.

ACKNOWLEDGEMENTS

A course of this scope is only possible with the assistance of many dedicated professionals committed to the advancement of real estate skills and knowledge. A special note of thanks is owed to the Ontario Real Estate Association for its ongoing forty-year commitment to excellence in real estate education.

A further debt of gratitude is owed to various government departments and agencies who assisted with information and published materials. Appropriate references are included within text materials.

The terms REALTOR® and MLS® are identified as design marks in this publication. No attempt has been made to designate all words or terms in which proprietary rights might exist. The inclusion, definition, or description of a word or term is provided for general information purposes only and is not intended to affect any legal status associated with the word or term as a trademark, service mark or proprietary item.

BEFORE YOU BEGIN...

The Hewlett Packard 10BII

Real Estate as a Professional Career, Land, Structures and Real Estate Trading, The Real Estate Transaction—General, The Residential Real Estate Transaction and *The Commercial Real Estate Transaction,* as well as various advanced programs, require detailed financial calculations. Calculations are illustrated using **HP 10BII** keystrokes. The use of the **HP 10BII** is not an endorsement of the product, but a practical decision for consistent content presentation. Students may select other calculators, but no assistance or support is provided. Students using such calculators are well advised to compare computational capabilities with required course calculations.

Examination

An examination follows completion of *The Residential Real Estate Transaction.* See College Program Standards in the *Student Handbook* for full details regarding examination locations, rules, policies and procedures.

Other Resources

Instructor Support Line   (866) 444-5557
Clarification regarding *course content only.*

Missing Course Materials   (416) 391-6732 (866) 411-6732
Course Administration Services

College Education Centre   (866) 411-6732 (Toronto)

My OREA Community—Education Forums

OREA encourages the use of the Education Forums as a learning tool. This can be found on our website at **www.orea.com**. Log in to "My Portfolio" using your student ID and password. Once logged in, click on the *My OREA Community (Discussion Forum for Courses)* link. If you do not already have a "My Portfolio" password, please contact the College Education Centre. This positive exchange of content information with an expert who will answer posted questions can be practical and extensive. Participation in the forum is specific to each course and fellow students are encouraged to join the discussions. Privacy is protected.

THE RESIDENTIAL
REAL ESTATE TRANSACTION
CONTENTS AT A GLANCE

TABLE OF CONTENTS

TABLE OF CONTENTS (continued)

TABLE OF CONTENTS (continued)

TABLE OF CONTENTS (continued)

TABLE OF CONTENTS (continued)

TABLE OF CONTENTS (continued)

TABLE OF CONTENTS (continued)

SECTION IV 375
Preparing For Your New Career

CHAPTER 10
Getting Started 376

TABLE OF CONTENTS (continued)

INTRODUCTION

 ## ABOUT THIS TEXT

The Residential Real Estate Transaction provides a detailed analysis of key topics and issues as they relate to specific types of residential real estate transactions. The course consists of four sections, each highlighting different perspectives on trading residential property, current trends and issues, common errors and omissions, and guidelines when preparing for a new career. Section I discusses various residential housing choices including important, new trends and opportunities for registrants such as gated communities, mature adult residences, land lease arrangements, co-operatives, co-ownership and timeshares. Subsequent chapters in the section are devoted to residential condominiums, residential leasing, cottage property, vacant land and new homes.

Section II addresses topical residential issues and trends including stigmatized property, grow houses, fraud, money laundering, auctions, home staging and brokerage operations. The second chapter expands awareness of environmental concerns when listing/selling property, environmental hazards commonly encountered in the marketplace, underground storage tanks and, lastly, green building and energy efficiency. Section III focuses on various contractual and title-related issues that are encountered in the residential marketplace.

Section IV is a hands-on tutorial and overview of what a prospective registrant can expect when working with a brokerage. Emphasis is placed on practical considerations when preparing for the first week, starting a new career at the brokerage, handling office dynamics and networking in the community. Lastly, helpful guidelines are included to assist in preparing for a new real estate career, developing effective time planning strategies and realistically addressing income/expense expectations.

Learning Features

Chapter content summaries and learning outcomes detail the learning journey in each chapter.

Illustrations simplify and summarize complex topics. A picture is worth a thousand words. Detailed subject matter often requires visual enhancements to ensure complete understanding.

Curiosities offer novel ideas or explanatory details, while satisfying the inquisitive nature in us all. The element of discovery can expand awareness and consolidate subject matter.

Market Memos are interspersed to bring reality to the subject matter. If a topic involves value, the memo may address new technologies that are revolutionizing the valuation process. If the topic details economic trends, the memo may highlight a specific indicator together with statistical data.

Perspectives bring fresh outlooks and consolidate complex topics, usually using a story line. Everyday occurrences of real estate registrants often complement the subject matter.

Cautions identify special concerns including situations where prudence is required and practices that can lead to dire consequences if pursued.

Each **Focus** concentrates on additional details for a particular topic. These informative descriptions bridge the gap between academic discussions and today's realities.

Study Aids

Notables highlight key topics in each chapter to assist students with review and study efforts, along with a summary of key glossary terms.

Strategic Thinking questions are included to assist in preparing for a new sales career.

A **Chapter Mini-Review** is provided with each chapter for personal review and assessment. The mini-review is a warm up for active learning exercises.

Active Learning Exercises are included at the end of each chapter. Various testing formats are used including multiple choice, fill-in-the-blanks, matching, short answer and form completion exercises.

The **Appendix** contains blank copies of OREA standard forms used in this course, OREA standard clauses and *all* solutions (for chapter mini-reviews and active learning exercises).

Additional Resources

 Web Links are provided for general interest regarding selected chapter topics. Knowledge of website content is not required for examination purposes.

Forms included in this text are copyrighted by the Ontario Real Estate Association and are included for illustration purposes. These forms have been developed by OREA for the use and reproduction of its members and licensees only and are reproduced with permission of the Ontario Real Estate Association. OREA forms, or portions thereof, are illustrated in various chapters. All OREA forms used in this course are reprinted in the *Appendix*.

Tips & Guidelines

Registration courses emphasize *learning by doing* through the mastery of practical real estate skills and knowledge. The course combines formal instruction, self evaluation and problem-solving with fictional characters and scenarios. Students must evaluate circumstances, make suggestions, correct errors and learn important lessons in preparation for the marketplace. Questions are posed that require introspection, strategic thinking, application of techniques and explanation of procedures.

HOW TO MAXIMIZE LEARNING

Make the Text Priority One	• Carefully review each chapter including every topic, illustration and example.
Follow the Learning Path	• Topics are logically sequenced by section and topics within chapters. • While creativity is encouraged, most students are advised to follow the pre-set order.
Access Additional Resources	• *Web Links* can be very helpful in clarifying and expanding chapter topics. *These resources are not required for examination purposes.*
Complete all Questions/ Exercises	• Practice makes perfect. Complete all chapter mini-reviews and exercises. Solutions are provided in the *Appendix*. • Suggestion: Use a blank sheet of paper as an answer sheet where feasible, leaving the chapter mini-reviews and exercises blank for follow-up review.
Continuously Review	• When in doubt, review. Repeat readings, mini-reviews and active learning exercises as often as required. • Don't move forward without fully understanding all content. • Learning has a lot in common with building blocks. Start with a good foundation and a sound structure will emerge. • Remember, knowledge is cumulative. Don't skip any chapters.
Prepare for the Exam	• The examination tests subject matter covered in the primary text. No surprises…if you diligently study the materials. • Exam questions vary, but not the underlying purpose. Emphasis is on understanding concepts, techniques and procedures. • Don't expect a mere recital of facts.

SECTION I

A CLOSER LOOK AT TRADING DIFFERENT TYPES OF PROPERTIES

Section 1 examines different types of residential properties traded in Ontario. In total, six chapters are included focusing on residential housing (including key niche markets), residential condominium, residential rentals, cottage property, farm property and vacant land, and new homes.

In each chapter, registrants gain a better understanding of unique attributes and special circumstances that must be addressed when working with these properties, including drafting clauses for agreements of purchase and sale. Chapter content will vary. Topics include construction variations, zoning and planning considerations, applicable regulatory requirements particularly concerning condominiums (*Condominium Act*) and residential rentals (*Residential Tenancies Act),* special considerations such as permits for waterfront improvements involving seasonal or year-round cottages and key provisions involving Tarion warranty coverage when discussing new homes.

The chapter on farm property and vacant land focuses on general farming and rural property discussions, including the growing popularity of hobby farming. Full-fledged commercial farming operations are typically addressed in advanced commercial courses.

CHAPTER 1

Residential Housing

Introduction

Residential housing has been analyzed from many perspectives in previous courses including ownership, planning, financing, appraisal and drafting agreements. This chapter expands on housing choices and new trends that are now dictating what configurations and housing arrangements are appearing or anticipated for the future.

The chapter also expands knowledge of specific housing uses with a detailed discussion of home-based businesses including zoning, insurance and taxation considerations. Further, new planning perspectives and legislation are focusing on intensification and infill, which directly impact how communities are developed now and in the future. Other housing options worthy of discussion include gated communities and mature adult housing choices. In particular, life lease developments and land lease communities are highlighted with particular emphasis on drafting agreements for homes on leased land.

New approaches to house construction is also highlighted with reference to the growing popularity of factory-built houses in new house developments, particularly land lease communities. The chapter concludes with new trends in alternative ownership options, including co-operatives and co-ownership, with a brief overview of timeshare arrangements and associated legislative protection provided under the *Consumer Protection Act*.

Learning Outcomes

At the conclusion of this chapter, students will be able to:

- Identify and describe typical single-family dwelling configurations, typical zoning restrictions and applicable clauses when drafting an agreement.
- Identify and describe multi-family dwellings (up to 4 units) including zoning, construction and tenancy considerations.
- Discuss home-based businesses with particular focus on zoning requirements, insurance considerations, taxation and business licensing.
- Discuss current planning initiatives involving intensification, infill and the pursuit of sustainable communities.
- Describe the typical structure of a gated community with reference to examples from the Ontario marketplace.
- Explain various housing options available for the mature adult market in Ontario.
- Outline the basic structure and characteristics of a life lease community.
- Outline the basic structure, characteristics and regulatory requirements of land lease communities including the role of factory-built housing in these and other residential developments.
- Analyze an agreement of purchase and sale for a dwelling in a land lease community.
- Outline the basic structure, characteristics and regulatory requirements relating to a co-operative.
- Analyze an agreement of purchase and sale for a residential housing co-operative.
- Briefly describe selected ownership options involving co-ownership and timeshare.

RESIDENTIAL HOUSING CHOICES

Residential real estate offers many choices by way of both ownership and rental arrangements. Traditional emphasis on bungalows, splits and two-stories has given way to new housing options better suited to today's environment. Planning authorities have demonstrated a keen interest in new housing approaches that maximize the efficient use of land and offer attractive options to various segments of the population.

The chapter begins with a detailed look at residential dwelling types including multi-family, current zoning provisions, home-based businesses, the trend toward increased densities and recent government planning initiatives regarding intensification. The balance of the chapter is devoted to innovative residential developments and designs, particularly in regard to the mature adult segment of the population.

Single-Family Homes

Land, Structures and Real Estate Trading introduced various housing styles from the 1950's to present. However, real estate registrants require a more indepth knowledge of zoning provisions as they impact selected housing types, the impact of zoning regulations in increasing densities and the more efficient use of land resources.

Zoning terminologies for residential properties vary significantly throughout the province. The fundamental residential housing unit for zoning purposes is the *dwelling unit.* A dwelling unit can be broadly described as a housing unit that has one or more habitable rooms as self-contained living quarters; i.e., generally analogous to a single-family home. The dwelling unit would normally consist of sanitary facilities, accommodation for sleeping and one kitchen. Multiple unit dwelling units, including apartment dwelling units, are not addressed in this course, as they are more appropriately classified under commercial enterprises.

TYPICAL CONFIGURATIONS

Many different, single-family dwelling types are possible with the focus in this course on seven basic configurations. Wordings generally parallel those found in zoning by-laws, but exact phraseology will differ.

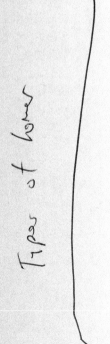

Types of homes

- A single family **detached dwelling** is best described as a building comprised of one dwelling unit.
- A **duplex dwelling** is one that is divided horizontally or vertically into two attached dwelling units on a single lot, each of which has a private entrance or is accessible directly from a common vestibule.
- A **linked dwelling** involves two or more buildings each consisting of not more than one dwelling unit each, attached below grade by a concrete wall. Height/thickness wall specifications are typically set in the zoning by-law.
- A **semi-detached** involves two attached dwelling units on separately deeded lots that are divided vertically above grade by way of a party wall. Height/thickness specifications are typically set out in the zoning by-law, with detailed requirements under *party walls* in the Ontario Building Code.
- A **street townhouse** involves one of more than two attached dwelling units that are divided vertically above grade by party walls. Once again, zoning by-law and Ontario Building Code requirements apply. A street townhouse must have frontage on a public street and have a yard abutting at least two exterior walls of each unit.
- A **CEC private road townhouse**, as with a street townhouse, involves one of more than two attached dwelling units that are divided vertically. However, this townhouse has

frontage on a private road that is a common element condominium. Condominiums are discussed in a subsequent chapter.

- A **triplex dwelling** is a building that is divided either horizontally and/or vertically into three separate dwelling units, each having a separate entrance or accessible through a common vestibule.

- A **fourplex dwelling** is a building that is divided either horizontally and/or vertically into four separate dwelling units, each having a separate entrance or accessible through a common vestibule.

NOTE: The scope of housing choices is limited to 4 units, as structures larger than this are viewed as commercial in nature.

Demand for Land and Creative Planning	CURIOSITY

The lack of serviced land and heightened consumer demand necessitate higher densities in residential areas. Here are some creative housing and lot designs that are intended to address the need while offsetting rising development costs. Not all concepts are currently found in Ontario.

Cluster Homes	A multiple unit residential development on a single lot. Cluster homes can consist of one and/or two unit buildings divided vertically from adjoining units.
Stacked Townhouse	Living units are layered over each other, while maintaining a street entrance for each unit. As a result, a large variety of configurations is possible ranging from two and three bedroom units combined with small bachelor units.
Quattroplex	This variation on the traditional fourplex can, with an appealing design, resemble a large single-family home having four units with either two in the front and two in the back or stacked in a vertical arrangement (often referred to as a coach house).
Secondary Suites	These self-contained units have gained popularity whether located within the unit (an accessory apartment) or beyond (a granny or garden flat) in the rear yard.

Lot design has also caught the eye of urban planners.

Wide/Shallow Lot	The wide shallow lot creates an illusion of size from the street, but sacrifices rear yard area to do so. Typical depths are 75 feet, as compared to traditional depths of 100 to 110 feet.
Zero Lot Line	The zero lot line approach provides that one side of a home is directly adjacent to the lot line (no side yard requirement), leaving more room to side yard on the remaining side and improved spacing between houses.

Residential Zoning Restrictions

Within Municipalities, detached dwellings are divided into three or more categories (e.g., R1, R2, R3 and so forth). Each category is then set out in relation to specific zoning regulations, such as setbacks and coverages. The successive zoning classifications provide for increasingly higher densities. Differences in zoning requirements for corner versus interior lots should be noted.

NOTE: Municipalities may designate dwelling other than detached with higher classification numbers (e.g., R7, R8 and so forth) or provide a different designation to distinguish urban and rural (e.g., RM for Residential Multiple or RR for Residential Rural).

A CLOSER LOOK AT TRADING DIFFERENT TYPES OF PROPERTIES    SECTION I

Sample Zoning Regulations—Detached Dwellings

ZONE	R1	R2	R3	R4
MINIMUM LOT AREA				
Interior Lot	750 m²	695 m²	550 m²	365 m²
Corner Lot	835 m²	810 m²	720 m²	500 m²
MINIMUM LOT FRONTAGE				
Interior Lot	22.5 m	18.0 m	15.0 m	12.0 m
Corner Lot	22.5 m	21.0 m	19.5 m	16.5 m
Maximum Lot Coverage	25%	30%	35%	40%
MINIMUM FRONT YARD				
Interior Lot	9.0 m	9.0 m	7.5 m	6.0 m
Corner Lot	7.5 m	7.5 m	6.0 m	6.0 m
MINIMUM INTERIOR SIDE YARD				
Interior Lot	1.8 m on one side of the lot and 4.2 m on the other side	1.8 m + 0.61 m for each additional storey or portion thereof above one storey	1.2 m + 0.61 m for each additional storey or portion thereof above one storey	1.2 m
Corner Lot	3.0 m	3.0 m	1.2 m + 0.61 m for each additional storey above one storey	1.2 m
Minimum Exterior Side Yard	7.5 m	7.5 m	6.0 m	4.5 m
MINIMUM REAR YARD				
Interior Lot	7.5 m	7.5 m	7.5 m	7.5 m
Corner Lot	3.0 m	3.0 m	3.0 m	7.5 m
Maximum Height	10.7 m	10.7 m	10.7 m	10.7 m
ATTACHED GARAGE, PARKING AND DRIVEWAY				
Attached Garage	Permitted	Permitted	Permitted	Permitted
Minimum Parking Spaces	✔ (see By-Law)	✔ (see By-Law)	✔ (see By-Law)	✔ (see By-Law)
Maximum Driveway Width	Lesser of 8.5 m or 50% of lot frontage	Lesser of 8.5 m or 50% of lot frontage	Lesser of 8.5 m or 50% of lot frontage	Lesser of 8.5 m or 50% of lot frontage
Accessory Buildings and Structures	✔ (see By-Law)	✔ (see By-Law)	✔ (see By-Law)	✔ (see By-Law)

The illustrated table provides for more or less standard lots. Additional provisions for special areas such as flood plains and frequently numerous exceptions (non-conforming uses) are also detailed in the zoning by-law.

DRAFTING ZONING CLAUSES

When drafting an agreement, the preprinted *Clause 8: Title Search* in the *Agreement of Purchase and Sale* (OREA Form 100) includes a reference to the fact that the present use of the property can be continued. As a reminder, registrants may insert the current use (e.g., single-family residential), but do not need to refer to the specific zoning. Current zoning may conflict with the present use. Registrants may elect to leave this line blank. If nothing is inserted, the preprinted wording applies; i.e., *that it's present use can be lawfully continued.*

If the intended future use is other than specified under Clause 8, a condition is typically inserted to protect the buyer; e.g., buyer seeking to expand use beyond single-family to two or more self contained rental units or a commercial conversion.

Conditional wording would typically focus on the buyer obtaining re-zoning or confirming that present zoning would accommodate the intended purposes.

SCENARIO	CLAUSE
Condition Regarding Re-Zoning A buyer is submitting an offer and wants to rezone the property from R1 to RM1 in order to obtain a higher density for the property.	**ZONING–2 Condition—Re-zoning with Seller's Consent** *This Offer is conditional upon the Buyer obtaining at the Buyer's expense, a re-zoning of the property to permit _____ for the said property. Both Buyer and Seller agree to proceed in a diligent manner to obtain the re-zoning. Unless the Buyer gives notice in writing delivered to the Seller personally or in accordance with any other provisions for the delivery of notice in this Agreement of Purchase and Sale or any Schedule thereto not later than _____ p.m. on the _____ day of _____, 20___, that this condition has been fulfilled, this Offer shall become null and void and the deposit shall be returned to the Buyer in full without deduction. This condition is included for the benefit of the Buyer and may be waived at the Buyer's sole option by notice in writing to the Seller as aforesaid within the time period stated herein.* *The Seller agrees, upon written notice, to execute applications and all other documents required for the Buyer to change the official plan, if necessary, and to re-zone the lands to a zoning suitable to the Buyer, or to amend any by-laws, and to support such application or applications for re-zoning or amending of by-laws, and to co-operate with the Buyer, in all reasonable respects, provided that the Buyer pay all costs of said re-zoning.*

SCENARIO	CLAUSE
Warranty Regarding Re-Zoning A buyer is submitting an offer and wants assurances that the lands are zoned as stated.	**ZONING–6 Zoning—Warranty** *The Seller warrants that the lands are zoned as _____ under by-law _____ for the municipality of _____.*

Multi-Family Dwellings (up to 4 Units)

Multi-family is a commonly used term referring to more than one dwelling unit on a specific property; e.g., triplex, fourplex and some townhouses.

ZONING RESTRICTIONS

Residential multiple zoning (RM or similar designations) provides differing requirements for multi-family dwellings. A sample set of zoning restrictions for semi-detached is provided. Similar requirements apply to three and four-unit buildings. (Note the lower requirements in RM2 (in the following diagram) to allow for increased density.)

*Sample Zoning Regulations—**Semi-Detached** Dwellings*

ZONE	RM1	RM2
MINIMUM LOT AREA		
Interior Lot	340 m²	200 m²
Corner Lot	400 m²	280 m²
MINIMUM LOT FRONTAGE		
Interior Lot	9.0 m	6.8 m
Corner Lot	12.0 m	9.8 m
Maximum Lot Coverage	35%	45%
Minimum Front Yard	6.0 m	4.5 m
Minimum Exterior Side Yard	6.0 m	4.5 m
MINIMUM INTERIOR SIDE YARD		
Attached Side	0.0 m	0.0 m
Unattached Side	1.8 m	0.9 m
Attached Garage—Unattached Side	1.2 m	0.9 m
Minimum Rear Yard	7.5 m	7.5 m
Maximum Height	10.7 m	10.7 m
Minimum Landscaped Area	25% of lot area	25% of lot area
ATTACHED GARAGE, PARKING AND DRIVEWAY		
Attached Garage	Permitted	Permitted
Minimum Parking Spaces	✔ (see By-Law)	✔ (see By-Law)
Maximum Driveway Width	5.2 m	5.2 m
Accessory Buildings and Structures	✔ (see By-Law)	✔ (see By-Law)

CONSTRUCTION

Smaller multi-family units, as with all new construction, are subject to the Ontario Building Code. The Code has been addressed in previous course materials. Most construction techniques mirror those for single-detached homes and are governed by Part 9 of the Code for smaller residential structures three stories and under. However, additional requirements apply concerning such things as fire separation, construction of common hallways, stairwells and party walls.

MULTI-FAMILY TENANCIES

Tenancies in multi-family units must adhere to residential rental requirements as set out in the *Residential Tenancies Act*. A detailed discussion of statutory requirements is set out in *Chapter 3: Residential Leasing*. The *Agreement of Purchase and Sale* (OREA Form 100) can be used for smaller residential buildings (i.e., up to 4 units). Clause 2 provides for other than vacant possession (i.e., assuming existing tenancies): *Upon completion, vacant possession of the property shall be given to the Buyer unless otherwise provided for in this Agreement.*

DRAFTING TENANCY CLAUSES

See *Chapter 3: Residential Leasing* concerning offer preparation and applicable clauses.

HOME-BASED BUSINESSES

Home-based businesses now represent a significant part of the overall economy. The combination of residential and business usage not only advances more efficiency in land, but has proven very effective for several reasons. Home businesses have gained widespread popularity as efficient business units given lower fixed costs in relation to a commercial office space. Further, business owners point to the time and cost saved by not commuting to and from work (not to mention environmental considerations), the ability to be at home for family, minimize child care expenses and generally be more independent in setting priorities and time scheduling for your career.

However, the decision to open a home-based business is not without certain downsides. The home-based individual may be unable to physically separate the work area from household interruptions. Lastly, a person operating a home office may unnecessarily isolate himself or herself from outside business contacts, lack the camaraderie of an office environment and not be in continuous contact with peer groups to stay informed.

ZONING PROVISIONS

Home-based businesses are generally allowed in both residential detached as well as multiple dwelling units (e.g., semi-detached and townhouses). Municipalities are generally concerned that the business does not interrupt or detract from the overall residential environment in which it is situated.

- **Typical Requirements**   The zoning will typically stipulate a maximum floor area (e.g., 25% of the dwelling unit), no outside storage of business-related equipment, deliveries be limited to courier and related services (i.e., no large trucks), no exterior alterations, a limited number of business visitors to the home, no signage (subject to certain exceptions) and number of employees limited to those persons who are permanent residents in the dwelling unit. In some municipalities, the by-law may provide for one or two non-residents to be permitted to operate from the residential location.

  Typical provisions are highlighted for illustration purposes only. As a general guideline, zoning provisions in larger communities appear more restrictive than smaller centres. Registrants should contact the local municipality for guidance.

- **Special Rules**   Municipalities may enact rules pertaining to health professionals (e.g., doctors and dentists) allowing them to operate an office within a detached home, along with appropriate provision for such things as signage, separate entrance and parking facilities. (See example on the following page.)

- **Type of Business Restrictions**   Municipalities may set out various enterprises that cannot be operated as a home-based business. These typically include certain activities that would not be consistent with a residential area, such as manufacturing or repairs, fabrication and food preparation.

EXAMPLE *Special Rules—Setting Up the Home Office*

Salesperson James is setting up a small real estate home office in her home. James is seeking both the flexibility of having a home office, while also having an office at her employing brokerage to meet clients and not miss out on the camaraderie and knowledge so frequently shared in the office. At the same time, a secondary home office just makes good sense for those days when visiting the office isn't necessary or she is going direct to meetings with clients and customers.

James inquires at the Anycity municipal office regarding current home-based business provisions. Restrictions include the following:

- No external advertising signs are permitted and there shall be no indication on the exterior of the dwelling that a home-based business is carried on.

- Only residents of the dwelling in which the home-based business is situated can be engaged and working from the dwelling.

- The use is restricted to the dwelling unit and may not be conducted in whole or in part in any accessory building.

- Not more than 25% of the gross floor area of the dwelling unit to a maximum of 28 square metres (300 square feet) can be used for the home-based office.

- No accessory outside storage is permitted.

- The use is clearly secondary to the main residential use and does not change the residential character of the dwelling unit nor create a nuisance, in particular, in regards to noise, traffic, parking or vibration.

- The maximum number of clients attending a home-based business is limited to two at any one time.

- Only one home-based business shall be permitted within a detached dwelling.

INSURANCE

Individuals contemplating a home-based business should check with their insurance broker regarding coverage. The typical homeowner's policy does not normally cover for such things as:

- Business equipment and related improvements to the property;
- Business-related supplies and inventory (including any separate structures that may be used to store such items).
- Personal liability for injuries sustained by clients/customers, employees, suppliers and maintenance people.

TAXATION

Selected business deductions for home offices are permitted by Canada Revenue Agency including occupancy expense based on the portion of total square footage within the residence used exclusively for business purposes. Contact Canada Revenue Agency directly for current taxation rules.

BUSINESS LICENSING

Certain businesses operating within a municipality will require a business license. Contact the local municipality for types of businesses and applicable fees.

PERMITS

In additional to confirming that an enterprise can be operated as a home-based business and determining whether or not a license is required, other permits will be required for renovations/alterations including a building permit and separate permit for electrical installations.

NEW PERSPECTIVES: RESIDENTIAL HOUSING

The Ontario housing landscape, once dominated by detached residential housing in suburban neighbourhoods, is rapidly changing to face an increasingly diverse population with differing housing needs.

The Need for Intensification

Intensification, a term coined in urban planning and government circles, involves the expanded use of buildings and serviced land to provide additional housing stock and more effectively utilize existing municipal services, as opposed to the creation of new housing stock through outlying subdivision developments. Intensification has various dimensions including the increased use of existing housing stock through additional dwelling units. Essentially, this planning approach seeks to increase density through effective urban redevelopment.

Intensification has traditionally been identified with additional second units (accessory apartments) in houses. However, the concept goes much further in the advocacy of creative housing options including mixed-use developments along arterial roads within urban areas and the redevelopment of existing industrial lands for residential purposes.

Current government policy includes major intensification initiatives (See *Focus: Places to Grow*). These policies will help to revitalize neighbourhoods and downtown areas, make more efficient use of existing infrastructure (e.g., transportation and servicing), reduce pressures on remaining agricultural lands and provide a wider variety of housing choices.

EXAMPLE   *Intensification*

Seller Smith operates a small retail business in a two-storey block structure. For years, the upper floor has been used for storage, however, the area would be much better utilized for residential tenancies. Upon contacting the local municipality, Smith is informed that there are zoning provisions for residential intensification within existing commercial areas.

Specifically, residential units are permitted both above commercial sites and/or integrated with commercial development on the same site. The scale of development is subject to various building height, lot coverage, density and building setback requirements. The municipal official with whom Smith speaks is optimistic, but cautions Smith that applications are reviewed based on, but not limited to, such things as proximity to similar types of usages, vehicular accessibility/parking, proximity of the existing structure to the street, suitability of the site in terms of size and shape to accommodate the intensification, and any adverse impact on adjacent property.

Urban Infill

Infill refers to any project that creates new housing within an existing, established neighbourhood. Infill could include the demolition of one detached dwelling with its replacement being two semi-detached units, the construction of townhouses where one or more single-family homes previously existed, the building of additional housing units on existing vacant lands or major additions and/or renovations to existing housing stock.

EXAMPLE   *Residential Infill*

Seller Smith has a 100 x 160 foot lot together with a single-family home. The current zoning is R2, classified as a low density residential designation and permits detached, semi-detached, duplex or other attached dwelling; e.g., an accessory apartment. Smith wants to renovate the existing structure on the westerly portion into a duplex, while severing the remaining 50 x 160 foot lot for a single, detached home. The municipality agrees with the duplex conversion subject to compliance with all fire, building code and municipal regulations. The severance application would also be viewed favourably given that it is appropriate infill consistent with housing in the immediate area.

Places to Grow	FOCUS

The *Places to Grow Act, 2005* provides for growth plans which establish long term strategies for identified growth areas. This legislation requires that all decisions under the *Planning Act* or *Condominium Act, 1998* conform to a growth plan as soon as the growth plan is effective.

On June 16, 2006, the Government of Ontario released its first growth plan for the Greater Golden Horseshoe. The Greater Golden Horseshoe (GGH) includes the cities of Toronto, Hamilton, Kawartha Lakes, Guelph, Peterborough, Barrie, Orillia and Brantford, the regional municipalities of Halton, Peel, York, Durham, Waterloo and Niagara, and the counties of Haldimand, Brant, Wellington, Dufferin, Simcoe, Northumberland and Peterborough.

The Growth Plan for the Greater Golden Horseshoe, 2006:

- Establishes coordinated population and job growth forecasts for municipalities as the basis for planning.

- Encourages revitalization of downtowns and city centres, making them more vibrant, people-oriented and attractive.

- Reduces development pressures on agricultural lands and natural areas by directing more growth to existing urban areas.

- Ensures that new development is planned to create complete communities that offer more choices in housing, better transit and a range of amenities like shops, schools, entertainment and services that are closer to where people live.

- Identifies 25 downtown locations in the GGH that will be focal points for accommodating people and jobs, through initiatives that offer attractive new living options within easy access to shops and services. These centres will also support transit and the economy of the surrounding area.

- Complements the province's Greenbelt Plan that protects 1.8 million acres of valuable farmland and natural areas at the heart of the Greater Golden Horseshoe.

- Establishes an integrated transportation network that will offer more transportation choices for getting from place to place, reducing congestion on our roads.

- Links planning for growth with planning for infrastructure, so that the roads, sewers, schools and other infrastructure is in place to meet the needs of growing communities.

In 2008, the Ministry of Public Infrastructure Renewal introduces a refinement of the GGH growth plan by introducing a built boundary as a fixed line representing built up areas. The built boundary is part of an overall plan to monitor intensification, as well as subsequent suburban development beyond that line.

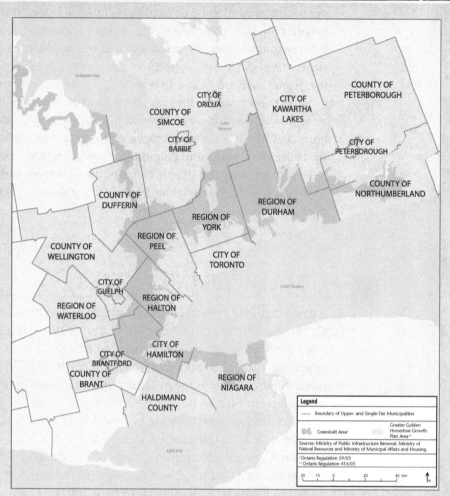

Source: *Build Boundary for the Growth Plan for the Greater Golden Horseshoe, 2006,* (Ministry of Public Infrastructure Renewal, 2008).

BUILT FORM AND THE PLANNING PROCESS

Built form refers to the height, shape, appearance and internal configuration/design of existing structures within a particular area. Municipalities, in reviewing existing densities, property uses and zoning requirements, take built form into consideration as part of the official planning review process.

Built form shapes our impression of a city, a neighbourhood or a specific development. At the development level, the built form is a significant factor in creating spatial relationships between buildings and people, including parklands, street design and community amenities. Built form affects many facets of urban planning. For example, zoning provisions that permit reverse lots (fenced rear yards facing public thoroughfares) will lessen neighbourhood integration with abutting streets, just as intensification using modernistic designs will not merge well with existing traditional housing in adjacent areas.

Legislative initiatives such as *Places to Grow* demand that new built forms enhance the community, the existing spatial structure, transportation and open space. Current population growth demands that built form complement compact urban design, as opposed to sprawl. To that end, municipalities are trying to have types of built form that are appropriate for our changing society and in support of sustainable communities.

SUSTAINABLE COMMUNITIES

The term *sustainable* generally refers to the desire to address today's current needs without compromising those of future generations. Uppermost is ensuring that communities properly integrate social, economic and environmental considerations. Above all, sustainable communities identify a sense of identity and belonging. These communities emphasize care and diligent stewardship of the environment, minimizing pollution and developing cleaner, safer neighbourhoods.

Sustainable communities are noted for their design and layout, as fundamental planning principles emphasize sufficient range, diversity, affordability and accessibility of housing. Overall design must include proper transportation services, business links with the wider community and community services to meet people's needs.

To achieve more sustainable communities, planners and developers are seeking creative ways to fashion urban neighbourhoods that will serve Ontario's needs both today and in the future.

GATED COMMUNITIES

A gated community is an enclosed residential development with controlled access points for cars, pedestrians and others. The community is typically surrounded by fences or other barricades/barriers (constructed or natural). Gated communities have proven very popular in the United States, as well as other countries in Europe and South America. Interestingly, a recent surge in gated residential developments has occurred in the Orient, particularly in China.

Gated developments have not been widely accepted within the Ontario marketplace. As of August 2003, the University of Dalhousie in Nova Scotia documented 241 gated developments in Canada, with approximately 15% in Ontario. British Columbia accounted for 71% of the total (Source: *Planning Responses to Gated Communities in Canada*, Jill Grant, School of Planning, Dalhousie University, 2003).

Overview

Gated communities vary based on local planning and regulatory requirements. As an overview, given that few Ontario gated communities exist, descriptive material is included regarding a typical larger US gated community. Canadian and Ontario gated communities are addressed later under this topic.

Gated communities in the United States are typically created through phased condominium projects; i.e., the development is built in successive stages with each phase consisting of a separate condominium. Several housing types are normally found within such communities including detached, semi-detached, townhouse, garden homes, villas, low rise and high rise. Similar housing types are usually grouped as neighbourhoods and generally align with the separate condominium phases within the overall project.

MASTER ASSOCIATION

Every owner within the gated community must be a member of the master association and pay applicable fees. The master community association owns and operates the common roadways, parking improvements and other common areas which are used by all owners in condominium phases (neighbourhoods). The master community, as a non-profit corporation, is responsible for general upkeep and will enter into various service and maintenance agreements relating to the overall development. The master community association has overall jurisdiction of the entire development, including implementing community wide standards.

NEIGHBOURHOOD ASSOCIATIONS

Individual communities are established which represent a group of units designated as a separate neighbourhood. These neighbourhoods may align with the original condominium phases, but need not. Each neighbourhood has a neighbourhood association (or committee) that delivers selected benefits not performed by the master association. The neighbourhood association oversees common elements identified as part of that local neighbourhood and assess unit owners for applicable expenses. For example, the neighbourhood association may be responsible for neighbourhood parkland, a pool, change room and surrounding areas that serves unit owners within that specific neighbourhood.

Neighbourhood associations typically have the right to establish heightened standards, while ensuring adherence to minimum standards set by the master association. These associations may decide to offer additional amenities upon approval of their respective unit owners. For example, a particular neighbourhood may have a separate gated access within the overall community. Accordingly, unit owners within that specific neighbourhood would be responsible for additional costs incurred for installation and maintenance of that gate.

The neighborhood association typically would maintain the exterior landscape portions of units within the neighbourhood including lawns, shrubs, trees and other landscaping, except those areas enclosed within fenced areas adjacent to units or otherwise not readily accessible. The association is also typically responsible for water resources (e.g., ponds or wetlands) within the neighbourhood including signage, landscaping, fencing, regulatory environmental requirements and related maintenance.

The neighbourhood association is directly involved in the enforcement of rules and regulations pertaining to that specific neighbourhood. A neighbourhood may enter into agreements with other neighbourhoods in the interest of adding needed amenities or sharing costs regarding common elements. A representative (or representatives) of that association has voting rights at duly convened meetings of the master association.

COMMON VS. PRIVATE AMENITIES

Gated community amenities can be owned and managed by the master association, a neighbourhood association or a private enterprise (usually involving recreational and related activities). Typical amenities include golf courses and associated golf clubhouses, club houses, fitness gyms, tennis courts, playgrounds and pools.

EXAMPLE   *River Estates*

Buyer Johnson has decided to purchase a condominium unit in River Estates, a gated community in the United States. The main gate provides automatic access (windshield electronic card) for residents and 24-hour manned security for visitors and others. River Estates consists of five neighbourhood communities: two consisting of detached homes, two with semi-detached, townhouse and low-rise housing and one with two high-rise buildings.

In addition to the master association, five neighbourhood associations oversee general maintenance within their respective communities. Each neighbourhood has selective common elements including a neighbourhood pool, change room and landscaped areas with barbecue facilities. The two neighbourhoods with detached homes have additional security gates that are accessible by code at their respective entrance.

The development also contains three private amenities. The first, an 18-hole professional course is operated as a separate business, available only to resident members of the gated community. A separate initial fee and ongoing membership fees apply, over and above any fees paid to the master association and neighbourhood association.

The second private amenity is a large, waterfront club house containing an exclusive member-only restaurant, ballroom facilities and an exercise gym. This amenity is also operated as a separate business with associated fees. Lastly, River Estates boasts a 80-boatslip marina. This separate condominium development provides for dock ownership and operates as a separate entity, but is bound by general regulations established by the master association.

The Canadian Experience

Gated communities in Canada have had limited success to date in comparison to the United States. The American appeal rests in part on gated access (somewhat comparable to walled cities of medieval times) offering additional security given much higher American crime rates. Further, the high concentration of gated communities in Arizona and Florida reflects in part an aging population of empty nesters and retirees seeking security in their older years behind guarded entrances and high walls.

The Canadian planning community has not been as receptive to gated communities. Opponents point out that such large scale developments create an elitism for those inside the walls (particularly the wealthy), adversely impact the sense of sustainable communities that planners have so avidly pursued in new developments. Planners involved with new housing developments, as well as intensification and infill projects, emphasize the need for *community* and *integration* rather than exclusionary, inward looking, distinct developments.

Municipalities have also not demonstrated a keen interest in considering such developments. In some instances, zoning by-laws may limit or discourage gated communities, restrict the use of gates (e.g., requirement to provide emergency access at all times), limit the use of reverse lots, require public access over private roads and restrict types of fences or other barricades that can be used in residential developments. In others, fundamental planning principles associated with sustainable communities and current built form considerations are in conflict with gated community developments. While official plans and other planning documents make no reference to gated communities, the matter would undoubtedly be critically addressed at point of draft plan approval or within site plan agreements.

Further, condominium developments have largely filled the need for security in many communities by providing restricted access at building entrances, while adhering to overall planning initiatives for an open community. Interestingly, some condominium developments that might be labelled as *gated communities* are simply condominium buildings with perimeter fencing and controlled access external to the main entry door into the structure. Interestingly, many condominium projects are fully enclosed by fencing, however they have an open but limited vehicle entrance to control and direct any vehicular or pedestrian traffic to the main concierge/security area.

The Ontario Marketplace

Gated communities are found scattered throughout the province. No formal study has been completed, but research involving various municipalities reveals a patchwork approach with little overall consistency. The majority appear aimed at the mature adult market and are predominantly condominium or land lease communities—both of which are addressed in more detail later in this and a subsequent chapter.

EXAMPLES	DESCRIPTION
Condominium— *Suburban Toronto*	The development contains approximately 600, primarily low density, condominium units. Nine different condominiums are registered within the overall community with a co-ordinating committee (similar to the US *master association* concept), including representatives from each of the nine registered condominiums. The condominiums have contractual sharing arrangements regarding amenities and have special arrangements for emergency and related services to gain quick access through the gate house.
Urban Land Lease Community— *Southwestern Ontario*	A privately-owned land lease community consisting of approximately 400 housing units appealing to the 50+ empty nester. Occupancy restrictions apply (i.e., two persons per unit). The property boasts 24-hour controlled access via a gatehouse with private roads throughout. Leases can be either 49 or 99 years in length. The development contains both single homes and townhomes. A residents' association represents the general interests of residents and assists in administrative issues regarding the community.
Urban Land Lease Community— *West of Toronto*	A 492-unit land lease community consisting of single-family detached homes and townhomes. Mid-rise condominiums are currently under construction on the site. Occupancy is restricted to two persons per residence. Residents pay for a monthly service fee (e.g., snow removal and road maintenance) relating to the private roads, over and above city taxes.
Condominium Complex— *Downtown Ottawa*	High-rise condominium towers on nine acres within 10 minutes drive of the downtown begun in the late 80's. Three towers are accessible through a front security gate. The development includes extensive gardens with outdoor pool, waterfalls, pathways, ponds, picnic and barbecue areas, tennis courts and squash courts, as well as indoor facilities typical of higher end condominium projects.
Rural Gated Community— *Guelph Area*	A resident-owned, not-for-profit corporation owns the land and leases sites to owner residents. The member-driven corporation manages the property which will ultimately include 400 sites, with a maximum of 800 residents. Residents use pass cards for access through the controlled gate.

MATURE ADULT RESIDENCES

Adult retirement/lifestyle communities are found throughout the province. In the past three decades, the market has grown from small, gated land lease communities (patterned after similar projects in Florida) to a wide range of freehold, condominium and tenancy developments with a variety of housing styles and amenities that appeal to golfers, skiers, boaters, nature lovers and a host of other leisure pursuits.

Today's seniors have many choices including freehold subdivisions with housing designs conducive to empty nesters, life lease projects (a lease arrangement for the duration of the tenant's life), land lease communities (ownership of the structure/lease of the land), retirement residences and mature adult communities offering independent, assisted living and long term care facilities.

Mature Adult Housing Choices

Ontario offers a wide range of retirement housing options for mature adults and seniors. Assume that an aging individual has a single-family detached home and is seeking alternative accommodation.

NOTE: The examples provided are by no means exhaustive; many variations are found in the marketplace.

Remain in Existing Home	Stay in the existing home, modify the property as needed to meet ongoing personal requirements (e.g., accessibility issues) and secure appropriate *at home* services. Interestingly, economic factors have resulted in two or more family generations residing in a single home.
Purchase a Condominium	Move into a condominium and avoid many maintenance demands found in single-family homes, while enjoying added security, organized social activities and other amenities.
Buy or Rent in a Retirement Community	Select a community specifically designed to meet the needs of mature adults/seniors. Many variations exist including land lease communities, life lease housing options, condominium and freehold ownership.
Choose to Live in a Retirement Residence	Select a retirement residence and rent a suite that best suits individual circumstances. Choose what services that you need. Most retirement residences offer an independent living arrangement (accommodation plus meal package) and an assisted living package (which includes selected medical and related services, provided by either on-site personnel or off-site contracted services).
Long Term Care	Select a private retirement residence that offers long term care or be approved for a long term facility (historically referred to as a nursing home) overseen by the government.

EXISTING HOME

Mature adults deciding to remain in their existing home must address long term issues, such as arranging for house maintenance, making necessary renovations to accommodate accessibility issues as they arise, taking care of routine housekeeping and related activities, or hiring others to provide those services as needed. However, for those with special needs, renovations to include such things as a stair lift or residential elevator can prove expensive, along with the challenge of securing adequate, trained help on an ongoing basis.

Just as economics has driven the rise in home-based businesses, those same factors are playing into family arrangements. Frequently, aging parents move in with their children often necessitating significant changes to accommodate privacy needs and some degree of separation within the family home.

Flex-Housing   CURIOSITY

Flex-housing is a new approach to building in response to changing requirements of Canadian families. The term *flex-housing,* introduced and promoted by Canada Mortgage and Housing Corporation, emphasizes versatility in residential construction to meet everyone's needs from young singles to aging parents. The key concept is to build structures that readily adapt to changing generational needs without costly renovations.

Flex-housing is not any particular architectural design, but rather a compilation of individual features that can be easily installed cost effectively at initial construction whether using levered door handles (rather than knobs) for older people, wider hallways and doorways for handicapped persons, hi-tech wiring in key rooms, pre-installation of alarm and surveillance systems, and energy efficient, mechanical systems. Flex-housing is all about adaptability, convertibility and flexibility.

Think of the cost savings if new homes had one no step entrance, all doors were at least 32" or 34" wide and all hallways were at least 36" wide. These enhancements not only benefit seniors, but also young families with baby carriages, families moving furniture to accommodate changing needs and persons with special accessibility needs.

The central idea underlying flex-housing is to ensure that residential structures not become functionally obsolete, necessitating costly updating. In the long run, proper construction methods and housing features will make such properties more desirable to consumers and a better investment in the long haul.

CONDOMINIUM

Condominium, a popular choice of maturing adults for several decades, offers a wide variety of housing styles from bungalow and two or three storey townhouses to high rise complexes. The condominium bungalow is particularly well suited to seniors seeking ground level living and no stairs (except to access the basement). Interestingly, while such developments are not adult only, the built form of many new developments are more conducive to mature adults; e.g., a single master bedroom on the main level, a low basement (crawl space) or situated on a concrete pad, and perhaps a guest suite in a loft area for visitors. High-rise condominiums have also proven attractive to empty nesters given elevator access, security, concierge services and amenities.

Condominium developments represent a significant housing component for mature adults and seniors. *Chapter 2: Residential Condominium* provides a detailed discussion of condominium types, legislative requirements and offer drafting.

RETIREMENT COMMUNITIES

Mature adults face numerous retirement community choices, the most popular of which appear to be land lease communities and life lease projects. These adult communities typically include selected restrictions regarding occupancy. Detailed discussions of both life lease and land lease options are included later in the chapter given their increased popularity in the marketplace.

RETIREMENT RESIDENCES

A retirement residence operates under a private pay system offering accommodation and various lifestyle options, depending on individual circumstances. Most retirement residences offer two levels of service: independent living and assisted living. Residents enter into a residency agreement setting out specifics of the accommodation and level of care services provided. Retirement residences fall under requirements for care homes, as set out in the *Residential Tenancies Act*.

INDEPENDENT LIVING	ASSISTED LIVING	LONG TERM CARE
The base monthly fee typically includes accommodation, house-keeping, meals, group programs and activities, selected transportation (e.g., to and from a local mall) and use of all common amenities. The scope of such services and amenities will vary depending on the residence selected.	Assisted living is designed for those requiring personalized care in addition to services and amenities provided under the base package. This extended package provides for emergency call services, nursing care, medication management and additional services such as scheduled or unscheduled transportation for additional care levels.	Selected retirement residences also offer long term care facilities on a private pay basis, but the majority limit provision of care services to assisted living levels, as they are not a hospital or long term care facility within the meaning of the laws of Ontario and are, consequently, limited in how much care can be provided. Deterioration of health would necessitate a transfer to a more suitable facility; i.e., long term care.

LONG TERM CARE FACILITIES

Long term care facilities provide accommodation, care, services and programs in accordance with legislation and policies/standards of the Ministry of Health & Long Term Care. Admission to a long term care facility must be authorized by a placement co-ordinator pursuant to the *Nursing Home Act*.

Most basic services in long term care facilities are paid by the government including accommodation, all meals, social/recreational activities, laundry, limited furnishings and nursing care. Other services (referred to as unfunded services) are payable by the resident. For example, basic accommodation may include a ward, but not the additional cost for a private room. Further, unfunded services could include medications, dental services, vision care and transportation depending on individual circumstances. A resident trust account is set up and funded by the resident or others to handle these additional costs.

Care Home Legislation

Various matters concerning the operation of care homes fall under the provisions of the *Residential Tenancies Act* . A care home is generally described as a residential complex in which residents receive care services including health, therapeutic or rehabilitative services, or services that assist with daily living activities. *Not all rehabilitative or therapeutic accommodation fall under the general provisions for care homes.*

The Regulations set out a range of such services as a guideline including nursing care, assistance with bathing, feeding, dressing, ambulatory and personal hygiene assistance and personal emergency response services. Registrants do not commonly encounter situations involving care homes. Certain key provisions, however, should be reviewed for general knowledge:

- A written tenancy agreement involving a care home must be provided setting out care services and meals, including the related costs.
- Every tenancy agreement must have a statement outlining that the prospective tenant:

    · has the right to seek third party advice; and

    · may cancel the agreement within five days after the agreement has been entered into.

- The *Residential Tenancies Act* contemplates that a landlord may have both care-related, as well as non care-related tenancies, within the same residential complex. In such instances, the former are referred to as care attached units and fall under the provisions set out for care homes.

- An information package must be provided to all prospective tenants setting out particulars including, but not limited to, alternative packages of care services, information regarding staffing, and emergency, fire and medical response systems. The Regulations set out minimum requirements concerning materials to be provided in the package.

LIFE LEASE COMMUNITIES

Life lease communities (also known as life equity or life estate communities) are relatively new to the Ontario marketplace, but have been in existence in the United States for several decades. Life lease projects allow the prospective resident to purchase the right to occupy a unit within the project during the life of that occupant or the life of the survivor of them if there are two occupants named in the life lease occupancy agreement.

Regulatory Requirements

Those individuals contemplating a life lease arrangement should be aware that many variations exist and a detailed review of the occupancy agreement by legal counsel is strongly recommended. Life lease arrangements are governed by contract law and common law, but not by either the *Condominium Act* or the *Residential Tenancies Act*. However, the Ministry of Municipal Affairs and Housing is taking a leading role in identifying best practices and improving consumer protection. However, general planning and building laws do apply such as the *Planning Act*, Building Code and municipal zoning by-laws.

Structure and Characteristics

Life lease communities are typically developed by not-for-profit service clubs, religious organizations and ethnic communities. Most life lease communities are market price based; i.e., the occupant pays the full market value at time of occupancy. A deposit is required at time of signing the life lease occupancy agreement. In the case of new construction, the occupant usually pays a reservation fee (deposit) and then is required to make advances as construction proceeds; e.g., 25% on obtaining the building permit, 25% upon completion of the foundation and so forth. Life lease units are not covered under the Tarion new home warranty coverage. Therefore, no coverage applies regarding construction defects and related problems, unless provided by the developer. Similarly, no deposit protection exists unless the developer has made appropriate arrangements; e.g., deposit monies held in trust.

    The occupant pays a monthly fee to the community to cover such things as lawn care, landscaping, snow and garbage removal, building insurance, property taxes, exterior repairs, and maintenance. Occupants are usually responsible for insurance coverage for personal effects and liability. Typically, the sponsoring organization sets up a reserve fund for ongoing repairs and maintenance, but no statutory regulation currently exists (as is the case under the *Condominium Act*) as to the minimum amount to be placed in reserve.

Termination

Provisions vary regarding the circumstances under which an occupant can terminate the occupancy agreement and how financial matters concerning the unit are addressed. In the event that an occupant vacates the unit, the unit is typically listed for re-occupation in *as is* condition at the then current market values. When a new occupancy agreement is signed, the previous occupant or his estate receives that amount less *resale fees*. Resale fees usually amounting to 5 to 15% of the sale price are deducted to handle administrative costs. This fee is in addition to any real estate commission or other fees related to the disposition.

 WEB LINKS
Ministry of Municipal Affairs and Housing   For more information concerning life lease communities, recent activities and consumer-related considerations, go to ***www.mah.gov.on.ca***.

LAND LEASE COMMUNITIES

Land lease communities have become a popular option for mature adults. Lease terms typically vary from 20 to 99 years. Historically, manufactured homes predominated in land lease communities, but in recent years modular homes and on-site built homes are now frequently found. Some land lease communities have also integrated condominium projects within the overall development and, as mentioned earlier, some land lease communities are gated.

Residents are responsible for various services relating to the community including snow removal, lawn care, maintenance of irrigation systems and so forth. The community may include amenities such as a clubhouse, recreational facilities, nature walkways and parkland. Owners pay a monthly maintenance fee, as well as a land lease. The land lease is typically calculated based on the lot size, location and view.

The entire community is operated by a corporation and residents normally have a council or advisory group to interface with the corporation on administrative matters and decisions affecting the community as a whole.

Legislative Requirements

Legislative requirements concerning mobile home parks or land lease communities are set out in the *Residential Tenancies Act*. For purposes of the Act, a mobile home park or a land lease community is a community in which the landlord retains possession of the land, structures, services and facilities for the common use and enjoyment of the tenants. Mobile home parks and land lease communities are covered by the general rules contained in the Act, as well as by special rules which recognize their unique nature.

A *land lease home* is a permanent structure, as opposed to a mobile home. A land lease community generally has sites that are rented by tenants who own the home on the site. The Act applies to a land lease home site, unless it is used by travelers or persons on vacation.

A *mobile home park* may have a mix of dwellings built without wheels or trailers built with wheels on sites that are covered by the Act. The Act *may apply* whether the site is used permanently or seasonally. However, the Act does not apply to a site that is intended for use by a person who is travelling or on vacation, or in a resort, tourist camp, campground or trailer park that is occupied for only a seasonal or temporary period.

NOTE: The terms mobile home park and land lease community are used interchangeably in the Act.

RIGHTS AND RESPONSIBILITIES

Registrants are increasingly involved with mobile and land lease homes as a consequence of the aging Canadian population and certain pricing advantages that are associated with land leases. Legislative requirements from the *Residential Tenancies Act* of particular interest to real estate registrants, are highlighted.

Landlord Responsibilities	**Tenant Responsibilities**
• Keeping the land lease community in good repair; • Meeting health, safety and maintenance standards; • Providing a means of garbage disposal; • Keeping the water supply, sewage disposal, fuel, drainage and electrical systems in good repair; • Maintaining the grounds, and all buildings and equipment intended for common use by residents.	• Keeping the premises clean; • Repairing any damage caused by them or their guests.

Sale or Lease of Mobile Home/Land Lease Home

• A tenant has the right to sell or lease the mobile home or land lease home without the landlord's consent;
• Any agreement that requires the tenant to use the landlord as an agent is void;
• The landlord may act as an agent of the tenant in negotiations for the lease or sale of the mobile home or land lease home with a written agency contract for the purpose of beginning those negotiations.

Signage

• The tenant, in selling his/her mobile or land lease home, may place a sign in the window of the home unless prohibited by the landlord. The landlord can only prevent such signage if all of the following conditions are met:
  · the landlord's prohibition regarding signs applies to all tenants;
  · the landlord provides a bulletin board for placement of *for sale* advertisements; and
  · the bulletin board is provided to all tenants free of charge and located in a prominent place accessible to the public at all times.

Landlord First Right of Refusal

If the tenancy agreement provides the landlord with the right of first refusal when a tenant is selling his or her land lease home, the landlord is given 72 hours, from the time that the seller receives an acceptable offer from a buyer, to purchase the land lease home on the same price and conditions. If the landlord does not agree, the tenant can proceed to sell to the initial buyer.

Drafting the Agreement of Purchase and Sale

A unique agreement of purchase and sale format is required for mobile, modular and manufactured homes, as the sale is limited to the dwelling, not including the land. The agreement must identify dwelling specifics such as the manufacturer, model and serial number (if applicable) and its location on the site (e.g., address and/or lot/site number).

PROVISION REGARDING RULES AND REGULATIONS

The agreement states that the buyer agrees to accept and comply with any rules and regulations for the community. The *Residential Tenancies Act* requires that if a landlord of a mobile home park or land lease community has rules, they must give a written copy of those rules to each tenant.

PROVISIONS CONCERNING LEASE ASSIGNMENT

The agreement also provides that the lease document is attached as Schedule B and that the seller agrees to assign the seller's interest in the lease to the buyer. Further, the agreement states that if the agreement includes a required consent by the landlord, the seller agrees to apply immediately for such a consent. The agreement is null and void if such consent is not received.

The tenant should write the landlord to obtain such consent. The *Residential Tenancies Act* provides that the landlord cannot refuse to consent to assign without permission of the Landlord and Tenant Board.

A sample *Agreement of Purchase and Sale—Mobile/Modular/Manufactured Home on Leased Premises* (OREA Form 110) is provided.

OREA Ontario Real Estate Association

Form 110
for use in the Province of Ontario

Agreement of Purchase and Sale
Mobile/Modular/Manufactured Home on Leased Premises

This Agreement of Purchase and Sale dated this ......15th...... day of .... June .... 20 XX ....

BUYER, ...Arthur James Bennett and Ruth Alice Bennett........................, agrees to purchase from
(Full legal names of all Buyers)

SELLER, ...Elizabeth Anne McDougall..................., the following
(Full legal names of all Sellers)

PROPERTY:

The .... Mobile .... building (the"Dwelling") more fully described as:
(Mobile/Modular/Manufactured)

Manufacturer .... Acme Industries Inc. ....

Model (if applicable) .... Southbreeze ....

Serial Number .... A17264H17 .... Year .... 2002 ....

Length .... 42 Feet .... Width .... 12 feet ....

Located At: (address, lot/site number, etc.) .... Site Number 52 .... (the "Land")

Name of Mobile Home Park (if applicable) .... Windy Hill Resort ....

The parties agree that the Land on which the Dwelling is located is not the property of the Seller and is not included as part of this Agreement.

PURCHASE PRICE: Dollars (CDN$) ....$38,000.00....

Thirty-Eight Thousand--- Dollars

DEPOSIT: Buyer submits .... Upon Acceptance ....
(Herewith/Upon Acceptance/as otherwise described in this Agreement)

Three Thousand--- Dollars (CDN$) ....$3,000.00....

by negotiable cheque payable to .... ABC Realty Inc. .... "Deposit Holder" to be held in trust pending completion or other termination of this Agreement and to be credited toward the Purchase Price on completion. For the purposes of this Agreement, "Upon Acceptance" shall mean that the Buyer is required to deliver the deposit to the Deposit Holder within 24 hours of the acceptance of this Agreement. The parties to this Agreement hereby acknowledge that, unless otherwise provided for in this Agreement, the Deposit Holder shall place the deposit in trust in the Deposit Holder's non-interest bearing Real Estate Trust Account and no interest shall be earned, received or paid on the deposit.

Buyer agrees to pay the balance as more particularly set out in Schedule A attached.

SCHEDULE(S) A, B (Lease) .... **attached hereto form(s) part of this Agreement.**

1. **IRREVOCABILITY:** This offer shall be irrevocable by .... Buyer .... until 11:50 ~~a.m.~~/p.m. on the 17th day of .... June .... 20 XX ...., after which time, if not accepted, this offer shall be null and void and the deposit shall be returned to the Buyer in full without interest.

INITIALS OF BUYER(S): *AB RB*   **INITIALS OF SELLER(S):** *EM*

Form 110   Revised 2015   **Page 1 of 6**

Fully Completed Sample   Agreement of Purchase and Sale—Mobile/Modular/Manufactured Home, Page 2 of 6

2.   COMPLETION DATE: This Agreement shall be completed by no later than 6:00 p.m. on the **31st** day of .... **July** ....

20. **XX** .... Upon completion, vacant possession of the Dwelling shall be given to the Buyer unless otherwise provided for in this Agreement.

3.   NOTICES: The Seller hereby appoints the Listing Brokerage as agent for the Seller for the purpose of giving and receiving notices pursuant to this Agreement. Where a Brokerage (Buyer's Brokerage) has entered into a representation agreement with the Buyer, the Buyer hereby appoints the Buyer's Brokerage as agent for the purpose of giving and receiving notices pursuant to this Agreement. **Where a Brokerage represents both the Seller and the Buyer (multiple representation), the Brokerage shall not be appointed or authorized to be agent for either the Buyer or the Seller for the purpose of giving and receiving notices.** Any notice relating hereto or provided for herein shall be in writing. In addition to any provision contained herein and in any Schedule hereto, this offer, any counter-offer, notice of acceptance thereof or any notice to be given or received pursuant to this Agreement or any Schedule hereto (any of them, "Document") shall be deemed given and received when delivered personally or hand delivered to the Address for Service provided in the Acknowledgement below, or where a facsimile number or email address is provided herein, when transmitted electronically to that facsimile number or email address, respectively, in which case, the signature(s) of the party (parties) shall be deemed to be original.

FAX No.: .... **N/A** ....   FAX No.: .... **N/A** ....
             (For delivery of Documents to Seller)   (For delivery of Documents to Buyer)

Email Address: .... **N/A** ....   Email Address: .... **N/A** ....
                  (For delivery of Documents to Seller)   (For delivery of Documents to Buyer)

4.   CHATTELS INCLUDED: In addition to the Dwelling, the following are included in the Purchase Price:

Ace Model 500 refrigerator, Ace Model 300 stove, Ace Model 200 built-in microwave oven

See Schedule A

Unless otherwise stated in this Agreement or any Schedule hereto, Seller agrees to convey all fixtures and chattels included in the Purchase Price free from all liens, encumbrances or claims affecting the said fixtures and chattels.

5.   FIXTURES EXCLUDED: The following items are not included in the Purchase Price:

N/A

6.   RENTAL ITEMS (Including Lease, Lease to Own): The following equipment is rented and **not** included in the Purchase Price. The Buyer agrees to assume the rental contract(s), if assumable:

N/A

The Buyer agrees to co-operate and execute such documentation as may be required to facilitate such assumption.

INITIALS OF BUYER(S): (*AB RB*)   INITIALS OF SELLER(S): (*EM*)

Form 110   Revised 2015   **Page 2 of 6**

SECTION I   A CLOSER LOOK AT TRADING DIFFERENT TYPES OF PROPERTIES

Fully Completed Sample   Agreement of Purchase and Sale—Mobile/Modular/Manufactured Home, Page 3 of 6

7. **HST:** I If the sale of the property (Real Property as described above) is subject to Harmonized Sales Tax (HST) then such tax shall be **in addition to** the Purchase Price. If the sale of the property is not subject to HST, Seller agrees to certify on or before closing, that the sale of the property is not subject to HST. Any HST on chattels, if applicable, is not included in the Purchase Price.

8. **RULES AND REGULATIONS:** The Buyer acknowledges that the Land lease may include Rules and Regulations for the occupancy of the Land and the Buyer agrees to accept and comply with said Rules and Regulations.

9. **LEASE:** The Buyer acknowledges that Dwelling is currently situate upon the Land pursuant to a Lease as more particularly set out in Schedule B attached hereto. The Seller agrees to assign the Seller's interest in the Lease to the Buyer and the Buyer agrees to accept the assignment of the Lease. If the said Lease contains a provision requiring that the Landlord consent to the assignment of the Lease, then Seller will apply forthwith for the requisite consent, and provide a copy in writing of the consent, and if such consent is refused and the Buyer does not enter into a new lease agreement with the Landlord, then this Agreement shall be null and void at the option of the Buyer and the deposit monies shall be refunded without interest or other penalty to the Buyer. The Buyer agrees to cooperate and provide such information and documentation as may be within control of the Buyer in order to obtain said assignment of Lease.

10. **TITLE:** Provided that the title to the Dwelling is good and free from all charges, liens, and encumbrances except as otherwise specifically provided

in this Agreement. Buyer shall be allowed until 6:00 p.m. on the ....15th.... day of..................July.................., 20..XX.., (Requisition Date) to examine the title to the Dwelling at Buyer's own expense and until thirty days from the Requisition Date or the date on which the conditions in this

Agreement are fulfilled or otherwise waived to satisfy Buyer that its present use (............Single family residential mobile............) may be lawfully continued and that the Dwelling may be insured against risk of fire. Seller hereby consents to the Landlord of the Land, the municipality or other governmental agencies releasing to Buyer details of all matters affecting the Dwelling, and Seller agrees to execute and deliver such further authorizations in this regard as Buyer may reasonably require. If within the specified times referred to above any valid objection to title or to the fact the said present use may not lawfully be continued, or that the Dwelling may not be insured against risk of fire is made in writing to Seller and which Seller is unable or unwilling to remove, remedy or satisfy and which Buyer will not waive, this Agreement notwithstanding any intermediate acts or negotiations in respect of such objections, shall be at an end and all monies paid shall be returned without interest or deduction and Seller, Listing Brokerage and Co-operating Brokerage shall not be liable for any costs or damages. Save as to any valid objection so made by such day and except for any objection going to the root of the title, Buyer shall be conclusively deemed to have accepted Seller's title to the Dwelling.

11. **FUTURE USE:** Seller and Buyer agree that there is no representation or warranty of any kind that the future intended use of the Dwelling by Buyer is or will be lawful except as may be specifically provided for in this Agreement.

12. **DOCUMENTS AND DISCHARGE:** Buyer shall not call for the production of any prior Bills of Sale or other evidence of title to the Dwelling except such as are in the possession or control of Seller. If requested by Buyer, Seller will deliver any sketch or plans of the Dwelling, including informational material from the manufacturer, within Seller's control to Buyer as soon as possible and prior to the Requisition Date. If a discharge of any security interest held by a corporation incorporated pursuant to the Trust And Loan Companies Act (Canada), Chartered Bank, Trust Company, Credit Union, Caisse Populaire or Insurance Company and which is not to be assumed by Buyer on completion, is not available in registrable form on completion, Buyer agrees to accept Seller's lawyer's personal undertaking to obtain, out of the closing funds, a registrable discharge and to register same, or cause same to be registered within a reasonable period of time after completion, provided that on or before completion Seller shall provide to Buyer a statement prepared by the security interest holder setting out the balance required to obtain the discharge, and, where a real-time electronic cleared funds transfer system is not being used, a direction executed by Seller directing payment to the holder of the amount required to obtain the discharge out of the balance due on completion.

13. **INSPECTION:** Buyer acknowledges having had the opportunity to inspect the Dwelling and understands that upon acceptance of this offer there shall be a binding agreement of purchase and sale between Buyer and Seller.

INITIALS OF BUYER(S): (*AB RB*)   **INITIALS OF SELLER(S):** (*EM*)

Form 110   Revised 2015   **Page 3 of 6**

Fully Completed Sample   *Agreement of Purchase and Sale—Mobile/Modular/Manufactured Home, Page 4 of 6*

14. INSURANCE: The Dwelling and all buildings on the Land and all other things being purchased shall be and remain until completion at the risk of Seller. Pending completion, Seller shall hold all insurance policies, if any, and the proceeds thereof in trust for the parties as their interests may appear and in the event of substantial damage, Buyer may either terminate this Agreement and have all monies paid returned without interest or deduction or else take the proceeds of any insurance and complete the purchase. No insurance shall be transferred on completion. If Seller is taking back a Security Interest, or Buyer is assuming a Security Interest, Buyer shall supply Seller with reasonable evidence of adequate insurance to protect Seller's or other security holder's interest on completion.

15. DOCUMENT PREPARATION: The Bill of Sale shall be prepared in registrable form at the expense of Seller, and any Security Interest to be given back by the Buyer to Seller at the expense of the Buyer.

16. RESIDENCY: (a) Subject to (b) below, the Seller represents and warrants that the Seller is not and on completion will not be a non-resident under the non-residency provisions of the Income Tax Act which representation and warranty shall survive and not merge upon the completion of this transaction and the Seller shall deliver to the Buyer a statutory declaration that Seller is not then a non-resident of Canada;
(b) provided that if the Seller is a non-resident under the non-residency provisions of the Income Tax Act, the Buyer shall be credited towards the Purchase Price with the amount, if any, necessary for Buyer to pay to the Minister of National Revenue to satisfy Buyer's liability in respect of tax payable by Seller under the non-residency provisions of the Income Tax Act by reason of this sale.Buyer shall not claim such credit if Seller delivers on completion the prescribed certificate.

17. ADJUSTMENTS: Any rents, security deposits, security interest, realty taxes including local improvement rates, unmetered public or private utility charges and unmetered cost of fuel, as applicable, shall be apportioned and allowed to the day of completion, the day of completion itself to be apportioned to Buyer.

18. TIME LIMITS: Time shall in all respects be of the essence hereof provided that the time for doing or completing of any matter provided for herein may be extended or abridged by an agreement in writing signed by Seller and Buyer or by their respective lawyers who may be specifically authorized in that regard.

19. TENDER: Any tender of documents or money hereunder may be made upon Seller or Buyer or their respective lawyers on the day set for completion.Money shall be tendered with funds drawn on a lawyer's trust account in the form of a bank draft, certified cheque or wire transfer using the Large Value Transfer System.

20. FAMILY LAW ACT: Seller warrants that spousal consent is not necessary to this transaction under the provisions of the Family Law Act, unless Seller's spouse has executed the consent hereinafter provided.

21. UFFI: Seller represents and warrants to Buyer that during the time Seller has owned the Dwelling, Seller has not caused the Dwelling or any structure on the property to be insulated with insulation containing ureaformaldehyde, and that to the best of Seller's knowledge no building on the property contains or has ever contained insulation that contains ureaformaldehyde. This warranty shall survive and not merge on the completion of this transaction.

22. LEGAL, ACCOUNTING AND ENVIRONMENTAL ADVICE: The parties acknowledge that any information provided by the brokerage is not legal, tax or environmental advice.

23. CONSUMER REPORTS: The Buyer is hereby notified that a consumer report containing credit and/or personal information may be referred to in connection with this transaction.

24. AGREEMENT IN WRITING: If there is conflict or discrepancy between any provision added to this Agreement (including any Schedule attached hereto) and any provision in the standard pre-set portion hereof, the added provision shall supersede the standard pre-set provision to the extent of such conflict or discrepancy. This Agreement including any Schedule attached hereto, shall constitute the entire Agreement between Buyer and Seller. There is no representation, warranty, collateral agreement or condition, which affects this Agreement other than as expressed herein. For the purposes of this Agreement, Seller means vendor and Buyer means purchaser. This Agreement shall be read with all changes of gender or number required by the context.

25. TIME AND DATE: Any reference to a time and date in this Agreement shall mean the time and date where the Dwelling is located.

INITIALS OF BUYER(S): *AB RB*   INITIALS OF SELLER(S): *EM*

Form 110 Revised 2015   **Page 4 of 6**

SECTION I   A CLOSER LOOK AT TRADING DIFFERENT TYPES OF PROPERTIES

26. SUCCESSORS AND ASSIGNS: The heirs, executors, administrators, successors and assigns of the undersigned are bound by the terms herein.

SIGNED, SEALED AND DELIVERED in the presence of: IN WITNESS whereof I have hereunto set my hand and seal:

Frank Danchuk
(Witness)

Arthur James Bennett
(Buyer)
●
(Seal)
DATE *June 15/xx*

Frank Danchuk
(Witness)

Ruth Alice Bennett
(Buyer)
●
(Seal)
DATE *June 15/xx*

I, the Undersigned Seller, agree to the above offer. I hereby irrevocably instruct my lawyer to pay directly to the brokerage(s) with whom I have agreed to pay commission, the unpaid balance of the commission together with applicable Harmonized Sales Tax (and any other taxes as may hereafter be applicable), from the proceeds of the sale prior to any payment to the undersigned on completion, as advised by the brokerage(s) to my lawyer.

SIGNED, SEALED AND DELIVERED in the presence of: IN WITNESS whereof I have hereunto set my hand and seal:

Wayne Strauss
(Witness)

Elizabeth Anne McDougall
(Seller)
●
(Seal)
DATE *June 16/xx*

(Witness)

(Seller)
●
(Seal)
DATE

SPOUSAL CONSENT: The Undersigned Spouse of the Seller hereby consents to the disposition evidenced herein pursuant to the provisions of the Family Law Act, R.S.O.1990, and hereby agrees with the Buyer that he/she will execute all necessary or incidental documents to give full force and effect to the sale evidenced herein.

(Witness)

(Spouse)
●
(Seal)
DATE

CONFIRMATION OF ACCEPTANCE: Notwithstanding anything contained herein to the contrary, I confirm this Agreement with all changes both typed and written was finally accepted by all parties at *6:00* a.m./p.m. this *16th* day of *June*, 20.*xx*

Elizabeth Anne McDougall
(Signature of Seller or Buyer)

INFORMATION ON BROKERAGE(S)

Listing Brokerage ..... **ABC Realty Inc.** Tel.No.(416) 238-4745

123 Main Street, Anycity, Anyregion L4H 6P6 **Frank Danchuk**
(Salesperson / Broker Name)

Co-op/Buyer Brokerage ..... Tel.No.(.....)

(Salesperson / Broker Name)

ACKNOWLEDGEMENT

I acknowledge receipt of my signed copy of this accepted Agreement of Purchase and Sale and I authorize the Brokerage to forward a copy to my lawyer.

Elizabeth Anne McDougall
(Seller)
DATE *June 16/xx*

(Seller)
DATE

Address for Service *18 Wellington Street East*

Anycity, Anyregion B5T 8N9 Tel.No.(416) 555-5632

Seller's Lawyer *Jack Burns and Associates*

Address *155 Maple Street, Anycity, Anyregion B4N 7K9*

Email .....

(416) 555-1212 (416) 555-2121
Tel.No. FAX No.

I acknowledge receipt of my signed copy of this accepted Agreement of Purchase and Sale and I authorize the Brokerage to forward a copy to my lawyer.

Arthur James Bennett
(Buyer)
DATE *June 16/xx*

Ruth Alice Bennett
(Buyer)
DATE *June 16/xx*

Address for Service *137 Beachwood Drive, Anycity, Anyregion*

N4G 6P7 Tel.No.(905) 666-1243

Buyer's Lawyer *John Smith and Associates*

Address *23 Southwood Crt., Anycity, Anyregion N5C 8L9*

Email .....

(905) 666-5656 (905) 666-6565
Tel.No. FAX No.

FOR OFFICE USE ONLY **COMMISSION TRUST AGREEMENT**

To: Co-operating Brokerage shown on the foregoing Agreement of Purchase and Sale:
In consideration for the Co-operating Brokerage procuring the foregoing Agreement of Purchase and Sale, I hereby declare that all moneys received or receivable by me in connection with the Transaction as contemplated in the MLS® Rules and Regulations of my Real Estate Board shall be receivable and held in trust. This agreement shall constitute a Commission Trust Agreement as defined in the MLS® Rules and shall be subject to and governed by the MLS® Rules pertaining to Commission Trust.
DATED as of the date and time of the acceptance of the foregoing Agreement of Purchase and Sale. Acknowledged by:

(Authorized to bind the Listing Brokerage)

(Authorized to bind the Co-operating Brokerage)

Form 110 Revised 2015 **Page 5 of 6**

Fully Completed Sample   Agreement of Purchase and Sale—Mobile/Modular/Manufactured Home, Page 6 of 6

OREA Ontario Real Estate Association

Form 110
for use in the Province of Ontario

Schedule A – Agreement of Purchase and Sale
Mobile/Modular/Manufactured Home on Leased Premises

This Schedule is attached to and forms part of the Agreement of Purchase and Sale between:

BUYER, ... Arthur James Bennett and Ruth Alice Bennett .... , and

SELLER, ... Elizabeth Anne McDougall ....

for the purchase and sale of .... Mobile building on Site Number 52 in Windy Hill Resort ....

.... dated the ...... 15th ...... day of .... June .... , 20 XX ....

Buyer agrees to pay the balance as follows:

The Buyer agrees to pay a further sum of Thirty-Five Thousand Dollars ($35,000.00), subject to adjustments, to the Seller on completion of this transaction, with funds drawn on a lawyer's trust account in the form of a bank draft, certified cheque, or wire transfer using the Large Value Transfer System.

The Buyer and Seller agree that in addition to the appliances listed above, the purchase price includes the following chattels as viewed with the property at the time of the showing:

- All bedroom furniture, including headboard, box spring and mattress, 1 night table, and 1 dresser
- Kitchen set, including table and 4 chairs, toaster, dishes, and cutlery
- Living room furniture, including sofa, chair, bookcase, coffee table, and 2 end tables
- All window coverings and exterior awning
- Charbroil barbecue and 2 propane tanks
- Metal storage shed

This form must be initialed by all parties to the Agreement of Purchase and Sale.

INITIALS OF BUYER(S):   INITIALS OF SELLER(S):

Form 110   Revised 2015   **Page 6 of 6**

FACTORY-BUILT HOUSING

Land, Structures and Real Estate Trading emphasized on-site building methods, but factory-built homes (FBH), including modular and manufactured homes, are a small but growing component of the overall Canadian housing marketplace. Off-site assembly of factory-built homes is gaining increased acceptance, but still represents less than 1 in 10 houses built in Canada, with the balance constructed using the traditional on-site, *stick-by-stick* method. A notable market niche for these homes has been and continues to be land lease communities, but in recent years growth is attributed to modular homes in new house subdivisions.

The image of factory-built homes in the consumer's mind has been a challenge. Many Ontario residents still associate prefabricated construction with 10 or 12-foot wide mobile homes transported to their destination behind trucks with *oversize load* signs, flags and escort cars. However, today's factory-built homes have come a long way from those early beginnings. Factories now produce everything from large fully-completed two-storey homes on near-site subdivision locations to large custom-designed homes manufactured partially on the factory floor and then erected in modular fashion on a permanent foundation.

The near-site factory warrants particular emphasis. Two recent Mattamy home developments in Cambridge and Milton involve complete houses being built near the subdivision and then transported and placed on poured basements. Homes proceed through an assembly line process involving various workstations. The homes, complete with all mechanical systems and interior finishes, are then transported by a specially designed transport vehicle and delivered for placement on the basement with only the exterior finish, porches and landscaping to be added following installation.

Types of Factory-Built Homes

Terminology regarding factory-built homes differs somewhat in the marketplace. Factory-built refers to homes built at an alternate site and delivered to the final building location, as distinct from on-site building. Factory-built homes can be divided into two broad categories: modular and manufactured. Manufactured homes include mobile homes, as well as other related housing options. Note: In some literature, *manufactured* and *factory built* are viewed as synonymous. Also, the term *prefabricated* is used to generally describe off-site construction.

- **Modular Homes**   A *modular home* is built in sections at a factory, transported on truck beds and assembled at their destination. Local building inspectors make certain that the structure meets requirements and that all finished work is done properly. Modular homes typically have truss floors designed to go on a basement or foundation. As mentioned earlier, the most recent innovation involves near-site factories that assemble virtually the entire structure and then transport the house on a special truck bed the short distance to the subdivision.

- **Manufactured Homes**   The term *manufactured home* traditionally referred to mobile homes and trailers built on non-removable chassis (including wheels), transported to the site using those wheels and often placed on concrete blocking piers or cement pylons. However, the range of options has expanded over the years. Now, manufactured homes include greater options including separate units that are transported, as with modular homes, on truck beds rather than their own wheels. Manufactured homes, including mobile homes, are built to a different standard than modular homes. However, manufactured homes can be upgraded to modular standards.

Construction

Computer-aided design (CAD) has been a major factor in the increasing sophistication of modular home construction. A detailed computer software design can determine the exact location of every construction component including studs, trusses, nailing locations, wiring, plumbing and other mechanical features. Most interior finishes and features are also installed. Advocates point to many advantages of factory-built homes and, more particularly, modular homes.

- Homes are constructed in an indoor, climate-controlled environment protected from weather extremes. This same protection provides an advantage in that construction personnel can work more efficiently and effectively.

- Indoor construction provides for greater precision and straightness. Wooden building products can be twisted or warped by rain, snow and prolonged sunshine.

- Interior damage due to weather can be also be avoided; e.g., snow melting and rain that penetrates the structure before the building envelope is fully sealed.

- Higher quality control is possible, as construction activity takes place within a factory environment, rather than individual crews appearing at different times at work sites. Further, all construction personnel can be more effectively managed, trained and supervised.

- Home construction proceeds at a pre-determined pace with little opportunity for delays which are often encountered in on-site building due to weather conditions.

Other benefits include increased worker safety as most components are built at factory floor level rather than on a raised foundation with associated open lower stairways, uneven ground around the perimeter and the perils of working on wet or slippery frozen surfaces. As well, theft of site materials including tools is all but eliminated and small wood lengths and other components, often discarded on the site, are now retrieved and used within the manufacturing process.

 # CO-OPERATIVE HOUSING

Co-operatives were generally described as an ownership option in *Land, Structures and Real Estate Trading*, but warrant more detailed analysis including a specific agreement of purchase and sale form required for this type of ownership. Co-ops in Ontario can either be equity co-operatives (with share capital) or non-profit co-operatives (without share capital). Interestingly, older residential equity co-operatives in Toronto were originally structured based on one vote per unit, but the share arrangement in equity co-ops now reflect the actual square footage of the unit in relation to the overall structure. Non-profit co-ops operate in part through federal and provincial funding.

Co-operative Corporations Act

The Financial Services Commission of Ontario (FSCO) regulates registration of organizations who conduct business as co-operatives under the *Co-operative Corporations Act*. The FSCO is an arm's length agency of the Ministry of Finance that became operational in July 1998 under the *Financial Services Commission of Ontario Act, 1997*.

Co-operatives are member-owned and controlled corporations. The Act does not regulate the day-to-day business of a co-operative, including the by-laws that are established for its operation. The legislation does require that one member equals one vote, regardless of the amount invested. The Act also sets out statutory requirements concerning offering statements and related disclosures; e.g., when securities are sold beyond basic membership shares and when surplus distribution occurs at point of termination.

REGISTRATION

Sections 4, 5 and 6 of the *Co-operative Corporations Act* detail registration requirements. The procedure for real estate co-operatives requires that a specific number of individuals (corporations or persons) file the articles of incorporation and other prescribed documents, and pay required fees to FSCO. FSCO then issues a certificate of incorporation. Detailed registration procedures, filing and record-keeping requirements, and information concerning offering statements can be obtained from the Credit Union and Co-operatives Branch.

Types of Co-operatives

While housing co-operatives are emphasized in this text, various other types of co-operatives exist. The Financial Services Commission of Ontario lists the following:

- Service Co-ops
- Consumer Co-ops
- Supply Co-ops
- Worker Co-ops
- Marketing Co-ops
- Producer Co-ops
- Child Care Co-ops
- Housing and Housing Development Co-ops
- Financing Co-ops
- Farming and Supply Co-ops
- Milk Transport Co-ops

Some co-operatives issue securities to their members and, in certain instances, to restricted categories of non-members. Co-operatives can be incorporated with or without share capital. Individuals investing in a co-operative normally do so to realize certain personal goals, for example the availability of goods or jobs.

Co-operatives in Canada have various support organizations. In the case of housing co-ops, regional, provincial and national associations exist, as well as various agencies providing development and management services. Registrants are strongly advised to seek legal advice on all matters associated with housing co-operatives.

Equity co-ops present special financing challenges because the entire property must be mortgaged, as opposed to condominium units with distinct ownership. The co-op mortgage is effectively a blanket mortgage over the entire property with joint liability of owners in relation to their proportionate share of ownership. This poses several complications:

- When acquiring a suite in an equity co-op, the buyer must assume the applicable liability for the proportionate share of any mortgage on the property and then secure secondary financing. Often lenders are reluctant to advance funds based on the pledge of security (the share) and assignment of collateral security (the occupancy agreement). In addition, the mortgagee will often require a personal guarantee.

- Cash purchases pose another challenge. The buyer must be assured that any obligation of the previous shareholder relating to the share is paid.

- A co-op typically provides for approval by the board of directors for any pledge of a share or assignment of an occupancy agreement, thereby introducing another element into the transaction process.

- Co-op owners are responsible for the proportionate share of any blanket mortgage and also potentially for obligations of other owners should these individuals fail to meet their financial commitments to the co-operative.

Agreement of Purchase and Sale

The *Agreement of Purchase and Sale* (OREA Standard Form 100) cannot be used in the acquisition of an equity co-operative, as a suitable agreement must address a two-fold process: a share is sold and an occupancy agreement is created or assigned. The *Agreement of Purchase and Sale—Co-operative Building Resale Agreement* (OREA Form 102) sets out the real property being granted by means of exclusive right to occupy and use, together with any parking spaces or lockers and the appropriate shares being purchased in the corporation. The agreement also requires that the purchaser, on or before closing, enter into an occupancy agreement with the co-operative corporation and abide by the rules and regulations of that corporation. A sample *Agreement of Purchase and Sale—Co-operative Building Resale Agreement* (OREA Form 102) is provided on the following pages.

Searches associated with the sale include a full search of title to the property, as well as the co-operative corporation. As no interest in land is being transferred, the new owner is provided documents in support of the new ownership, namely:

- new share certificate;
- assumption of occupancy agreement;
- other particulars concerning rights being acquired (e.g., the specific suite and other exclusive use areas);
- amount of the mortgage;
- rules/regulations; and
- by-laws (including a statement that the seller has complied with same).

The *Business Corporations Act* permits corporations (including co-operative corporations) to place restrictions on the transfer of shares. Consequently, anyone contemplating the purchase or sale of a unit should be aware of what restrictions exist, the process required to obtain approval if such do exist, and associated time lines and costs.

Land transfer tax applies to the purchase of co-ops, despite the fact that a share is being sold, not an interest in land. The government refers to such a disposition as a beneficial interest in land for taxation purposes.

Fully Completed Sample   Agreement of Purchase and Sale—Co-operative Building Resale Agreement, Page 1 of 6

OREA Ontario Real Estate Association

Agreement of Purchase and Sale
Co-operative Building Resale Agreement

Form 102
for use in the Province of Ontario

This Agreement of Purchase and Sale dated this ......**14th**.... day of ....**May**....................... 20.**XX**....

BUYER, ...**Harold Stephen Adamson**.............................., agrees to purchase from
(Full legal names of all Buyers)

SELLER, ...**Margaret June Shaeffer**.............................., the following
(Full legal names of all Sellers)

REAL PROPERTY AND SHARES:

The exclusive right to occupy and use ....**Suite 709**.............................. (the "Unit")

in the Co-operative Apartment Building located at: ....**259 Elgin Avenue**..............................

in the ....**City of Anycity, Region of Anyregion**..............................

Parking Space(s) ....**B27**.......... Locker ....**A16**.......... (the "Property")

and ....**96**.......... shares (the "shares") in the Capital of ....**Elgin Residences Ltd.**.......... (the "Corporation")

PURCHASE PRICE: Dollars (CDN$) **$92,000.00**

Ninety-Two Thousand-- Dollars

DEPOSIT: Buyer submits ....**Upon Acceptance**..............................
(Herewith/Upon Acceptance/as otherwise described in this Agreement)

Six Thousand-- Dollars (CDN$) **$6,000.00**

by negotiable cheque payable to ....**ABC Realty Inc.**.............................. "Deposit Holder" to be held in
trust pending completion or other termination of this Agreement and to be credited toward the Purchase Price on completion. For the purposes of this
Agreement, "Upon Acceptance" shall mean that the Buyer is required to deliver the deposit to the Deposit Holder within 24 hours of the acceptance of
this Agreement. The parties to this Agreement hereby acknowledge that, unless otherwise provided for in this Agreement, the Deposit Holder shall place
the deposit in trust in the Deposit Holder's non-interest bearing Real Estate Trust Account and no interest shall be earned, received or paid on the deposit

Buyer agrees to pay the balance as more particularly set out in Schedule A attached.

SCHEDULE(S) A..............................**attached hereto form(s) part of this Agreement.**

1. **IRREVOCABILITY:** This offer shall be irrevocable by ....**Buyer**.......... until ......**8:00**...... a.m./p.m. on the
(Seller/Buyer)

..**15th**.. day of ....**May**.......... 20 **XX**......, after which time, if not accepted, this offer shall be null and
void and the deposit shall be returned to the Buyer in full without interest.

2. **COMPLETION DATE:** This Agreement shall be completed by no later than 6:00 p.m. on the ..**31st**.. day of ....**July**..........

20 .**XX**......... Upon completion, vacant possession of the property shall be given to the Buyer unless otherwise provided for in this Agreement.

INITIALS OF BUYER(S): (*HA*)   **INITIALS OF SELLER(S):** (*MS*)

Fully Completed Sample Agreement of Purchase and Sale—Co-operative Building Resale Agreement, Page 2 of 6

3. NOTICES: The Seller hereby appoints the Listing Brokerage as agent for the Seller for the purpose of giving and receiving notices pursuant to this Agreement. Where a Brokerage (Buyer's Brokerage) has entered into a representation agreement with the Buyer, the Buyer hereby appoints the Buyer's Brokerage as agent for the purpose of giving and receiving notices pursuant to this Agreement. **Where a Brokerage represents both the Seller and the Buyer (multiple representation), the Brokerage shall not be appointed or authorized to be agent for either the Buyer or the Seller for the purpose of giving and receiving notices.** Any notice relating hereto or provided for herein shall be in writing. In addition to any provision contained herein and in any Schedule hereto, this offer, any counter-offer, notice of acceptance thereof or any notice to be given or received pursuant to this Agreement or any Schedule hereto (any of them, "Document") shall be deemed given and received when delivered personally or hand delivered to the Address for Service provided in the Acknowledgement below, or where a facsimile number or email address is provided herein, when transmitted electronically to that facsimile number or email address, respectively, in which case, the signature(s) of the party (parties) shall be deemed to be original.

FAX No.: .... 416-238-4700 ....
(For delivery of Documents to Seller)

FAX No.: .... 416-626-9980 ....
(For delivery of Documents to Buyer)

Email Address: .... admin@abcrealty.com ....
(For delivery of Documents to Seller)

Email Address: .... notices@xyzrealestate.com ....
(For delivery of Documents to Buyer)

4. CHATTELS INCLUDED: Acme Model 300 refrigerator, Acme Model 330 stove, Excelsior Model 280 dishwasher, all existing window coverings, bookshelves in living room

Unless otherwise stated in this Agreement or any Schedule hereto, Seller agrees to convey all fixtures and chattels included in the Purchase Price free from all liens, encumbrances or claims affecting the said fixtures and chattels.

5. FIXTURES EXCLUDED: N/A

6. RENTAL ITEMS (Including Lease, Lease to Own): The following equipment is rented and **not** included in the Purchase Price. The Buyer agrees to assume the rental contract(s), if assumable:

N/A

The Buyer agrees to co-operate and execute such documentation as may be required to facilitate such assumption.

7. MAINTENANCE EXPENSES: Seller warrants that the maintenance expenses presently payable to the Corporation in respect of the property are

approximately $ .... 575.00 .... per month and include: .... property taxes, building insurance, heat, hydro, water

INITIALS OF BUYER(S): (*HA*)

INITIALS OF SELLER(S): (*MS*)

Form 102 Revised 2015 **Page 2 of 6**

Fully Completed Sample   Agreement of Purchase and Sale—Co-operative Building Resale Agreement, Page 3 of 6

8. **PARKING AND LOCKERS:** Parking and Lockers are as described above or assigned as follows: ......N/A..

.... at an additional cost of: ....

9. **HST:** If the sale of the Property (Real Property as described above) is subject to Harmonized Sales Tax (HST), then such tax shall be

...................**included in**...................... the Purchase Price. If the sale of the Property is not subject to HST, Seller agrees to certify on or before
(included in/in addition to)

closing, that the sale of the Property is not subject to HST. Any HST on chattels, if applicable, is not included in the Purchase Price.

10. **APPROVAL:** This Agreement is subject to Seller, at the Seller's own expense, obtaining approval of the Board of Directors of the Corporation to the
sale and transfer of the Seller's shares in the capital of the Corporation to the Buyer and approval of the Buyer as shareholder and occupant of the

Unit, and if such approval is not obtained by 11:59 p.m. on the ...**25th**... day of ....**June**.........., 20..**XX**...... this agreement shall
become null and void and the Buyer's deposit shall be returned to the Buyer in full without deduction. The buyer agrees to cooperate and provide such
information and documentation as may be within control of the Buyer in order to obtain said approval.

11. **TITLE SEARCH:** Buyer shall be allowed until 6:00 p.m. on the ...**15th**... day of ....**July**.........., 20..**XX**.., (Requisition Date) to
examine the Corporation's title to the Property at the Buyer's expense and until the earlier of: (i) thirty days from the later of the Requisition Date or the
date on which the conditions in this Agreement are fulfilled or otherwise waived or; (ii) five days prior to completion, to satisfy the Buyer that there are

no outstanding work orders or deficiency notices affecting the Property, and that its present use (.....**Single family residential**.....) may be
lawfully continued. If within that time any valid objection to title or to any outstanding work order or deficiency notice, or to the fact the said present use
may not lawfully be continued, is made in writing to Seller and which Seller is unable or unwilling to remove, remedy or satisfy and which Buyer will
not waive, this Agreement notwithstanding any intermediate acts or negotiations in respect of such objections, shall be at an end and all monies paid
shall be returned without interest or deduction and Seller, Listing Brokerage and Co-operating Brokerage shall not be liable for any costs or damages.
Save as to any valid objection so made by such day and except for any objection going to the root of the title, Buyer shall be conclusively deemed
to have accepted Seller's title to the Property. Seller hereby consents to the municipality or other governmental agencies releasing to Buyer details of
all outstanding work orders affecting the Property, and Seller agrees to execute and deliver such further authorizations in this regard as Buyer may
reasonably require.

12. **CORPORATION DOCUMENTATION:** The Seller shall deliver to the Buyer on or before closing:
(a) a certified copy of the Resolution of the Board of Directors of the Corporation approving the Buyer as a shareholder and as an occupant of the Unit;
(b) a share certificate for the Seller's shares in the capital of the Corporation endorsed in favour of the Buyer;
(c) a certificate or letter from the Corporation confirming:
(i) with respect to the Property, that all charges and obligations have been paid or discharged as of the date of closing;
(ii) with respect to the Corporation that the affairs of the Corporation are in order and that there are no legal actions pending against the
Corporation or contemplated by the Corporation, that there are no special assessments contemplated by the Corporation, that there are no orders or
complaints against the real property by the Building, Health or Fire Departments, that no sale of real property is contemplated, and the Building is not
and never has been insulated with Urea-Formaldehyde Foam Insulation.

13. **OCCUPANCY AGREEMENT:** The Buyer agrees on or before closing to enter into an Occupancy Agreement with the Corporation and to abide by
the rules and regulations of the Corporation.

14. **TITLE:** Buyer agrees to accept the Corporation's title to the Property subject to all rights and easements registered against title for the supply and
installation of telephone services, electricity, gas, sewers, water, television cable facilities and other related services; provided that title to the Property
is otherwise good and free from all encumbrances except: (a) as herein expressly provided; (b) any registered restrictions, conditions or covenants
that run with the land provided such have been complied with; and (c) any existing municipal agreements, zoning by-laws and/or regulations and
utility or service contracts.

15. **DOCUMENTS AND DISCHARGE:** Buyer shall not call for the production of any title deed, abstract, survey or other evidence of title to the Property
except such as are in the possession or control of Seller. If a discharge of any Charge/Mortgage, lien or other encumbrance held by a corporation
incorporated pursuant to the Trust And Loan Companies Act (Canada), Chartered Bank, Trust Company, Credit Union, Caisse Populaire or Insurance
Company and which is not to be assumed by Buyer on completion, is not available in registrable form on completion, Buyer agrees to accept Seller's
lawyer's personal undertaking to obtain, out of the closing funds, a discharge in registrable form and to register same, or cause same to be registered,
on title within a reasonable period of time after completion, provided that on or before completion Seller shall provide to Buyer a statement prepared
by the mortgagee, lienholder or encumbrancer setting out the balance required to obtain the discharge, and, where a real-time electronic cleared
funds transfer system is not being used, a direction executed by Seller directing payment to the mortgagee, lienholder or encumbrancer of the amount
required to obtain the discharge out of the balance due on completion.

INITIALS OF BUYER(S): (*HA*)   **INITIALS OF SELLER(S):** (*MS*)

Fully Completed Sample   Agreement of Purchase and Sale—Co-operative Building Resale Agreement, Page 4 of 6

16. MEETINGS: Seller represents and warrants to Buyer that at the time of the acceptance of this Offer the Seller has not received a notice convening a special or general meeting of the Corporation respecting; (a) the termination of the government of the property; (b) the winding up or dissolution of the Corporation; (c) any substantial alteration in or substantial addition to the property or the renovation thereof; OR (d) any substantial change in the assets or liabilities of the Corporation; and Seller covenants that if the Seller receives any such notice prior to the date of completion the Seller shall forthwith notify Buyer in writing and the Buyer may thereupon at the Buyer's option declare this Agreement to be null and void and all monies paid by Buyer shall be refunded without interest or deduction.

17. INSPECTION: Buyer acknowledges having had the opportunity to inspect the Property and understands that upon acceptance of this offer there shall be a binding agreement of purchase and sale between Buyer and Seller. **The Buyer acknowledges having the opportunity to include a requirement for a property inspection report in this Agreement and agrees that except as may be specifically provided for in this Agreement, the Buyer will not be obtaining a property inspection or property inspection report regarding the Property.**

18. INSURANCE: The Unit and all other things being purchased shall be and remain at the risk of the Seller until completion. In the event of substantial damage to the real property Buyer may at the Buyer's option either permit the proceeds of insurance to be used for repair of such damage in accordance with the provisions of the Insurance Trust Agreement or other insurance arrangement, or terminate this Agreement and all deposit monies paid by Buyer hereunder shall be refunded without interest or deduction. If Seller is taking back a Charge/Mortgage, or Buyer is assuming a Charge/Mortgage, Buyer shall supply Seller with reasonable evidence of adequate insurance to protect Seller's or other mortgagee's interest on completion.

19. RESIDENCY: (a) Subject to (b) below, the Seller represents and warrants that the Seller is not and on completion will not be a non-resident under the non-residency provisions of the Income Tax Act which representation and warranty shall survive and not merge upon the completion of this transaction and the Seller shall deliver to the Buyer a statutory declaration that Seller is not then a non-resident of Canada;
(b) provided that if the Seller is a non-resident under the non-residency provisions of the Income Tax Act, the Buyer shall be credited towards the Purchase Price with the amount, if any, necessary for Buyer to pay to the Minister of National Revenue to satisfy Buyer's liability in respect of tax payable by Seller under the non-residency provisions of the Income Tax Act by reason of this sale. Buyer shall not claim such credit if Seller delivers on completion the prescribed certificate.

20. ADJUSTMENTS: Maintenance expenses and, where billed to the Unit and not the Corporation, realty taxes, including local improvement rates; mortgage interest; rentals; unmetered public or private utilities and fuel; are to be apportioned and allowed to the day of completion, the day of completion itself to be apportioned to the Buyer. There shall be no adjustment for the Seller's share of any reserve or contingency fund to which the Seller may have contributed prior to the date of completion.

21. TIME LIMITS: Time shall in all respects be of the essence hereof provided that the time for doing or completing of any matter provided for herein may be extended or abridged by an agreement in writing signed by Seller and Buyer or by their respective lawyers who may be specifically authorized in that regard.

22. TENDER: Any tender of documents or money hereunder may be made upon Seller or Buyer or their respective lawyers on the day set for completion. Money shall be tendered with funds drawn on a lawyer's trust account in the form of a bank draft, certified cheque or wire transfer using the Large Value Transfer System

23. FAMILY LAW ACT: Seller warrants that spousal consent is not necessary to this transaction under the provisions of the Family Law Act, R.S.O.1990 unless Seller's spouse has executed the consent hereinafter provided.

24. LEGAL, ACCOUNTING AND ENVIRONMENTAL ADVICE: The parties acknowledge that any information provided by the brokerage is not legal, tax or environmental advice.

25. CONSUMER REPORTS: The Buyer is hereby notified that a consumer report containing credit and/or personal information may be referred to in connection with this transaction.

26. AGREEMENT IN WRITING: If there is conflict or discrepancy between any provision added to this Agreement (including any Schedule attached hereto) and any provision in the standard pre-set portion hereof, the added provision shall supersede the standard pre-set provision to the extent of such conflict or discrepancy. This Agreement including any Schedule attached hereto, shall constitute the entire Agreement between Buyer and Seller. There is no representation, warranty, collateral agreement or condition, which affects this Agreement other than as expressed herein. For the purposes of this Agreement, Seller means vendor and Buyer means purchaser. This Agreement shall be read with all changes of gender or number required by the context.

27. TIME AND DATE: Any reference to a time and date in this Agreement shall mean the time and date where the property is located.

INITIALS OF BUYER(S): (*HA*)   **INITIALS OF SELLER(S):** (*MS*)

Form 102   Revised 2015   **Page 4 of 6**

SECTION I   A CLOSER LOOK AT TRADING DIFFERENT TYPES OF PROPERTIES

28. SUCCESSORS AND ASSIGNS: The heirs, executors, administrators, successors and assigns of the undersigned are bound by the terms herein.

SIGNED, SEALED AND DELIVERED in the presence of: IN WITNESS whereof I have hereunto set my hand and seal:

John Vogel   *Harold Stephen Adamson*   ●   DATE *May 14/xx*
(Witness)   (Buyer)   (Seal)

    ●   DATE
(Witness)   (Buyer)   (Seal)

I, the Undersigned Seller, agree to the above offer. I hereby irrevocably instruct my lawyer to pay directly to the brokerage(s) with whom I have agreed to pay commission, the unpaid balance of the commission together with applicable Harmonized Sales Tax (and any other taxes as may hereafter be applicable), from the proceeds of the sale prior to any payment to the undersigned on completion, as advised by the brokerage(s) to my lawyer.

SIGNED, SEALED AND DELIVERED in the presence of: IN WITNESS whereof I have hereunto set my hand and seal:

Lee Waciuk   *Margaret June Shaeffer*   ●   DATE *May 15/xx*
(Witness)   (Seller)   (Seal)

    ●   DATE
(Witness)   (Seller)   (Seal)

SPOUSAL CONSENT: The Undersigned Spouse of the Seller hereby consents to the disposition evidenced herein pursuant to the provisions of the Family Law Act, R.S.O.1990, and hereby agrees with the Buyer that he/she will execute all necessary or incidental documents to give full force and effect to the sale evidenced herein.

    ●   DATE
(Witness)   (Spouse)   (Seal)

CONFIRMATION OF ACCEPTANCE: Notwithstanding anything contained herein to the contrary, I confirm this Agreement with all changes both typed and written was finally accepted by all parties at *5:00* ~~a.m.~~/p.m. this *15th* day of *May*, 20.*xx*.

Margaret June Shaeffer
(Signature of Seller or Buyer)

INFORMATION ON BROKERAGE(S)

Listing Brokerage **ABC Realty Inc.**   Tel.No.(416) 238-4745
123 Main Street, Anycity, Anyregion L4H 6P5   **Lee Waciuk**
(Salesperson / Broker Name)

Co-op/Buyer Brokerage **XYZ Real Estate Ltd.**   Tel.No.(416) 625-9983
29 Maple Drive, Anycity, Anyregion L2J 7K6   **John Vogel**
(Salesperson / Broker Name)

ACKNOWLEDGEMENT

I acknowledge receipt of my signed copy of this accepted Agreement of Purchase and Sale and I authorize the Brokerage to forward a copy to my lawyer.

Margaret June Shaeffer   DATE *May 15/xx*
(Seller)

  DATE
(Seller)
Address for Service *55 South Lane, Anycity, Anyregion*
N8N 2K2   Tel.No.(416) 666-1121
Seller's Lawyer *Cindy Jones and Associates*
Address *565 Pine Street, Anycity, Anyregion R4K 8L9*
Email
(416) 666-5544   (416) 666-5454
Tel.No.   FAX No.

I acknowledge receipt of my signed copy of this accepted Agreement of Purchase and Sale and I authorize the Brokerage to forward a copy to my lawyer.

Harold Stephen Adamson   DATE *May 15/xx*
(Buyer)

  DATE
(Buyer)
Address for Service *75 Pim Street, Anycity, Anyregion*
B6L 7J9   Tel.No.(416) 646-3344
Buyer's Lawyer *George Roberts and Associates*
Address *15 Concession Street, Anyregion B5D 3P9*
Email
(416) 656-5353   (416) 656-5454
Tel.No.   FAX No.

Property Manager: **Anycity Property Management   30 Welland Drive, Anycity, ON K0N 1P0   905-999-1212/905-999-2121**
(Name)   (Address)   (Tel No.,FAX No.)

FOR OFFICE USE ONLY   **COMMISSION TRUST AGREEMENT**

To: Co-operating Brokerage shown on the foregoing Agreement of Purchase and Sale:
In consideration for the Co-operating Brokerage procuring the foregoing Agreement of Purchase and Sale, I hereby declare that all moneys received or receivable by me in connection with the Transaction as contemplated in the MLS® Rules and Regulations of my Real Estate Board shall be receivable and held in trust. This agreement shall constitute a Commission Trust Agreement as defined in the MLS® Rules and shall be subject to and governed by the MLS® Rules pertaining to Commission Trust.

DATED as of the date and time of the acceptance of the foregoing Agreement of Purchase and Sale.   Acknowledged by:

Lee Waciuk   *John Vogel*
(Authorized to bind the Listing Brokerage)   (Authorized to bind the Co-operating Brokerage)

Form 102   Revised 2015   **Page 5 of 6**

 **Ontario Real Estate Association**

Form 102
for use in the Province of Ontario

Schedule A
Agreement of Purchase and Sale –
Co-operative Building Resale

This Schedule is attached to and forms part of the Agreement of Purchase and Sale between:

BUYER, ... Harold Stephen Adamson ...., and

SELLER, ... Margaret June Shaeffer ....

for the purchase and sale of .... Suite 709, 259 Elgin Avenue, Anycity, Anyregion ....

.... dated the ...14th... day of .... May ...., 20..XX..

Buyer agrees to pay the balance as follows:

The Buyer agrees to pay a further sum of Eighty-Six Thousand Dollars ($86,000.00), subject to adjustments, to the Seller on completion of this transaction, with funds drawn on a lawyer's trust account in the form of a bank draft, certified cheque, or wire transfer using the Large Value Transfer System.

This Offer is conditional upon the inspection of the subject property by a home inspector at the Buyer's own expense, and the obtaining of a report satisfactory to the Buyer in the Buyer's sole and absolute discretion. Unless the Buyer gives notice in writing delivered to the Seller personally or in accordance with any other provisions for the delivery of notice in this Agreement of Purchase and Sale or any Schedule thereto not later than 5 p.m. on the 21st day of May, 20xx, that this condition is fulfilled, this Offer shall be null and void and the deposit shall be returned to the buyer in full without deduction The Seller agrees to co-operate in providing access to the property for the purpose of this inspection. This condition is included for the benefit of the Buyer and may be waived at the Buyer's sole option by notice in writing to the Seller as aforesaid within the time period stated herein.

This form must be initialed by all parties to the Agreement of Purchase and Sale.

INITIALS OF BUYER(S): (*HA*)   INITIALS OF SELLER(S): (*MS*)

Form 102   Revised 2015   **Page 6 of 6**

CO-OWNERSHIP

Co-ownership, briefly introduced in *Land, Structures and Real Estate Trading*, involves the ownership of a property directly by two or more individuals as tenants in common.

Co-ownership involves individuals as tenants in common and places ownership/control directly in the hands of those tenant in common owners. As an example of a basic co-ownership arrangement, four individuals may elect to buy a large cottage, as none individually can afford the purchase price for a prime recreational property. As a group, they establish rules concerning maintenance, occupancy times and cost sharing, as well as procedures to dispose of the property should the tenants in common wish to disband the arrangement.

Many co-ownership variations exist in the marketplace. In recent years, co-ownership arrangements in cottage areas have become more formalized. A typical configuration involves ten owners acquiring a five-week occupancy during each year. All ten owners are registered on title in accordance with their proportionate interest in the property. Rules and procedures are set out by way of agreement between the tenants in common. The two remaining weeks are used for general upkeep and refurbishing the property. Marketing materials typically refer to such arrangements as fractional ownership.

More formalized, complex co-ownership buildings exist in urban areas; i.e., multi-unit co-ownership building. The tenants in common owners have exclusive right to occupy and use a specific unit and are issued a share certificate in the co-ownership corporation reflecting their proportionate interest. A specific agreement of purchase and sale has been developed for the resale of such co-ownership arrangements—a copy is provided on the following pages.

NOTE: Co-ownership should be clearly distinguished from condominium and co-operative ownership. In the case of a condominium, the overall property is owned by a condominium corporation created upon condominium registration with titles for individual units held by the applicable unit owners. The common elements are owned by the corporation. A co-operative is owned by a corporation with shares issued in the capital stock of the corporation. The individual receives a share certificate for the corporation when buying into the co-operative, along with a right to occupy a specific unit.

Fully Completed Sample   Agreement of Purchase and Sale—Co-ownership Building Resale Agreement, Page 1 of 6

OREA Ontario Real Estate Association

Form 115
for use in the Province of Ontario

Agreement of Purchase and Sale
Co-ownership Building Resale Agreement

This Agreement of Purchase and Sale dated this ..... **12th** ..... day of ..... **May** ..... 20 **XX**

BUYER, ... **Mario J. Sardelis and Marie E. Sardelis** ..... , agrees to purchase from
(Full legal names of all Buyers)

SELLER, ... **Wendy M.Y. Liu and Steven C. P. Liu** ..... , the following
(Full legal names of all Sellers)

REAL PROPERTY AND SHARES: A ..... **1.502** ..... percentage in the property legally described as:

..... **Block B, Plan M416** .....

as tenant-in-common with all the other co-owners that are the co-owners from time to time, together with the exclusive right to occupy and

use ..... **Suite 604** ..... (the "Unit")

in the Co-ownership Building located at: ..... **45 Brookstar Lane** .....

in the ..... **City of Anycity, Region of Anyregion** .....

Parking Space(s) ..... **#220** ..... Locker ..... **#74** ..... (the "Property")

and ..... **15.02** ..... shares (the "shares") in the Capital of ..... **2357103 Ontario Ltd.** ..... (the "Corporation")

PURCHASE PRICE: Dollars (CDN$) ..... **$127,500.00** .....

..... **One Hundred and Twenty-Seven Thousand Five Hundred**--Dollars

DEPOSIT: Buyer submits ..... **As otherwise described in this Agreement** .....
(Herewith/Upon Acceptance/as otherwise described in this Agreement)

..... **Five Thousand**--- Dollars (CDN$) ..... **$5,000.00** .....

by negotiable cheque payable to ..... **ABC Realty Inc.** ..... "Deposit Holder" to be held in
trust pending completion or other termination of this Agreement and to be credited toward the Purchase Price on completion. For the purposes of this
Agreement, "Upon Acceptance" shall mean that the Buyer is required to deliver the deposit to the Deposit Holder within 24 hours of the acceptance of
this Agreement. The parties to this Agreement hereby acknowledge that, unless otherwise provided for in this Agreement, the Deposit Holder shall place
the deposit in trust in the Deposit Holder's non-interest bearing Real Estate Trust Account and no interest shall be earned, received or paid on the deposit
Buyer agrees to pay the balance as more particularly set out in Schedule A attached.

SCHEDULE(S) A ..... **attached hereto form(s) part of this Agreement.**

1. **IRREVOCABILITY:** This offer shall be irrevocable by ..... **Buyer** ..... until **8:00** a.m./p.m. on the **14th**
    (Seller/Buyer)

    day of ..... **May** ..... 20 **XX** , after which time, if not accepted, this offer shall be null and void and the deposit shall be
    returned to the Buyer in full without interest.

2. **COMPLETION DATE:** This Agreement shall be completed by no later than 6:00 p.m. on the **30th** day of ..... **June** ..... 20 **XX**
    Upon completion, vacant possession of the property shall be given to the Buyer unless otherwise provided for in this Agreement.

INITIALS OF BUYER(S): (*MS MS*)   **INITIALS OF SELLER(S):** (*WL SL*)

Form 115   Revised 2015   **Page 1 of 6**

Fully Completed Sample   Agreement of Purchase and Sale—Co-ownership Building Resale Agreement, Page 2 of 6

3. **NOTICES:** The Seller hereby appoints the Listing Brokerage as agent for the Seller for the purpose of giving and receiving notices pursuant to this Agreement. Where a Brokerage (Buyer's Brokerage) has entered into a representation agreement with the Buyer, the Buyer hereby appoints the Buyer's Brokerage as agent for the purpose of giving and receiving notices pursuant to this Agreement. **Where a Brokerage represents both the Seller and the Buyer (multiple representation), the Brokerage shall not be appointed or authorized to be agent for either the Buyer or the Seller for the purpose of giving and receiving notices.** Any notice relating hereto or provided for herein shall be in writing. In addition to any provision contained herein and in any Schedule hereto, this offer, any counter-offer, notice of acceptance thereof or any notice to be given or received pursuant to this Agreement or any Schedule hereto (any of them, "Document") shall be deemed given and received when delivered personally or hand delivered to the Address for Service provided in the Acknowledgement below, or where a facsimile number or email address is provided herein, when transmitted electronically to that facsimile number or email address, respectively, in which case, the signature(s) of the party (parties) shall be deemed to be original.

(Fax # of Buyer)

FAX No.: .... 416-238-4760 ....   FAX No.: .... 604-709-1446 ....
(For delivery of Documents to Seller)   (For delivery of Documents to Buyer)

Email Address: ....   Email Address: ....
(For delivery of Documents to Seller)   (For delivery of Documents to Buyer)

4. **CHATTELS INCLUDED:** Coldspot refrigerator Model 320, Apex stove Model 19, Whirlpool dishwasher Model X15, garburator, all existing drapery tracking, drapes, curtain rods, and window coverings.

Unless otherwise stated in this Agreement or any Schedule hereto, Seller agrees to convey all fixtures and chattels included in the Purchase Price free from all liens, encumbrances or claims affecting the said fixtures and chattels.

5. **FIXTURES EXCLUDED:** Tiffany-style light fixture in entrance hall

6. **RENTAL ITEMS (Including Lease, Lease to Own):** The following equipment is rented and **not** included in the Purchase Price. The Buyer agrees to assume the rental contract(s), if assumable:

N/A

The Buyer agrees to co-operate and execute such documentation as may be required to facilitate such assumption.

7. **MAINTENANCE EXPENSES:** Seller warrants that the maintenance expenses presently payable to the Corporation in respect of the property are approximately $.......... 620.00 .... per month and include:.......... property taxes, building insurance, heat, hydro, water charges, security and maintenance expenses

8. **PARKING AND LOCKERS:** Parking and Lockers are as described above or assigned as follows:.......... as described above .... at an additional cost of:.......... N/A

9. **HST:** If the sale of the Property (Real Property as described above) is subject to Harmonized Sales Tax (HST), then such tax shall be .... included in .... the Purchase Price. If the sale of the Property is not subject to HST, Seller agrees to certify on or before
(included in/in addition to)
closing, that the sale of the Property is not subject to HST. Any HST on chattels, if applicable, is not included in the Purchase Price.

INITIALS OF BUYER(S): (*MS MS*)   INITIALS OF SELLER(S): (*WL SL*)

Form 115   Revised 2015   **Page 2 of 6**

Fully Completed Sample   Agreement of Purchase and Sale—Co-ownership Building Resale Agreement, Page 3 of 6

10. APPROVAL: This Agreement is subject to Seller, at the Seller's own expense, obtaining approval of the Board of Directors of the Corporation to the sale and transfer of the Seller's shares in the capital of the Corporation to the Buyer and approval of the Buyer as shareholder and occupant of the

Unit, and if such approval is not obtained by 11:59 p.m. on the ....5th.. day of ....June................., 20.XX. this agreement shall become null and void and the Buyer's deposit shall be returned to the Buyer in full without deduction. The buyer agrees to cooperate and provide such information and documentation as may be within control of the Buyer in order to obtain said approval.

11. TITLE SEARCH: Buyer shall be allowed until 6:00 p.m. on the ...12th.. day of...............June................., 20.XX., (Requisition Date) to examine the title to the Property at Buyer's own expense and until the earlier of: (i) thirty days from the later of the Requisition Date or the date on which the conditions in this Agreement are fulfilled or otherwise waived or; (ii) five days prior to completion, to satisfy Buyer that there are no outstanding

work orders or deficiency notices affecting the Property, and that its present use (...............single family residential....................) may be lawfully continued. If within that time any valid objection to title or to any outstanding work order or deficiency notice, or to the fact the said present use may not lawfully be continued, is made in writing to Seller and which Seller is unable or unwilling to remove, remedy or satisfy or obtain insurance save and except against risk of fire (Title Insurance) in favour of the Buyer and any mortgagee, (with all related costs at the expense of the Seller), and which Buyer will not waive, this Agreement notwithstanding any intermediate acts or negotiations in respect of such objections, shall be at an end and all monies paid shall be returned without interest or deduction and Seller, Listing Brokerage and Co-operating Brokerage shall not be liable for any costs or damages. Save as to any valid objection so made by such day and except for any objection going to the root of the title, Buyer shall be conclusively deemed to have accepted Seller's title to the Property. Seller hereby consents to the municipality or other governmental agencies releasing to Buyer details of all outstanding work orders and deficiency notices affecting the Property, and Seller agrees to execute and deliver such further authorizations in this regard as Buyer may reasonably require.

12. CORPORATION DOCUMENTATION: The Seller shall deliver to the Buyer on or before closing:
(a) a certified copy of the Resolution of the Board of Directors of the Corporation approving the Buyer as a shareholder and as an occupant of the Unit;
(b) a share certificate for the Seller's shares in the capital of the Corporation endorsed in favour of the Buyer.
(c) a certificate or letter from the Corporation confirming:
   (i) with respect to the Property, that all charges and obligations have been paid or discharged as of the date of closing;
   (ii) with respect to the Corporation that the affairs of the Corporation are in order and that there are no legal actions pending against the Corporation or contemplated by the Corporation, that there are no special assessments contemplated by the Corporation, that there are no orders or complaints against the real property by the Building, Health or Fire Departments, and the Building is not and never has been insulated with Urea-Formaldehyde Foam Insulation.

13. OCCUPANCY AGREEMENT: The Buyer agrees on or before closing to enter into an Occupancy Agreement with the Corporation and to abide by the rules and regulations of the Corporation.

14. TITLE: The Buyer agrees to accept the title to the Property subject to all rights and easements registered against title for the supply and installation of telephone services, electricity, gas, sewers, water, television cable facilities and other related services; provided that title to the Property is otherwise good and free from all encumbrances except: (a) as herein expressly provided; (b) any registered restrictions, conditions or covenants that run with the land provided such have been complied with; and (c) any existing municipal agreements, zoning by-laws and/or regulations and utility or service contracts.

15. DOCUMENTS AND DISCHARGE: Buyer shall not call for the production of any title deed, abstract, survey or other evidence of title to the Property except such as are in the possession or control of Seller. If a discharge of any Charge/Mortgage, lien or other encumbrance held by a corporation incorporated pursuant to the Trust And Loan Companies Act (Canada), Chartered Bank, Trust Company, Credit Union, Caisse Populaire or Insurance Company and which is not to be assumed by Buyer on completion, is not available in registrable form on completion, Buyer agrees to accept Seller's lawyer's personal undertaking to obtain, out of the closing funds, a discharge in registrable form and to register same, or cause same to be registered, on title within a reasonable period of time after completion, provided that on or before completion Seller shall provide to Buyer a statement prepared by the mortgagee, lienholder or encumbrancer setting out the balance required to obtain the discharge, and, where a real-time electronic cleared funds transfer system is not being used, a direction executed by Seller directing payment to the mortgagee, lienholder or encumbrancer of the amount required to obtain the discharge out of the balance due on completion.

16. MEETINGS: Seller represents and warrants to Buyer that at the time of the acceptance of this Offer the Seller has not received a notice convening a special or general meeting of the Corporation respecting; (a) the termination of the government of the property; (b) the winding up or dissolution of the Corporation; (c) any substantial alteration in or substantial addition to the property or the renovation thereof; OR (d) any substantial change in the assets or liabilities of the Corporation; and Seller covenants that if the Seller receives any such notice prior to the date of completion the Seller shall forthwith notify Buyer in writing and the Buyer may thereupon at the Buyer's option declare this Agreement to be null and void and all monies paid by Buyer shall be refunded without interest or deduction.

INITIALS OF BUYER(S): (*MS MS*)   INITIALS OF SELLER(S): (*WL SL*)

Form 115   Revised 2015   **Page 3 of 6**

Fully Completed Sample   *Agreement of Purchase and Sale—Co-ownership Building Resale Agreement, Page 4 of 6*

17. INSPECTION: Buyer acknowledges having had the opportunity to inspect the Property and understands that upon acceptance of this offer there shall be a binding agreement of purchase and sale between Buyer and Seller. **The Buyer acknowledges having the opportunity to include a requirement for a property inspection report in this Agreement and agrees that except as may be specifically provided for in this Agreement, the Buyer will not be obtaining a property inspection or property inspection report regarding the Property.**

18. INSURANCE: The Unit and all other things being purchased shall be and remain at the risk of the Seller until completion. In the event of substantial damage to the real property Buyer may at the Buyer's option either permit the proceeds of insurance to be used for repair of such damage in accordance with the provisions of the Insurance Trust Agreement or other insurance arrangement, or terminate this Agreement and all deposit monies paid by Buyer hereunder shall be refunded without interest or deduction. If Seller is taking back a Charge/Mortgage, or Buyer is assuming a Charge/Mortgage, Buyer shall supply Seller with reasonable evidence of adequate insurance to protect Seller's or other mortgagee's interest on completion.

19. DOCUMENT PREPARATION: The Transfer/Deed shall, save for the Land Transfer Tax Affidavit, be prepared in registrable form at the expense of Seller, and any Charge/Mortgage to be given back by the Buyer to Seller at the expense of the Buyer.

20. RESIDENCY: (a) Subject to (b) below, the Seller represents and warrants that the Seller is not and on completion will not be a non-resident under the non-residency provisions of the Income Tax Act which representation and warranty shall survive and not merge upon the completion of this transaction and the Seller shall deliver to the Buyer a statutory declaration that Seller is not then a non-resident of Canada;
(b) provided that if the Seller is a non-resident under the non-residency provisions of the Income Tax Act, the Buyer shall be credited towards the Purchase Price with the amount, if any, necessary for Buyer to pay to the Minister of National Revenue to satisfy Buyer's liability in respect of tax payable by Seller under the non-residency provisions of the Income Tax Act by reason of this sale. Buyer shall not claim such credit if Seller delivers on completion the prescribed certificate.

21. ADJUSTMENTS: Maintenance expenses and, where billed to the Unit and not the Corporation, realty taxes, including local improvement rates; mortgage interest; rentals; unmetered public or private utilities and fuel; are to be apportioned and allowed to the day of completion, the day of completion itself to be apportioned to the Buyer. There shall be no adjustment for the Seller's share of any reserve or contingency fund to which the Seller may have contributed prior to the date of completion.

22. PROPERTY ASSESSMENT: The Buyer and Seller hereby acknowledge that the Province of Ontario has implemented current value assessment and properties may be re-assessed on an annual basis. The Buyer and Seller agree that no claim will be made against the Buyer or Seller, or any Brokerage, Broker or Salesperson, for any changes in property tax as a result of a re-assessment of the Property, save and except any property taxes that accrued prior to the completion of this transaction.

23. TIME LIMITS: Time shall in all respects be of the essence hereof provided that the time for doing or completing of any matter provided for herein may be extended or abridged by an agreement in writing signed by Seller and Buyer or by their respective lawyers who may be specifically authorized in that regard.

24. TENDER: Any tender of documents or money hereunder may be made upon Seller or Buyer or their respective lawyers on the day set for completion. Money shall be tendered with funds drawn on a lawyer's trust account in the form of a bank draft, certified cheque or wire transfer using the Large Value Transfer System.

25. FAMILY LAW ACT: Seller warrants that spousal consent is not necessary to this transaction under the provisions of the Family Law Act, R.S.O.1990 unless Seller's spouse has executed the consent hereinafter provided.

26. LEGAL, ACCOUNTING AND ENVIRONMENTAL ADVICE: The parties acknowledge that any information provided by the brokerage is not legal, tax or environmental advice.

27. CONSUMER REPORTS: The Buyer is hereby notified that a consumer report containing credit and/or personal information may be referred to in connection with this transaction.

28. AGREEMENT IN WRITING: If there is conflict or discrepancy between any provision added to this Agreement (including any Schedule attached hereto) and any provision in the standard pre-set portion hereof, the added provision shall supersede the standard pre-set provision to the extent of such conflict or discrepancy. This Agreement including any Schedule attached hereto, shall constitute the entire Agreement between Buyer and Seller. There is no representation, warranty, collateral agreement or condition, which affects this Agreement other than as expressed herein. For the purposes of this Agreement, Seller means vendor and Buyer means purchaser. This Agreement shall be read with all changes of gender or number required by the context.

29. TIME AND DATE: Any reference to a time and date in this Agreement shall mean the time and date where the Property is located.

INITIALS OF BUYER(S): (*MS MS*)   INITIALS OF SELLER(S): (*WL SL*)

Form 115   Revised 2015   **Page 4 of 6**

30. SUCCESSORS AND ASSIGNS: The heirs, executors, administrators, successors and assigns of the undersigned are bound by the terms herein.

SIGNED, SEALED AND DELIVERED in the presence of: IN WITNESS whereof I have hereunto set my hand and seal:

A. Fernandes	*Mario J. Sardelis* ● (Seal)	DATE *May 12/xx*
(Witness)	(Buyer)	
A. Fernandes	*Marie E. Sardelis* ● (Seal)	DATE *May 12/xx*
(Witness)	(Buyer)	

I, the Undersigned Seller, agree to the above offer. I hereby irrevocably instruct my lawyer to pay directly to the brokerage(s) with whom I have agreed to pay commission, the unpaid balance of the commission together with applicable Harmonized Sales Tax (and any other taxes as may hereafter be applicable), from the proceeds of the sale prior to any payment to the undersigned on completion, as advised by the brokerage(s) to my lawyer.

SIGNED, SEALED AND DELIVERED in the presence of: IN WITNESS whereof I have hereunto set my hand and seal:

W. Palm	*Wendy M.Y. Liu* ● (Seal)	DATE *May 12/xx*
(Witness)	(Seller)	
W. Palm	*Steven C.P. Liu* ● (Seal)	DATE *May 12/xx*
(Witness)	(Seller)	

SPOUSAL CONSENT: The Undersigned Spouse of the Seller hereby consents to the disposition evidenced herein pursuant to the provisions of the Family Law Act, R.S.O.1990, and hereby agrees with the Buyer that he/she will execute all necessary or incidental documents to give full force and effect to the sale evidenced herein.

	● (Seal)	DATE
(Witness)	(Spouse)	

CONFIRMATION OF ACCEPTANCE: Notwithstanding anything contained herein to the contrary, I confirm this Agreement with all changes both typed and written was finally accepted by all parties at ....*6:00*.... a.m./p.m. this *12th* day of........*May*........, 20.*xx*....

Wendy M.Y. Liu
(Signature of Seller or Buyer)

INFORMATION ON BROKERAGE(S)

Listing Brokerage ...... **ABC Realty Inc.** ...... Tel.No.(**416**) **555-1212**

123 Main Street, Anycity, Anyregion L4H 6P5   **William Palm**
(Salesperson / Broker Name)

Co-op/Buyer Brokerage ...... **XYZ Real Estate Limited** ...... Tel.No.(**416**) **666-1212**

25 Maple Drive, Anycity, Anyregion L2J 7P6   **A. Fernandes**
(Salesperson / Broker Name)

ACKNOWLEDGEMENT

I acknowledge receipt of my signed copy of this accepted Agreement of Purchase and Sale and I authorize the Brokerage to forward a copy to my lawyer.	I acknowledge receipt of my signed copy of this accepted Agreement of Purchase and Sale and I authorize the Brokerage to forward a copy to my lawyer.
Wendy M.Y. Liu DATE *May 12/xx*	*Mario. J. Sardelis* DATE *May 12/xx*
(Seller)	(Buyer)
Steven C.P. Liu DATE *May 12/xx*	*Marie. J. Sardelis* DATE *May 12/xx*
(Seller)	(Buyer)
Address for Service ...*Unit 604, 45 Brookstar Lane*	Address for Service ...*27 Langton Drive, Suite 101*
Anycity N3K 5P6 Tel.No.(*416*) *827-1313*	*Anycity V3Y 4K7* Tel.No.(*416*) *709-1446*
Seller's Lawyer ...*Jane Pierce, c/o Pierce and Lyons*	Buyer's Lawyer *Thomas Rowley, c/o Steward Millard and Stoltz*
Address ...*327 Centre Avenue, Anycity K0T 3B2*	Address ...*291 Westside Drive, Anycity K9C 4B2*
Email	Email
(*416*) *888-1212* (*416*) *888-2121*	(*416*) *333-1212* (*416*) *333-2121*
Tel.No. FAX No.	Tel.No. FAX No.

Property Manager: **John McIntyre**   **1556 Weston Avenue, Anycity K8T 3Y6**   **905-222-2121**
(Name)   (Address)   (Tel No.,FAX No)

FOR OFFICE USE ONLY   **COMMISSION TRUST AGREEMENT**

To: Co-operating Brokerage shown on the foregoing Agreement of Purchase and Sale:
In consideration for the Co-operating Brokerage procuring the foregoing Agreement of Purchase and Sale, I hereby declare that all moneys received or receivable by me in connection with the Transaction as contemplated in the MLS® Rules and Regulations of my Real Estate Board shall be receivable and held in trust. This agreement shall constitute a Commission Trust Agreement as defined in the MLS® Rules and shall be subject to and governed by the MLS® Rules pertaining to Commission Trust.

DATED as of the date and time of the acceptance of the foregoing Agreement of Purchase and Sale.   Acknowledged by:

W. Palm   *A. Fernandes*
(Authorized to bind the Listing Brokerage)   (Authorized to bind the Co-operating Brokerage)

Form 115   Revised 2015   **Page 5 of 6**

SECTION I   A CLOSER LOOK AT TRADING DIFFERENT TYPES OF PROPERTIES

 **Ontario Real Estate Association**

Form 115
for use in the Province of Ontario

Schedule A
Agreement of Purchase and Sale –
Co-ownership Building Resale

This Schedule is attached to and forms part of the Agreement of Purchase and Sale between:

BUYER, ... Mario E. Sardelis and Marie E. Sardelis ...., and

SELLER, ... Wendy M. Y. Liu and Steven C.P. Liu ....

for the purchase and sale of .... Suite 604, 45 Brookstar Lane, City of Anycity, Region of Anyregion ....

.... dated the ...12th... day of .... May ...., 20.XX...

Buyer agrees to pay the balance as follows:

The Buyer agrees to pay a further sum of One Hundred and Twenty-two Thousand Five Hundred Dollars ($122,500.00), subject to adjustments, to the Seller on completion of this transaction, with funds drawn on a lawyer's trust account in the form of a bank draft, certified cheque, or wire transfer using the Large Value Transfer System.

The Buyer and Seller agree that the deposit will be delivered to the listing Brokerage within seven (7) days from the Confirmation of Acceptance of this Agreement.

This form must be initialed by all parties to the Agreement of Purchase and Sale.

INITIALS OF BUYER(S): (*MS MS*)   INITIALS OF SELLER(S): (*WL SL*)

Form 115   Revised 2015   **Page 6 of 6**

TIMESHARE

Timeshare is the division of property rights into fractional interests based on time. Timeshare ownership is a logical extension of the creative division of ownership interests found in condominium, co-operatives and co-ownership and has been included in this chapter as a matter of general interest.

Timeshare is proven most popular in the sale of recreational properties, particularly in the case of southern vacation resorts. Most timeshare interests in this province are concentrated in Collingwood and vicinity

Fee Ownership Interest

Fee simple ownership is probably the most straight-forward method to acquire an interest in timeshare. Initially, a condominium corporation is created and registered in the condominium corporations index of the applicable land registration office, with appropriate pages for each time interval. Individual weeks are registered under the unit, with all 52 weeks being displayed with the percentage interest in each of the periods. The sum of interests must total 100%.

The initial transfer from the developer/owner is typically accompanied by a notice of agreement to each of the timeshare owners. This agreement generally binds each owner to the restrictive covenants, rules, regulations and by-laws of the timeshare condominium project. When the fee simple ownership is conveyed, the new owner must also sign a notice of agreement ensuring continuance of such compliance. Procedures will vary somewhat by individual project.

Right-to-Use Interest

Given certain legal complexities with fee simple timeshare ownership, many timeshare ventures have moved toward right-to-use agreements. Essentially, the buyer of the right enters a contractual arrangement to enjoy the use of the property, while the title to the land and improvements rests with the developer, corporation or association. This type of ownership has become extremely attractive in many countries. It currently accounts for a significant portion of today's vacation timeshare industry.

Unlike fee simple arrangements, the creation of condominium is not required. Essentially, the owners obtain their interest through a notice of lease that designates the specific week being acquired. As with fee simple ownership, the right can be conveyed to others or encumbered subject to regulations included in the original timeshare documentation. The conveyance is accomplished through a notice of assignment of lease.

Consumer Protection Act

Consumers have certain rights under the *Consumer Protection Act* when acquiring an interest in a timeshare. The Act reads as follows:

Requirements for time share agreements

27.   Every time share agreement shall be in writing, shall be delivered to the consumer and shall be made in accordance with the prescribed requirements. 2002, c. 30, Sched. A, s. 27.

Cancellation: cooling-off period

28. (1) A consumer may, without any reason, cancel a time share agreement at any time from the date of entering into the agreement until 10 days after receiving the written copy of the agreement. 2002, c. 30, Sched. A, s. 28 (1).

Cancellation: failure to meet requirements

(2) In addition to the right under subsection (1), a consumer may cancel a time share agreement within one year after the date of entering into the agreement if the consumer does not receive a copy of the agreement that meets the requirements under section 27. 2002, c. 30, Sched. A, s. 28 (2).

Source: *Consumer Protection Act*, Sec. 27 and Subsec 28 (1) and (2).

This protection does not apply to Ontario residents when acquiring a timeshare interest outside of either the province or the country.

KNOWLEDGE INTEGRATION

Notables

- Dwelling types include, but are not limited to, detached, duplex, linked, semi-detached, townhouse, triplex and fourplex.
- Municipalities have various residential zoning restrictions providing for successively higher density development.
- Home-based businesses must comply with zoning provisions. The scope of these provisions varies by municipality.
- Intensification involves the expanded use of existing buildings and serviced land to provide additional housing stock and more effectively utilize existing municipal services.
- The term *sustainable* refers to the desire to address today's current needs without compromising those of future generations.
- Gated communities have not been widely accepted in Ontario, but examples are scattered throughout the province.
- Mature adults have expanding choices in terms of suitable residences. Several options are discussed in chapter materials.

- Life lease communities have gained significant prominence in the Ontario marketplace.
- Land lease communities are found throughout the province. Special legislative requirements apply and a specific agreement of purchase and sale can be used for transactions involving homes on leased land.
- Factory-built housing, including modular and manufactured homes, is gaining wider acceptance in the Ontario marketplace.
- The residential agreement of purchase and sale cannot be used in selling a co-operative, as the agreement must address two circumstances: a share is sold and an occupancy agreement is created or assigned.
- Co-ownership is a growing option for those seeking alternative housing arrangements. Co-ownership is currently proving most popular in recreational areas.

Web Links

Web links are included for general interest regarding selected chapter topics.

Ministry of Municipal Affairs and Housing   For more information concerning life lease communities, recent activities and consumer-related considerations, go to ***www.mah.gov.on.ca***.

Strategic Thinking For Your Career

Questions are included to assist in developing your new career. No answers are provided.

1. What specific zoning provisions apply to various housing types within the local community?

2. Do I fully understand local requirements concerning home-based businesses?

3. Are there any gated communities within my local market area and, if so, what particular market niche(s) do they serve?

4. Are there any land lease communities within my local market area and what provisions do they have regarding signage when listing a home within the community?

5. Are there any residential co-operatives (other than non-profit co-operatives) or co-ownership arrangements in my local market areas?

Chapter Mini-Review

Solutions are located in the Appendix.

1. For zoning purposes, a detached dwelling is best described as a building consisting of one dwelling unit.

    ⦿ True   ◯ False

2. The blank space for present use in the *Title Search* clause (Clause 8) in the *Agreement of Purchase and Sale* (OREA Form 100) must be filled out when drafting an agreement.

    ◯ True   ⦿ False

3. Zoning provisions concerning home-based businesses will typically set out restrictions as to signage and number of non-resident employees.

    ◯ True   ◯ False

4. The term *built form* refers to the design, appearance and configuration of existing structures within a community.

    ◯ True   ◯ False

5. A private amenity in a gated community is typically a recreational facility or clubhouse that is not part of the common amenities within a gated community, and is operated as a separate business.

    ◯ True   ◯ False

6. Flex-housing is a term introduced by the Ontario Building Code to describe new requirements that now apply to new residential construction.

    ◯ True   ◯ False

7. The *Residential Tenancies Act* includes provisions relating to care homes; i.e., various retirement residences offering accommodation and care to mature adults and seniors.

    ◯ True   ◯ False

8. A life lease community is a condominium project that provides the opportunity for mature adults to occupy a unit for the life of that individual (or individuals in the case of a couple).

    ◯ True   ◯ False

9. The owner of a land lease community must allow real estate brokerages to place for sale or for rent signs on the listed home within that community.

  ◯ True   ◯ False

10. Co-ownership places ownership and control directly in the hands of the tenant in common owners.

  ◯ True   ◯ False

Active Learning Exercises

Solutions are located in the Appendix.

▣ Exercise 1   Multiple Choice

1.1   A linked dwelling is best described as a:

  a.   Dwelling consisting of one dwelling unit.

  b.   Dwelling connected below grade by a concrete wall.

  c.   Dwelling that is attached by a party wall.

  d.   Dwelling that is one of three or four separate dwelling units divided horizontally or vertically.

1.2   Which of the following is a correct statement regarding home-based businesses?

  a.   Signage restrictions are rarely imposed on these businesses.

  b.   No business deductions are available for taxation purposes involving home-based businesses.

  c.   Special rules may apply for health professionals operating a home-based office.

  d.   Business licenses are required for all home-based businesses.

1.3   Gated communities:

  a.   Are found only in United States.

  b.   Are restricted to land lease communities in Ontario.

  c.   Must have security personnel at the entrance.

  d.   Have not been widely accepted in Ontario at this time.

1.4   Which of the following statements is correct?

  a.   A unique agreement of purchase and sale has been developed for modular or manufactured homes in land lease communities.

  b.   Life lease communities are governed by the *Residential Tenancies Act.*

  c.   For legislative purposes, requirements for a land lease home are different than those for a mobile home.

  d.   Tarion warranty coverage applies to residential dwellings in life lease communities.

1.5 In a land lease community:

a. The landlord cannot include a right of first refusal in a tenancy agreement.

b. Can include a right of first refusal, but such a right is subject to additional requirements under the Act.

c. Must include a right of first refusal in all tenancy agreements.

d. A landlord must act for the tenant in selling his or her home.

1.6 Which of the following is a correct statement?

a. The *Agreement of Purchase and Sale—Co-operative Building Resale* provides that both a share is sold and an occupancy agreement is created or assigned.

b. Modular homes are not largely constructed in a controlled environment, as is the case with manufactured homes.

c. *Places to Grow* legislation primarily promotes expansion of existing municipal boundaries.

d. Section 9 of the Building Code focuses on building requirements for large, multi-story buildings.

■ **Exercise 2   Matching**

Match the phrase/word in the left column with the appropriate description in the right column (not all descriptions are used).

____ Street Townhouse	a. Private Pay Mature Adult Accommodation
____ Intensification	b. Modular Home
____ Built Form	c. Expanded Use of Existing Land and Services
____ Retirement Residence	d. Flex Housing
____ Factory-Built Housing	e. Alpha Track Detector
____ Co-ownership	f. Right to Occupy for Occupant's Life
____ Timeshare	g. Two or More Attached Dwellings Divided Vertically
____ Life Lease	h. Fractional Interest Based on Time Intervals
	i. Tenants in Common
	j. Sustainable Community
	k. Height, Shape and Appearance of Existing Buildings

■ **Exercise 3   Offer Drafting**

Vincent A. Rogato wants you to draft an offer on a co-operative unit located at 3397 West Shore Blvd., Suite 205. The seller is Sharon W. Wingate. Various details are included below. Insert any additional details necessary to complete the offer. A blank *Agreement of Purchase and Sale—Co-operative Building Resale Agreement* (OREA Form 102) is provided on the following pages.

> The co-operative unit, Suite 205, is located at 3397 West Shore Blvd. in the City of Anycity, Region of Anyregion. The exclusive right to occupy and use this unit includes a single parking space (B05) and a locker (A27). The sale involves 87 shares in the capital of 3397 West Shore Blvd. Inc.
>
> The offered price is $238,900 with a deposit of $12,000, and the balance is due on completion date. The $12,000 is to be deposited with the listing brokerage upon acceptance of the agreement. No additional schedules are needed beyond Schedule A. Vincent Rogato requires that the offer be conditional on a home inspection. A 10-day time frame is sufficient for the condition precedent.
>
> The completion date will be August 20th (a normal business day) with today's date being June 1st, 20xx. The offer, dated at Anycity, will be irrevocable until 6 p.m. on June 2nd. Notices cannot be delivered by fax or email. The sale includes kitchen appliances (Acme Model R320 refrigerator, Acme Model S500 stove and Acme Model D200 dishwasher) and a stacking Acme Model S550 washer/dryer. The dining room fixture is excluded and no equipment rentals apply.
>
> Maintenance expenses are currently $625.00 per month and include property taxes, building insurance, heat, hydro and water. No additional costs apply to the parking space and locker, which are included in the purchase price. If any HST applies to this sale, it is deemed to be included in the purchase price. The board of directors of the corporation have until June 15th to approve the transfer of the seller's shares. An appropriate title search period would be until July 20th.
>
> Insert necessary dates and signatures as required for a fully completed agreement ready for presentation. The listing brokerage is ABC Realty Inc. representing the seller and the co-operating brokerage is XYZ Real Estate Limited representing the buyer. The property management company is Anycity Property Management, located at 30 Welland Drive, Anycity.

Have the buyer sign the offer today. The offer is presented to the seller tomorrow and accepted by her. Complete all necessary signatures and information to make this an accepted Agreement of Purchase and Sale that would be retained in the listing brokerage's files.

OREA Ontario Real Estate Association

Form 102
for use in the Province of Ontario

Agreement of Purchase and Sale
Co-operative Building Resale Agreement

This Agreement of Purchase and Sale dated this .... day of .... 20.............

BUYER, ..., agrees to purchase from
(Full legal names of all Buyers)

SELLER, ..., the following
(Full legal names of all Sellers)

REAL PROPERTY AND SHARES:

The exclusive right to occupy and use .... (the "Unit")

in the Co-operative Apartment Building located at: ....

in the ....

Parking Space(s) .... Locker ....(the "Property")

and .... shares (the "shares") in the Capital of .... (the "Corporation")

PURCHASE PRICE: Dollars (CDN$) ....

.... Dollars

DEPOSIT: Buyer submits ....
(Herewith/Upon Acceptance/as otherwise described in this Agreement)

.... Dollars (CDN$) ....

by negotiable cheque payable to .... "Deposit Holder" to be held in trust pending completion or other termination of this Agreement and to be credited toward the Purchase Price on completion. For the purposes of this Agreement, "Upon Acceptance" shall mean that the Buyer is required to deliver the deposit to the Deposit Holder within 24 hours of the acceptance of this Agreement. The parties to this Agreement hereby acknowledge that, unless otherwise provided for in this Agreement, the Deposit Holder shall place the deposit in trust in the Deposit Holder's non-interest bearing Real Estate Trust Account and no interest shall be earned, received or paid on the deposit

Buyer agrees to pay the balance as more particularly set out in Schedule A attached.

SCHEDULE(S) A..**attached hereto form(s) part of this Agreement.**

1.   **IRREVOCABILITY:** This offer shall be irrevocable by .... until .... a.m./p.m. on the
(Seller/Buyer)

.... day of .... 20 ...., after which time, if not accepted, this offer shall be null and void and the deposit shall be returned to the Buyer in full without interest.

2.   **COMPLETION DATE:** This Agreement shall be completed by no later than 6:00 p.m. on the .... day of ....

20 .... Upon completion, vacant possession of the property shall be given to the Buyer unless otherwise provided for in this Agreement.

INITIALS OF BUYER(S): (⬭)   **INITIALS OF SELLER(S):** (⬭)

Form 102   Revised 2015   **Page 1 of 6**

3. **NOTICES:** The Seller hereby appoints the Listing Brokerage as agent for the Seller for the purpose of giving and receiving notices pursuant to this Agreement. Where a Brokerage (Buyer's Brokerage) has entered into a representation agreement with the Buyer, the Buyer hereby appoints the Buyer's Brokerage as agent for the purpose of giving and receiving notices pursuant to this Agreement. **Where a Brokerage represents both the Seller and the Buyer (multiple representation), the Brokerage shall not be appointed or authorized to be agent for either the Buyer or the Seller for the purpose of giving and receiving notices.** Any notice relating hereto or provided for herein shall be in writing. In addition to any provision contained herein and in any Schedule hereto, this offer, any counter-offer, notice of acceptance thereof or any notice to be given or received pursuant to this Agreement or any Schedule hereto (any of them, "Document") shall be deemed given and received when delivered personally or hand delivered to the Address for Service provided in the Acknowledgement below, or where a facsimile number or email address is provided herein, when transmitted electronically to that facsimile number or email address, respectively, in which case, the signature(s) of the party (parties) shall be deemed to be original.

FAX No.: ....   FAX No.: ....

(For delivery of Documents to Seller)   (For delivery of Documents to Buyer)

Email Address: ....   Email Address: ....

(For delivery of Documents to Seller)   (For delivery of Documents to Buyer)

4. **CHATTELS INCLUDED:** ....

....

....

....

Unless otherwise stated in this Agreement or any Schedule hereto, Seller agrees to convey all fixtures and chattels included in the Purchase Price free from all liens, encumbrances or claims affecting the said fixtures and chattels.

5. **FIXTURES EXCLUDED:** ....

....

....

....

6. **RENTAL ITEMS (Including Lease, Lease to Own):** The following equipment is rented and **not** included in the Purchase Price. The Buyer agrees to assume the rental contract(s), if assumable:

....

....

....

The Buyer agrees to co-operate and execute such documentation as may be required to facilitate such assumption.

7. **MAINTENANCE EXPENSES:** Seller warrants that the maintenance expenses presently payable to the Corporation in respect of the property are

approximately $ .... per month and include: ....

....

....

....

INITIALS OF BUYER(S): (   )   INITIALS OF SELLER(S): (   )

Form 102   Revised 2015   **Page 2 of 6**

Exercise 3   Agreement of Purchase and Sale—Co-operative Building Resale Agreement, Page 3 of 6

8. **PARKING AND LOCKERS:** Parking and Lockers are as described above or assigned as follows: ....

.... at an additional cost of: ....

9. **HST:** If the sale of the Property (Real Property as described above) is subject to Harmonized Sales Tax (HST), then such tax shall be

.... the Purchase Price. If the sale of the Property is not subject to HST, Seller agrees to certify on or before
   (included in/in addition to)

closing, that the sale of the Property is not subject to HST. Any HST on chattels, if applicable, is not included in the Purchase Price.

10. **APPROVAL:** This Agreement is subject to Seller, at the Seller's own expense, obtaining approval of the Board of Directors of the Corporation to the sale and transfer of the Seller's shares in the capital of the Corporation to the Buyer and approval of the Buyer as shareholder and occupant of the

Unit, and if such approval is not obtained by 11:59 p.m. on the .... day of ...., 20............. this agreement shall become null and void and the Buyer's deposit shall be returned to the Buyer in full without deduction. The buyer agrees to cooperate and provide such information and documentation as may be within control of the Buyer in order to obtain said approval.

11. **TITLE SEARCH:** Buyer shall be allowed until 6:00 p.m. on the .... day of ...., 20......., (Requisition Date) to examine the Corporation's title to the Property at the Buyer's expense and until the earlier of: (i) thirty days from the later of the Requisition Date or the date on which the conditions in this Agreement are fulfilled or otherwise waived or; (ii) five days prior to completion, to satisfy the Buyer that there are

no outstanding work orders or deficiency notices affecting the Property, and that its present use (...) may be lawfully continued. If within that time any valid objection to title or to any outstanding work order or deficiency notice, or to the fact the said present use may not lawfully be continued, is made in writing to Seller and which Seller is unable or unwilling to remove, remedy or satisfy and which Buyer will not waive, this Agreement notwithstanding any intermediate acts or negotiations in respect of such objections, shall be at an end and all monies paid shall be returned without interest or deduction and Seller, Listing Brokerage and Co-operating Brokerage shall not be liable for any costs or damages. Save as to any valid objection so made by such day and except for any objection going to the root of the title, Buyer shall be conclusively deemed to have accepted Seller's title to the Property. Seller hereby consents to the municipality or other governmental agencies releasing to Buyer details of all outstanding work orders affecting the Property, and Seller agrees to execute and deliver such further authorizations in this regard as Buyer may reasonably require.

12. **CORPORATION DOCUMENTATION:** The Seller shall deliver to the Buyer on or before closing:
    (a) a certified copy of the Resolution of the Board of Directors of the Corporation approving the Buyer as a shareholder and as an occupant of the Unit;
    (b) a share certificate for the Seller's shares in the capital of the Corporation endorsed in favour of the Buyer;
    (c) a certificate or letter from the Corporation confirming:
        (i) with respect to the Property, that all charges and obligations have been paid or discharged as of the date of closing;
        (ii) with respect to the Corporation that the affairs of the Corporation are in order and that there are no legal actions pending against the Corporation or contemplated by the Corporation, that there are no special assessments contemplated by the Corporation, that there are no orders or complaints against the real property by the Building, Health or Fire Departments, that no sale of real property is contemplated, and the Building is not and never has been insulated with Urea-Formaldehyde Foam Insulation.

13. **OCCUPANCY AGREEMENT:** The Buyer agrees on or before closing to enter into an Occupancy Agreement with the Corporation and to abide by the rules and regulations of the Corporation.

14. **TITLE:** Buyer agrees to accept the Corporation's title to the Property subject to all rights and easements registered against title for the supply and installation of telephone services, electricity, gas, sewers, water, television cable facilities and other related services; provided that title to the Property is otherwise good and free from all encumbrances except: (a) as herein expressly provided; (b) any registered restrictions, conditions or covenants that run with the land provided such have been complied with; and (c) any existing municipal agreements, zoning by-laws and/or regulations and utility or service contracts.

15. **DOCUMENTS AND DISCHARGE:** Buyer shall not call for the production of any title deed, abstract, survey or other evidence of title to the Property except such as are in the possession or control of Seller. If a discharge of any Charge/Mortgage, lien or other encumbrance held by a corporation incorporated pursuant to the Trust And Loan Companies Act (Canada), Chartered Bank, Trust Company, Credit Union, Caisse Populaire or Insurance Company and which is not to be assumed by Buyer on completion, is not available in registrable form on completion, Buyer agrees to accept Seller's lawyer's personal undertaking to obtain, out of the closing funds, a discharge in registrable form and to register same, or cause same to be registered, on title within a reasonable period of time after completion, provided that on or before completion Seller shall provide to Buyer a statement prepared by the mortgagee, lienholder or encumbrancer setting out the balance required to obtain the discharge, and, where a real-time electronic cleared funds transfer system is not being used, a direction executed by Seller directing payment to the mortgagee, lienholder or encumbrancer of the amount required to obtain the discharge out of the balance due on completion.

INITIALS OF BUYER(S): ⬭   **INITIALS OF SELLER(S):** ⬭

Form 102   Revised 2015   **Page 3 of 6**

16. **MEETINGS:** Seller represents and warrants to Buyer that at the time of the acceptance of this Offer the Seller has not received a notice convening a special or general meeting of the Corporation respecting; (a) the termination of the government of the property; (b) the winding up or dissolution of the Corporation; (c) any substantial alteration in or substantial addition to the property or the renovation thereof; OR (d) any substantial change in the assets or liabilities of the Corporation; and Seller covenants that if the Seller receives any such notice prior to the date of completion the Seller shall forthwith notify Buyer in writing and the Buyer may thereupon at the Buyer's option declare this Agreement to be null and void and all monies paid by Buyer shall be refunded without interest or deduction.

17. **INSPECTION:** Buyer acknowledges having had the opportunity to inspect the Property and understands that upon acceptance of this offer there shall be a binding agreement of purchase and sale between Buyer and Seller. **The Buyer acknowledges having the opportunity to include a requirement for a property inspection report in this Agreement and agrees that except as may be specifically provided for in this Agreement, the Buyer will not be obtaining a property inspection or property inspection report regarding the Property.**

18. **INSURANCE:** The Unit and all other things being purchased shall be and remain at the risk of the Seller until completion. In the event of substantial damage to the real property Buyer may at the Buyer's option either permit the proceeds of insurance to be used for repair of such damage in accordance with the provisions of the Insurance Trust Agreement or other insurance arrangement, or terminate this Agreement and all deposit monies paid by Buyer hereunder shall be refunded without interest or deduction. If Seller is taking back a Charge/Mortgage, or Buyer is assuming a Charge/Mortgage, Buyer shall supply Seller with reasonable evidence of adequate insurance to protect Seller's or other mortgagee's interest on completion.

19. **RESIDENCY:** (a) Subject to (b) below, the Seller represents and warrants that the Seller is not and on completion will not be a non-resident under the non-residency provisions of the Income Tax Act which representation and warranty shall survive and not merge upon the completion of this transaction and the Seller shall deliver to the Buyer a statutory declaration that Seller is not then a non-resident of Canada;
(b) provided that if the Seller is a non-resident under the non-residency provisions of the Income Tax Act, the Buyer shall be credited towards the Purchase Price with the amount, if any, necessary for Buyer to pay to the Minister of National Revenue to satisfy Buyer's liability in respect of tax payable by Seller under the non-residency provisions of the Income Tax Act by reason of this sale. Buyer shall not claim such credit if Seller delivers on completion the prescribed certificate.

20. **ADJUSTMENTS:** Maintenance expenses and, where billed to the Unit and not the Corporation, realty taxes, including local improvement rates; mortgage interest; rentals; unmetered public or private utilities and fuel; are to be apportioned and allowed to the day of completion, the day of completion itself to be apportioned to the Buyer. There shall be no adjustment for the Seller's share of any reserve or contingency fund to which the Seller may have contributed prior to the date of completion.

21. **TIME LIMITS:** Time shall in all respects be of the essence hereof provided that the time for doing or completing of any matter provided for herein may be extended or abridged by an agreement in writing signed by Seller and Buyer or by their respective lawyers who may be specifically authorized in that regard.

22. **TENDER:** Any tender of documents or money hereunder may be made upon Seller or Buyer or their respective lawyers on the day set for completion. Money shall be tendered with funds drawn on a lawyer's trust account in the form of a bank draft, certified cheque or wire transfer using the Large Value Transfer System

23. **FAMILY LAW ACT:** Seller warrants that spousal consent is not necessary to this transaction under the provisions of the Family Law Act, R.S.O.1990 unless Seller's spouse has executed the consent hereinafter provided.

24. **LEGAL, ACCOUNTING AND ENVIRONMENTAL ADVICE:** The parties acknowledge that any information provided by the brokerage is not legal, tax or environmental advice.

25. **CONSUMER REPORTS: The Buyer is hereby notified that a consumer report containing credit and/or personal information may be referred to in connection with this transaction.**

26. **AGREEMENT IN WRITING:** If there is conflict or discrepancy between any provision added to this Agreement (including any Schedule attached hereto) and any provision in the standard pre-set portion hereof, the added provision shall supersede the standard pre-set provision to the extent of such conflict or discrepancy. This Agreement including any Schedule attached hereto, shall constitute the entire Agreement between Buyer and Seller. There is no representation, warranty, collateral agreement or condition, which affects this Agreement other than as expressed herein. For the purposes of this Agreement, Seller means vendor and Buyer means purchaser. This Agreement shall be read with all changes of gender or number required by the context.

27. **TIME AND DATE:** Any reference to a time and date in this Agreement shall mean the time and date where the property is located.

INITIALS OF BUYER(S): ⬭   **INITIALS OF SELLER(S):** ⬭

Form 102   Revised 2015   **Page 4 of 6**

Exercise 3   Agreement of Purchase and Sale—Co-operative Building Resale Agreement, Page 5 of 6

28. SUCCESSORS AND ASSIGNS: The heirs, executors, administrators, successors and assigns of the undersigned are bound by the terms herein.

SIGNED, SEALED AND DELIVERED in the presence of: IN WITNESS whereof I have hereunto set my hand and seal:

....   ● DATE ....
(Witness)   (Buyer)   (Seal)

....   ● DATE ....
(Witness)   (Buyer)   (Seal)

I, the Undersigned Seller, agree to the above offer. I hereby irrevocably instruct my lawyer to pay directly to the brokerage(s) with whom I have agreed to pay commission, the unpaid balance of the commission together with applicable Harmonized Sales Tax (and any other taxes as may hereafter be applicable), from the proceeds of the sale prior to any payment to the undersigned on completion, as advised by the brokerage(s) to my lawyer.

SIGNED, SEALED AND DELIVERED in the presence of: IN WITNESS whereof I have hereunto set my hand and seal:

....   ● DATE ....
(Witness)   (Seller)   (Seal)

....   ● DATE ....
(Witness)   (Seller)   (Seal)

SPOUSAL CONSENT: The Undersigned Spouse of the Seller hereby consents to the disposition evidenced herein pursuant to the provisions of the Family Law Act, R.S.O.1990, and hereby agrees with the Buyer that he/she will execute all necessary or incidental documents to give full force and effect to the sale evidenced herein.

....   ● DATE ....
(Witness)   (Spouse)   (Seal)

CONFIRMATION OF ACCEPTANCE: Notwithstanding anything contained herein to the contrary, I confirm this Agreement with all changes both typed

and written was finally accepted by all parties at .... a.m./p.m. this .... day of.., 20..........

....
(Signature of Seller or Buyer)

INFORMATION ON BROKERAGE(S)

Listing Brokerage .... Tel.No.(..............)....................................

....
(Salesperson / Broker Name)

Co-op/Buyer Brokerage .... Tel.No.(..............)....................................

....
(Salesperson / Broker Name)

ACKNOWLEDGEMENT

I acknowledge receipt of my signed copy of this accepted Agreement of Purchase and Sale and I authorize the Brokerage to forward a copy to my lawyer. | I acknowledge receipt of my signed copy of this accepted Agreement of Purchase and Sale and I authorize the Brokerage to forward a copy to my lawyer.

.... DATE .... DATE ....
(Seller)   (Buyer)

.... DATE .... DATE ....
(Seller)   (Buyer)
Address for Service ....   Address for Service ....

.... Tel.No.(..........)...   .... Tel.No.(..........)...
Seller's Lawyer ....   Buyer's Lawyer ....

Address ....   Address ....

Email ....   Email ....

(..........)........................... (..........)...........   (..........)........................... (..........)...........
    Tel.No.   FAX No.   Tel.No.   FAX No.

Property Manager: ....
                    (Name)   (Address)   (Tel No.,FAX No.)

FOR OFFICE USE ONLY   **COMMISSION TRUST AGREEMENT**

To: Co-operating Brokerage shown on the foregoing Agreement of Purchase and Sale:
In consideration for the Co-operating Brokerage procuring the foregoing Agreement of Purchase and Sale, I hereby declare that all moneys received or receivable by me in connection with the Transaction as contemplated in the MLS® Rules and Regulations of my Real Estate Board shall be receivable and held in trust. This agreement shall constitute a Commission Trust Agreement as defined in the MLS® Rules and shall be subject to and governed by the MLS® Rules pertaining to Commission Trust.

DATED as of the date and time of the acceptance of the foregoing Agreement of Purchase and Sale.   Acknowledged by:

....
(Authorized to bind the Listing Brokerage)   (Authorized to bind the Co-operating Brokerage)

Form 102   Revised 2015   **Page 5 of 6**

OREA Ontario Real Estate Association

Form 102
for use in the Province of Ontario

Schedule A
Agreement of Purchase and Sale –
Co-operative Building Resale

This Schedule is attached to and forms part of the Agreement of Purchase and Sale between:

BUYER, ..., and

SELLER, ...

for the purchase and sale of ....

.... dated the .... day of ...., 20.............

Buyer agrees to pay the balance as follows:

This form must be initialed by all parties to the Agreement of Purchase and Sale.

INITIALS OF BUYER(S): ⬭   **INITIALS OF SELLER(S):** ⬭

Form 102   Revised 2015   **Page 6 of 6**

CHAPTER 2

Residential Condominium

Introduction

Condominium ownership represents a major sector of the Ontario real estate market. Condos have broad-based appeal ranging from luxury downtown accommodations to recreational lakeside suites and seniors' retirement villas.

As a creature of statute, condominiums are understandably burdened with complexities. This chapter introduces fundamentals necessary to understand how condominiums are created, what condominium types are found in rural and urban markets, and essential knowledge when drafting agreements.

In recent years, legislation has dramatically expanded the types of condominiums available to consumers in Ontario. Prior to the current legislation, only standard condominiums could be registered, but now both leasehold and freehold condominiums are available, including creative options relating to common element, vacant land and phased condominium projects.

This chapter provides condominium fundamentals for anyone involved in the listing, marketing and sale of this property type. However, advanced courses are strongly recommended for those seeking to concentrate on this expanding sector of the Ontario real estate marketplace.

Learning Outcomes

At the conclusion of this chapter, students will be able to:

- Describe basic concepts and legal structures underlying condominium creation.
- Describe planning and construction considerations relevant to condominium creation.
- Identify and describe different types of condominium corporations.
- Discuss the role/responsibilities of the board of directors in governing condominiums.
- Compare the *Agreement of Purchase and Sale* (OREA Form 100) with the *Agreement of Purchase and Sale–Condominium Resale* (OREA Form 101).
- Outline the overall structure and purpose of the status certificate in marketing resale condominiums.
- Identify selected issues impacting the listing and selling of resale condominiums, including use restrictions, owner alterations and reserve funds.
- Analyze situations involving the listing and sale of residential resale circumstances, including appropriate agreements.

CREATING A CONDOMINIUM

A condominium is created at law through the registration of a declaration (often referred to as the condominium constitution) and a description; i.e., a diagrammatic presentation of the property.

DECLARATION	DESCRIPTION
The declaration contains both required and optional information as set out in the *Condominium Act*. Required information includes: <ul><li>Statement that the *Condominium Act* governs.</li><li>Consent of registered mortgagees.</li><li>Proportionate share of common elements appurtenant to each unit.</li><li>Proportionate contribution of unit owners to common expenses.</li><li>Corporation address for service.</li><li>Common elements for designated units (exclusive use common element), if applicable.</li><li>Any conditions required by approving authority.</li></ul>	The description contains a series of plans, surveys and specifications describing the property and structures, together with certificates attesting to compliance and accuracy, for example: <ul><li>Plan of survey.</li><li>Architectural plans and Certificate of Architect.</li><li>Unit boundaries.</li><li>Unit shape, dimension and location.</li><li>Structural plans (if any) and Certificate of Engineer.</li><li>Certificate of Ontario Land Surveyor.</li><li>All interests appurtenant to the land that is included in the property.</li></ul> Documentation will vary based on individual projects.

Planning Act Requirements

The initial step in the development process involves obtaining the necessary approvals under the *Planning Act*. Such approvals are given either by the municipality, or the Minister of Municipal Affairs and Housing where the municipality is not authorized to grant such approvals. Essentially, condominium projects go through much the same process from a planning perspective, as do plans of subdivision (discussed in *Land, Structures and Real Estate Trading*).

APPLICATION PROCESS

Applications for condominiums are processed under Section 51 of the *Planning Act* and in accordance with Ontario Regulation 544/06. Exact procedures can vary by municipality. The following description is by way of example only.

The application must be completed either by the owner of the lands or an authorized agent. The applicant must ensure that the site and the proposal is consistent with the health, safety and welfare of future residents, with sufficient studies included to properly support the application. Municipalities typically require a pre-submission consultation to ensure that the project is reasonable and aligns with established planning parameters.

DRAFT PLAN AND FINAL APPROVAL

A draft plan is submitted with the application and circulated to appropriate persons and public agencies that may have an interest in the application. These stakeholders may require additional studies in support of the application; e.g., traffic, environmental and noise impact. The range of studies required is normally addressed at the pre-submission consultation. A site audit is required detailing grading, drainage, landscaping and lighting plans, along with the detailed scope of work for the project. Draft approval is granted upon successful completion of the planning and approval process.

Registration occurs when the Ministry of Municipal Affairs and Housing and the local municipality (including the regional municipality, if applicable) are satisfied that:

- everything has been completed in accordance with the Ontario Building Code and Ontario Fire Code; and
- that everything contained in the declaration and description has been provided.

Once completed, the final plan is approved and registered. Registrants interested in detailed procedures for draft approval, final approval and registration should contact the local municipality.

Construction Requirements

All condominiums must comply with the Ontario Building Code. If a residential condominium is being built, the developer must meet various requirements set out by the Tarion Warranty Corporation. If the building is a high-rise condominium project that falls under Part 3 of the Ontario Building Code, the developer must comply with design and site review requirements set out by Tarion. This may also apply when building a low-rise condominium, which has elements falling under Part 3 of the Building Code, at the discretion of the Registrar.

As clarification, Part 3 of the Ontario Building Code focuses on construction components involved in high-rise buildings, while Part 9 relates to housing and small buildings.

Condominium Registration

Condominium legal structure, as mentioned earlier, is established through a declaration, aptly referred to as the condominium constitution and the description (diagrammatic representations including surveys of the land and improvements).

A condominium is created in law when both the declaration and the description are registered. The individual who holds the freehold or leasehold interest in the land is known as the declarant. The declarant invokes the *Condominium Act* through this registration process. Registered encumbrancers, such as mortgagees and lien holders, must consent in the declaration to the invocation of the Act.

A corporation without share capital is automatically formed upon incorporation in which members are the unit owners (excepting a *common elements condominium* discussed later). The land registrar for the applicable land registry office gives the corporation a name and sequential number; e.g., Waterloo South Condominium Corporation 986. The objects of the corporation centre on management of the property and corporation assets. These functions are paid for by unit owners through common expenses, in proportions specified in the declaration.

The corporation has a duty to effect unit owner compliance under the Act, the declaration and the by-laws and has the power to own, acquire, encumber and dispose of real and personal property according to the by-laws. The corporation does not provide limited liability. The unit owners are personally liable for all the debts and obligations of the condominium corporation.

CONDOMINIUM STRUCTURE AND TYPES

The condominium corporation is divided into units and common elements (except with the common elements condominiums). Owners exclusively occupy their respective units, while being tenants in common in the common elements. Parking and/or storage areas may or may not be included with the unit.

If parking and/or storage areas are provided, owners may own such facilities, lease them, be granted exclusive rights to use or simply be assigned such facilities on a discretionary basis. Most parking and storage areas in Ontario condominiums are either owned or exclusively used.

Unit

A unit is that portion of the property so designated in the description and broadly described as the space defined by boundaries including all the land, structures and fixtures within that defined space. For purposes of the Act, all units are deemed to be property with each owner having exclusive ownership and use of his/her unit. Units are clearly differentiated from common elements, which are held by the owners (as tenants in common (undivided interest)), in proportions as set out in the declaration. A common elements condominium does not have any units.

Common Elements

The common elements consist of all property within the condominium corporation, except the units. The clear delineation of units vs. common elements is essential. Registrants must understand the scope of ownership when listing and selling condominiums. Common elements are held by the owners, as tenants in common (undivided interest), in proportions as set out in the declaration. One or more owners may have exclusive use of selected common elements, such as parking spaces and balconies.

The board of directors may make an addition, alteration or improvement to the common elements without owner approval, unless the owners requisition a meeting and vote against the proposed work. Additions, alterations and improvements of a substantial nature require approval of the owners who own 66 % of the units. Owners may make additions, alterations and improvements to the common elements (e.g., installing a patio area or fence on an exclusive use common area) but are subject to board approval, a formal agreement and other criteria as set out in the Act.

Units vs. Common Elements   CURIOSITY

The effect of condominium registration is to divide the property into units and common elements. Appurtenant to each unit is a proportionate ownership share of the common elements. The proportions of such shares are specified in the declaration. Each unit owner owns his/her unit separately, together with an undivided interest in the common elements.

Each unit owner is responsible for a proportionate share of common expenses, which is also set out in the declaration. As a general guideline, the allocation of ownership and responsibility for common expenses are in direct proportion to the unit size in relation to the total size of all units, but variations exist. Further, the allocations for ownership and common expenses can differ. Expert advice is required on such matters.

Parking

Parking may be allowed in or on a unit, on the common elements or on an exclusive area within those common elements, depending on the declaration established for a condominium. Parking arrangements, along with any restrictions, are fully documented. Information about visitor parking is detailed including availability, what costs (if any) apply and, if no visitor parking is available, what other facilities exist and where.

Registrants most frequently encounter parking issues in resale units. Buyers need to carefully review all documentation provided with the status certificate to determine which type of parking is provided and what parking spaces, if any, are included with the unit. Also, restrictions may apply regarding the parking of recreational vehicles, commercial vehicles, small utility trailers and boats. Ceiling clearances may be a factor as well in underground garages, depending on the size of vehicle(s) driven.

Parking spaces can generally be grouped under the following four types:

Freehold	The unit owner owns the parking space, either within the unit description or separately titled. If the latter, the unit owner is typically permitted to sell the space(s) to another owner in the complex at fair market value, however, restrictions regarding such matters should be fully investigated.
Leasehold	The condominium corporation retains parking spaces and leases them to unit owners.
Exclusive Use Common Element	The condominium corporation owns the parking spaces, but grants the rights to use specific spaces as set out in the declaration.
Allocated/ Assigned	The condominium corporation owns the parking spaces and assigns spaces to unit owners on a discretionary basis.

Storage (Locker)

Storage lockers, as with parking spaces, can be grouped under four categories:

- freehold in which the unit owner owns the storage locker;
- leasehold in which the condominium corporation retains ownership and leases to unit owners;
- exclusive use common elements in which a right to specific locker space is set out in the declaration; and
- allocated/assigned in which lockers are assigned on a discretionary basis by the corporation.

Condominium Types

Condominium corporations can be broadly grouped into leasehold (leasehold condominium) or freehold (standard, common element, vacant land and phased condominiums). Only standard condominiums could be registered prior to the new Act. Each new type has its own specific market appeal.

LEASEHOLD

A leasehold condominium is a condominium corporation in which all units and their appurtenant common interests are subject to leasehold interests by the owners. All leasehold interests in units, along with common interests, must be for the same term.

Market Focus

A leasehold interest in land can be divided into units and common elements and, subject to registration of a declaration and description, be described as a leasehold condominium. Each leasehold interest and its appurtenant common interest is valid even if the lessor is the owner of that interest. Leasehold interests and appurtenant common interests are for the same term. Leasehold terms cannot be less than 40 years (less a day) nor more than 99 years. Owners of units do not require consent to transfer, mortgage, lease or otherwise deal with their interest.

FREEHOLD—STANDARD

A standard condominium is a freehold condominium that is not a common elements or a vacant land condominium. Condominium corporations created prior to the new *Condominium Act* coming into force are classified as standard condominiums.

FREEHOLD—COMMON ELEMENTS

A common elements condominium corporation consists of common interests only held by owners in those common elements, but having no units. All references to *unit* or *proposed unit* in the Act are deemed to be references to a common interest in the corporation.

Market Focus

The common elements condominium corporation represents a significant advance in condominium legislation. Such corporations must be freehold, and not a vacant land or a phased condominium. Each owner of an interest in the common elements must own a freehold parcel of land to which his or her common interest attaches.

Upon registration of the declaration and description, the common interest of an owner attaches to that owner's parcel of land (e.g., a home located nearby) and remains attached even if that home is subsequently sold (the home is referred to as a POTL or Parcel of Tied Land). A golf course, ski hill, park or road might be a common elements condominium in which owners are required to pay for maintenance, repair and modifications.

FREEHOLD—VACANT LAND

The vacant land condominium is a condominium providing for the development and sale of units (i.e., land), without the necessity of immediately completing structures.

Market Focus

Developers can market condominium ownership, complete services and related infrastructure, sell land to buyers subject to building requirements and register the condominium corporation—all prior to any construction occurring on individual land units.

Titles are transferred to buyers with homes and/or other structures to be built later. The declaration contains restrictions concerning future construction; e.g., building size, design, standards and commencement/completion time frames. Ownership interests are based on land size. The unit owner must provide insurance for buildings and structures on the unit. By-laws can be passed regarding minimum maintenance requirements for units.

The declarant must construct any buildings and structures on common elements prior to registration or provide a bond or other acceptable security for subsequent construction. The security is released once all buildings, structures, facilities and services are completed and approved.

SECTION I   A CLOSER LOOK AT TRADING DIFFERENT TYPES OF PROPERTIES

FREEHOLD—PHASED

A phased condominium is a condominium corporation operating as a freehold corporation in which the declarant may create additional units or common elements within the corporation. The term phase refers to additional units and common elements that are created in accordance with the Act, upon the registration of an amendment to both the original declaration and the description.

Market Focus

The phased condominium provides flexibility for declarants in the development process by permitting the registration of an initial development as a condominium and then being permitted to bring in successive units/common elements under that single condominium corporation. Under the previous Act, declarants involved with large developments had to register individual condominium corporations when involved with large projects involving several buildings and/or phases.

The ability to bring successive units/common elements under a single corporation produces economy of scale; e.g., avoids the need for several board of directors within a larger development. Further, the grouping of several phases offers bulk buying advantages when purchasing services (e.g., utilities).

CONDOMINIUM GOVERNANCE

Board of Directors

A board of directors is elected in accordance with the Act and by-laws. The board consists of at least three persons or a greater number as specified in the by-laws. Directors are required to be a minimum age of 18 years and cannot be undischarged bankrupts or mentally incompetent persons.

A director ceases to be a director if either of the two latter events occur, or the individual concerned does not obtain a discharge for a lien (relating to the payment of common expenses), within 90 days of the registration of that lien. Directors are appointed for three years or such lesser period as specified in the by-laws. All business of the corporation is conducted at meetings of the board of directors.

STANDARD OF CARE

Directors must adhere to a standard of care in their role by acting honestly and in good faith while exercising care, diligence and skill of a reasonable person in carrying out their function. Directors can rely in good faith on financial statements, reports or opinions of relevant experts (e.g., accountants, lawyers or engineers) and not be liable should a breach of duty occur. Directors may be indemnified and saved harmless by the corporation and the corporation may acquire appropriate insurance. However, such protections do not apply if the director acts dishonestly and/or not in good faith.

FIRST BOARD

A board of directors, appointed by the declarant, is required within 10 days following condominium registration. The first board consists of at least three persons, who hold office until the turn-over meeting. The first board must call a meeting before the later of:

- the 30th day after the declarant transfers 20% of the units; or
- the 90th day after the first unit is transferred.

At this meeting, the owners may elect two directors who hold office, in addition to those appointed by the declarant. The first board must call a turn-over meeting to elect a new board.

TURNOVER MEETING

The turnover meeting relates to the transfer of control from declarant to owners. The turnover meeting must be called not more than 21 days following the time when the declarant ceases to be the registered owner of the majority of units. Four objectives are addressed in a turnover meeting.

1. ELECTION OF NEW BOARD

2. DECLARANT DELIVERY OF DOCUMENTS (AT MEETING)

- Seal of the Corporation.
- Minute book (including the registered declaration, registered by-laws, current rules and minutes of owners' and board meetings).
- Copies of all agreements entered into by the corporation, the declarant or the declarant's representatives (includes management contracts, deeds, leases, licenses and easements).
- Copies of all insurance policies, insurance trust agreements, memoranda and related items.
- Bills of sale or transfers for items that are assets of the corporation, but not part of the property.
- Records concerning owners and mortgagees.
- Records regarding leasing of units.
- Any other records relating to units and employees of the corporation.

3. DECLARANT DELIVERY OF DOCUMENTS (WITHIN 30 DAYS FOLLOWING MEETING)

- As-built architectural, structural, engineering, mechanical, electrical and plumbing plans.
- Existing warranties/guarantees concerning equipment, fixtures and chattels included in the sale of units or common elements not protected by warranties/guarantees given directly to the unit purchaser.
- As-built specifications including any substantive changes from original plans.
- All existing plans for underground site services, site grading, drainage, landscaping and telecommunications services, along with any other plans or information not already referenced.
- Documentation relating to the *Ontario New Home Warranties Plan Act* (if applicable).
- Owner/corporation responsibilities concerning repair after damage and maintenance.
- Details of what constitutes a standard unit.
- Corporation financial records.
- All reserve fund studies completed or required to be completed at the time that the meeting is held. If the meeting is held after nine months following registration, first year reserve study must be provided.
- Most current disclosure statement.
- Any other materials as required by the Regulations.

4. DECLARANT DELIVERY OF DOCUMENTS (WITHIN 60 DAYS FOLLOWING MEETING)

- Audited financial statements, at the corporation's expense, as of the last day of the month in which the meeting is held.

The corporation may make application to the Ontario Court (General Division) if materials are not supplied. Non-compliance by the declarant can result in an order by the Court to comply, along with the possibility of damages, court costs and fines.

By-Laws

By-laws are documented standard procedures and requirements regarding a condominium's internal operations that involve governance; e.g., establishing procedures for borrowing funds, setting director remuneration and other regulatory matters. By-laws are made, amended or repealed by the board of directors and must be consistent with the Act and the declaration. By-laws are not effective unless the owners of the majority of units vote in favour. A copy must be registered in the land registry office. Registered by-laws made by the declarant (i.e., the owner/developer) are valid until replaced.

Rules

Rules are directives and regulations developed by a condominium corporation that promote the safety, security and welfare of owners, as well as the property and assets of the corporation. Rules also prevent unreasonable interference with the use and enjoyment of common elements.

Registrants should be aware of rules impacting condominiums being marketed, as they can directly impact the purchaser. The board of directors can make, amend or repeal rules that are reasonable concerning the common elements. The board must provide owners with a copy of the rules (made, amended or repealed), the effective date and notice that they may requisition a meeting. Rules are not effective until approved by the owners at a requisitioned meeting within 30 days. If no meeting is requisitioned within that period, the rules become effective.

| *Enforcing the Declaration* | RESIDENTIAL CASE LAW |

In 2001, a condominium buyer was seeking a residential condominium complex that permitted dogs. Ultimately, that buyer entered into an agreement to purchase a unit through a real estate salesperson who was aware that the buyer had a dog. The condominium corporation clearly stated in its Declaration that no animals...including those usually considered pets could be kept or allowed in the units. The agreement made no reference to the pet prohibition, which had been passed by the condominium corporation approximately 10 months earlier in 2000. The offer also did not include a condition allowing the buyer time to satisfy herself that a dog would be permitted.

The sale closed approximately one month later on May 1st, 2001. Fifteen days following closing, the condominium corporation's solicitors wrote to the new owner stating that having a dog in the complex was contrary to the Declaration. In a subsequent letter, the corporation advised the owner that it would consider an amendment to the Declaration if other owners agreed. The new owner and other unit owners lobbied, but the resulting poll was insufficient to amend the Declaration. In March 2002, a follow-up letter once again warned that legal action would be taken if the dog was not removed. The action commenced approximately six months later.

The owner asked the Court to dismiss the action by exercising its discretion to exempt the dog from applicable provisions in the Declaration. Further, the owner argued that the condominium corporation did not take action quickly enough and, therefore, laches applies. Laches refers to negligent or unreasonable delay in pursuing a legal remedy. Lastly, the owner argued that the pet prohibition would be an act of discrimination pursuant to the Ontario Human Rights Code, as she suffered from an identified mental disorder involving depression.

The Court found in favour of the condominium corporation stating that the prohibition was reasonable, the buyer employed both a real estate representative and a lawyer to provide guidance and the Estoppel Certificate (now referred to as a Status Certificate) highlighted the restriction. Interestingly, the Judge commented:

...perhaps her quarrel is with one of the professionals advising her.

On the matter of discrimination, the Court found that not having the dog did constitute a form of stress relating to her depression, but that such would not constitute a disability within the meaning of the Ontario Human Rights Code. The owner was ordered to permanently remove the dog from the unit and comply with the Declaration.

continued...

COMMENTARY

Several points warrant close attention by real estate registrants involved with condominium properties.

Declaration/ Enforcement	Documentation is key to any condominium sale. Provisions in the Declaration are presumed valid and will be enforced. This document is fundamental to the corporation and inextricably tied to title acquired by a unit owner. Further, the condominium corporation has a duty to take necessary steps in its enforcement.
Salesperson Involvement	In this instance, the owner dispute centred on the condominium corporation. However, all registrants should make special note of the Judge's comment: *...perhaps her quarrel is with one of the professionals advising her.*
Ontario Human Rights Code	Salespersons are reminded that while this particular owner's argument concerning the Ontario Human Rights Code failed, no pet provisions are subject to exceptions involving disabilities; e.g., seeing-eye dogs for the blind, as defined under that Code.
Exclusions/ Restrictions	Don't assume anything when marketing residential condominiums. Pet exclusions and restrictions can be readily located in the Declaration, By-laws and/or Rules. Do your home-work. Also, while pets may be permitted in various complexes, make certain buyers are aware of other restrictions and provisions that apply, for example: <ul><li>Size (weight) and number of pets.</li><li>Unit owners are responsible for damage caused by their pets.</li><li>Pets must be carried in lobbies, hallways and internal walkways.</li><li>Dogs must be on a leash at all times.</li><li>All pets must be registered with the condominium corporation.</li><li>Any noise or objectionable behaviour will require the pet's removal from the complex.</li></ul>

THE RESALE CONDOMINIUM AGREEMENT

Resale condominium units pose distinct challenges. Numerous rules, procedures, by-laws and other documents impact both ownership rights and day-to-day activities. Further, the buyer is not only acquiring a unit, but also the common elements and associated common expenses. Buyers must carefully consider the financial well-being of the condominium corporation, as well as how effectively it is being managed.

Sale of Resale Units

The *Agreement of Purchase and Sale–Condominium Resale*, a standard OREA form, is designed for resale condominium transactions. In addition to pre-printed clauses unique to this form, real estate registrants should clearly delineate what is included with the property; i.e., storage lockers and/or parking spaces. Further, any improvements or additions completed by the owner should be discussed and duly noted.

The status certificate, issued by the condominium corporation, sets out important details regarding the resale condominium unit and the condominium corporation.

Drafting the Agreement

The *Agreement of Purchase and Sale–Condominium Resale* (OREA Form 101) differs in several respects from its residential resale counterpart (OREA Form 100). A fully completed condominium agreement is illustrated as an example and to highlight additional clauses.

Carefully Review All Clauses	CAUTION	

Additional clauses are highlighted in this chapter, but not all wording variations. For example, pre-printed wordings involving *Title* and *Title Search* vary to reflect condominium-specific requirements, including statutory compliance with the *Condominium Act* requirements. Further, the clause found in the *Agreement of Purchase and Sale* relating to compliance with subdivision control has understandably been deleted.

Registrants are expected to be fully conversant with all pre-printed wordings in the *Agreement of Purchase and Sale— Condominium Resale*. An exercise is included at the end of the chapter regarding both major and minor differences.

Major Differences:
OREA Form 101 (compared to OREA Form 100)

PROPERTY DESCRIPTION
Details property particulars including parking and locker details.

> **SELLER,** ...., the following
> (Full legal names of all Sellers)
>
> **PROPERTY:**
> a unit in the condominium property known as .... No.........................
> (Apartment/Townhouse/Suite/Unit)
>
> located at ....
>
> in the ....
>
> being .... Condominium Plan No ....
> (Legal Name of Condominium Corporation)
>
> Unit Number .... Level No. .... Building No. .... together with ownership
>
> or exclusive use of Parking Space(s) ...., together with ownership or exclusive use of
> (Number(s), Level(s))
>
> Locker(s) ...., together with Seller's proportionate undivided tenancy-in-common interest
> (Number(s), Level(s))
> in the common elements appurtenant to the Unit as described in the Declaration and Description including the exclusive right to use such other parts of the common elements appurtenant to the Unit as may be specified in the Declaration and Description: the Unit, the proportionate interest in the common elements appurtenant thereto, and the exclusive use portions of the common elements, being herein called the "Property".
>
> **PURCHASE PRICE:**   Dollars (CDN$) ....

CLAUSE 7: COMMON EXPENSES
Seller warranty regarding amount of common expenses payable.

> The Buyer agrees to co-operate and execute such documentation as may be required to facilitate such assumption.
>
> 7. **COMMON EXPENSES:** Seller warrants to Buyer that the common expenses presently payable to the Condominium Corporation in respect of the
>
> Property are approximately $ .... per month, which amount includes the following: ....
>
> ....
>
> ....

CLAUSE 8: PARKING AND LOCKERS
Applicable if parking and lockers are assigned and at what additional cost.

> **8. PARKING AND LOCKERS:** Parking and Lockers are as described above or assigned as follows: ....
>
> .... at an additional cost of: ....

CLAUSE 13: STATUS CERTIFICATE AND MANAGEMENT OF CONDOMINIUM
Seller represents and warrants that there are no special assessments contemplated or legal actions pending. Seller gives consent to obtain status certificate. Buyer acknowledges that the condominium corporation may have entered into a management agreement.

> Titles Office or such other location agreeable to both lawyers.
>
> **13. STATUS CERTIFICATE AND MANAGEMENT OF CONDOMINIUM:** Seller represents and warrants to Buyer that there are no special assessments contemplated by the Condominium Corporation, and there are no legal actions pending by or against or contemplated by the Condominium Corporation. The Seller consents to a request by the Buyer or the Buyer's authorized representative for a Status Certificate from the Condominium Corporation. Buyer acknowledges that the Condominium Corporation may have entered into a Management Agreement for the management of the condominium property.
>
> **14. DOCUMENTS AND DISCHARGE:** Buyer shall not call for the production of any title deed, abstract, survey or other evidence of title to the Property

CLAUSE 15: MEETINGS
Seller represents and warrants that no special meeting has been convened for condominium termination or any substantial changes or alterations.

> funds transfer system is not being used, a direction executed by Seller directing payment to the mortgagee of the amount required to obtain the discharge out of the balance due on completion.
>
> **15. MEETINGS:** Seller represents and warrants to Buyer that at the time of the acceptance of this Offer the Seller has not received a notice convening a special or general meeting of the Condominium Corporation respecting; (a) the termination of the government of the condominium property; (b) any substantial alteration in or substantial addition to the common elements or the renovation thereof; OR (c) any substantial change in the assets or liabilities of the Condominium Corporation; and Seller covenants that if Seller receives any such notice prior to the date of completion Seller shall forthwith notify Buyer in writing and Buyer may thereupon at Buyer's option declare this Agreement to be null and void and all monies paid by Buyer shall be refunded without interest or deduction.
>
> INITIALS OF BUYER(S): ( )   INITIALS OF SELLER(S): ( )

CLAUSE 17: APPROVAL OF THE AGREEMENT
Agreement is null and void if approval (if required) is not given by the condominium corporation.

> this Agreement, the Buyer will not be obtaining a property inspection or property inspection report regarding the Property.
>
> **17. APPROVAL OF THE AGREEMENT:** In the event that consent to this sale is required to be given by the Condominium Corporation or the Board of Directors, the Seller will apply forthwith for the requisite consent, and if such consent is refused, then this Agreement shall be null and void and the deposit monies paid hereunder shall be refunded without interest or other penalty to the Buyer.
>
> **18. INSURANCE:** The Unit and all other things being purchased shall be and remain at the risk of the Seller until completion. In the event of substantial

Sample Agreement
A fully completed *Agreement of Purchase and Sale—Condominium Resale* is illustrated on the following pages.

OREA Ontario Real Estate Association

Agreement of Purchase and Sale
Condominium Resale

Form 101
for use in the Province of Ontario

This Agreement of Purchase and Sale dated this .... **8th** .... day of .... **February** .... 20 **XX**

BUYER, ... **Derek William Trotter and Deborah Anne Cormier** .... , agrees to purchase from
(Full legal names of all Buyers)

SELLER, ... **Mary Ellen Rose and John Daniel Rose** .... , the following
(Full legal names of all Sellers)

PROPERTY:
a unit in the condominium property known as .... **Unit** .... No. **901**
(Apartment/Townhouse/Suite/Unit)

located at .... **2072 Marsland Drive** ....

in the .... **City of Anycity, Regional Municipality of Anyregion** ....

being .... **Anyregion** .... Condominium Plan No **288**
(Legal Name of Condominium Corporation)

Unit Number .... **1** .... Level No. .... **9** .... Building No. .... together with ownership

or exclusive use of Parking Space(s) .... **123 Level A** .... , together with ownership or exclusive use of
(Number(s), Level(s))

Locker(s) .... **123 Level B** .... , together with Seller's proportionate undivided tenancy-in-common interest
(Number(s), Level(s))

in the common elements appurtenant to the Unit as described in the Declaration and Description including the exclusive right to use such other parts of the common elements appurtenant to the Unit as may be specified in the Declaration and Description: the Unit, the proportionate interest in the common elements appurtenant thereto, and the exclusive use portions of the common elements, being herein called the "Property".

PURCHASE PRICE: Dollars (CDN$) **$218,000.00**

.... **Two Hundred and Eighteen Thousand**-- Dollars

DEPOSIT: Buyer submits .... **Herewith** ....
(Herewith/Upon Acceptance/as otherwise described in this Agreement)

.... **Eight Thousand**-- Dollars (CDN$) **$8,000.00**

by negotiable cheque payable to .... **ABC Realty Inc.** .... "Deposit Holder" to be held in trust pending completion or other termination of this Agreement and to be credited toward the Purchase Price on completion. For the purposes of this Agreement, "Upon Acceptance" shall mean that the Buyer is required to deliver the deposit to the Deposit Holder within 24 hours of the acceptance of this Agreement. The parties to this Agreement hereby acknowledge that, unless otherwise provided for in this Agreement, the Deposit Holder shall place the deposit in trust in the Deposit Holder's non-interest bearing Real Estate Trust Account and no interest shall be earned, received or paid on the deposit.

Buyer agrees to pay the balance as more particularly set out in Schedule A attached.

SCHEDULE(S) A .... **attached hereto form(s) part of this Agreement.**

1. **IRREVOCABILITY:** This offer shall be irrevocable by .... **Buyer** .... until **5:00** ~~a.m.~~/p.m. on the **10th**
(Seller/Buyer)

day of .... **February** .... 20 **XX** , after which time, if not accepted, this offer shall be null and void and the deposit shall be returned to the Buyer in full without interest.

2. **COMPLETION DATE:** This Agreement shall be completed by no later than 6:00 p.m. on the **31st** day of .... **March** .... ,

20 **XX** Upon completion, vacant possession of the property shall be given to the Buyer unless otherwise provided for in this Agreement.

INITIALS OF BUYER(S): (*DT DC*)   **INITIALS OF SELLER(S):** (*MR JR*)

Form 101   Revised 2015   **Page 1 of 6**

3. NOTICES: The Seller hereby appoints the Listing Brokerage as agent for the Seller for the purpose of giving and receiving notices pursuant to this Agreement. Where a Brokerage (Buyer's Brokerage) has entered into a representation agreement with the Buyer, the Buyer hereby appoints the Buyer's Brokerage as agent for the purpose of giving and receiving notices pursuant to this Agreement. **Where a Brokerage represents both the Seller and the Buyer (multiple representation), the Brokerage shall not be appointed or authorized to be agent for either the Buyer or the Seller for the purpose of giving and receiving notices.** Any notice relating hereto or provided for herein shall be in writing. In addition to any provision contained herein and in any Schedule hereto, this offer, any counter-offer, notice of acceptance thereof or any notice to be given or received pursuant to this Agreement or any Schedule hereto (any of them, "Document") shall be deemed given and received when delivered personally or hand delivered to the Address for Service provided in the Acknowledgement below, or where a facsimile number or email address is provided herein, when transmitted electronically to that facsimile number or email address, respectively, in which case, the signature(s) of the party (parties) shall be deemed to be original.

FAX No.: .... 519-555-2121 ....

(For delivery of Documents to Seller)

FAX No.: .... 519-444-2121 ....

(For delivery of Documents to Buyer)

Email Address: .... admin@abcrealty.com ....

(For delivery of Documents to Seller)

Email Address: .... notices@xyzrealestate.com ....

(For delivery of Documents to Buyer)

4. CHATTELS INCLUDED: All wall-to-wall carpeting, all window coverings including drapery rods, teak spice rack located in the kitchen, electric stove (Dominion Model 250, black), refrigerator/freezer (Dominion Model 330, black), dishwasher (WhisperQuiet, Model 360, black), and stacking washer/dryer (Luxor Fountain Model 550).

Unless otherwise stated in this Agreement or any Schedule hereto, Seller agrees to convey all fixtures and chattels included in the Purchase Price free from all liens, encumbrances or claims affecting the said fixtures and chattels.

5. FIXTURES EXCLUDED: Ebony-framed mirror in hallway, shelf unit in study

6. RENTAL ITEMS (Including Lease, Lease to Own): The following equipment is rented and **not** included in the Purchase Price. The Buyer ` agrees to assume the rental contract(s), if assumable:

N/A

The Buyer agrees to co-operate and execute such documentation as may be required to facilitate such assumption.

7. COMMON EXPENSES: Seller warrants to Buyer that the common expenses presently payable to the Condominium Corporation in respect of the Property are approximately $ .... 478.25 .... per month, which amount includes the following: heat, hydro, hot water, water charges, central air conditioning and insurance (common elements)

8. PARKING AND LOCKERS: Parking and Lockers are as described above or assigned as follows: .... N/A .... at an additional cost of: ....

INITIALS OF BUYER(S): (*DT DC*)

INITIALS OF SELLER(S): (*MR JR*)

Form 101   Revised 2015   **Page 2 of 6**

Fully Completed Sample   Agreement of Purchase and Sale—Condominium Resale, Page 3 of 6

9. **HST:** If the sale of the Property (Real Property as described above) is subject to Harmonized Sales Tax (HST), then such tax shall be .... **included in** .... the Purchase Price. If the sale of the Property is not subject to HST, Seller agrees to certify on or before
(included in/in addition to)
closing, that the sale of the Property is not subject to HST. Any HST on chattels, if applicable, is not included in the Purchase Price.

10. **TITLE SEARCH:** Buyer shall be allowed until 6:00 p.m. on the ..**15th**.. day of ....**March**................, 20**XX**.., (Requisition Date) to examine the title to the Property at Buyer's own expense and until the earlier of: (i) thirty days from the later of the Requisition Date or the date on which the conditions in this Agreement are fulfilled or otherwise waived or; (ii) five days prior to completion, to satisfy Buyer that there are no

outstanding work orders or deficiency notices affecting the Property, and that its present use (..**condominium apartment, single-family residential**..) may be lawfully continued. If within that time any valid objection to title or to any outstanding work order or deficiency notice, or to the fact the said present use may not lawfully be continued, is made in writing to Seller and which Seller is unable or unwilling to remove, remedy or satisfy or obtain insurance save and except against risk of fire (Title Insurance) in favour of the Buyer and any mortgagee, (with all related costs at the expense of the Seller), and which Buyer will not waive, this Agreement notwithstanding any intermediate acts or negotiations in respect of such objections, shall be at an end and all monies paid shall be returned without interest or deduction and Seller, Listing Brokerage and Co-operating Brokerage shall not be liable for any costs or damages. Save as to any valid objection so made by such day and except for any objection going to the root of the title, Buyer shall be conclusively deemed to have accepted Seller's title to the Property. Seller hereby consents to the municipality or other governmental agencies releasing to Buyer details of all outstanding work orders and deficiency notices affecting the Property, and Seller agrees to execute and deliver such further authorizations in this regard as Buyer may reasonably require.

11. **TITLE:** Buyer agrees to accept title to the Property subject to all rights and easements registered against title for the supply and installation of telephone services, electricity, gas, sewers, water, television cable facilities and other related services; provided that title to the Property is otherwise good and free from all encumbrances except: (a) as herein expressly provided; (b) any registered restrictions, conditions or covenants that run with the land provided such have been complied with; (c) the provisions of the Condominium Act and its Regulations and the terms, conditions and provisions of the Declaration, Description and By-laws, Occupancy Standards By-laws, including the Common Element Rules and other Rules and Regulations; and (d) any existing municipal agreements, zoning by-laws and/or regulations and utilities or service contracts.

12. **CLOSING ARRANGEMENTS:** Where each of the Seller and Buyer retain a lawyer to complete the Agreement of Purchase and Sale of the Property, and where the transaction will be completed by electronic registration pursuant to Part III of the Land Registration Reform Act, R.S.O. 1990, Chapter L4 and the Electronic Registration Act, S.O. 1991, Chapter 44, and any amendments thereto, the Seller and Buyer acknowledge and agree that the exchange of closing funds, nonregistrable documents and other items (the "Requisite Deliveries") and the release thereof to the Seller and Buyer will (a) not occur at the same time as the registration of the transfer/deed (and any other documents intended to be registered in connection with the completion of this transaction) and (b) be subject to conditions whereby the lawyer(s) receiving any of the Requisite Deliveries will be required to hold same in trust and not release same except in accordance with the terms of a document registration agreement between the said lawyers. The Seller and Buyer irrevocably instruct the said lawyers to be bound by the document registration agreement which is recommended from time to time by the Law Society of Upper Canada. Unless otherwise agreed to by the lawyers, such exchange of the Requisite Deliveries will occur in the applicable Land Titles Office or such other location agreeable to both lawyers.

13. **STATUS CERTIFICATE AND MANAGEMENT OF CONDOMINIUM:** Seller represents and warrants to Buyer that there are no special assessments contemplated by the Condominium Corporation, and there are no legal actions pending by or against or contemplated by the Condominium Corporation. The Seller consents to a request by the Buyer or the Buyer's authorized representative for a Status Certificate from the Condominium Corporation. Buyer acknowledges that the Condominium Corporation may have entered into a Management Agreement for the management of the condominium property.

14. **DOCUMENTS AND DISCHARGE:** Buyer shall not call for the production of any title deed, abstract, survey or other evidence of title to the Property except such as are in the possession or control of Seller. Seller agrees to deliver to Buyer, if it is possible without incurring any costs in so doing, copies of all current condominium documentation of the Condominium Corporation, including the Declaration, Description, By-laws, Common Element Rules and Regulations and the most recent financial statements of the Condominium Corporation. If a discharge of any Charge/Mortgage held by a corporation incorporated pursuant to the Trust And Loan Companies Act (Canada), Chartered Bank, Trust Company, Credit Union, Caisse Populaire or Insurance Company and which is not to be assumed by Buyer on completion, is not available in registrable form on completion, Buyer agrees to accept Seller's lawyer's personal undertaking to obtain, out of the closing funds, a discharge in registrable form and to register same, or cause same to be registered, on title within a reasonable period of time after completion, provided that on or before completion Seller shall provide to Buyer a mortgage statement prepared by the mortgagee setting out the balance required to obtain the discharge, and, where a real-time electronic cleared funds transfer system is not being used, a direction executed by Seller directing payment to the mortgagee of the amount required to obtain the discharge out of the balance due on completion.

15. **MEETINGS:** Seller represents and warrants to Buyer that at the time of the acceptance of this Offer the Seller has not received a notice convening a special or general meeting of the Condominium Corporation respecting; (a) the termination of the government of the condominium property; (b) any substantial alteration in or substantial addition to the common elements or the renovation thereof; OR (c) any substantial change in the assets or liabilities of the Condominium Corporation; and Seller covenants that if Seller receives any such notice prior to the date of completion Seller shall forthwith notify Buyer in writing and Buyer may thereupon at Buyer's option declare this Agreement to be null and void and all monies paid by Buyer shall be refunded without interest or deduction.

INITIALS OF BUYER(S): ⬭*DT DC*⬭   INITIALS OF SELLER(S): ⬭*MR JR*⬭

Form 101   Revised 2015   **Page 3 of 6**

16. **INSPECTION:** Buyer acknowledges having had the opportunity to inspect the Property and understands that upon acceptance of this offer there shall be a binding agreement of purchase and sale between Buyer and Seller. **The Buyer acknowledges having the opportunity to include a requirement for a property inspection report in this Agreement and agrees that except as may be specifically provided for in this Agreement, the Buyer will not be obtaining a property inspection or property inspection report regarding the Property.**

17. **APPROVAL OF THE AGREEMENT:** In the event that consent to this sale is required to be given by the Condominium Corporation or the Board of Directors, the Seller will apply forthwith for the requisite consent, and if such consent is refused, then this Agreement shall be null and void and the deposit monies paid hereunder shall be refunded without interest or other penalty to the Buyer.

18. **INSURANCE:** The Unit and all other things being purchased shall be and remain at the risk of the Seller until completion. In the event of substantial damage to the Property Buyer may at Buyer's option either permit the proceeds of insurance to be used for repair of such damage in accordance with the provisions of the Insurance Trust Agreement, or terminate this Agreement and all deposit monies paid by Buyer hereunder shall be refunded without interest or deduction. If Seller is taking back a Charge/Mortgage, or Buyer is assuming a Charge/Mortgage, Buyer shall supply Seller with reasonable evidence of adequate insurance to protect Seller's or other mortgagee's interest on completion.

19. **DOCUMENT PREPARATION:** The Transfer/Deed shall, save for the Land Transfer Tax Affidavit, be prepared in registrable form at the expense of Seller, and any Charge/Mortgage to be given back by the Buyer to Seller at the expense of the Buyer.

20. **RESIDENCY:** (a) Subject to (b) below, the Seller represents and warrants that the Seller is not and on completion will not be a non-resident under the non-residency provisions of the Income Tax Act which representation and warranty shall survive and not merge upon the completion of this transaction and the Seller shall deliver to the Buyer a statutory declaration that Seller is not then a non-resident of Canada; (b) provided that if the Seller is a non-resident under the non-residency provisions of the Income Tax Act, the Buyer shall be credited towards the Purchase Price with the amount, if any, necessary for Buyer to pay to the Minister of National Revenue to satisfy Buyer's liability in respect of tax payable by Seller under the non-residency provisions of the Income Tax Act by reason of this sale. Buyer shall not claim such credit if Seller delivers on completion the prescribed certificate.

21. **ADJUSTMENTS:** Common Expenses; realty taxes, including local improvement rates; mortgage interest; rentals; unmetered public or private utilities and fuel where billed to the Unit and not the Condominium Corporation; are to be apportioned and allowed to the day of completion, the day of completion itself to be apportioned to the Buyer. There shall be no adjustment for the Seller's share of any assets or liabilities of the Condominium Corporation including any reserve or contingency fund to which Seller may have contributed prior to the date of completion.

22. **PROPERTY ASSESSMENT:** The Buyer and Seller hereby acknowledge that the Province of Ontario has implemented current value assessment and properties may be re-assessed on an annual basis. The Buyer and Seller agree that no claim will be made against the Buyer or Seller, or any Brokerage, Broker or Salesperson, for any changes in property tax as a result of a re-assessment of the Property, save and except any property taxes that accrued prior to the completion of this transaction.

23. **TIME LIMITS:** Time shall in all respects be of the essence hereof provided that the time for doing or completing of any matter provided for herein may be extended or abridged by an agreement in writing signed by Seller and Buyer or by their respective lawyers who may be specifically authorized in that regard.

24. **TENDER:** Any tender of documents or money hereunder may be made upon Seller or Buyer or their respective lawyers on the day set for completion. Money shall be tendered with funds drawn on a lawyer's trust account in the form of a bank draft, certified cheque or wire transfer using the Large Value Transfer System.

25. **FAMILY LAW ACT:** Seller warrants that spousal consent is not necessary to this transaction under the provisions of the Family Law Act, R.S.O. 1990 unless Seller's spouse has executed the consent hereinafter provided.

26. **UFFI:** Seller represents and warrants to Buyer that during the time Seller has owned the Property, Seller has not caused any building on the Property to be insulated with insulation containing ureaformaldehyde, and that to the best of Seller's knowledge no building on the Property contains or has ever contained insulation that contains ureaformaldehyde. This warranty shall survive and not merge on the completion of this transaction, and if the building is part of a multiple unit building, this warranty shall only apply to that part of the building which is the subject of this transaction.

27. **LEGAL, ACCOUNTING AND ENVIRONMENTAL ADVICE:** The parties acknowledge that any information provided by the brokerage is not legal, tax or environmental advice.

28. **CONSUMER REPORTS: The Buyer is hereby notified that a consumer report containing credit and/or personal information may be referred to in connection with this transaction.**

29. **AGREEMENT IN WRITING:** If there is conflict or discrepancy between any provision added to this Agreement (including any Schedule attached hereto) and any provision in the standard pre-set portion hereof, the added provision shall supersede the standard pre-set provision to the extent of such conflict or discrepancy. This Agreement including any Schedule attached hereto, shall constitute the entire Agreement between Buyer and Seller. There is no representation, warranty, collateral agreement or condition, which affects this Agreement other than as expressed herein. For the purposes of this Agreement, Seller means vendor and Buyer means purchaser. This Agreement shall be read with all changes of gender or number required by the context.

30. **TIME AND DATE:** Any reference to a time and date in this Agreement shall mean the time and date where the Property is located.

INITIALS OF BUYER(S): (*DT DC*)   INITIALS OF SELLER(S): (*MR JR*)

Fully Completed Sample   Agreement of Purchase and Sale—Condominium Resale, Page 5 of 6

31. SUCCESSORS AND ASSIGNS: The heirs, executors, administrators, successors and assigns of the undersigned are bound by the terms herein.

SIGNED, SEALED AND DELIVERED in the presence of: IN WITNESS whereof I have hereunto set my hand and seal:

Linda Ward
(Witness)
    Derek Trotter
(Buyer)   (Seal)   DATE *Feb. 8/xx*

Linda Ward
(Witness)
    Deborah Cormier
(Buyer)   (Seal)   DATE *Feb. 8/xx*

I, the Undersigned Seller, agree to the above offer. I hereby irrevocably instruct my lawyer to pay directly to the brokerage(s) with whom I have agreed to pay commission, the unpaid balance of the commission together with applicable Harmonized Sales Tax (and any other taxes as may hereafter be applicable), from the proceeds of the sale prior to any payment to the undersigned on completion, as advised by the brokerage(s) to my lawyer.

SIGNED, SEALED AND DELIVERED in the presence of: IN WITNESS whereof I have hereunto set my hand and seal:

Albert Lee
(Witness)
    Mary Rose
(Seller)   (Seal)   DATE *Feb. 9/xx*

Albert Lee
(Witness)
    John Rose
(Seller)   (Seal)   DATE *Feb. 9/xx*

SPOUSAL CONSENT: The Undersigned Spouse of the Seller hereby consents to the disposition evidenced herein pursuant to the provisions of the Family Law Act, R.S.O.1990, and hereby agrees with the Buyer that he/she will execute all necessary or incidental documents to give full force and effect to the sale evidenced herein.

(Witness)   (Spouse)   (Seal)   DATE

CONFIRMATION OF ACCEPTANCE: Notwithstanding anything contained herein to the contrary, I confirm this Agreement with all changes both typed and written was finally accepted by all parties at *4:30* a.m./p.m. this *9th* day of *February* , 20 *xx* .

John Rose
(Signature of Seller or Buyer)

INFORMATION ON BROKERAGE(S)

Listing Brokerage .... **ABC Realty Inc.**   Tel.No.(**519**) **555-1212**
   123 Main Street, Anycity, Anyregion L4H 6P5   **Albert Lee**
(Salesperson / Broker Name)

Co-op/Buyer Brokerage .... **XYZ Real Estate Ltd.**   Tel.No.(**519**) **444-1212**
   29 Maple Drive, Anycity, Anyregion L2J 7K6   **Linda Ward**
(Salesperson / Broker Name)

ACKNOWLEDGEMENT

I acknowledge receipt of my signed copy of this accepted Agreement of Purchase and Sale and I authorize the Brokerage to forward a copy to my lawyer.

Mary Rose
(Seller)   DATE *Feb. 9/xx*

John Rose
(Seller)   DATE *Feb. 9/xx*

Address for Service *Unit 901, 2072 Marsland Drive*
Anycity, K0B 1Z0   Tel.No.(*519*) *555-2675*

Seller's Lawyer *Brooks and Duncan*

Address *138 Commercial Vista, Anycity, K8C 1B2*

Email

(*519*) *666-1212*
Tel.No.
   (*519*) *666-2121*
FAX No.

I acknowledge receipt of my signed copy of this accepted Agreement of Purchase and Sale and I authorize the Brokerage to forward a copy to my lawyer.

Derek Trotter
(Buyer)   DATE *Feb. 9/xx*

Deborah Cormier
(Buyer)   DATE *Feb. 9/xx*

Address for Service *Apt. 326, 17 Pine Drive, Anycity*
K9C 3B5   Tel.No.(*519*) *777-1212*

Buyer's Lawyer *Marchand and Jenkins*

Address *392 Douglas Drive*

Email

(*519*) *444-1212*
Tel.No.
   (*519*) *444-2121*
FAX No.

Property Manager: **Advanced Mgmt. Corp.**   **1382 Main Street, Anycity K9B 3C7**   **519-999-1212 519-999-2121**
(Name)   (Address)   (Tel No.,FAX No)

FOR OFFICE USE ONLY   **COMMISSION TRUST AGREEMENT**

To: Co-operating Brokerage shown on the foregoing Agreement of Purchase and Sale:
In consideration for the Co-operating Brokerage procuring the foregoing Agreement of Purchase and Sale, I hereby declare that all moneys received or receivable by me in connection with the Transaction as contemplated in the MLS® Rules and Regulations of my Real Estate Board shall be receivable and held in trust. This agreement shall constitute a Commission Trust Agreement as defined in the MLS® Rules and shall be subject to and governed by the MLS® Rules pertaining to Commission Trust.

DATED as of the date and time of the acceptance of the foregoing Agreement of Purchase and Sale.   Acknowledged by:

Albert Lee
(Authorized to bind the Listing Brokerage)
    Linda Ward
(Authorized to bind the Co-operating Brokerage)

Form 101   Revised 2015   **Page 5 of 6**

Fully Completed Sample   Agreement of Purchase and Sale—Condominium Resale, Page 6 of 6

 **Ontario Real Estate Association**

Form 101
for use in the Province of Ontario

Schedule A
Agreement of Purchase and Sale –
Condominium Resale

This Schedule is attached to and forms part of the Agreement of Purchase and Sale between:

BUYER, ... Derek William Trotter and Deborah Anne Cormier ...., and

SELLER, ... Mary Ellen Rose and John Daniel Rose ....

for the purchase and sale of .... Unit 901, 2072 Marsland Drive, Anycity ....

.... dated the ...... 8th ...... day of .... February ...., 20 XX ......

Buyer agrees to pay the balance as follows:

The Buyer agrees to pay a further sum of Two Hundred and Ten Thousand Dollars ($210,000.00), subject to adjustments, to the Seller on completion of this transaction, with funds drawn on a lawyer's trust account in the form of a bank draft, certified cheque, or wire transfer using the Large Value Transfer System.

This offer is conditional upon the Buyer arranging, at the Buyer's own expense, a new first charge/ mortgage for not less than One Hundred and Ninety-Eight Thousand Dollars ($198,000.00), bearing interest at a rate of not more than 6% per annum, calculated semi-annually not in advance, repayable in blended monthly payments of about One Thousand Two Hundred and Sixty-Six Dollars and Eighty-Two Cents ($1,266.82), including principal and interest, and to run for a term of not less than 3 years from the date of completion of this transaction. Unless the Buyer gives notice in writing delivered to the Seller personally or in accordance with any other provisions for the delivery of notice in this Agreement of Purchase and Sale or any Schedule thereto not later than 8:00 p.m. on the 28th day of February, 20xx, that this condition is fulfilled, this Offer shall be null and void and the deposit shall be returned to the Buyer in full without deduction. This condition is included for the benefit of the Buyer and may be waived at the Buyer's sole option by notice in writing to the Seller as aforesaid within the time period stated herein.

This Offer is conditional upon the Buyer's Solicitor reviewing the following Condominium Corporation's documentation: a Status Certificate and attachments, and finding all of the foregoing satisfactory in the Buyer's Solicitor's sole and absolute discretion. Unless the Buyer gives notice in writing delivered to the Seller personally or in accordance with any other provisions for the delivery of notice in this Agreement of Purchase and Sale or any Schedule thereto not later than 8:00 p.m. on the 28th of February, 20xx, that this condition is fulfilled, this Offer shall be null and void and the deposit shall be returned to the Buyer in full without deduction. The Buyer or the Buyer's Solicitor agrees to request the foregoing documentation within 4 days after acceptance of this Agreement. This condition is included for the benefit of the buyer and may be waived at the Buyer's sole option by notice in writing to the Seller as aforesaid within the time period stated herein.

This form must be initialed by all parties to the Agreement of Purchase and Sale.

INITIALS OF BUYER(S): (*DT DC*)   INITIALS OF SELLER(S): (*MR JR*)

Form 101   Revised 2015   **Page 6 of 6**

KEY CONSIDERATIONS: RESALE UNITS

Common Expenses

Common expenses involve costs relating to the performance of the objects and duties of the corporation, including all expenses specified as common expenses in the Act or in a declaration. The payment of common expenses and the amount of such expenses is an important consideration when purchasing a condominium. Owners contribute common expenses in proportions outlined in the declaration. Any default can result in a lien against the owner's unit (including legal costs and other expenses), which can be enforced in the same manner as a mortgage. No owner is exempt from this requirement, even if he/she has waived or abandoned the right to use the common elements, is making a claim against the corporation or is restricted from using such common elements.

The right to register a lien for common expense arrears, previously limited to residential condominiums in prior legislation, now includes non-residential condominiums.

EXAMPLE   *Common Expenses*

Owner James purchases a resale condominium unit in a 230-suite complex. The corporation has just finalized budget estimates for the upcoming year and established a total budget of $2,137,216. The common expense allocation is based on individual unit square footage as a percentage of total square footage of all units. James' unit represents 0.3467% (.003467) of the total area of all units. Accordingly, James will be responsible to pay the following:

$2,137,216 x .003467 =
$7,409.73 annually or $617.48 per month

If James' 3-bedroom unit consisted of 1,850 square feet, his common expenses (commonly quoted by real estate registrants on a per square foot basis) would be $0.33 per square foot ($617.48 ÷ 1,850). Condominium common expenses can range significantly based on amenities offered.

NOTE: If James held title to a parking space (as opposed to having the exclusive right to occupy that parking space; i.e., an exclusive use common element), the proportionate share of the parking space would also be calculated. Assume that the parking space accounted for 0.0231% (.000231), then the added cost would be:

$2,137,216 x .000231 =
$493.70 (annually) or $41.14 per month

As previously noted, the agreement of purchase and sale provides a representation and warranty by the seller that no special assessments are contemplated.

LIEN (COMMON EXPENSES)

The *Condominium Act* provides that when a unit owner is in default regarding common expenses, the corporation has an automatic unregistered lien. The lien expires three months after the default occurs unless a certificate of lien is registered by the corporation. The owner must be given written notice of the certificate of lien ten days prior to registration.

Procedures   Registrants may not be directly involved with liens, but should be aware of basic procedures. The lien, when registered, covers the amount of the default, the amount that the owner is in default following the registration of the lien, interest, legal costs and other reasonable expenses incurred by the condominium in collecting the debt.

If the debt is paid, the corporation must register a discharge and provide notice of same to the unit owner. A lien has priority over every registered or unregistered encumbrance except a claim of the Crown, a claim for taxes, charges, rates or assessments under various provincial statutes or a lien that is prescribed. Regulation 49/01 details procedures and applicable forms; see *Form 6: Certificate of Lien* and *Form 7: Discharge of Lien*.

Reserve Fund

The reserve fund is used solely for major repair and replacement of common elements and corporation assets; e.g., roofs, building exterior finishes, roads, sidewalks, electrical, heating and plumbing systems, and recreational/parking facilities.

Funds are collected from common expenses and must be held in trust. Interest or other income from the reserve fund forms part of that fund. If repair costs to common elements exceeds monies in reserve, a special assessment may be required to meet such expenses. Repayment terms can vary considerably, but essentially the unit owners are required to contribute a specified sum in addition to normal monthly common expenses.

STATUTORY FUND REQUIREMENTS

When a condominium is first registered, and until a first reserve fund study and associated plan is completed, the reserve amount is the greater of money reasonably required for major repairs and replacements based on life expectancies and replacement costs, or 10% of the budgeted amount for contributions to the common expenses exclusive of the reserve fund.

Corporations are, thereafter, required to undertake reserve fund studies in accordance with prescribed time limits. Such ongoing studies, among other things, determine whether the existing funds in reserve and contributions collected are adequate. For new condominiums following proclamation of the *Condominium Act* in 2001, a reserve fund study must be completed in the year following registration. Within 120 days of receipt, the board must establish the plan for future funding; within 15 days provide owners (and the auditor) with a summary; and within 30 days following, implement the plan.

PERFORMANCE AUDIT

A performance audit involves detailed examination and scrutiny of the common elements by an individual (with qualifications as set out in the Act). This audit includes inspecting major building components, reviewing condominium documentation and conducting a survey of owners concerning damage or defects. The individual then prepares/submits a written report to the board of directors.

Requirement: Selected Condominiums   Requirements concerning performance audits apply to condominium corporations with one or more units used for residential purposes and common elements condominium corporations. The person conducting the audit must hold a Certificate of Authorization (*Professional Engineers Act*) or Certificate of Practice (*Architects Act*).

The audit is designed to reveal deficiencies that might give rise to a new home warranty claim, whether or not the corporation falls under that program. The reader is reminded that new home coverage provided by Tarion Warranty Corporation is restricted to new residential condominiums and is further subject to other qualifying criteria.

The auditor may enter the property at reasonable times either alone or accompanied by appropriate experts, require the production of relevant documents and make examinations, tests or inquiries deemed reasonable. The performance audit must be completed no later than ten months following the registration of the declaration and description.

Status Certificate

The status certificate provides a wealth of information for the resale buyer. This certificate is a document containing information regarding the operational, legal and financial dimensions of the condominium corporation. The corporation is required to give each person, so requesting, a status certificate with respect to a unit in the corporation.

Registrants should be familiar with all aspects of the status certificate. The certificate must be provided within ten days by the corporation to anyone who requests this document. A prescribed fee, not to exceed $100 inclusive of all applicable taxes, can be charged.

CONTENTS

The information contained within the status certificate and the accompanying documents are vital from a buyer's perspective in fully understanding both the status of an individual unit and the overall operation of the condominium corporation.

Certificate content includes, but is not limited to:

- Corporation's address for service; directors'/officers' names and addresses for service.
- Statement of common expenses (including default for the unit, if any).
- Amount payable by the unit for common expenses.
- Particulars of any increase in common expenses for the unit since the date of the current year budget. Reasons for the increase must also be provided.
- Statement concerning any assessments relating to the reserve fund since the date of the budget for the current year (including reasons for such assessments).
- Information concerning any applications regarding amendments to the declaration.
- Details of outstanding judgments.
- Status of any legal actions being taken against the condominium corporation.
- Current budget and the most recent audited statement, including the auditor's report.
- Copy of the current declaration, by-laws and rules.
- A listing of various current agreements; e.g., management and insurance.
- Statement that the person requesting the status certificate has the right to inspect agreements.
- Owner compliance with current agreements regarding modifications that relate to the unit; e.g., additions or changes to exclusive use common elements.
- Particulars concerning the most recent reserve fund study and the amount of the fund (no earlier than the end of the month within 90 days of the certificate), including any current plans to increase the fund.
- Number of units leased for the fiscal year preceding the status certificate date.
- Certificate or memorandum of current insurance policies.
- Any planned or proposed additions, alterations or improvements to the common elements; other assets of the corporation; or services.
- A statement if a court has appointed an inspector pursuant to the Act.

OTHER AGREEMENTS

Persons paying the fee for the certificate can, upon written request, also inspect certain agreements; e.g., management and insurance. Copies will be furnished for a fee. Upon written request, the name and address for service of the corporation, directors and officers, the person responsible for management and the individual delegated to provide status certificates can also be obtained.

CERTIFICATE NOT PROVIDED/INFORMATION OMITTED

The Act also sets out requirements in the event that information is omitted or a certificate is not provided, when requested. If any information is omitted, the statute provides that the certificate states there is no such information.

When a status certificate is requested and not provided within the required time limit (ten days), the Act states that a certificate is deemed to have been provided and:

- no default in common expenses has occurred;
- no increase in common expenses has occurred (since the date of the current year's budget); and
- no levies have been assessed against the unit.

STATUS CERTIFICATE CLAUSE

SCENARIO	CLAUSE

A buyer has submitted an offer on a condominium, but wants his or her lawyer to fully review the status certificate and attachments to ensure that these are satisfactory from the lawyer's perspective.	**CONDO–1 Condition–Review of Condominium Documents— By Specific Date**
	
	This offer is conditional upon the Buyer's lawyer reviewing the Status Certificate and Attachments and finding the Status Certificate and Attachments satisfactory in the Buyer's Lawyer's sole and absolute discretion. The (buyer or seller) _____ agrees to request at the (buyer's or seller's) _____ expense, the Status Certificate and Attachments within _____ days after acceptance of this Offer.
	
	   Unless the buyer gives notice in writing to the Seller personally or in accordance with any other provisions for the delivery of notice in this Agreement of Purchase and Sale or any Schedule thereto not later than 5:00 p.m. on the ___ day of _____ 20 ___ , that this condition is fulfilled, this Offer shall be null and void and the deposit shall be returned to the Buyer in full without deduction.
	
	   This condition is included for the benefit of the Buyer and may be waived at the Buyer's sole option by notice in writing to the Seller as aforesaid within the time period stated herein.

NOTE: An alternate wording is provided; *'within a specific number of days'* rather than *'within a specific time limit'*.

Use Restrictions

Use restrictions generally refer to limitations placed on unit owners as found in the declaration, by-laws and/or rules. Such restrictions are established initially by the declarant and modified by the condominium corporation, as needed. The *Condominium Act* requires that the current declaration, by-laws and rules be included with the status certificate.

Use restrictions vary significantly in condominiums. The following examples have been taken from restrictions found in condominium documentation to represent the range of possibilities.

- No pets (or restrictions on pets; e.g., weight limit).
- White backing on exterior drapery materials with temporary draperies allowed during initial move-in period only.
- No outside installations; e.g., antennae, clotheslines, satellite dishes or other exterior telecommunication/radio devices.

- Parking restricted to private passenger vehicles only; i.e., no commercial vehicles in driveways.
- No alterations with respect to the unit, exclusive use common areas or common elements requiring condominium corporation consent can be made without the appropriate written consent.
- No signs permitted other than those approved by the corporation; e.g., name and/or address plate.
- No temporary structures or incidental permanent outside structures or improvements.
- No artificial vegetation, sculptures, weather vanes, birdbaths, flagpoles or fountains.
- No outside storage of garbage/trash/refuse containers.
- No awnings, canopies or shutters, unless approved by the corporation.
- Garage doors shall be closed at all times (other than entering/exiting).

Owner Alterations and Additions	CAUTION

Alterations and additions to common elements (particularly exclusive use common elements) have proven troublesome in the resale market.

While the *Condominium Act* is quite specific regarding approval processes and required agreements, changes to balconies, privacy fences/decking and interior renovations in older condos may lack such approvals. In some instances, documentation regarding ownership and ongoing repair responsibilities may be vague or non-existent.

Such issues can pose problems at closing, if not addressed in advance.

USE RESTRICTION CLAUSES

SCENARIO	*CLAUSE*
Scenario 1 A buyer is drafting an offer and wants to ensure that the seller has not made any improvements, additions, alterations or repairs (that require consent of the condominium corporation) without having received such consent.	**CONDO–3** **Alterations by Owner** *The Seller represents and warrants that, with respect to the unit, the Condominium Act, Declaration, By-laws and Rules of the Condominium Corporation have been complied with, and that no improvements, additions, alterations or repairs that require the consent of the Condominium Corporation have been carried out in the said unit, the exclusive use areas or the common elements, unless the required consent has been obtained from the Condominium Corporation. This warranty shall survive and not merge on the completion of this transaction.*
Scenario 2 A seller wants assurances that the buyer, guests and family members will abide by the declaration, by-laws and rules of the condominium corporation.	**CONDO–5** **Compliance by Buyers, Guests and Family Members** *The Buyer hereby covenants with the Seller and with the Condominium Corporation that the Buyer, members of the household, and guests, will comply with the Condominium Act, the Declaration, the By-laws and all Rules and Regulations, in using the unit and the common elements, and will be subject to the same duties imposed by the above as those applicable to other individual unit owners.*

Scenario 3	CONDO–10	Tenant to Occupy Property
A seller wants assurances that tenants of the new buyer will comply with the declaration, by-laws and rules of the condominium corporation.	*The Buyer agrees to abide by the Declaration, By-laws, Rules and Regulations of the Condominium Corporation and, if the property is to be rented, the Buyer agrees to inform all tenants of the Rules and Regulations and receive written acknowledgement of the tenants regarding their willingness to abide by same within the rental document. It is clearly understood that all rental agreements shall conform with the Rules and Regulations as passed from time to time by the Board of Directors of the Condominium Corporation.*	

Special Clause: Common Elements Condominium

A clause has been developed for use with the *Agreement of Purchase and Sale* (OREA Form 100) when a freehold property is being sold and that property (referred to as a POTL or Parcel of Tied Land) includes an interest in a common elements condominium. For example, a seller may be selling his or her home and that home is tied to an ownership interest in a nearby golf course that is a common elements condominium.

As an alternative, a new form has been created especially for the sale of a POTL. A sample of Form 111, *Agreement of Purchase and Sale—POTL Common Elements Condominium* can be found in the *Appendix* section.

CLAUSE

CONDO/POTL	Schedule B: Common Elements Condominium (POTL)

PROPERTY: The property shall be deemed to include a common interest in the Condominium Corporation being _____ Condominium Plan No. _____ as more particularly set out on the Declaration and Description.

COMMON EXPENSES: Seller warrants to Buyer that the common expenses presently payable to the Condominium Corporation in respect of the Property are approximately $ _____ per month.

STATUS CERTIFICATE AND MANAGEMENT OF CONDOMINIUM: Seller represents and warrants to Buyer that there are no special assessments contemplated by the Condominium Corporation, and there are no legal actions pending by or against or contemplated by the Condominium Corporation. The Seller consents to a request by the Buyer or the Buyer's authorized representative for a Status Certificate from the Condominium Corporation. Buyer acknowledges that the Condominium Corporation may have entered into a Management Agreement for the management of the condominium property.

MEETINGS: Seller represents and warrants to Buyer that at the time of the acceptance of this Offer the Seller has not received a notice convening a special or general meeting of the Condominium Corporation respecting (a) the termination of the government of the condominium property; (b) any substantial alteration in or substantial addition to the common elements or the renovation thereof; OR (c) any substantial change in the assets or liabilities of the Condominium Corporation; and Seller covenants that if the Seller receives any such notice prior to the date of completion Seller shall forthwith notify the Buyer in writing and Buyer may thereupon at the Buyer's option declare the Agreement null and void and all monies paid by the Buyer shall be refunded without interest or deduction.

TITLE: Buyer agrees to accept title to the Property subject to the provisions of the Condominium Act and its Regulations and the terms, conditions and provisions of the Declaration, Description and By-laws, Occupancy Standards By-laws, including the Common Element Rules and other Rules and Regulations.

The True Cost of Condominium

Looking for creativity when promoting condominium in the marketplace? Here's some ideas from a condo believer to counter those who say that condominium is expensive.

Condominium is a powerful group event. It's all about financial synergism. In a condo, the sum of the parts is greater than the whole. Where else can a buyer with limited resources have home ownership, use top notch facilities, stroll in a private park, have a prime view, use professionally decorated entertainment rooms and much more …often in the best location in town?

Some people say that condo living is expensive. But buyers often erroneously compare condos to detached homes. The problem rests in looking at direct costs only; that is, actual home repair costs versus common expense fees.

The overall picture is different—if true comparisons are made. I tell all my potential buyers to compare apples to apples. Don't forget to add in:

- *the real cost of a proper home maintenance program;*
- *the establishment of a home reserve fund for sudden unexpected and often significant repairs; and*
- *the cost of labour—your labour to get things done around the house.*

Make a fair comparison:

Home Insurance	*The common expense fee typically includes building and standard unit coverage. The condo owner only insures the upgrades, non-standard items and personal belongings.*
Equipment	*Consider costs for the purchase and repair of lawnmowers, gardening equipment, snow-blowers, lawn watering equipment and incidental tools.*
Maintenance	*Don't forget the bits and pieces; e.g., exterior paint, driveway sealant, fertilizer, annual flowers, shrubs, sprays, light bulbs, cleaning solvents and deck painting. It all adds up.*
Future Reserves	*Allocate funds for maintenance of major items: roof, windows, garage floor, pool and landscaping. New condominiums set aside funds for this purpose that are reflected in the common expense payments.*
Security Monitoring	*Add home monitoring costs comparable to security provided by the condo.*
Labour Cost	*Don't forget to charge for your time…even when it appears free. In condominium, you pay others but gain personal freedom. Hard to put a price on, but definitely valuable.*
Professional Management	*Well-managed properties don't happen by accident. Someone has to be paid so you don't have to worry.*

SELLER PROPERTY INFORMATION STATEMENT AND SCHEDULE

Many issues covered in this chapter can be effectively addressed at point of listing by using the *Seller Property Information Statement* (OREA Form 220) and the associated *Seller Property Information Statement–Schedule for Condominium* (OREA Form 221). This schedule, attached to and forming part of the SPIS, addresses matters such as fees, special assessments, pending lawsuits and other key matters impacting resale condominiums.

Seller Property Information Statement
Schedule for Condominium

Form 221
for use in the Province of Ontario

This Schedule is attached to and forms part of the Seller Property Information Statement (Form 220) for:

PROPERTY:		**SELLER(S) TO INITIAL**		
SELLER(S):		**EACH APPLICABLE BOX**		

CONDOMINIUM CORPORATION: (Provide Applicable ADDITIONAL COMMENTS)	**YES**	**NO**	**UNKNOWN**	**NOT APPLICABLE**
1. **(a)** Condominium fee $..				
(b) Condominium fee includes:				
(c) Cost for amenities not included in Condominium fee $............................ Details				
2. Are there any special assessments approved or contemplated?				
3. Have you received any written notice of lawsuit(s) pending?				
4. Have you been informed of any notices, claims, work orders or deficiency notices affecting the common elements received from any person or any public body?				
5. **(a)** Has a reserve fund study been completed? Date of Study...................				
(b) Approximate amount of reserve fund as of last notification $...................				
6. **(a)** Are there any restrictions on pets?				
(b) Are there any restrictions on renting the property?				
(c) Are there any other restrictions on the use of the property?				
7. **(a)** If any renovations, additions or improvements were made to the unit and/or common elements, was approval of the Condominium Corporation obtained?				
(b) Is approval of any prospective buyer required by the Condominium Corporation?				
(c) Are any other approvals required by the Condominium Corporation or Property Manager? If yes, specify:				
(d) Name of Property Management Company				
8. Are there any pending rule or by-law amendments which may alter or restrict the uses of the property?				
9. Is the Condominium registered?				
10. Parking: Number of Spaces .... ☐Owned ☐Exclusive Use ☐Leased or Licensed Parking space number(s)..				
11. Locker:.. ☐ Owned ☐ Exclusive Use Locker number(s)...				
12. **(a)** Amenities: ☐ Pool ☐ Sauna ☐ Exercise ☐ Room ☐ Meeting/Party Room ☐ Boat Docking ☐ Guest Parking ☐ Other...................................				
(b) Are you aware of any problems with any of the common element amenities? If yes, specify:				

ADDITIONAL COMMENTS:...

....

....

INITIALS OF BUYER(S): ⬭

Form 221   Revised 2014   **Page 1 of 1**

Condominium Termination

Condominium corporations can be terminated in four ways: consent, sale of property, substantial damage and court application.

CONSENT

Consent is required of owners of at least 80% of the units. Further, at least 80% of persons having registered claims against the property (created following registration of the declaration and description) must also give their consent.

SALE OF PROPERTY

The Act ceases to govern the condominium if the property as a whole is sold. If a part is sold, the Act ceases to govern that part. An 80% majority vote is required; i.e., the owners of at least 80% of the units. If the common elements being sold are only for the use of owners of specific units, then those owners may consent to the sale, subject to other provisions in the Act.

When the property is sold, the unit owners share net sale proceeds, as per their proportionate ownership share outlined in the declaration. Proceeds from common areas, designated as exclusive use elements for specific owners, are divided between the owners in proportion to their respective ownership.

SUBSTANTIAL DAMAGE

If the condominium suffers damage, the board of directors will assess the scope of such damage and determine if it is substantial. Substantial, for purposes of the Act, is when the cost of repair equals or exceeds 25% of the replacement cost of all buildings and structures on the property.

The owners are then notified accordingly. Upon receipt of such notice, the owners can requisition a meeting within 30 days. If the owners of at least 80% of the units consent, a notice of termination must be registered with 30 days. If no vote occurs in favour of termination, the corporation is obligated to make the necessary repairs.

COURT APPLICATION

The Ontario Court (General Division), upon application by an owner, a mortgagee (or other encumbrancer) or the corporation, may terminate a condominium corporation according to criteria set out in the Act. When a court ordered termination occurs, the property ceases to be governed by the Act. The corporation's assets are then applied against all claims. The remaining funds are distributed among the owners in accordance with their proportionate interest in the common elements, as set out in the declaration.

KNOWLEDGE INTEGRATION

Notables

- The declaration and description are key documents in condominium registration.
- Condominiums go through much the same process from a planning perspective as do plans of subdivision.
- All newly built condominiums must comply with the Ontario Building Code. Residential condominiums must also comply with Tarion Warranty Corporation requirements.
- A condominium consists of units exclusively occupied by owners (except in the case of common element condominiums) and common elements held by owners as tenants in common.
- Use/ownership of parking and storage areas varies. Owned and exclusive use common elements are most typically found in Ontario.
- Condominiums can be broadly divided into leasehold and freehold. Freehold includes standard, common element, vacant land and phased condominium corporations.

- The board of directors, elected in accordance with the *Condominium Act*, must adhere to a standard of care when performing their duties.
- Primary documents for governance purposes include the declaration, the by-laws and the rules.
- The *Agreement of Purchase and Sale— Condominium Resale* (OREA Form 101) generally parallels the *Agreement of Purchase and Sale*, but important clauses have been added.
- Reserve fund creation and management are statutorily set out in the Act.
- The status certificate must be provided within ten days of a request and payment of the appropriate fee.
- Buyers should carefully review all condominium documentation, particularly use restrictions in the declaration, by-laws and rules.
- Owner alterations/additions can prove troublesome at point of closing, if proper procedures have not been followed.

Strategic Thinking For Your Career

Questions are included to assist in developing your new career. No answers are provided.

1. What new condominium corporations are under development within the local marketplace?

2. Is there potential to specialize in condominium sales or at least make such activity a significant component of my overall career?

3. What are major niche markets for condominium (e.g., retirement, young singles or families) within my immediate trading area?

4. Which local resale residential condominium properties best fit my personal strategy? What benefits and features do each have? Should I consider requesting status certificates to be better informed?

Chapter Mini-Review

Solutions are located in the Appendix.

1. When seeking approval for a condominium, an application (including a draft plan) is typically delivered to the local municipality, who in turn circulates the materials to persons and public agencies having an interest in the application.

    ◯ True   ◯ False

2. If a high-rise residential condominium is constructed that falls under Part 9 of the Ontario Building Code, the developer must comply with design and site review requirements of the Tarion Warranty Corporation.

    ◯ True   ◯ False

3. The declaration sets out the proportionate amount for each unit in order to determine each unit's contribution to common expenses.

    ◯ True   ◯ False

4. The declarant must hold a freehold interest in the land in order for a condominium corporation to be formed pursuant to the *Condominium Act*.

    ◯ True   ◯ False

5. The directors of a condominium corporation must adhere to a standard of care in carrying out their functions, unless otherwise instructed by the management company that handles day-to-day affairs of the corporation.

    ◯ True   ◯ False

6. Rules cannot be made, amended or repealed by the board of directors without holding a general meeting of owners.

    ◯ True   ◯ False

7. Ownership interests in a vacant land condominium are based on the size of individual land units.

    ◯ True   ◯ False

8. A unit owner, who owns a separately-titled parking space, may be permitted to sell the space to another owner at fair market value depending on provisions set out in the declaration, by-laws and/or rules.

    ◯ True   ◯ False

9. A common element condominium is generally referred to as a standard condominium pursuant to the *Condominium Act*.

    ⚪ True   ⚪ False

10. In the *Condominium Resale Agreement* (OREA Form 101), the preprinted wording provides that the agreement is subject to the buyer's approval of the status certificate within the title search requisition period.

    ⚪ True   ⚪ False

11. Use restrictions in condominium documentation are always detailed in the rules, as opposed to the by-laws or the declaration.

    ⚪ True   ⚪ False

12. If repair costs exceed monies available in the reserve fund, a special assessment may be levied against unit owners to meet such expenses.

    ⚪ True   ⚪ False

Active Learning Exercises

Solutions are located in the Appendix.

▣ Exercise 1   Common Expenses

Buyer Rochelle has reviewed the declaration for Suite 2106 and discovered that the unit's proportionate share of ownership is 0.2758%. Two separately-titled parking spaces are 0.0196% and 0.0179% respectively. If the total budget for this corporation is $2,871,500, what is Rochelle's monthly common expense payment, assuming that common expense payments are in direct proportion to ownership share?

▣ Exercise 2   Condominium Facts

For each of the following, identify whether the statement is correct or not correct, detailing reason(s) in support of your decision.

2.1 The board of directors is obligated to terminate the condominium when substantial damage occurs to a condominium (exceeding 25% of the replacement cost of buildings and other structures).

◯ Correct   ◯ Not Correct

Reason:

2.2 A minimum of 10% of the budgeted amount for common expense contributions must be held in the reserve fund at all times.

◯ Correct   ◯ Not Correct

Reason:

2.3 A phased condominium can make sound economic sense, particularly with larger condominium projects.

◯ Correct   ◯ Not Correct

Reason:

2.4 In the *Agreement of Purchase and Sale—Condominium Resale* (OREA Form 101), the seller only represents and warrants that there are no special assessments, but does not make any other representations/warranties concerning the condominium corporation.

◯ Correct   ◯ Not Correct

Reason:

2.5 A seller could obtain a status certificate to assist in the listing process and make such document available to the buyer. The buyer would then not need to request a status certificate when making an offer.

◯ Correct   ◯ Not Correct

Reason:

2.6 If a status certificate is not issued by a condominium corporation when requested by a buyer, a certificate is deemed to be provided stating certain facts regarding common expenses.

◯ Correct   ◯ Not Correct

Reason:

▣ Exercise 3   Form Comparison

Key clause differences exist between the *Agreement of Purchase and Sale—Condominium Resale* and the *Agreement of Purchase and Sale*, but other wordings are also affected. Based on a close scrutiny of both forms (see *Appendix*), identify eight or more differences in the OREA Form 101 as compared to OREA Form 100.

CLAUSE	WORDING DIFFERENCE

■ **Exercise 4   Analyzing the Condominium Resale Agreement**

Salesperson Hui drafted an offer for $278,000 for his clients regarding a condominium resale property owned by Michael Sharma (see the following pages). Michael and Natalie Sharma have occupied the property as their principal residence for the past two years. The Sharmas made a counter offer with various changes, including an amended price of $285,000. The buyers, Brenda Cheung and Raymond Ng, agreed to the counter offer. The existing mortgage with Anycity Trust has a remaining term of two years. Critically analyze the agreement identifying all errors and potential problems.

OREA Ontario Real Estate Association

Agreement of Purchase and Sale
Condominium Resale

Form 101
for use in the Province of Ontario

This Agreement of Purchase and Sale dated this ..... **10th** ..... day of ..... **May** ..... 20 **XX**

BUYER, ... **Brenda Cheung and Raymond Ng** ..... , agrees to purchase from
(Full legal names of all Buyers)

SELLER, ... **Michael Sharma** ..... , the following
(Full legal names of all Sellers)

PROPERTY:
a unit in the condominium property known as ..... **Suite** ..... No. **2807**
(Apartment/Townhouse/Suite/Unit)

located at ..... **2827 Lakeside Drive** .....

in the ..... **City of Anycity, Region of Anyregion** .....

being ..... **Anyregion** ..... Condominium Plan No ..... **398** .....
(Legal Name of Condominium Corporation)

Unit Number ..... **5** ..... Level No. ..... **26** ..... Building No. ..... **A** ..... together with ownership

or exclusive use of Parking Space(s) ..... **A23, Level P3** ..... , together with ownership or exclusive use of
(Number(s), Level(s))

Locker(s) ..... **A88, Level P2** ..... , together with Seller's proportionate undivided tenancy-in-common interest
(Number(s), Level(s))

in the common elements appurtenant to the Unit as described in the Declaration and Description including the exclusive right to use such other parts of the common elements appurtenant to the Unit as may be specified in the Declaration and Description: the Unit, the proportionate interest in the common elements appurtenant thereto, and the exclusive use portions of the common elements, being herein called the "Property".

PURCHASE PRICE: *BC MS*   Dollars (CDN$) ..... **$285,000.00** *BC MS*
Two Hundred and Eighty-Five Thousand   ~~$278,000.00~~
~~Two Hundred and Seventy Eight Thousand~~-- Dollars

DEPOSIT: Buyer submits ..... **Upon Acceptance** .....
(Herewith/Upon Acceptance/as otherwise described in this Agreement)

..... **Six Thousand**-- Dollars (CDN$) **$6,000.00**

by negotiable cheque payable to ..... **ABC Realty Inc.** ..... "Deposit Holder" to be held in trust pending completion or other termination of this Agreement and to be credited toward the Purchase Price on completion. For the purposes of this Agreement, "Upon Acceptance" shall mean that the Buyer is required to deliver the deposit to the Deposit Holder within 24 hours of the acceptance of this Agreement. The parties to this Agreement hereby acknowledge that, unless otherwise provided for in this Agreement, the Deposit Holder shall place the deposit in trust in the Deposit Holder's non-interest bearing Real Estate Trust Account and no interest shall be earned, received or paid on the deposit.

Buyer agrees to pay the balance as more particularly set out in Schedule A attached.

SCHEDULE(S) A ..... **attached hereto form(s) part of this Agreement.**

1. **IRREVOCABILITY:** This offer shall be irrevocable by ..... **Buyer** ..... until ..**5:00**.. ~~a.m.~~/p.m. on the ..... *BC* **11th** *MS* ~~10th~~
(Seller/Buyer)

   day of ..... **May** ..... 20 **XX** , after which time, if not accepted, this offer shall be null and void and the deposit shall be returned to the Buyer in full without interest.

2. **COMPLETION DATE:** This Agreement shall be completed by no later than 6:00 p.m. on the **31st** day of ..... **June** ..... ,

   20 **XX** Upon completion, vacant possession of the property shall be given to the Buyer unless otherwise provided for in this Agreement.

INITIALS OF BUYER(S): (*BC*)   INITIALS OF SELLER(S): (*MS*)

Form 101   Revised 2015   **Page 1 of 6**

3. **NOTICES:** The Seller hereby appoints the Listing Brokerage as agent for the Seller for the purpose of giving and receiving notices pursuant to this Agreement. Where a Brokerage (Buyer's Brokerage) has entered into a representation agreement with the Buyer, the Buyer hereby appoints the Buyer's Brokerage as agent for the purpose of giving and receiving notices pursuant to this Agreement. **Where a Brokerage represents both the Seller and the Buyer (multiple representation), the Brokerage shall not be appointed or authorized to be agent for either the Buyer or the Seller for the purpose of giving and receiving notices.** Any notice relating hereto or provided for herein shall be in writing. In addition to any provision contained herein and in any Schedule hereto, this offer, any counter-offer, notice of acceptance thereof or any notice to be given or received pursuant to this Agreement or any Schedule hereto (any of them, "Document") shall be deemed given and received when delivered personally or hand delivered to the Address for Service provided in the Acknowledgement below, or where a facsimile number or email address is provided herein, when transmitted electronically to that facsimile number or email address, respectively, in which case, the signature(s) of the party (parties) shall be deemed to be original.

FAX No.: .... 905-555-2121 ....   FAX No.: .... 905-444-2121 ....
(For delivery of Documents to Seller)   (For delivery of Documents to Buyer)

Email Address: .... admin@abcrealty.com ....   Email Address: .... notices@xyzrealestate.com ....
(For delivery of Documents to Seller)   (For delivery of Documents to Buyer)

4. **CHATTELS INCLUDED:** washer & dryer, fridge, stove, dishwasher, Matrix ceiling fans (LR and DR)

   broadloom in all rooms excluding kitchen and baths, ~~security system~~ *BC* *MS*

   ....

   ....

   ....

   Unless otherwise stated in this Agreement or any Schedule hereto, Seller agrees to convey all fixtures and chattels included in the Purchase Price free from all liens, encumbrances or claims affecting the said fixtures and chattels.

5. **FIXTURES EXCLUDED:** None

   ....

   ....

   ....

6. **RENTAL ITEMS (Including Lease, Lease to Own):** The following equipment is rented and **not** included in the Purchase Price. The Buyer `agrees to assume the rental contract(s), if assumable:

   None

   ....

   ....

   The Buyer agrees to co-operate and execute such documentation as may be required to facilitate such assumption.

7. **COMMON EXPENSES:** Seller warrants to Buyer that the common expenses presently payable to the Condominium Corporation in respect of the

   Property are approximately $ .... 618.30 .... per month, which amount includes the following: .... heat, hydro, hot water, ...

   water charges, central air conditioning, and insurance (common elements)

   ....

8. **PARKING AND LOCKERS:** Parking and Lockers are as described above or assigned as follows: .... N/A *BC* *MS* **Additional parking**

   space assigned by condominium corp (A33, P3) ... at an additional cost of: .... **To Be Determined** ....

   INITIALS OF BUYER(S): (*BC*)   INITIALS OF SELLER(S): (*MS*)

Form 101   Revised 2015   **Page 2 of 6**

Exercise 4   Agreement of Purchase and Sale—Condominium Resale, Page 3 of 6

9. HST: If the sale of the Property (Real Property as described above) is subject to Harmonized Sales Tax (HST), then such tax shall be
...............**included in**...................... the Purchase Price. If the sale of the Property is not subject to HST, Seller agrees to certify on or before
   (included in/in addition to)
closing, that the sale of the Property is not subject to HST. Any HST on chattels, if applicable, is not included in the Purchase Price.

10. TITLE SEARCH: Buyer shall be allowed until 6:00 p.m. on the ....**31st**.. day of ....**May**............., 20**XX**., (Requisition Date)
to examine the title to the Property at Buyer's own expense and until the earlier of: (i) thirty days from the later of the Requisition Date or the date
on which the conditions in this Agreement are fulfilled or otherwise waived or; (ii) five days prior to completion, to satisfy Buyer that there are no

outstanding work orders or deficiency notices affecting the Property, and that its present use (...**condominium apartment - single family residential**..)
may be lawfully continued. If within that time any valid objection to title or to any outstanding work order or deficiency notice, or to the fact the said
present use may not lawfully be continued, is made in writing to Seller and which Seller is unable or unwilling to remove, remedy or satisfy or obtain
insurance save and except against risk of fire (Title Insurance) in favour of the Buyer and any mortgagee, (with all related costs at the expense of the
Seller), and which Buyer will not waive, this Agreement notwithstanding any intermediate acts or negotiations in respect of such objections, shall be
at an end and all monies paid shall be returned without interest or deduction and Seller, Listing Brokerage and Co-operating Brokerage shall not be
liable for any costs or damages. Save as to any valid objection so made by such day and except for any objection going to the root of the title, Buyer
shall be conclusively deemed to have accepted Seller's title to the Property. Seller hereby consents to the municipality or other governmental agencies
releasing to Buyer details of all outstanding work orders and deficiency notices affecting the Property, and Seller agrees to execute and deliver such
further authorizations in this regard as Buyer may reasonably require.

11. TITLE: Buyer agrees to accept title to the Property subject to all rights and easements registered against title for the supply and installation of telephone
services, electricity, gas, sewers, water, television cable facilities and other related services; provided that title to the Property is otherwise good and
free from all encumbrances except: (a) as herein expressly provided; (b) any registered restrictions, conditions or covenants that run with the land
provided such have been complied with; (c) the provisions of the Condominium Act and its Regulations and the terms, conditions and provisions of
the Declaration, Description and By-laws, Occupancy Standards By-laws, including the Common Element Rules and other Rules and Regulations; and
(d) any existing municipal agreements, zoning by-laws and/or regulations and utilities or service contracts.

12. CLOSING ARRANGEMENTS: Where each of the Seller and Buyer retain a lawyer to complete the Agreement of Purchase and Sale of the Property,
and where the transaction will be completed by electronic registration pursuant to Part III of the Land Registration Reform Act, R.S.O. 1990, Chapter
L4 and the Electronic Registration Act, S.O. 1991, Chapter 44, and any amendments thereto, the Seller and Buyer acknowledge and agree that
the exchange of closing funds, nonregistrable documents and other items (the "Requisite Deliveries") and the release thereof to the Seller and Buyer
will (a) not occur at the same time as the registration of the transfer/deed (and any other documents intended to be registered in connection with the
completion of this transaction) and (b) be subject to conditions whereby the lawyer(s) receiving any of the Requisite Deliveries will be required to hold
same in trust and not release same except in accordance with the terms of a document registration agreement between the said lawyers. The Seller
and Buyer irrevocably instruct the said lawyers to be bound by the document registration agreement which is recommended from time to time by the
Law Society of Upper Canada. Unless otherwise agreed to by the lawyers, such exchange of the Requisite Deliveries will occur in the applicable Land
Titles Office or such other location agreeable to both lawyers.

13. STATUS CERTIFICATE AND MANAGEMENT OF CONDOMINIUM: Seller represents and warrants to Buyer that there are no special assessments
contemplated by the Condominium Corporation, and there are no legal actions pending by or against or contemplated by the Condominium
Corporation. The Seller consents to a request by the Buyer or the Buyer's authorized representative for a Status Certificate from the Condominium
Corporation. Buyer acknowledges that the Condominium Corporation may have entered into a Management Agreement for the management of the
condominium property.

14. DOCUMENTS AND DISCHARGE: Buyer shall not call for the production of any title deed, abstract, survey or other evidence of title to the Property
except such as are in the possession or control of Seller. Seller agrees to deliver to Buyer, if it is possible without incurring any costs in so doing,
copies of all current condominium documentation of the Condominium Corporation, including the Declaration, Description, By-laws, Common Element
Rules and Regulations and the most recent financial statements of the Condominium Corporation. If a discharge of any Charge/Mortgage held by a
corporation incorporated pursuant to the Trust And Loan Companies Act (Canada), Chartered Bank, Trust Company, Credit Union, Caisse Populaire
or Insurance Company and which is not to be assumed by Buyer on completion, is not available in registrable form on completion, Buyer agrees to
accept Seller's lawyer's personal undertaking to obtain, out of the closing funds, a discharge in registrable form and to register same, or cause same
to be registered, on title within a reasonableperiod of time after completion, provided that on or before completion Seller shall provide to Buyer a
mortgage statement prepared by the mortgagee setting out the balance required to obtain the discharge, and, where a real-time electronic cleared
funds transfer system is not being used, a direction executed by Seller directing payment to the mortgagee of the amount required to obtain the
discharge out of the balance due on completion.

15. MEETINGS: Seller represents and warrants to Buyer that at the time of the acceptance of this Offer the Seller has not received a notice convening
a special or general meeting of the Condominium Corporation respecting; (a) the termination of the government of the condominium property; (b)
any substantial alteration in or substantial addition to the common elements or the renovation thereof; OR (c) any substantial change in the assets or
liabilities of the Condominium Corporation; and Seller covenants that if Seller receives any such notice prior to the date of completion Seller shall
forthwith notify Buyer in writing and Buyer may thereupon at Buyer's option declare this Agreement to be null and void and all monies paid by Buyer
shall be refunded without interest or deduction.

INITIALS OF BUYER(S):   (*BC*)   INITIALS OF SELLER(S):   (*MS*)

    Form 101   Revised 2015   **Page 3 of 6**

16. **INSPECTION:** Buyer acknowledges having had the opportunity to inspect the Property and understands that upon acceptance of this offer there shall be a binding agreement of purchase and sale between Buyer and Seller. **The Buyer acknowledges having the opportunity to include a requirement for a property inspection report in this Agreement and agrees that except as may be specifically provided for in this Agreement, the Buyer will not be obtaining a property inspection or property inspection report regarding the Property.**

17. **APPROVAL OF THE AGREEMENT:** In the event that consent to this sale is required to be given by the Condominium Corporation or the Board of Directors, the Seller will apply forthwith for the requisite consent, and if such consent is refused, then this Agreement shall be null and void and the deposit monies paid hereunder shall be refunded without interest or other penalty to the Buyer.

18. **INSURANCE:** The Unit and all other things being purchased shall be and remain at the risk of the Seller until completion. In the event of substantial damage to the Property Buyer may at Buyer's option either permit the proceeds of insurance to be used for repair of such damage in accordance with the provisions of the Insurance Trust Agreement, or terminate this Agreement and all deposit monies paid by Buyer hereunder shall be refunded without interest or deduction. If Seller is taking back a Charge/Mortgage, or Buyer is assuming a Charge/Mortgage, Buyer shall supply Seller with reasonable evidence of adequate insurance to protect Seller's or other mortgagee's interest on completion.

19. **DOCUMENT PREPARATION:** The Transfer/Deed shall, save for the Land Transfer Tax Affidavit, be prepared in registrable form at the expense of Seller, and any Charge/Mortgage to be given back by the Buyer to Seller at the expense of the Buyer.

20. **RESIDENCY:** (a) Subject to (b) below, the Seller represents and warrants that the Seller is not and on completion will not be a non-resident under the non-residency provisions of the Income Tax Act which representation and warranty shall survive and not merge upon the completion of this transaction and the Seller shall deliver to the Buyer a statutory declaration that Seller is not then a non-resident of Canada; (b) provided that if the Seller is a non-resident under the non-residency provisions of the Income Tax Act, the Buyer shall be credited towards the Purchase Price with the amount, if any, necessary for Buyer to pay to the Minister of National Revenue to satisfy Buyer's liability in respect of tax payable by Seller under the non-residency provisions of the Income Tax Act by reason of this sale. Buyer shall not claim such credit if Seller delivers on completion the prescribed certificate.

21. **ADJUSTMENTS:** Common Expenses; realty taxes, including local improvement rates; mortgage interest; rentals; unmetered public or private utilities and fuel where billed to the Unit and not the Condominium Corporation; are to be apportioned and allowed to the day of completion, the day of completion itself to be apportioned to the Buyer. There shall be no adjustment for the Seller's share of any assets or liabilities of the Condominium Corporation including any reserve or contingency fund to which Seller may have contributed prior to the date of completion.

22. **PROPERTY ASSESSMENT:** The Buyer and Seller hereby acknowledge that the Province of Ontario has implemented current value assessment and properties may be re-assessed on an annual basis. The Buyer and Seller agree that no claim will be made against the Buyer or Seller, or any Brokerage, Broker or Salesperson, for any changes in property tax as a result of a re-assessment of the Property, save and except any property taxes that accrued prior to the completion of this transaction.

23. **TIME LIMITS:** Time shall in all respects be of the essence hereof provided that the time for doing or completing of any matter provided for herein may be extended or abridged by an agreement in writing signed by Seller and Buyer or by their respective lawyers who may be specifically authorized in that regard.

24. **TENDER:** Any tender of documents or money hereunder may be made upon Seller or Buyer or their respective lawyers on the day set for completion. Money shall be tendered with funds drawn on a lawyer's trust account in the form of a bank draft, certified cheque or wire transfer using the Large Value Transfer System.

25. **FAMILY LAW ACT:** Seller warrants that spousal consent is not necessary to this transaction under the provisions of the Family Law Act, R.S.O. 1990 unless Seller's spouse has executed the consent hereinafter provided.

26. **UFFI:** Seller represents and warrants to Buyer that during the time Seller has owned the Property, Seller has not caused any building on the Property to be insulated with insulation containing ureaformaldehyde, and that to the best of Seller's knowledge no building on the Property contains or has ever contained insulation that contains ureaformaldehyde. This warranty shall survive and not merge on the completion of this transaction, and if the building is part of a multiple unit building, this warranty shall only apply to that part of the building which is the subject of this transaction.

27. **LEGAL, ACCOUNTING AND ENVIRONMENTAL ADVICE:** The parties acknowledge that any information provided by the brokerage is not legal, tax or environmental advice.

28. **CONSUMER REPORTS: The Buyer is hereby notified that a consumer report containing credit and/or personal information may be referred to in connection with this transaction.**

29. **AGREEMENT IN WRITING:** If there is conflict or discrepancy between any provision added to this Agreement (including any Schedule attached hereto) and any provision in the standard pre-set portion hereof, the added provision shall supersede the standard pre-set provision to the extent of such conflict or discrepancy. This Agreement including any Schedule attached hereto, shall constitute the entire Agreement between Buyer and Seller. There is no representation, warranty, collateral agreement or condition, which affects this Agreement other than as expressed herein. For the purposes of this Agreement, Seller means vendor and Buyer means purchaser. This Agreement shall be read with all changes of gender or number required by the context.

30. **TIME AND DATE:** Any reference to a time and date in this Agreement shall mean the time and date where the Property is located.

INITIALS OF BUYER(S): (*BC*)　　　　INITIALS OF SELLER(S): (*MS*)

Form 101   Revised 2015   **Page 4 of 6**

Exercise 4   Agreement of Purchase and Sale—Condominium Resale, Page 5 of 6

31. SUCCESSORS AND ASSIGNS: The heirs, executors, administrators, successors and assigns of the undersigned are bound by the terms herein.

SIGNED, SEALED AND DELIVERED in the presence of: IN WITNESS whereof I have hereunto set my hand and seal:

Steven Hui ....   *Brenda Cheung* ....   ● DATE ...*May 10/xx*.....
(Witness)   (Buyer)   (Seal)

Steven Hui ....   *Raymond Ng* ....   ● DATE ...*May 10/xx*.....
(Witness)   (Buyer)   (Seal)

I, the Undersigned Seller, agree to the above offer. I hereby irrevocably instruct my lawyer to pay directly to the brokerage(s) with whom I have agreed to pay commission, the unpaid balance of the commission together with applicable Harmonized Sales Tax (and any other taxes as may hereafter be applicable), from the proceeds of the sale prior to any payment to the undersigned on completion, as advised by the brokerage(s) to my lawyer.

SIGNED, SEALED AND DELIVERED in the presence of: IN WITNESS whereof I have hereunto set my hand and seal:

Julie Ramos ....   *Michael Sharma* ....   ● DATE ...*May 10/xx*.....
(Witness)   (Seller)   (Seal)

....   ● DATE ....
(Witness)   (Seller)   (Seal)

SPOUSAL CONSENT: The Undersigned Spouse of the Seller hereby consents to the disposition evidenced herein pursuant to the provisions of the Family Law Act, R.S.O.1990, and hereby agrees with the Buyer that he/she will execute all necessary or incidental documents to give full force and effect to the sale evidenced herein.

....   ● DATE ....
(Witness)   (Spouse)   (Seal)

CONFIRMATION OF ACCEPTANCE: Notwithstanding anything contained herein to the contrary, I confirm this Agreement with all changes both typed

and written was finally accepted by all parties at ...*4:30*... a.m./p.m. this ...*12th*... day of.......................*May*....................., 20.*XX*....

Brenda Cheung
(Signature of Seller or Buyer)

INFORMATION ON BROKERAGE(S)

Listing Brokerage ....**ABC Realty Inc.**................... Tel.No.(.905.) .555-1212..

..**123 Main Street, Anycity, Anyregion L4H 6P5**...... **Julio Ramos**........
(Salesperson / Broker Name)

Co-op/Buyer Brokerage ....**XYZ Real Estate Ltd.**................ Tel.No.(.905.) .444-1212..

..**29 Maple Drive, Anycity, Anyregion L2J 7K6**...... **Steven Hui**........
(Salesperson / Broker Name)

ACKNOWLEDGEMENT

I acknowledge receipt of my signed copy of this accepted Agreement of Purchase and Sale and I authorize the Brokerage to forward a copy to my lawyer.	I acknowledge receipt of my signed copy of this accepted Agreement of Purchase and Sale and I authorize the Brokerage to forward a copy to my lawyer.
Michael Sharma .... DATE *May 12/xx* (Seller)	*Brenda Cheung* .... DATE *May 12/xx* (Buyer)
.... DATE .... (Seller)	*Raymond Ng* .... DATE *May 12/xx* (Buyer)
Address for Service ..*Suite 2807, 2827 Lakeside Drive* ..*Anycity K0N 1P0*.... Tel.No.(.905.) .666-1212.	Address for Service ..*Apt. 1850, 3871 Victoria Drive, Anycity* ..*K9C 3B5*.... Tel.No.(.905.) .777-1212.
Seller's Lawyer ..*Gupta and Sohi*....	Buyer's Lawyer ..*Hanna, Martin, and Anders*....
Address ..*138 Wentworth Drive, Anycity K3C 1B2*....	Address ..*Suite 300, First Place Centre, Anycity K2B 2C7*....
Email	Email ....
(.905.) .666-1212. Tel.No. (.905.) .666-2121. FAX No.	(.905.) .222-1212. Tel.No. (.905.) .222-2121. FAX No.

Property Manager: ..**McGowan Mgmt.**.... **142 John Street, Anycity K0N 1P0**   905-999-1212 905-999-2121
(Name)   (Address)   (Tel No.,FAX No)

FOR OFFICE USE ONLY   **COMMISSION TRUST AGREEMENT**

To: Co-operating Brokerage shown on the foregoing Agreement of Purchase and Sale:
In consideration for the Co-operating Brokerage procuring the foregoing Agreement of Purchase and Sale, I hereby declare that all moneys received or receivable by me in connection with the Transaction as contemplated in the MLS® Rules and Regulations of my Real Estate Board shall be receivable and held in trust. This agreement shall constitute a Commission Trust Agreement as defined in the MLS® Rules and shall be subject to and governed by the MLS® Rules pertaining to Commission Trust.

DATED as of the date and time of the acceptance of the foregoing Agreement of Purchase and Sale.   Acknowledged by:

Julie Ramos ....   *Steven Hui* ....
(Authorized to bind the Listing Brokerage)   (Authorized to bind the Co-operating Brokerage)

Form 101   Revised 2015   **Page 5 of 6**

OREA Ontario Real Estate Association

Form 101
for use in the Province of Ontario

Schedule A
Agreement of Purchase and Sale –
Condominium Resale

This Schedule is attached to and forms part of the Agreement of Purchase and Sale between:

BUYER, ... Brenda Cheung and and Raymond Ng ...., and

SELLER, ... Michael Sharma ....

for the purchase and sale of ...... Unit 2807, 2827 Lakeside Drive, Anycity, Regional Municipality of Anyregion

.... dated the ...10th... day of .... May ...., 20 XX ...

Buyer agrees to pay the balance as follows:

The Buyer agrees to pay a further sum of Twenty-Nine Thousand Dollars ($29,000.00), subject to adjustments, to the Seller on completion of this transaction, with funds drawn on a lawyer's trust account in the form of a bank draft, certified cheque, or wire transfer using the Large Value Transfer System.

The Buyer agrees to assume the existing first charge/mortgage held by Anycity Trust for approximately One Hundred and Ninety-Five Thousand Dollars ($195,000.00), bearing interest at the rate of 4.3% per annum, calculated semi-annually not in advance, repayable in blended monthly payments of One Thousand Two Hundred and Thirty-Six Dollars and Thirty-Eight Cents ($1,236.38), including both principal and interest, and due on September 30, 20xx.

The Seller agrees to take back a second mortgage in the amount of Sixty Thousand Dollars ($60,000.00), bearing interest at the rate of 4.5% per annum, calculated semi-annually not in advance, repayable in blended monthly payments of Three Hundred and Thirty-Two Dollars and Eight Cents ($332.08), including both principal and interest, and to run for a term of four years from the date of completion of this transaction.

The Buyer shall have the right to inspect the property one further time prior to completion, at a mutually agreed upon time, provided that written notice is given to the Seller. The Seller agrees to provide access to the property for the purpose of this inspection.

This form must be initialed by all parties to the Agreement of Purchase and Sale.

INITIALS OF BUYER(S): (*BC*)   **INITIALS OF SELLER(S):** (*MS*)

Form 101   Revised 2015   **Page 6 of 6**

■ Exercise 5   SPIS—Unit 4, 17 Manor Hill Road

A Seller Property Information Statement is illustrated for Unit 4, 17 Manor Hill Road (see following page). Identify ten possible problems or areas of concern (in point form) that may require further clarification or additional information, from either the seller's or buyer's perspective. Provide a short explanation or brief action plan regarding each.

SECTION	LINE	CONCERN	BRIEF EXPLANATION/ACTION PLAN
e.g., General	22	HST Status Unknown	Confirm with accountant.

OREA Ontario Real Estate Association

Form 220
for use in the Province of Ontario

Seller Property Information Statement
Residential

ANSWERS MUST BE COMPLETE AND ACCURATE This statement is designed in part to protect Sellers by establishing that correct information concerning the property is being provided to buyers. All of the information contained herein is provided by the Sellers to the brokerage/broker/salesperson. Any person who is in receipt of and utilizes this Statement acknowledges and agrees that **the information is being provided for information purposes only and is not a warranty as to the matters recited hereinafter even if attached to an Agreement of Purchase and Sale.** The brokerage/broker/salesperson shall not be held responsible for the accuracy of any information contained herein.

BUYERS MUST STILL MAKE THEIR OWN ENQUIRIES Buyers must still make their own enquiries notwithstanding the information contained on this statement. Each question and answer must be considered and where necessary, keeping in mind that the Sellers' knowledge of the property may be inaccurate or incomplete, additional information can be requested from the Sellers or from an independent source such as the municipality. Buyers can hire an independent inspector to examine the property to determine whether defects exist and to provide an estimate of the cost of repairing problems that have been identified. **This statement does not provide information on psychological stigmas that may be associated with a property.**

For the purposes of this Seller Property Information Statement, a "Seller" includes a landlord or a prospective landlord and a "buyer" includes a tenant, or a prospective tenant.

PROPERTY: Unit 4, 17 Manor Road	SELLER(S) TO **INITIAL** EACH APPLICABLE BOX			
SELLER(S): Janet Wong				
GENERAL: (Provide Applicable ADDITIONAL COMMENTS)	YES	NO	UNKNOWN	NOT APPLICABLE
1. I have occupied the property from..........20xx..............to......present..............				
2. Does any other party have an ownership or spousal interest in the property?		JW		
3. Is the property a condominium or a freehold property that includes an interest in a common elements condominium, (POTL)? (If yes, Schedule 221 to be completed.)	JW			
4. Does ownership of this property require membership in an Association and payment of Association fees? If yes, specify...		JW		
5. Is the property subject to first right of refusal, option, lease, rental agreement or other listing?		JW		
6. Are there any encroachments, registered easements, or rights-of-way?				JW
7. Is there a plan of survey? Date of survey..........N/A Condominium..............................				
8. Are there any disputes concerning the boundaries of the property?		JW		
9. Are you aware of any non-compliance with zoning regulations?		JW		
10. Are you aware of any pending developments, projects or rezoning applications in the neighbourhood? Additional townhouses - Phase 2, See Condo Documents	JW			
11. Are there any public projects planned for the neighbourhood? eg: road widenings, new highways, expropriations etc.		JW		
12. Are there any restrictive covenants that run with the land?				
13. Are there any drainage restrictions?			JW	
14. Are there any local levies or unusual taxes being charged at the present time or contemplated? If so, at what cost? .... Expiry date.......................................			JW	
15. Have you received any notice, claim, work order or deficiency notice affecting the property from any person or any public body?			JW	
16. (a) Is the property connected to municipal water? (If not, Schedule 222 to be completed.)	JW			
(b) Is the property connected to municipal sewer? (If not, Schedule 222 to be completed.)	JW			
17. Are there any current or pending Heritage restrictions for the property or the area?		JW		

INITIALS OF BUYER(S): ◯

Form 220   Revised 2016   **Page 1 of 3**

Exercise 5   Seller Property Information Statement—Page 2 of 4

GENERAL (cont'd): (Provide Applicable ADDITIONAL COMMENTS)

	YES	NO	UNKNOWN	NOT APPLICABLE
18. Are there any conditional sales contracts, leases, rental agreements or service contracts? eg: furnace, alarm system, hot water tank, propane tank, etc. Specify....... **Appliances $132/month**.. Are they assignable or will they be discharged?...	*JW*			
19. Are there any defects in any appliances or equipment included with the property?		*JW*		
20. Do you know the approximate age of the building(s)?Age....**15**........................... Any additions: Age........................				
21. Are you aware of any past or pending claims under the Tarion Warranty Corporation (formerly ONHWP)? Tarion Warranty Corporation/ONHWP Registration No..		*JW*		
22. Will the sale of this property be subject to HST?			*JW*	

ADDITIONAL COMMENTS: **New townhouses scheduled for Phase 2 - directly adjacent. Will impact parking and**

....**partially obstruct water view.**..

....

....

....

ENVIRONMENTAL: (Provide Applicable ADDITIONAL COMMENTS)

	YES	NO	UNKNOWN	NOT APPLICABLE
1. Are you aware of possible environmental problems or soil contamination of any kind on the property or in the immediate area? eg: radon gas, toxic waste, underground gasoline or fuel tanks etc.		*JW*		
2. Are there any existing or proposed waste dumps, disposal sites or land fills in the immediate area?		*JW*		
3. Are there any hydro generating projects planned for the immediate area? eg: Wind Turbines		*JW*		
4. Is the property subject to flooding?		*JW*		
5. Is the property under the jurisdiction of any Conservation Authority or Commission?		*JW*		
6. Are you aware of any excessive erosion, settling, slippage, sliding or other soil problems?		*JW*		
7. Does the property have any abandoned or de-commissioned ☐ well ☐ septic system ☐ swimming pool ☐ foundation ☐ other, specify..		*JW*		
8. (a) Is there a fuel oil tank on the property? If yes, complete the following: ☐ Underground. Date for required upgrading or removal.. ☐ Aboveground. Age of tank.......................... Date of last inspection..........................		*JW*		
(b) Does the fuel oil tank comply with the Technical Standards and Safety Authority requirements and any other requirements for fuel to be delivered?				*JW*
9. Has the use of the property ever been for the growth or manufacture of illegal substances?		*JW*		

ADDITIONAL COMMENTS:..

....

....

....

....

INITIALS OF BUYER(S): ⬭

Form 220   Revised 2016   **Page 2 of 3**

IMPROVEMENTS AND STRUCTURAL: (Provide Applicable ADDITIONAL COMMENTS)	YES	NO	UNKNOWN	NOT APPLICABLE
1. Are you aware of any structural problems? **Leaking windows - see note**	JW			
2. (a) Have you made any renovations, additions or improvements to the property? **See below**	JW			
(b) Was a building permit obtained?		JW		
(c) Has the final building inspection been approved or has a final occupancy permit been obtained?		JW		
3. To the best of your knowledge have the building(s) ever contained ureaformaldehyde insulation?		JW		
4. Is there vermiculite insulation on the property? If yes, has it been tested for asbestos?...		JW		
5. (a) Are you aware of any deficiencies or non-compliance with the Ontario Fire Code?		JW		
(b) Is your property equipped with operational smoke detectors?	JW			
(c) Is the property equipped with operational carbon monoxide detectors?	JW			
6. (a) Is the woodstove(s)/chimney(s)/fireplace(s)/insert(s) in good working order?				JW
(b) Has the wood energy system been **WETT** inspected? (Wood Energy Technology Transfer)				JW
7. Are you aware of any problems with the central air conditioning system?		JW		
8. Are you aware of any problems with the heating system?		JW		
9. (a) Are you aware of any moisture and/or water problems?		JW		
(b) Are you aware of any roof leakage or unrepaired damage? Age of roof covering		JW		
(c) Are you aware of any damage due to wind, fire, flood, insects, termites, rodents, pets or wood rot?		JW		
(d) Have any repairs been carried out to correct any past or present problems related to (a), (b) and/or (c)? If yes, explain in additional comments below.		JW		
10.(a) Are you aware of any problems with the electrical system? Size of service...................................		JW		
(b) Type of wiring: ☐copper ☐aluminium ☐knob-and-tube ☐other..............................			JW	
11. Are you aware of any problems with the plumbing system?		JW		
12. Is there any lead, galvanized metal, cast iron or Kitec plumbing on the property?		JW		
13. Are you aware of any problems with the swimming pool, sauna, hot tub, jet bathtub or lawn sprinkler system?		JW		

ADDITIONAL COMMENTS: ....**Leaking windows in several units - repairs may require special assessment.**

....**Owner altered pass-through between dining room and kitchen, and added small rear deck.**

....

....

Schedule(s) attached hereto and forming part of this Statement include:..... Schedule for Condominium (Form 221) ....

The Sellers state that the above information is true, based on their current actual knowledge as of the date below. Any important changes to this information known to the Sellers will be disclosed by the Sellers prior to closing. Sellers are responsible for the accuracy of all answers. Sellers further agree to indemnify and hold the Brokerage/Broker/Salesperson harmless from any liability incurred as a result of any buyer relying on this information. The Sellers hereby authorize the Brokerage to post a copy of this Seller Property Information Statement into the database(s) of the appropriate MLS® system and that a copy of this Seller Property Information Statement be delivered by their agent or representative to prospective buyers or their agents or representatives. The Sellers hereby acknowledge receipt of a true copy of this statement.

Janet Wong.......................... DATE *May 1/xx* .... DATE................
(Signature of Seller)   (Signature of Seller)

I acknowledge that the information provided herein is not warranted and hereby acknowledge receipt of a copy of the above information including any applicable Schedule(s).

....   DATE...
(Signature of Buyer or Authorized Representative)

....   DATE...
(Signature of Buyer)

Form 220   Revised 2016   **Page 3 of 3**

Exercise 5   Seller Property Information Statement—Page 4 of 4

OREA Ontario Real Estate Association

Form 221
for use in the Province of Ontario

Seller Property Information Statement
Schedule for Condominium

This Schedule is attached to and forms part of the Seller Property Information Statement (Form 220) for:

PROPERTY: Unit 4, 17 Manor Road	SELLER(S) TO **INITIAL**
SELLER(S): Janet Wong	EACH APPLICABLE BOX

CONDOMINIUM CORPORATION: (Provide Applicable ADDITIONAL COMMENTS)	YES	NO	UNKNOWN	NOT APPLICABLE
1. **(a)** Condominium fee $ 327.50/month				
(b) Condominium fee includes: utilities, parking and cable television				
(c) Cost for amenities not included in Condominium fee $ ...... Details				JW
2. Are there any special assessments approved or contemplated?		JW		
3. Have you received any written notice of lawsuit(s) pending?		JW		
4. Have you been informed of any notices, claims, work orders or deficiency notices affecting the common elements received from any person or any public body?		JW		
5. **(a)** Has a reserve fund study been completed? Date of Study......			JW	
(b) Approximate amount of reserve fund as of last notification $			JW	
6. **(a)** Are there any restrictions on pets? See below	JW			
(b) Are there any restrictions on renting the property? See below	JW			
(c) Are there any other restrictions on the use of the property?		JW		
7. **(a)** If any renovations, additions or improvements were made to the unit and/or common elements, was approval of the Condominium Corporation obtained?	JW			
(b) Is approval of any prospective buyer required by the Condominium Corporation?		JW		
(c) Are any other approvals required by the Condominium Corporation or Property Manager? If yes, specify:		JW		
(d) Name of Property Management Company Manor Hill Road Property Management				
8. Are there any pending rule or by-law amendments which may alter or restrict the uses of the property?	JW	See below		
9. Is the Condominium registered?	JW			
10. Parking: Number of Spaces ...2... ☐ Owned ☑ Exclusive Use ☐ Leased or Licensed Parking space number(s) 37 & 52				
11. Locker: ...... ☐ Owned ☑ Exclusive Use Locker number(s) 4				
12. **(a)** Amenities: ☑ Pool ☐ Sauna ☑ Exercise ☐ Room ☐ Meeting/Party Room ☐ Boat Docking ☐ Guest Parking ☐ Other......				
(b) Are you aware of any problems with any of the common element amenities? If yes, specify:		JW		

ADDITIONAL COMMENTS: No pet bylaw being considered at next board meeting. Rentals restricted to minimum six-month duration.

Bylaw amended approximately six months ago. Owner recently installed satellite dish on rear exterior wall.

INITIALS OF BUYER(S):

Form 221   Revised 2014   **Page 1 of 1**

■ Exercise 6   The Partially-Completed Offer

A partially-completed condominium offer is illustrated (see following pages). Insert all necessary dates and other information required for a fully-completed, accepted agreement of purchase and sale based on the following:

> The buyer submits the offer September 8, 20xx with an irrevocable date of September 9th at 5 p.m. Include an appropriate condition regarding a home inspection, the arranging of a new first mortgage for not less than $180,000 @ 5.5%, amortized over 25 years with bi-weekly payments and due in two years and the buyer's solicitor's review of a status certificate. The conditions should be fulfilled no later than 11:59 p.m. on September 30th. Also include a clause permitting the buyer to reinspect the premises one more time prior to closing.
>
> Allow until October 30th for title search, with a completion date set for December 1st. ABC Realty Inc. is representing both the buyer and the sellers. Insert your name as witness where appropriate. The sellers counter on the 9th for $215,000, with a revised irrevocable of September 10th at 5 p.m. The counter offer is accepted by the buyer at 10:30 a.m. on September 10th.

Fill in any other information on the offer as required.

Exercise 6   Agreement of Purchase and Sale—Condominium Resale, Page 1 of 6

OREA Ontario Real Estate Association

Agreement of Purchase and Sale
Condominium Resale

Form 101
for use in the Province of Ontario

This Agreement of Purchase and Sale dated this .... day of .... 20..........

BUYER, ... Barbara Lopez .... , agrees to purchase from
(Full legal names of all Buyers)

SELLER, ... Victoria Anne Cooper and Joseph Alan Cooper .... , the following
(Full legal names of all Sellers)

PROPERTY:
a unit in the condominium property known as .... Townhouse .... No....7..............
(Apartment/Townhouse/Suite/Unit)

located at .... 394 Highland Road ....

in the .... City of Anycity, Regional Municipality of Anyregion ....

being .... Anyregion .... Condominium Plan No ....210..............
(Legal Name of Condominium Corporation)

Unit Number ....7................. Level No. ....1................. Building No. ....1................. together with ownership

or exclusive use of Parking Space(s) .... 16 and 17   Level A .... , together with ownership or exclusive use of
(Number(s), Level(s))

Locker(s) ....N/A................. , together with Seller's proportionate undivided tenancy-in-common interest
(Number(s), Level(s))

in the common elements appurtenant to the Unit as described in the Declaration and Description including the exclusive right to use such other parts of the common elements appurtenant to the Unit as may be specified in the Declaration and Description: the Unit, the proportionate interest in the common elements appurtenant thereto, and the exclusive use portions of the common elements, being herein called the "Property".

PURCHASE PRICE: Dollars (CDN$) ....$209,000.00..............

.......Two Hundred and Nine Thousand-- Dollars

DEPOSIT: Buyer submits .... Upon Acceptance ....
(Herewith/Upon Acceptance/as otherwise described in this Agreement)

.......Five Thousand-- Dollars (CDN$) ....$5,000.00..............

by negotiable cheque payable to .... ABC Realty Inc. .... "Deposit Holder" to be held in trust pending completion or other termination of this Agreement and to be credited toward the Purchase Price on completion. For the purposes of this Agreement, "Upon Acceptance" shall mean that the Buyer is required to deliver the deposit to the Deposit Holder within 24 hours of the acceptance of this Agreement. The parties to this Agreement hereby acknowledge that, unless otherwise provided for in this Agreement, the Deposit Holder shall place the deposit in trust in the Deposit Holder's non-interest bearing Real Estate Trust Account and no interest shall be earned, received or paid on the deposit.

Buyer agrees to pay the balance as more particularly set out in Schedule A attached.

SCHEDULE(S) A..**attached hereto form(s) part of this Agreement.**

1. **IRREVOCABILITY:** This offer shall be irrevocable by .... until .... a.m./p.m. on the ....
(Seller/Buyer)

    day of .... 20 ...., after which time, if not accepted, this offer shall be null and void and the deposit shall be returned to the Buyer in full without interest.

2. **COMPLETION DATE:** This Agreement shall be completed by no later than 6:00 p.m. on the .... day of ....,

    20 .... Upon completion, vacant possession of the property shall be given to the Buyer unless otherwise provided for in this Agreement.

    INITIALS OF BUYER(S): ( )   **INITIALS OF SELLER(S):** ( )

Form 101   Revised 2015   **Page 1 of 6**

Exercise 6   Agreement of Purchase and Sale—Condominium Resale, Page 2 of 6

3. NOTICES: The Seller hereby appoints the Listing Brokerage as agent for the Seller for the purpose of giving and receiving notices pursuant to this Agreement. Where a Brokerage (Buyer's Brokerage) has entered into a representation agreement with the Buyer, the Buyer hereby appoints the Buyer's Brokerage as agent for the purpose of giving and receiving notices pursuant to this Agreement. **Where a Brokerage represents both the Seller and the Buyer (multiple representation), the Brokerage shall not be appointed or authorized to be agent for either the Buyer or the Seller for the purpose of giving and receiving notices.** Any notice relating hereto or provided for herein shall be in writing. In addition to any provision contained herein and in any Schedule hereto, this offer, any counter-offer, notice of acceptance thereof or any notice to be given or received pursuant to this Agreement or any Schedule hereto (any of them, "Document") shall be deemed given and received when delivered personally or hand delivered to the Address for Service provided in the Acknowledgement below, or where a facsimile number or email address is provided herein, when transmitted electronically to that facsimile number or email address, respectively, in which case, the signature(s) of the party (parties) shall be deemed to be original.

FAX No.: ....   FAX No.: ....

               (For delivery of Documents to Seller)   (For delivery of Documents to Buyer)

Email Address: ....   Email Address: ....

               (For delivery of Documents to Seller)   (For delivery of Documents to Buyer)

4. CHATTELS INCLUDED: Sun Glamour patio set including four chairs, table, and umbrella; mirror located in foyer; and broadloom in living room, dining room, family room, and three bedrooms

Unless otherwise stated in this Agreement or any Schedule hereto, Seller agrees to convey all fixtures and chattels included in the Purchase Price free from all liens, encumbrances or claims affecting the said fixtures and chattels.

5. FIXTURES EXCLUDED: Dining room chandelier

6. RENTAL ITEMS (Including Lease, Lease to Own): The following equipment is rented and **not** included in the Purchase Price. The Buyer ` agrees to assume the rental contract(s), if assumable:

Hot water tank and water softener @ $51.20 per month (plus applicable taxes)

The Buyer agrees to co-operate and execute such documentation as may be required to facilitate such assumption.

7. COMMON EXPENSES: Seller warrants to Buyer that the common expenses presently payable to the Condominium Corporation in respect of the Property are approximately $ $189.05 per month, which amount includes the following: Water charges, lawn and road maintenance, garbage pickup, and insurance (common elements)

8. PARKING AND LOCKERS: Parking and Lockers are as described above or assigned as follows: N/A

.... at an additional cost of: ....

INITIALS OF BUYER(S): (⬭)   INITIALS OF SELLER(S): (⬭)

Form 101   Revised 2015   **Page 2 of 6**

Exercise 6   Agreement of Purchase and Sale—Condominium Resale, Page 3 of 6

9. **HST:** If the sale of the Property (Real Property as described above) is subject to Harmonized Sales Tax (HST), then such tax shall be .... included in .... the Purchase Price. If the sale of the Property is not subject to HST, Seller agrees to certify on or before
(included in/in addition to)
closing, that the sale of the Property is not subject to HST. Any HST on chattels, if applicable, is not included in the Purchase Price.

10. **TITLE SEARCH:** Buyer shall be allowed until 6:00 p.m. on the .... day of ...., 20......., (Requisition Date) to examine the title to the Property at Buyer's own expense and until the earlier of: (i) thirty days from the later of the Requisition Date or the date on which the conditions in this Agreement are fulfilled or otherwise waived or; (ii) five days prior to completion, to satisfy Buyer that there are no

outstanding work orders or deficiency notices affecting the Property, and that its present use (...) may be lawfully continued. If within that time any valid objection to title or to any outstanding work order or deficiency notice, or to the fact the said present use may not lawfully be continued, is made in writing to Seller and which Seller is unable or unwilling to remove, remedy or satisfy or obtain insurance save and except against risk of fire (Title Insurance) in favour of the Buyer and any mortgagee, (with all related costs at the expense of the Seller), and which Buyer will not waive, this Agreement notwithstanding any intermediate acts or negotiations in respect of such objections, shall be at an end and all monies paid shall be returned without interest or deduction and Seller, Listing Brokerage and Co-operating Brokerage shall not be liable for any costs or damages. Save as to any valid objection so made by such day and except for any objection going to the root of the title, Buyer shall be conclusively deemed to have accepted Seller's title to the Property. Seller hereby consents to the municipality or other governmental agencies releasing to Buyer details of all outstanding work orders and deficiency notices affecting the Property, and Seller agrees to execute and deliver such further authorizations in this regard as Buyer may reasonably require.

11. **TITLE:** Buyer agrees to accept title to the Property subject to all rights and easements registered against title for the supply and installation of telephone services, electricity, gas, sewers, water, television cable facilities and other related services; provided that title to the Property is otherwise good and free from all encumbrances except: (a) as herein expressly provided; (b) any registered restrictions, conditions or covenants that run with the land provided such have been complied with; (c) the provisions of the Condominium Act and its Regulations and the terms, conditions and provisions of the Declaration, Description and By-laws, Occupancy Standards By-laws, including the Common Element Rules and other Rules and Regulations; and (d) any existing municipal agreements, zoning by-laws and/or regulations and utilities or service contracts.

12. **CLOSING ARRANGEMENTS:** Where each of the Seller and Buyer retain a lawyer to complete the Agreement of Purchase and Sale of the Property, and where the transaction will be completed by electronic registration pursuant to Part III of the Land Registration Reform Act, R.S.O. 1990, Chapter L4 and the Electronic Registration Act, S.O. 1991, Chapter 44, and any amendments thereto, the Seller and Buyer acknowledge and agree that the exchange of closing funds, nonregistrable documents and other items (the "Requisite Deliveries") and the release thereof to the Seller and Buyer will (a) not occur at the same time as the registration of the transfer/deed (and any other documents intended to be registered in connection with the completion of this transaction) and (b) be subject to conditions whereby the lawyer(s) receiving any of the Requisite Deliveries will be required to hold same in trust and not release same except in accordance with the terms of a document registration agreement between the said lawyers. The Seller and Buyer irrevocably instruct the said lawyers to be bound by the document registration agreement which is recommended from time to time by the Law Society of Upper Canada. Unless otherwise agreed to by the lawyers, such exchange of the Requisite Deliveries will occur in the applicable Land Titles Office or such other location agreeable to both lawyers.

13. **STATUS CERTIFICATE AND MANAGEMENT OF CONDOMINIUM:** Seller represents and warrants to Buyer that there are no special assessments contemplated by the Condominium Corporation, and there are no legal actions pending by or against or contemplated by the Condominium Corporation. The Seller consents to a request by the Buyer or the Buyer's authorized representative for a Status Certificate from the Condominium Corporation. Buyer acknowledges that the Condominium Corporation may have entered into a Management Agreement for the management of the condominium property.

14. **DOCUMENTS AND DISCHARGE:** Buyer shall not call for the production of any title deed, abstract, survey or other evidence of title to the Property except such as are in the possession or control of Seller. Seller agrees to deliver to Buyer, if it is possible without incurring any costs in so doing, copies of all current condominium documentation of the Condominium Corporation, including the Declaration, Description, By-laws, Common Element Rules and Regulations and the most recent financial statements of the Condominium Corporation. If a discharge of any Charge/Mortgage held by a corporation incorporated pursuant to the Trust And Loan Companies Act (Canada), Chartered Bank, Trust Company, Credit Union, Caisse Populaire or Insurance Company and which is not to be assumed by Buyer on completion, is not available in registrable form on completion, Buyer agrees to accept Seller's lawyer's personal undertaking to obtain, out of the closing funds, a discharge in registrable form and to register same, or cause same to be registered, on title within a reasonableperiod of time after completion, provided that on or before completion Seller shall provide to Buyer a mortgage statement prepared by the mortgagee setting out the balance required to obtain the discharge, and, where a real-time electronic cleared funds transfer system is not being used, a direction executed by Seller directing payment to the mortgagee of the amount required to obtain the discharge out of the balance due on completion.

15. **MEETINGS:** Seller represents and warrants to Buyer that at the time of the acceptance of this Offer the Seller has not received a notice convening a special or general meeting of the Condominium Corporation respecting; (a) the termination of the government of the condominium property; (b) any substantial alteration in or substantial addition to the common elements or the renovation thereof; OR (c) any substantial change in the assets or liabilities of the Condominium Corporation; and Seller covenants that if Seller receives any such notice prior to the date of completion Seller shall forthwith notify Buyer in writing and Buyer may thereupon at Buyer's option declare this Agreement to be null and void and all monies paid by Buyer shall be refunded without interest or deduction.

INITIALS OF BUYER(S): (⬭)   INITIALS OF SELLER(S): (⬭)

Form 101   Revised 2015   **Page 3 of 6**

16. INSPECTION: Buyer acknowledges having had the opportunity to inspect the Property and understands that upon acceptance of this offer there shall be a binding agreement of purchase and sale between Buyer and Seller. **The Buyer acknowledges having the opportunity to include a requirement for a property inspection report in this Agreement and agrees that except as may be specifically provided for in this Agreement, the Buyer will not be obtaining a property inspection or property inspection report regarding the Property.**

17. APPROVAL OF THE AGREEMENT: In the event that consent to this sale is required to be given by the Condominium Corporation or the Board of Directors, the Seller will apply forthwith for the requisite consent, and if such consent is refused, then this Agreement shall be null and void and the deposit monies paid hereunder shall be refunded without interest or other penalty to the Buyer.

18. INSURANCE: The Unit and all other things being purchased shall be and remain at the risk of the Seller until completion. In the event of substantial damage to the Property Buyer may at Buyer's option either permit the proceeds of insurance to be used for repair of such damage in accordance with the provisions of the Insurance Trust Agreement, or terminate this Agreement and all deposit monies paid by Buyer hereunder shall be refunded without interest or deduction. If Seller is taking back a Charge/Mortgage, or Buyer is assuming a Charge/Mortgage, Buyer shall supply Seller with reasonable evidence of adequate insurance to protect Seller's or other mortgagee's interest on completion.

19. DOCUMENT PREPARATION: The Transfer/Deed shall, save for the Land Transfer Tax Affidavit, be prepared in registrable form at the expense of Seller, and any Charge/Mortgage to be given back by the Buyer to Seller at the expense of the Buyer.

20. RESIDENCY: (a) Subject to (b) below, the Seller represents and warrants that the Seller is not and on completion will not be a non-resident under the non-residency provisions of the Income Tax Act which representation and warranty shall survive and not merge upon the completion of this transaction and the Seller shall deliver to the Buyer a statutory declaration that Seller is not then a non-resident of Canada; (b) provided that if the Seller is a non-resident under the non-residency provisions of the Income Tax Act, the Buyer shall be credited towards the Purchase Price with the amount, if any, necessary for Buyer to pay to the Minister of National Revenue to satisfy Buyer's liability in respect of tax payable by Seller under the non-residency provisions of the Income Tax Act by reason of this sale. Buyer shall not claim such credit if Seller delivers on completion the prescribed certificate.

21. ADJUSTMENTS: Common Expenses; realty taxes, including local improvement rates; mortgage interest; rentals; unmetered public or private utilities and fuel where billed to the Unit and not the Condominium Corporation; are to be apportioned and allowed to the day of completion, the day of completion itself to be apportioned to the Buyer. There shall be no adjustment for the Seller's share of any assets or liabilities of the Condominium Corporation including any reserve or contingency fund to which Seller may have contributed prior to the date of completion.

22. PROPERTY ASSESSMENT: The Buyer and Seller hereby acknowledge that the Province of Ontario has implemented current value assessment and properties may be re-assessed on an annual basis. The Buyer and Seller agree that no claim will be made against the Buyer or Seller, or any Brokerage, Broker or Salesperson, for any changes in property tax as a result of a re-assessment of the Property, save and except any property taxes that accrued prior to the completion of this transaction.

23. TIME LIMITS: Time shall in all respects be of the essence hereof provided that the time for doing or completing of any matter provided for herein may be extended or abridged by an agreement in writing signed by Seller and Buyer or by their respective lawyers who may be specifically authorized in that regard.

24. TENDER: Any tender of documents or money hereunder may be made upon Seller or Buyer or their respective lawyers on the day set for completion. Money shall be tendered with funds drawn on a lawyer's trust account in the form of a bank draft, certified cheque or wire transfer using the Large Value Transfer System.

25. FAMILY LAW ACT: Seller warrants that spousal consent is not necessary to this transaction under the provisions of the Family Law Act, R.S.O. 1990 unless Seller's spouse has executed the consent hereinafter provided.

26. UFFI: Seller represents and warrants to Buyer that during the time Seller has owned the Property, Seller has not caused any building on the Property to be insulated with insulation containing ureaformaldehyde, and that to the best of Seller's knowledge no building on the Property contains or has ever contained insulation that contains ureaformaldehyde. This warranty shall survive and not merge on the completion of this transaction, and if the building is part of a multiple unit building, this warranty shall only apply to that part of the building which is the subject of this transaction.

27. LEGAL, ACCOUNTING AND ENVIRONMENTAL ADVICE: The parties acknowledge that any information provided by the brokerage is not legal, tax or environmental advice.

28. CONSUMER REPORTS: The Buyer is hereby notified that a consumer report containing credit and/or personal information may be referred to in connection with this transaction.

29. AGREEMENT IN WRITING: If there is conflict or discrepancy between any provision added to this Agreement (including any Schedule attached hereto) and any provision in the standard pre-set portion hereof, the added provision shall supersede the standard pre-set provision to the extent of such conflict or discrepancy. This Agreement including any Schedule attached hereto, shall constitute the entire Agreement between Buyer and Seller. There is no representation, warranty, collateral agreement or condition, which affects this Agreement other than as expressed herein. For the purposes of this Agreement, Seller means vendor and Buyer means purchaser. This Agreement shall be read with all changes of gender or number required by the context.

30. TIME AND DATE: Any reference to a time and date in this Agreement shall mean the time and date where the Property is located.

INITIALS OF BUYER(S): ⬭   INITIALS OF SELLER(S): ⬭

Form 101   Revised 2015   **Page 4 of 6**

Exercise 6   Agreement of Purchase and Sale—Condominium Resale, Page 5 of 6

31. SUCCESSORS AND ASSIGNS: The heirs, executors, administrators, successors and assigns of the undersigned are bound by the terms herein.

SIGNED, SEALED AND DELIVERED in the presence of: IN WITNESS whereof I have hereunto set my hand and seal:

.... ● DATE ....
(Witness)   (Buyer)   (Seal)

.... ● DATE ....
(Witness)   (Buyer)   (Seal)

I, the Undersigned Seller, agree to the above offer. I hereby irrevocably instruct my lawyer to pay directly to the brokerage(s) with whom I have agreed to pay commission, the unpaid balance of the commission together with applicable Harmonized Sales Tax (and any other taxes as may hereafter be applicable), from the proceeds of the sale prior to any payment to the undersigned on completion, as advised by the brokerage(s) to my lawyer.

SIGNED, SEALED AND DELIVERED in the presence of: IN WITNESS whereof I have hereunto set my hand and seal:

.... ● DATE ....
(Witness)   (Seller)   (Seal)

.... ● DATE ....
(Witness)   (Seller)   (Seal)

SPOUSAL CONSENT: The Undersigned Spouse of the Seller hereby consents to the disposition evidenced herein pursuant to the provisions of the Family Law Act, R.S.O.1990, and hereby agrees with the Buyer that he/she will execute all necessary or incidental documents to give full force and effect to the sale evidenced herein.

.... ● DATE ....
(Witness)   (Spouse)   (Seal)

CONFIRMATION OF ACCEPTANCE: Notwithstanding anything contained herein to the contrary, I confirm this Agreement with all changes both typed and written was finally accepted by all parties at .... a.m./p.m. this .... day of.., 20..........

....
(Signature of Seller or Buyer)

INFORMATION ON BROKERAGE(S)

Listing Brokerage .... Tel.No.(................)..............................

....
(Salesperson / Broker Name)

Co-op/Buyer Brokerage .... Tel.No.(................)..............................

....
(Salesperson / Broker Name)

ACKNOWLEDGEMENT

I acknowledge receipt of my signed copy of this accepted Agreement of Purchase and Sale and I authorize the Brokerage to forward a copy to my lawyer. | I acknowledge receipt of my signed copy of this accepted Agreement of Purchase and Sale and I authorize the Brokerage to forward a copy to my lawyer.

.... DATE .... | .... DATE ....
(Seller) | (Buyer)

.... DATE .... | .... DATE ....
(Seller) | (Buyer)

Address for Service .... | Address for Service ....

.... Tel.No.(..........)..................... | .... Tel.No.(..........).....................

Seller's Lawyer .... | Buyer's Lawyer ....

Address .... | Address ....

Email .... | Email ....

(..........)..................... (..........)..................... | (..........)..................... (..........).....................
   Tel.No.   FAX No. | Tel.No.   FAX No.

Property Manager: **Anycity Property Management**   **30 Welland Drive, Anycity K0N 1P0**   **705-999-1212 705-999-2121**
                    (Name)   (Address)   (Tel No.,FAX No)

FOR OFFICE USE ONLY   **COMMISSION TRUST AGREEMENT**

To: Co-operating Brokerage shown on the foregoing Agreement of Purchase and Sale:
In consideration for the Co-operating Brokerage procuring the foregoing Agreement of Purchase and Sale, I hereby declare that all moneys received or receivable by me in connection with the Transaction as contemplated in the MLS® Rules and Regulations of my Real Estate Board shall be receivable and held in trust. This agreement shall constitute a Commission Trust Agreement as defined in the MLS® Rules and shall be subject to and governed by the MLS® Rules pertaining to Commission Trust.

DATED as of the date and time of the acceptance of the foregoing Agreement of Purchase and Sale.   Acknowledged by:

....
(Authorized to bind the Listing Brokerage)   (Authorized to bind the Co-operating Brokerage)

Form 101   Revised 2015   **Page 5 of 6**

Form 101
for use in the Province of Ontario

Schedule A
Agreement of Purchase and Sale –
Condominium Resale

This Schedule is attached to and forms part of the Agreement of Purchase and Sale between:

BUYER, ... Barbara Lopez ...., and

SELLER, ... Victoria Anne Cooper and Joseph Alan Cooper ....

for the purchase and sale of .. Unit 7, 394 Highland Road, City of Anycity, Regional Municipality of Anyregion ..

.... dated the .... day of ...., 20 ....

Buyer agrees to pay the balance as follows:

This form must be initialed by all parties to the Agreement of Purchase and Sale.

INITIALS OF BUYER(S): ⬭   INITIALS OF SELLER(S): ⬭

    Form 101   Revised 2015   **Page 6 of 6**

CHAPTER 3

Residential Leasing

Introduction

More than 30% of all private Ontario dwellings are occupied by renters. Total rental-occupied dwellings in this province exceed 1.3 million. Rental markets, sometimes over-looked by seasoned registrants, can represent solid opportunities for newly-registered salespersons. Demand is typically high given traditionally low vacancy factors in the active Ontario marketplace. Further, young rental clients grow with your new sales career, as they move-up to home ownership, expand assets and acquire different lifestyles.

The rental market also brings new salespeople into direct contact with investors holding income property who routinely seek out renters. These same investors acquire or dispose of rental properties and require brokerage services. Make a sound strategic decision —include rental activity in your career design.

This chapter identifies key differences between residential and commercial real estate, most notably regarding regulatory requirements that affect both landlords and tenants under the *Residential Tenancies Act*. Chapter materials then focus on the agreement to lease, as differentiated from a lease, key provisions contained within the *Agreement to Lease—Residential* (OREA Form 400), a typical rental application (OREA Form 410) and selected clauses commonly used when preparing an agreement to lease.

The balance of the chapter highlights the role of the Landlord and Tenant Board, along with key regulatory requirements in the *Residential Tenancies Act* commonly encountered by registrants when dealing with landlords and tenants in the marketplace.

Learning Outcomes

At the conclusion of this chapter, students will be able to:

- Discuss and provide examples of four major types of tenancy, including fixed term, periodic, tenancy at will and tenancy at sufferance.
- Differentiate between residential and commercial tenancies, with particular regard to use issues and statutory exemptions under the *Residential Tenancies Act*.
- Detail the essential elements of a legally enforceable lease, with particular reference to the *Agreement to Lease—Residential* (OREA Form 400).
- Discuss key provisions of the *Agreement to Lease—Residential* (OREA Form 400), including typical clauses used when drafting such agreements.
- Outline the role of the Landlord and Tenant Board with particular emphasis on mediation and adjudication processes when resolving landlord/tenant disputes.
- Discuss selected provisions of the *Residential Tenancies Act* as they impact commencing a residential tenancy, the concept of lawful rent and associated guidelines concerning rent increases, access and entry rights, and assignments and subletting.
- Discuss specific provisions in the *Residential Tenancies Act* concerning termination by the landlord and by the tenant.
- Discuss the role that the *Residential Tenancies Act* has in addressing special provisions concerning the conversion of rental premises into condominiums.

LEASEHOLD INTEREST

A residential tenancy is legally derived from a *leasehold estate* (interest) in property. Rights associated with this interest have gradually evolved from feudal times to present practices. The primary distinguishing characteristic, compared to freehold, is time. Whereas a *freehold estate* (ownership) is indefinite in time, leasehold is either certain or capable of being made so. Over hundreds of years, common law has refined the granting of lease-hold interests and associated legal practices; e.g., essential lease elements, creation, registration, assignment and subletting.

Ontario residential tenancies are heavily impacted by the *Residential Tenancies Act* (RTA). Statutory knowledge is vital in addressing tenancy matters. Conversely, commercial tenancies in this province rely primarily on common law principles and case law, given the less focal role of the *Commercial Tenancies Act.*

Types of Tenancy

Four major types of tenancy have evolved from feudal times: *fixed term, periodic, tenancy at will* and *tenancy at sufferance*—each with accompanying common law rights and remedies for landlords and tenants, including termination. However, notwithstanding this fact, the *Residential Tenancies Act* ensures security of tenure (subject to termination provisions set out in the legislation). For example, if a residential fixed term lease expires, the landlord/tenant relationship automatically converts to a periodic tenancy; e.g., month-to-month. Landlords may only terminate for specific causes detailed in the Act.

Similarly, an unwritten tenancy at will has legal status regardless of whether a lease ever existed or not. If the parties agree verbally and all statutory provisions are complied with, such a relationship becomes a periodic tenancy enforceable under the RTA. The bottom line…any registrant dealing with residential tenancies requires familiarity with key *Residential Tenancies Act* provisions to diligently serve landlord and tenant clients.

FIXED TERM

A fixed term tenancy provides the tenant with exclusive possession for a specific term, which is normally agreed to in a written contract. In a fixed term lease, both the commencement and expiry dates must be determined before the lease takes effect. In a commercial fixed term tenancy, the tenancy ends on the expiry date and no notice is required, however, it is not unusual for the tenancy to continue on a periodic basis. In residential tenancies, if the tenant remains in possession of the property following the expiry date, the tenancy is deemed to continue on a month-to-month basis pursuant to provincial tenancy legislation.

PERIODIC TENANCY

A periodic tenancy is for a fixed period but indefinite length that can be made certain by notice of termination. In other words, the periodic tenancy automatically renews itself (usually on a weekly, monthly or yearly basis), unless notice is given to the contrary.

In residential tenancies, a periodic tenancy can be either in writing or oral and may simply state that the tenancy is on a month-to-month basis. If a residential tenant remains in a property following the expiration of a fixed term tenancy, the tenancy relationship normally converts into a periodic tenancy automatically.

> **EXAMPLE**   *Periodic Tenancy*
>
> Owner Smith enters into a commercial tenancy agreement with Jones whereby Jones has a monthly tenancy beginning on the first of each month. This tenancy will automatically renew itself for the same duration as the original period unless either Smith or Jones gives notice to terminate (a notice to quit) to the other.

TENANCY AT WILL

Tenancy at will can arise when, after expiration of a lease, or when no lease exists, the tenant remains in possession with the consent of the landlord or the person entitled to possession.

Real estate registrants should be aware that a tenancy agreement can occur by contract or by implication from the acts of the parties. An implied tenancy at will may arise when a tenant occupies premises without rent. An express tenancy at will may arise when a real estate transaction does not close on the scheduled date and possession is granted in anticipation of a future closing.

EXAMPLE — *Tenancy at Will*

Seller Smith sells his commercial property to Buyer Jones, but Jones has to wait for the closing of another property on the same day that is now delayed. The solicitors for Jones and Smith agree to allow Jones to take possession of the commercial property, provided that he agrees to vacate the premises without notice if the other transaction does not close in a short period of time.

While there are certain risks involved in such arrangements, the lawyers, as well as Jones and Smith, are confident that closing is a certainty. If this were not the case, Smith could well demand that Jones secure interim financing to close the sale. Further, the parties are comfortable with the arrangement as the property involves commercial usage and does not invoke legislative requirements that would normally be considered in a residential tenancy; e.g., specific notice periods and related requirements. Accordingly, the buyer and seller enter into a tenancy agreement to suit the circumstances.

TENANCY AT SUFFERANCE

This type of tenancy (also referred to as an *over-holding tenancy*) could occur if a person has possession without the consent of the owner and without paying rent. It arises by implication of law in situations where the tenancy has been terminated but the tenant does not vacate. Tenancy at sufferance might typically arise if the tenant did not vacate after a proper notice to quit, or did not vacate after the fixed term tenancy expired. In certain circumstances, a tenant may be liable for damages or for double rent.

EXAMPLE — *Tenancy at Sufferance*

Owner Smith, a commercial landlord, gives Tenant Jones a notice to vacate. Jones has occupied the property for several years. Smith, in giving notice, currently resides at a distant location and has no immediate use for the property, which is scheduled for redevelopment. Jones, while accepting the notice, remains on the property without paying any rent.

Residential vs. Commercial Tenancies

Residential tenants have more statutory rights than their commercial counterparts. Consequently, clearly distinguishing the two is vital. Principal use is the primary consideration (i.e., what the premises are being used for) in distinguishing residential from commercial tenants, but registrants must also be aware of RTA exemptions; e.g., occupants sharing a bathroom or kitchen facility.

The line between commercial and residential tenancies is often blurred by legislative considerations impacting both landlords and tenants. Registrants must first understand the *Residential Tenancies Act* to gain a full perspective on the issue of whether a lease falls to residential tenancy legislation or to the *Commercial Tenancies Act*. This determination can have significant impact, as the residential statute affords tenants a wide range of rights not found in its commercial counterpart.

PRINCIPAL USE

A commercial lease can be identified as any lease involving a property that is principally used for business activity. The operative word *principally* should be emphasized and, in most instances, common sense prevails. For example, a small home office within a residential structure would not affect the residential status of the property. A structure containing a main level commercial enterprise and two upper apartments would be identified as commercial for the lower units and residential for the upper units.

Registrants should normally determine if a property is residential and subject to the *Residential Tenancies Act*. However, certain hybrid situations can cause problems. Consider a tenant renting a home located on 30-acre rural property and also renting the barns and balance of the property as a riding stable. If the individual occupied the home prior to the riding stable operation and leased the business operation under a separate lease, the RTA would undoubtedly apply to the residential tenancy. If the person became a tenant coincident with renting the barns for a riding stable operation under a single lease (in other words the occupancy of the house was required to carry on the business), the property would undoubtedly be judged as principally used for commercial purposes.

Establishing whether a residential or commercial tenancy exists can have a significant impact, particularly in regard to notices concerning termination, rent charged and rights of access by the landlord (or his/her agent) to show the property and to make repairs.

STATUTORY EXEMPTIONS

In addition to principal use considerations, registrants should also be aware of key exclusions for certain types of rental arrangements set out in the *Residential Tenancies Act*. The following is descriptive in nature only to highlight the scope of exemptions. Exact wordings in the *Residential Tenancies Act* should be accessed when analyzing specific circumstances.

- Accommodation for the travelling or vacationing public.
- Seasonal or temporary accommodation; e.g., hotel, motel, lodge, campground, trailer park and tourist home.
- Farm employee whose occupancy is conditional on continued employment.
- Non-profit housing co-operatives.
- Penal or correctional facility.
- Accommodation subject to selected Acts. Specific exemptions include accommodation that is subject to the *Public Hospitals Act, Private Hospitals Act, Community Psychiatric Hospitals Act, Mental Hospitals Act, Homes for the Aged and Rest Homes Act, Nursing Homes Act, Ministry of Correctional Service Act, Charitable Institutions Act* and *Child and Family Services Act*. Exemptions concerning municipal, provincial and federal housing programs are detailed in the Regulations.
- Emergency shelter.
- Accommodation provided to students by an educational institution under specific circumstances.
- An employee with accommodation in the same building or project used in part, or in whole, for a non-residential purpose and accommodation is contingent on continuing employment.

- Occupants sharing a bathroom or kitchen facility with the owner, the owner's spouse/same-sex partner/child/parent or the spouse or same-sex partner's child/parent and where any of these individuals live in the same building. Roomers/boarders who occupy a room in a rooming, boarding or lodging house and share facilities with each other (i.e., not related to each other as detailed above) are not exempt from the provisions of the Act.
- Premises occupied for business or agricultural purposes with living accommodation attached and under one lease.
- Accommodation involving rehabilitative or therapeutic services subject to certain restrictions.

A landlord or tenant may apply to the Landlord and Tenant Board to determine if the *Residential Tenancies Act* applies to their particular rental unit or rental complex. Further discussion of both the Board and the Act is included later in this chapter.

LEASE

A lease is defined as a contract between a landlord (lessor) and a tenant (lessee) for the occupation or use of the landlord's property by the tenant, for a specified time and for a specified consideration. Under the terms of a lease, the lawful owner of the property (the landlord) transfers the rights of use, possession and enjoyment to another (the tenant) for a specified period of time, or at will for a consideration (rent). A lease may also be referred to as a *tenancy agreement*.

Purpose

The purpose of a lease is to establish a written record of an agreement between the parties for a tenancy arrangement within a defined period. A lease document is a detailed document setting out the responsibilities of the parties, rents payable and obligations of both landlord and tenant, along with a wide range of provisions concerning notices, remedies and termination.

A lease can be verbal or written, express or implied by a person's conduct. Its terms are found in common law and in provincial statutes concerning commercial or residential tenancies. Normally, the parties will enter into a written signed lease or tenancy agreement in order to precisely describe their relationship. A wide range of lease forms and associated wordings are found in the marketplace.

When a property owner agrees to lease property, the tenant acquires an interest in that property and may register applicable documents in the land registration office giving notice of this interest. Methods will vary based on whether the property is registered under land titles or registry and upon specific registration requirements set out under either the *Land Titles Act* or the *Registry Act*.

Essential Elements

Lease forms differ substantially, but whether for residential, commercial or industrial purposes, all must contain the following elements to make them legally enforceable:

Legal Names	The full legal name, correctly spelled, of the individual(s) and/or corporation(s) that are party to the lease must appear.
Legally Competent	The person signing must be legally competent. This is particularly important in the management of retirement and nursing homes, and the signatures of spouses and guarantors are obtained, where applicable.
Readily Identifiable Description	Legal description of the leased premises should ideally be entered. However, as long as the description allows the space and specific property to be readily identifiable (including address, dimensions and a floor plan), this requirement can be considered fulfilled.
Consideration	Consideration, that is, the exchange of something of value. In a lease, the amount of rent, method of payment and to whom the payment is due are detailed.
Legal Purpose	A lease must include a description of the legal purpose for which the premise is to be used. By virtue of this clause, for example, tenants can be controlled in the particular type of business being carried on, thereby permitting exclusive use within a retail complex and providing assurance that other tenants will not be in direct competition.
Start/End Dates	Commencement and expiration dates must be included since, if these two dates were omitted, the lease would be so vague as to be unenforceable. Any renewal privileges should be spelled out in detail.
What is Expected	Rules and regulations, policies, procedures and generally what is expected of each party must be clearly delineated.

Lease vs. Agreement to Lease

An *agreement to lease* is technically referred to as an *agreement for lease without settled form of lease*. An agreement to lease generally sets out fundamental, material aspects of the agreement between the parties, but contemplates the execution of a formal, detailed lease. An agreement to lease covers substantive issues and is best described as a consensus leading to final agreement (the lease).

DRAFTING AN AGREEMENT TO LEASE

Registrants, when drafting an agreement to lease, must ensure that all essential elements of the lease are included, namely, the parties, a description of the premises to be leased (often formally referred to as the demised premises), the commencement of the lease, the term of the lease and the amount of rent. All other material matters in a lease, other than specific exceptions, reservations, covenants or special conditions, are implied by law.

The agreement to lease must also address all other material issues in order that a lease can be correctly drawn as a consequence of the agreement. Salespersons are well advised to ensure that every agreement to lease is complete in all respects. Any confusion can result in legal ramifications. A clause can be inserted in an agreement to lease stating that the lease will include other reasonable conditions and terms as the landlord may require. The issue of what constitutes reasonable will ultimately fall to judicial interpretation should problems arise. While courts would undoubtedly strictly interpret this term as being anything of a non-substantive nature, the entire matter is best avoided by registrants.

Prudence suggests that a blank copy of the lease be attached to the agreement to lease in order to eliminate any confusion and ensure that the tenant fully appreciates the true scope of the document. Landlords dealing with complex leases often require this procedure.

AGREEMENT TO LEASE (OREA FORM 400)

The *Agreement to Lease—Residential* (Form 400) sets out lease fundamentals and substantive terms. This document may constitute the entire agreement between landlord and tenant, if a detailed lease is not prepared. The complete lease expands the terms and details provisions, rights and responsibilities consistent with the agreement to lease.

RENTAL APPLICATION (OREA FORM 410)

The rental application sets out acceptable information that can be asked to a prospective residential tenant including details about the renters and other occupants, last two places of residence, present employment, financial obligations and personal references. The form complies with the *Privacy Act* and also informs the applicant that a consumer report containing credit and/or personal information may be referred to in connection with the rental.

Sample Agreement & Application

A fully completed *Agreement to Lease—Residential* and *Rental Application—Residential* are illustrated on the following pages.

OREA Ontario Real Estate Association

Form 400
for use in the Province of Ontario

Agreement to Lease
Residential

This Agreement to Lease dated this .... **28th** .... day of .... **May** ...., 20 **XX**

TENANT (Lessee), ... **Robert James Hudson and Tanya Louise Hudson** ....
(Full legal names of all Tenants)

LANDLORD (Lessor), ... **Mark David Chandra** ....
(Full legal name of Landlord)

ADDRESS OF LANDLORD .... **Suite 321, 3271 West Ridge Place, Anycity K9C 2V4** ....
(Legal address for the purpose of receiving notices)

The Tenant hereby offers to lease from the Landlord the premises as described herein on the terms and subject to the conditions as set out in this Agreement.

1. **PREMISES:** Having inspected the premises and provided the present tenant vacates, I/we, the Tenant hereby offer to lease, premises known as:
   289 Western Crescent, Anycity (Legal Description: Lot 93, Plan M-294, City of Anycity)

2. **TERM OF LEASE:** The lease shall be for a term of .... **Two Years** .... commencing .... **August 1, 20xx** ....

3. **RENT:** The Tenant will pay to the said Landlord monthly and every month during the said term of the lease the sum of .... **One Thousand Eight Hundred and Seventy-Five**--- Canadian Dollars (CDN$ **1,875.00** ....),
   payable in advance on the first day of each and every month during the currency of the said term. First and last months' rent to be paid in advance upon completion or date of occupancy, whichever comes first.

4. **DEPOSIT AND PREPAID RENT:** The Tenant delivers........ **Upon Acceptance** ....
   (Herewith/Upon acceptance/as otherwise described in this Agreement)

   by negotiable cheque payable to........ **ABC Realty Inc.** .... "Deposit Holder"

   in the amount of .... **Three Thousand Seven Hundred and Fifty**---

   Canadian Dollars (CDN$ .... **3,750.00** ....) as a deposit to be held in trust as security for the faithful performance by the Tenant of all

   terms, covenants and conditions of the Agreement and to be applied by the Landlord against the .... **first** .... and .... **last** .... month's rent. If the Agreement is not accepted, the deposit is to be returned to the Tenant without interest or deduction.

   For the purposes of this Agreement, "Upon Acceptance" shall mean that the Tenant is required to deliver the deposit to the Deposit Holder within 24 hours of the acceptance of this Agreement. The parties to this Agreement hereby acknowledge that, unless otherwise provided for in this Agreement, the Deposit Holder shall place the deposit in trust in the Deposit Holder's non-interest bearing Real Estate Trust Account and no interest shall be earned, received or paid on the deposit.

5. **USE:** The Tenant and Landlord agree that unless otherwise agreed to herein, only the Tenant named above and any person named in a Rental Application completed prior to this Agreement will occupy the premises.

   Premises to be used only for:........ **single-family residential** ....

6. **SERVICES AND COSTS:** The cost of the following services applicable to the premises shall be paid as follows:

	LANDLORD	TENANT		LANDLORD	TENANT
Gas	☐	☑	Cable TV	☐	☑
Oil	☐	☐	Condominium/Cooperative fees	☐	☐
Electricity	☐	☑	Garbage Removal	☐	☐
Hot water heater rental	☐	☑	Other:	☐	☐
Water and Sewerage Charges	☑	☐	Other:	☐	☐

The Landlord will pay the property taxes, but if the Tenant is assessed as a Separate School Supporter, Tenant will pay to the Landlord a sum sufficient to cover the excess of the Separate School Tax over the Public School Tax, if any, for a full calendar year, said sum to be estimated on the tax rate for the current year, and to be payable in equal monthly installments in addition to the above mentioned rental, provided however, that the full amount shall become due and be payable on demand on the Tenant.

INITIALS OF TENANT(S): *RH TH*   INITIALS OF LANDLORD(S): *MC*

Form 400   Revised 2015   **Page 1 of 4**

7. **PARKING:** Paved side drive and double-car garage

8. **ADDITIONAL TERMS:** See Schedule A

9. **SCHEDULES:** The schedules attached hereto shall form an integral part of this Agreement to Lease and consist of: **Schedule(s) A**

10. **IRREVOCABILITY:** This offer shall be irrevocable by .... Tenant .... until .... 5:00 .... ~~a.m.~~/p.m. on the .... 31st ....
    (Landlord/Tenant)

    day of.......... May ....,20.XX..........after which time if not accepted, this Agreement shall be null and void and all monies paid thereon shall be returned to the Tenant without interest or deduction.

11. **NOTICES:** The Landlord hereby appoints the Listing Brokerage as agent for the Landlord for the purpose of giving and receiving notices pursuant to this Agreement. Where a Brokerage (Tenant's Brokerage) has entered into a representation agreement with the Tenant, the Tenant hereby appoints the Tenant's Brokerage as agent for the purpose of giving and receiving notices pursuant to this Agreement. **Where a Brokerage represents both the Landlord and the Tenant (multiple representation), the Brokerage shall not be appointed or authorized to be agent for either the Tenant or the Landlord for the purpose of giving and receiving notices.** Any notice relating hereto or provided for herein shall be in writing. In addition to any provision contained herein and in any Schedule hereto, this offer, any counter-offer, notice of acceptance thereof or any notice to be given or received pursuant to this Agreement or any Schedule hereto (any of them, "Document") shall be deemed given and received when delivered personally or hand delivered to the Address for Service provided in the Acknowledgement below, or where a facsimile number or email address is provided herein, when transmitted electronically to that facsimile number or email address, respectively, in which case, the signature(s) of the party (parties) shall be deemed to be original.

    FAX No.: .... 613-555-2121 ....   FAX No.: .... 613-444-2121 ....
    (For delivery of Documents to Landlord)   (For delivery of Documents to Tenant)

    Email Address: .... admin@abcrealty.com ....   Email Address: .... notices@xyzrealestate.com ....
    (For delivery of Documents to Landlord)   (For delivery of Documents to Tenant)

12. **EXECUTION OF LEASE:** Lease shall be drawn by the Landlord on the Landlord's standard form of lease, and shall include the provisions as contained herein and in any attached schedule, and shall be executed by both parties before possession of the premises is given. The Landlord shall provide the tenant with information relating to the rights and responsibilities of the Tenant and information on the role of the Landlord and Tenant Board and how to contact the Board. (Information For New Tenants as made available by the Landlord and Tenant Board and available at www.ltb.gov.on.ca)

13. **ACCESS:** The Landlord shall have the right, at reasonable times to enter and show the demised premises to prospective tenants, purchasers or others. The Landlord or anyone on the Landlord's behalf shall also have the right, at reasonable times, to enter and inspect the demised premises.

14. **INSURANCE:** The Tenant agrees to obtain and keep in full force and effect during the entire period of the tenancy and any renewal thereof, at the Tenant's sole cost and expense, fire and property damage and public liability insurance in an amount equal to that which a reasonably prudent Tenant would consider adequate. The Tenant agrees to provide the Landlord, upon demand at any time, proof that said insurance is in full force and effect and to notify the Landlord in writing in the event that such insurance is cancelled or otherwise terminated.

15. **RESIDENCY:** The Landlord shall forthwith notify the Tenant in writing in the event the Landlord is, at the time of entering into this Agreement, or, becomes during the term of the tenancy, a non-resident of Canada as defined under the Income Tax Act, RSC 1985, c.1 (ITA) as amended from time to time, and in such event the Landlord and Tenant agree to comply with the tax withholding provisions of the ITA.

16. **USE AND DISTRIBUTION OF PERSONAL INFORMATION:** The Tenant consents to the collection, use and disclosure of the Tenant's personal information by the Landlord and/or agent of the Landlord, from time to time, for the purpose of determining the creditworthiness of the Tenant for the leasing, selling or financing of the premises or the real property, or making such other use of the personal information as the Landlord and/or agent of the Landlord deems appropriate.

17. **CONFLICT OR DISCREPANCY:** If there is any conflict or discrepancy between any provision added to this Agreement (including any Schedule attached hereto) and any provision in the standard pre-set portion hereof, the added provision shall supersede the standard pre-set provision to the extent of such conflict or discrepancy. This Agreement, including any Schedule attached hereto, shall constitute the entire Agreement between Landlord and Tenant. There is no representation, warranty, collateral agreement or condition, which affects this Agreement other than as expressed herein. This Agreement shall be read with all changes of gender or number required by the context.

18. **CONSUMER REPORTS:** The Tenant is hereby notified that a consumer report containing credit and/or personal information may be referred to in connection with this transaction.

INITIALS OF TENANT(S): (RH TH)   INITIALS OF LANDLORD(S): (MC)

19. BINDING AGREEMENT: This Agreement and acceptance thereof shall constitute a binding agreement by the parties to enter into the Lease of the Premises and to abide by the terms and conditions herein contained.

SIGNED, SEALED AND DELIVERED in the presence of: IN WITNESS whereof I have hereunto set my hand and seal:

Carol Bennett ....   *Bob Hudson* .... ● DATE *May 28/xx* ....
(Witness)   (Tenant or Authorized Representative)   (Seal)

Carol Bennett ....   *Tanya Hudson* .... ● DATE *May 28/xx* ....
(Witness)   (Tenant or Authorized Representative)   (Seal)

.... ● DATE ....
(Witness)   (Guarantor)   (Seal)

We/I the Landlord hereby accept the above offer, and agree that the commission together with applicable HST (and any other tax as may hereafter be applicable) may be deducted from the deposit and further agree to pay any remaining balance of commission forthwith.

SIGNED, SEALED AND DELIVERED in the presence of: IN WITNESS whereof I have hereunto set my hand and seal:

Jamie Silverman ....   *Mark Chandra* .... ● DATE *May 29/xx* ....
(Witness)   (Landlord or Authorized Representative)   (Seal)

.... ● DATE ....
(Witness)   (Landlord or Authorized Representative)   (Seal)

CONFIRMATION OF ACCEPTANCE: Notwithstanding anything contained herein to the contrary, I confirm this Agreement with all changes both typed and written was

finally acceptance by all parties at .. *5:00* .. a.m./p.m. this .. *29* .. day of .... *May* ...., 20.. *xx* .....   *Mark Chandra* ....
                                                                                                           (Signature of Landlord or Tenant)

INFORMATION ON BROKERAGE(S)

Listing Brokerage .... ABC Realty Inc. .... Tel.No.(.. 613 ..) 555-1212

...123 Main Street, Anycity, Anyregion L4H 6P5........ Jamie Silverman.....................
                                                                        (Salesperson / Broker Name)

Co-op/Buyer Brokerage .... XYZ Real Estate Ltd. .... Tel.No.(.. 613 ..) 444-1212

...29 Maple Drive, Anycity, Anyregion L2J 7K6........ Carol Bennett.................
                                                                        (Salesperson / Broker Name)

ACKNOWLEDGEMENT

I acknowledge receipt of my signed copy of this accepted Agreement of Lease and I authorize the Brokerage to forward a copy to my lawyer.

Mark Chandra .... DATE *May 29/xx* ......
(Landlord)

.... DATE ....
(Landlord)

Address for Service ... *Ste. 321, 3271 West Ridge Place*

Anycity K9C 2V4 .... Tel.No.(.. 613 ..) 333-1212

Landlord's Lawyer ... *Ms. J Dobson c/o Dobson Reilly*

Address ... *Westgate Mall, Anycity K9C 3V8*

Email ....

(.. 613 ..) 222-1212 .... (.. 613 ..) 222-2121
Tel.No.   FAX No.

I acknowledge receipt of my signed copy of this accepted Agreement of Lease and I authorize the Brokerage to forward a copy to my lawyer.

Bob Hudson .... DATE *May 29/xx* ......
(Tenant)

Tanya Hudson .... DATE *May 29/xx* ......
(Tenant)

Address for Service ... *7 Granite Lane, Anycity K2V 2B8*

.... Tel.No.(.. 613 ..) 666-1212

Tenant's Lawyer ... *J. Hartwick c/o Dicillo & Hartwick*

Address ... *3218 East Mall Court, Anycity K3C 5B7*

Email ....

(.. 613 ..) 888-1212 .... (.. 613 ..) 888-2121
Tel.No.   FAX No.

FOR OFFICE USE ONLY   **COMMISSION TRUST AGREEMENT**

To: Co-operating Brokerage shown on the foregoing Agreement to Lease:
In consideration for the Co-operating Brokerage procuring the foregoing Agreement to Lease, I hereby declare that all moneys received or receivable by me in connection with the Transaction as contemplated in the MLS Rules and Regulations of my Real Estate Board shall be receivable and held in trust. This agreement shall constitute a Commission Trust Agreement as defined in the MLS Rules and shall be subject to and governed by the MLS Rules pertaining to Commission Trust.

DATED as of the date and time of the acceptance of the foregoing Agreement to Lease.   Acknowledged by:

Jamie Silverman ....   *Carol Bennett* ....
(Authorized to bind the Listing Brokerage)   (Authorized to bind the Co-operating Brokerage)

Form 400   Revised 2015   **Page 3 of 4**

SECTION I   A CLOSER LOOK AT TRADING DIFFERENT TYPES OF PROPERTIES

OREA Ontario Real Estate Association

Form 400
for use in the Province of Ontario

Schedule A
Agreement to Lease - Residential

This Schedule is attached to and forms part of the Agreement to Lease between:

TENANT (Lessee), ... Robert James Hudson and Tanya Louise Hudson ...., and

LANDLORD (Lessor), ... Mark David Chandra ....

for the lease of .... 289 Western Crescent , Anycity ....

.... dated the ...28th... day of .... May ...., 20 **xx** ....

The Landlord and Tenant agree that the Tenant shall have the use of all existing drapery rods and window coverings; fireplace screen and accessories; KitchenDesign Pro Series stove, refrigerator, and dishwasher; MaxLoad washer and dryer; QuickFreeze freezer; and EasyLight gas barbecue.

The Landlord agrees to have the carpets professionally cleaned prior to the commencement of the lease at the Landlord's cost and the Tenant shall have the carpets professionally cleaned at the end of the lease term at the Tenant's cost. Tenant agrees not to make any decorating changes to the premises without the express written consent of the Landlord or his authorized agent.

This form must be initialled by all parties to the Agreement to Lease.

INITIALS OF TENANT(S): *RH TH*

INITIALS OF LANDLORD(S): *MC*

Form 400   Revised 2015   **Page 4 of 4**

OREA Ontario Real Estate Association

Form 410
for use in the Province of Ontario

Rental Application
Residential

I/We hereby make application to rent .... 289 Western Crescent, Anycity K9V 2L3

from the ...... 1st ...... day of ...... August ...... 20 XX .... at a monthly rental of $ 1,875.00

to become due and payable in advance on the .... 1st .... day of each and every month during my tenancy.

1. **Name** ..... Robert James Hudson .... Date of birth ... 05/21/66 ...... SIN No. (Optional) ... 123 456 789

   Drivers License No ..... C-23456-81326-60521 ... Occupation ...... Regional Sales Manager

2. **Name** ..... Tanya Louise Hudson .... Date of birth ... 04/23/69 ... SIN No. (Optional) ... 234 567 890

   Drivers License No ... C-82983-82926-90423 ... Occupation ...... Teacher

3. **Other Occupants:** Name ... Jason Hudson .... Relationship ... Son .... Age ... 13

   Name ... Amanda Hudson .... Relationship ... Daughter .... Age ... 9

   Name ... Belinda Hudson .... Relationship ... Daughter .... Age ... 6

   Do you have any pets? .... Yes ... If so, describe ...... Miniature Poodle

   Why are you vacating your present place of residence? ... Relocating nearer to regional high school and closer to work.

LAST TWO PLACES OF RESIDENCE

Address ..... 7 Granite Lane, Anycity K2V 2B8   Address ..... 45 Maple Crescent, Anycity, K3V 9D5

From ..... September 1994 ... To ...... Present   From ..... August 1990 ... To ..... August 1994

Name of Landlord ..... Wendell Bartram   Name of Landlord ..... Anycity Investments Inc.

Telephone: (613) 999-1212   Telephone: (613) 777-1212

PRESENT EMPLOYMENT   **PRIOR EMPLOYMENT**

Employer ..... TABA Shoes Ltd.   ˈExquisite Shoes Inc.

Business address ..... 50 Commercial Drive, Anycity   ˈEastgate Mall, 2918 Main Street West, Anycity K3B 2T2

Business telephone 613-666-1212   ˈ613-333-1212

Position held ..... Regional Sales Manager   ˈStore Manager

Length of employment ..... 2 years   ˈ10 Years

Name of supervisor ..... Catherine Wilson   ˈSteve Madden

Current salary range: Monthly $ ..... 8,200 + bonuses

Form 410   Revised 2009   **Page 1 of 2**

Fully Completed Sample   *Rental Application—Residential, Page 2 of 2*

SPOUSE'S PRESENT EMPLOYMENT

Employer ..Anycity School Board.......................

Business address ..20 Confederation Boulevard, Anycity K3T 8B2.....

Business telephone ..613-979-9912.............................

Position held ..Grade 5 Teacher................................

Length of employment ..15 Years..............................

Name of supervisor ..Fraser Morse.............................

Current salary range: Monthly $ ..5,100.......

PRIOR EMPLOYMENT

..N/A...

....

....

....

....

....

Name of Bank ..Anycity Trust.... Branch ..Eastgate Mall.. Address ..2918 Main Street West, Anycity K3B 2T2..

Chequing Account # ..213684.......... Savings Account # ..193282..........

FINANCIAL OBLIGATIONS

Payments to ..Anycity Trust - Line of Credit.................. Amount: $ ..475.00..

Payments to ..VISA.. Amount: $ ..200.00..

PERSONAL REFERENCES

Name ..Brent Reid.......... Address ..344 Bankside Drive, Anycity, K5Y 3B9..

Telephone: (..613..) 222-2121.... Length of Acquaintance ..20 Years.. Occupation ..Retail Merchant..

Name ..Dr. Edward Chan.... Address ..92 Orchard Heights Blvd.........

Telephone: (..613..) 888-2121.... Length of Acquaintance..15 Years.. Occupation..Doctor..

AUTOMOBILE(S)

Make ..Dodge.... Model ..Caravan.. Year ..20xx.. Licence No ..234-ANC..

Make ..Toyota.... Model ..Camry.. Year ..20xx.. Licence No ..183-CBA..

The Applicant consents to the collection, use and disclosure of the Applicant's personal information by the Landlord and/or agent of the Landlord, from time to time, for the purpose of determining the creditworthiness of the Applicant for the leasing, selling or financing of the premises or the real property, or making such other use of the personal information as the Landlord and/or agent of the Landlord deems appropriate.

The Applicant represents that all statements made above are true and correct. **The Applicant is hereby notified that a consumer report containing credit and/or personal information may be referred to in connection with this rental.** The Applicant authorizes the verification of the information contained in this application and information obtained from personal references. This application is not a Rental or Lease Agreement. In the event that this application is not accepted, any deposit submitted by the Applicant shall be returned.

Bob Hudson   *05/28/xx*
Signature of Applicant   Date

Tanya Hudson   *05/28/xx*
Signature of Applicant   Date

Telephone: (.*613*.) *666-1212*   Telephone: (.*613*.) *666-1212*

Form 410   Revised 2009   **Page 2 of 2**

AGREEMENT TO LEASE—CLAUSES

Registrants will face various situations involving rental property that should be properly set out in the agreement to lease. Selected clauses are highlighted for general guidance only.

Credit Check

In some instances, a landlord may not use a formal rental application form, but still require that credit check be performed in accordance with the *Consumer Reporting Act*. As a reminder regarding statutory requirements, if the landlord refuses to grant a lease due to information contained in the consumer report, he or she must give notice that refusal was due to the information received. The landlord is also obligated to inform the prospective tenant of the nature and source of information received, if the tenant so requests in writing within 60 days of the refusal notice.

SCENARIO	*CLAUSE*
A landlord wishes to conduct a credit check on a prospective tenant.	**LEASE/RES–1** **Condition—Credit Check** *This Offer to Lease is conditional upon the Landlord satisfying the Landlord concerning the personal and/or credit worthiness of the Tenant. The Tenant hereby consents to having the Landlord conduct or cause to be conducted a personal and/or credit investigation in respect to the Tenant. Unless the Landlord gives notice in writing delivered to the Tenant personally or in accordance with any other provisions for the delivery of notice in this Agreement to Lease or any Schedule thereto not later than _____p.m. on the _____day of _____, 20____, that this condition is fulfilled, this Offer shall be null and void and the deposit shall be returned to the Tenant in full without deduction. This condition is included for the benefit of the Landlord and may be waived at the Landlord's sole option by notice in writing to the Tenant as aforesaid within the time period stated herein.*

No Lease to be Signed

In some instances, the landlord and tenant may decide that the agreement to lease is sufficient and a formal lease document is not necessary. The clause *LEASE/RES–2 Agreement to Lease Only/No Lease to be Signed* can be inserted:

CLAUSE
LEASE/RES–2   **Agreement to Lease Only/No Lease to be Signed**
Tenant and Landlord agree that an accepted Agreement to Lease shall form a completed lease and no other lease will be signed between the Parties.

If this clause is used, ensure that *Clause 12: Execution of Lease* in the Agreement to Lease is ruled out and initialled by the parties.

Chattels, Maintenance and Related Issues

As with all real estate negotiations, registrants face unique circumstances that must be addressed in agreements to lease, such as alterations/improvements, appliances included, cleaning of carpets at commencement by landlord and by tenant at termination, maintenance of grounds and swimming pool (if applicable) and so forth. Three of several clause wordings are highlighted by way of example. See the *Appendix* for others.

SCENARIO	CLAUSE
The landlord and tenant have agreed that chattels left by the owner can be stored in the basement and that the tenant will maintain the grounds. Further, pets will be on the premises but the tenant agrees to be responsible for any resulting repairs or replacements.	**LEASE/RES–6** **Chattels Left by Owner** *Tenant agrees that any chattels left on the rented premises, and not specifically mentioned herein, may remain and be stored on the premises at no cost to, and shall remain at the risk of, the Landlord.* **LEASE/RES–11** **Maintenance of Grounds** *The Tenant shall keep the lawns in good condition and shall not injure or remove the shade trees, shrubbery, hedges or any other tree or plant which may be in, upon or about the premises, and shall keep the sidewalks in front and at the sides of the premises free of snow and ice.* **LEASE/RES–15** **Pets** *Tenant agrees to be responsible for any repair or replacement cost due to the presence of any pets on the premises. Tenant further agrees that if pets are kept on the premises, Tenant shall, at lease termination, have the carpets professionally cleaned and make any repairs that may be necessary to restore any damages caused by pets.*

First Right of Refusal

A first right of refusal (also referred to as a right of first refusal) is a contractual right that can involve any asset. In this example, the tenant is obtaining a first right of refusal for the leased premises. The first right of refusal provides that, before the seller can enter into a transaction with a third party, he or she must first allow the tenant a specified period to submit an offer on the same terms and conditions.

SCENARIO	CLUSE
The tenant is interested in potentially buying the property, but lacks sufficient funds at this time. The landlord, anxious to retain this prospect as a tenant, offers a first right of refusal.	**LEASE/RES–20** **Tenant's First Right of Refusal** *The Landlord covenants and agrees with the Tenant that, during the term of the lease or any renewal thereof, the Landlord will give the Tenant three (3) business days to submit an Offer upon the same terms and conditions as any bona fide Offer to purchase the leased property that the Landlord has received and is willing to accept, and any Lease executed by the Landlord and Tenant shall include this first right of refusal.* *The Landlord shall give the Tenant written notice of such bona fide Offer and a copy of such Offer to the Tenant. In the event that the Tenant submits to the Landlord, within the time period described above, a written and signed Offer to purchase the property upon the same terms and conditions as the Offer initially received by the Landlord, the Landlord shall accept the Offer submitted by the Tenant. In the event that the Tenant fails to deliver to the Landlord, within the time limit described above, a written and signed Offer to purchase the property on the same terms and conditions as the initial Offer, the Landlord shall be at liberty to sell the property to the Buyer who submitted the initial Offer. Should the Tenant exercise the said first right of refusal, the Landlord agrees to pay the Agents so named in this Agreement, (or their successor companies) a fee of _____..*

LANDLORD AND TENANT BOARD

The Landlord and Tenant Board (formerly the Ontario Rental Housing Tribunal) has two key roles. The Board provides information about the *Residential Tenancies Act* and resolves disputes between most residential landlords and tenants. The Board is best described as quasi-judicial in that it generally operates like a court of law, but not in all respects.

Members of the Board are appointed by the provincial government. The Board operates in terms of rules of practice and interpretation guidelines and makes such rules and guidelines, as well as approved forms, available to the public. The Landlord and Tenant Board is involved in various activities that include determining matters pursuant to applications made by parties, making findings (e.g., that a capital expenditure is reasonable), making and issuing orders, mediating situations, and adjudicating (i.e., holding hearings).

Mediation vs. Adjudication

Mediation is generally described as a process of bringing about some form of agreement or reconciliation between opposing parties. This process has proven particularly effective in resolving a wide variety of disputes that might otherwise extend into lengthy hearings and/or legal actions.

The Board often mediates issues that arise as a consequence of applications made by either landlords or tenants. Mediation is not mandatory (with one exception involving transferral of a tenant in a care home to a new facility). The Board will not become involved in a mediation process concerning tenancy disputes, unless an application is received.

Further, even with an application, the decision may be made not to mediate if resolution by this means appears impractical.

Conversely, adjudication is the process of deciding or settling by law issues arising between landlords and tenants pursuant to the *Residential Tenancies Act*. With adjudication, a hearing is typically held. Based on evidence presented by the tenant and landlord, a member of the Board issues an order. An order is the final, written version of the Board Member's decision.

WEB LINKS
Landlord and Tenant Board   Go to the Landlord and Tenant Board website (*www.ltb.gov.on.ca*) for detailed information regarding the structured process for handling landlord/tenant disputes. Downloadable forms and explanatory notes are available on the site. Forms can be broadly divided into notices (notices made by landlords to tenants and vice versa; e.g., notice of termination), applications to resolve disputes and miscellaneous forms relating to the dispute resolution process.

RESIDENTIAL TENANCIES ACT

The *Residential Tenancies Act* is a complex piece of legislation spanning numerous provisions that not only impact residential premises, but also care homes and land lease properties as discussed in Chapter 1. Selected, commonly encountered topics are outlined. Information provided has been excerpted (or modified) from a residential tenancy reference text, reprinted with permission of the author. Summaries are included for descriptive purposes only and the Act should be consulted directly on all tenancy matters. The Landlord and Tenant Board also provides helpful brochures and downloadable information for landlords and tenants.

WEB LINKS
Residential Tenancies Act   Go to the *www.e-laws.gov.on.ca* for a current version of the legislation. Always refer directly to the Act and Regulations for up-to-date information regarding residential tenancies.

Starting a Residential Tenancy

Various statutory provisions relate directly or indirectly to the tenant application and selection process. Selected topics are highlighted that typically impact negotiations involving landlords and tenants:

RENTAL HISTORY/CREDIT REFERENCES

Regulation 290/98 under the Ontario Human Rights Code sets out permissible landlord practices, including tenant credit references and rental history information. A landlord may request credit references and/or rental history information, an authorization to conduct a credit check and a guarantee for the rent, in addition to a rent deposit, in order to assess and subsequently select or refuse a tenant.

A landlord may request income information only if items detailed above (credit references and rental history) are also requested.

- If such details are obtained, income information must be used in conjunction with that information to assess and subsequently select or refuse a tenant.
- If such details are requested but not obtained, the income information can be considered on its own merit when selecting or refusing a prospective tenant.

A final provision under this regulation warrants emphasis:

> *Nothing in this Regulation authorizes a landlord to refuse accommodation to any person because of race, ancestry, place of origin, colour, ethnic origin, citizenship, creed, sex, sexual orientation, age, marital status, family status, handicap or the receipt of public assistance.*
>
> Source: Sec. 4, Ontario Regulation 290/98: Business Practices Permissible to Landlords in Selecting Prospective Tenants for Residential Accommodation.

PET PROVISIONS

Any provision in a tenancy agreement that forbids animals (frequently referred to as the *no pet* provision) is in violation of the Act. In other words, a *no pet* provision in a tenancy agreement is void. However, exceptions do apply; e.g., provisions in the Ontario Human Rights Code and pet restrictions in condominiums (subject to certain qualifications). A condominium declaration may contain enforceable provisions (e.g., no pet provisions) relating to the occupation and use of units and common elements.

Registrants commonly encounter questions regarding pets in rental accommodation. Any tenant or landlord wishing detailed information or currently involved in a dispute concerning animals is strongly advised to contact the Landlord and Tenant Board and/or seek expert advice.

The landlord may make application for an order to terminate the tenancy and evict the tenant under selected circumstances concerning animals; e.g., where the animal causes substantial interference with reasonable enjoyment, causes a serious allergic reaction or the animal is inherently dangerous.

RENT DEPOSIT

The landlord can require a rent deposit, but it must not be more than the lesser of the amount of rent for one rental period or one month. Any reference to a security deposit is automatically deemed to be a rent deposit for purposes of the Act and the maximum rent deposit is one month's rent.

Registrants should be aware of certain important requirements regarding rent deposits:

- If the lawful rent increases, the landlord may require the tenant to pay the appropriate additional amount concerning the rent deposit.
- The landlord is required to pay the tenant interest annually on the rent deposit. Such interest is calculated on the percentage change from year to year in the Consumer Price Index for Ontario for prices of goods and services as reported monthly by Statistics Canada, averaged over the 12-month period that concludes at the end of May of the previous calendar year, rounded to the first decimal point.
- The rent deposit is applied to the last rent period prior to the termination of the tenancy.
- A tenant is not required to provide a landlord with postdated cheques or agree to automatic debit payments from an account, to a credit card or similar automatic withdrawal for rent payment. Any landlord stipulation to that effect in a tenancy agreement is in violation of the Act.
- The landlord must provide receipts relating to rents and rent deposits upon request by the tenant.

Rent Provisions

LAWFUL RENT

The *Residential Tenancies Act* provides that no charge of rent, or increase of rent, is allowed greater than the lawful rent permitted. Lawful rent for a new tenant is the first rent charged to that new tenant, subject to certain qualifications outlined in the Act; e.g., selected provisions relating to rent premiums and discounts.

The topic of lawful rents has understandable complexities. As a general statement, the landlord can only increase rent in accordance with the Act if 12 months have elapsed since: (1) the last rent increase; or (2) since the day the rental unit was first rented by the tenant. Special provisions apply to existing tenants previously falling under the *Rent Control Act, 1992*.

RENT INCREASE—GENERAL PROVISIONS

Various rent increase procedures are detailed in the Act. Only summary points are included in the following. Registrants seeking detailed knowledge of rental provisions should access the *Residential Tenancies Act*.

- The landlord must give at least 90 days notice on an approved form for any rent increase. This includes an increase involving higher operating costs or capital expenditures.
- An increase is void if the notice is not provided in accordance with the Act. A new notice must be issued.
- No landlord may increase the rent by more than the guideline, except in accordance with the Act.

NOTE: An added cost relating to the addition of a parking space or a prescribed service, facility, privilege, accommodation or thing agreed to by the tenant and landlord is not deemed to be an increase for purposes of rent increases under the Act. If the parking space or prescribed service is no longer provided, the rent must be reduced accordingly.

RENT GUIDELINE

Increases in rent are not permitted for a tenant or assignee, except in accordance with the Act. The Minister for the Ministry of Municipal Affairs and Housing determines and publishes a *rent guideline* for the following year no later than the 31st day of August of the current year.

The rent guideline is the percentage change from year to year in the Consumer Price Index for Ontario for prices of goods and services as reported monthly by Statistics Canada, averaged over the 12-month period that concludes at the end of May of the previous calendar year, rounded to the first decimal point.

INCREASES ABOVE GUIDELINE

Increases above the guideline can be effected in various ways. The Act sets out detailed procedures, some of which are summarized below for illustrative purposes. Registrants should advise landlords and tenants to access the Act directly and/or seek expert advice.

- The landlord and tenant may agree to increase rent if new or additional services are provided. The Regulations set out various items that fall under the parameters of a service. The Act also provides flexibility on related issues; e.g., rent adjustment for increase/decrease in unit size and discontinued services.
- Landlord and tenant may agree to increase rent if capital expenditures are provided in exchange for a rent increase, subject to certain qualifications and restrictions. If the rent increase application is for capital expenditures or security services, there is

a limit of three percent above the guideline for a maximum of three years. Once the capital expenditure is fully paid for, the rent must go down for any tenants who were living there at the time of the increase.

- The Act sets out provisions for rent increases based on capital expenditures relating to the rental property that are incurred by the landlord. The landlord must make application to the Landlord and Tenant Board for such an increase.
- The landlord may also apply to the Board for an order to increase rents relating to certain extraordinary costs involving such areas as municipal taxes, utilities and certain services. The Act also provides for reductions if taxes are lowered (below a prescribed level), utility costs associated with the increase are subsequently reduced or services are discontinued.

Procedures and calculations relating to rent guidelines are complex. Expert advice is strongly recommended.

NEW RENTAL UNITS (AND OTHER PARTIALLY EXEMPTED UNITS)

The Act provides partial exemption (for new rental units and other units) relating to selected portions of the Act.

RULES RELATING TO RENT   `RESIDENTIAL TENANCIES ACT`

6.   (2)   Sections 104, 111, 112, 120, 121, 122, 126 to 133, 165 and 167 do not apply with respect to a rental unit if,

   (a) it was not occupied for any purpose before June 17, 1998;

   (b) it is a rental unit no part of which has been previously rented since July 29, 1975; or

   (c) no part of the building, mobile home park or land lease community was occupied for residential purposes before November 1, 1991. 2006, c. 17, s. 6 (2).

Subsec. 6(2) is specific regarding the partial exemption for *a rental unit not occupied* [*i.e., new*] *for any purpose before June 17, 1998*. Registrants should exercise appropriate caution regarding any matters relating to *partially exempt* units. The portions of the Act exempted are, most notably, provisions concerning rent rules, lawful rent and the amount of rent charged. Other sections of the Act are also exempted due to their linkage with the main topic of lawful rents and rent guidelines.

Detailed review of the Act and Regulations is required. In particular, it should be noted that, despite various rent-related exemptions, the 12-month rule regarding rent increases is not exempted.

Access and Entry Rights

Quiet enjoyment is fundamental to any tenancy, which includes the non-interference of the landlord or his/her agents. Alternatively, the Act also provides that the tenant cannot interfere with landlord rights. Real estate registrants should be particularly mindful of provisions regarding access to tenanted properties.

GENERAL ACCESS/LOCKING SYSTEMS

The right to access or gain admittance to rental premises, as set out in *Residential Tenancies Act*, must be clearly understood by all salespersons involved in the showing and/ or rental of residential property. The right of quiet possession by tenants is well established in both common and statutory law. Consequently, registrants must be knowledgeable of and demonstrate prudence regarding entry requirements.

The Act sets out selected access-related issues:

- The landlord may not restrict reasonable access by election candidates (or their authorized representatives) for any federal, provincial or municipal office.
- The landlord cannot change the entry locking system to a residential unit without providing replacement keys to the tenant. The tenant can apply to the Landlord and Tenant Board for an order to regain possession of their unit if they have been illegally locked out.
- The tenant cannot change, or have someone else change, the entry locking system to a residential unit without the landlord's consent.

LANDLORD RIGHT OF ENTRY

Right of entry by the landlord is broadly divided into two scenarios: entry with written 24-hour notice and entry without notice.

ENTRY WITH WRITTEN 24-HOUR NOTICE	ENTRY WITHOUT WRITTEN NOTICE
Entry by the landlord with proper written notice is permitted provided that the notice sets out the reason for the request and the day and time of the requested entry. The landlord may enter between 8 a.m. and 8 p.m.: • to carry out repairs or do work in the rental unit; • to allow a potential mortgagee or insurer of the residential complex to view that particular rental unit; • to allow a potential purchaser to view the rental unit; • to inspect for purposes of ensuring that the property is in a good state of repair and meets health, safety, housing and maintenance standards, consistent with the landlord's obligations; or • for any other reasonable grounds specified in the tenancy agreement.	Entry is permitted without written notice in the following specific situations: • in the case of an emergency or the tenant consents at the time of entry; • if the tenancy agreement provides for regular cleaning by the landlord and if: · entry is made at times specified; or · between 8 a.m. and 8 p.m. when no times are specified. • if the landlord wants to show a prospective tenant and if: · the landlord and tenant have agreed to a termination or either has given notice of termination; · the landlord enters the rental unit between 8 a.m. and 8 p.m.; and · the landlord, before entering, makes a reasonable effort to inform the tenant of his/her intention to enter.

Assignments and Subletting

ASSIGNMENT

Assignment provisions apply to all tenancies whether periodic, fixed, contractual or statutory, but not to the tenant of a superintendent's premises (which is specifically excluded under the Act).

- If a tenant requests an assignment, the landlord can either consent or refuse consent.
- If a tenant requests an assignment to a specific assignee, the landlord can consent or refuse consent based on that assignee.

A refusal regarding an assignee cannot be arbitrary or unreasonable. It should be noted that the landlord may consent to an assignment and subsequently refuse an assignment to a specific assignee. The landlord may charge reasonable out-of-pocket expenses in giving consent.

If an assignment is requested by a tenant and the landlord refuses or does not respond within seven days of the request, the tenant may give notice of termination within 30 days of the request.

If an assignment is made, the terms and conditions of the tenancy agreement continue to apply. Both assignee and tenant (now former tenant) are liable to the landlord and have rights under the tenancy agreement as follows: (1) the former tenant for the period up to the assignment; and (2) the assignee for the period following assignment.

SUBLETTING

Subletting provisions apply to all tenancies whether periodic (e.g., month-to-month), fixed (e.g., lease with exact term), contractual (specifically detailed by contract) or statutory (provided under the Act, for example, a fixed tenancy becomes a periodic tenancy if the tenant remains following the term).

The Act sets out various requirements and restrictions concerning subletting. Selected items are highlighted for descriptive purposes only. Registrants should access the Act directly for exact wordings.

- Subletting provisions do not apply to the tenant of a superintendent's premises.
- The landlord cannot arbitrarily or unreasonably withhold consent to a sublet.
- The landlord may charge reasonable out-of-pocket expenses relating to the consent.
- The tenant remains entitled to benefits and liable for breaches under the tenancy agreement during the subtenancy period.
- The subtenant is entitled to benefits and is liable to the tenant for breaches of the subtenant's obligations.
- The subtenant has no right to occupy the rental unit after the end of the subtenancy.
- The tenant may apply to the Landlord and Tenant Board for an order for compensation from an overholding subtenant, if the subtenant is in possession of the rental unit at the time of the application.
- Various rights given to the landlord concerning termination apply to the tenant/subtenant relationship as if the tenant were landlord and the subtenant were tenant (e.g., damage, reasonable enjoyment and too many persons).
- If a subtenant overholds and the original tenant has vacated the rental unit, the landlord may negotiate a new tenancy agreement with that person.
- The unauthorized occupation shall be deemed to be an assignment with landlord consent if:
    · a new tenancy agreement is not entered into within 60 days; and
    · no application is made to evict the person or the subtenant.

Termination (By Landlord)

Termination of a tenancy agreement is only possible in accordance with the Act. A notice of termination must identify the rental unit, the date of the tenancy termination and be signed (by the person giving the notice or his/her agent). In the case of the landlord, the notice must also set out the reasons and details respecting the termination.

The Act outlines appropriate notices to be used based on a range of circumstances. A notice of termination is not required if the tenant and landlord agree to terminate. Registrants should consult the Act directly on such matters.

BEFORE END OF PERIOD

The landlord may proceed with a notice of termination either before the end of the tenancy period or at the end of the term, based on specific reasons set out in the Act. Notice periods and procedures vary. Reasons for termination include:

- non-payment of rent;
- termination for cause (e.g., illegal act, misrepresentation of income, damage, interference with reasonable enjoyment of other tenants, impairing of safety and too many persons occupying the rental unit); and
- the Act also provides for termination for repeat of selected causes.

A change under the *Residential Tenancies Act* from the previous Act is of particular note. A shorter notice period is now provided to landlords in the case of tenants who cause wilful or excessive damage to a rental unit or building. This notice period (reduced from 20 to 10 days) also applies to tenants who cause a disturbance in a small rental building where the landlord also resides.

AT END OF PERIOD/TERM

Termination procedures at the end of the term depend on the reason for termination. Possession and sale of property are most frequently encountered by real estate registrants.

Demolition, Conversion of Use, Extensive Renovations	The notice period is 120 days subject to certain qualifications regarding such activities.
Possession Required	A landlord may, by notice, terminate a tenancy if possession of the rental unit is for residential occupation by the landlord, the landlord's spouse or a child or parent of one of them. This also applies if the person provides or will provide care services to the landlord, the landlord's spouse, or a child or parent of the landlord or the landlord's spouse. Termination is 60 days after notice and is the day a period of the tenancy ends, or in the case of a fixed term, the end of the term. Upon receiving a notice, the tenant may then terminate earlier than the date provided in the landlord's notice of termination, but not earlier than ten days following notice.

Sale of Property	A landlord of a residential complex, containing no more than three residential units, may give notice if: • The landlord has entered into an agreement of purchase and sale to sell the complex; and • The purchaser, the purchaser's spouse, a child or parent of one of them, or a person who provides care services to the purchaser, the purchaser's spouse, or a child or parent of the purchaser or the purchaser's spouse requires possession of the complex or a unit within the complex. • The termination is 60 days following the notice and is the day a period of the tenancy ends, or in the case of a fixed term, the end of the term. Upon notice, the tenant may terminate earlier than the landlord's notice, but not earlier than ten days following notice. The same provisions apply to a condominium.
Other Specified Reasons	**Rent** The tenant persistently fails to pay rent on the due date. **Qualifications** The tenant ceases to meet qualifications in selected government owned, operated or administered rental units, federal or provincial non-profit housing projects, non-profit housing co-operative non-member units, education institution rental units and religious institution charitable non-profit units. **Tenant/Employee** An employee's employment has been terminated and the rental unit was provided during the employment. **Condominium** The tenancy arose pursuant to an agreement of purchase and sale for a proposed unit and the agreement of purchase and sale has been terminated.

Termination provisions by landlords are complex. Registrants should refer to the Act regarding both procedures and applications to the Landlord and Tenant Board.

Termination (By Tenant)

Termination of a tenancy agreement is only possible in accordance with the Act. A notice of termination must identify the rental unit, the date of the tenancy termination and be signed by the person giving the notice or his/her agent. A notice of termination is not required if the tenant and landlord agree to terminate.

Registrants should be particularly aware of notice periods relating to terminations by tenants. The tenant may give notice at the end of a rental period or at the end of a tenancy for a fixed term.

DAILY OR WEEKLY TENANCY	MONTHLY OR YEARLY TENANCY	FIXED TERM TENANCY
28 days before effective date of termination; i.e., last day of the rental period.	60 days before effective date of termination; i.e., last day of the rental period.	60 days before specified expiration date to be effective on the expiration date.

ABANDONED

The term abandoned is defined as the act of leaving a rental premises completely and finally. The *Residential Tenancies Act* sets out provisions concerning the abandonment of a rental unit and landlord rights concerning the disposal of tenant property. A unit is not considered abandoned if the tenant is still paying rent.

A landlord must proceed cautiously regarding a seemingly abandoned unit. A unit is not abandoned when the rent is paid. However, confusion can arise when the unit appears vacated and the rent is not paid.

Substantial evidence should precede any action by the landlord. Clear evidence must exist that the tenant has left; e.g., all possessions are gone and the door is left open. Evidence should be cumulative in support of taking any action. Such evidence might include the fact that the tenant informed the landlord of his/her intent to leave, the mail has remained uncollected and a neighbour spoke with the tenant and saw the individual loading personal effects.

The landlord should also make attempts to contact the tenant and, at minimum, keep records of such attempts. Notwithstanding these guidelines, any landlord can take on substantial risk by re-renting a unit, or taking other action (e.g., disposing of any tenant's possessions) without an order by the Landlord and Tenant Board.

Special Tenancy Situations

As a reminder, the *Residential Tenancies Act* not only covers various residential rental arrangements as detailed in the Act, but also addresses special circumstances. Provisions concerning care homes and mobile home parks were discussed in a previous chapter. Other provisions of note concern condominium conversion.

CONDOMINIUM CONVERSION

The *Residential Tenancies Act* provides for tenants' security of tenure in the event that a residential complex is converted to condominium. The landlord cannot demand that tenants move out in order to convert a rental building into a condominium.

The tenant, in most instances, can continue to live in the rental unit after the property becomes registered as a condominium. As such, the tenant is protected under the *Residential Tenancies Act*. The Act sets out various exceptions and qualifications that should be read in detail.

Expert advice is required concerning all matters involving condominium conversions. Registrants should also be reminded that local municipalities may have restrictions concerning such conversions.

KNOWLEDGE INTEGRATION

Notables

- Four types of tenancy have evolved including fixed term, periodic, tenancy at will and tenancy at sufferance.

- Principal use is the primary distinguishing characteristic between residential and commercial tenancies, but exemptions under the *Residential Tenancies Act* must also be carefully reviewed for a complete perspective.

- A lease must contain certain elements to make it legally enforceable.

- An agreement to lease can constitute a formal agreement between landlord and tenant in the absence of a fully documented lease.

- The *Agreement to Lease—Residential* (OREA Form 400) sets out lease particulars and substantive terms and may constitute the entire agreement if a detailed lease is not prepared.

- Tenants are assured security of tenure. When a lease expires, the tenancy automatically becomes month-to-month until terminated pursuant to the *Residential Tenancies Act.*

- The *Residential Tenancies Act* provides that verbal tenancy agreements have legal status; i.e., the landlord allows possession, the tenant pays rent, but no formal document is signed.

- The Landlord and Tenant Board is responsible for mediation and adjudication of landlord/tenant disputes relating to the *Residential Tenancies Act.*

- Various tenancy common law principles are pre-empted by statutory provisions set out in the *Residential Tenancies Act*; e.g., assignment, entry and termination provisions.

- Landlord access/entry falls under two categories: written 24-hour notice and entry without notice.

- The Act requires that lawful rent must be charged. New units are exempt from some, but not all, rent-related provisions.

- The *Residential Tenancies Act* also addresses special tenancy situations involving care homes, mobile home parks/land lease communities and condominium conversions.

Web Links

Web links are included for general interest regarding selected chapter topics.

Landlord and Tenant Board   Go to the Landlord and Tenant Board website (*www.ltb.gov.on.ca*) for detailed information regarding the structured process for handling landlord/tenant disputes. Downloadable forms and explanatory notes are available on the site. Forms can be broadly divided into notices (notices made by landlords to tenants and vice versa; e.g., notice of termination), applications to resolve disputes and miscellaneous forms relating to the dispute resolution process.

Residential Tenancies Act   Go to the *www.e-laws.gov.on.ca* for a current version of the legislation. Always refer directly to the Act and Regulations for up-to-date information regarding residential tenancies.

Strategic Thinking For Your Career

Questions are included to assist in developing your new career. No answers are provided.

1. How are rental properties marketed in the local area? Does an opportunity exist; e.g., does a large percentage of rental ads involve owners attempting to rent apartments by themselves?

2. What is the local vacancy factor and current demand for apartments? What long-term forecasts are available?

3. Are brokerages in the local marketplace actively involved with residential rentals and what added services can I provide to gain a competitive advantage?

4. What information is available on the Landlord and Tenant Board website that could assist me in better understanding rental provisions set out in the *Residential Tenancies Act*?

Chapter Mini-Review

Solutions are located in the Appendix.

1. A fixed term tenancy is best described as a tenancy with a fixed period, but indefinite length; that is, the tenancy automatically renews itself unless notice is provided to the contrary.

    ◯ True   ◯ False

2. Predominant use is an important consideration in establishing if a tenancy is residential or commercial.

    ◯ True   ◯ False

3. A legally enforceable lease only requires that the parties to the lease are identified by full legal names and the leased premises is sufficiently described to be readily identifiable.

    ◯ True   ◯ False

4. A tenant may register his/her leasehold interest at the land registration office.

    ◯ True   ◯ False

5. A preprinted blank lease must be attached to the *Agreement to Lease—Residential* (OREA Form 400) in order to make the agreement legally enforceable.

    ◯ True   ◯ False

6. Adjudication is used by the Landlord and Tenant Board to resolve all disputes between landlords and tenants.

    ◯ True   ◯ False

7. According to the *Residential Tenancies Act*, the former tenant is not liable to the landlord for any obligations under the lease following an assignment of that lease to another party.

    ◯ True   ◯ False

8. A *no pet* provision in a residential lease is void, subject to certain exceptions, most notably a lease involving a residential condominium in which pet restrictions are properly documented and enforced.

    ◯ True   ◯ False

9. A landlord must provide written 24-hour notice when planning to carry out repairs or do work in a rental unit.

    ◯ True   ◯ False

10. A residential landlord must give 60 days written notice of any increase in rent.

    ◯ True   ◯ False

11. The *Residential Tenancies Act* provides that a landlord may make application to terminate a residential tenancy before the end of the term if a tenant has substantially interfered with the reasonable enjoyment of other tenants.

    ◯ True   ◯ False

12. Any residential landlord may give notice of termination to an existing tenant(s) at the end of a term if he or she has accepted an offer to sell the property.

    ◯ True   ◯ False

Active Learning Exercises

Solutions are located in the Appendix.

■ Exercise 1   Multiple Choice

1.1   An agreement to lease is technically referred to as:

    a.   An agreement of purchase and sale.

    b.   An agreement for lease without settled form of lease.

    c.   An agreement for lease subject to formal lease signing.

    d.   An agreement to lease with lease affixed.

1.2   Which of the following is NOT an exemption under the *Residential Tenancies Act*?

    a.   Living accommodation for the travelling or vacationing public.

    b.   Living accommodation provided for rehabilitative or therapeutic services.

    c.   Premises occupied by an individual for business or agricultural purposes, with living accommodation attached for that person.

    d.   Living accommodation provided to a landlord's spouse, parent or child on a daily or weekly basis.

1.3   If possession of a rental unit is required by the landlord:

    a.   The landlord must give 120 days notice to the tenant.

    b.   Such possession must be for a minimum term of one year.

    c.   Such possession can only be obtained at the end of the term.

    d.   The landlord can only gain possession if the property has more than three residential units.

1.4   Termination by a tenant:

    a.   Requires 60 days notice, if tenancy is monthly.

    b.   Must be made in writing.

    c.   Is only possible in accordance with the *Residential Tenancies Act*.

    d.   All of the above.

1.5   Which of the following statements is correct?

    a.   Seasonal or temporary accommodation is exempt under the *Residential Tenancies Act*.

    b.   Members of the Landlord and Tenant Board are appointed by the Court.

    c.   The rent control guideline published annually must be 2% or higher.

    d.   Salespersons are exempted from entry requirements and associated notice periods set out in the *Residential Tenancies Act*.

1.6   When a tenant is subletting a residential unit:

    a.   He/she must pay reasonable out-of-pocket expenses to the landlord relating to the sublet.

    b.   He/she is no longer liable under the original tenancy agreement.

    c.   The landlord can arbitrarily withhold consent to the sublet.

    d.   The landlord cannot make application to terminate the subtenancy due to the subtenant damaging the unit.

1.7   A landlord may make application to terminate a tenancy before the end of the term if:

    a.   Possession is required by the landlord.

    b.   The property is being sold.

    c.   Too many persons are occupying the rental unit in contravention of local by-laws.

    d.   Demolition or extensive renovations are being undertaken.

1.8   Which of the following is a correct statement?

    a.   A landlord can require that a tenant provide post-dated rent cheques.

    b.   A landlord must pay 4% annual interest on tenants' rent deposits.

    c.   A landlord is required to collect a rent deposit.

    d.   The maximum rent deposit is one month's rent.

▣ Exercise 2   Rent Calculations

NOTE: Guideline increases in this exercise are fictitious. Go to the Landlord and Tenant Board (www.ltb.gov.on.ca) for current permissible percentage increases based on changes in the Consumer Price Index for Ontario.

2.1   A salesperson lists a fully-occupied duplex with the following lawful monthly rents: Apartment 1: $1,125.00 and Apartment 2: $1,250.00. What would be the maximum projected annual lawful rent for these apartments if a 2.9% rent guideline increase is permitted for the upcoming year, based on changes in the Consumer Price Index for Ontario?

2.2   A landlord is considering increasing the rent based on the published rent guideline for 20xx. If the notice is given to the tenant on August 1, 20xx, what is the first month that the actual rent increase would be effective?

2.3   A tenant submits a rent deposit of $875.00 (one month's rent) for a month-to-month tenancy. Over two successive years, the landlord increases the rent using published rent guidelines of 2.4% and 2.7% respectively. What increases in rent deposit could the landlord require for each of those successive years?

2.4   A small residential complex containing six two-bedroom units was constructed last year. The landlord originally asked and obtained $1,450.00 per month for each unit. In each instance, a one-year lease was signed. One unit has now come vacant at the end of the lease. If the rent guideline for the current year is 1.9%, what is the maximum lawful rent that can be charged for a new tenant occupying the vacant unit?

■ Exercise 3   Residential Tenancies Act

Briefly respond to each of the following statements based on your knowledge of the *Residential Tenancies Act.*

3.1   Landlord: *I haven't seen that tenant for about three weeks now. Most of his things are gone. I'll sign a listing …go ahead and rent the apartment for me.*

3.2   Tenant: *I know that a no pet provision in a residential rental agreement is void. That means that the landlord can't force me to get rid of an animal once I'm in possession of the rental unit.*

3.3   Salesperson: *If a tenant wants to assign his or her lease, it's really straightforward. The landlord can either accept the assignment or refuse. If the landlord refuses, then the tenant can give notice of termination.*

3.4   Landlord: *When you have a prospective buyer, just drop by the building and use my passkey to enter the units. Both tenants know that the property is up for sale …I told them earlier this week.*

3.5   Tenant: *I just noticed that the rent guideline for next year is 1.7%. That's great. I currently pay $1,000, so the maximum monthly increase possible is $17.00.*

■ Exercise 4   Drafting an Agreement to Lease—Residential

Draft the initial offer, prepare the counter offer (amend original) and finalize the accepted agreement based on the following information. Include additional details as necessary.

> Barbara Ellen Forsyth and Raymond Steven Forsyth want to lease 10 Roxway Drive, Anycity from Mario Galletta for two years. This residential, single-family house is currently listed through your brokerage, ABC Realty Inc. The legal description is Lot 10, Plan M-2983.
>
> The prospective tenants, as customers, ask that an offer be drafted for $2,300.00 per month with first and last months' rent to be submitted upon acceptance. The tenant is responsible for gas, electricity, hot water heater rental, cable TV and the monthly security system fee. The landlord pays for water/sewerage charges and property taxes. The Roxway house has a single-car garage and paved drive. All existing drapery rods, window coverings in the kitchen, dining room, living room and three bedrooms, and the following appliances are included: WestRange stove and refrigerator, Fountain Deluxe dishwasher, Durability Plus washer and dryer, and EasyLight gas barbecue.
>
> The prospective tenants want the tenancy to begin on October 1st. The offer date is August 25th with an irrevocable of 11:59 p.m. on August 26th. Both landlord and tenant agree that the accepted Agreement to Lease—Residential will form the completed lease. No other lease will be signed.
>
> Mario Galletta, upon reviewing the offer on the 26th, counters at $2,650.00 per month and provides a further day for the Forsyth's to consider the counter offer. Barbara and Ray Forsyth accept the terms at 3:30 p.m. on the 27th.
>
> Mr. and Mrs. Forsyth currently reside in Apt. 207, 32 Stanwood Crescent, Anycity K8T 8B3 and their lawyer is Ms. A. Willman of Bartlett, Winslow & Phillip, 385 Vanier Drive, Anycity K9T 3C7. Mario Galletta's address for service is 39 Elizabeth Crescent, Anytown, K7E 8O7. His lawyer is G. Myers of Myers and Smallwood, 15 Melrose Blvd., Anycity, K9C 3T4.

OREA Ontario Real Estate Association

Agreement to Lease
Residential

Form 400
for use in the Province of Ontario

This Agreement to Lease dated this .... day of.., 20.................

TENANT (Lessee), ...
(Full legal names of all Tenants)

LANDLORD (Lessor), ...
(Full legal name of Landlord)

ADDRESS OF LANDLORD ....
(Legal address for the purpose of receiving notices)

The Tenant hereby offers to lease from the Landlord the premises as described herein on the terms and subject to the conditions as set out in this Agreement.

1. **PREMISES:** Having inspected the premises and provided the present tenant vacates, I/we, the Tenant hereby offer to lease, premises known as:

    ....

2. **TERM OF LEASE:** The lease shall be for a term of .... commencing ....

3. **RENT:** The Tenant will pay to the said Landlord monthly and every month during the said term of the lease the sum of ....

    .... Canadian Dollars (CDN$..................................),
    payable in advance on the first day of each and every month during the currency of the said term. First and last months' rent to be paid in advance upon completion or date of occupancy, whichever comes first.

4. **DEPOSIT AND PREPAID RENT:** The Tenant delivers...
    (Herewith/Upon acceptance/as otherwise described in this Agreement)

    by negotiable cheque payable to.. "Deposit Holder"

    in the amount of..

    Canadian Dollars (CDN$..) as a deposit to be held in trust as security for the faithful performance by the Tenant of all

    terms, covenants and conditions of the Agreement and to be applied by the Landlord against the .... and ....
    month's rent. If the Agreement is not accepted, the deposit is to be returned to the Tenant without interest or deduction.

    For the purposes of this Agreement, "Upon Acceptance" shall mean that the Tenant is required to deliver the deposit to the Deposit Holder within 24 hours of the acceptance of this Agreement. The parties to this Agreement hereby acknowledge that, unless otherwise provided for in this Agreement, the Deposit Holder shall place the deposit in trust in the Deposit Holder's non-interest bearing Real Estate Trust Account and no interest shall be earned, received or paid on the deposit.

5. **USE:** The Tenant and Landlord agree that unless otherwise agreed to herein, only the Tenant named above and any person named in a Rental Application completed prior to this Agreement will occupy the premises.

    Premises to be used only for:..

    ....

    ....

    ....

6. **SERVICES AND COSTS:** The cost of the following services applicable to the premises shall be paid as follows:

	LANDLORD	TENANT		LANDLORD	TENANT
Gas	☐	☐	Cable TV	☐	☐
Oil	☐	☐	Condominium/Cooperative fees	☐	☐
Electricity	☐	☐	Garbage Removal	☐	☐
Hot water heater rental	☐	☐	Other:	☐	☐
Water and Sewerage Charges	☐	☐	Other:	☐	☐

The Landlord will pay the property taxes, but if the Tenant is assessed as a Separate School Supporter, Tenant will pay to the Landlord a sum sufficient to cover the excess of the Separate School Tax over the Public School Tax, if any, for a full calendar year, said sum to be estimated on the tax rate for the current year, and to be payable in equal monthly installments in addition to the above mentioned rental, provided however, that the full amount shall become due and be payable on demand on the Tenant.

INITIALS OF TENANT(S): ( )   **INITIALS OF LANDLORD(S):** ( )

Exercise 4   Agreement to Lease—Residential, Page 2 of 4

7. PARKING: ....

....

....

8. ADDITIONAL TERMS: ....

....

....

....

9. SCHEDULES: The schedules attached hereto shall form an integral part of this Agreement to Lease and consist of: **Schedule(s) A** ....

....

10. IRREVOCABILITY: This offer shall be irrevocable by .... until .... a.m./p.m. on the ....
(Landlord/Tenant)

day of..,20...................after which time if not accepted, this Agreement shall be null and void and all monies paid thereon shall be returned to the Tenant without interest or deduction.

11. NOTICES: The Landlord hereby appoints the Listing Brokerage as agent for the Landlord for the purpose of giving and receiving notices pursuant to this Agreement. Where a Brokerage (Tenant's Brokerage) has entered into a representation agreement with the Tenant, the Tenant hereby appoints the Tenant's Brokerage as agent for the purpose of giving and receiving notices pursuant to this Agreement. **Where a Brokerage represents both the Landlord and the Tenant (multiple representation), the Brokerage shall not be appointed or authorized to be agent for either the Tenant or the Landlord for the purpose of giving and receiving notices.** Any notice relating hereto or provided for herein shall be in writing. In addition to any provision contained herein and in any Schedule hereto, this offer, any counter-offer, notice of acceptance thereof or any notice to be given or received pursuant to this Agreement or any Schedule hereto (any of them, "Document") shall be deemed given and received when delivered personally or hand delivered to the Address for Service provided in the Acknowledgement below, or where a facsimile number or email address is provided herein, when transmitted electronically to that facsimile number or email address, respectively, in which case, the signature(s) of the party (parties) shall be deemed to be original.

FAX No.: ....   FAX No.: ....
(For delivery of Documents to Landlord)   (For delivery of Documents to Tenant)

Email Address: ....   Email Address: ....
(For delivery of Documents to Landlord)   (For delivery of Documents to Tenant)

12. EXECUTION OF LEASE: Lease shall be drawn by the Landlord on the Landlord's standard form of lease, and shall include the provisions as contained herein and in any attached schedule, and shall be executed by both parties before possession of the premises is given.The Landlord shall provide the tenant with information relating to the rights and responsibilities of the Tenant and information on the role of the Landlord and Tenant Board and how to contact the Board. (Information For New Tenants as made available by the Landlord and Tenant Board and available at www.ltb.gov.on.ca)

13. ACCESS: The Landlord shall have the right, at reasonable times to enter and show the demised premises to prospective tenants, purchasers or others. The Landlord or anyone on the Landlord's behalf shall also have the right, at reasonable times, to enter and inspect the demised premises.

14. INSURANCE: The Tenant agrees to obtain and keep in full force and effect during the entire period of the tenancy and any renewal thereof, at the Tenant's sole cost and expense, fire and property damage and public liability insurance in an amount equal to that which a reasonably prudent Tenant would consider adequate. The Tenant agrees to provide the Landlord, upon demand at any time, proof that said insurance is in full force and effect and to notify the Landlord in writing in the event that such insurance is cancelled or otherwise terminated.

15. RESIDENCY: The Landlord shall forthwith notify the Tenant in writing in the event the Landlord is, at the time of entering into this Agreement, or, becomes during the term of the tenancy, a non-resident of Canada as defined under the Income Tax Act, RSC 1985, c.1 (ITA) as amended from time to time, and in such event the Landlord and Tenant agree to comply with the tax withholding provisions of the ITA.

16. USE AND DISTRIBUTION OF PERSONAL INFORMATION: The Tenant consents to the collection, use and disclosure of the Tenant's personal information by the Landlord and/or agent of the Landlord, from time to time, for the purpose of determining the creditworthiness of the Tenant for the leasing, selling or financing of the premises or the real property, or making such other use of the personal information as the Landlord and/or agent of the Landlord deems appropriate.

17. CONFLICT OR DISCREPANCY: If there is any conflict or discrepancy between any provision added to this Agreement (including any Schedule attached hereto) and any provision in the standard pre-set portion hereof, the added provision shall supersede the standard pre-set provision to the extent of such conflict or discrepancy. This Agreement, including any Schedule attached hereto, shall constitute the entire Agreement between Landlord and Tenant. There is no representation, warranty, collateral agreement or condition, which affects this Agreement other than as expressed herein. This Agreement shall be read with all changes of gender or number required by the context.

18. CONSUMER REPORTS: The Tenant is hereby notified that a consumer report containing credit and/or personal information may be referred to in connection with this transaction.

INITIALS OF TENANT(S): (⬭)   INITIALS OF LANDLORD(S): (⬭)

Form 400   Revised 2015   **Page 2 of 4**

19. BINDING AGREEMENT: This Agreement and acceptance thereof shall constitute a binding agreement by the parties to enter into the Lease of the Premises and to abide by the terms and conditions herein contained.

SIGNED, SEALED AND DELIVERED in the presence of: IN WITNESS whereof I have hereunto set my hand and seal:

....   (Seal)   DATE ....
(Witness)   (Tenant or Authorized Representative)

....   (Seal)   DATE ....
(Witness)   (Tenant or Authorized Representative)

....   (Seal)   DATE ....
(Witness)   (Guarantor)

We/I the Landlord hereby accept the above offer, and agree that the commission together with applicable HST (and any other tax as may hereafter be applicable) may be deducted from the deposit and further agree to pay any remaining balance of commission forthwith.

SIGNED, SEALED AND DELIVERED in the presence of: IN WITNESS whereof I have hereunto set my hand and seal:

....   (Seal)   DATE ....
(Witness)   (Landlord or Authorized Representative)

....   (Seal)   DATE ....
(Witness)   (Landlord or Authorized Representative)

CONFIRMATION OF ACCEPTANCE: Notwithstanding anything contained herein to the contrary, I confirm this Agreement with all changes both typed and written was

finally acceptance by all parties at .... a.m./p.m. this .... day of ...., 20.......... ....
                (Signature of Landlord or Tenant)

INFORMATION ON BROKERAGE(S)

Listing Brokerage .... Tel.No.(...............)...........................

....
(Salesperson / Broker Name)

Co-op/Buyer Brokerage .... Tel.No.(...............)...........................

....
(Salesperson / Broker Name)

ACKNOWLEDGEMENT

I acknowledge receipt of my signed copy of this accepted Agreement of Lease and I authorize the Brokerage to forward a copy to my lawyer.	I acknowledge receipt of my signed copy of this accepted Agreement of Lease and I authorize the Brokerage to forward a copy to my lawyer.
.... DATE .... (Landlord)	.... DATE .... (Tenant)
.... DATE .... (Landlord)	.... DATE .... (Tenant)
Address for Service	Address for Service ....
.... Tel.No.(..........).................	.... Tel.No.(..........).................
Landlord's Lawyer	Tenant's Lawyer ....
Address	Address ....
Email	Email ....
(..........)................. (..........)................. Tel.No. FAX No.	(..........)................. (..........)................. Tel.No. FAX No.

FOR OFFICE USE ONLY   **COMMISSION TRUST AGREEMENT**

To: Co-operating Brokerage shown on the foregoing Agreement to Lease:
In consideration for the Co-operating Brokerage procuring the foregoing Agreement to Lease, I hereby declare that all moneys received or receivable by me in connection with the Transaction as contemplated in the MLS Rules and Regulations of my Real Estate Board shall be receivable and held in trust. This agreement shall constitute a Commission Trust Agreement as defined in the MLS Rules and shall be subject to and governed by the MLS Rules pertaining to Commission Trust.

DATED as of the date and time of the acceptance of the foregoing Agreement to Lease.   Acknowledged by:

....
(Authorized to bind the Listing Brokerage)   (Authorized to bind the Co-operating Brokerage)

Form 400   Revised 2015   **Page 3 of 4**

SECTION I   A CLOSER LOOK AT TRADING DIFFERENT TYPES OF PROPERTIES

Exercise 4   Agreement to Lease—Residential, Page 4 of 4

 **Ontario Real Estate Association**

Form 400
for use in the Province of Ontario

Schedule A
Agreement to Lease - Residential

This Schedule is attached to and forms part of the Agreement to Lease between:

TENANT (Lessee), ..., and

LANDLORD (Lessor), ...

for the lease of ....

.... dated the .... day of ...., 20.................

This form must be initialled by all parties to the Agreement to Lease.

INITIALS OF TENANT(S):   **INITIALS OF LANDLORD(S):**

Form 400   Revised 2015   **Page 4 of 4**

CHAPTER 4

Cottage Property

Introduction

The field of cottage sales is an exciting, demanding and increasingly complicated facet of real estate sales. Originally, the concept of rural sales including cottages was viewed as a basic extension of the urban residential market. In recent years, registrants in the rural marketplace have needed to acquire specialized knowledge to deal with unique issues faced by cottage sellers and buyers.

The proliferation of legislative controls has been a driving force. Few would remember the time when constructing a cottage involved a hasty visit to the township office for a building permit. Now complex issues face anyone developing, building or renovating cottage and rural properties. In particular, environmental controls affecting waterfront properties have increased dramatically given the environmental movement and the associated government agencies and a host of planners involved in the process.

In previous pre-registration courses, most notably *Land, Structures and Real Estate Trading*, many topics were covered that affect both rural and urban registrants such as property ownership, planning and land use, and structural types/components. This chapter takes a closer look at specific issues when targeting the cottage marketplace. Some overlap with previous subject matter is unavoidable.

Chapter 4 focuses on unique considerations in cottage construction, an overview of water well and waste disposal issues affecting recreational properties, waterfront improvements, and associated regulatory requirements concerning boat houses, docks, dredging waterfront areas and aquatic plant control. Applicable clauses are highlighted when drafting offers. The discussion then centres on access challenges particularly with properties located on private roads, typical zoning restrictions that apply to cottages and, lastly, various servicing issues (hydro, telephone and municipal services) that must be investigated as such services may be limited or unavailable. Registrants contemplating a career in cottage and rural recreational sales should pursue advanced courses that meet their specific needs.

Learning Outcomes

At the conclusion of this chapter, students will be able to:

- Identify significant construction issues involving cottages, with particular reference to structural movements, sagging roofs, decks/porches, drainage and winterization.
- Discuss key considerations involving water wells and sewage systems, including appropriate clause drafting.
- Identify key approval procedures and related requirements concerning the installation of boathouses and docks, including appropriate clause drafting.
- Outline regulatory provisions concerning dredging and aquatic plant control.
- Explain key issues regarding cottage access from the perspective of both public roads and private deeded or undeeded access.
- Outline typical zoning provisions that relate to waterfront cottages, as distinct from requirements for other residential uses.
- Identify and discuss important limitations that may be encountered when trying to obtain hydro or telephone services in recreational areas.
- Identify and discuss municipal services that may or may not be available to recreational properties.
- Review the cottage and recreational property checklist.

COTTAGES AND THE RECREATIONAL MARKET

The term *cottage* conjures up an image of an idyllic Muskoka or Haliburton waterfront retreat, but various types of property fulfill the same urge to escape the urban commotion and seek solitude, whether by a lake or simply on a remote lot. The recreational market contains many alternatives, the most notable of which are:

Seasonal Cottages

The largest category of recreational property involves non-winterized structures used during the summer months (although increasingly year-round use is favoured given escalating prices and increasing services and facilities offered to the rural recreational home). In many cases, however, terrain, water access only, uncleared road access during winter and snow/ice conditions make such winterization unrealistic or impossible. The most expensive and popular cottages are those that border a lake or river.

Winterized/Year Round Cottages/Homes

This expanding category involves a greater investment with buyers often investing funds in expanding, renovating or building a permanent home for either full or part-time use. The typical scenario involves a couple with children who convert a cottage into a winterized home for seasonal use, with the ultimate plan to retire and move there permanently.

Country Homes

At one time, affluent city dwellers enjoyed the benefit of a fully furnished country home, but the trend now encompasses many middle income families seeking the solitude of an off-water acreage beyond the hustle and bustle of urban life.

Chalets

These fully equipped homes are typically purchased for winter sports use. Skiing is a major attraction, but the growth of these developments in Barrie, Collingwood and Huntsville areas in particular, have given rise to a wide range of facilities and services for the chalet owner. Ownership options now range into condominium, timeshare and co-ownership.

Hobby Farms

Hobby farms were originally purchased to further a personal hobby, such as training animals, and growing a limited variety of crops. The stereotyped purchaser was typically a full-time professional seeking the exercise and enjoyment of pursing a small enterprise. In recent years, hobby farms are often simply country homes in disguise. While purchased with the intent of an enterprise, many become simply a second home away from urban congestion.

The focus in this chapter is on cottages (seasonal and year round), but many of the topics discussed apply equally to other types of recreational housing.

 CONSTRUCTION

The listing and sale of cottage property necessitates specialized knowledge regarding construction issues not frequently encountered in most urban markets. Cottages must meet all requirements of the Ontario Building Code, as do all other new structures, but older structures may suffer from various defects, problems and deficiencies given the time period in which they were constructed and now largely fall beyond the scope of municipal inspectors, unless modifications are made.

Structural Movement

Many recreational properties have been built on perimeter walls and not full foundations. As a result, some structures may have cracks in walls or other visual signs of building

movement and settling, such as uneven floors. Often, seasonal cottages are built using concrete block and telltale cracks appear in foundation walls.

FOOTINGS

The problem may involve inadequate footings, which can be expensive to repair. Older cottages are particularly prone to this problem as the footings may have been installed on weak soil or were of an insufficient size/depth to support structural weight. Also, the footing may not have extended below the frost line, resulting in heaving following the winter period and the spring thaw.

PIERS

Given local terrain, some cottages are constructed using piers. Structural movement may occur because the piers used are not adequate, deterioration (e.g., wood rot) has occurred or the span between the piers is too large. Once again, signs of movement include structural cracks, sagging and piers that are out of alignment. The problem may also be due to inadequate footings below the piers.

Roof Construction/Pitch

Older cottages may suffer from inadequate roof construction, such as insufficient roof trusses, large spacing between trusses and/or generally poor construction quality resulting in sagging. Further, cottage roofs may have been built or extended with a low pitch, resulting in deterioration as a result of heavy snow load or ice damming.

Low pitch roofs are particularly prone to ice damming as snow and ice collect in a certain area of the roof, often the eaves. Melting snow on the upper roof areas cannot be drained properly, as the thawing and runoff is prevented by the ice accumulation. Water then backs up under the shingles, penetrates the underlying roof structure and ultimately leaks into the exterior walls and main building structure. Interior ceiling or wall stains are a telltale sign that ice damming is occurring.

Decks/Porches

Deficiencies in the main structure are also found with decks and porches, given improperly constructed footings and piers. In some instances, cottage owners may have improved the structure from a living perspective (e.g., enclosed the deck or porch area) or expanded the area without taking into consideration the added load and needed structural modifications.

Drainage

Many older cottages were built on low lands near the water's edge with poor drainage. Often, the original owner was not overly concerned as no basement was ever contemplated and the entire structure was built on concrete block pilings or a perimeter wall with a crawl space. However, the lack of drainage can result not only in long term moisture damage to the structure, but also erosion near or under the structure and damage due to spring runoff from higher elevations surrounding the building area.

Improper drainage can also pose a health hazard should surface water enter a well that is located in a low, wet area. Further, poor drainage surrounding the absorption bed for a sewage (septic) system located in a similar area may create significant problems. See additional discussion later is this chapter.

Do It Yourself Work

Prospective buyers should be particularly cautious when investigating any cottage regarding structural or other changes. Often, weekend owners spend their time altering or adding to the existing cottage. Appropriate approvals may not have been obtained, workmanship can be substandard and improper materials may have been used.

Wood Stoves

Wood burning appliances in existing cottages may not have been installed according to the Ontario Building Code and Ontario Fire Code. Prospective buyers are well advised to have these appliances inspected by a certified member of the Wood Energy Technology Transfer Inc. (WETT Inc.). WETT is a non-profit training and education association that promotes the safe and effective use of wood burning systems in Canada.

WEB LINKS

WETT   Go to the Wood Energy Technology Transfer Inc. (WETT Inc.) site for additional information (*www.wettinc.ca*).

Winterization

No clear definition exists for the term *winterizing* and yet it is commonly used in reference to cottages that have been converted from seasonal to year round use. Unfortunately, the phrase *a fully-winterized cottage* is relative to the person making the statement. For example, one person may be speaking of a cottage that is occupied year round, while another may refer to one that is occupied during specific weeks in the winter and otherwise left unheated during the balance of that season.

As there are no universally accepted standards, cottage buyers should carefully consider the following:

Varying Amounts of Insulation	The cottage may be considered by the seller to be winterized (i.e., he or she could spend winter weekends there), but some areas of the cottage may be insulated, while others are not.
Windows	Cottage owners may winterize without replacing windows. Often, the original windows were sliders (glass sliders in tracks) with limited insulation value and prone to leakage. A new owner would undoubtedly face a costly replacement program involving casement windows with double or triple glazing. Further, extensive use of glass (e.g., a solarium) may forewarn of potential heating and ventilation problems unless proper construction methods and materials were used. The same applies to skylights which are prone to leakage, unless professionally installed.
Unheated Areas/Cold Areas	Floors above certain unheated areas (such as a crawl space) may not be insulated. Keep in mind that corrective action will require adequate space to install insulation, improve ventilation and install heating ducts (if applicable). Proper ventilation and vapour barriers are typically needed to reduce the potential for damage due to moisture build-up. As a further caution, the owner may have added insulation, but not installed the vapour barriers given the difficulty of doing so on a retrofit basis.

Water/ Septic Systems	Even though the owners may use the cottage in the winter, it still begs the question as to what extent of water and waste disposal winterization has occurred. If the cottage is an unheated structure during most of the winter, water lines must be carefully drained to avoid freezing and anti-freeze placed in traps leading to the sewage system.
	Also, where are the pumps located and what procedures must be followed for these during winter months? Other pertinent questions include:
	• How deep are the water lines between the cottage and well? • Are heated water lines used?
	Heated water lines are specially designed water pipes for recreational property to facilitate year round water supply. The lines normally consist of an automatic thermostatic control combined with a heating element that extends through the plastic water line. For temporary installations, these lines lay on the ground, however, the heating elements can also be installed in existing buried water lines.
Vaulted Ceilings	The structural design of uninsulated vaulted ceilings may prevent the cost-effective installation of proper insulation. A significant retrofit project may be the only way to resolve this problem.

Retaining Walls

Retaining walls are often used for shore areas, landscaping and driveways due to challenging terrain. The difficulty for buyers lies in assessing the quality of construction because the important components are buried in the wall itself. Well constructed retaining walls must have adequate drainage (proper gravel behind the wall with outlets at the base), adequate footings and quality materials.

DRAFTING CLAUSES

Buyers will typically seek out expert advice on matters regarding the structural integrity of a cottage and other matters such as outside decks, degree of winterization and related matters. A sample clause is shown on the following page.

SCENARIO	CLAUSE
Condition Regarding Inspection A buyer is submitting an offer and wants an inspection completed by a specific individual who is a builder in the area and is very familiar with cottage properties.	INSP–7 Condition—Inspection of Property–Third Party *This Offer is conditional upon the inspection of the subject property by _____ and the obtaining of a report satisfactory to the Buyer at the Buyer's own expense. Unless the Buyer gives notice in writing delivered to the Seller personally or in accordance with any other provisions for the delivery of notice in this Agreement of Purchase and Sale or any Schedule thereto not later than ____p.m. on the _____day of _____, 20____, that this condition is fulfilled, this Offer shall be null and void and the deposit shall be returned to the Buyer in full without deduction. The Seller agrees to co-operate in providing access to the property for the purpose of this inspection. This condition is included for the benefit of the Buyer and may be waived at the Buyer's sole option by notice in writing to the Seller as aforesaid within the time period stated herein.*

WATER WELLS AND
WASTE DISPOSAL SYSTEMS

NOTE: *Land, Structures and Real Estate Trading* contained detailed discussions regarding wells, including installation requirements and bacteriological testing, as well as classifications of waste disposal systems (Classes 1 through 6). Current content expands this resource material in relation to cottages.

Water Quality

The protection of water quality and quantity primarily falls under two statutes and associated regulations; i.e., the *Ontario Water Resources Act* and the *Safe Drinking Water Act*. Real estate registrants most commonly encounter water quality issues relating to private well systems in rural and cottage areas. Matters involving a private system for use by a residential household including a cottage fall under the *Ontario Water Resources Act*.

The Ministry of the Environment licenses well contractors under the *Ontario Water Resources Act* and all work must meet minimum well construction requirements. Once constructed, the well owner is responsible for monitoring, maintaining and preventing contamination of the well (including the aquifer). An aquifer refers to a water-bearing formation that is capable of transmitting water in sufficient quantities to serve as a source of water supply. Well records are maintained by the Ministry of the Environment.

WEB LINKS
Water Quality/Well Records   Go to the Ministry of the Environment site (*www.ene.gov.on.ca*) for additional information about drinking water systems and water quality.

WATER SOURCES

Cottages rely on various water sources. Newer cottage wells are typically either drilled or bored. Dug wells may be found in older cottages. Drilled wells involve small diameter pipes, while a bored well can be two to three feet in diameter and considerably more shallow that the drilled well. Registrants may also encounter shared systems in which a well is located on one cottage property, but shared with others nearby. A buyer facing this situation should have a clear understanding of the sharing arrangement (i.e., a written agreement) and associated rights, responsibilities and maintenance costs.

Cottages may also rely on a shore well that is located near the water's edge. Such wells are particularly prone to contamination. Alternatively, river or lake water may be pumped though an above ground or below ground pipe from the shore to the building. Obviously, the risk of contamination is much higher and water purification equipment is typically installed. Alternatively, some cottage owners may rely on a well for drinking water and restrict lake water use for other daily needs.

CONTAMINATION/TESTING

Water well contamination is generally due to two factors: poor construction (e.g., lack of proper depth and inadequate application of sealing materials) and surface water contamination often arising from drainage problems. As a consequence, continuous bacteriological testing of private well systems is strongly recommended. Such testing is typically done by the local health authorities, but private laboratories also provide this service.

Three separate samples are recommended and should be collected one to three weeks apart. Following initial testing, one or two tests per year appear adequate, unless some occurrence has taken place that would affect the water supply. For seasonal properties, two or three samples are recommended during any particular season, with the first being conducted at the start of the season.

PREVENTATIVE MEASURES

Various measures should be taken by cottagers to ensure high water quality and prevent contamination from leaking into the well:

- Seal from the outside any openings to the well using durable sealing materials. Further, check that all connections (e.g., electrical lines, water lines and pumps) are water-tight and properly sealed.
- Ensure that the sanitary well seal and well cap are firmly situated and watertight.
- Make certain that well vent pipes are properly screened or otherwise protected so that foreign matter does not enter the well.
- The well casing should be visible to ensure easy access if repair work is required. If the existing well is below ground level, it is advisable to have the casing raised to a minimum of 40 cm above ground surface.

WELL DISINFECTING

Water disinfecting can be accomplished using chlorine. Chlorine is a greenish-yellow, incombustible, water soluble poisonous gas. Chlorination is used with new or reworked wells (dug or drilled), cisterns, springs, pumps and pipes. Disinfecting the water by chlorination extends to electrical cables, ropes, pipes, well, well cap, and plumbing lines and fixtures in the house presently drawing water from the well. Bacteria may get into the water supply during construction or repair.

Disinfecting is the final step after all defects in location and construction have been corrected and before samples are collected for bacterial examination. Typically, a predetermined amount of chlorinated household bleach is poured into the well based on water depth, then all taps are opened until a chlorine odour is detected. The water in the pipes is then left to stand for a minimum of six hours and subsequently flushed. It is recommended that residents store enough clean water for three days for drinking, washing and watering plants before well disinfecting. Another option is to boil all water used from the source. A bacteriological retesting of the water follows after several days. Meanwhile, all water used from that source must be boiled.

Cottagers may elect to pour bleach (chlorine) into an existing well given that a bacteriological test has indicated contamination. While this immediate chlorine infusion will undoubtedly produce a *safe water* test, the underlying problem (such as ground water seepage) remains. The chlorine has temporarily removed the bacteria, but the bacteria will likely return.

PRIVATE WELL—WATER TREATMENT

Two of several water treatment systems for private wells are included for general description purposes. The method used will vary based on particular water issues. Registrants should research other common systems used in the local area.

Chlorination Injector Unit

This water treatment device is used primarily in recreational property that feeds a weak solution of chlorine into the water distribution system immediately after it comes from the well. The water must then be pumped into a pressure or storage tank that is large enough to ensure that the water will be stored for a specified period of time to effectively destroy any bacteria. An alternative treatment device called a super chlorination unit is installed either before, or immediately after, the pump. As the water pump is activated, the unit feeds a strong solution of chlorine into the water. The water is then passed through an activated carbon filter to dechlorinate the treated water.

Reverse Osmosis

This procedure involves the removal of dissolved solids and minerals (e.g., chloride and sulphate) from a water supply that is frequently used in recreational properties. Reverse osmosis entails forcing water through a semi-permeable membrane. The membrane passes fresh water, leaving behind minerals and other solid content. Such units have limited gallonage-per-day capacities.

DRAFTING CLAUSES

SCENARIO	CLAUSE
Condition Regarding Private Well A buyer is submitting an offer on a cottage and wants to ensure that the water well provides both a sufficient quantity and quality of water. In addition, the condition must include a provision that the pump and related equipment is in proper working order.	**SEWER/WATER–2 Condition—Water Supply—All Well Types** *This Offer is conditional upon the Buyer determining, at the Buyer's own expense, that:* *(1) there is an adequate water supply to meet the Buyer's household needs;* *(2) the pump and all related equipment serving the property are in proper operating condition; and* *(3) the Buyer can obtain a Bacteriological Analysis of Drinking Water from the authority having jurisdiction indicating that there is no significant evidence of bacterial contamination.* *Unless the Buyer gives notice in writing delivered to the Seller personally or in accordance with any other provisions for the delivery of notice in this Agreement of Purchase and Sale or any Schedule thereto not later than _____ p.m. on the _____ day of _____, 20____ that these conditions have been fulfilled, this Offer shall become null and void and the deposit shall be returned to the Buyer in full without deduction. These conditions are included for the benefit of the Buyer and may be waived at the Buyer's sole option by notice in writing to the Seller as aforesaid within the time period stated herein. The Seller agrees to allow access to the subject property to the Buyer or the Buyer's agent for the purpose of satisfying this condition.*

IMPORTANT: The following note is included in the *Guidelines for Residential & Commercial Clauses* (OREA, 2009):

> *Sale of Property with a well and/or septic system involves specific knowledge of the system. There is a difference in a well's performance depending on many variables; e.g. the amount of available water, the delivery capacity of the well system, the amount of water that can be delivered over a certain period of time and seasonable variables. The type of well, drilled, bored or dug, can also affect performance. Expert advice should be sought.*

Sewage (Septic) System

Sewage systems may be outdated, inadequate to handle current demands or otherwise not operating properly (e.g., due to poor drainage). New septic tank installations fall under the Ontario Building Code. An approval certificate is required (Certificate of Installation and Approval) and an appropriate permit issued before the system can be operated. This applies both in the case of new structures as well as additions. A buyer should insist on seeing this documentation. With older cottages, no paperwork may exist.

Buyers should be aware that cottages were frequently built as seasonal residences, but then were expanded and modernized. For example, the septic system might have been originally built for one kitchen, one bath and two bedrooms, but a much larger winterized home now boasts three bathrooms, three bedrooms and a guest cottage—all reliant on that original system. Installation of a new sewage system may be required. The size of the system is determined by the total fixtures within the cottage, total finished area and number of bedrooms.

Most septic problems involve the absorption (leaching) bed. Specifics regarding waste disposal systems were addressed in *Land, Structures and Real Estate Trading*, but special emphasis should be focused on raised absorption beds, as often a raised bed is needed given rocky locations, inadequate drainage or poor percolation due to soil conditions often found in northern recreational areas.

RAISED ABSORPTION BED

A raised absorption bed is constructed on or above the existing terrain as part of a sewage system using approved, imported soil and/or special filters. Given special absorption qualities of approved filter sand, the overall leaching bed size is reduced in comparison to conventional leaching beds used with a sewage system. Clearances from adjacent wells and structures are increased by an amount equal to two units horizontal for each unit vertical height of the surface of the leaching bed above natural grade. For example, if the clearance to a well was 15 metres for a standard leaching bed, a raised absorption bed might require a minimum clearance of 30 metres or more.

Raised absorption beds are frequently encountered where there is a lack of soil depth to accommodate a standard leaching system, such as in rocky terrain typical in many northern recreational areas. Raised absorption beds have a life expectancy of between 25 and 35 years, as is the case with standard leaching beds, however, this can vary depending on circumstances.

Details are provided for education purposes only. Contact the building department of the local municipality for guidance. Information can be obtained concerning installation requirements and minimum distribution pipe clearances from structures, property lines, wells and other water sources such as a lake, river, pond, stream or reservoir. Information is also available at local health units.

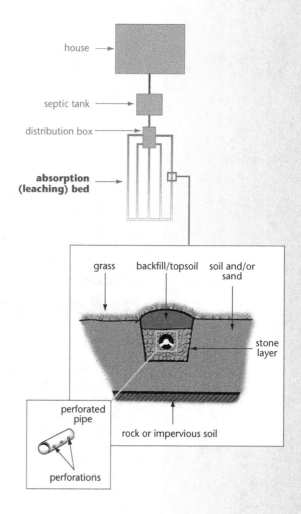

DRAFTING CLAUSES

SCENARIO	CLAUSE
Condition Regarding Sewage System A buyer is submitting an offer on a cottage and wants to ensure that the sewage system meets all requirements and is in good working order.	**SEWER/WATER–1 Condition—Sewage Systems—Approvals** *This Offer is conditional upon the Buyer determining, at the Buyer's own expense, that at the time of installation:* *(1) all sewage systems serving the property are wholly within the setback requirements of the said property and had received all required Certificates of Installation and Approval pursuant to the Environmental Protection Act;* *(2) all sewage systems serving the property had been constructed in accordance with the said Certificates of Installation and Approval;* *(3) all sewage systems serving the property had received all required use permits under the said Act or any other legislation; and further, that on inspection, the septic bed is in good working order.* *The Buyer shall be allowed to retain at the Buyer's own expense, a professional in the septic business to make an examination of the septic system.* *Seller agrees to allow access to the property for the purposes of a septic inspection and agrees to allow the Buyer to request information as outlined above from the appropriate authorities having jurisdiction.* *Unless the Buyer gives notice in writing delivered to the Seller personally or in accordance with any other provisions for the delivery of notice in this Agreement of Purchase and Sale or any Schedule thereto not later than _____ p.m. on the _____ day of _____, 20____, that these conditions have been fulfilled, this Offer shall become null and void and the deposit shall be returned to the Buyer in full without deduction. These conditions are included for the benefit of the Buyer and may be waived at the Buyer's sole option by notice in writing to the Seller as aforesaid within the time period stated herein.*

An additional warranty from the seller regarding working order should also be added to the agreement of purchase and sale.

CLAUSE
SEWER/WATER–4   Sewage System—Good Working Order—Warranty
The Seller represents and warrants, to the best of the Seller's knowledge and belief, that, during the Seller's occupancy of the building, the sewage system has been and will be in good working order on closing. The Parties agree that this representation and warranty shall survive and not merge on completion of this transaction, but apply only to the state of the property existing at completion of this transaction.

WATERFRONT IMPROVEMENTS

Waterfront cottage owners may have constructed boat houses, docks or other improvements on the bed of a lake or river that is not owned. An overview of relevant legislation is necessary to fully understand this issue,

Public Lands Act

Public lands, pursuant to the *Public Lands Act*, are administered by the Ministry of Natural Resources and Forestry (MNR) and involve the management and disposition of public lands and forests. The Act and Regulations set out requirements for issuance of work permits regarding public lands, sale or lease of such lands, roads on public lands, alterations affecting these lands and the construction of dams or other water-related improvements.

Real estate registrants most frequently encounter public lands and the MNR in relation to work permits and shoreline ownership issues. The Act provides that no person shall, without a permit, carry on logging, mineral exploration or industrial operations on public lands, construct or place a building, structure or thing on public lands, clear or cause to be cleared any public lands, dredge or cause to be dredged any shore lands and fill or cause to be filled any shore lands. Shore lands, for purposes of the Act, refer to public or private lands covered by the waters of a lake, river, stream or pond and include adjacent lands that are seasonally inundated by water.

Registrants are reminded that waterfront properties may also fall under both provincial and federal jurisdictions; e.g., federally-controlled canals/waterways such as the Rideau or Trent-Severn systems. Further, such properties will be subject to zoning provisions relating to their waterfront location (e.g., setbacks) and possibly flood plan restrictions imposed locally by the conservation authority.

WEB LINKS

Ministry of Natural Resources and Forestry   Go to the Ministry of Natural Resources and Forestry website (***www.mnr.gov.on.ca***) for detailed information regarding the administration of public lands and requirements specifically focused on cottages.

Boathouses/Docks

The construction of boathouses/docks can impact both shoreline waters and fish habitat. Permits for construction of these structures fall to the Ministry of Natural Resources and Forestry, as such structures are normally built on public lands as defined under the *Public Lands Act*; i.e., lands that fall below the high water mark for most water bodies in Ontario. As mentioned above, if a property fronts on the Rideau or Trent-Severn Waterway, in-water or shoreline works must also be approved by federal authorities. Currently, the appropriate federal contact is the Department of Canadian Heritage, Parks Canada. Zoning provisions will also apply regarding location and size of the structure, along with appropriate approval by the relevant municipality. See subsequent discussion in this chapter.

Work Permit   The requirement for a work permit from the Ministry of Natural Resources and Forestry will depend on the type of work being completed. Buyers and sellers should contact the MNR for guidance and specifics regarding permits. The following is provided as a general discussion for education purposes only. All matters concerning permits must be directed to the Ministry.

PERMIT NOT REQUIRED	PERMIT REQUIRED
Docks and boathouses DO NOT normally need a work permit for the following: • Cantilever docks where the footings are located off the shore lands. • Floating docks and floating boathouses. • Docks and/or boathouses supported by posts, stilts, poles, cribs or other supporting structure—provided that the area of the supporting structure on the bed of the lake or river does not exceed 15 square metres. • Boat lifts and marine railways where the occupied area of the bed of the water body is less than 15 square metres. • Removal of an old dock or boathouse.	Docks and boathouses that DO require a work permit: • Any docks and/or boathouses where the total surface area of cribs, or other supporting structures, to be constructed or placed on the bed of the water body exceeds 15 square metres.

Shore lands are defined in regulation as *lands covered or seasonally inundated by the water of a lake, river, stream or pond.* All docks and boathouses must be located directly in front of the applicant's property and must not interfere with his or her neighbours' use or enjoyment of their property. *Reminder:* Municipal zoning and related requirements still apply.

TWO-STOREY OR SINGLE-STOREY BOATHOUSE WITH LIVING ACCOMMODATION

Land use occupational authority is required under the *Public Lands Act.* Property owners considering boathouses or docks should contact the ministry for detailed information and current regulations. Individuals contemplating such projects are also reminded that the federal *Fisheries Act* provides for the protection of fish habitat. Violations can involve substantial fines. The MNR provides a range of guidelines to assist and to better ensure that boathouse/dock projects minimize environmental harm.

Registrants are also reminded that most alterations/additions to such structures must comply with municipal regulations (e.g., the Ontario Building Code and building/property restrictions found in zoning by-laws).

Boathouse Lease Program	CAUTION

In 2006, the Ministry of Natural Resources and Forestry reinstituted its boathouse lease program and demanded rent for boathouses that are situated on public lands. The Ministry requires that the property owner enter into a lease agreement to confirm the lease arrangements and fees payable. The MNR also requires that the owner pay for registering the lease on title and associated legal costs. The Ministry is particularly focusing its attention on boathouses with a second storey and/or having living accommodation.

DRAFTING CLAUSES

SCENARIO	CLAUSE
Condition Regarding Boat House or Dock A buyer wants to purchase a cottage with an existing boathouse. Accordingly, she submits an offer with the following clause to ensure that the boat-house has received all necessary approvals and permits.	**DOCKS–1** Condition—Docks/Boathouses *This Offer is conditional upon the Buyer determining, at the Buyer's own expense, that the* [boathouse, dock, pier, etc.], *used in conjunction with the property, and passing to the Buyer on completion,* [has/have] *received all necessary approvals and permits from the Ministry of Natural Resources, the Federal Government under the Navigable Waters Protection Act, Canada, from* [insert appropriate conservation or canal authority as required], *and from all other relevant authorities. Unless the Buyer gives notice in writing delivered to the Seller personally or in accordance with any other provisions for the delivery of notice in this Agreement of Purchase and Sale or any Schedule thereto not later than ____ p.m. on the _____ day of _____, 20____, that this condition has been fulfilled, this Offer shall become null and void and the deposit shall be returned to the Buyer in full without deduction. This condition is included for the benefit of the Buyer and may be waived at the Buyer's sole option by notice in writing to the Seller as aforesaid within the time period stated herein.*

Dredging and Related Activities

Dredging is broadly classified as any activity that involves the removal or displacement of material from a lake, river or stream bed. As mentioned previously, the beds of most bodies of water are legally public land and fall under the *Public Lands Act*. The following is provided as a general educational discussion only. All matters concerning permits must be directed to the Ministry of Natural Resources and Forestry.

PERMIT NOT REQUIRED	PERMIT REQUIRED
• Installation of a cable, water line or heat loop for private use; e.g., a single cottage or residence. • Submarine cables where laid on a lake or river bottom.	• Boat channels or swimming areas. • Installation of a cable, water line or heat loop for commercial purposes; e.g., a marina or large scale development. • Removal of rocks/boulders from shore-lands or the bottom of lakes/streams to fill a crib or create a beach.

Individuals contemplating dredging should contact the Ministry of Natural Resources and Forestry for detailed information, current regulations and permit applications. The MNR may need to visit the site and, accordingly, adequate time should be allowed for the application process. Local conservation authorities may also be involved in the approval process if projects fall within regulated areas.

Individuals contemplating dredging should also be reminded that the federal *Fisheries Act* provides for the protection of fish habitat. The MNR provides a range of guidelines to assist in that regard and to better ensure that a dredging project minimizes harm to fish habitat. The quantity of material to be removed, the maintenance of bankside and shoreline vegetation, the protection of aquatic plants and the disposal of dredged materials are all taken into consideration when reviewing dredging proposals.

Summary: When a Work Permit is Required

The following is reprinted from the Ministry of Natural Resources and Forestry website as further clarification on work permits.

WORK PERMITS

A work permit is required to:

- fill shore lands such as creating a beach and constructing shoreline protection works (e.g. break wall, groyne, seawall);
- dredge shore lands such as:
  - creating a boat slip, boating channel or swimming area;
  - installing a water line, heat loop or cable for commercial use (i.e. marina, resort or large scale development); and
  - removal of rocks/boulders from shore lands or the bottom of a lake or stream;
- construct a dock or boathouse where the total surface area of the supporting structure (e.g. pipes, cribs) placed on the bed of the water body exceeds 15 square metres;
- construct a building on public land;
- construct a road on public land, except where constructed under the authority of the *Crown Forest Sustainability Act*;
- construct a trail on public land, except where constructed under the authority of the *Crown Forest Sustainability Act* or for purpose of mineral exploration;
- construct a water crossing (e.g. bridge, culvert and causeway) on public land, except where constructed under the authority of the *Crown Forest Sustainability Act*; and remove aquatic vegetation.

Some types of activities do not require a work permit including:

- minor road maintenance on public land;
- cantilever docks where the footings are located off the shore lands;
- floating docks and floating boathouses;
- docks or boathouses where the total surface area of the supporting structure (e.g. pipes, cribs) placed on the bed of the water body is less than 15 square metres;
- removal of an old dock or boathouse;
- ice fishing huts; and
- installation of a water line, submarine cable or heat loop for private use.

For detailed information on the Ministry's requirements for work permits, please refer to *Policy PL 3.03.04—Public Lands Act Work Permits* (Section 14).

If in doubt about whether a work permit is required or not—applicants are encouraged to contact their local Ministry of Natural Resources and Forestry office well in advance and make an appointment to speak with a Ministry staff person.

Please note that while some boathouses or floating docks may not require a work permit, they may require permission for occupational authority (e.g. land use permit, lease) from the Ministry because they are located on Crown lake bed, or they may need to be reviewed by Transport Canada for potential impacts on navigation. Public Lands Act work permit approvals do not apply to federal waterbodies such as the Trent-Severn and Rideau Canal waterways. For further information on approval requirements for these waterbodies, please contact:

Trent-Severn Waterway Office
P.O. Box 567
2155 Ashburnham Drive
Peterborough Ontario K9J 626
705-755-4900

Rideau Canal Waterway Office
34A Beckwith Street
Smith Falls Ontario K7A 2B3
613-283-5170

Aquatic Plant Control

Waterfront cottage owners have used various control methods for aquatic plants that include raking, mechanical harvesting, removal by hand, the placement of barriers (e.g., mats or blankets placed on the river or lake bottom), cutter-bar devices that mow the plants and the use of chemicals (e.g., herbicide). The underlying regulatory concern is that such practices will in some way harm fish habitat. Procedures are established based on the type of control process being used; i.e., chemical or physical/mechanical. The approach taken will dictate which ministry is most directly involved in the approval process.

Acid Rain/Lake Acidity — FOCUS

Acid rain refers to the influx of airborne acids entering bodies of water through precipitation and ground water runoff. Such acids can directly impact vegetation, fish and the entire ecosystem. Acid sensitivity refers to the ability of any lake to overcome acidic deposits that occur as a result of acid rain.

Acidity in lakes is measured using a pH scale that ranges from 0 to 14; the lower the pH, the greater the acidity. In Ontario, the Ministry of the Environment categorizes the lake's ability to neutralize a certain amount of acid based on the following rating system:

Level 1	Lakes have zero or negative alkalinity and have already become acidic.
Level 2	Lakes have very low alkalinity and are sensitive to heavy acid loadings by way of precipitation (or such things as spring run off).
Level 3	Lakes are moderately sensitive to heavy acid loadings.
Level 4	Lakes are of low sensitivity, but have experienced some damage due to acid rain.
Level 5	Lakes are not sensitive to acid loadings.

Reference   Contact the offices of Environment Canada and the Ministry of the Environment for more details about your market area and current initiatives, measurements guidelines and regulations concerning acid rain.

CHEMICALS (HERBICIDES)

The Ministry of the Environment oversees the control of underwater plant growth through the use of chemicals (e.g., herbicides) pursuant to the *Pesticides Act* and a permit (Permit to Purchase and/or Perform a Water Extermination) must be obtained from the Ministry. Properties fronting on the Rideau Canal or Trent-Severn Waterway fall under federal jurisdiction and Parks Canada (Department of Canadian Heritage) should also be contacted. Removal of aquatic plants is seasonally restricted owing to fish spawning periods and exact time frames will be set out in the permit.

Approvals do not in any way relieve the responsibility of the person using such chemicals from recourse by others (e.g., neighbours) for undesirable effects. Clearly, expert advice is required when considering the use of chemicals.

PHYSICAL/MECHANICAL

The requirement for a work permit from the Ministry of Natural Resources and Forestry involving physical or mechanical means will depend on the location of the property and size of the project. A permit is not required for removal of up to 100 square metres of aquatic vegetation annually from any lake or stream south of the line formed by Highway 7 from Lake Huron (Sarnia) to Sharbot Lake at Highway 38 and the area south of Highway 401 from Kingston to the Quebec border.

A work permit is required if any amount of aquatic plant removal is planned in the area north of Highway 7 from Lake Huron (Sarnia) to Sharbot Lake at Highway 38 and the area north of Highway 401 from Kingston to the Quebec border. A permit is required for work involving more than 100 square metres of aquatic vegetation annually from any lake or stream south of the line formed by Highway 7 from Lake Huron (Sarnia) to Sharbot Lake at Highway 38 and the area south of Highway 401 from Kingston to the Quebec border. This general discussion is for education purposes only. Contact the Ministry of Natural Resources and Forestry for current requirements and guidance.

Access and Road Allowances

Access is a key issue when a potential buyer is considering the purchase of a cottage. He or she should determine:

- That the property can be accessed by a public road or a private road.
- If the road is private, who owns the road, what costs are involved (e.g., access and/or maintenance fees) and is there is a registered and permanent right to access the property using that road?
- If the road is public, is it open year round and what services/maintenance are provided? Contact the municipality regarding this matter, particularly when the area is zoned as seasonal residential (or similar wording), as restricted maintenance (i.e., maintenance in non-winter months only) may apply in some jurisdictions. Further, what services does the municipality provide to rectify various road-related problems: e.g., washouts, fallen trees, poor drainage, loss of gravel topping and so forth.

If the cottage is on an island, the potential buyer should determine where a car can be parked and a boat docked.

ROAD ALLOWANCES (OPEN AND UNOPENED)

Certain basic facts about legal access by public road should be outlined. (Note: Additional information regarding roads including private access is provided under title-related issues in a subsequent chapter.)

Unless a public road allowance set down originally by Crown surveyors has been closed by municipal decree, it remains open (despite the fact that it has never been used). Interestingly, this rule also applies to roads that are dedicated and accepted within a plan of subdivision. As a point of clarification, subdivision developers will dedicate certain parts of a draft plan of subdivision as *public roads*. However, these do not technically become *public* until the time that the municipality accepts such dedications in accordance with provisions set out in the *Planning Act* and agrees to maintain these roads.

As a further point of interest, a road may become part of the municipal road system if municipal money is regularly spent on that road for its repair and maintenance. Also, a property owner may wish to open an unopened road allowance at private expense. Municipal approval is required and the owner must bring the road up to acceptable standards or provide financial assurances that such costs will be paid should the municipality do the work.

SHORE ROAD ALLOWANCE

The initial laying out of road allowances in Ontario includes the establishment of shore road allowances, which were 66' in width from the high water mark of navigable rivers and shores of lakes. Such roads were rarely opened, but intended for commercial pursuits and public passage. The fact that these have never been opened does not affect their legal status or the right of the public to use them.

Townships surveyed prior to 1850 (primarily eastern and southwestern Ontario) do not contain these road allowances. The existence of a road allowance will normally appear in the deed to the property. Shore road allowances are discussed in more detail under title-related issues in a subsequent chapter.

Buyers should be aware that structures on many waterfront lots (e.g., boathouses and docks) are built on road allowances. In fact, the actual cottage may encroach on part of the shore road allowance. Clearly, the only way to accurately determine such matters is to obtain legal expertise and ensure that a survey is prepared by an Ontario Land Surveyor setting out the location of all structures on the lot.

PRIVATE ROADS/RIGHTS-OF-WAY

Registrants should proceed with caution regarding any property that is accessed by a private road or right-of-way. Such rights-of-way may be deeded or undeeded. Even in the case of deeded right-of-way, the registered description may be vague or the paper trail from one owner to another may not have been completed properly and the legal status of that right-of-way could be called into question.

If the cottage is accessible only by crossing Crown land, the prospective buyer should contact the Ministry of Natural Resources and Forestry directly to ensure that such access can be continued and obtain appropriate written confirmation.

Over many years (dating from the 1930s), various owners on a northern lake had accessed their property using a road crossing the property of the defendants. On June 6 and 7, 2001, the defendants locked a gate and erected a chain effectively closing off both east and west access points. The other owners commenced an action, seeking a declaration that they were entitled to an easement to access their properties. As background, the defendants, approximately one month earlier, sent letters to the various owners. Their concerns centred on high vehicular speeds and traffic volume. Following the letter, speed warning signs were posted, as well as speed bumps. While some improvement occurred relating to speed, the defendants wanted to impose a speed limit of 5 km/hr (3 mph).

The defendant's lawyer pointed out by letter that (a) the defendants had every right to stop access as the property is in land titles and no rights would accrue by usage, (b) the *Road Access Act* does not apply, as it relates to blocking all access. (Note: The various owners had a deeded right-of-way adjacent to the defendants' property that, while not easy to use, was nevertheless available to them). Given the circumstances, the owners engaged a building contractor who provided an affidavit that this unopened road allowance was not a viable alternative.

The Judge, in arriving at a decision, focused on two key arguments advanced by counsel. First, the exceptions do apply to land titles on the issue of easements and rights-of-way that are not registered on title; i.e., an easement arising by implication that is necessary for the reasonable enjoyment of the property. Second, the lawyer for the owners emphasized that these owners would suffer irreparable harm. In particular, they pointed out the current lack of an access route for emergencies or service vehicles (e.g., septic tank truck.).

The Judge granted an Interim Order that the defendants remove all fences and barricades on the land in question, along with an Interim Injunction prohibiting the defendants from impeding or obstructing the owners access to and from their respective properties, pending any subsequent trial of that action.

Reference   Harry Peters et al. v. Edward and Deanna Morrison, Ontario Superior Court of Justice, Released November 20, 2001.
Digested from full text judgment.

COMMENTARY

Issues concerning private roads and accessibility to property can result in serious disputes and litigation.

Fully investigate and disclose matters concerning easements and rights-of-way. In many instances, accesses in rural areas are poorly described or have never been formally documented. Further, arrangements concerning repairs and associated costs are often either poorly documented or involve a verbal understanding only.

Never allow uncertainty or confusion to creep into negotiations, as the result can prove costly, time-consuming and worse. Seek expert advice on all such matters.

QUESTIONS TO PONDER
- Assume that one of the cottages described above has just been listed for sale. How would you handle this situation with a prospective client who is interested in buying?

- What information should be obtained when a listing salesperson discovers that the property to be listed has a right-of-way or easement?

 # ZONING REQUIREMENTS

Zoning by-laws are intended to implement overall policies as set down in the official plan. Common provisions applying to all properties have been detailed (along with overall planning concepts) in *Land, Structures and Real Estate Trading*. However, some provisions understandably vary based on specific uses.

Cottages and, more specifically, waterfront homes and cottages, come under closer scrutiny as they are situated on lands in the close vicinity of natural features and environmentally-sensitive areas that the municipality wants to protect. Therefore, added restrictions are often imposed on cottages regarding land use, the erection/location of buildings/ structures, required frontages and depths, setbacks, lot coverage and type of construction.

The *Planning Act* provides clear direction to municipalities concerning protection of environmentally sensitive areas:

A municipality can create zoning provisions relating to:

MARSHY LANDS, ETC.

3.   For prohibiting the erection of any class or classes of buildings or structures on land that is subject to flooding or on land with steep slopes, or that is rocky, low-lying, marshy, unstable, hazardous, subject to erosion or to natural or artificial perils.

CONTAMINATED LANDS; SENSITIVE OR VULNERABLE AREAS

3.1   For prohibiting any use of land and the erecting, locating or using of any class or classes of buildings or structures on land,

   i.   that is contaminated,

   ii.   that contains a sensitive groundwater feature or a sensitive surface water feature, or

   iii.   that is within an area identified as a vulnerable area in a drinking water source protection plan that has taken effect under the Clean Water Act, 2006.

NATURAL FEATURES AND AREAS

3.2   For prohibiting any use of land and the erecting, locating or using of any class or classes of buildings or structures within any defined area or areas,

   i.   that is a significant wildlife habitat, wetland, woodland, ravine, valley or area of natural and scientific interest,

   ii.   that is a significant corridor or shoreline of a lake, river or stream, or

   iii.   that is a significant natural corridor, feature or area.

Cottage Zoning: Examples

Zoning requirements and wordings vary by municipality. Selected examples are included to illustrate typical restrictions placed on waterfront cottages. Registrants should access local zoning provisions.

SETBACK—HIGH WATER MARK

Municipalities may use the high water mark to determine setbacks and other lot related rules, notwithstanding legal debates as to the establishment of a high water mark on an inland lake or river (particularly when water levels are controlled).

NOTE: Many municipalities now typically establish a specific benchmark for bodies of water within their jurisdiction and notify property owners accordingly.

Example Wording

No building or structure shall be located within the minimum required setback of 20 metres from the high water mark of any waterbody or watercourse or within 30 metres of any environmental protection zone (flood plain).

BOATHOUSES, BOAT PORTS AND DOCKS

Various requirements are established regarding how far such structures can extend into a navigable waterway. Once again, the high water mark is the defining benchmark.

NOTE: A boat port is best described as a temporary boat storage facility open on at least two sides that is typically supported by posts.

Example Wording

Boathouses, boat ports and docks must;

- *Be located no closer than 5 metres to a side lot line;*
- *Project into the water no more than 15 meters from the high water mark;*
- *Be used for boat storage only and not for human habitation; and*
- *Must not exceed 4.5 metres in height, nor 6.7 metres from the high water mark to the main roof peak.*

WATERFRONT DECKS (CONNECTED TO THE BOATHOUSE, BOAT PORT OR DOCK)

The municipality typically controls the extent of improvements at the waterfront, including structures. In this example, the wording specifically relates to sundecks.

Example Wording

A sundeck on the land extending from the boathouse, boat port or dock must:

- *Be located no closer than 5 metres from any side lot line;*
- *Not extend further inland that 5 meters from the high water mark; and*
- *Not exceed 25% of the lot frontage.*

TOTAL COVERAGE

The municipality would also set total coverage limits on both structures referred to above.

Example Wording

The total portion of a shoreline occupied by boathouses, boat ports, sundecks and docks, on or connected to a lot, shall not exceed the lesser of 25% of the lot frontage or 22 metres.

Non-Conforming Uses

Municipalities are introducing more restrictive zoning provisions in the interest of improved environmental protection and proper planning. However, most Southern Ontario lakefront developments were established many decades ago. Consequently, recreational zoning by-laws typically contain lists of non-conforming lots, given that they existed prior to the effective date of the present by-laws. Such lots may be used and buildings erected, enlarged, modified or repaired provided that they comply with all other provisions of the zoning by-law (save and except for the special provisions cited).

Environmental Zones/Flood Plains

Cottage owners, as with all owners, should fully investigate what provisions apply to their particular lots and should not operate on the assumption that buildings can be erected or existing structures modified in line with typical requirements. If some portion of the land in question falls within an environmental zone, additional restrictions can apply as to the building setbacks, total building coverage and location of a building on that land. Check with the local municipality for current requirements.

SERVICES

Cottage owners face other challenges given that their properties are sometimes in distant locations in recreational areas. The following information is provided to assist registrants in understanding limitations on services availability.

Hydro One and Telephone Services

As a general guideline, Hydro One Networks Inc. will provide 30 metres of free wire (secondary line) from the last pole location (primary line) on a dedicated, accepted road allowance. The company should be contacted directly involving situations where the primary line is at a distance and must be brought some distance to the owner's property. For example, a group of currently unserviced cottages may be located on a private access road that is 500 metres from the dedicated road allowance where the primary line is located. Cottagers should also be aware that services may not be available given that the installation of primary and secondary lines are not economically feasible.

In the case of telephone service, Bell Canada will extend an existing service to a new customer, but (as with Hydro One) provision of services that exceed a specified distance must be borne by that customer. Interestingly, the fact that hydro has already provided services to a cottage or cottages does not automatically assure the provision of telephone services. The telephone company will undertake an independent analysis of demand and the economic viability of installing telephone facilities in a certain area. Bell Canada normally utilizes Hydro One poles to string telephone lines.

The prospective buyer of a cottage should contact Hydro One and Bell Canada directly. It should also be noted that independent telephone companies operate within certain jurisdictions in the province. Rules and procedures may vary.

Municipal Services

Garbage Collection   Buyers should ascertain from the municipality whether or not garbage services are provided. Typically, the municipality provides such service on dedicated roads, but either limits or offers no service in the case of more distant recreational areas. In such instances, the property owner may have to take garbage to a landfill site or to bins provided by the municipality at certain points within its geographic boundaries. Cottagers on private access roads typically must pay for a private service or deliver their garbage to a landfill site. Delivery to landfill sites now commonly involve tipping fees (which commonly apply only beyond a certain basic weight limit per visit).

Fire Protection   Cottages within a reasonable distance of larger communities are normally serviced by a staffed fire department. However, small rural communities and surrounding areas may rely on volunteers. Even more remote areas will have no service. Registrants are reminded that proximity to a fire hall can impact the rate charged for fire insurance. Typically, insurance companies focus on whether the structure is within five miles of a responding fire hall. In certain locales, insurers may not provide coverage given lack of adequate fire protection.

School Buses   Typically, school bus routes are restricted to main public roads. The buyer should contact the applicable Board of Education directly to determine availability. When contacting the Board, be prepared to provide the legal description, municipal address (if available) and the current owner's name. Potential buyers should also be aware that areas consisting of primarily seasonal users may not be serviced by school buses. Policies on this matter vary in recreational areas across the province.

An OREA article (EDGE, July/August, 2007) is reprinted, as it addresses confusion that can arise regarding ownership of hydro poles.

When your clients buy a rural property do you think they know they might be buying hydro poles, too? A recent court case highlights the importance of uncovering all the facts in a real estate transaction—especially when dealing with rural property. The case involved a buyer who purchased a home on four acres in Pembroke and discovered, after the fact, that he owned and was responsible for replacing two decaying hydro poles on the property. Neither the real estate lawyer nor the REALTOR® involved in the case had ever heard of hydro pole ownership prior to this case. According to Hydro One, their policy regarding ownership of the hydro poles is standard procedure.

Hydro One's customer communication department confirmed that it is policy that, if the property is more than 30 metres from the main line, the homeowner is financially responsible for the transmission wire and poles to carry the power over any additional distance. They were unable, however, to provide any written policy regarding how they determine ownership of the equipment.

A section on Hydro One's web site **http://www.hydroonenetworks.com** refers to the company's *Conditions of Service*. It states:

Your Electrical Equipment   Customers may own the power lines supplying their premises. In this situation, you're responsible for the installation and maintenance of those power lines. You must comply with all applicable laws, including (but not limited to) the Ontario Electrical Safety Code and ensure that your equipment is properly identified and connected for metering and operation purposes. You must take all necessary steps to correct any deficiencies in a timely fashion. If you don't complete the work in a timely manner, we have the right to disconnect your electrical service.

Our Electrical Equipment   We will repair or replace, at our expense, any of our equipment on your property that fails due to ordinary wear and tear. For any other damage, you are responsible for paying us the value of our equipment or the cost to repair or replace the equipment.

CASE BY CASE

In response to an e-mail inquiry for more precision regarding the policy, a representative from Hydro One's customer communication department replied: *"Please be advised that the main lines and poles (typically along the roadside) are owned and maintained by Hydro One Networks. Secondary lines and poles (from the roadside to the building/home) are the responsibility of the property owner. It is important to note that for tree trimming on secondary lines, Hydro One offers to provide a temporary disconnect/reconnect, once per year, free of charge for this type of maintenance. Additionally, Hydro One Networks will always respond to an emergency situation, even where the secondary lines are involved. Our crew will make it a safe situation (disconnect the lines where necessary) in order to allow the customer the opportunity to make arrangements for the necessary repairs."*

But, a clerk in Hydro One's real estate department confirmed that the policy regarding poles is not cut and dry and that they deal with each case individually. *"If the pole is feeding only one property, it's usually customer owned,"* said real estate clerk, Diane Gauvreau. *"But if it crosses someone else's property or serves more than one property, Hydro One has to take an easement in order to access the line and takes ownership of the pole(s)."* Gauvreau added that since April 1999, all easements are registered so it's only the unregistered easements prior to that date where ownership of the poles and/or lines could be unclear.

The best advice for REALTORS® when dealing with rural real estate transactions is to always request an unregistered easement search. When conducting a search, Hydro One suggests that whenever possible, enter the former municipality name as it will yield more accurate results. Since there is a history of municipalities across the province amalgamating or changing names, prior or original names are important. For example: A search for unregistered easements in the current Town of Clarington might have to be conducted under any or all of; Town of Newcastle, Town of Bowmanville, Township of Darlington, etc. Hydro One offers a self-serve online unregistered easement search for $28.25 per search at **http://www.services.hydroone.com/lvr/welcome.html** or call their real estate department at 1-800-387-1946.

CHECKLIST

A cottage and recreational property checklist is included for further reference. Registrants may find it helpful when posing questions to sellers when listing cottage and recreational property.

COTTAGE AND RECREATIONAL CHECKLIST

1. ACCESS TO PROPERTY

a. Name of Nearest Highway:

b. Name of Nearest County Road:

c. Name of Nearest Municipal Road:

d. Is this property serviced by a private road?

   If so, is access seasonal? Year round?

   What are the maintenance requirements related to private road?

   Is the driveway private? Mutual?

   Do you cross private property to access your driveway? If so, is the right of way deeded?

Water Access

Is your property water access only?

   If so, where is parking available?

   Where are launching facilities?

   Name of Lake or Waterway:

   Is this water navigable?

   Name the Connecting Waterways:

2. TITLE AND LEGAL MATTERS

Name of Owner(s):

Full Legal Description:

a. Do you have a survey?

   Date:

   Is it a building location?

   If not, are you willing to provide one?

b. Is there a survey of road easements/rights of way?

c. Is there a survey indicating ownership under water?

d. Do any other persons have beneficial interest in this property?

e. Are there easements or encroachments on this property?

2. TITLE AND LEGAL MATTERS (continued)

f. Are there any legal restrictions or rights (recorded on title or otherwise within the knowledge of the seller)?

g. Are there any agreements concerning road easements, rights of way?

h. Are there any disputes concerning the property boundaries?

i. Is a copy of the deed available?

j. Is there any ownership of fences?

k. Are there any restrictions associated with crown patent?

l. Are any improvements on the property encroaching over or on the property line?

Lot Size

   Frontage:

   Depth:

   Acreage:

3. SHORELINE

a. Is the shoreline owned privately? By the Crown?

b. Are there any current negotiations to close the shoreline road allowance?

c. Have there been any improvements to the natural shoreline? If so, describe.

d. Are there any pending applications for shoreline improvement?

e. Are there any disputes concerning the shoreline?

f. Are any structures or docks on the shoreline allowance?

g. Is the shoreline measurement included in the lot size?

h. Are there any problems with ice packs? Wave action? Boat traffic?

continued

COTTAGE AND RECREATIONAL CHECKLIST (continued)

4. ZONING/PLANNING

a. Current Zoning of Property:

b. Does the zoning conform with local zoning by-laws? If not, explain.

c. Are there any building or zoning restrictions affecting the property?

d. Are all set backs in accordance with zoning?

e. Are there any room additions, structural modifications or other alterations?

f. Are there any applications for severance pending?

g. Are there any applications for minor variance pending?

h. Is this property subject to a site plan agreement?

5. WASTE DISPOSAL

a. Is this property serviced by sewers?

b. Is this property serviced by a septic system?

   If so, what size?

   Type:

   Age:

   When was it last pumped?

   Is there a copy of the septic location permit?

c. Are there any holding tanks?

   Privy(s)?

   Cesspools?

   Pits?

d. Are there any negotiations with the Ministry of Environment concerning the waste disposal system?

e. Is the system, including the bed, entirely on the property?

   With proper clearances?

f. Does the Seller grant permission to the Salesperson to obtain information from the Ministry of Environment?

6. WATER SUPPLY

What type of water system supplies this property?

a. Drilled well?

   Depth:

   Water Flow:

   Copy of well certificate available?

6. WATER SUPPLY (continued)

b. Dug well?

   Depth:

c. Water Line?

   Buried?

   Depth:

   Above ground?

   Pyrotenex?

   How far into lake?

d. Date of Most Recent Water Sample:

e. Existence of any water treatment devices?

f. Are any water lines shared with adjoining properties?

   If so, is the agreement in writing?

   Is it registered on title?

g. Type of Pumping System:

   Age:

   Location:

7. ENVIRONMENTAL

a. What is the acid sensitivity of lake?

b. If your property is located on the Great Lakes or canal system, are any additional approvals needed?

c. Are there chemicals used in the beach area, and do you have appropriate permits?

d. Are there any pending applications concerning the use of chemicals by neighbours?

e. Is this property located within conservation authority jurisdiction?

f. Is this property near a designated flood plain?

   Is this property subject to flooding?

g. Has there been any landfill activity undertaken on the property?

   Is there any pending?

   Location:

   Appropriate Approvals:

h. Are there any pending notices, disputes, claims or other negotiations to be carried out with Ministries, Municipalities or other authorities concerning environmental or related issues?

continued

COTTAGE AND RECREATIONAL CHECKLIST (continued)

8. STRUCTURE/IMPROVEMENTS

a. Are there any foundation related problems that you are aware of?

b. Do you consider the foundation seasonal? Winterized? Partially winterized? Able to be winterized?

c. *Siding*

Type:

Facia and Soffit:

Roof, Type:

Age:

d. *Windows*

Thermal *(# and Location)*

Double Glaze *(# and Location)*

Single Glaze *(# and Location)*

Further Comments on Windows:

e. *Doors*

Thermal *(# and Location)*

Wood *(# and Location)*

Metal *(# and Location)*

Sliding *(# and Location)*

Winterized *(# and Location)*

Further Comments on Doors:

f. *Decks*

Size:

Type:

Stained:

9. FUSES/CIRCUIT BREAKERS

a. *Electricity*

Amps:

Access Into Property:

Approximate Cost:

b. *Heating*

Type:

Approximate Cost:

c. Central Vac?

d. Laundry?

e. Appliances Included?

f. Fireplace?

g. Telephone?

10. STRUCTURAL MEASUREMENTS

a. *Main Building*

Type:

Age:

Winterized:

Partially Winterized:

Seasonal:

Size of Building:

Living Room:

Dining Room:

Family Room:

Kitchen: Size:

Finish:

Style of Cupboards:

Appliances Included:

Porch:

Deck:

Den:

Laundry:

Bedrooms:

Bathrooms *(Include Type)*:

Extras:

b. Garage:

c. Boathouses:

Age:

Conforming:

d. Docks, Number:

Docks, Type:

Docks, Conforming:

continued

COTTAGE AND RECREATIONAL CHECKLIST (continued)

11. OTHER

a. *Type of Building Foundation*

Full Basement:

Block:

Poured Concrete:

   Height:

   Depth Below Ground:

Perimeter Wall:

Crawl Space:

Poured Concrete Floor:

   Piers:

   Type:

   Depth Into Ground:

b. Name of contractors that built or supplied maintenance on any of the land and buildings.

12. TAXES/MUNICIPAL SERVICES/UTILITIES

a. Current Taxes on Property:

b. Assessment & Year:

c. Provision for Garbage Collection:

d. Location of Nearest Dump and Hours of Operation:

e. Provision of School Bus Service:

f. *Provision of Snowplowing*

   Municipal:

   Private (Name and Cost):

g. Extension of Fire Protection:

h. Existence of Submarine Cables:

13. MORTGAGES

a. Copy of Current Mortgage:

b. Details of Mortgage:

c. Any Special Prepayment Arrangements or Provisions:

d. Amount Outstanding and Verification:

e. Availability of Seller Take Back:

14. PERSONAL PROPERTY/FIXTURES

Please provide a detailed list of the following

   Personal Property Included

   Personal Property Excluded

   Fixtures Included

   Fixtures Not Included

   Negotiable Items

15. AMENITIES OF YOUR LAKE

a. Are there any Marinas?

b. Are there any stores?

c. Is there a cottager's association?

   If so, what does it cost to belong?

   Who is the contact person?

16. ADDITIONAL INFORMATION

Please provide any other information that you feel would be useful.

KNOWLEDGE INTEGRATION

Notables

- Cottages are broadly grouped into seasonal or year round use.

- Cottages must meet requirements of the Ontario Building Code, but many older structures may suffer from various defects, problems and deficiencies.

- Structural movement is a key consideration, as many cottages have been built on perimeter walls or piers that may not meet current standards.

- No clear definition of winterization exists. Buyers must be careful to fully understand the extent of winterization and associated challenges in correcting potential problems.

- An appropriate conditional clause should be inserted in the agreement of purchase and sale to permit the buyer adequate time to have the property professionally inspected.

- Water quality and quantity are primary considerations for cottage buyers. Draft an appropriate condition that addresses both the mechanical system and the ability to have a bacteriological analysis.

- A raised absorption bed may be required given terrain and/or soil conditions.

- As with water wells, an appropriate condition should be included relating to the sewage system including a seller's warranty regarding its good working order.

- The requirement for a boathouse or dock permit will depend on circumstances surrounding the scope of the project.

- A potential cottage buyer should firmly establish what access is provided to the cottage.

- Be particularly cautious with undeeded rights-of-way, while also noting that deeded rights-of-way are not without problems.

- Waterfront cottages come under tighter scrutiny concerning zoning provisions given their proximity to environmentally sensitive areas.

- Cottage buyers should be aware that additional costs may be incurred to obtain hydro and telephone services.

Web Links

Web links are included for general interest regarding selected chapter topics.

WETT	Go to the Wood Energy Technology Transfer Inc. (WETT Inc.) site for additional information (*www.wettinc.ca*).
Water Quality/ Well Records	Go to the Ministry of the Environment site (*www.ene.gov.on.ca*) for additional information about drinking water systems and water quality.
Ministry of Natural Resources and Forestry	Go to the Ministry of Natural Resources and Forestry website (*www.mnr.gov.on.ca*) for detailed information regarding the administration of public lands and requirements specifically focused on cottages.

Strategic Thinking For Your Career

Questions are included to assist in developing your new career. No answers are provided.

1. What brochures should I collect from the municipality and government agencies for current information on topics covered in this chapter?

2. If I plan to focus on cottage property, what specific zoning provisions apply to seasonal and year-round cottages and, more particularly, waterfront cottages.

3. What services are provided in cottage areas within my local marketplace?

4. What items can I add to the checklist provided in this chapter to address unique local circumstances?

Chapter Mini-Review

Solutions are located in the Appendix.

1. A low pitch on a cottage roof can pose problems during thawing periods following winter months.

    ◯ True   ◯ False

2. Cottage owners, when winterizing existing cottages, must follow mandatory procedures set by the municipality regarding amount of insulation.

    ◯ True   ◯ False

3. A buyer wishing to have a prospective cottage inspected must use the services of a home inspector.

    ◯ True   ◯ False

4. Chlorine disinfecting is used following construction of a new well to remove bacteria that may reside in the water and well equipment during the installation process.

    ◯ True   ◯ False

5. Cottage owners must use a raised absorption bed according to requirements set out in the Ontario Building Code.

    ◯ True   ◯ False

6. The *Public Lands Act* is administered by the Ministry of the Environment.

    ◯ True   ◯ False

7. The Ministry responsible for aquatic plant control varies based on whether the cottage owner is using chemicals or mechanical means.

    ◯ True   ◯ False

8. Shore road allowances are found on inland lakes throughout Ontario.

    ◯ True   ◯ False

9. A public road allowance set out by the original Crown surveyors remains open, unless it has not been used for the last 50 years.

    ◯ True   ◯ False

10. A cottage building lot that falls within an environmentally-sensitive area may be subject to more stringent zoning requirements than other properties within that particular municipality.

⭕ True   ⭕ False

11. The cost of obtaining hydro service in a recreational area is in part dependent on the cottage's distance from an existing primary line.

⭕ True   ⭕ False

Active Learning Exercises

Solutions are located in the Appendix.

▣ Exercise 1   Multiple Choice

1.1   The Ontario Building Code:

    a.   Applies to new year-round cottages, but not new seasonal cottages.

    b.   Sets out requirements regarding aquatic plant control.

    c.   Regulates the installation of septic tanks.

    d.   Regulates requirements regarding hydro and telephone services provided in recreational areas.

1.2   A raised absorption bed:

    a.   Can only be used in new cottage installations and not with older cottages.

    b.   Must be used in all new cottage installations.

    c.   Uses imported soil and approved filter sand.

    d.   Cannot be used in rocky areas.

1.3   The construction of a boathouse on an Ontario inland lake:

    a.   Is prohibited as it could affect fish habitat.

    b.   Is not subject to local zoning provisions.

    c.   Cannot be built on lands falling under the *Public Lands Act*.

    d.   Can be subject to obtaining a work permit from the Ministry of Natural Resources and Forestry.

1.4   Which of the following is correct?

    a.   A two-storey boathouse is prohibited on Ontario inland lakes.

    b.   Cottage buyers should enquire about the access road to the prospective cottage to ensure that it aligns with their expectations.

    c.   Inadequate footings are rarely the cause of structural movement in older cottages.

    d.   Acid rain has not been a problem in Ontario's cottage areas.

1.5 A zoning provision relating to a boat dock may:

    a. Detail location of the dock in relation to the side lot line.

    b. Limit the distance that the dock projects into the waterway.

    c. Restrict the size of a land-based sundeck or other structure joined to the dock.

    d. All of the above.

1.6 Which of the following is a correct statement?

    a. A vaulted ceiling in an older cottage may prove difficult to properly insulate.

    b. One bacteriological test every three or four years is sufficient for cottage wells.

    c. If hydro service is provided to a seasonal cottage, then telephone service is assured.

    d. Seasonal cottage owners do not receive municipal garbage pickup and must deliver garbage to a central landfill.

■ Exercise 2   Mini-Scenarios

2.1 The prospective buyer notices a crack in the cottage's perimeter concrete block wall that extends from the top block to the ground level. What could be the problem?

2.2 A buyer, upon closing the sale of a seasonal cottage built on a perimeter wall, discovers that the main level floor areas seem cold despite having the furnace working. He purchased the cottage with the understanding that it was winterized. What could be the problem?

2.3 A buyer is seriously considering a cottage on a private access road. He intends on using the property year round. What relevant questions should he ask about this access?

2.4   An owner wants to open part of an unopened road allowance to access a cottage. What should he do?

2.5   A prospective buyer is considering a distant, seasonal cottage and wants to know about obtaining fire insurance. How would you respond to this inquiry?

CHAPTER 5

Vacant Land

Introduction

This chapter highlights important considerations when acquiring vacant land, along with a limited analysis of agricultural land/farm property. The farm property discussion is an overview only, without reference to operational and financial dimensions of farming operations and related agri-businesses. Such topics are best left for advanced courses and individuals specializing in large farm sales.

Registrants marketing vacant land work with many buyers including those wishing to build a home, those starting a hobby farm and others seeking additional acreage to add to an existing land base. Course materials introduce key considerations when purchasing vacant land with an emphasis on smaller acreages and rural lots. Guidelines are provided when drafting offers and addressing such matters as lot dimensions, calculation of purchase price (e.g., price per acre) and include appropriate wordings when dealing with

severances, provision of services and building permits. Cautions regarding building location on the site are also addressed. The discussion also extends into key considerations about forested land/bush lots and larger acreages.

The farm property overview emphasizes the changing farm scene, farm classifications, recent legislative initiatives regarding nutrient management and key issues to consider when drafting offers for properties that are near farming operations. The final topic has become a key issue for rural residential registrants given the continuing exodus of urban dwellers seeking rural locations in close proximity to existing farming operations.

Learning Outcomes

At the conclusion of this chapter, students will be able to:

- Outline selected factors to consider when acquiring vacant land.
- Identify and explain key elements to consider in the purchase of vacant land for building purposes including lot dimensions, purchase price calculation, severances, provision of service, obtaining a building permit and determining the building location.
- Outline typical clauses to be considered when drafting an offer involving vacant land for building purposes.
- Discuss the tax incentive program available to lower property taxes on forested land.
- Briefly describe key features and issues to consider in larger rural acreages.
- Discuss farm property with particular emphasis on the changing farm scene, farming classifications, and recent legislation affecting the listing and sale of farming operations.
- Explain the ramifications of normal farm practices protection on nearby properties, including an appropriate clause wording to be inserted in the agreement of purchase and sale.

VACANT LAND

Buyers acquire vacant land for many reasons. The prospective purchaser may intend on building a home, setting aside land for future plans, securing a rural hideaway or simply investing in hopes of selling as land prices increase. Regardless, certain key factors need to be considered when acquiring vacant land.

NOTE: Vacant land acquired for commercial and land development purposes is covered in *The Commercial Real Estate Transaction*.

Location

As with all real estate, make certain that the location meets personal or investment needs. If the purchase is for investment, carefully assess land potential for future development. Detailed research is necessary to discover the true opportunities and the variety of uses possible.

Physical Attributes

Parcel size and natural features such as hills, forests or streams are all factors in selecting the right property. Pay particular attention to aesthetics of the land, as these can play a key role in future value.

Boundaries/Survey

Insist on an up-to-date survey from the seller or, if unavailable, include an appropriate clause to require the seller to provide a new one.

Access/Easements/Restrictions

Important questions to consider: how is the property accessed, what utilities are available, are there any easements registered against the property that will affect future plans, do any regulatory agencies control how the land is used or whether a structure can be built (e.g., conservation authority) and what zoning restrictions will impact intended uses?

Initial/Ongoing Costs

Buyers may seek investment return by holding vacant land for future sale. Proper budgeting is essential. Vacant land purchases require all cash or some form of financing (typically a seller take back). Ongoing expenses for this financing, along with taxes, any maintenance (e.g., fence repairs) and liability insurance, must be taken into consideration. Vacant land can involve a long holding period to realize a return and cash flow is a key consideration.

Revenue

When acquiring property for long term investment, carefully consider uses that may generate some income to offset expenses. Check zoning for permitted uses. Revenue might be realized by using the property as a car park, storage location for equipment or temporary rental for cash crops.

Market Trends/Activity

Buying vacant land for investment is all about timing. Carefully analyze market trends. Go beyond sales activities and look at underlying causes. Assess what social and economic pressures will affect land in specific locations. Watch where the public dollars are being spent. For example, many successful investors track long-term municipal planning including forecasted and budgeted funds for infrastructure (i.e., sewer, water and transportation services).

Vacant Land/Residential Building Lot

Smaller acreages and lots in rural areas are popular, as many buyers plan to build a residential home on a rural building lot that affords them more lot size, amenities such as a woods or stream, and increased privacy. Know the exact dimensions of the lot, how

the purchase price is determined, if the sale is subject to a severance, what services (e.g., hydro and telephone) are available to the lot, whether or not a building permit can be obtained and what limitations exist concerning the site location for the building.

LOT DIMENSIONS

Lot dimensions should be precise and an up-to-date survey is essential.

Frontage	That side of a lot that abuts a public street or highway.
Depth	Distance between front and rear lot lines.
Width	Distance between the side lines of a lot.
Shape	Determined by the frontage, depth and width.
Area	Size measured in square feet, square metres, hectares or acres. (Square feet/metres measurements are most commonly found with commercial properties.)
Irregular Shapes	Include all dimensions based on above terminology. Include survey to avoid any confusion.

The Building Lot | **RESIDENTIAL CASE LAW**

The buyers entered into an agreement to buy an irregularly-shaped lot. The agreement described the property, being purchased for $1,110,000, as having a frontage of AS PER SURVEY and approximately 1.5 acres in size. The offer of $1,110,000 was also conditional upon obtaining a building permit.

The seller did not furnish the survey that he agreed to provide within 72 hours. The buyers then had a survey completed and discovered, just a few days prior to the requisition date, that the property was only 1.15 acres. As a consequence, they would be unable to build a large home (16,000 square feet), due to lot coverage restrictions set out in local zoning and building by-laws.

Upon realizing that the property was significantly less than described, the buyers essentially took the position that the land was other than described and did nothing further, allowing both the requisition and closing dates to go by with no further action. The issue at trial involved the return of the deposit and the matter of whether or not the buyers could rescind the contract based on the incorrect lot size. Given evidence submitted, the Judge found that the smaller than promised lot size was a material and substantial fact. Accordingly, the Court declared that the agreement was void ab initio (Latin for *from the beginning*), and ordered that the deposit money (plus accumulated interest) be réleased to the buyers.

Reference   Olszewski v. Trapman, Manchella and Re/Max (2000) 35 RPR (3d) 316

COMMENTARY

Accuracy in describing lot size and dimensions is vital to any listing. However, debates can arise in real estate circles concerning the term *more or less,* as it relates to real estate transactions. In other words, is there any room for minor variation and when does a difference become significant? This case involved a significant difference between what was represented and what existed on the ground. In fact, the actual lot was 23.33% smaller than represented and the Judge deemed this to be a significant variation. As a point of interest, another case cited involved a lot that was 6.541% smaller than promised and was also judged to be substantial. While very minor variations might be legally tolerated, the issue becomes one of interpretation by the Courts. Prudent registrants should always strive for complete accuracy in all details concerning listed property and emphasize the need for an up-to-date survey.

PURCHASE PRICE (LOT PRICE VS. PER ACRE)

Smaller vacant land parcels are typically purchased on a *per lot* basis. However, larger acreages may be transacted using a *per acre* arrangement.

SCENARIO	CLAUSE
Clause Regarding Price	**DEV–6** **Price Based Upon Acreage**
A buyer is submitting an offer on rural vacant land based on the price per acre.	*The Seller acknowledges that the Buyer is acquiring the property for development, and the purchase price is calculated on the basis of _____ ($_____) per acre. In the event of a discrepancy in area, the purchase price will be adjusted accordingly at time of completion.*
	NOTE: Survey or other acceptable confirmation of exact acreage is required and an appropriate condition or similar wording is needed; e.g., seller to provide up-to-date survey.

SALE SUBJECT TO SEVERANCE

Land severance procedures were detailed in *Land, Structures and Real Estate Trading*. A seller may be offering vacant land for sale prior to final severance approval. In such instances, an appropriate condition should be included in the agreement of purchase and sale.

SCENARIO	CLAUSE
Condition Regarding Severance	**DEV–2** **Condition—Severance— Seller Undertakes Expense and Completion**
A buyer is submitting an offer on a vacant residential lot. As the lot is not yet severed, the buyer includes an appropriate condition making the offer conditional upon the seller completing the severance.	*This Offer is conditional upon the Buyer obtaining, at the Seller's expense, a consent to sever the property as follows: (provide description of proposed severance). Unless the Buyer gives notice in writing delivered to the Seller personally or in accordance with any other provisions for the delivery of notice in this Agreement of Purchase and Sale or any Schedule thereto not later than ____ p.m. on the _____ day of _____, 20 ____, that this condition is fulfilled, this Offer shall become null and void and the deposit shall be returned to the Buyer in full without deduction. The Seller agrees to sign any requisite documents required for the above condition and do all things reasonably necessary in support of the satisfaction of the condition.* *The Seller understands and acknowledges that the Seller shall be responsible for satisfying any conditions imposed for approval of the severance, and if such conditions give the Seller options in the manner of compliance, the Buyer shall determine which option will be selected. The Seller shall obtain a reference plan prepared by an Ontario Land Surveyor suitable for registration purposes in the Land Registry Office in which the said property is located.*
	NOTE: Additional wording may be inserted concerning the extension of the completion date if the severance is not completed, along with limiting cost relating to obtaining said severance. The buyer would also want to ensure that a building permit could be available for the severed lot.

PROVISION OF SERVICES

In some instances, the land being purchased may not fall within the Hydro One Networks Inc. guidelines; i.e., a specified number of metres of free wire (secondary line) from the last pole location (primary line) on a dedicated, accepted road allowance. Given this situation, the buyer may also incur costs regarding telephone installation.

SCENARIO	CLAUSE
Condition Regarding Costs A buyer is submitting an offer on a vacant residential lot. Given the lack of a primary line in close proximity to where the house will be built, the buyer includes an appropriate condition making the offer conditional upon the cost of hydro and telephone service.	**DEV–1** **Condition—Services—Hydro/Telephone** *This Offer is conditional upon the Buyer determining, at the Buyer's own expense, that the provision of service by hydro and telephone to the said property shall not exceed a cost of _____ ($_____). Unless the Buyer gives notice in writing delivered to the Seller personally or in accordance with any other provisions for the delivery of notice in this Agreement of Purchase and Sale or any Schedule thereto not later than ____ p.m. on the _____ day of _____, 20___, that this condition is fulfilled, this Offer shall become null and void and the deposit shall be returned to the Buyer in full without deduction. This condition is included for the benefit of the Buyer and may be waived at the Buyer's sole option by notice in writing to the Seller as aforesaid within the time period stated herein.*

OBTAINING A BUILDING PERMIT

Building permits were covered in *Land, Structures and Real Estate Trading*. A brief overview of the permit process is provided. Caution is advised as exact procedures will vary by municipality.

STEP 1	**Application** The application contains mandatory information as to the exact project (the who, what, where and how), along with a specified number of building plans, the survey and building permit fee.
STEP 2	**Review** The municipality will then review the permit application and associated documents from three perspectives: *Zoning* — Ensure conformance with applicable zoning by-laws. *Architectural/Structural* — Compliance with structural, fire and life safety requirements of the Ontario Building Code. *Mechanical* — Compliance with heating, ventilating and air conditioning (HVAC) and plumbing requirements of the Ontario Building Code.
STEP 3	**Receive Permit** If the review is successful, the application is approved giving the legal authority to start construction. *Note:* Any changes to the original design may require a subsequent review and approval.
STEP 4	**Inspection** Each major phase of construction must be inspected by the municipal building department. If the inspections are not requested as scheduled, completed work may have to be uncovered and remedied as determined by the inspector.

BUILDING LOCATION

The buyer must also take into consideration various zoning provisions, which can impact building location and size. Beyond normal zoning setbacks, special requirements may apply concerning environmentally-sensitive areas, buildings in close proximity to navigable waterways, setbacks to public highways and established building lines in built-up areas. Rural building location may also be affected by soil conditions, extent of rock outcroppings and minimum drainage clearances when installing a private sewage system.

The Building Location	RESIDENTIAL CASE LAW

The buyers wanted a lot with particular features and were shown several by the salesperson. The salesperson indicated that the structure could be built on a specific location on the lot to meet the buyers' requirements. The transaction proceeded in the usual manner with the buyers' lawyer searching title and closing the transaction. The lawyer did not meet with the clients and did not review their building plans.

The buyers later discovered that they could not build as planned and needed several municipal approvals for any construction. Further, the ultimate location for the structure was closer to the road and, as a result, the view was significantly different than originally anticipated. To compound matters, delays and additional construction costs were encountered.

The salesperson, the real estate brokerage, the lawyer and the law firm were found liable for damages. The salesperson was liable because he had held himself out to have special knowledge knowing that buyers would rely on his expertise and on his knowledge of local zoning by-laws. Accordingly, his advice concerning the location was negligent.

The lawyer was negligent for not pointing out to the client the zoning requirements for setback and other significant matters that would impact their plans. The process of checking zoning and other municipal requirements is a significant part of legal practice in rural areas. Further, explaining the legal significance of various documents relating to such matters is a prime function of lawyers.

Reference　Harela v. Powell 163 DLR (4th) 365

COMMENTARY

While this case involved a cottage lot, the same legal principles apply to other similar situations. Whatever personal experience and expertise is provided, the simple question is: *Did you lead the buyers to believe that they could do something that could not be done?* Often matters fall beyond the expertise of real estate professionals. Indeed, the RECO Code of Ethics requires that registrants refer consumers to others for expert advice when unable to provide services with reasonable knowledge and skill (*Code of Ethics, Sec. 8: Service From Others*). Keep in mind that any brokerage and its authorized representatives must exercise a degree of care and skill in representing the principal that would be expected from the average person in that occupation. By advancing additional skills and expertise, the registrant is raising the level of expectation and can be called to account for any problems that arise as a consequence of that heightened expectation.

Vacant Land/Waterfront

Registrants focusing on vacant land in recreational areas will encounter vacant land with frontage of rivers and lakes. Issues already addressed under *Vacant Land/Building Lot* apply, plus additional factors relating to waterfront. Topics concerning waterfront lots, improvements near the shoreline, shore road allowances and wells/private sewage systems were highlighted in *Chapter 4: Cottage Property*.

Forested Land/Bush Lot

Smaller forested properties are found in Southern Ontario, with large bush lots located in northern areas. In some instances, the smaller properties may be part of a farm, hobby farm, or merely an acreage set aside for tree farming of maple, oak, hemlock and birch, the production of firewood and the growing of Christmas trees. Still other forested areas are maintained and preserved by individuals for aesthetic reasons, including environmental considerations and wildlife protection.

MANAGED FOREST TAX INCENTIVE PROGRAM (MFTIP)

This tax incentive program provides for lower property taxes if owners agree to conserve woodlands that consist of not less than four hectares (approximately ten acres), excluding residences. As part of the application process, the owner must prepare a managed forest plan with a long term horizon (i.e., 20 years or more), along with a ten-year plan of activities and have it approved by a Managed Forest Plan Approver. The application deadline is June 30th for consideration relating to the subsequent taxation year.

Selling a Managed Forest Property

Registrants should be aware of various procedures set out under this program. When listing a managed forest property, confirm with the seller and with the Municipal Property Assessment Corporation (MPAC) that the property is assessed as a managed forest and not as a residential property. The Managed Forest Plan is the property of the landowner and properties that are sold are removed from the program by MPAC. Also, associations involved with this program will not provide copies of documents without the seller's permission.

The seller can assist by providing a copy of the Managed Forest Plan and his/her Notice of Property Assessment. The owner may also have a copy of the Ontario Managed Forest Tax Incentive Program (MFTIP) Guide or A Guide for Stewardship Planning for Natural Areas (or similar publications), provided by the Ministry of Natural Resources and Forestry (MNR). These guides set out exact procedures to be followed. Essentially, when the property is sold, the owner must complete the Landowner Report form and send a copy of the Report of Activities to the Ministry of Natural Resources and Forestry.

Buying a Managed Forest Property

When purchasing a managed forest property, the buyer should verify that the property is currently classified as a managed forest. The buyer should be informed that the property will automatically be removed from the managed forest tax class at point of sale, unless the buyer applies to the program. The buyer should also be advised that if he/she does not apply for the program, property taxes may increase as a result. An application must be received by the MNR within 90 days of the closing of the sale.

The buyer must also be aware that he/she is responsible for any taxes owing up to five years back if the property was classified as a managed forest, but is later found not to have been eligible for the applicable tax class. The agreement of purchase and sale should contain a clause, or other provision as the buyer's lawyer may require, protecting the buyer regarding any re-assessment because the property was ineligible under the program while under the seller's ownership.

Buyer Wishes to Continue Program

The buyer should obtain and carefully read a copy of the Ontario Managed Forest Tax Incentive Program (MFTIP) Guide for full program details. He/she should also review the previous owner's approved managed forest plan, with particular regard to planned management activities. The buyer should walk the forest to view and discuss the management of that forest (preferably with the previous owner), should consider whether the current plan's objectives and outlined activities are consistent with personal objectives and whether he/she is comfortable continuing to manage according to the plan. A new plan might be more appropriate based on the review of existing circumstances.

As previously mentioned, buyers wishing to continue in the program must make application within prescribed time limits (i.e., prior to 90 days after sale closing). Buyers wanting to keep the property in the MFTIP program should also:

- review the program guide;
- attempt to get a copy of the Managed Forest Plan from the seller;
- update the current plan or prepare a new one; and
- have the plan approved by a Managed Forest Plan Approver.

The above description is for general guidance and education purposes only, as procedures and requirements are subject to change.

WEB LINKS

Managed Forest Tax Incentive Program   For more information concerning this program, contact the Ministry of Natural Resources and Forestry (***www.mnr.gov.on.ca.***). For questions regarding how the MFTIP program impacts property assessment, contact the Municipal Property Assessment Corporation (***www.mpac.ca***).

Larger Acreages

Large acreages can attract buyers seeking add-ons to existing farming operations, hobby farmers, and those seeking a country retreat and/or secluded building site. Some include existing structures (typically older farm buildings). Most are a mixture of tillable, working acres for cash crops, as well as small bushlots and rolling grasslands. Agricultural portions may include either random tiling (selected wet areas) or systematic tiling every 40 to 60 feet.

As with other vacant land, the buyer should exercise caution to ensure that the property is accessible for a serviced road, conduct research into any lowlands, wetland areas or frontages on lakes, rivers and streams regarding how these lands are impacted by conservation and other authorities.

Sample Agreement

A fully completed agreement of purchase and sale for vacant land is provided on the following pages.

Executors of an estate sold a farm that purportedly contained 98 acres more or less. The farm, which had been in the family since 1950, originally consisted of a half of a concession lot (100 acres), less two 3/4 acre parcels that had been severed for family members. The 98-acre representation made by the executors was consistent with 1990 documents including a real estate valuation, notice of property assessment and a farm land class property tax application. These documents were submitted by the executors to the Court in the ensuing litigation.

The property was initially offered to prospective buyers by the 'yet-to-be' appointed executors, but offers received during that time period were rejected. The property was subsequently listed twice through a brokerage but no offers were received. After expiration of the listing, the ultimate buyer concluded an acceptable agreement. Some months after closing, the new owner retained the services of a surveyor while installing a new irrigation system. The property was found to contain only 85.77 acres. It should be noted that the new buyer introduced evidence in court that an application to sever, made by one of the family members in 1989, showed a total acreage of 85.77 acres.

Testimony presented in Court revealed that the buyer had purchased the property *as is* and that the sellers had clearly stated that no survey was available. If the buyer wanted a survey, it had to be completed at his expense. The buyer also walked the property and at no time suggested that the land was being purchased on a 'per acre' basis. Lastly, shortly before closing, the buyer gave a direction to his solicitor which essentially acknowledged that he was accepting title subject to:

> *such title deficiencies, encroachments, zoning infractions and other matters as would be revealed by an up-to-date survey of the property. I acknowledge that I elected not to obtain an up-to-date survey.*

The solicitor for the buyer also stated in the ensuing reporting letter that:

> *You also agreed to waive the requirement for any survey and to pay the vendor's legal costs.*

The Court dismissed the action finding that the buyer had received what he bargained for and the sellers' mis-representations were innocent and in full accordance with their knowledge and belief and not actionable.

Reference: John Beattie Farms Limited v. Stevenson; Superior Court of Justice; Docket #02–B4833–SR

COMMENTARY

While this case involved rural property, issues concerning lot dimensions can impact any transaction. Registrants should note key points surrounding this case.

Executors	• Made innocent representations based on documents that they believed were reliable.
	• Clearly indicated to the buyer that no survey was available and if one was needed it would be at the buyer's cost.
Agreement of Purchase and Sale	• Stated that the purchaser waives any survey requirements.
Buyer	• Bought the property as a whole and did not expressly state that it was being purchased on a per acre basis.
	• Failed to have a survey completed which would have revealed the discrepancy.
	• Provided a direction to close stating that no survey would be obtained.
Buyer's Solicitor	• Confirmed in the reporting letter that the buyer had waived any survey requirements.

Fully Completed Sample   Agreement of Purchase and Sale (for Vacant Land), Page 1 of 6

OREA Ontario Real Estate Association   **Agreement of Purchase and Sale**

Form 100
for use in the Province of Ontario

This Agreement of Purchase and Sale dated this ....**26th**.... day of ....**February**................ 20.**XX**....

BUYER, ...**Charles Edward Morgan**................, agrees to purchase from
(Full legal names of all Buyers)

SELLER, ...**Sylvia Ruth Davies and Wayne Scott Davies**................, the following
(Full legal names of all Sellers)

REAL PROPERTY:

Address ....**32A Cambridge Drive**........

fronting on the ....**North**........ side of ....**Cambridge Drive**........

in the ....**Town of Anytown, Regional Municipality of Anyregion**........

and having a frontage of ....**62.8 feet**........ more or less by a depth of ....**121.45 feet**........ more or less

and legally described as ....**Part of Lot 21, Plan 365, more particularly described as Part 2 on 52R-873**........

.... (the "property")
(Legal description of land including easements not described elsewhere)

PURCHASE PRICE: Dollars (CDN$) ....**$63,000.00**....

Sixty-Three Thousand-- Dollars

DEPOSIT: Buyer submits ....**Herewith**................
(Herewith/Upon Acceptance/as otherwise described in this Agreement)

Five Thousand-- Dollars (CDN$) ....**$5,000.00**....

by negotiable cheque payable to ....**ABC Realty Inc.**................ "Deposit Holder" to be held
in trust pending completion or other termination of this Agreement and to be credited toward the Purchase Price on completion. For the purposes of this
Agreement, "Upon Acceptance" shall mean that the Buyer is required to deliver the deposit to the Deposit Holder within 24 hours of the acceptance of
this Agreement. The parties to this Agreement hereby acknowledge that, unless otherwise provided for in this Agreement, the Deposit Holder shall place
the deposit in trust in the Deposit Holder's non-interest bearing Real Estate Trust Account and no interest shall be earned, received or paid on the deposit.

Buyer agrees to pay the balance as more particularly set out in Schedule A attached.

SCHEDULE(S) A........**attached hereto form(s) part of this Agreement.**

1. **IRREVOCABILITY:** This offer shall be irrevocable by ....**Buyer**................ until ....**8:00**.... ~~a.m.~~/p.m. on the ....**28th**....
    (Seller/Buyer)

    day of ....**February**................ 20 **XX**...., after which time, if not accepted, this offer shall be null and void and the deposit
    shall be returned to the Buyer in full without interest.

2. **COMPLETION DATE:** This Agreement shall be completed by no later than 6:00 p.m. on the ....**24th**.... day of ....**July**................

    20 **XX**.......... Upon completion, vacant possession of the property shall be given to the Buyer unless otherwise provided for in this Agreement.

INITIALS OF BUYER(S): (*CM*)   INITIALS OF SELLER(S): (*SD WD*)

SECTION I   A CLOSER LOOK AT TRADING DIFFERENT TYPES OF PROPERTIES

Fully Completed Sample   Agreement of Purchase and Sale (for Vacant Land), Page 2 of 6

3. **NOTICES:** The Seller hereby appoints the Listing Brokerage as agent for the Seller for the purpose of giving and receiving notices pursuant to this Agreement. Where a Brokerage (Buyer's Brokerage) has entered into a representation agreement with the Buyer, the Buyer hereby appoints the Buyer's Brokerage as agent for the purpose of giving and receiving notices pursuant to this Agreement. **Where a Brokerage represents both the Seller and the Buyer (multiple representation), the Brokerage shall not be appointed or authorized to be agent for either the Buyer or the Seller for the purpose of giving and receiving notices.** Any notice relating hereto or provided for herein shall be in writing. In addition to any provision contained herein and in any Schedule hereto, this offer, any counter-offer, notice of acceptance thereof or any notice to be given or received pursuant to this Agreement or any Schedule hereto (any of them, "Document") shall be deemed given and received when delivered personally or hand delivered to the Address for Service provided in the Acknowledgement below, or where a facsimile number or email address is provided herein, when transmitted electronically to that facsimile number or email address, respectively, in which case, the signature(s) of the party (parties) shall be deemed to be original.

FAX No.: .... 416-555-2121 ....
(For delivery of Documents to Seller)

FAX No.: .... 416-666-2121 ....
(For delivery of Documents to Buyer)

Email Address: .... admin@abcrealty.com ....
(For delivery of Documents to Seller)

Email Address: .... notices@xyzrealestate.com ....
(For delivery of Documents to Buyer)

4. **CHATTELS INCLUDED:** .... N/A ....

....

....

....

....

Unless otherwise stated in this Agreement or any Schedule hereto, Seller agrees to convey all fixtures and chattels included in the Purchase Price free from all liens, encumbrances or claims affecting the said fixtures and chattels.

5. **FIXTURES EXCLUDED:** .... N/A ....

....

....

....

....

6. **RENTAL ITEMS (Including Lease, Lease to Own):** The following equipment is rented and **not** included in the Purchase Price. The Buyer agrees to assume the rental contract(s), if assumable:

.... N/A ....

....

....

The Buyer agrees to co-operate and execute such documentation as may be required to facilitate such assumption.

7. **HST:** If the sale of the Property (Real Property as described above) is subject to Harmonized Sales Tax (HST), then such tax shall be

.... in addition to .... the Purchase Price. If the sale of the Property is not subject to HST, Seller agrees to certify on or before
(included in/in addition to)

closing, that the sale of the Property is not subject to HST. Any HST on chattels, if applicable, is not included in the Purchase Price.

INITIALS OF BUYER(S): (*CM*)   INITIALS OF SELLER(S): (*SD WD*)

Form 100   Revised 2015   **Page 2 of 6**

8. **TITLE SEARCH:** Buyer shall be allowed until 6:00 p.m. on the .....**24th**..... day of ....**June**...................................., 20.**XX**..., (Requisition Date) to examine the title to the Property at Buyer's own expense and until the earlier of: (i) thirty days from the later of the Requisition Date or the date on which the conditions in this Agreement are fulfilled or otherwise waived or; (ii) five days prior to completion, to satisfy Buyer that there are no outstanding

    work orders or deficiency notices affecting the Property, and that its present use (...............**residential vacant land**...............) may be lawfully continued and that the principal building may be insured against risk of fire. Seller hereby consents to the municipality or other governmental agencies releasing to Buyer details of all outstanding work orders and deficiency notices affecting the property, and Seller agrees to execute and deliver such further authorizations in this regard as Buyer may reasonably require.

9. **FUTURE USE:** Seller and Buyer agree that there is no representation or warranty of any kind that the future intended use of the property by Buyer is or will be lawful except as may be specifically provided for in this Agreement.

10. **TITLE:** Provided that the title to the property is good and free from all registered restrictions, charges, liens, and encumbrances except as otherwise specifically provided in this Agreement and save and except for (a) any registered restrictions or covenants that run with the land providing that such are complied with; (b) any registered municipal agreements and registered agreements with publicly regulated utilities providing such have been complied with, or security has been posted to ensure compliance and completion, as evidenced by a letter from the relevant municipality or regulated utility; (c) any minor easements for the supply of domestic utility or telephone services to the property or adjacent properties; and (d) any easements for drainage, storm or sanitary sewers, public utility lines, telephone lines, cable television lines or other services which do not materially affect the use of the property. If within the specified times referred to in paragraph 8 any valid objection to title or to any outstanding work order or deficiency notice, or to the fact the said present use may not lawfully be continued, or that the principal building may not be insured against risk of fire is made in writing to Seller and which Seller is unable or unwilling to remove, remedy or satisfy or obtain insurance save and except against risk of fire (Title Insurance) in favour of the Buyer and any mortgagee, (with all related costs at the expense of the Seller), and which Buyer will not waive, this Agreement notwithstanding any intermediate acts or negotiations in respect of such objections, shall be at an end and all monies paid shall be returned without interest or deduction and Seller, Listing Brokerage and Co-operating Brokerage shall not be liable for any costs or damages. Save as to any valid objection so made by such day and except for any objection going to the root of the title, Buyer shall be conclusively deemed to have accepted Seller's title to the property.

11. **CLOSING ARRANGEMENTS:** Where each of the Seller and Buyer retain a lawyer to complete the Agreement of Purchase and Sale of the property, and where the transaction will be completed by electronic registration pursuant to Part III of the Land Registration Reform Act, R.S.O. 1990, Chapter L4 and the Electronic Registration Act, S.O. 1991, Chapter 44, and any amendments thereto, the Seller and Buyer acknowledge and agree that the exchange of closing funds, non-registrable documents and other items (the "Requisite Deliveries") and the release thereof to the Seller and Buyer will (a) not occur at the same time as the registration of the transfer/deed (and any other documents intended to be registered in connection with the completion of this transaction) and (b) be subject to conditions whereby the lawyer(s) receiving any of the Requisite Deliveries will be required to hold same in trust and not release same except in accordance with the terms of a document registration agreement between the said lawyers. The Seller and Buyer irrevocably instruct the said lawyers to be bound by the document registration agreement which is recommended from time to time by the Law Society of Upper Canada. Unless otherwise agreed to by the lawyers, such exchange of the Requisite Deliveries will occur in the applicable Land Titles Office or such other location agreeable to both lawyers.

12. **DOCUMENTS AND DISCHARGE:** Buyer shall not call for the production of any title deed, abstract, survey or other evidence of title to the property except such as are in the possession or control of Seller. If requested by Buyer, Seller will deliver any sketch or survey of the property within Seller's control to Buyer as soon as possible and prior to the Requisition Date. If a discharge of any Charge/Mortgage held by a corporation incorporated pursuant to the Trust And Loan Companies Act (Canada), Chartered Bank, Trust Company, Credit Union, Caisse Populaire or Insurance Company and which is not to be assumed by Buyer on completion, is not available in registrable form on completion, Buyer agrees to accept Seller's lawyer's personal undertaking to obtain, out of the closing funds, a discharge in registrable form and to register same, or cause same to be registered, on title within a reasonable period of time after completion, provided that on or before completion Seller shall provide to Buyer a mortgage statement prepared by the mortgagee setting out the balance required to obtain the discharge, and, where a real-time electronic cleared funds transfer system is not being used, a direction executed by Seller directing payment to the mortgagee of the amount required to obtain the discharge out of the balance due on completion.

13. **INSPECTION:** Buyer acknowledges having had the opportunity to inspect the Property and understands that upon acceptance of this offer there shall be a binding agreement of purchase and sale between Buyer and Seller. **The Buyer acknowledges having the opportunity to include a requirement for a property inspection report in this Agreement and agrees that except as may be specifically provided for in this Agreement, the Buyer will not be obtaining a property inspection or property inspection report regarding the Property.**

14. **INSURANCE:** All buildings on the property and all other things being purchased shall be and remain until completion at the risk of Seller. Pending completion, Seller shall hold all insurance policies, if any, and the proceeds thereof in trust for the parties as their interests may appear and in the event of substantial damage, Buyer may either terminate this Agreement and have all monies paid returned without interest or deduction or else take the proceeds of any insurance and complete the purchase. No insurance shall be transferred on completion. If Seller is taking back a Charge/Mortgage, or Buyer is assuming a Charge/Mortgage, Buyer shall supply Seller with reasonable evidence of adequate insurance to protect Seller's or other mortgagee's interest on completion.

INITIALS OF BUYER(S): (*CM*)   INITIALS OF SELLER(S): (*SD WD*)

Form 100   Revised 2015   **Page 3 of 6**

Fully Completed Sample   *Agreement of Purchase and Sale (for Vacant Land), Page 4 of 6*

15. **PLANNING ACT:** This Agreement shall be effective to create an interest in the property only if Seller complies with the subdivision control provisions of the Planning Act by completion and Seller covenants to proceed diligently at Seller's expense to obtain any necessary consent by completion.

16. **DOCUMENT PREPARATION:** The Transfer/Deed shall, save for the Land Transfer Tax Affidavit, be prepared in registrable form at the expense of Seller, and any Charge/Mortgage to be given back by the Buyer to Seller at the expense of the Buyer. If requested by Buyer, Seller covenants that the Transfer/Deed to be delivered on completion shall contain the statements contemplated by Section 50(22) of the Planning Act, R.S.O.1990.

17. **RESIDENCY:** (a) Subject to (b) below, the Seller represents and warrants that the Seller is not and on completion will not be a non-resident under the non-residency provisions of the Income Tax Act which representation and warranty shall survive and not merge upon the completion of this transaction and the Seller shall deliver to the Buyer a statutory declaration that Seller is not then a non-resident of Canada; (b) provided that if the Seller is a non-resident under the non-residency provisions of the Income Tax Act, the Buyer shall be credited towards the Purchase Price with the amount, if any, necessary for Buyer to pay to the Minister of National Revenue to satisfy Buyer's liability in respect of tax payable by Seller under the non-residency provisions of the Income Tax Act by reason of this sale. Buyer shall not claim such credit if Seller delivers on completion the prescribed certificate.

18. **ADJUSTMENTS:** Any rents, mortgage interest, realty taxes including local improvement rates and unmetered public or private utility charges and unmetered cost of fuel, as applicable, shall be apportioned and allowed to the day of completion, the day of completion itself to be apportioned to Buyer.

19. **PROPERTY ASSESSMENT:** The Buyer and Seller hereby acknowledge that the Province of Ontario has implemented current value assessment and properties may be re-assessed on an annual basis. The Buyer and Seller agree that no claim will be made against the Buyer or Seller, or any Brokerage, Broker or Salesperson, for any changes in property tax as a result of a re-assessment of the property, save and except any property taxes that accrued prior to the completion of this transaction.

20. **TIME LIMITS:** Time shall in all respects be of the essence hereof provided that the time for doing or completing of any matter provided for herein may be extended or abridged by an agreement in writing signed by Seller and Buyer or by their respective lawyers who may be specifically authorized in that regard.

21. **TENDER:** Any tender of documents or money hereunder may be made upon Seller or Buyer or their respective lawyers on the day set for completion. Money shall be tendered with funds drawn on a lawyer's trust account in the form of a bank draft, certified cheque or wire transfer using the Large Value Transfer System.

22. **FAMILY LAW ACT:** Seller warrants that spousal consent is not necessary to this transaction under the provisions of the Family Law Act, R.S.O.1990 unless Seller's spouse has executed the consent hereinafter provided.

23. **UFFI:** Seller represents and warrants to Buyer that during the time Seller has owned the property, Seller has not caused any building on the property to be insulated with insulation containing ureaformaldehyde, and that to the best of Seller's knowledge no building on the property contains or has ever contained insulation that contains ureaformaldehyde. This warranty shall survive and not merge on the completion of this transaction, and if the building is part of a multiple unit building, this warranty shall only apply to that part of the building which is the subject of this transaction.

24. **LEGAL, ACCOUNTING AND ENVIRONMENTAL ADVICE:** The parties acknowledge that any information provided by the brokerage is not legal, tax or environmental advice.

25. **CONSUMER REPORTS: The Buyer is hereby notified that a consumer report containing credit and/or personal information may be referred to in connection with this transaction.**

26. **AGREEMENT IN WRITING:** If there is conflict or discrepancy between any provision added to this Agreement (including any Schedule attached hereto) and any provision in the standard pre-set portion hereof, the added provision shall supersede the standard pre-set provision to the extent of such conflict or discrepancy. This Agreement including any Schedule attached hereto, shall constitute the entire Agreement between Buyer and Seller. There is no representation, warranty, collateral agreement or condition, which affects this Agreement other than as expressed herein. For the purposes of this Agreement, Seller means vendor and Buyer means purchaser. This Agreement shall be read with all changes of gender or number required by the context.

27. **TIME AND DATE:** Any reference to a time and date in this Agreement shall mean the time and date where the property is located.

INITIALS OF BUYER(S): ⬭ *CM* ⬭   **INITIALS OF SELLER(S):** ⬭ *SD WD* ⬭

Form 100   Revised 2015   **Page 4 of 6**

28. SUCCESSORS AND ASSIGNS: The heirs, executors, administrators, successors and assigns of the undersigned are bound by the terms herein.

SIGNED, SEALED AND DELIVERED in the presence of: IN WITNESS whereof I have hereunto set my hand and seal:

D. Samuels	*Charles Morgan*	●	DATE *Feb. 26/xx*
(Witness)	(Buyer)	(Seal)	
		●	DATE
(Witness)	(Buyer)	(Seal)	

I, the Undersigned Seller, agree to the above offer. I hereby irrevocably instruct my lawyer to pay directly to the brokerage(s) with whom I have agreed to pay commission, the unpaid balance of the commission together with applicable Harmonized Sales Tax (and any other taxes as may hereafter be applicable), from the proceeds of the sale prior to any payment to the undersigned on completion, as advised by the brokerage(s) to my lawyer.

SIGNED, SEALED AND DELIVERED in the presence of: IN WITNESS whereof I have hereunto set my hand and seal:

W. Jones	*Sylvia Davies*	●	DATE *Feb. 26/xx*
(Witness)	(Seller)	(Seal)	
W. Jones	*Wayne Davies*	●	DATE *Feb. 26/xx*
(Witness)	(Seller)	(Seal)	

SPOUSAL CONSENT: The Undersigned Spouse of the Seller hereby consents to the disposition evidenced herein pursuant to the provisions of the Family Law Act, R.S.O.1990, and hereby agrees with the Buyer that he/she will execute all necessary or incidental documents to give full force and effect to the sale evidenced herein.

		●	DATE
(Witness)	(Spouse)	(Seal)	

CONFIRMATION OF ACCEPTANCE: Notwithstanding anything contained herein to the contrary, I confirm this Agreement with all changes both typed and written was finally accepted by all parties at ....*6:00*.... a.m./p.m. this ...*26th*... day of.................*February*.................., 20..*xx*....

....
Wayne Davies
(Signature of Seller or Buyer)

INFORMATION ON BROKERAGE(S)

Listing Brokerage ....**ABC Realty Inc.**............   Tel.No.(..*416*..) *555-1212*
123 Main Street, Anycity, Anyregion L4H 6P5   **W. Jones**
(Salesperson / Broker Name)

Co-op/Buyer Brokerage ....**XYZ Real Estate Ltd.**............   Tel.No.(..*416*..) *666-1212*
29 Maple Drive, Anycity, Anyregion L2J 7K6   **D. Samuels**
(Salesperson / Broker Name)

ACKNOWLEDGEMENT

I acknowledge receipt of my signed copy of this accepted Agreement of Purchase and Sale and I authorize the Brokerage to forward a copy to my lawyer.	I acknowledge receipt of my signed copy of this accepted Agreement of Purchase and Sale and I authorize the Brokerage to forward a copy to my lawyer.
Sylvia Davies .... DATE *Feb. 26/xx* (Seller)	*Charles Morgan* .... DATE *Feb. 26/xx* (Buyer)
Wayne Davies .... DATE *Feb. 26/xx* (Seller)	.... DATE (Buyer)
Address for Service *54 Hillcrest Blvd., Anytown, Anyregion* *N8H 2C3* .... Tel.No.(..*416*..) *777-1212*	Address for Service *104 Sunnyside Court, Anytown, Anyregion* *B6R 9L8* .... Tel.No.(..*416*..) *888-1212*
Seller's Lawyer *Cindy Jones and Associates*	Buyer's Lawyer *George Roberts and Associates*
Address *565 Pine Street, Anytown, Anyregion R4K 8L9*	Address *15 Concession Street, Anytown, Anyregion B5D 3P9*
Email	Email ....
(..*416*..) *666-5544* (..*416*..) *666-5454* Tel.No. FAX No.	(..*416*..) *777-5353* (..*416*..) *777-5454* Tel.No. FAX No.

FOR OFFICE USE ONLY   **COMMISSION TRUST AGREEMENT**

To: Co-operating Brokerage shown on the foregoing Agreement of Purchase and Sale:
In consideration for the Co-operating Brokerage procuring the foregoing Agreement of Purchase and Sale, I hereby declare that all moneys received or receivable by me in connection with the Transaction as contemplated in the MLS® Rules and Regulations of my Real Estate Board shall be receivable and held in trust. This agreement shall constitute a Commission Trust Agreement as defined in the MLS® Rules and shall be subject to and governed by the MLS® Rules pertaining to Commission Trust.

DATED as of the date and time of the acceptance of the foregoing Agreement of Purchase and Sale.   Acknowledged by:

W. Jones   *D. Samuels*
....
(Authorized to bind the Listing Brokerage)   (Authorized to bind the Co-operating Brokerage)

Form 100   Revised 2015   **Page 5 of 6**

SECTION I   A CLOSER LOOK AT TRADING DIFFERENT TYPES OF PROPERTIES

Fully Completed Sample   *Agreement of Purchase and Sale (for Vacant Land), Page 6 of 6*

OREA Ontario Real Estate Association

Form 100
for use in the Province of Ontario

Schedule A
Agreement of Purchase and Sale

This Schedule is attached to and forms part of the Agreement of Purchase and Sale between:

BUYER, ... Charles Edward Morgan ...., and

SELLER, ... Sylvia Ruth Davies and Wayne Scott Davies ....

for the purchase and sale of .... 32A Cambridge Drive, Town of Anytown, Region of Anyregion ....

.... dated the ..26th.. day of .... February ...., 20.xx.....

Buyer agrees to pay the balance as follows:

The Buyer agrees to pay a further sum of Fifty-Eight Thousand Dollars ($58,000.00), subject to adjustments, to the Seller on completion of this transaction, with funds drawn on a lawyer's trust account in the form of a bank draft, certified cheque, or wire transfer using the Large Value Transfer System.

This Offer is conditional upon the Seller obtaining, at the Seller's expense, a consent to sever the above described property, Part 2 on Reference Plan 52R 873, from the Seller's existing property. Unless the Seller gives notice in writing delivered to the Buyer personally or in accordance with any other provisions for the delivery of notice in this Agreement of Purchase and Sale or any Schedule thereto not later than 5:00 p.m. on the 31st day of May, 20xx, that this condition is fulfilled, this Offer shall become null and void and the deposit shall be returned to the Buyer in full without deduction. The Seller agrees to proceed immediately with all steps necessary to attempt to satisfy the foregoing condition.

This Offer is conditional on the Buyer determining, in the Buyer's sole and absolute discretion, that the zoning of the property will permit the construction of a single-family 2-storey home with a minimum of 3,400 square feet plus a 2-car attached garage in accordance with the plans and drawings now in possession of the Buyer, and that municipal services and utilities are available to the property. Unless the Buyer gives notice in writing delivered to the Seller personally or in accordance with any other provisions for the delivery of notice in this Agreement of Purchase and Sale or any Schedule thereto not later than 5:00 p.m. on the 3rd day of April, 20xx, that this condition is fulfilled, this Offer shall be null and void and the deposit shall be returned to the Buyer in full without deduction. This condition is included for the benefit of the Buyer and may be waived at the Buyer's sole option by notice in writing to the Seller as aforesaid within the time period stated herein.

Buyer and Seller agree the Seller is responsible for all costs related to the severance, including costs to comply with any conditions imposed for the consent, and the Buyer is responsible to pay H.S.T. payable on this transaction and all costs related to building permits, the provision of municipal services and utilities, and any developmental changes.

This form must be initialed by all parties to the Agreement of Purchase and Sale.

INITIALS OF BUYER(S): (CM)   **INITIALS OF SELLER(S):** (SD WD)

Form 100   Revised 2015   **Page 6 of 6**

FARM PROPERTY: OVERVIEW

A farm may be defined as a tract of land forming a single property devoted to agriculture. Within this definition fall many kinds of activities, including the small farm close to a city and the huge western ranch containing thousands of acres. Farm property includes land, buildings and equipment used on any kind of farm, regardless of its basic purpose. Selling farms requires extensive knowledge that goes beyond the scope of this introductory topic, but an overview is helpful for registrants contemplating a career in rural sales. This overview does not include operational and financial considerations regarding farming operations and related agri-businesses.

Selling Farm Property

What makes good farm sales representatives? Obviously they must be sales-minded with a thorough general knowledge of real estate. It is also essential that they be able to talk intelligently to farmer-clients about relevant issues. This requires a working knowledge of the types of farming common to their areas, as well as a recognition that every farm is peculiar in its physical characteristics and its potential best use.

To negotiate successfully with prospective purchasers they must also be well informed about the following:

- Soil types including drainage problems, fertility and fertilizer use;
- Kinds of livestock and/or crops (heat units] best suited to the area;
- Problems of seeding and harvesting;
- Machinery and equipment required;
- Farm buildings;
- Operating capital: how to obtain it and potential cash flow;
- Marketing of farm produce;
- Sources of advice and financial assistance; and
- Discovering the best use for an individual farm unit.

The Changing Farm Scene

The farming situation in Ontario, and in Canada for that matter, is constantly changing. Some of the more obvious changes are listed:

- Decreasing number of farms, farmers, farm labourers and total farm population;
- Fewer family farms;
- Increasing farm size;
- Tougher domestic and international competition;
- Increasing technological change and efficiency;
- Stronger marketing boards that are increasingly national in scope;
- Less independence for individuals;
- Increasing planning and contractual arrangements;
- Increase in computer centred data processing systems and management assistance plans;
- Better forecasting of markets and prices;
- More sophisticated marketing strategies;

- Constant improvement in quality of management;
- Greater reliance on and use of planning; and
- Improved research, training, education and management.

THE SMALL FARM

Small farms continue to be a significant component of the overall farming scene, but the incidence of off-farm work is prevalent. In some cases, small farmers with part-time jobs could be much better off financially than many full-time farmers. Some advantages accrue to the small farmer with a part-time job. For example, a small farm owner who has a part-time job can outlast a prolonged period of low prices or poor market conditions better than a full-time farmer.

Some farmers establish themselves by taking part-time employment while they build up sufficient resources to go into full-time farming. In addition, the income of many part-time and small farm families is supplemented by the income of spouses and/or other family members having full or part-time off the farm jobs.

Presently, many noted experts visualize only two solutions to farm problems: the establishment of viable farm units and the withdrawal from agriculture of farms that cannot be made viable. Obviously, there may be a third solution namely part-time farming.

THE FARM CORPORATION

For some years now there seems to have been a trend to larger and larger farms in order to provide a viable operation. This trend has come about because of rising labour costs, rising food cost and increasingly larger investments in equipment. In order to maintain a reasonable return from a farm operation, the management team has to be more sophisticated looking for new ways to cuts costs. One way to do this is to make the operation larger. This means that more dollars must be invested, a different type of financing created and more individual people involved, with the end result being the formation of the farm corporation. With non-farming personnel part of such a corporation, increased emphasis is placed on the farm as a business and the need for profit.

THE VIABLE FARM

Regardless of size, the objective is a viable farm. Such a farm can be described as a business that, under good management, is able to yield adequate returns on the resources, land, labour and capital employed in the farming enterprise. The Ministry of Agriculture, Food and Rural Affairs is a primary resource for farmers achieving that objective.

WEB LINKS

Ministry of Agriculture, Food and Rural Affairs   This chapter provides an overview of farming only. Registrants seeking detailed information about recent farming initiatives should go to the Ministry's website (*www.omafra.gov.on.ca*).

Farming Classifications

Most farms can be classified into the following three types.

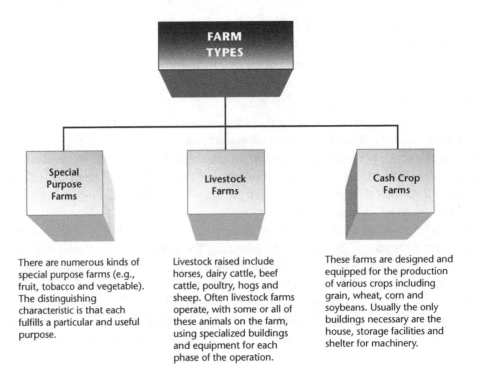

FARM TYPES

Special Purpose Farms

There are numerous kinds of special purpose farms (e.g., fruit, tobacco and vegetable). The distinguishing characteristic is that each fulfills a particular and useful purpose.

Livestock Farms

Livestock raised include horses, dairy cattle, beef cattle, poultry, hogs and sheep. Often livestock farms operate, with some or all of these animals on the farm, using specialized buildings and equipment for each phase of the operation.

Cash Crop Farms

These farms are designed and equipped for the production of various crops including grain, wheat, corn and soybeans. Usually the only buildings necessary are the house, storage facilities and shelter for machinery.

Farming and Nutrient Management

Farms are coming under increasing scrutiny from an environmental perspective and registrants should be generally aware of relevant legislation. Nutrient management broadly refers to regulatory controls as to how nutrients are applied to land or generally managed in an environmentally responsible manner.

Nutrient sources are found in manure, commercial fertilizers, biosolids generated by municipal sewage treatment facilities, and pulp and paper sludge. Such management has been addressed in a patchwork of provincial regulations, municipal by-laws and other regulatory provisions that demanded consolidation under province-wide standards.

NUTRIENT MANAGEMENT ACT

A comprehensive approach to nutrient management is required to protect water, the environment and the well-being of Ontario communities, while ensuring that various affected operations (i.e., farms and other agricultural operations) can effectively operate within such a framework.

The *Nutrient Management Act, 2002* introduced new standards for land-applied materials containing nutrients, including new inspection and compliance measures, authorities for remedial action and provincial enforcement.

The Act, best described as an enabling statute, sets the stage for future regulatory provisions and includes a two-tiered conceptual framework:

Nutrient Management Plan (NMP)

Plans are established for different types of operations that are involved with land-applied materials containing nutrients. Accordingly, varying requirements are then in place depending on whether the plan applies, for example, to a farming operation or a municipal sewage treatment plant.

Nutrient Management Strategy (NMS)

The strategy sets out in detail how such operations manage nutrient materials on a day-to-day basis.

The legislation reinforces authorities and regulatory provisions currently contained in the *Environmental Protection Act*, the *Highway Traffic Act*, the *Ontario Water Resources Act* and the *Pesticides Act*.

IMPACT ON LISTING/SELLING

The *Nutrient Management Act*, from a registrant's perspective, has the most impact on farm and other agricultural operations particularly regarding:

- Storage, handling, use and transportation of commercial fertilizers;
- Requirements to develop, document and retain records relating to nutrient management plans and strategies;
- Required qualifications for farmers and others applying such materials; and
- Establishment of minimum distance requirements regarding land applications to protect adjacent land and watersheds/sources.

Registrants involved with listing and selling agricultural and related operations should keep fully informed about ongoing developments relating to this Act and its Regulations.

 WEB LINKS

Nutrient Management Act   The *Nutrient Management Act* was jointly developed by the Ministry of the Environment and the Ministry of Agriculture, Food and Rural Affairs. Additional details are available on their respective web sites: ***www.ene.gov.on.ca*** and ***www.omafra.gov.on.ca***.

DRAFTING OFFERS: PROPERTIES NEAR FARMS

The accelerating migration of urban dwellers to rural parts of the province has, in some cases, created a conflict between those who farm for a living and those who use property for purely residential purposes. This has resulted in complaints surrounding noise, odour and dust arising from farm operations.

The Ontario Ministry of Agriculture, Food and Rural Affairs (OMAFRA) is responsible for the *Farming and Food Production Protection Act* (FFPPA), passed on May 11, 1998. This legislation replaces the previous *Farm Practices Protection Act*. The guiding principle of the legislation is set out below:

> *It is in the provincial interest that in agricultural areas, agricultural uses and normal farm practices be promoted and protected in a way that balances the needs of the agricultural community with provincial health, safety and environmental concerns.*

Protection for Farmers

Registrants involved with agricultural operations and rural residential properties should clearly understand the intent and scope of this legislation. The FFPPA is designed to give farmers protection from nuisance complaints and subsequent lawsuits or injunctions. The FFPPA also ensures that the farming and food production industry is protected from restrictive municipal by-laws that constrain normal farm practices.

The underlying principle in the Act is generally consistent with other provincial environmental legislation such as the *Environmental Protection Act*, the *Pesticides Act*, the *Health Protection and Promotion Act* and the *Ontario Water Resources Act*.

Municipal By-Law Challenge

The *Farming and Food Production Protection Act* contains provisions for a municipal by-law to be challenged, if it is deemed to restrict a normal farm practice being carried out as part of an agricultural operation. A person or a municipality may apply to the Normal Farm Practices Board for a determination as to whether a practice is considered to be a normal farm practice. If so, such practice would not fall within the scope of a restrictive municipal by-law. The Act also applies to by-laws implemented before the FFPPA came into force.

The strategy in dealing with municipal by-laws is a multi-staged approach. Education programs by Ministry staff and farm groups provide municipalities with an understanding of what constitutes a normal farming practice. Municipalities are encouraged to consult with OMAFRA, farm groups and farmers prior to creating by-laws that might impact the farming community. If a Board hearing is required, the Board will determine if the farm practice is considered to be normal pursuant to the Act.

Normal Farm Practices Protection Board

The Normal Farm Practices Protection Board (NFPPB), established under the FFPPA, is composed of members appointed by the Minister of Agriculture, Food and Rural Affairs. Hearings before the NFPPB are similar to court hearings, however, less formal. Parties before the Board do not require representation by a lawyer or an agent.

The proceedings are heard by a minimum of three Board members; the Chair or Vice-Chair and two other members. When the need arises, the Board may summon one or more persons having technical or special knowledge of the matter before it. Upon hearing a nuisance matter, the Board may:

- dismiss the complaint if the disturbance results from a normal farm practice; or
- order the farmer to cease the practice causing the disturbance if it is not considered to be normal farm practice; or
- order the farmer to modify the practice to be consistent with normal farm practice.

Upon hearing a by-law challenge, the Board will state whether it is of the opinion that:

- the farm practice is a normal farm practice; or
- the farm practice will be a normal farm practice if specific modifications are made within a time frame set out in the decision.

Following the hearing, the NFPPB reviews all information before it and makes its decision. The written decision, together with an explanation, is typically forwarded to the parties within 30 days of the hearing. The Board operates in terms of several important definitions, three of which are highlighted:

Disturbance	Under the FFPPA, disturbance includes odour, dust, flies, light, smoke, noise and vibration.
Agricultural Operation	Agricultural operations include: new activities involving ratites (e.g., ostrich and emu), bees, maple syrup, tree farms, deer and elk; on-farm processing; activities that are necessary but an ancillary part of an agricultural operation, such as movement of transport vehicles for the purpose of an agricultural operation.
Normal Farm Practice	A practice that is conducted in a manner consistent with proper and acceptable customs and standards; and a normal farm practice makes use of innovative technology in a manner consistent with proper farm management practices.

The NFPPB is authorized to rule on three types of cases:

- A nuisance case involving a disturbance that arises that may or may not be a normal farm practice. If a normal farm practice, a decision to that effect protects the farmer from further similar complaints.
- A by-law case in which a municipal by-law restricts some farm practice. The board determines if such a practice is a normal farm practice. If so, the practice is exempt from the municipal by-law.
- A by-law case specifically involving vehicular movement in which a by-law is restricting such vehicular movement. The board will rule on whether the farm practice requiring such movement is a normal farm practice. If so, the specific vehicular movement is exempt from the by-law.

Drafting Offers

Registrants marketing rural residential properties near areas used for agricultural and food production activities should include an appropriate clause in any offer informing the potential buyer that normal farm practices and associated issues (which may involve dust, noise, flies, light, odour, etc.) have protection in Ontario under the *Farming and Food Production Protection Act*.

SCENARIO	CLAUSE
Acknowledgement Regarding Nearby Farm A buyer is submitting an offer with the understanding that a large farming operation is located nearby and that normal farming activities occur that can cause discomfort or inconveniences.	**ENV–6** **Agricultural Activities Acknowledgement** *The Buyer acknowledges that the property lies within, partially within, adjacent to or within two kilometres of an area zoned, used or identified for agricultural and food production activities and that such activities occur in the area. These activities may include intensive operations that cause discomfort and inconveniences that involve, but not limited to dust, noise, flies, light, odour, smoke, traffic, vibration, operating of machinery during any 24 hour period, storage and utilization of manure and the application by spraying or otherwise of chemical fertilizers, soil amendments, herbicides and pesticides. One or more of these inconveniences have protection in Ontario under the Farming and Food Production Protection Act.*

KNOWLEDGE INTEGRATION

Notables

- Vacant land buyers should take various factors into consideration including location, physical attributes, boundaries, access/easements/restrictions, market trends and initial/ongoing costs.

- Accurate lot dimensions and an up-to-date survey are essential.

- Lot purchased on a *per acre* basis typically provides that any discrepancy in area will be adjusted on closing.

- Conditions relating to vacant land include sale subject to severance, provision of services and obtaining a building permit.

- Buyers of forested land/bush lots may be interested in advantages provided under the Managed Forest Tax Incentive Program, which offers lower taxes for those who agree to conserve woodlands.

- Registrants involved with forested land should inquire as to current requirements under the Managed Forest Tax Incentive Program.

- A farm property overview is provided including skills needed in selling farm property and fundamental farming changes taking place at this time.

- Farms can be broadly classified into special purpose, livestock and cash crop farms.

- Farms fall under various legislative requirements. The recent *Nutrient Management Act* warrants special mention given the expanding concern over environmental issues in the marketplace.

- Registrants should exercise caution when marketing rural residential properties in close proximity to an operating farm. The *Farming and Food Production Protection Act* includes provisions to protect farmers from nuisance complaints and lawsuits resulting from disturbances such as odour, dust, flies, light, smoke, noise and vibration.

Web Links

Web links are included for general interest regarding selected chapter topics.

Managed Forest Tax Incentive Program
For more information concerning this program, contact the Ministry of Natural Resources and Forestry (*www.mnr.gov.on.ca.*). For questions regarding how the MFTIP program impacts property assessment, contact the Municipal Property Assessment Corporation (*www.mpac.org*).

Ministry of Agriculture, Food and Rural Affairs
This chapter provides an overview of farming only. Registrants seeking detailed information about recent farming initiatives should go to the Ministry's website (*www.omafra.gov.on.ca*).

Nutrient Management Act
The *Nutrient Management Act* was jointly developed by the Ministry of the Environment and the Ministry of Agriculture, Food and Rural Affairs. Additional details are available on their respective web sites: *www.ene.gov.on.ca* and *www.omafra.gov.on.ca.*

Strategic Thinking For Your Career

Questions are included to assist in developing your new career. No answers are provided.

1. Should I consider focusing my efforts on vacant land and farms and what brokerages within my local marketplace concentrate on these types of property?

2. If I am planning on marketing vacant land, what types of revenue sources are available to offset ongoing costs of rural vacant land?

3. What helpful information can I obtain from the Ministry of Agriculture, Food and Rural Affairs to expand my knowledge of rural land and farm property?

Chapter Mini-Review

Solutions are located in the Appendix.

1. An important consideration in buying vacant land is to determine whether any easements or other restrictions impact the property.

    ◯ True   ◯ False

2. Vacant rural land is typically sold based on the square footage of the land.

    ◯ True   ◯ False

3. Costs relating to the severance of a property are normally the responsibility of the seller, not the buyer.

    ◯ True   ◯ False

4. An owner can readily make significant design changes to a residential structure during construction without the need for further municipal approval relating to the building permit.

    ◯ True   ◯ False

5. The Managed Forest Tax Incentive Program only applies to wooded land situated in Northern Ontario.

    ◯ True   ◯ False

6. Only very large farm corporations can be viewed as viable farms.

    ◯ True   ◯ False

7. A farm specializing in fruit is best described as a special purpose farm.

    ◯ True   ◯ False

8. The *Nutrient Management Act* is focused on various environmental considerations involving farms, including the storage and handling of commercial fertilizers.

    ◯ True   ◯ False

Active Learning Exercises

Solutions are located in the Appendix.

▣ Exercise 1   Multiple Choice

1.1   A farm that produces soybean only is best described as a:

a.   Cash crop farm.

b.   Viable farm.

c.   Livestock farm.

d.   Farm corporation.

1.2   Which of the following is a correct statement regarding important factors to consider when buying vacant land?

a.   Buyers need not be concerned about access or easement considerations, as these rarely impact the purchase of vacant land.

b.   An offer cannot be accepted by the seller until a land severance for the land in question is finalized.

c.   Regulatory agencies, such as a conservation authority, can directly impact land use.

d.   The municipality reviews a building permit application from a zoning perspective only.

1.3   The Managed Forest Tax Incentive Program:

a.   States that the buyer need not be approved, provided that the seller has previously been approved.

b.   Is overseen by the Municipal Property Assessment Corporation.

c.   Applies only to forested areas of less than 10 acres.

d.   Requires that a Managed Forest Plan be prepared.

1.4   Which of the following statements is correct?

a.   A major trend in farming is the increasing number of family farms.

b.   Availability/installation cost of services is rarely a consideration when considering the purchase of rural land.

c.   The *Nutrient Management Act* introduced new standards for land-applied materials containing nutrients; e.g., fertilizers.

d.   The *Nutrient Management Act* applies only to special purpose farms.

1.5 The *Farming and Food Production Protection Act*:

   a. States that an individual cannot build a rural residence in close proximity to an operating farm.

   b. Provides legislative protection for operating farms from restrictive municipal by-laws concerning normal farm practices.

   c. Protects farmers from complaints regarding all types of farming disturbances.

   d. Protects rural residential owners from disturbances caused by farmers relating to odour, dust, flies, light, smoke, noise and vibrations.

■ Exercise 2   Matching

Match the phrase/word in the left column with the appropriate description in the right column (not all descriptions are used).

____ *Frontage*	*a. Marketing Boards*
____ *Secondary Line*	*b. Prepared by Seller*
____ *Managed Forest Tax Incentive Program*	*c. Not Less Than Four Hectares*
____ *Disturbance*	*d. Land Severance*
____ *Building Location*	*e. Hydro One Networks Inc.*
____ *Vacant Land—Ongoing Costs*	*f. Building Permit*
____ *Landowner Report*	*g. Odour, Dust and Flies*
	h. Taxes, Fencing and Liability Insurance
	i. Setback from Public Road
	j. Abuts a Public Street or Highway.

◼ Exercise 3   The Agreement of Purchase and Sale

James B. Witnell wants you to draft an offer on a three-acre parcel of vacant land situated in a rural area of the Township of Anytownship owned by Mary V. Goldman. Witnell plans to build a new home on the property. Various details are included below. Insert any additional information necessary to complete an accepted agreement of purchase and sale. A blank *Agreement of Purchase and Sale* (OREA Form 100) is provided on the following pages.

> The vacant land is located at 3477 West Concession Road (north side) in the Township of Anytownship, Regional Municipality of Anyregion. The property is approximately three acres in size with a frontage of 300 feet and a depth of 435 feet, and is legally described as *Part of Lot 10, Plan 270, more particularly described as Part 2 on Reference Plan 99R2320.*
>
> The offered price is $135,000 with a deposit of $10,000, and the balance is due on completion date. The $10,000 is to be deposited with the listing brokerage upon acceptance of the agreement. In addition to the usual Schedule A, an additional schedule is required (illustrating the type of structure to be built on the land). Buyer Witnell has asked that the offer be conditional on satisfying himself that a building permit for the structure illustrated in Schedule B will be available. A further condition is required concerning the cost of providing hydro and telephone services, which is not to exceed $2,000. Allow until September 15th, 20xx as a time limit for both conditions precedent. The seller has agreed to provide a new survey within the same time frame.
>
> The completion date will be October 20th (a normal business day) with today's date being August 12th, 20xx. The offer, dated at Anycity, will be irrevocable until 8 p.m. on the 13th. An appropriate title search period would be until September 30th, 20xx. Notices cannot be delivered by fax or email. No chattels are included, no fixtures excluded and the clause concerning rental items does not apply. If any HST applies to this sale, it is deemed to be in addition to the purchase price.
>
> Insert necessary dates and signatures as required for a fully completed agreement ready for presentation. The listing brokerage is ABC Realty Inc., representing the seller and the co-operating brokerage is XYZ Real Estate Limited, representing the buyer.
>
> When presenting the offer, the seller signs back the offer at $143,500 and extends the irrevocable date by one additional day (i.e., August 14th). The increased price is acceptable to the buyer, who signs the agreement on the 14th. Fully complete all necessary details for this accepted agreement including initials, signatures, acknowledgements and the commission trust agreement.
>
> **NOTE:** The additional schedule relating to the building permit condition is referred to on page 1, but not attached to the agreement for purposes of this learning exercise.

OREA Ontario Real Estate Association   # Agreement of Purchase and Sale

Form 100
for use in the Province of Ontario

This Agreement of Purchase and Sale dated this .... day of .... 20............

BUYER, ..., agrees to purchase from
(Full legal names of all Buyers)

SELLER, ..., the following
(Full legal names of all Sellers)

REAL PROPERTY:

Address ....

fronting on the .... side of ....

in the ....

and having a frontage of .... more or less by a depth of .... more or less

and legally described as ....

.... (the "property")
(Legal description of land including easements not described elsewhere)

PURCHASE PRICE: Dollars (CDN$) ....

.... Dollars

DEPOSIT: Buyer submits ....
(Herewith/Upon Acceptance/as otherwise described in this Agreement)

.... Dollars (CDN$) ....

by negotiable cheque payable to .... "Deposit Holder" to be held
in trust pending completion or other termination of this Agreement and to be credited toward the Purchase Price on completion. For the purposes of this
Agreement, "Upon Acceptance" shall mean that the Buyer is required to deliver the deposit to the Deposit Holder within 24 hours of the acceptance of
this Agreement. The parties to this Agreement hereby acknowledge that, unless otherwise provided for in this Agreement, the Deposit Holder shall place
the deposit in trust in the Deposit Holder's non-interest bearing Real Estate Trust Account and no interest shall be earned, received or paid on the deposit.

Buyer agrees to pay the balance as more particularly set out in Schedule A attached.

SCHEDULE(S) A...**attached hereto form(s) part of this Agreement.**

1. **IRREVOCABILITY:** This offer shall be irrevocable by .... until .... a.m./p.m. on the ....
(Seller/Buyer)

    day of .... 20 ...., after which time, if not accepted, this offer shall be null and void and the deposit
    shall be returned to the Buyer in full without interest.

2. **COMPLETION DATE:** This Agreement shall be completed by no later than 6:00 p.m. on the .... day of ....

    20 .... Upon completion, vacant possession of the property shall be given to the Buyer unless otherwise provided for in this Agreement.

INITIALS OF BUYER(S): ⬭   **INITIALS OF SELLER(S):** ⬭

Form 100   Revised 2015   **Page 1 of 6**

3. **NOTICES:** The Seller hereby appoints the Listing Brokerage as agent for the Seller for the purpose of giving and receiving notices pursuant to this Agreement. Where a Brokerage (Buyer's Brokerage) has entered into a representation agreement with the Buyer, the Buyer hereby appoints the Buyer's Brokerage as agent for the purpose of giving and receiving notices pursuant to this Agreement. **Where a Brokerage represents both the Seller and the Buyer (multiple representation), the Brokerage shall not be appointed or authorized to be agent for either the Buyer or the Seller for the purpose of giving and receiving notices.** Any notice relating hereto or provided for herein shall be in writing. In addition to any provision contained herein and in any Schedule hereto, this offer, any counter-offer, notice of acceptance thereof or any notice to be given or received pursuant to this Agreement or any Schedule hereto (any of them, "Document") shall be deemed given and received when delivered personally or hand delivered to the Address for Service provided in the Acknowledgement below, or where a facsimile number or email address is provided herein, when transmitted electronically to that facsimile number or email address, respectively, in which case, the signature(s) of the party (parties) shall be deemed to be original.

FAX No.: ....   FAX No.: ....
                   (For delivery of Documents to Seller)   (For delivery of Documents to Buyer)

Email Address: ....   Email Address: ....
                   (For delivery of Documents to Seller)   (For delivery of Documents to Buyer)

4. **CHATTELS INCLUDED:**..

....

....

....

....

Unless otherwise stated in this Agreement or any Schedule hereto, Seller agrees to convey all fixtures and chattels included in the Purchase Price free from all liens, encumbrances or claims affecting the said fixtures and chattels.

5. **FIXTURES EXCLUDED:**..

....

....

....

....

6. **RENTAL ITEMS (Including Lease, Lease to Own):** The following equipment is rented and **not** included in the Purchase Price. The Buyer agrees to assume the rental contract(s), if assumable:

....

....

....

The Buyer agrees to co-operate and execute such documentation as may be required to facilitate such assumption.

7. **HST:** If the sale of the Property (Real Property as described above) is subject to Harmonized Sales Tax (HST), then such tax shall be

.... the Purchase Price. If the sale of the Property is not subject to HST, Seller agrees to certify on or before
         (included in/in addition to)

closing, that the sale of the Property is not subject to HST. Any HST on chattels, if applicable, is not included in the Purchase Price.

INITIALS OF BUYER(S): ⬭   **INITIALS OF SELLER(S):** ⬭

8. **TITLE SEARCH:** Buyer shall be allowed until 6:00 p.m. on the .... day of ...., 20..........., (Requisition Date) to examine the title to the Property at Buyer's own expense and until the earlier of: (i) thirty days from the later of the Requisition Date or the date on which the conditions in this Agreement are fulfilled or otherwise waived or; (ii) five days prior to completion, to satisfy Buyer that there are no outstanding

work orders or deficiency notices affecting the Property, and that its present use (...) may be lawfully continued and that the principal building may be insured against risk of fire. Seller hereby consents to the municipality or other governmental agencies releasing to Buyer details of all outstanding work orders and deficiency notices affecting the property, and Seller agrees to execute and deliver such further authorizations in this regard as Buyer may reasonably require.

9. **FUTURE USE:** Seller and Buyer agree that there is no representation or warranty of any kind that the future intended use of the property by Buyer is or will be lawful except as may be specifically provided for in this Agreement.

10. **TITLE:** Provided that the title to the property is good and free from all registered restrictions, charges, liens, and encumbrances except as otherwise specifically provided in this Agreement and save and except for (a) any registered restrictions or covenants that run with the land providing that such are complied with; (b) any registered municipal agreements and registered agreements with publicly regulated utilities providing such have been complied with, or security has been posted to ensure compliance and completion, as evidenced by a letter from the relevant municipality or regulated utility; (c) any minor easements for the supply of domestic utility or telephone services to the property or adjacent properties; and (d) any easements for drainage, storm or sanitary sewers, public utility lines, telephone lines, cable television lines or other services which do not materially affect the use of the property. If within the specified times referred to in paragraph 8 any valid objection to title or to any outstanding work order or deficiency notice, or to the fact the said present use may not lawfully be continued, or that the principal building may not be insured against risk of fire is made in writing to Seller and which Seller is unable or unwilling to remove, remedy or satisfy or obtain insurance save and except against risk of fire (Title Insurance) in favour of the Buyer and any mortgagee, (with all related costs at the expense of the Seller), and which Buyer will not waive, this Agreement notwithstanding any intermediate acts or negotiations in respect of such objections, shall be at an end and all monies paid shall be returned without interest or deduction and Seller, Listing Brokerage and Co-operating Brokerage shall not be liable for any costs or damages. Save as to any valid objection so made by such day and except for any objection going to the root of the title, Buyer shall be conclusively deemed to have accepted Seller's title to the property.

11. **CLOSING ARRANGEMENTS:** Where each of the Seller and Buyer retain a lawyer to complete the Agreement of Purchase and Sale of the property, and where the transaction will be completed by electronic registration pursuant to Part III of the Land Registration Reform Act, R.S.O. 1990, Chapter L4 and the Electronic Registration Act, S.O. 1991, Chapter 44, and any amendments thereto, the Seller and Buyer acknowledge and agree that the exchange of closing funds, non-registrable documents and other items (the "Requisite Deliveries") and the release thereof to the Seller and Buyer will (a) not occur at the same time as the registration of the transfer/deed (and any other documents intended to be registered in connection with the completion of this transaction) and (b) be subject to conditions whereby the lawyer(s) receiving any of the Requisite Deliveries will be required to hold same in trust and not release same except in accordance with the terms of a document registration agreement between the said lawyers. The Seller and Buyer irrevocably instruct the said lawyers to be bound by the document registration agreement which is recommended from time to time by the Law Society of Upper Canada. Unless otherwise agreed to by the lawyers, such exchange of the Requisite Deliveries will occur in the applicable Land Titles Office or such other location agreeable to both lawyers.

12. **DOCUMENTS AND DISCHARGE:** Buyer shall not call for the production of any title deed, abstract, survey or other evidence of title to the property except such as are in the possession or control of Seller. If requested by Buyer, Seller will deliver any sketch or survey of the property within Seller's control to Buyer as soon as possible and prior to the Requisition Date. If a discharge of any Charge/Mortgage held by a corporation incorporated pursuant to the Trust And Loan Companies Act (Canada), Chartered Bank, Trust Company, Credit Union, Caisse Populaire or Insurance Company and which is not to be assumed by Buyer on completion, is not available in registrable form on completion, Buyer agrees to accept Seller's lawyer's personal undertaking to obtain, out of the closing funds, a discharge in registrable form and to register same, or cause same to be registered, on title within a reasonable period of time after completion, provided that on or before completion Seller shall provide to Buyer a mortgage statement prepared by the mortgagee setting out the balance required to obtain the discharge, and, where a real-time electronic cleared funds transfer system is not being used, a direction executed by Seller directing payment to the mortgagee of the amount required to obtain the discharge out of the balance due on completion.

13. **INSPECTION:** Buyer acknowledges having had the opportunity to inspect the Property and understands that upon acceptance of this offer there shall be a binding agreement of purchase and sale between Buyer and Seller. **The Buyer acknowledges having the opportunity to include a requirement for a property inspection report in this Agreement and agrees that except as may be specifically provided for in this Agreement, the Buyer will not be obtaining a property inspection or property inspection report regarding the Property.**

14. **INSURANCE:** All buildings on the property and all other things being purchased shall be and remain until completion at the risk of Seller. Pending completion, Seller shall hold all insurance policies, if any, and the proceeds thereof in trust for the parties as their interests may appear and in the event of substantial damage, Buyer may either terminate this Agreement and have all monies paid returned without interest or deduction or else take the proceeds of any insurance and complete the purchase. No insurance shall be transferred on completion. If Seller is taking back a Charge/Mortgage, or Buyer is assuming a Charge/Mortgage, Buyer shall supply Seller with reasonable evidence of adequate insurance to protect Seller's or other mortgagee's interest on completion.

INITIALS OF BUYER(S): (   )   INITIALS OF SELLER(S): (   )

Form 100   Revised 2015   **Page 3 of 6**

SECTION I   A CLOSER LOOK AT TRADING DIFFERENT TYPES OF PROPERTIES

Exercise 3   Agreement of Purchase and Sale—Page 4 of 6

15. **PLANNING ACT:** This Agreement shall be effective to create an interest in the property only if Seller complies with the subdivision control provisions of the Planning Act by completion and Seller covenants to proceed diligently at Seller's expense to obtain any necessary consent by completion.

16. **DOCUMENT PREPARATION:** The Transfer/Deed shall, save for the Land Transfer Tax Affidavit, be prepared in registrable form at the expense of Seller, and any Charge/Mortgage to be given back by the Buyer to Seller at the expense of the Buyer. If requested by Buyer, Seller covenants that the Transfer/Deed to be delivered on completion shall contain the statements contemplated by Section 50(22) of the Planning Act, R.S.O.1990.

17. **RESIDENCY:** (a) Subject to (b) below, the Seller represents and warrants that the Seller is not and on completion will not be a non-resident under the non-residency provisions of the Income Tax Act which representation and warranty shall survive and not merge upon the completion of this transaction and the Seller shall deliver to the Buyer a statutory declaration that Seller is not then a non-resident of Canada; (b) provided that if the Seller is a non-resident under the non-residency provisions of the Income Tax Act, the Buyer shall be credited towards the Purchase Price with the amount, if any, necessary for Buyer to pay to the Minister of National Revenue to satisfy Buyer's liability in respect of tax payable by Seller under the non-residency provisions of the Income Tax Act by reason of this sale. Buyer shall not claim such credit if Seller delivers on completion the prescribed certificate.

18. **ADJUSTMENTS:** Any rents, mortgage interest, realty taxes including local improvement rates and unmetered public or private utility charges and unmetered cost of fuel, as applicable, shall be apportioned and allowed to the day of completion, the day of completion itself to be apportioned to Buyer.

19. **PROPERTY ASSESSMENT:** The Buyer and Seller hereby acknowledge that the Province of Ontario has implemented current value assessment and properties may be re-assessed on an annual basis. The Buyer and Seller agree that no claim will be made against the Buyer or Seller, or any Brokerage, Broker or Salesperson, for any changes in property tax as a result of a re-assessment of the property, save and except any property taxes that accrued prior to the completion of this transaction.

20. **TIME LIMITS:** Time shall in all respects be of the essence hereof provided that the time for doing or completing of any matter provided for herein may be extended or abridged by an agreement in writing signed by Seller and Buyer or by their respective lawyers who may be specifically authorized in that regard.

21. **TENDER:** Any tender of documents or money hereunder may be made upon Seller or Buyer or their respective lawyers on the day set for completion. Money shall be tendered with funds drawn on a lawyer's trust account in the form of a bank draft, certified cheque or wire transfer using the Large Value Transfer System.

22. **FAMILY LAW ACT:** Seller warrants that spousal consent is not necessary to this transaction under the provisions of the Family Law Act, R.S.O.1990 unless Seller's spouse has executed the consent hereinafter provided.

23. **UFFI:** Seller represents and warrants to Buyer that during the time Seller has owned the property, Seller has not caused any building on the property to be insulated with insulation containing ureaformaldehyde, and that to the best of Seller's knowledge no building on the property contains or has ever contained insulation that contains ureaformaldehyde. This warranty shall survive and not merge on the completion of this transaction, and if the building is part of a multiple unit building, this warranty shall only apply to that part of the building which is the subject of this transaction.

24. **LEGAL, ACCOUNTING AND ENVIRONMENTAL ADVICE:** The parties acknowledge that any information provided by the brokerage is not legal, tax or environmental advice.

25. **CONSUMER REPORTS: The Buyer is hereby notified that a consumer report containing credit and/or personal information may be referred to in connection with this transaction.**

26. **AGREEMENT IN WRITING:** If there is conflict or discrepancy between any provision added to this Agreement (including any Schedule attached hereto) and any provision in the standard pre-set portion hereof, the added provision shall supersede the standard pre-set provision to the extent of such conflict or discrepancy. This Agreement including any Schedule attached hereto, shall constitute the entire Agreement between Buyer and Seller. There is no representation, warranty, collateral agreement or condition, which affects this Agreement other than as expressed herein. For the purposes of this Agreement, Seller means vendor and Buyer means purchaser. This Agreement shall be read with all changes of gender or number required by the context.

27. **TIME AND DATE:** Any reference to a time and date in this Agreement shall mean the time and date where the property is located.

INITIALS OF BUYER(S): ⬭   INITIALS OF SELLER(S): ⬭

Form 100   Revised 2015   **Page 4 of 6**

28. SUCCESSORS AND ASSIGNS: The heirs, executors, administrators, successors and assigns of the undersigned are bound by the terms herein.

SIGNED, SEALED AND DELIVERED in the presence of: IN WITNESS whereof I have hereunto set my hand and seal:

....   ●   DATE ....
(Witness)   (Buyer)   (Seal)

....   ●   DATE ....
(Witness)   (Buyer)   (Seal)

I, the Undersigned Seller, agree to the above offer. I hereby irrevocably instruct my lawyer to pay directly to the brokerage(s) with whom I have agreed to pay commission, the unpaid balance of the commission together with applicable Harmonized Sales Tax (and any other taxes as may hereafter be applicable), from the proceeds of the sale prior to any payment to the undersigned on completion, as advised by the brokerage(s) to my lawyer.

SIGNED, SEALED AND DELIVERED in the presence of: IN WITNESS whereof I have hereunto set my hand and seal:

....   ●   DATE ....
(Witness)   (Seller)   (Seal)

....   ●   DATE ....
(Witness)   (Seller)   (Seal)

SPOUSAL CONSENT: The Undersigned Spouse of the Seller hereby consents to the disposition evidenced herein pursuant to the provisions of the Family Law Act, R.S.O.1990, and hereby agrees with the Buyer that he/she will execute all necessary or incidental documents to give full force and effect to the sale evidenced herein.

....   ●   DATE ....
(Witness)   (Spouse)   (Seal)

CONFIRMATION OF ACCEPTANCE: Notwithstanding anything contained herein to the contrary, I confirm this Agreement with all changes both typed and written was finally accepted by all parties at .... a.m./p.m. this .... day of..., 20...........

....
(Signature of Seller or Buyer)

INFORMATION ON BROKERAGE(S)

Listing Brokerage .... Tel.No.(...............)................................

....
(Salesperson / Broker Name)

Co-op/Buyer Brokerage .... Tel.No.(...............)................................

....
(Salesperson / Broker Name)

ACKNOWLEDGEMENT

I acknowledge receipt of my signed copy of this accepted Agreement of Purchase and Sale and I authorize the Brokerage to forward a copy to my lawyer.	I acknowledge receipt of my signed copy of this accepted Agreement of Purchase and Sale and I authorize the Brokerage to forward a copy to my lawyer.
.... DATE .... (Seller)	.... DATE .... (Buyer)
.... DATE .... (Seller)	.... DATE .... (Buyer)
Address for Service	Address for Service ....
.... Tel.No.(...........)........................	.... Tel.No.(...........)........................
Seller's Lawyer	Buyer's Lawyer ....
Address	Address ....
Email	Email ....
(...........)................ (........)............... Tel.No. FAX No.	(...........)................ (........)............... Tel.No. FAX No.

FOR OFFICE USE ONLY   **COMMISSION TRUST AGREEMENT**

To: Co-operating Brokerage shown on the foregoing Agreement of Purchase and Sale:
In consideration for the Co-operating Brokerage procuring the foregoing Agreement of Purchase and Sale, I hereby declare that all moneys received or receivable by me in connection with the Transaction as contemplated in the MLS® Rules and Regulations of my Real Estate Board shall be receivable and held in trust. This agreement shall constitute a Commission Trust Agreement as defined in the MLS® Rules and shall be subject to and governed by the MLS® Rules pertaining to Commission Trust.

DATED as of the date and time of the acceptance of the foregoing Agreement of Purchase and Sale.   Acknowledged by:

....
(Authorized to bind the Listing Brokerage)   (Authorized to bind the Co-operating Brokerage)

Form 100   Revised 2015   **Page 5 of 6**

Exercise 3   Agreement of Purchase and Sale—Page 6 of 6

 **Ontario Real Estate Association**

Form 100
for use in the Province of Ontario

Schedule A
Agreement of Purchase and Sale

This Schedule is attached to and forms part of the Agreement of Purchase and Sale between:

BUYER, ..., and

SELLER, ...

for the purchase and sale of ....

.... dated the .... day of ...., 20...............

Buyer agrees to pay the balance as follows:

This form must be initialed by all parties to the Agreement of Purchase and Sale.

INITIALS OF BUYER(S):   **INITIALS OF SELLER(S):**

Form 100   Revised 2015   **Page 6 of 6**

CHAPTER 6

New Homes

Introduction

New homes pose distinct challenges for registrants. Frequently, on-site model home attendance is required to market house styles, floor plans and amenities. Knowledge of specifications, features and options is essential. While detailed new home technical skills go beyond this initial course, all real estate salespeople should possess a general appreciation for the new house market, and the processes associated with new home construction such as obtaining a building permit, compliance with zoning requirements, construction standards and financing considerations.

In this chapter, Tarion Warranty Corporation coverages and procedures are detailed including one, two and seven year warranty protection, exclusions to coverage, deposit protection, and procedures regarding delays and substitutions. Related documents, when taking possession of a new home, are also described, along with customer service standards and performance guidelines when submitting warranty requests.

No standard new home agreement presently exists. The *Agreement of Purchase and Sale* (OREA Form 100) can be adapted but registrants should seek advice from the broker of record or manager.

Learning Outcomes

At the conclusion of this chapter, students will be able to:

- Outline the salesperson's role in marketing new homes, including establishing builder relationships and acquiring adequate product knowledge.
- Describe the application process and required documentation involved in obtaining a building permit.
- Briefly outline the building inspection procedure, zoning compliance requirements, construction standards for new homes and construction loans for new homes (including condominiums).
- Identify major warranty coverages provided for new homes by the Tarion Warranty Corporation.
- Outline selected warranty provisions regarding deposit protection, important coverage exclusions, and procedures in the event of delays and substitutions.
- Outline procedures regarding possession of a new home and associated documentation, including the warranty certificate and pre-delivery inspection form.
- Detail clauses, schedules and statements required to adapt the resale *Agreement of Purchase and Sale* (OREA Form 100) when drafting an offer for a new house.

NEW HOME MARKET

The new home market is a major sector of the Ontario economy. For example, the Greater Toronto Home Builders' Association (now renamed the Building Industry and Land Development Association) reported in 2003 that the employment of nearly 240,000 people was directly attributable to the residential construction industry. One new home created the equivalent of 2.8 jobs for a full year. This expanding market offers many opportunities for those seeking a market niche beyond traditional resale activities.

The Salesperson's Role

The salesperson's role is difficult to precisely describe, as new home sales activities range from individual custom-built residences to multiple model home, mega-subdivision sites. The latest technologies have further complicated the picture. Today's advanced housing development can include an on-site, all season building facility where homes are constructed within a temperature-controlled plant and transported to the nearby chosen lot.

Given such diversity, new home salespeople's duties range from detailed interaction with the custom builder to model home representatives working with professional brochures, sales office hours, front elevation pictures, optional floor plans, builder's samples, upgrades, incentives, development phases, base prices, prepackaged financing, sequential deposits and standard schedules.

Builder Relationships

Relationships between real estate brokerages and builders can vary from signed exclusive authorities to informal registration procedures (notification that a prospect has been introduced and a commission owed if a sale occurs).

In exclusive relationships, brokerage involvement can range from traditional marketing (e.g., brokerage advertising and open houses) to on-site contracted services where the builder's image and marketing strategy dominates. Such contracts typically set out responsibilities, cost sharing arrangements, model home staffing, reporting procedures (e.g., feedback and sales tracking) and customer service standards.

Prospect registration systems require completion of a form when a salesperson introduces a prospective buyer at the sales centre. Typically, builder advertisements clearly state *Brokers Protected*. Such arrangements usually set out a commission for introducing the prospect, assuming a successful closing.

FORMALIZED ARRANGEMENTS

In recent years, more formalized arrangements have been established between builders and real estate boards. For example, selected builder associations and real estate boards are strengthening ties through co-operation agreements. Board members may register a prospect prior to that individual's first visit to a sales centre of any builder within that building association.

Exact terms will vary, but typically the member must continue to be involved in the selling process and be present when the agreement is signed (unless other arrangements are made). The builder's sales staff co-operate fully by showing the home, answering questions and preparing appropriate builder forms during the negotiating process.

The registration is documented and valid for a specified period; e.g., 60 days, but can be renewed. During that period, the salesperson is protected against a direct sale by the builder to the registered prospect at the specified sales centre location.

REMINDER   Builders may employ salaried staff not registered under REBBA 2002 to handle sales activity involving their owned new home inventory. (See full-time salaried employee exemption under REBBA, Sec. 5(f).)

Marketing A New Home Development   **PERSPECTIVE**

ABC Realty Inc. just landed a new home contract in Meadowland Springs—a new upscale 700-home subdivision planned for suburban Anycity. Meadowland Springs brings the latest housing innovations, energy efficiency standards, design elements and construction techniques to prospective buyers. ABC Realty Inc. will be handling all sales for the builder. The sales centre (ultimately including five model homes) is now under construction. Broker Hobson shared some insight into what the contract contains. ABC is required to:

- Establish a MeadowLand Springs sales team including recruiting, training and managing registered salespeople in accordance with REBBA 2002, and enforcing quality control standards established by the builder.

- Provide regular ongoing training regarding Meadowland Springs models, elevations, alternate floor plans, basic prices, builder-included finishings, upgrade options/costs, allowances, Tarion warranty provisions, procedures in the event of construction delays and adjustments/closing costs.

- Fully explain all sales documentation to buyers and draft clear, concise purchase agreements, including schedules.

- Assist on a cost-sharing basis in all signage, promotional materials and media advertising.

- Staff the builder-constructed Sales Centre on the following timetable: Mon. through Thurs.—12 Noon to 8 p.m.; Fridays—12 Noon to 6 p.m. and Sat., Sun. & Holidays 11 a.m. to 6 p.m.

- Assist the builder as necessary in creating and modifying the competitive strategy within the local marketplace through the use of market data, customer feedback, demographic prospect profiles and other relevant information as required by the builder.

- Assist the builder in selecting appropriate advertising media (e.g., billboards, signage, flyers, television, radio, newspaper and web site) and evaluating effectiveness in relation to targeted audiences.

- Maintain all sales documents in strict accordance with REBBA 2002 and provide monthly summary reports of all pending sale transactions to the builder.

- Ensure the proper tracking of all sales centre activities; e.g., expense status reports, market reports, staffing reports, customer feedback and traffic reports.

Product Knowledge

Salespersons contemplating new home sales should start with consumer basics. Visit model homes, review promotional packages including floor plans, specification sheets, financing arrangements, prices, options and deposit requirements. Find out what type of contracts are used, time-lines for home completions, subdivision requirements and/or restrictions impacting house construction (i.e., architectural controls), and features that set developments apart from each other.

Develop a keen eye for quality construction and finishes. Scrutinize layouts and design features that maximize living space. Discover what brand name products are provided and what new innovations, energy efficient systems and hi-tech features are either packaged or optional as upgrades. Carefully assess what design flexibility exists to modify house plans to meet individual consumer needs.

Look beyond the house and lot. What will be built nearby? What future plans will impact the development in terms of traffic, access, allocation for green space and recreational areas. Remember, buyers not only purchase a home, but also a community. Get specifics about shopping malls, schools, child care, places of worship and public transportation. Being well informed is the first step in building a successful new home sales career. Do your homework.

NEW HOME CONSTRUCTION

New home construction begins with application for a building permit. The granting of this permit is subject to zoning compliance and documented assurances that construction standards will be rigidly maintained in accordance with the Ontario Building Code. Students can review structural components in residential construction, as well as details regarding the planning process, subdividing of land, land severances and general building code standards in *Land, Structures and Real Estate Trading*.

This topic expands the discussion in terms of specifics about building permits, the application process, zoning requirements, construction standards and new construction financing, including the use of holdbacks in relation to the *Construction Lien Act*.

Building Permit

An individual contemplating new home construction must obtain a building permit from the local municipality. A building permit application is required in order for municipal staff to ensure that planned construction meets the Ontario Building Code, zoning provisions for the land in question, any site control provisions that may apply and other special requirements; e.g., property located within a flood prone area regulated by the local conservation authority.

APPLICATION/DOCUMENTATION

Building permit applications submitted to municipalities must use the provincial building permit application, which cannot be altered (other than converting it into electronic format). However, a municipality may require additional documents, specifications and plans in line with municipal building by-laws. Documentation accompanying a building permit application typically includes:

- architectural drawings, drawn to an acceptable scale (e.g., 1 :50 metric scale (¼ inch equals 1 foot));
- floor plan layout and foundation/basement layout. The floor plan layout typically includes house layout, a foundation/basement plan, a framing plan for each floor and a roof framing plan;
- elevations for front, sides and rear of structure;
- detailed cross sections of the structure. Cross sections depict building components concealed in walls, floors and ceilings;
- site plan showing location of structure, setbacks, easements/rights-of-way, landscaping and hard surfaces (e.g., driveways);
- heating, ventilation and air conditioning drawings. These drawings also typically require heat loss/heat gain calculations and duct calculations to ensure proper sizing and adequate heating/ventilation, including furnace capacity; and
- the applicable building permit fee for the specific municipality.

NOTE: Special requirements including appropriate qualifications apply when a designer is involved in preparing the house design. Check with the local municipality.

For convenience, larger municipalities may provide online secure access to track the process from initial application to permit issuance.

BUILDING CODE: INSPECTION PROCEDURE

The municipality will require that construction start within a specified time following building permit issuance. The permit must be posted on the site and drawings related to the project must be maintained on the site at all times. The individual building the structure must notify the building inspection department at specified points during construction; e.g., completion of footings, backfill of foundation, outside services, plumbing rough-in, framing, insulation and so forth.

A building inspector can enter on the land and inspect the structure at any reasonable time. If deficiencies are noted and not corrected, a stop order may be issued. An occupancy permit is issued once all inspections are completed and Ontario Building Code requirements are met.

OTHER INSPECTIONS

Inspection requirements, over and above the Ontario Building Code, can vary based on municipal requirements and specific housing features. The following are illustrative only. Check with the local municipality.

Site Plan Control	If the property is subject to site plan control, then additional inspections will typically be required for grading, sodding and landscaping.
	NOTE: Grading inspection is normally required even when the property is not subject to site plan control. The inspection may also involve trees if the municipality has a tree by-law.
Electrical Inspection	The Electrical Safety Authority will require an inspection. An appropriate residential application must be completed containing applicant and site information.
Gas Inspection	Installations of gas equipment and appliances also require an appropriate inspection.

Zoning Requirements

A building permit will not be issued unless an applicant complies with all zoning regulations. If the applicant cannot meet one or more zoning by-law requirements, he or she may make separate application to the Committee of Adjustment. The Committee of Adjustment is authorized under the *Planning Act* to grant minor variances. The decision for such a variance is based on the merits of each application. In granting a minor variance, the zoning regulation for that specific property is amended.

Construction Standards

New homes must be constructed in accordance with the Ontario Building Code. Part 9 of the Code applies to residential occupancies in which the structure has area greater than ten square metres (108 square feet), does not exceed 600 square metres (6,460 square feet) and is 3 storeys or less in building height. Part 3 applies to business and personal services occupancies, mercantile occupancies, and medium and low hazard industrial occupancies that meet the above criteria. Larger structures (i.e., those exceeding three storeys in building height and 600 square metres in building size) must comply with Parts 3, 4, 5 and 6.

Part 9 of the Code sets out detailed requirements regarding materials, systems and equipment. Only selected requirements are highlighted:

- Structural requirements regarding floor loads, allowable deflections and foundation conditions.
- Area/space design for interior rooms and hallways, along with ceiling heights.
- Required doors, doorway sizes, external doors and use of glass.
- Stairs, ramps, handrails and guards.
- Means of egress and fire protection.
- Excavation, damp-proofing and drainage including specifications for footings, foundations, columns and crawl spaces.
- Masonry including chimneys, flues and fireplaces.
- Wood framing, flooring, interior finishes, roofing and exterior cladding.
- Electrical, plumbing and heating systems.

Construction Loans (New Homes)

A construction loan is a mortgage typically involving sequential advances by the lender to the borrower during pre-determined stages of construction. The timing and amounts of mortgage advances for new home construction will vary depending upon the lender's policies. A five-stage schedule is illustrated, but many variations exist in the marketplace.

FIRST DRAW 15%	SECOND DRAW 20%	THIRD DRAW 20%	FOURTH DRAW 25%	FIFTH DRAW 20%
Primary excavation, lot grading and construction of foundation.	Concrete block wall complete, trusses placed and roof sheathed.	Rough plumbing, electrical and mechanical, and installation of windows and doors.	Drywall, trim and painting completed.	Installation of all equipment, landscaping, utility connections and appropriate occupancy permits.

STAGE OF CONSTRUCTION

Some lenders operate with as few as three draws (advances). Inspections are normally necessary at each draw and holdbacks are usually required.

EXAMPLE   *New Home Construction Loan*

Smith is building a new home on his existing lot and has arranged a $100,000 conventional mortgage with a local lender. The lender requires that advances be made at three points during construction. The first draw (33.333%) can be taken when the primary excavation and full basement are completed, the trusses placed and the roof sheathed. The next 33.333% draw occurs when all rough plumbing, electrical and mechanical items are installed, doors and windows are in place, and drywall and trim completed. The final draw of 33.333% occurs upon completion of the house and receipt of appropriate municipal approvals and occupancy permit. With each draw, an amount equal to 10% of the draw is withheld in recognition of the applicable provincial construction (lien) act. This holdback is released following the expiration of rights for claims under that act. Therefore, Smith will receive the following amounts during construction:

Total Amount of Mortgage	$100,000
First Advance (33.3% of $90,000)	−30,000
Second Advance (33.3% of $90,000)	−30,000
Third Advance (33.3% of $90,000)	−30,000
Total Holdback (10%)	**$10,000**

SECTION I   A CLOSER LOOK AT TRADING DIFFERENT TYPES OF PROPERTIES

Construction Loans (New Condominiums)

Construction loans for condominiums are typically viewed from two perspectives: the blanket mortgage and the unit mortgage. A blanket mortgage is registered during project development with loan advances provided coincident with progressive stages of construction. This mortgage is then typically fractured or splintered into individual mortgages that can be assumed by buyers at the point of completion and final registration. The fracturing or splintering process creates unit mortgages and, at the same time, provides partial releases for the builder as individual units are registered to buyers. Unit owners receive marketable title, are then assessed individually for taxes, become responsible for mortgage payments and are required to remit their proportionate share of common expenses.

Construction Liens and Holdbacks

A construction lien can be filed in the land registry office against a property by a person or corporation for labour, services or materials supplied. Formerly referred to as a mechanic's lien under the *Mechanics' Lien Act*, such claims now fall under the *Construction Lien Act*. The claim for a construction lien must be registered in the land registration office, must be verified by affidavit and the owner must be notified regarding the claim. Liens must be registered within 45 days of specified events set out in the Act.

A summary of major provisions concerning basic and finishing holdbacks is provided as holdbacks can impact real estate registrants, particularly in the listing and selling of new homes. A contract, for purposes of this Act, includes any amendments and a contractor refers to a person who is contracted or employed directly by the owner, or an agent of the owner, to supply services or materials to an improvement. The legislation also covers subcontracts; i.e., any agreement between the contractor and a subcontractor or between two or more subcontractors relating to the supply of services or materials.

BASIC HOLDBACK

The *Construction Lien Act* provides for two different types of holdbacks: basic and finishing. Under the basic holdback, the Act states that 10% of the price of all services and materials provided under a contract or a subcontract be withheld by the owner. This amount is retained until the period for all liens that can be claimed under the Act has expired; i.e., up to and including the point of substantial completion. Substantial completion is defined as the point when the improvement being made pursuant to a contract, or a substantial portion thereof, is ready for use or is being used for the purposes for which it was intended.

EXAMPLE   *Basic Holdback: New Home*

Smith is having a new home built. The detached home costs $240,000 and Smith has agreed to pay the contractor with three equal payments, less the basic holdback of 10%. Accordingly, the three payments are $72,000 each (80,000–8,000), to be paid successively starting with the completion of the foundation, then the framing and roof and finally the interior finishing. Smith will withhold the $8,000 amount at each stage until the periods for all liens that can be claimed under the *Construction Lien Act* have expired.

FINISHING HOLDBACK

A holdback under the *Construction Lien Act* involves a circumstance in which a contract has been certified or declared to be substantially performed, but various services or materials are required to complete that particular contract. The payer, under the contract or a subcontract, can retain a separate holdback of 10% of the price of the remaining services or materials until all liens that may be claimed against the holdback have expired, been satisfied, are discharged or otherwise provided for under the Act. If a notice of lien is received, the payer may also retain an additional amount, sufficient to satisfy that lien.

> **EXAMPLE**   *Finishing Holdback: Addition*
>
> Smith is having an addition constructed on the rear elevation of his recently-purchased home. The total contract price for this new main floor family room with a full basement is $87,500. At the point of substantial completion, several small unfinished items remain (eavestrough and fascia), owing to back order problems. These items amount to $3,000. Accordingly, Smith withholds $300 as a finishing holdback against the final $3,000 payment in the event that a lien arises (pursuant to time limits as set out in the Act) following the completion of this unfinished work.

NEW HOME WARRANTY

Overview

The Tarion Warranty Corporation, a not-for-profit corporation, administers warranty coverage for most new homes in the province, pursuant to provisions set out in the *Ontario New Home Warranties Plan Act*. Warranty provisions can impact new homes, as well as existing housing stock to which coverage still applies. Primary warranty coverage is broken down into one, two and seven-year segments. New home buyers also obtain protection relating to deposits, delayed closings and substitutions. However, it is important to note that not all new homes and not all damages are covered.

All builders and sellers must be registered to sell new homes (including condominiums) in Ontario. Each home must be enrolled prior to construction. Builders and sellers enroll new homes by submitting enrollment forms, along with prescribed fees. Tarion provides a pre-printed Certificate of Completion and Possession (along with an attached Warranty Certificate), which is fully completed at point of buyer possession and pre-delivery inspection.

Salespersons should ask the builder/seller for its registration number and the home's enrollment number. If the seller and builder are different (often found in condominium properties), obtain registration numbers for both. Warranty coverage remains with the home to the end of the warranty period. Coverage information is available on the Tarion sticker located on the electrical panel, the Warranty Certificate or by contacting Tarion directly. An ONHWP (Ontario New Home Warranty Program) sticker may be found representing warranties that were placed before the name change to Tarion Warranty Corporation.

Ontario New Home Warranties Plan Act

This Act governs most new home construction. Anyone building or selling new homes must be registered, enroll the homes and provide certain warranties as detailed later under this topic. Selling in this context does not refer to a real estate brokerage selling property on behalf of an owner. All new homes must be enrolled in the program, but there are exemptions.

The *Ontario New Home Warranties Plan Act (ONHWPA, R.S.O. 1990, c. O.31. Sec.1)* defines vendor as *any person who sells on his, her, or its own behalf a home not previously occupied to an owner and includes a builder who constructs a home under a contract with the owner.* Home, according to the Act, is defined as:

- *A self-contained single-family dwelling, either detached or attached by a common wall to one or more others.*
- *A building consisting of two self-contained one-family dwellings under single ownership.*
- *A condominium unit, including the common elements.*
- *Any dwelling that meets the definition of a home according to Regulations under the Act, and includes additional structures or appurtenances relating to the home.*

Basically, the warranty provided requires every vendor to warrant that a home is constructed in a workmanlike manner, free from defects in material, fit for habitation, constructed in accordance with the Ontario Building Code, free of major structural defects and subject to any other warranties as prescribed by the Regulations. Selective features of the plan concerning residential homes are provided for illustration purposes. The Act should be read in its entirety concerning all warranty and procedural matters. Additional provisions apply to condominium properties.

Tarion Warranty Corporation

Tarion Warranty Corporation (previously known as the Ontario New Home Warranty Program) is a private corporation established in 1976 that administers the *Ontario New Home Warranties Plan Act.* This legislation outlines warranty coverage for new homes and condominiums (subject to selected exclusions) in the Province of Ontario. The corporation regulates the new home building industry and is funded entirely by builder registration, renewal and home enrollment fees.

Tarion ensures that homeowners receive the warranty coverage that is provided under the Act (usually referred to as statutory warranty coverage). Further, the corporation is responsible for ensuring that builders meet minimum service standards when fixing or otherwise resolving warranted items under the statutory warranty coverage.

Real estate registrants involved in the marketing and sale of new homes require detailed warranty information offered through Tarion. Information in this publication is summary only and intended as a general education guide only. Brokerages, brokers and salespersons must obtain current information by contacting the Tarion Warranty Corporation.

WEB LINKS

Tarion Warranty Corporation   Go to the Tarion Warranty Corporation website (*www.tarion.com*) for current information regarding warranty coverages and related details. The site provides extensive information for consumers.

Warranty Protection

The total coverage available on each home or condominium unit is capped at $300,000. A maximum of $15,000 applies to warranted damage that involves environmentally harmful substances. Claims involving septic systems are subject to a $25,000 limit. Lastly, condominium common elements are covered for a total of $50,000 times the number of units, to a maximum of $2.5 million.

Several types of warranties exist with differing warranty periods. The program includes three warranties with specific coverages for one, two and seven year periods. Each warranty period begins on the date of possession, except for the warranty on a condominium's common elements, which begins on the registration of the condominium declaration and description.

Homeowners and condominium corporations must use the applicable statutory warranty forms during the warranty period. Forms include a 30-Day Form (used during the first 30 days of possession), a Year-End form relating to outstanding warranty items, a Second-Year Form regarding outstanding warranty items in the two-year warranty period and the Major Structural Defect Form during the third year and no later than the seventh year of possession.

Builders will pass on to the buyer any warranties given by manufacturers, suppliers and subcontractors that extend beyond the first year. In these cases, the buyer should make any claims directly to the manufacturer or distributor.

ONE-YEAR WARRANTY PROTECTION

The builder warrants for one year from the date of possession that the home is free from defects in workmanship and materials, is fit to live in, meets the Ontario Building Code requirements and has no major structural defects (see additional discussion under the sub-topic *Seven Year Warranty*).

TWO-YEAR WARRANTY PROTECTION

The two-year warranty covers such items as:

- Water seepage through the basement or foundation walls. (In condominiums, this protection includes all below-ground areas such as parking garages.)
- Defects in materials and work, including caulking windows and doors so that the building envelope prevents water penetration.
- Defects in materials and work in the electrical, plumbing and heating delivery/distribution systems.
- Defects in materials and work that result in the detachment, displacement or deterioration of exterior cladding, leading to detachment or serious deterioration.
- Ontario Building Code violations in relation to health and safety provisions.
- Major structural defects (see additional discussion under the sub-topic *Seven Year Warranty*).

SEVEN-YEAR WARRANTY PROTECTION

The seven-year warranty covers major structural defects as defined in the *Ontario New Home Warranties Plan Act* as:

- any defect in materials or work that results in the failure of a load-bearing part of the home's structure; or
- any defect in materials or work that significantly and adversely affects the buyer's use of the building as a home.

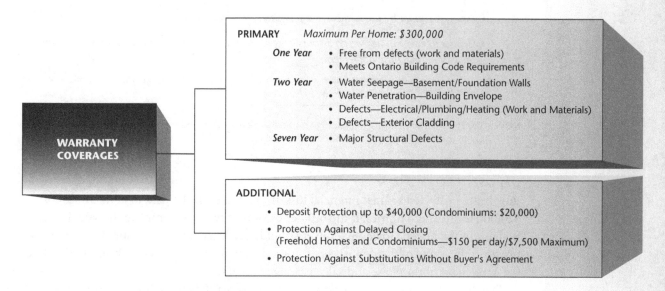

WARRANTY COVERAGES

PRIMARY   *Maximum Per Home: $300,000*

One Year
- Free from defects (work and materials)
- Meets Ontario Building Code Requirements

Two Year
- Water Seepage—Basement/Foundation Walls
- Water Penetration—Building Envelope
- Defects—Electrical/Plumbing/Heating (Work and Materials)
- Defects—Exterior Cladding

Seven Year
- Major Structural Defects

ADDITIONAL
- Deposit Protection up to $40,000 (Condominiums: $20,000)
- Protection Against Delayed Closing (Freehold Homes and Condominiums—$150 per day/$7,500 Maximum)
- Protection Against Substitutions Without Buyer's Agreement

WARRANTY COVERAGE—EXCLUSIONS

Real estate registrants should be aware of important exclusions relating to the statutory warranty coverage. The following has been reprinted from the Tarion Warranty Corporation publication titled *Homeowner Information Package: A Guide to Your New Home Warranty* to ensure that this information is accurately and fully conveyed.

The following conditions and/or items are not covered by the statutory warranty:

- *Damage resulting from improper maintenance, such as dampness or condensation caused by the homeowner's failure to maintain proper ventilation levels or improper operation of a humidifier, hot tub or any other moisture producing device.*

- *Alterations, deletions or additions made by the homeowner (such as changes to the direction of the grading or the slope of the ground away from the house).*

- *Defects in materials, design and work supplied or installed by the homeowner/purchaser.*

- *Secondary damage caused by defects under warranty. While the defects themselves are covered, the personal or property damage they cause is not. However, your homeowner insurance may cover secondary damage.*

- *Normal wear and tear, such as scuffs and scratches to floor and wall surfaces caused by homeowners moving, decorating and/or day-to-day use of the home.*

- *Normal shrinkage of materials that dry out after construction (such as nail "pops" or minor concrete cracking).*

continued...

- *Settling soil around the house or along utility lines.*

- *Damage from floods, "acts of God", wars, riots or vandalism.*

- *Damage from insects or rodents, unless it is the result of construction that does not meet the Ontario Building Code.*

- *Damage caused by municipal services or other utilities.*

- *Surface defects in work and materials noted and accepted in writing by the homeowner at the time of possession.*

- *Damage caused by the homeowner or visitors.*

- *Contractual warranties which lie outside the Act. You may have recourse for these warranties under your purchase agreement.*

Source: *Homeowner Information Package: A Guide to Your New Home Warranty (For all homes with a date of possession on or after September 1, 2005), August 2005.*

NOTE: The Homeowner Information Package is updated periodically by the Tarion Warranty Corporation. Go to *www.tarion.com* to access the latest version.

DEPOSIT PROTECTION

Buyers are protected against financial loss, limited to their deposit, to a maximum of $40,000 for freehold homes, if the builder cannot or will not complete the sale through no fault of the buyer. However, a buyer should seek legal advice to ensure that he or she is within the scope of the deposit protection; i.e., that the buyer is legally entitled to treat the agreement of purchase and sale as being at an end.

The deposit protection for condominium units is $20,000, as buyers are covered for deposits above that amount by excess deposit insurance provisions of the *Condominium Act.*

CONFIRMING COVERAGE

NEW HOMES	RESALE HOMES
Registrants should ask the builder for its registration number and the home's enrollment number. Condominiums should have an enrollment number for each unit, as well as a number for the common elements. The Act prohibits a builder from contracting out of the warranties. In addition, the Addendum under the Act, which limits the builder's right to extend closing (excluding condominium units), prevails over any conflicting provision in the agreement of purchase and sale. Registrants should be aware of these restrictions when preparing offers.	When a home changes owners, the warranty stays with the home up to the end of the warranty period. Thus, a subsequent buyer may inherit any remaining warranties. Real estate registrants should check details of the original purchase (e.g., name of builder, enrollment number and warranty start date) to determine whether statutory warranty coverage remains for a resale home. This information is available on the Tarion sticker on the electrical panel, the Warranty Certificate or by contacting the Tarion Warranty Corporation.

Excluded Properties

Real estate registrants should be familiar with various property exclusions under the *Ontario New Home Warranty Plan Act.* The following list has been developed for illustration purposes and is not exhaustive.

- Temporary or seasonal homes; e.g., cottages not built on permanent foundations and not insulated sufficiently to enable year-round living.
- Homes built on existing footings/foundations or otherwise converted, such as a converted industrial building registered as a residential condominium.
- Homes that have been lived in or rented, prior to the sale to the original owner. This would include converted residential rental buildings registered as residential condominiums.
- Residential properties held for investment purposes by limited partnerships in which investors purchase interests or units. The purchase of a partnership interest does not fall under the definition of a home.
- Homes in which the contractor only erects the shell and the owner completes/finishes the interior work.
- An owner owning a vacant lot and contracting the building of a home through subcontractors, as the owner is not deemed to be a builder. (See additional discussion below under *Caution: Contract or Custom Built Homes.*)
- As a general guideline, homes purchased from a trustee or receiver do not have coverage, but as with all exclusions, Tarion should be contacted directly for guidance.

Registrants should be aware that a new home or condominium purchased for rental purposes is covered, as the new owner is not required to occupy the home. Purchasers considering new residential properties not covered by ONHWP may wish to pursue private contractual warranties. Alternatively, contractors may furnish such warranties; e.g., large-scale building conversion projects.

Contract or Custom Built Homes	CAUTION

Coverage on contract or custom built homes will generally depend on the particular circumstances:

- The home *is covered* if a consumer hires one contractor to build a custom home from foundation to finish.
- The home *is not covered* if a consumer hires more than one contractor to build various parts of the home.

A consumer should seek legal advice and contact Tarion Warranty Corporation regarding coverage on contract or custom built homes prior to entering into a formal contract with the builder.

Delayed Closing

Tarion Warranty Corporation recently amended warranty provisions concerning delayed closing for both new freehold homes and new condominiums. A statement relating to the delayed closing warranty must be attached to all agreements of purchase and sale for new houses. Builders are required to provide a specific closing date and inform the buyer whether the date is firm or tentative. Four separate statements have been developed depending on whether the agreement is freehold (firm or tentative) or condominium (firm or tentative).

A copy of the freehold statement for a firm closing date is illustrated later in this chapter. Applicable delayed closing procedures are included in each form.

Substitutions

The buyer is protected against substitutions of items of construction or finishings as set out in the agreement of purchase and sale. The builder can substitute any items not specifically selected but included in the agreement of purchase and sale (e.g., items listed in a standard features sheet), but only with items of equal or better quality.

The agreement of purchase and sale may also give the buyer the right to make selections of certain features, such as style and colour of kitchen cabinets. Examples include:

- interior and exterior paint colours (not shadings);
- design and colour of cabinets and counter tops;
- colour and type of kitchen and bath fixtures;
- floor finishes; and
- style of interior trim.

If the builder cannot supply the buyer's choice of colour or finish, he/she must notify the buyer in writing and give him/her the opportunity to make a new selection. If the buyer does not make a new selection within seven days of the notice, the builder has the right to substitute options of equal or better quality. If the builder fails to give notice, he/she cannot substitute these chosen items without the buyer's consent. If this occurs, the buyer can require the builder to change the item back to the original selection or a cash settlement can be reached with the builder.

Most new home agreements of purchase and sale allow the builder to modify certain design features, such as reversing house plans or changing the home's elevation. Such changes are not covered under the Act.

Warranty Certificate/Pre-Delivery Inspection

New home buyers taking possession of homes after October 1, 2003 encounter two important documents. The Certificate of Completion and Possession (CCP)/Warranty Certificate marks the official date of possession and establishes when the warranty coverage starts. The builder and buyer must complete the CCP/Warranty Certificate on or before possession.

The CCP is completed coincident with the Pre-Delivery Inspection (PDI) form. The PDI form affords the buyer the opportunity to describe incomplete, damaged, missing or non-operational items within and outside the home. Tarion provides a standard PDI form, however, builders may use their own forms provided advance approval is obtained.

The buyer must be thorough and precise when completing the inspection and take the necessary time to fully review the new home. Buyers do not automatically lose coverage when a problem is not itemized, as some items might be overlooked or not readily apparent during the pre-delivery inspection.

During the walk-through, the builder will remove the warranty sticker from the CCP form and place it on the electrical panel. This sticker contains registration information and enrollment numbers.

The buyer of a condominium unit completes a CCP/Warranty Certificate at interim occupancy, which establishes the warranty start date for that particular unit. Once the condominium corporation is registered, the builder and condominium corporation sign a separate CCP/Warranty Certificate for the common elements and this establishes the start date for the common elements.

Builders must forward copies of the completed CCP, PDI form and Confirmation of Receipt for the Homeowner Information Package to Tarion no later than 15 days following the possession date.

Customer Service Standard

All homes with a possession date on or after October 1, 2003 are subject to the Customer Service Standard. The Standard was introduced for consistency in providing homeowners and builders with warranty program specifics. The Standard consists of four parts:

PART A
HOMEOWNER INFORMATION PACKAGE

Builders must provide a homeowner information package on or before the pre-delivery inspection date. This information package details warranty rights of the new home purchaser. A provision must be included in every purchase agreement that this package is available and will be delivered to the buyer at, or before, the pre-delivery inspection.

PART B
PRE-DELIVERY INSPECTION (PDI)

Builders must conduct a pre-delivery inspection of the home with the buyer (or his/her designee), complete a Certificate of Completion and Possession/Warranty Certificate (see previous description) and complete a PDI Form which outlines deficiencies at time of possession. A provision must be included in every purchase agreement that the parties agree to meet on or before possession to conduct a PDI.

PART C
WARRANTY SERVICE RULES

This part details warranty rules concerning how buyers request warranty service, time frames for builder response and Tarion involvement in the process.

PART D
WARRANTY REVIEW: BUILDER-REQUESTED CONCILIATION

This part outlines procedures when a builder-originated request is received by Tarion regarding a warranty dispute between a homeowner and the builder.

Warranty Requests

The Ontario New Home Warranty Program has detailed procedures for handling warranty issues. Registrants are not typically involved in such matters and should direct any questions to the Tarion Warranty Corporation. Fortunately, all buyers receive a *Homeowner Information Package* offering detailed information about the warranty coverage and how warranty service requests are made.

PERFORMANCE GUIDELINES

Tarion Warranty Corporation provides Construction Performance Guidelines to assist homeowners in understanding how various disputed items will be resolved. The guidelines are built on historical claims data setting out various problem areas; e.g., cracks in basement floors, leaky basements and what specific items are either covered or not. Visit the Tarion website at **www.tarion.com**.

DRAFTING A NEW HOME AGREEMENT

Agreement of Purchase and Sale (OREA Form 100)

A standardized new home agreement is not currently available in Ontario. The *Agreement of Purchase and Sale* (OREA Form 100) can be adapted for new homes. However, registrants are cautioned that its use is intended for resale properties. If the form is being used for a new home purchase, the registrant should seek guidance from the broker of record or manager regarding appropriate clauses, amendments to pre-printed wordings and relevant schedules. The Ontario Real Estate Association has developed selected clauses to assist in the process.

SCENARIO

Buyer Purchasing New Home

A buyer is submitting an offer using the *Agreement of Purchase and Sale* (OREA Form 100). The salesperson has consulted with the broker of record. The broker of record provides several recommendations to the salesperson, including the need for selected clauses and schedules.

CLAUSES

NEW–1   Builder Registered

The Seller represents and warrants, to the best of the Seller's knowledge and belief, that the said home and its builder are both registered under the Ontario New Home Warranty Program. The Parties agree that this representation and warranty shall form an integral part of this Agreement and survive the completion of this transaction. Documents attesting to these registrations are attached as Schedule "__" and form part of this Agreement of Purchase and Sale.

NEW–2   Completion of Construction

The Seller agrees to complete the house, the (itemize any other structures), and grounds in a good and workmanlike manner, in accordance with all the specifications outlined in Schedule "__" attached hereto and forming part of this Agreement of Purchase and Sale.

NEW–3   HST—New Homes

The Buyer and the Seller acknowledge and agree that the HST payable in connection with the purchase and sale transaction contemplated by this Agreement of Purchase and Sale is included in the purchase price subject to the provisions hereinafter set out.

Notwithstanding that the purchase price payable by the Buyer includes HST, the Buyer hereby assigns and transfers to the Seller all of the Buyer's rights, title and interest in any rebates, refunds or credits available, including Federal Sales Tax rebates and HST rebates to which the Buyer is entitled in connection with the payment of HST payable on the transfer to the Buyer of ownership or possession of the property. The Buyer further appoints and authorizes the Seller or the Seller's agents to be the Buyer's authorized representative and attorney for the purposes of applying for and collecting such tax rebates. The Buyer agrees to execute, at no cost to the Seller, any and all documents required to give effect to this provision.

The Buyer represents and warrants to the Seller that the Buyer shall personally occupy the property or cause one or more of the Buyer's relations to occupy the property as the Buyer's or the Buyer's relation's primary place of residence upon completion and agrees to deliver to the Seller on closing a Statutory Declaration in the Seller's form in which the Buyer declares that the property being purchased by the Buyer is for use as the Buyer's or the Buyer's relation's primary place of residence and will be so occupied forthwith upon completion.

In the event that the Buyer breaches the warranty or any of the provisions referred to above which results in the Buyer being ineligible or the Seller being unable to obtain the rebates referred to herein then the Buyer shall pay to the Seller forthwith an amount equal to the amount which the Buyer would have been eligible to obtain were it not for such breach or failure to carry out the Buyer's obligations.

NOTE: *Definition of Relation as set out in the Excise Tax Act.*

Relation—A relation means an individual related to you by blood, marriage, common-law partnership, or adoption within the meaning of the Income Tax Act. "Blood relation" is limited to parents, children, or other descendants or siblings. "Marriage relation" includes your spouse or a person who is connected to your spouse by blood or adoption. A relation includes a common-law partner, a former spouse or a former common-law partner.

SCHEDULE: TARION WARRANTY CORPORATION

In Ontario, the Tarion Warranty Corporation requires that, when a new home is sold, the Agreement must include the standard Tarion form of Addendum, exactly as published by Tarion and the form must be completed without any revisions or deletions. The required Addendum (Schedule) is statutorily deemed to be part of the agreement of purchase and sale.

Four versions are available and the registrant must select the correct one for the transaction. Two of the four forms relate to new freehold homes and two concern new condominiums:

- Freehold Firm Closing Date—Statement of Critical Dates and Addendum
- Freehold Tentative Closing Date—Statement of Critical Dates and Addendum
- Condominium Firm Occupancy Date—Statement of Critical Dates and Addendum
- Condominium Tentative Occupancy Date—Statement of Critical Dates and Addendum

The schedule titled *Freehold Firm Closing Date—Statement of Critical Dates and Addendum* is illustrated. Additional information concerning these schedules is available on the Tarion Warranty Corporation website (**www.tarion.com**). Go to *Policies and Guidelines* under the *New Home Builder* tab.

TARION
PROTECTING ONTARIO'S NEW HOME BUYERS

Freehold Form
(Firm Closing Date)

Property _____

_____

Statement of Critical Dates
Delayed Closing Warranty

This Statement of Critical Dates forms part of the Addendum to which it is attached, which in turn forms part of the agreement of purchase and sale between the Vendor and the Purchaser relating to the Property. **The Vendor must complete all blanks set out below. Both the Vendor and Purchaser must sign this page.**

NOTE TO HOME BUYERS: *Please visit Tarion's website: www.tarion.com for important information about all of Tarion's warranties including the Delayed Closing Warranty, the Pre-Delivery Inspection and other matters of interest to new home buyers. You can also obtain a copy of the Homeowner Information Package which is strongly recommended as essential reading for all home buyers. The website features a calculator which will assist you in confirming the various Critical Dates related to the Closing of your purchase.*

VENDOR _____
                Full Name(s)

PURCHASER _____
                Full Name(s)

1. Critical Dates

The **Firm Closing Date**, which is the date that the Vendor anticipates the home will be completed and ready to move in, is: the ___ day of _____, 20___.

If the Vendor cannot close by the Firm Closing Date, then the Purchaser is entitled to delayed closing compensation (see section 7 of the Addendum) and the Vendor must set a Delayed Closing Date.

The Vendor can set a Delayed Closing Date that is up to 365 days after the Firm Closing Date: This **Outside Closing Date** could be as late as: the ___ day of _____, 20___.

2. Purchaser's Termination Period

If the purchase of the home is not completed by the Outside Closing Date, then the Purchaser can terminate the transaction during a period of **30 days** thereafter (the **"Purchaser's Termination Period"**), which period, unless extended by mutual agreement, will end on: the ___ day of _____, 20___.

If the Purchaser terminates the transaction during the Purchaser's Termination Period, then the Purchaser is entitled to delayed closing compensation and to a full refund of all monies paid plus interest (*see sections 7, 10 and 11 of the Addendum*).

Note: *Any time a Critical Date is set or changed as permitted in the Addendum, other Critical Dates may change as well. At any given time the parties must refer to: the most recent revised Statement of Critical Dates; or agreement or written notice that sets a Critical Date, and calculate revised Critical Dates using the formulas contained in the Addendum. Critical Dates can also change if there are unavoidable delays (see section 5 of the Addendum).*

Acknowledged this ____ day of _____, 20___.

VENDOR: _____   PURCHASER: _____

_____   _____

FREEHOLD FIRM - 2012   Page 1 of 11

Freehold Form
(Firm Closing Date)

Addendum to Agreement of Purchase and Sale
Delayed Closing Warranty

This addendum, including the accompanying Statement of Critical Dates (the "**Addendum**"), forms part of the agreement of purchase and sale (the "**Purchase Agreement**") between the Vendor and the Purchaser relating to the Property. This Addendum is to be used for a transaction where the home purchase is in substance a purchase of freehold land and residential dwelling. This Addendum contains important provisions that are part of the delayed closing warranty provided by the Vendor in accordance with the *Ontario New Home Warranties Plan Act* (the "ONHWP Act"). If there are any differences between the provisions in the Addendum and the Purchase Agreement, then the Addendum provisions shall prevail. **PRIOR TO SIGNING THE PURCHASE AGREEMENT OR ANY AMENDMENT TO IT, THE PURCHASER SHOULD SEEK ADVICE FROM A LAWYER WITH RESPECT TO THE PURCHASE AGREEMENT OR AMENDING AGREEMENT, THE ADDENDUM AND THE DELAYED CLOSING WARRANTY.**

Tarion recommends that Purchasers register on Tarion's **MyHome** on-line portal and visit Tarion's website – **tarion.com**, to better understand their rights and obligations under the statutory warranties.

The Vendor shall complete all blanks set out below.

VENDOR

Full Name(s)

Tarion Registration Number	Address

Phone	City	Province	Postal Code

Fax	Email*

PURCHASER

Full Name(s)

Address	City	Province	Postal Code

Phone

Fax	Email*

PROPERTY DESCRIPTION

Municipal Address

City	Province	Postal Code

Short Legal Description

Number of Homes in the Freehold Project _____ (if applicable – see Schedule A)

INFORMATION REGARDING THE PROPERTY

The Vendor confirms that:

(a) The Property is within a plan of subdivision or a proposed plan of subdivision.   O Yes   O No

If yes, the plan of subdivision is registered.   O Yes   O No

If the plan of subdivision is not registered, approval of the draft plan of subdivision has been given.   O Yes   O No

(b) The Vendor has received confirmation from the relevant government authorities that there is sufficient:

(i) water capacity; and (ii) sewage capacity to service the Property.   O Yes   O No

If yes, the nature of the confirmation is as follows:

If the availability of water and sewage capacity is uncertain, the issues to be resolved are as follows:

(c) A building permit has been issued for the Property.   O Yes   O No

(d) Commencement of Construction: O has occurred; or O is expected to occur by the ____ day of _____, 20__.

The Vendor shall give written notice to the Purchaser within 10 days after the actual date of Commencement of Construction.

Note: Since important notices will be sent to this address, it is essential that you ensure that a reliable email address is provided and that your computer settings permit receipt of notices from the other party.

FREEHOLD FIRM - 2012   Page 2 of 11

Freehold Form
(Firm Closing Date)

SETTING AND CHANGING CRITICAL DATES

1. Setting the Firm Closing Date

(a) **Completing Construction Without Delay**: The Vendor shall take all reasonable steps to complete construction of the home on the Property and to Close without delay.

(b) **Firm Closing Date:** The Vendor shall set a Firm Closing Date, which shall be set out in the Statement of Critical Dates at the time the Purchase Agreement is signed.

2. Changing the Firm Closing Date – Three Ways

(a) The Firm Closing Date, can be changed only:
    (i) by the Vendor setting a Delayed Closing Date in accordance with section 3;
    (ii) by the mutual written agreement of the Vendor and Purchaser in accordance with section 4; or
    (iii) as the result of an Unavoidable Delay of which proper written notice is given in accordance with section 5.

(b) If a new Firm Closing Date is set in accordance with section 4 or 5, then the new date is the "Firm Closing Date" for all purposes in this Addendum.

3. Changing the Firm Closing Date – By Setting a Delayed Closing Date

(a) If the Vendor cannot Close on the Firm Closing Date and sections 4 and 5 do not apply, the Vendor shall select and give written notice to the Purchaser of a Delayed Closing Date in accordance with this section, and delayed closing compensation is payable in accordance with section 7.

(b) The Delayed Closing Date may be any Business Day after the date the Purchaser receives written notice of the Delayed Closing Date but not later than the Outside Closing Date.

(c) The Vendor shall give written notice to the Purchaser of the Delayed Closing Date as soon as the Vendor knows that it will be unable to Close on the Firm Closing Date, and in any event at least 10 days before the Firm Closing Date, failing which delayed closing compensation is payable from the date that is 10 days before the Firm Closing Date, in accordance with paragraph 7(c). If notice of a new Delayed Closing Date is not given by the Vendor before the Firm Closing Date, then the new Delayed Closing Date shall be deemed to be the date which is 90 days after the Firm Closing Date.

(d) After the Delayed Closing Date is set, if the Vendor cannot Close on the Delayed Closing Date, the Vendor shall select and give written notice to the Purchaser of a new Delayed Closing Date, unless the delay arises due to Unavoidable Delay under section 5 or is mutually agreed upon under section 4, in which case the requirements of those sections must be met. Paragraphs (b) and (c) above apply with respect to the setting of the new Delayed Closing Date.

(e) Nothing in this section affects the right of the Purchaser or Vendor to terminate the Purchase Agreement on the bases set out in section 10.

4. Changing Critical Dates – By Mutual Agreement

(a) This Addendum sets out a framework for setting, extending and/or accelerating Critical dates, which cannot be altered contractually except as set out in this section 4. Any amendment not in accordance with this section is voidable at the option of the Purchaser.

(b) The Vendor and Purchaser may at any time, after signing the Purchase Agreement, mutually agree in writing to accelerate or extend any of the Critical Dates. Any amendment which accelerates or extends any of the Critical Dates must include the following provisions:

    (i) the Purchaser and Vendor agree that the amendment is entirely voluntary – the Purchaser has no obligation to sign the amendment and each understands that this purchase transaction will still be valid if the Purchaser does not sign this amendment;

    (ii) the amendment includes a revised Statement of Critical Dates which replaces the previous Statement of Critical Dates;

    (iii) the Purchaser acknowledges that the amendment may affect delayed closing compensation payable; and

    (iv) if the change involves extending either the Firm Closing Date or the Delayed Closing Date, then the amending agreement shall:

        i. disclose to the Purchaser that the signing of the amendment may result in the loss of delayed closing compensation as described in section 7;

        ii. unless there is an express waiver of compensation, describe in reasonable detail the cash amount, goods, services, or other consideration which the Purchaser accepts as compensation; and

        iii. contain a statement by the Purchaser that the Purchaser waives compensation or accepts the compensation referred to in clause ii above, in either case, in full satisfaction of any delayed closing compensation payable by the Vendor for the period up to the new Firm Closing Date or Delayed Closing Date.

    If the Purchaser for his or her own purposes requests a change of the Firm Closing Date or the Delayed Closing Date, then subparagraphs (b)(i), (iii) and (iv) above shall not apply.

(c) A Vendor is permitted to include a provision in the Purchase Agreement allowing the Vendor a one-time unilateral right to extend a Firm Closing Date or Delayed Closing Date, as the case may be, for one (1) Business Day to avoid the necessity of tender where a Purchaser is not ready to complete the transaction on the Firm Closing Date or Delayed Closing Date, as the case may be. Delayed closing compensation will not be payable for such period and the Vendor may not impose any penalty or interest charge upon the Purchaser with respect to such extension.

Freehold Form
(Firm Closing Date)

(d) The Vendor and Purchaser may agree in the Purchase Agreement to any unilateral extension or acceleration rights that are for the benefit of the Purchaser.

5. Extending Dates – Due to Unavoidable Delay

(a) If Unavoidable Delay occurs, the Vendor may extend Critical Dates by no more than the length of the Unavoidable Delay Period, without the approval of the Purchaser and without the requirement to pay delayed closing compensation in connection with the Unavoidable Delay, provided the requirements of this section are met.

(b) If the Vendor wishes to extend Critical Dates on account of Unavoidable Delay, the Vendor shall provide written notice to the Purchaser setting out a brief description of the Unavoidable Delay, and an estimate of the duration of the delay. Once the Vendor knows or ought reasonably to know that an Unavoidable Delay has commenced, the Vendor shall provide written notice to the Purchaser by the earlier of: 20 days thereafter; and the next Critical Date.

(c) As soon as reasonably possible, and no later than 20 days after the Vendor knows or ought reasonably to know that an Unavoidable Delay has concluded, the Vendor shall provide written notice to the Purchaser setting out a brief description of the Unavoidable Delay, identifying the date of its conclusion, and setting new Critical Dates. The new Critical Dates are calculated by adding to the then next Critical Date the number of days of the Unavoidable Delay Period (the other Critical Dates changing accordingly), provided that the Firm Closing Date or Delayed Closing Date, as the case may be, must be at least 10 days after the day of giving notice unless the parties agree otherwise. Either the Vendor or the Purchaser may request in writing an earlier Firm Closing Date or Delayed Closing Date, and the other party's consent to the earlier date shall not be unreasonably withheld.

(d) If the Vendor fails to give written notice of the conclusion of the Unavoidable Delay in the manner required by paragraph (c) above, then the notice is ineffective, the existing Critical Dates are unchanged, and any delayed closing compensation payable under section 7 is payable from the existing Firm Closing Date.

(e) Any notice setting new Critical Dates given by the Vendor under this section shall include an updated revised Statement of Critical Dates.

EARLY TERMINATION CONDITIONS

6. Early Termination Conditions

(a) The Vendor and Purchaser may include conditions in the Purchase Agreement that, if not satisfied, give rise to early termination of the Purchase Agreement, but only in the limited way described in this section.

(b) The Vendor is not permitted to include any conditions in the Purchase Agreement other than: the types of Early Termination Conditions listed in Schedule A; and/or the conditions referred to in paragraphs (j), (k) and (l) below. Any other condition included in a Purchase Agreement for the benefit of the Vendor that is not expressly permitted under Schedule A or paragraphs (j), (k) and (l) below is deemed null and void and is not enforceable by the Vendor, but does not affect the validity of the balance of the Purchase Agreement.

(c) The Vendor confirms that this Purchase Agreement is subject to Early Termination Conditions that, if not satisfied (or waived, if applicable), may result in the termination of the Purchase Agreement.   O Yes O No

(d) If the answer in (c) above is "Yes", then the Early Termination Conditions are as follows. The obligation of each of the Purchaser and Vendor to complete this purchase and sale transaction is subject to satisfaction (or waiver, if applicable) of the following conditions and any such conditions set out in an appendix headed "Early Termination Conditions":

Condition #1 (if applicable)
Description of the Early Termination Condition:

The Approving Authority (as that term is defined in Schedule A) is: _____
The date by which Condition #1 is to be satisfied is the _____ day of_____, 20 _____.

Condition #2 (if applicable)
Description of the Early Termination Condition:

The Approving Authority (as that term is defined in Schedule A) is: _____
The date by which Condition #2 is to be satisfied is the _____ day of _____, 20_____.

The date for satisfaction of any Early Termination Condition may be changed by mutual agreement provided in all cases it is set at least 90 days before the Firm Closing Date, and will be deemed to be 90 days before the Firm Closing Date if no date is specified or if the date specified is later than 90 days before the Firm Closing Date. This time limitation does not apply to the condition in subparagraph 1(b)(iv) of Schedule A which must be satisfied or waived by the Vendor within 60 days following the later of: (A) the signing of the Purchase Agreement; and (B) the satisfaction or waiver by the Purchaser of a Purchaser financing condition permitted under paragraph (l) below.

Note: The parties must add additional pages as an appendix to this Addendum if there are additional Early Termination Conditions.

III TARION
PROTECTING ONTARIO'S NEW HOME BUYERS

Freehold Form
(Firm Closing Date)

(e) There are no Early Termination Conditions applicable to this Purchase Agreement other than those identified in subparagraph (d) above and any appendix listing additional Early Termination Conditions.

(f) The Vendor agrees to take all commercially reasonable steps within its power to satisfy the Early Termination Conditions identified in subparagraph (d) above.

(g) For conditions under paragraph 1(a) of Schedule A the following applies:

   (i) conditions in paragraph 1(a) of Schedule A may not be waived by either party;

   (ii) the Vendor shall provide written notice not later than five (5) Business Days after the date specified for satisfaction of a condition that: (A) the condition has been satisfied; or (B) the condition has not been satisfied (together with reasonable details and backup materials) and that as a result the Purchase Agreement is terminated; and

   (iii) if notice is not provided as required by subparagraph (ii) above then the condition is deemed not satisfied and the Purchase Agreement is terminated.

(h) For conditions under paragraph 1(b) of Schedule A the following applies:

   (i) conditions in paragraph 1(b) of Schedule A may be waived by the Vendor;

   (ii) the Vendor shall provide written notice on or before the date specified for satisfaction of the condition that: (A) the condition has been satisfied or waived; or (B) the condition has not been satisfied nor waived, and that as a result the Purchase Agreement is terminated; and

   (iii) if notice is not provided as required by subparagraph (ii) above then the condition is deemed satisfied or waived and the Purchase Agreement will continue to be binding on both parties.

(i) If a Purchase Agreement or proposed Purchase Agreement contains Early Termination Conditions, the Purchaser has three (3) Business Days after the day of receipt of a true and complete copy of the Purchase Agreement or proposed Purchase Agreement to review the nature of the conditions (preferably with legal counsel). If the Purchaser is not satisfied, in the Purchaser's sole discretion, with the Early Termination Conditions, the Purchaser may revoke the Purchaser's offer as set out in the proposed Purchase Agreement, or terminate the Purchase Agreement, as the case may be, by giving written notice to the Vendor within those three Business Days.

(j) The Purchase Agreement may be conditional until Closing (transfer to the Purchaser of title to the home), upon compliance with the subdivision control provisions (section 50) of the *Planning Act,* which compliance shall be obtained by the Vendor at its sole expense, on or before Closing.

(k) The Purchaser is cautioned that there may be other conditions in the Purchase Agreement that allow the Vendor to terminate the Purchase Agreement due to the fault of the Purchaser.

(l) The Purchase Agreement may include any condition that is for the sole benefit of the Purchaser and that is agreed to by the Vendor (e.g., the sale of an existing dwelling, Purchaser financing or a basement walkout). The Purchase Agreement may specify that the Purchaser has a right to terminate the Purchase Agreement if any such condition is not met, and may set out the terms on which termination by the Purchaser may be effected.

MAKING A COMPENSATION CLAIM

7. Delayed Closing Compensation

(a) The Vendor warrants to the Purchaser that, if Closing is delayed beyond the Firm Closing Date (other than by mutual agreement or as a result of Unavoidable Delay as permitted under sections 4 and 5), then the Vendor shall compensate the Purchaser up to a total amount of $7,500, which amount includes: (i) payment to the Purchaser of a set amount of $150 a day for living expenses for each day of delay until the date of Closing; or the date of termination of the Purchase Agreement, as applicable under paragraph (b) below; and (ii) any other expenses (supported by receipts) incurred by the Purchaser due to the delay.

(b) Delayed closing compensation is payable only if: (i) Closing occurs; or (ii) the Purchase Agreement is terminated or deemed to have been terminated under paragraph 10(b) of this Addendum. Delayed closing compensation is payable only if the Purchaser's claim is made to Tarion in writing within one (1) year after Closing, or after termination of the Purchase Agreement, as the case may be, and otherwise in accordance with this Addendum. Compensation claims are subject to any further conditions set out in the ONHWP Act.

(c) If the Vendor gives written notice of a Delayed Closing Date to the Purchaser less than 10 days before the Firm Closing Date, contrary to the requirements of paragraph 3(c), then delayed closing compensation is payable from the date that is 10 days before the Firm Closing Date.

(d) Living expenses are direct living costs such as for accommodation and meals. Receipts are not required in support of a claim for living expenses, as a set daily amount of $150 per day is payable. The Purchaser must provide receipts in support of any claim for other delayed closing compensation, such as for moving and storage costs. Submission of false receipts disentitles the Purchaser to any delayed closing compensation in connection with a claim.

Freehold Form
(Firm Closing Date)

(e) If delayed closing compensation is payable, the Purchaser may make a claim to the Vendor for that compensation after Closing or after termination of the Purchase Agreement, as the case may be, and shall include all receipts (apart from living expenses) which evidence any part of the Purchaser's claim. The Vendor shall assess the Purchaser's claim by determining the amount of delayed closing compensation payable based on the rules set out in section 7 and the receipts provided by the Purchaser, and the Vendor shall promptly provide that assessment information to the Purchaser. The Purchaser and the Vendor shall use reasonable efforts to settle the claim and when the claim is settled, the Vendor shall prepare an acknowledgement signed by both parties which:

   (i)   includes the Vendor's assessment of the delayed closing compensation payable;

   (ii)   describes in reasonable detail the cash amount, goods, services, or other consideration which the Purchaser accepts as compensation (the "Compensation"), if any; and

   (iii) contains a statement by the Purchaser that the Purchaser accepts the Compensation in full satisfaction of any delay compensation payable by the Vendor.

(f) If the Vendor and Purchaser cannot agree as contemplated in paragraph 7(e), then to make a claim to Tarion the Purchaser must file a claim with Tarion in writing within one (1) year after Closing. A claim may also be made and the same rules apply if the sale transaction is terminated under paragraph 10(b), in which case, the deadline for a claim is one (1) year after termination.

8. Adjustments to Purchase Price

Only the items set out in Schedule B (or an amendment to Schedule B), shall be the subject of adjustment or change to the purchase price or the balance due on Closing. The Vendor agrees that it shall not charge as an adjustment or readjustment to the purchase price of the home, any reimbursement for a sum paid or payable by the Vendor to a third party unless the sum is ultimately paid to the third party either before or after Closing. If the Vendor charges an amount in contravention of the preceding sentence, the Vendor shall forthwith readjust with the Purchaser. This section shall not: restrict or prohibit payments for items disclosed in Part I of Schedule B which have a fixed fee; nor shall it restrict or prohibit the parties from agreeing on how to allocate as between them, any rebates, refunds or incentives provided by the federal government, a provincial or municipal government or an agency of any such government, before or after Closing.

MISCELLANEOUS

9. Ontario Building Code – Conditions of Closing

(a) On or before Closing, the Vendor shall deliver to the Purchaser:

   (i)   an Occupancy Permit (as defined in paragraph (d)) for the home; or

   (ii)   if an Occupancy Permit is not required under the Building Code, a signed written confirmation by the Vendor that all conditions of occupancy under the Building Code have been fulfilled and occupancy is permitted under the Building Code.

(b) Notwithstanding the requirements of paragraph (a), to the extent that the Purchaser and the Vendor agree that the Purchaser shall be responsible for one or more prerequisites to obtaining permission for occupancy under the Building Code, (the "Purchaser Occupancy Obligations"):

   (i)   the Purchaser shall not be entitled to delayed closing compensation if the reason for the delay is that the Purchaser Occupancy Obligations have not been completed;

   (ii)   the Vendor shall deliver to the Purchaser, upon fulfilling all prerequisites to obtaining permission for occupancy under the Building Code (other than the Purchaser Occupancy Obligations), a signed written confirmation that the Vendor has fulfilled such prerequisites; and

   (iii) if the Purchaser and Vendor have agreed that such prerequisites (other than the Purchaser Occupancy Obligations) are to be fulfilled prior to Closing, then the Vendor shall provide the signed written confirmation required by subparagraph (ii) on or before the date of Closing.

(c) If the Vendor cannot satisfy the requirements of paragraph (a) or subparagraph (b)(ii), the Vendor shall set a Delayed Closing Date (or new Delayed Closing Date) on a date that the Vendor reasonably expects to have satisfied the requirements of paragraph (a) or subparagraph (b)(ii), as the case may be. In setting the Delayed Closing Date (or new Delayed Closing Date), the Vendor shall comply with the requirements of section 3, and delayed closing compensation shall be payable in accordance with section 7. Despite the foregoing, delayed closing compensation shall not be payable for a delay under this paragraph (c) if the inability to satisfy the requirements of subparagraph (b)(ii) is because the Purchaser has failed to satisfy the Purchaser Occupancy Obligations.

(d) For the purposes of this section, an "Occupancy Permit" means any written or electronic document, however styled, whether final, provisional or temporary, provided by the chief building official (as defined in the *Building Code Act*) or a person designated by the chief building official, that evidences that permission to occupy the home under the Building Code has been granted.

10. Termination of the Purchase Agreement

(a) The Vendor and the Purchaser may terminate the Purchase Agreement by mutual written agreement. Such written mutual agreement may specify how monies paid by the Purchaser, including deposit(s) and monies for upgrades and extras are to be allocated if not repaid in full.

Freehold Form
(Firm Closing Date)

(b) If for any reason (other than breach of contract by the Purchaser) Closing has not occurred by the Outside Closing Date, then the Purchaser has 30 days to terminate the Purchase Agreement by written notice to the Vendor. If the Purchaser does not provide written notice of termination within such 30-day period then the Purchase Agreement shall continue to be binding on both parties and the Delayed Closing Date shall be the date set under paragraph 3(c), regardless of whether such date is beyond the Outside Closing Date.

(c) If: calendar dates for the applicable Critical Dates are not inserted in the Statement of Critical Dates; or if any date for Closing is expressed in the Purchase Agreement or in any other document to be subject to change depending upon the happening of an event (other than as permitted in this Addendum), then the Purchaser may terminate the Purchase Agreement by written notice to the Vendor.

(d) The Purchase Agreement may be terminated in accordance with the provisions of section 6.

(e) Nothing in this Addendum derogates from any right of termination that either the Purchaser or the Vendor may have at law or in equity on the basis of, for example, frustration of contract or fundamental breach of contract.

(f) Except as permitted in this section, the Purchase Agreement may not be terminated by reason of the Vendor's delay in Closing alone.

11. Refund of Monies Paid on Termination

(a) If the Purchase Agreement is terminated (other than as a result of breach of contract by the Purchaser), unless there is agreement to the contrary under paragraph 10(a), the Vendor shall refund all monies paid by the Purchaser including deposit(s) and monies for upgrades and extras, within 10 days of such termination, with interest from the date each amount was paid to the Vendor to the date of refund to the Purchaser. The Purchaser cannot be compelled by the Vendor to execute a release of the Vendor as a prerequisite to obtaining the refund of monies payable as a result of termination of the Purchase Agreement under this paragraph, although the Purchaser may be required to sign a written acknowledgement confirming the amount of monies refunded and termination of the purchase transaction. Nothing in this Addendum prevents the Vendor and Purchaser from entering into such other termination agreement and/or release as may be agreed to by the parties.

(b) The rate of interest payable on the Purchaser's monies is 2% less than the minimum rate at which the Bank of Canada makes short-term advances to members of Canada Payments Association, as of the date of termination of the Purchase Agreement.

(c) Notwithstanding paragraphs (a) and (b) above, if either party initiates legal proceedings to contest termination of the Purchase Agreement or the refund of monies paid by the Purchaser, and obtains a legal determination, such amounts and interest shall be payable as determined in those proceedings.

12. Definitions

"**Business Day**" means any day other than: Saturday; Sunday; New Year's Day; Family Day; Good Friday; Easter Monday; Victoria Day; Canada Day; Civic Holiday; Labour Day; Thanksgiving Day; Remembrance Day; Christmas Day; Boxing Day; and any special holiday proclaimed by the Governor General or the Lieutenant Governor; and where New Year's Day, Canada Day or Remembrance Day falls on a Saturday or Sunday, the following Monday is not a Business Day, and where Christmas Day falls on a Saturday or Sunday, the following Monday and Tuesday are not Business Days; and where Christmas Day falls on a Friday, the following Monday is not a Business Day.

"**Closing**" means the completion of the sale of the home including transfer of title to the home to the Purchaser and "**Close**" has a corresponding meaning.

"**Commencement of Construction**" means the commencement of construction of foundation components or elements (such as footings, rafts or piles) for the home.

"**Critical Dates**" means the Firm Closing Date, the Delayed Closing Date, the Outside Closing Date and the last day of the Purchaser's Termination Period.

"**Delayed Closing Date**" means the date, set in accordance with section 3, on which the Vendor agrees to Close, in the event the Vendor cannot Close on the Firm Closing Date.

"**Early Termination Conditions**" means the types of conditions listed in Schedule A.

"**Firm Closing Date**" means the firm date on which the Vendor agrees to Close as set in accordance with this Addendum.

"**Outside Closing Date**" means the date which is 365 days after the Firm Closing Date or such other date as may be mutually agreed upon in accordance with section 4.

"**Property**" or "**home**" means the home including lands being acquired by the Purchaser from the Vendor.

"**Purchaser's Termination Period**" means the 30-day period during which the Purchaser may terminate the Purchase Agreement for delay, in accordance with paragraph 10(b).

"**Statement of Critical Dates**" means the Statement of Critical Dates attached to and forming part of this Addendum (in form to be determined by Tarion from time to time), and, if applicable, as amended in accordance with this Addendum.

"**The ONHWP Act**" means the *Ontario New Home Warranties Plan Act* including regulations, as amended from time to time.

"**Unavoidable Delay**" means an event which delays Closing which is a strike, fire, explosion, flood, act of God, civil insurrection, act of war, act of terrorism or pandemic, plus any period of delay directly caused by the event, which are beyond the reasonable control of the Vendor and are not caused or contributed to by the fault of the Vendor.

"**Unavoidable Delay Period**" means the number of days between the Purchaser's receipt of written notice of the commencement of the Unavoidable Delay, as required by paragraph 5(b), and the date on which the Unavoidable Delay concludes.

FREEHOLD FIRM - 2012   Page 7 of 11

Freehold Form
(Firm Closing Date)

13. Addendum Prevails

The Addendum forms part of the Purchase Agreement. The Vendor and Purchaser agree that they shall not include any provision in the Purchase Agreement or any amendment to the Purchase Agreement or any other document (or indirectly do so through replacement of the Purchase Agreement) that derogates from, conflicts with or is inconsistent with the provisions of this Addendum, except where this Addendum expressly permits the parties to agree or consent to an alternative arrangement. The provisions of this Addendum prevail over any such provision.

14. Time Periods, and How Notice Must Be Sent

(a) Any written notice required under this Addendum may be given personally or sent by email, fax, courier or registered mail to the Purchaser or the Vendor at the address/contact numbers identified on page 2 or replacement address/contact numbers as provided in paragraph (c) below. Notices may also be sent to the solicitor for each party if necessary contact information is provided, but notices in all events must be sent to the Purchaser and Vendor, as applicable. If email addresses are set out on page 2 of this Addendum, then the parties agree that notices may be sent by email to such addresses, subject to paragraph (c) below.

(b) Written notice given by one of the means identified in paragraph (a) is deemed to be given and received: on the date of delivery or transmission, if given personally or sent by email or fax (or the next Business Day if the date of delivery or transmission is not a Business Day); on the second Business Day following the date of sending by courier; or on the fifth Business Day following the date of sending, if sent by registered mail. If a postal stoppage or interruption occurs, notices shall not be sent by registered mail, and any notice sent by registered mail within 5 Business Days prior to the commencement of the postal stoppage or interruption must be re-sent by another means in order to be effective. For purposes of this section 14, Business Day includes Remembrance Day, if it falls on a day other than Saturday or Sunday, and Easter Monday.

(c) If either party wishes to receive written notice under this Addendum at an address/contact number other than those identified on page 2 of this Addendum, then the party shall send written notice of the change of address, fax number, or email address to the other party in accordance with paragraph (b) above.

(d) Time periods within which or following which any act is to be done shall be calculated by excluding the day of delivery or transmission and including the day on which the period ends.

(e) Time periods shall be calculated using calendar days including Business Days but subject to paragraphs (f), (g) and (h) below.

(f) Where the time for making a claim under this Addendum expires on a day that is not a Business Day, the claim may be made on the next Business Day.

(g) Prior notice periods that begin on a day that is not a Business Day shall begin on the next earlier Business Day, except that notices may be sent and/or received on Remembrance Day, if it falls on a day other than Saturday or Sunday, or Easter Monday.

(h) Every Critical Date must occur on a Business Day. If the Vendor sets a Critical Date that occurs on a date other than a Business Day, the Critical Date is deemed to be the next Business Day.

(i) Words in the singular include the plural and words in the plural include the singular.

(j) Gender-specific terms include both sexes and include corporations.

15. Disputes Regarding Termination

(a) The Vendor and Purchaser agree that disputes arising between them relating to termination of the Purchase Agreement under section 11 shall be submitted to arbitration in accordance with the *Arbitration Act, 1991* (Ontario) and subsection 17(4) of the ONHWP Act.

(b) The parties agree that the arbitrator shall have the power and discretion on motion by the Vendor or Purchaser or any other interested party, or of the arbitrator's own motion, to consolidate multiple arbitration proceedings on the basis that they raise one or more common issues of fact or law that can more efficiently be addressed in a single proceeding. The arbitrator has the power and discretion to prescribe whatever procedures are useful or necessary to adjudicate the common issues in the consolidated proceedings in the most just and expeditious manner possible. The *Arbitration Act, 1991* (Ontario) applies to any consolidation of multiple arbitration proceedings.

(c) The Vendor shall pay the costs of the arbitration proceedings and the Purchaser's reasonable legal expenses in connection with the proceedings unless the arbitrator for just cause orders otherwise.

(d) The parties agree to cooperate so that the arbitration proceedings are conducted as expeditiously as possible, and agree that the arbitrator may impose such time limits or other procedural requirements, consistent with the requirements of the *Arbitration Act, 1991* (Ontario), as may be required to complete the proceedings as quickly as reasonably possible.

(e) The arbitrator may grant any form of relief permitted by the *Arbitration Act, 1991* (Ontario), whether or not the arbitrator concludes that the Purchase Agreement may properly be terminated.

For more information please visit www.tarion.com

**Freehold Form
(Firm Closing Date)**

SCHEDULE A

Types of Permitted Early Termination Conditions

1. **The Vendor of a home is permitted to make the Purchase Agreement conditional as follows:**

(a) upon receipt of Approval from an Approving Authority for:
   (i)   a change to the official plan, other governmental development plan or zoning by-law (including a minor variance);
   (ii)   a consent to creation of a lot(s) or part-lot(s);
   (iii)   a certificate of water potability or other measure relating to domestic water supply to the home;
   (iv)   a certificate of approval of a septic system or other measure relating to waste disposal from the home;
   (v)   completion of hard services for the property or surrounding area (i.e., roads, rail crossings, water lines, sewage lines, other utilities);
   (vi)   allocation of domestic water or storm or sanitary sewage capacity;
   (vii)   easements or similar rights serving the property or surrounding area;
   (viii) site plan agreements, density agreements, shared facilities agreements or other development agreements with Approving Authorities or nearby landowners, and/or any development Approvals required from an Approving Authority; and/or
   (ix)   site plans, plans, elevations and/or specifications under architectural controls imposed by an Approving Authority.
   The above-noted conditions are for the benefit of both the Vendor and the Purchaser and cannot be waived by either party.

(b) upon:
   (i)   subject to paragraph 1(c), receipt by the Vendor of confirmation that sales of homes in the Freehold Project have exceeded a specified threshold by a specified date;
   (ii)   subject to paragraph 1(c), receipt by the Vendor of confirmation that financing for the Freehold Project on terms satisfactory to the Vendor has been arranged by a specified date;
   (iii)   receipt of Approval from an Approving Authority for a basement walkout; and/or
   (iv)   confirmation by the Vendor that it is satisfied the Purchaser has the financial resources to complete the transaction.
   The above-noted conditions are for the benefit of the Vendor and may be waived by the Vendor in its sole discretion.

(c) the following requirements apply with respect to the conditions set out in subparagraph 1(b)(i) or 1(b)(ii):
   (i)   the 3 Business Day period in section 6(i) of the Addendum shall be extended to 10 calendar days for a Purchase Agreement which contains a condition set out in subparagraphs 1(b)(i) and/or 1(b)(ii);
   (ii)   the Vendor shall complete the Property Description on page 2 of this Addendum;
   (iii)   the date for satisfaction of the condition cannot be later than 9 months following signing of the purchase Agreement; and
   (iv)   until the condition is satisfied or waived, all monies paid by the Purchaser to the Vendor, including deposit(s) and monies for upgrades and extras: (A) shall be held in trust by the Vendor's lawyer pursuant to a deposit trust agreement (executed in advance in the form specified by Tarion Warranty Corporation, which form is available for inspection at the offices of Tarion Warranty Corporation during normal business hours), or secured by other security acceptable to Tarion and arranged in writing with Tarion, or (B) failing compliance with the requirement set out in clause (A) above, shall be deemed to be held in trust by the Vendor for the Purchaser on the same terms as are set out in the form of deposit trust agreement described in clause (A) above.

2. **The following definitions apply in this Schedule:**

"Approval" means an approval, consent or permission (in final form not subject to appeal) from an Approving Authority and may include completion of necessary agreements (i.e., site plan agreement) to allow lawful access to and use and Closing of the property for its intended residential purpose.
"Approving Authority" means a government (federal, provincial or municipal), governmental agency, Crown corporation, or quasi-governmental authority (a privately operated organization exercising authority delegated by legislation or a government).
"Freehold Project" means the construction or proposed construction of three or more freehold homes (including the Purchaser's home) by the same Vendor in a single location, either at the same time or consecutively, as a single coordinated undertaking.

3. **Each condition must:**

(a) be set out separately;
(b) be reasonably specific as to the type of Approval which is needed for the transaction; and
(c) identify the Approving Authority by reference to the level of government and/or the identity of the governmental agency, Crown corporation or quasi-governmental authority.

4. **For greater certainty, the Vendor is not permitted to make the Purchase Agreement conditional upon:**

(a) receipt of a building permit;
(b) receipt of an Closing permit; and/or
(c) completion of the home.

FREEHOLD FIRM - 2012   Page 9 of 11

**Freehold Form
(Firm Closing Date)**

SCHEDULE B

Adjustments to Purchase Price or Balance Due on Closing

PART I   Stipulated Amounts/Adjustments

These are additional charges, fees or other anticipated adjustments to the final purchase price or balance due on Closing, the dollar value of which is stipulated in the Purchase Agreement and set out below.

[Draft Note: List items with any necessary cross-references to text in the Purchase Agreement.]

1.

2.

3.

**Freehold Form
(Firm Closing Date)**

PART II   **All Other Adjustments – to be determined in accordance with the terms of the Purchase Agreement**

These are additional charges, fees or other anticipated adjustments to the final purchase price or balance due on Closing, which will be determined after signing the Purchase Agreement, all in accordance with the terms of the Purchase Agreement.

[Draft Note: List items with any necessary cross-references to text in the Purchase Agreement.]

1.

2.

3.

Agreement of Purchase and Sale (BILD)

The Building Industry and Land Development Association (BILD) has an agreement of purchase and sale that is widely used. BILD was formed through the merger of the Greater Toronto Home Builders' Association and Urban Development Institute/Ontario. Use of this agreement is restricted to Building Industry and Land Development Association members and Ontario Home Builders' Association members. Because of the complexity of this form, prudent buyers should seek legal counsel prior to making a firm commitment.

WEB LINKS

Building Industry and Land Development Association (BILD)   Go to the BILD website (*www.newhomes.org*) for detailed information about this association.

Ontario Home Builders' Association   The website for the provincial association for home builders is *www.ohba.ca*.

KNOWLEDGE INTEGRATION

Notables

- New home sales range from custom homes to mega-subdivisions. Salespersons' duties and activities are similarly diverse.

- Builder relationships can involve various arrangements from exclusive authorities to information registration cards with commission paid for prospect introduction.

- Building permit applications are standardized across the province, but support documentation may vary by municipality.

- A building permit will not be issued unless an applicant complies with all zoning requirements or an appropriate variance is granted by the Committee of Adjustment.

- Construction standards for new homes are set out in Part 9 of the Ontario Building Code.

- An exemption under the *Real Estate and Business Brokers Act, 2002* permits builders to employ full-time salaried staff when selling their owned new home inventory.

- The Tarion Warranty Corporation provides both primary and additional coverages. Primary defect coverage is based on three time periods: one year, two year and seven year. Additional coverages relate to deposit protection, delayed closings and protection against substitutions.

- All builders and sellers must be registered under Tarion to sell new homes (including condominiums).

- Not all new homes and not all damages within new homes are covered.

- No standardized new home agreement currently exists in Ontario.

- The *Agreement of Purchase and Sale—Residential* (OREA Form 100) can be used for new homes, assuming that appropriate changes are made including selected clauses and an appendix relating to the Tarion warranty coverage.

- The BILD *Agreement of Purchase and Sale* is widely used by builders throughout Ontario.

 ## Web Links

Web links are included for general interest regarding selected chapter topics.

Tarion Warranty Corporation

Go to the Tarion Warranty Corporation website (*www.tarion.com*) for current information regarding warranty coverages and related details. The site provides extensive information for consumers.

Building Industry and Land Development Association (BILD)

Go to the BILD website (*www.newhomes.org*) for detailed information about this association.

Ontario Home Builders' Association

The website for the provincial association for home builders is *www.ohba.ca*.

Strategic Thinking For Your Career

Questions are included to assist in developing your new career. No answers are provided.

1. Which builders in the local market-place will consider exclusive agency relationships and which operate on brokerage protected arrangements?

2. What opportunities are available with local, new home developments? What specifics about house plans, options, upgrades, financing, deposits, subdivision restrictions and related information is readily available?

3. What procedures must be followed in my local municipality when applying for a building permit and what inspections are typically required?

4. What agreements of purchase and sale are being used locally by builders and what schedules are typically attached?

5. Who do I know that has recently purchased a new home, so that I might better understand the Tarion warranty process from a consumer perspective?

Chapter Mini-Review

Solutions are located in the Appendix.

1. All salespersons selling new homes for a builder are exempt from registration under the *Real Estate and Business Brokers Act, 2002.*

    ○ True   ○ False

2. Real estate brokerages may be contracted by a new home builder to provide only specific services when marketing and selling new homes.

    ○ True   ○ False

3. A building permit application typically contains other support documentation, such as architectural drawings and a detailed site plan.

    ○ True   ○ False

4. Construction standards for homes is covered under Part 3 of the Ontario Building Code.

    ○ True   ○ False

5. Homes enrolled in the new home warranty program must, among other things, be in compliance with the Ontario Building Code.

    ○ True   ○ False

6. The new home warranty program is administered by the Ontario government.

    ○ True   ○ False

7. Under Tarion warranty coverages, all defects in workmanship are warrantied for a seven-year period.

    ○ True   ○ False

8. Every agreement for a new home (including a condominium) provides the buyer with a right to terminate if closing delay occurs.

    ○ True   ○ False

9. An ownership change concerning a resale home does not disrupt remaining warranty coverage, subject to when that home was initially enrolled with the Tarion Warranty Corporation.

◯ True   ◯ False

10. The Certificate of Completion and Possession is completed at the same time as the Pre-Delivery Inspection.

◯ True   ◯ False

11. Construction performance guidelines assist homeowners in understanding how disputed items will be resolved.

◯ True   ◯ False

12. In Ontario, an owner of a property is able to, for a given period of time, holdback 15% of the value of the services or materials that are supplied to an improvement under a contract with that owner.

◯ True   ◯ False

Active Learning Exercises

Solutions are located in the Appendix.

■ Exercise 1   Scenarios

NOTE: The following scenarios are inserted for learning purposes only. Any decision regarding the merits of a claim and associated warranty coverage rests solely with the Tarion Warranty Corporation.

1.1   Smith had a small, uninsulated seasonal cottage constructed by a local builder. Prior to completion, Smith asked for the builder's registration. The builder was not registered and claimed that, in any event, seasonal properties are excluded under Tarion warranty coverage. Smith wants to file a complaint. Does he have valid grounds?

1.2   Buyer Hatfield, upon purchasing his new home with Tarion warranty coverage, immediately faced problems with leakage in two casement windows. Also, some shelving in a home office that Hatfield installed collapsed under the weight of too many books. What would be Tarion's probable position on these matters, based on information provided in this chapter?

1.3 Buyer Khan accompanied the builder on the pre-delivery inspection and noted two defects: a defective door frame and a noticeable stain on one of the carpets apparently caused by tradespeople. These items appeared on the Certificate of Completion and Possession and were subsequently fixed. However, following closing, the buyer discovered that the carpet stain was only the external indication of a much larger problem involving staining in rooms immediately below the original damaged area. Would Kahn be covered? Support your answer with specific references to the warranty program.

1.4 Builder McCrae anticipates a minor delay to the firm closing date for a freehold home. Can McCrae accomplish this if the buyer agrees and, if so, what specific provision in the Tarion Freehold Form sets out the appropriate procedure?

1.5   Buyer Finlayson moved into his new home with warranty provided by the Tarion Corporation on April 20xx. Two months later, significant leakage in the roof flashing resulted in staining on an upper bedroom ceiling. However, water also dripped on a family heirloom—a mahogany chest of drawers. Repairs to the chest exceeded $1,000. What portions of the total damage would probably be covered under the warranty coverage?

1.6   Developer Reed is renovating an old factory for conversion into condominium lofts. In addition, the property contains eight existing row houses which will be retained, renovated and marketed as condominium townhouses within the same development. Will Tarion warranty cover the project if Developer Reed is a registered builder? Explain your answer with direct reference to the warranty program.

1.7   Buyer Owen discovers water bubbling through the front yard near the driveway. The two-year-old home has Tarion warranty coverage. Racing to the basement, he discovers that an apparent water main break, somewhere in the front yard, has allowed water to follow the water pipe into the basement and has seriously damaged lower-level family room carpets, baseboards and drywall. Does Tarion coverage apply or not and why?

1.8   A strike has delayed the completion of the buyer's home on Glenwood Circle. Builder Jenson, registered with Tarion, cannot finish the home by the firm closing date. What is the strike referred to in the Tarion Freehold Form and can the builder extend the original closing date?

▣ Exercise 2   New Home Warranty and the Resale Property

You are presenting ABC Realty Inc.'s marketing plan to Mr. and Mrs. Lam. Their home was purchased new 18 months ago from a Tarion registered builder and now must be sold given a corporate transfer to Western Canada.

The home is beautifully finished with fully decorated main and upper floors. Mr. Lam intended to complete the basement himself, but at the moment only framing and electrical/plumbing have been completed, along with some drywall. In one corner, kitchen cupboards have been installed, but most of the work remains unfinished. You casually move some plywood in the basement to discover efflorescence and some signs of dampness on the exterior concrete wall. Also, small cracks start at floor level and run upwards toward a rear basement window.

What questions should be asked of the sellers regarding improvements made, Tarion coverage and related issues affecting this resale home?

SECTION II

CURRENT TRENDS AND ISSUES IN RESIDENTIAL REAL ESTATE

Section II focuses on current trends and issues that can impact residential registrants in their day-to-day activities. Chapter 7 includes discussions of stigmatized property, the ongoing problems associated with grow houses, fraud relating to property including mortgages and money laundering. Recent initiatives to counter fraudulent practices and current amendments to money laundering legislation are emphasized. The balance of this chapter highlights marketing-relating trends including auctions, home staging and brokerage operations.

Chapter 8 emphasizes environmental concerns and the expanding role of environmental legislation, as it impacts real estate trading activity. Several key environmental hazards are discussed, along with energy conservation efforts and expanding opportunities in green building. Lastly, the federal EnerGuide and ENERGY STAR® programs are highlighted. Registrants need to continuously monitor new environmental initiatives that will benefit consumers in their quest for improved energy conservation and reduced energy costs.

CHAPTER 7

Stigmatized Property, Grow Operations and Other Topical Issues

Introduction

Real estate registrants are always faced with new trends and issues that impact the real estate marketplace. Six topics are included in this chapter, along with additional material in *Chapter 8: Environmental Concerns and Related Topics*. This chapter begins with the challenging topic of stigmatized property where value can be affected by what is perceived, rather than what may be real. The next topic involves grow houses and the illegal growing of marijuana in which operators use sophisticated methods to by-pass meters and tap into hydro, gas and water lines and generally disguise the entire operation within residential homes on typical suburban streets. Registrants must be clearly aware of possible indications of a previous grow house and take appropriate steps should one be discovered.

The third topic focuses on fraud with particular emphasis on mortgage fraud, how to identify possible circumstances that may indicate mortgage fraud and generally understand how such fraud is perpetrated on innocent consumers. An overview of federal requirements concerning money laundering is also included, with particular emphasis on suspicious transactions and terrorist financing.

The final three topics relate to trends in the marketplace that are worthy of discussion and provide a better understanding of key issues. Auctions are highlighted, along with the distinctive methods used in the auctioning process. Home staging, as a popular method to improve saleability is discussed, along with helpful guidelines to properly stage a home from both internal and external perspectives. Lastly, a brief discussion is included about brokerage operations and alternative brokerage remuneration methods.

Learning Outcomes

At the conclusion of this chapter, students will be able to:

- Describe how a stigma can impact the value of a residential property and differentiate between real and perceived risk.
- Outline possible indications that a home has been used as a grow operation and discuss appropriate clauses to include when drafting an agreement of purchase and sale.
- Differentiate between identity fraud and value fraud and discuss the growing problem of mortgage fraud.
- Discuss types of mortgage fraud, including key indicators that indicate the potential for fraud in the real estate marketplace.
- Detail various activities that real estate registrants can do to help detect and prevent mortgage fraud, with particular reference to regulatory requirements concerning the falsifying of information.
- Identify and discuss compliance requirements for brokerages, brokers and salespersons regarding money laundering.
- Outline key steps in the auction process including benefits of an auction from the seller's perspective, (along with guidelines to assist buyers in understanding the process).
- Describe how home staging works and detail staging guidelines from both interior and exterior perspectives.
- Briefly describe recent trends in brokerage operations and business models, including the growth in popularity of teams and the use of social media in marketing and lead generation.

STIGMATIZED PROPERTY

A stigma is generally defined as a mark of disgrace. For real estate purposes, a stigma is associated with potentially detrimental factors that negatively affect a property, given certain unfortunate events such as a murder or suicide in or on the property, or the purported existence of ghosts.

Intangible issues such as stigmas are difficult to quantify. Tangible problems can be alleviated or solved by direct action. Value adjustments are routinely made by appraisers to adjust for physical circumstances such as a run-down property adjacent to a new house, or a home abutting a busy neighbourhood convenience store. However, stigma goes beyond the physical. The unsettling reality of stigmas is that perception can also impact value. It is one thing to remedy the physical signs of a murder, but quite another to remove ongoing perceptions; i.e., the lingering memory of an incident occurring on the property, particularly when the event has gained widespread notoriety.

Real vs. Perceived Risk

Two primary issues come into play when discussing stigma: *real risk* and *perceived risk*. As an extreme example, the haunted house may have no real danger (if you don't believe in ghosts) but the perceived impact may arise when informed that the house just purchased is haunted. Some argue the value might increase (commercial value due to the haunting), while others see value loss (restriction on marketability and enjoyment of the property).

Stigmas come in many forms, but most attention centres on murders, suicides and hauntings. In fact, some US jurisdictions have statutory disclosure requirements. In California for example, real estate representatives must disclose any murder occurring on the property within the past three years. However, stigmas can arise from other perceived situations. For example, a negative perception may surface not because the listed property has ground contamination, but rather that a nearby property has had to undergo environmental remediation.

UFFI, urea formaldehyde foam insulation, is also a good example of intermingling real and perceived risk. Documented evidence now appears to suggest that little or no real danger exists assuming proper installation, yet the risk perception remains. Consequently, agreements of purchase and sale continue to include a UFFI clause.

Impact on Value

Estimating value loss due to stigmas is not easy. While some buyers may be willing to entertain certain risks, the available pool of buyers is often restricted due to negative perceptions. Limited research suggests that stigmas result in longer periods to sell the affected property, as well as negatively impact value. Few would argue that stigma does not affect value, but rather under what circumstances and by how much.

Many considerations come into play. For example, media exposure, rumours, hearsay evidence and technical jargon meld together into an intricate blend of fact and fiction. Just consider the impact of a large billboard that states "*Keep Metro Garbage Out*" placed on land adjacent to a listed property. What impact does the sign have . . . notwithstanding where the dump may ultimately be located?

Remedies

In many cases, time is the only viable remedy, as the stigma disappears from recent memory. Individuals have resorted to remodelling, changing the civic address and demolishing structures in an attempt to resolve the matter. Unfortunately, in some notorious cases, the properties become a tourist destination with all the nuisance factors associated with that celebrity status.

Disclosure

The most prudent approach to stigmas lies in disclosure. The key question: If a buyer knew about the circumstances, would he or she buy the property? In other words, from the buyer's perspective, is the stigma a material fact that would impact the buying decision. If the buyer is not given the opportunity to evaluate this information, salespeople leave themselves open to possible litigation.

One thing is certain. If a stigma is attached to a property and no disclosure is made, the salesperson can be assured of one thing. Neighbours bearing the bad news will make certain the buyer is fully aware when he or she moves in. If a registrant makes the conscious decision to deny the buyer of this information, the courts will undoubtedly side with the innocent consumer who could have otherwise made a rational decision on the matter before submitting an offer.

GROW HOUSE

The term grow house is commonly associated with residential properties used for illegal growing of marijuana. Such activity typically involves larger residential homes (i.e., 2,200 square feet or more) with unfinished basements that are purchased or rented. However, grow operations have been discovered in many different types of structures.

A typical residential operation involves equipment and seedling plants brought in through the garage and set up in the basement, main and/or upper levels. A basement can house approximately 400 plants which reach maturity in approximately three months. To mature quickly, the plants require heat, water, fertilizer and humidity. The electricity requirements, in particular, can be substantial.

Operators have sophisticated methods of by-passing existing meters and tapping into hydro, gas and water lines. Given the heat and water needed, condensation occurs that must be vented through holes cut in floors, ceilings and roofs. Existing chimneys and other flues (e.g., fireplaces) are also used.

Disclosure/Drafting Offers

Salespersons have a basic choice as to whether or not to list a property that has been used as a grow house. If a salesperson elects to do so, proper disclosure should be made. As a recommended procedure, listing brokerages should indicate on the listing to *Please contact listing broker prior to showing and/or preparing offers on this property.*

Full disclosure should be made by the listing brokerage and a list maintained of all co-operating brokerages to whom that disclosure has been made. A further suggestion is to put the warning in writing and fax it to those co-operating brokerages who were given full disclosure.

Buyer representatives should recommend that a proper inspection be made by the buyer. Presently, beyond visible damage done and repairs that may be required, the long term impact of excessive humidity, use of fertilizers and application of chemicals on structural components, damage to interior finishes, interior finishes (e.g., drywall, woodwork and carpeting) and indoor air quality have not been fully investigated. Potential health hazards remain a concern and appropriate caution is needed.

SCENARIO	CLAUSE
A buyer is submitting an offer and is aware that the property was used as a grow house in the past.	**ENV–10 Growth or Manufacture of Illegal Substances— Acknowledgement** *The Buyer acknowledges that the use of the property and buildings and structures thereon may have been for the growth or manufacture of illegal substances and acknowledges that the Seller makes no representations and/or warranties with respect to the state of repair of the premises and the Buyer accepts the property and the buildings and structures thereon in their present state and in an "as is" condition.*
A buyer is submitting an offer and is seeking confirmation from the seller that the property has not been used for the manufacture of illegal substances during that seller's occupancy.	**ENV–11 No Growth or Manufacture of Illegal Substances— Warranty** *The Seller represents and warrants that during the time the Seller has owned the property, the use of the property and the buildings and structures thereon has not been for the growth or manufacture of any illegal substances, and that to the best of the Seller's knowledge and belief, the use of the property and the buildings and structures thereon has never been for the growth or manufacture of illegal substances. This warranty shall survive and not merge on the completion of this transaction.*

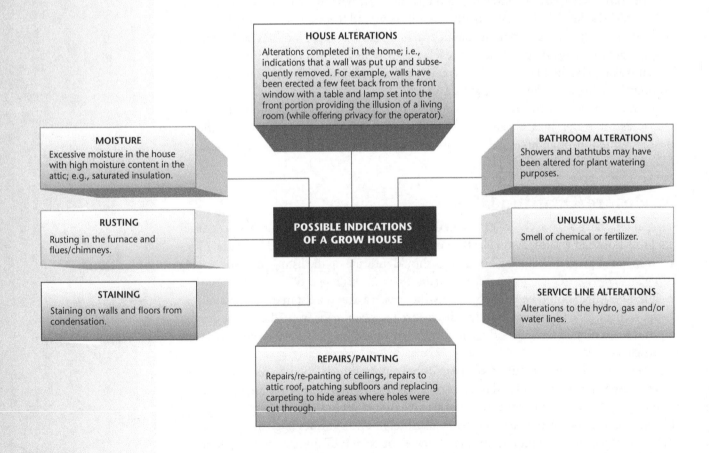

HOUSE ALTERATIONS
Alterations completed in the home; i.e., indications that a wall was put up and subsequently removed. For example, walls have been erected a few feet back from the front window with a table and lamp set into the front portion providing the illusion of a living room (while offering privacy for the operator).

MOISTURE
Excessive moisture in the house with high moisture content in the attic; e.g., saturated insulation.

BATHROOM ALTERATIONS
Showers and bathtubs may have been altered for plant watering purposes.

RUSTING
Rusting in the furnace and flues/chimneys.

POSSIBLE INDICATIONS OF A GROW HOUSE

UNUSUAL SMELLS
Smell of chemical or fertilizer.

STAINING
Staining on walls and floors from condensation.

SERVICE LINE ALTERATIONS
Alterations to the hydro, gas and/or water lines.

REPAIRS/PAINTING
Repairs/re-painting of ceilings, repairs to attic roof, patching subfloors and replacing carpeting to hide areas where holes were cut through.

Home Inspection

A complete home inspection will uncover problems relating to structural deficiencies; i.e., the integrity of any repairs to reverse the electrical wiring and seal any breaks in the foundation or other holes used for venting. Inspectors will be looking to ensure that wiring is safe, checking for any problems arising from excess moisture within the structure and verifying the integrity of the vapour barrier. However, chemical contamination and health risks are outside of the home inspector's expertise; e.g., visible mould will require the services of a mould investigator.

Working with Prospective Buyers/Tenants

Certain tell-tale signs may indicate an intention to operate a grow house. The following list is offered as a general guideline only.

- Seeking an unfinished basement and focusing on the basement during showing; i.e., not looking at the home as would a normal purchaser.
- Displaying a particular interest in the privacy of the house.
- Buying sight unseen and communicating only by fax, phone or e-mail.
- Willing to pay top dollar with no questions asked.
- Wanting immediate possession.

In addition, registrants should be wary of renters insisting on making rent payments in cash, having no known source of income yet seemingly affluent (e.g., expensive cars and sophisticated telecommunications devices), being reluctant to allow landlords to inspect their rented premises and making arrangements away from the property to pay rent and/or discuss problems.

Salespersons involved with rentals, as well as property managers, should also be aware that residential and commercial marijuana growing operations used in the past may be repeatedly used, as such properties are generally known by the criminal element.

Civil Liability

Although the potential for criminal and other legal ramifications involving real estate registrants who list and sell a grow house are unclear, the best line of defense is always full disclosure. Police departments, as part of their investigations of grow houses, will be interested in real estate registrants involved in properties that are subsequently turned into illegal grow operations.

When listing a property, registrants should consider the following if suspicions arise:

- Check with the local police to see if the property is a busted drug house.
- Disclose, disclose, disclose.
- Make sure to provide for a home inspection condition in the offer.
- If asked to find a tenant, carefully consider other factors as outlined previously.
- The listing does not have to be taken.

If a real estate registrant knows or reasonably should know that the buyer or tenant is planning on using the property as a grow house, he/she may wish to consult with the police or a criminal lawyer regarding the law relating to aiding and abetting a criminal activity. Issues may also arise concerning money laundering and the seizing of assets obtained with the proceeds of crime. For additional details concerning grow houses in a particular marketplace, contact the local police department.

The Grow House   **DISCIPLINE HEARING DECISION**

A home was used for the cultivation of marijuana plants in 2002. In 2003, the registrant represented the buyers of this home. At point of negotiations, she was advised of the prior use as a grow house. Accordingly, the 2003 *Agreement of Purchase and Sale* included the following written disclosure:

> *The Buyer acknowledges that the use of the property and buildings and structures thereon may have been for the growth or manufacture of illegal substances and acknowledges that the Seller makes no representations and/or warranties with respect to the state of repair of the premises and the Buyer accepts the property and the buildings and structures thereon in their present state and in an "as is" condition.*

In January, 2005 the registrant listed the property for sale on behalf of Seller A, acting under a Power of Attorney for Consumer A. The MLS® Listing, prepared at the authorization of the registrant, stated the following:

> *Lovely Home! Close To All Amenities, Street B and Street C, Street D, Close To Shopping Mall. All Electric Light Fixtures, Fridge, Stove, Washer, Dryer, B/I Dishwasher, B/I Microwave, California Shutters, Cac, Cvac, Gdo And Remotes, Interlocking Walkway. Entrance to House From Garage. No Disappointments. 24 Hours Notice To Tenants For Showings. Thanks For Showing!*

The registrant showed the property to buyer clients, who then entered into an agreement of purchase and sale. The registrant represented all parties to the transaction. The buyers, prior to closing, discovered that the home had been previously used as a grow house. The registrant had not, up to that point, disclosed this fact nor made the buyers aware that a written disclosure was provided in the 2003 transaction.

When asked why no disclosure was made, the registrant indicated that, while she was aware that a previous owner had been preparing the property to be a grow house, the operation was stopped by police before it began and she has merely forgotten to tell the buyers. After this conversation, the registrant faxed the buyers the written disclosure about the grow house which she had been provided in the 2003 transaction. The buyers requested a mutual release from the agreement of purchase and sale, including return of their deposit funds.

DECISION

The RECO Discipline Hearing Panel determined that the registrant acted in an unprofessional manner and breached Rules: 1, 2, 10, 11 and 21 (previous Code of Ethics under REBBA). The decision stated that she *failed to disclose what she had been told about the property and in light of that information failed to verify whether the property had been a grow house on behalf of her clients the buyers, when this information could have practically been obtained.*

Source: Discipline Decision, Burgess June 21, 2007

FRAUD

Fraud, best defined as a deception deliberately made to secure an unfair or unlawful advantage, takes on many forms in the Canadian marketplace. Fraud encompasses a broad spectrum ranging from telemarketing and Internet scams to elaborate schemes targeting insurance companies, credit card organizations and banking facilities. Recently, law enforcement and legislators have focused on the growth of real estate related fraud and, more specifically, mortgage fraud. Fraud, for real estate and mortgage financing purposes, is typically focused on identity and/or value fraud.

Identity Fraud

Identity fraud (often referred to as *identity theft*) has proven particularly difficult to control given the ingenuity of fraudsters. Perpetrators typically use stolen credit card numbers, social insurance numbers, bank account PINs and other confidential information to borrow large sums of money, make major purchases and/or empty bank accounts.

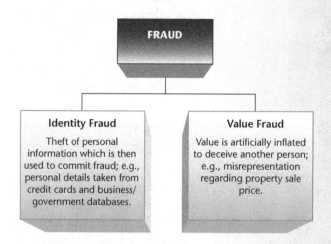

Thieves often gain access to personal information through relatively simple techniques such as diverting mail to a different address, rummaging through trash (dumpster diving) looking for items such as receipts, bank statements and pre-approved credit offerings, and stealing wallets/purses.

From a real estate perspective, a fraudster might obtain a diskette and password that allows access to the electronic property registration system. He or she could then potentially transfer title, register a discharge of the existing financing, place new financing on the property and pocket the funds. Many identity fraud variations are possible.

PHISHING

The phishing scam uses spam, pop-up messages and e-mail to deceive Internet users into disclosing personal information including credit card numbers, SINs and bank account details.

The message seemingly comes from a business or organization with which the consumer presently deals. The text involves a request for updating and/or validating account information. The individual is then directed to a web site that looks much like the legitimate organization's web site. The fraudster wants the person to divulge personal information so that he/she can steal his or her identity, charge amounts to credit cards or commit other fraud crimes using the person's name.

Avoid sending any personal information by e-mail (a non-secure method of transmitting information). When information is requested, contact the inquiring organization using a telephone number known to be correct and confirm the proper web address. Check all credit card and bank account statements immediately upon receipt for any unauthorized charges. If such mail is late, call the issuing company to verify billing address and balances.

Lastly, contact a computer representative to upgrade security measures and minimize exposure to Internet fraud.

Value Fraud

Value fraud involves schemes in which the true value of a product or service is either much less than presented or has no value. For example, with a telemarketing scheme, the scam artist may obtain an advance deposit from a consumer and never fulfil the terms of the agreement. With insurance fraud, the fraudster may claim and receive compensation for stated loss that far exceeds the actual loss.

In real estate, value fraud is most commonly associated with selling price. Many variations exist, but essentially the fraudster artificially inflates the selling price in order to secure a loan exceeding that property's true value. The fraudster pockets the difference, stops making mortgage payments and the lender absorbs an inevitable deficiency when power of sale action is taken.

Lenders may also suffer loss of all advanced funds. For example, a loan may be approved for a fictitious property (sometimes referred to as an *air loan*) or for a misrepresented situation; e.g., a storage locker or garage space sold as a condominium unit.

Value-based fraud often involves both the fraudster and willing participants who are encouraged to participate by providing cash incentives to use their names and/or credit histories to fraudulently obtain loans.

A Growing Problem

Stakeholders in the real estate industry now realize the full impact of fraud. Some loss estimates range as high as $600 million for 2004 for mortgage fraud alone, up from $150 million just three years earlier. When combined with other forms of fraud, the estimates grow into the billions.

Insiders generally acknowledge that mortgage fraud has been expanding at an alarming rate. Its growth seems closely linked to both the buoyant Canadian real estate market and the move to e-business and electronic platforms. Barriers to mortgage financing have been reduced given heightened marketplace competition. At the same time, the house buying process has become more *anonymized*. Face-to-face dealings have given way to online mortgage applications, appraisals based on computer-generated valuation models rather than direct property inspections and funds/title documents transferred by electronic registration.

Fail-safe measures built into traditional buying models are in jeopardy given fast-paced mortgage approvals and closings in the highly competitive real estate marketplace. Historically, consumers contacted known professionals to assist; e.g., the local bank manager who handled the borrower's accounts would also arrange a mortgage. Increasingly, consumers seek out those that can best expedite the deal. Familiarity has taken second place to expediency.

Deterring Fraud—A Concerted Effort   CURIOSITY

Many regulatory and professional organizations have joined in the battle to stem the growing fraud problem, including the Real Estate Council of Ontario (RECO), the Law Society of Upper Canada, Canada Mortgage and Housing Corporation, Teranet Inc., Mortgage Professionals Canada, the Independent Mortgage Brokers Association of Ontario (IMBA), and various title insurers.

To fight mortgage fraud, the Financial Services Commission of Ontario (FSCO) developed a checklist to help Ontario's mortgage brokering industry detect and prevent mortgage fraud. Some key practices in the checklist relate to:

- verifying a person has the legal right to mortgage the property
- confirming the accuracy of other information, such as employment and income
- validating a driver's licence with the Ministry of Transportation (MTO)
- confirming the source of the borrower's down payment
- confirming if the property will be occupied by the owner or a tenant
- detailing the reason for no appraisal, or an appraisal not signed by a real estate appraiser with a designation from the Appraisal Institute of Canada

RECO has launched various initiatives to counter this growing problem, such as introducing education materials, strengthening consumer awareness, expanding investigations, and pursuing additional remedies available under REBBA 2002.

SECTION II   CURRENT TRENDS AND ISSUES IN RESIDENTIAL REAL ESTATE

Mortgage Fraud

Mortgage fraud has attracted extensive media attention given its impact on innocent homeowners and lenders. Lending institutions, credit reporting agencies, title companies and origination services are placing increased emphasis on systems and procedures to counter this growing problem.

Fraudulent activities range from misrepresentation in a mortgage application to elaborate schemes for financial gain involving organized crime. Registrants, through diligent professional activities, can help minimize such fraud.

TYPES OF MORTGAGE FRAUD

Many forms of mortgage fraud are possible. Most people think in terms of misrepresentations involving documents in support of an application; e.g., falsifying employment letters, stating that the borrower will reside in the residence when such is not the case and providing false personal identification. These activities do not typically provide financial gain, but do advance personal interests to the detriment of others.

More complex, financial gain schemes involve contract falsification with one or more accomplices to make the deal work, together with sequential real estate transactions and escalating prices involving the same property. For example, a property flip might involve the fraudster, a straw buyer (i.e., a person buying a property for another, thereby concealing the real buyer's identity) who purchases the property, a fraudulent appraisal to establish a higher lending value and a salesperson to facilitate the initial and flip sales.

IDENTIFYING MORTGAGE FRAUD

Fraud is often difficult to casually detect, but telltale clues are present. Anyone involved with real estate or mortgage transactions should prudently watch for key signals. Warning signs are cumulative in nature. Obviously, no single factor will indicate fraud potential, but the more that appear, the more vigilant and diligent you need to be.

Unknown Persons	If persons are unknown to you, ask for photo identification.
Inconsistent Personal Details	Watch for inconsistencies or contradictions in personal information provided.
Things Don't Add Up	Be sensitive to situations that don't make sense; e.g., the buyer who has a significant downpayment but no tangible assets, or an individual with limited employment history who has accumulated significant assets.
Unusual Circumstances	Be aware of out-of-the-ordinary situations. Examples include one person acting on behalf of another in a real estate transaction, or a buyer not wishing to personally see the property nor have it appraised or inspected.
Close Connections	Large fraud schemes typically require complicity. Circumstances that might indicate this possibility involve a lawyer acting for both parties in the transaction or the salesperson repeatedly involved in multiple representation with a particular buyer. Further, a salesperson might participate directly as buyer or seller in several real estate transactions.
Activity Too Focused	Salesperson does majority of business with few clients and refers buyers/sellers to the same lawyer or appraiser.

Unusual Requests/Facts	Many possibilities exist. The buyer wants the property removed from MLS® immediately. Listing information doesn't align with the facts. The client requests that the deposit be held at other than the listing brokerage for no apparent reason. The buyer or seller instructs you not to speak to a particular party involved with the transaction.
Unusual Activity	Examples include several transactions involving the same property within a short time frame and a listing/sale price history that doesn't make sense based on market trends.

EXAMPLES: *MORTGAGE FRAUD*

The After Closing Second

Consumer Fraudster misrepresents the downpayment, arranges private financing for the downpayment, qualifies for the first mortgage based on false information and then registers a second mortgage on title after closing.

The Wrong Agreement

Salesperson Fraudster is buying a home from Seller Smith for $250,000. Smith hastily signs five copies of the agreement, not noticing the price change to $285,000 on one copy. The salesperson then uses the altered copy to arrange financing for the property.

Forged Documents

The fraudster arbitrarily selects the property at 1238 Maple Avenue, goes to the local land registry office and confirms property details including any mortgage on the property.

He completes a Discharge of Charge/Mortgage for the existing mortgage by forging appropriate bank officials' signatures. This document is registered on title. The property is now free and clear. The existing mortgagee remains unaware, as the property owner keeps remitting mortgage payments.

He then forges a Transfer/Deed of Land for its current value of $340,000, pays the land transfer tax and other registration costs, and registers his ownership on title.

As the new property owner, the fraudster then approaches a lender to obtain a 50% loan-to-value mortgage of $170,000. The lender, unaware of any risk given the sizeable equity position, orders a drive-by appraisal only. Consequently, no contact is made with the homeowner. The money is advanced to a lawyer accomplice and the fraudster makes off with $170,000 (less land transfer tax and incidental registration fees). The owner, unaware of the events, keeps paying the existing mortgage.

The Boost and Flip

The seller places her property on MLS® at $219,900 in a very buoyant real estate market. The fraudster quickly buys the property for $210,000 and asks that the property be immediately removed from MLS® (to minimize knowledge of the first listing).

The fraudster subsequently sells to a straw buyer for $249,000. The property is appraised by an accomplice for full value ($249,000) and a 95% mortgage is successfully arranged for $236,550. The property is then placed on MLS® with incorrect measurements (i.e., larger square footage to justify the new price) and is sold for $248,500 subject to assuming the $236,550 mortgage.

At minimum, the fraudster receives the $26,550 (difference between the original purchase price and the arranged mortgage), plus the final buyer's downpayment of $11,950. If the buyer qualifies for the mortgage payment but lacks sufficient downpayment, the fraudster may take back an undisclosed second mortgage which is registered after closing.

The False Statement

Borrower Fraudster provides forged employment letters (or other documentation) using desktop publishing software and submits details to the lender. The mortgage is approved based on false qualifying information.

SECTION II   CURRENT TRENDS AND ISSUES IN RESIDENTIAL REAL ESTATE

Rising prices and profits have also lured fraudsters into our midst. Media attention on rising real estate values over the past few years has caught the attention of those seeking to take advantage of any weak links in the transaction process.

Fraud has proven difficult to control in real estate transactions. The perpetrators are creative. By the time a particular scam is identified and controlled, the fraudsters have moved on to other weak points. Successful counter measures require the combined effort of those involved with legal, appraisal, real estate brokerage and financing sectors in concert with law enforcement agencies.

Detection & Prevention

Salespersons are a vital link in identifying potential fraud, but other stakeholders are also working diligently to develop improved methods to diminish fraud in real estate transactions and mortgage origination.

BEST PRACTICES/PROCEDURES

Various professional organizations are upgrading systems and procedures. As an example, the Canadian Association of Accredited Mortgage Professionals (CAAMP) has developed origination standards. Such standards include:

- Ensuring that mortgage applications have been fully completed and do not contain inconsistencies regarding borrower details.
- Establishing the identity of all applicants.
- Obtaining confirmation of downpayment with increased due diligence when a 'gift' is involved.
- Obtaining original documentation confirming employment.
- Providing a copy of the listing and agreement, along with any attachments or addenda.

EDUCATION

The Real Estate Council of Ontario, the Ontario Real Estate Association and real estate boards are all playing a role in disseminating up-to-date information on fraud issues and prevention techniques.

This activity is complemented by research reports, education courses, pamphlets and online resources to increase awareness both for registrants and consumers by organizations such as Ministry of Consumer and Business Services, CMHC, title insurers and lenders.

REGULATORY ACTIVITIES

Organizations directly responsible for regulating sectors of the real estate industry have taken proactive steps. The Real Estate Council of Ontario, the Financial Services Commission of Ontario and the Law Society of Upper Canada are underway with initiatives that identify and implement heightened standards to minimize fraud opportunities. At the same time, new legislation places greater focus on enforcement procedures.

REBBA 2002, for example, includes a specific provision in the Code of Ethics relating to error, misrepresentation and fraud. The Code not only requires the registrant to avoid misrepresentation (Code of Ethics, Sec. 37) but he/she also must take steps to prevent fraud, error or misrepresentation. See subsequent topic titled *RECO Initiatives*.

AUTOMATED DETECTION SYSTEMS

Computer-based detection systems are available for lenders, credit bureaus, high ratio financing insurers (e.g., Genworth Financial Canada and CMHC) and other mortgage service providers to detect unusual activity and circumstances that may indicate possible mortgage fraud.

Mortgage fraud systems generally look for suspicious events and activity based on historical research. Automated flagging has proven very effective in warning lenders of potential problems that warrant further investigation.

Fraud software varies significantly in the marketplace. Many programs alert the client concerning misused or false information based on continuously updated source data from government records, banks, telephone/cellular companies and Canada Post. For example, an alert would be issued if a social insurance number is invalid (SIN numeric range not yet created or the SIN is a retired number (deceased person)).

Certain addresses are identified (e.g., post office box, rental boxes and detention centres) as well as telephones (e.g., cell phones and public pay phones). Geographic overlays are also used in which two data elements are compared such as the telephone number and postal code to ensure that they coincide geographically.

Fraud software may also involve detailed property transaction analysis to identify unusual sales or mortgage activity, sale prices above the neighbourhood norm and reoccurrence of similar names in sequential transactions.

Personal Fraud Proofing PERSPECTIVE

Salespersons, as with all consumers, must be constantly vigilant regarding scams associated with identity fraud. Here are a few suggestions to help reduce your chances of being a victim:

- Avoid sharing or circulating personal information, wherever possible.
- Don't provide credit card numbers or other personal information unless you know that the communication channel is secure.
- Burn or shred all discarded personal information; never leave receipts behind (e.g., bank machines and self-serve gas pumps).
- Burn or shred pre-approved credit card applications.
- Take particular care when providing your SIN. This number is a key link to other information sources.
- Check your credit report annually to make certain that everything is accurate; i.e., no debts or unauthorized activities have taken place.
- Cancel unused credit cards.
- Watch billing dates for important mailings; e.g., credit card statements. If mail is not received, it may have been fraudulently redirected.
- Select difficult passwords for your accounts and change them frequently.
- Carry only limited identifying documents, credit cards and related items.

To learn more about identity fraud, go to the Privacy Commissioner of Canada web site at **www.privcom.gc.ca**, call toll-free at (800) 282–1376 or write: The Office of the Privacy Commissioner, 112 Kent Street, Ottawa, ON, K1A 1H3. Web sites for local police forces also typically provide useful information concerning fraud.

SECTION II CURRENT TRENDS AND ISSUES IN RESIDENTIAL REAL ESTATE

RECO Initiatives

The Real Estate Council of Ontario, as already mentioned, has taken a proactive approach to fraud. Initiatives include investigations previously under REBBA and now under REBBA 2002, enforcement, co-operation with other organizations, education for both registrants and consumers, and legislative reform.

REGISTRAR ACTIONS

Mortgage fraud, as a criminal offence, falls under the *Real Estate and Business Brokers Act, 2002*. The Real Estate Council of Ontario does not have the statutory authority to prosecute a registrant for criminal activity, but can refer the matter to the Registrar. Registrants are reminded that the Registrar, or an authorized representative, has the right under REBBA 2002 to fully investigate mortgage fraud and is afforded access to all books of account, cash, documents, bank accounts, vouchers, correspondence and records of the registrant being investigated.

The Registrar further has the right to refuse, suspend or revoke registration based on findings of criminal activity, subject to the right of appeal by the registrant to the Licence Appeal Tribunal (LAT). Two cases are cited in which appeals were heard by the LAT following a Notice of Proposal by the Registrar to revoke registration. In both instances, the Tribunal directed the Registrar to carry out the Proposal and revoke the applicable registration.

Registrants should note that any matters concerning fraud which come to the attention of RECO will be vigorously pursued.

Revocation of Registration: Inflating Prices | **LICENCE APPEAL TRIBUNAL DECISION**

The Registrar issued a Notice of Proposal to revoke a salesperson's registration given his participation in fraudulent activity, which involved the intentional inflating of selling prices involving five properties. The registrant appealed the Notice of Proposal to the Licence Appeal Tribunal.

In the ensuing Hearing, testimony confirmed that the salesperson convinced sellers to remove their unsold properties from the market. The prices were then substantially increased, the properties sold to individuals produced by the salesperson and financing was obtained based on the inflated prices.

Typically, upon execution of the agreement of purchase and sale, the salesperson produced a mutual agreement which was signed by the buyer and seller agreeing to redirect excess funds received from the mortgagee back to the seller and other parties who were involved in the dishonest transactions. At no point, was the mortgagee informed of the mutual agreement.

As pointed out in the Hearing, the salesperson had committed two frauds: the first against the mortgagees who were deceived into advancing mortgage funds based on inflated, untrue values and the second against other brokers and salespersons who might rely on such inflated prices in arriving at other listing prices, as well as consumers purchasing in the vicinity who might also be misled.

The Tribunal, upon hearing all evidence, determined that the Registrar's Proposal was well founded and directed the Registrar to revoke the salesperson's registration.

Source: Licence Appeal Tribunal, Reasons for Decision and Order, Released February 1, 2005

Revocation of Registration: Property Flips   LICENCE APPEAL TRIBUNAL DECISION

The Registrar issued a Notice of Proposal to revoke a salesperson's registration given his involvement in three transactions in which purchase prices were inflated by way of property flips. Mortgages were subsequently obtained that exceeded 100% of the original purchase prices.

In each instance, a power of sale property was involved. As an example, one such property was listed at $115,000 and sold for $112,000 to a buyer. However, the buyer's name was not registered on title, but rather another name (a relative of the registrant) appeared. The mortgage application showed the second individual as the prospective owner, with a purchase price of $145,000. A mortgage was obtained for $133,762.50.

The mortgagee, suspecting fraud when completing its own investigation, notified RECO. Based on evidence collected, the Registrar held that the past conduct of the registrant afforded reasonable grounds that the individual would not carry on business in accordance with the law and conduct himself with integrity and honesty.

The Tribunal upon hearing evidence from the mortgagee, RECO inspectors, a RECO registration officer, the Assistant Registrar and the registrant, concluded that the Registrar had reasonable grounds for the Notice of Proposal and directed that the Proposal be carried out.

Source: Licence Appeal Tribunal, Reasons for Decision and Order, Released March 31, 2005

MONEY LAUNDERING

The *Proceeds of Crime (Money Laundering) and Terrorist Financing Act* is a federal statute with three primary objectives:

- to implement specific measures to detect and deter money laundering and the financing of terrorist activities, and to facilitate investigations and prosecution of related offences;
- to respond to the threat posed by organized crime by providing law enforcement officials with the information they need to deprive criminals of the proceeds of their criminal activities, while protecting individual privacy; and
- to help fulfill Canada's international commitments to fight multinational crime.

The Financial Transactions and Reports Analysis Centre of Canada (FINTRAC) is the federal agency responsible for the collection, analysis and disclosure of information to assist in the detection, prevention, and deterrence of money laundering and the financing of terrorist activities in Canada and abroad.

Matters concerning identification verification and receipt of funds requirements under the legislation were discussed in *The Real Estate Transaction—General*, as compliance is directly related to drafting and negotiating offers. However, this Act covers a much broader scope involving suspicious transactions and terrorist property.

Compliance Overview

The Act, enacted in 2001, originally required reporting of suspicious transactions and related activities by various persons and entities, including real estate brokerages, brokers and salespersons. In 2008, compliance was significantly expanded to include identification verification and receipt of funds reports. All real estate registrants in Ontario are subject to these reporting requirements.

Published by the Real Estate Council of Ontario

Falsifying information

The *Real Estate and Business Brokers Act, 2002* (the "Act") which came into force on March 31, 2006 contained two new offences related to falsifying information. Sec. 34 and 35 of the Act state:

Falsifying information

34.   No registrant shall falsify, assist in falsifying or induce or counsel another person to falsify or assist in falsifying any information or document relating to a trade in real estate.

Furnishing false information

35.   No registrant shall furnish, assist in furnishing or induce or counsel another person to furnish or assist in furnishing any false or deceptive information or documents relating to a trade in real estate.

These provisions make it an explicit offence under the Act to falsify information, assist another person in falsifying information or furnish false information related to real estate transactions.

Registrants who contravene this section of the Act may have their registration suspended or revoked or be charged under the statute. If convicted of an offence under the Act, individual registrants may be fined up to $50,000 and are subject to prison terms of up to 2 years. Corporations are subject to fines of up to $250,000 for offences under the Act. In addition, a court may order a convicted person to pay compensation or restitution to affected parties.

These measures reflect the fact that falsifying information related to real estate transactions is a serious issue. Any registrant, for example, who counseled an individual to lie with respect to a mortgage application, would be guilty of an offence under these clauses.

Registrants also have an obligation not to provide any false information about a property during a transaction or to counsel a seller to falsify any information about a property.

These measures also strengthen the ability of enforcement officials to deal with real estate scams. Most if not all real estate scams, involve, at some point in the process, the falsification of information related to a real estate transaction. In some real estate scams individuals have sold properties without the true owners consent. Registrants or any persons who participate in this type of activity are obviously operating in violation of the Act.

Real Estate Council of Ontario
Tel: 416-207-4800 Toll Free: 1-800-245-6910 Fax: 416-207-4820

Office of the Registrar
AsktheRegistrar@reco.on.ca

REBBA*2002*
Real Estate & Business Brokers Act, 2002

For more information about RECO,
visit: www.reco.on.ca

Suspicious Transaction

As of 2001, all real estate brokers and salespersons had to report suspicious transactions. A suspicious transaction is a financial transaction for which there are reasonable grounds to suspect that it is related to the commission of a money laundering offence. Such an offence involves concealing or converting property or the proceeds of property (e.g. money), knowing or believing that these were derived from the commission of an offence referred to in Section 462.31 of the *Criminal Code*. A money laundering offence may also extend to property or proceeds derived from illegal activities that took place outside Canada.

TERRORIST ACTIVITY FINANCING

Terrorist financing provides funds for terrorist activity. The sums needed to mount terrorist attacks are not always large and the associated transactions are not necessarily complex. Methods used by terrorist groups to generate funds from illegal sources are often very similar to those used by traditional criminal organizations. Like criminal organizations, these groups must find ways to launder and use illicit funds without drawing attention of the authorities. For this reason, transactions related to terrorist financing may look a lot like those related to money laundering.

Effective June 12, 2002, suspicious transactions included financial transactions where reasonable grounds exist to suspect that such are related to the commission of a terrorist activity financing offence.

GUIDELINES

A suspicious transaction can involve several factors that may seem individually insignificant, but together may raise suspicion that the transaction is related to the commission of a money laundering offence. A transaction may be connected to money laundering when a broker or salesperson thinks that it (or a group of transactions) raises questions or gives rise to discomfort, apprehension or mistrust.

Transactions may give rise to reasonable grounds to suspect that they are related to money laundering regardless of the sum of money involved. No minimum dollar value applies to a suspicious transaction.

SPECIFIC INDICATORS

FINTRAC has developed both general and specific indicators of suspicious transactions to assist persons and entities affected by the Act. Taken together, these may point to a suspicious transaction. The following illustration contains these specific indicators (which can be useful to real estate brokers and salespersons).

Registrants are reminded that *behaviour is suspicious, not people*. The consideration of many factors, not just any one factor, can lead to a conclusion that reasonable grounds exist to suspect that a transaction is related to the commission of a money laundering offence.

INDICATORS—SUSPICIOUS TRANSACTION

- ❐ Client arrives at a real estate closing with a significant amount of cash.

- ❐ Client purchases property in the name of a nominee, such as an associate or a relative (other than a spouse).

- ❐ Client does not want to put his or her name on any document that would connect him/her with the property or uses different names on offers to purchase, closing documents and deposit receipts.

- ❐ Client inadequately explains the last minute substitution of the purchasing party's name.

- ❐ Client negotiates a purchase for market value or above asking price, but records a lower value on documents, paying the difference under the table.

- ❐ Client sells property below market value, with an additional amount under the table payment.

- ❐ Client pays initial deposit with a cheque from a third party, other than a spouse or a parent.

- ❐ Client pays substantial downpayment in cash and balance is financed by an unusual source or offshore bank.

- ❐ Client purchases personal use property under a corporate veil when this type of transaction is inconsistent with the ordinary business practice of the client.

- ❐ Client purchases property without inspecting it.

- ❐ Client purchases multiple properties in a short time period, and seems to have few concerns about the location, condition and anticipated repair costs, etc. of each property.

- ❐ Client pays rent or the amount of a lease in advance using a large amount of cash.

- ❐ Client is known to have paid large remodelling or home improvement invoices with cash, on a property for which property management services are provided.

Terrorist Property Reporting

Real estate brokers and salespersons are required to send a terrorist property report to FINTRAC, if property in their possession or control is known to be owned or controlled by or on behalf of a terrorist or a terrorist group. This includes information about any transaction or proposed transaction relating to that property. In this context, property means any type of real or personal property in the real estate broker's or salesperson's possession or control, and includes any deed or instrument giving title or right to property, or giving right to money or goods. For example, cash, bank accounts, insurance policies, money orders, real estate, securities and traveller's cheques, among other types of assets, are considered property.

A terrorist or a terrorist group includes anyone that has, as one of their purposes or activities, facilitated or carried out any terrorist activity. This can be an individual, a group, a trust, a partnership or a fund. It can also be an unincorporated association or organization.

Real estate brokerages are required to verify that the names of their clients are not on the Canadian or United Nations list of known terrorists. Relevant information is available through FINTRAC. Members of organized real estate can also access the Money Laundering Compliance Centre operated by The Canadian Real Estate Association.

WEB LINKS

FINTRAC   Go to the Financial Transactions and Reports Analysis Centre of Canada website (*www.fintrac-canafe.gc.ca*) for detailed information regarding all compliance issues.

REALTORLink®   Members of organized real estate can access the Money Laundering Compliance Centre through the REALTORLink® website. Go to *www.realtorlink.ca.*

Large Cash Transactions ($10,000 or More)

Individuals and corporations/entities have been required to report the following financial transactions since the Act came into effect. The third requirement applies to real estate brokers and salespersons.

- The sending or receiving of international electronic funds transfers of $10,000 or more through the SWIFT network;
- Other international electronic funds transfers of $10,000 or more (through non-SWIFT networks); and
- Large cash transactions involving amounts of $10,000 or more.

A record must be kept for every amount of cash of $10,000 or more that is received in a single transaction.

If a broker or salesperson is aware that two or more cash transactions of less than $10,000 each were made within a 24-hour period (i.e., 24 consecutive hours), by or on behalf of the same client, this would be viewed as a single large cash transaction if they add up to $10,000 or more and must be reported to FINTRAC as explained above. Large cash transaction records are not required if the cash is received from a financial entity or a public body.

Identification Verification

Identification verification, which came into effect in June 2008, expanded compliance to include identifying individuals and corporations/entities for every real estate transaction in which the real estate brokerage is involved. Detailed procedures and associated forms were discussed when addressing offer preparation and negotiations in *The Real Estate Transaction—General.*

Receipt of Funds

The requirement to complete a Receipt of Funds Record also came into effect in June 2008. This record must be prepared for every amount of funds that a registrant receives in the course of a single real estate transaction. Detailed procedures and associated forms were discussed when addressing offer preparation and negotiations in *The Real Estate Transaction—General.*

Compliance Regime

The following five elements must be included in a compliance regime developed by a real estate brokerage:

- The appointment of a compliance officer.
- The development and application of written compliance policies and procedures.

- The assessment and documentation of risks of money laundering and terrorist financing, and measures to mitigate high risks.
- Implementation and documentation of an ongoing compliance training program.
- A documented review of the effectiveness of policies and procedures, training program and risk assessment.

FINTRAC has prepared guidelines to assist brokerages in ongoing administration of their compliance regime, as well as providing interpretation notices that focus on technical interpretations regarding certain provisions contained in the *Proceeds of Crime (Money Laundering) and Terrorist Financing Act* and associated Regulations. Real estate brokerages are responsible to continuously develop, apply and update written compliance policies in accordance with requirements set out by the Financial Transactions and Reports Analysis Center.

RISK ASSESSMENT
Brokerages are also responsible to complete a review of policies every two years. The Canadian Real Estate Association has developed a Risk Assessment Form to assist in the process. The form is available to members on the Money Laundering Compliance Centre. Others should consult the FINTRAC website for detailed procedures. If a brokerage determines that the risk for money laundering or terrorist financing is high, the broker of record will need to take action to mitigate the risk.

The *Risk Assessment Form* developed by The Canadian Real Estate Association and published by the Ontario Real Estate Association has been included for information purposes in the *Appendix*.

Reporting/Record Keeping

Real estate brokerages are required to report suspicious (or attempted suspicious) transactions, large cash transactions and property in their possession or control that is owned or controlled by a terrorist or terrorist group. Reports filed with FINTRAC must be kept confidential. As well, the collection of personal information mandated under this Act places an added responsibility on brokerages, brokers and salespersons to be diligent regarding privacy issues and requirements set out in the *Personal Information Protection and Electronic Documents Act* (PIPEDA). FINTRAC also has obligations in regard to private information forwarded to the organization.

Brokerages must keep the following reports and records on file relating to real estate transactions:

- Large Cash Transaction Reports
- Receipt of Funds Records
- Suspicious Transaction Reports
- Individual Identification Information Records
- Corporation/Entity Identification Information Records
- Self-Assessed Risk Management Report (prepared every two years).

Applicable forms for brokerages are available from FINTRAC and OREA depending on the type of report required.

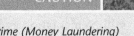
All registrants must be fully informed and up-to-date on all matters involving the *Proceeds of Crime (Money Laundering) and Terrorist Financing Act* and be in full compliance with procedures detailed by FINTRAC. Significant fines and possible imprisonment can result from failing to adhere to these requirements.

Topics included in this course are summary in nature, but ample resources are available when active in the marketplace. Make certain that you fully understand this important federal legislation by fully reviewing information on the FINTRAC website (**www.fintrac-canafe.gc.ca**). Members of organized real estate should also carefully review all material included in the CREA Money Laundering Compliance Center (**www.realtorlink.ca**). Lastly, discuss the matter in detail with the broker of record or manager to ensure a thorough knowledge of brokerage policies and procedures.

AUCTIONS

Auctions have been effective over the years in establishing real value of many products and services, including real estate. The success of an auction lies in the staging of an open, competitive environment to buy and sell. Proponents of real estate auctions frequently point to the widespread use of real estate auctions, particularly in Australia.

The real estate auction can be very effective under the right circumstances. Real estate auctions in Ontario have enjoyed success, particularly in niche markets such as estate sales. Auctions have also proven attractive to any seller faced with a short time line to dispose of property.

Auctioneers

An auctioneer can be generally described as anyone who engages in the business of selling or offering for sale by public auction goods, wares, merchandise or effects of any kind. Auctioneers are not licensed at a provincial level, but are required to obtain an auctioneer's license from the local municipality (if applicable). Not all municipalities have a by-law relating to such licensing.

The municipal by-law will set out various stipulations, including initial and renewal fees. Generally, the by-law includes a requirement that auctioneers prominently display their name and business address at each auction and in all advertising materials, maintain a proper set of books for all business transactions concluded and provide a detailed accounting relating to proceeds and associated commissions/charges.

EXEMPTION: REBBA 2002

The *Real Estate and Business Brokers Act, 2002* provides that auctioneers are exempted under the Act and may conduct sales of real property under certain circumstances:

EXEMPTIONS   REBBA

5.   (1)   Despite section 4, registration shall not be required in respect of any trade in real estate by . . .

        (b) an auctioneer if the trade is made in the course of and as part of the auctioneer's duties as auctioneer;

Real estate brokerages may conduct auctions of real property provided they comply with local municipal regulations.

The Auction Process

Auctioneers point to various benefits of auctioning real estate, but generally emphasize the competitive bidding environment, the removal of an artificial ceiling on the asking price and the immediate binding contract that can flow from an auction. Normally, the auctioneer operates under an auction authority that is an agreement between the seller and auctioneer. This document sets out the conditions under which a fee is earned and the length of the agreement.

In addition, auctioneers usually prepare an auctioning plan or strategy regarding advertising and promotion, the plan for showings, the type of information to be contained in the bidder's information package and auction location.

PREVIEW/MARKETING

For real estate auctions, the auctioneer typically develops a pre-view marketing campaign including advertising and showings scheduled for the two or three week period prior to the auction date. Interested buyers receive bidder registration packages at that time. The sellers typically set a reserve price (reserve bid) that is unknown to the bidders, but need not. The decision to do so or not is a function of strategy, market conditions, auction strategy and specific seller needs.

TYPES OF AUCTIONS

Generally, three types of auctions exist in the real estate marketplace:

- The *absolute auction* is without a minimum reserve bid for the seller. This type of auction normally attracts the widest interest since a sale is virtually guaranteed with no restrictions or limitations on the final selling price.
- The *minimum bid* auction provides a safety net for the seller. He/she can establish the minimum acceptable sale price. Obviously, the amount of interest in the sale is many times directly related to the minimum bid. A minimum well below market value should attract proportionately more interest.
- The *auction by confirmation* permits the seller to reject any final high bid price.

THE AUCTION

The sellers, in conjunction with the auctioneer, set a time and date for the auction. For discussion purposes, assume that a minimum bid auction is being held:

- If the reserve price is not met at the auction, the sellers would seek out other ways to market the property. Further, the sellers might approach active bidders to see if an acceptable price could be negotiated.
- If the reserve price is met or exceeded, the property is sold.

Under this form of auction, the seller has more than one opportunity to sell the property. He or she may receive an acceptable offer before the auction, sell the property at auction or negotiate with one or more bidders for an agreeable price if the reserve price is not met. Conversely, this type of auction may not attract widespread interest as would an absolute auction.

SELLER PERSPECTIVE	BUYER PERSPECTIVE
Sale with No Conditions The seller is given the opportunity to have a quick sale with no conditions.	**Preparation** Ensure that all the necessary preparation is done in order to make an informed bid at the auction. Register your interest in the property so that you will be kept informed about any important developments as the auction date nears. Attend various auctions to get a better understanding of the process.
Timing The total time consumed from start to finish can be 45 to 50 days or less, depending on circumstances.	
Seller in Control The seller is in control, as he or she sets the time period for pre-marketing (including bidder inspections) and establishes the auction date to suit personal circumstances. The seller may dictate other conditions to meet personal circumstances.	**Inspection** Take the time to carefully inspect the property. Involve an appropriate expert in the process (e.g., home inspector, builder, architect, etc.).
	Legal Have legal counsel check the title and any other non-title search items prior to the auction.
Market Value An auction is a good method to produce a sale at market value, assuming adequate marketing efforts are undertaken prior to auction date.	**Lender** Select a lender who is prepared to inspect the auction property at the preview stage and give a commitment based on that inspection.
Unique Properties Auctions have proven effective when sellers are dealing with unique properties or those that have special value to particular buyers.	**Market Data** Seek professional assistance to obtain detailed information on existing sales activity involving comparable properties over the past several months.
	The buyer may wish to be represented by a real estate brokerage to ensure that his or her interests are protected.
	Insurance Arrange suitable insurance, if successful at the auction, to ensure that your investment is adequately protected.

HOME STAGING

Home staging can be generally described as the process of making a home attractive to potential buyers. The goal of staging is to sell a home quickly and for the most money possible by attracting the highest amount of potential buyers. Home staging, originally associated with model homes, has gained widespread popularity in residential resale market.

A seller has several options when staging a property. He/she might use a professional home stager to spotlight their home, obtain guidance from a real estate professional trained in staging concepts or rely on the many do-it-yourself home staging guides. Regardless of the method, the key objective is to make the home stand out against the competition by spotlighting its key features and benefits, conveying a positive visual impression to potential buyers and generally making an attractive marketing package. It is important to note that home staging is not a regulated field and there are no industry standards.

Staging is all about creating an effective living space that is appealing to the buyer. Staging is not about decorating, as this is a personalized activity. In actual fact, staging seeks to depersonalize the property, while also removing clutter, cleaning, organizing rooms for maximum impact, maximizing features and minimizing flaws. An effective home staging draws the buyer's interest to key selling points, be it the meticulously clean, neat kitchen, the unobstructed patio view from the family room, the sense of roominess in even the smallest bedroom and the enviable impression left from a spotless master bathroom.

Interior Rooms

Most consumers can achieve some success in home staging by following certain basic tips. Beyond that, home staging books and courses are available or a home staging professional can assist in finessing the property ready for sale.

Bright and Airy Trumps Dark and Dismal	Buyers want to see bright, inviting rooms. They are buying impression as much as reality.
Clean is the Only Option	A good rule of thumb: *if it can be seen, it has to be cleaned.* Not just once, but routinely when selling the home. If some things require a professional (e.g., carpet cleaning), hire an expert.
Get Rid of Clutter	Whether it's clothes closets, the childrens' rooms or the lower room, the clutter has to go. If you can't bear to part with the bits and pieces, rent a storage unit.
If It's Broken, Fix It	Even the smallest things can translate into *they don't take care of the place.* It's amazing how much information a burned out light bulb and a broken screen conveys about the owner.
If It's Had Better Days, Replace It	The worn stairway carpet may have sentimental value, but it won't help your staging efforts. Replace worn items, assuming that its economically feasible to do so.
It's About the Buyer, Not the Seller	Depersonalizing the home can make all the difference. Allow the buyer to view the property on his or her terms, not yours. It's very difficult to visualize living in a home when it's crammed with the seller's personal mementos. Pack away the photos and memorabilia. Save it for your next home.
Clear the Traffic Areas	Homes with ample space to move around in are more appealing. Too much furniture? Rearrange for more space, get rid of it or store it.
Floors are Important Too	Floors should be spotless. Always highlight flooring features such as creative mosaics and hardwood flooring. Make them a focal point and they will catch the buyer's attention.
Don't Ignore Empty Areas	For example, don't by-pass the basement when staging. Get rid of all the clutter and increase amount of lighting. Let the buyer see the potential for this large, often underutilized asset.
Smells Don't Sell Well	Eliminate odours of all kinds—they probably won't be appreciated by the buyer. Make certain that all household garbage is removed from the kitchen and other receptacles. Pets and nurseries can also be a challenge. Use room deodorizers, open windows for ventilation and run exhaust fans before showings. If a significant problem exists, get professional help.

| Get the Garage in Shape | Cluttered garages are out. Take the time to clean it out, clean it up, organize the tools and paint the floor (if necessary). The garage can become a focal feature of a well-staged home with a little diligent effort. |

Curb Appeal

Staging tends to emphasize improving the *look and feel* of internal rooms, but complete staging also involves exterior appearance, including landscaping. Curb appeal should not be underestimated. Often, homes are half sold before the buyer even reaches the front door. A well-manicured lawn, appealing entrance and freshly painted asphalt driveway all leave a lasting impression. Here's a few outside staging tips:

It's More Than a Mowed Lawn	Make certain that planting beds are neat, all edges carefully trimmed and re-mulch to give a lasting impression.
Flowers, Flowers	You don't necessary have to invest in window boxes (although it can definitely help with some houses). Just make certain that there are plenty of well-tended flowers.
Painting Can Be a Real Plus	If the home exterior is drab, colours are not well-matched or the old paint job is fading, seriously consider repainting exterior trim, front door and garage doors. Get a professional involved to advise on a new colour scheme. It's amazing what a difference a new paint job can make.
Clean, Clean, Clean	If cleaning works inside your staged home, it's a must on the outside. Pressure wash all exterior surfaces including driveways, walkways and so forth, clean all windows and screens and take extra time with the entrance way and front door.
Improve Your Green Perspective	In some instances, home stagers may involve tree professionals (arborists), but you can make real gains by clearing out overgrowth and raising the tree canopy (removing lower limbs) to make the home more visible.
The New and Improved Patio	Cut back overgrown plants, re-set uneven pavers, replace outdated lighting fixtures, conceal wires to 12-volt landscaping lighting systems, remove clutter (e.g., old flower pots and planters) and freshen up the decor as budget permits. Anything that ought to be thrown away, should be.

What About the Vacant House?   CURIOSITY

The difference between a house and a home is the furnishings. A vacant house can be staged with limited furniture and accessories to give it that 'homey' feeling. Discount furniture retailers may provide the answer, if furniture rental is too much for the pocket book. It isn't necessary to fully furnish, simply include the basics to help the buyer visualize living in the property. Retailers often package inexpensive room groupings that will do the trick. A few accent towels in bathrooms and decorative touches in the kitchen can add even more to the staging process.

RECENT TRENDS IN BROKERAGE OPERATIONS

Most real estate brokerages have and continue to operate under traditional bricks and mortar, full service business models. However, change is everywhere and registrants, including prospective brokers of record, should be aware of key trends that can impact decisions about the ongoing structure and operation of a new or existing brokerage.

Expanding Franchise Options

Franchising remains a solid option for many brokerages. When real estate franchising first gained widespread popularity approximately forty years ago, the primary attractions were brand awareness, proprietary marketing materials, national advertising and referrals. Over the years, the main players have broadened service mixes to include administrative systems, which assist brokerages in management functions, performance reporting/ tracking and web-enhanced online features/services.

In recent years, new franchises have appeared that widen appeal by providing innovative methods such as profit sharing based on franchisee performance (i.e., each brokerage is viewed as a profit centre), as well as sponsoring and residual income sharing to registrants who bring others into the brokerage.

Market niche franchising has also entered the Canadian market, for example, brokerages focused solely on luxury homes. Limited service franchises have existed for many years, but have taken on new prominence in the face of recent MLS® developments involving the Competition Bureau.

Virtual vs. Bricks and Mortar

Virtual brokerage operations, while contemplated with much fanfare during the initial days of the internet, have not gained a significant presence. However, technologies flowing from those days have impacted traditional bricks and mortar operations, particularly those searching for lower overhead and improved efficiencies.

EXAMPLE *Virtual Technologies and Fixed Costs*

Assume a broker of record wants to open a new brokerage with 25 registrants, receptionists and support staff. To house this sales force, she estimates 100 square feet per person (based on both individual and shared offices). To this total, she adds 950 square feet for a reception area, administrative offices, meeting room and storage/kitchen facilities. This brings the total area to 3,450 square feet.

Alternatively, the broker of record might consider acquiring technology, which allows registrants to operate off-site, both on the road and at home. This alternate plan calls for four 100 square foot, small conference rooms and a larger meeting room for on demand scheduling. When adding receptionist and administrative space, the total is 1,400 square feet—a 59% reduction in space and associated occupancy costs.

Home-Based Registrants

The trend to home-based registrants has come about in large part due to new technologies, particularly mobile communication (including mobile internet), smart phones and the latest advances in GPS/location-based services (i.e., locating property on a smart phone by its GPS location). Voice over internet protocol (VOIP) is also a leading innovation that allows registrants to communicate from anywhere with seamless interface back to the main brokerage. Registrants with home offices do not have to register as a branch office under REBBA 2002, provided that the public is not invited to those home offices.

Teams

Real estate teams, ranging from husband and wife sharing duties to specialized teams with several registered persons, have gained significant popularity. Proponents point to the ability to focus efforts and gain efficiencies through a team approach, the ability to provide 24/7 service that a single registrant would find difficult to attain, and the benefit of shared advertising and marketing expenses. Real estate teams have no stature under REBBA 2002.

Social Media and Live Data Exchange

Registrants can now generate leads and communicate with other registrants and clients/customers on a real-time basis using various social media tools that blend lead generation, client communication and advertising. Examples include email accounts, professional blogs, Twitter, Facebook, LinkedIn, and various video and audio sharing facilities.

Connectivity using social media tools provides registrants with greater mobility, immediate access to data and the ability to instantly notify clients/customers of market information, recent changes, legislative items and newsworthy real estate events. Advocates believe that social media and live data are helping to consolidate the registrant's focal role in the real estate transaction. All social media activity must be REBBA 2002 compliant.

Limited Service Offerings and Mere Postings

Recent developments regarding MLS® and the Competition Bureau have resulted in renewed interest in these business models, particularly the *mere posting* of an MLS® listing by members of organized real estate. The full impact of this option has not been fully assessed, but clearly will have an impact on *a la carte* service options, flat fee business models and other limited service arrangements.

Registrants should note that when a brokerage has a limited service agreement with the seller under which the seller will receive offers directly from the buyer or the buyer's representative (i.e., the seller's brokerage will not receive or convey offers), then the offer retention requirements under REBBA 2002, including those pertaining to unsuccessful offers, do not apply.

KNOWLEDGE INTEGRATION

Notables

- A stigma is typically associated with a perceived risk, as distinct from a real risk.

- A key issue is whether or not a particular stigma is a material fact that would impact a buyer's decision to acquire a specific property.

- Homes used as grow houses can have long term problems given the heat, water, fertilizer and humidity required to cultivate the plants.

- A home inspection may uncover certain irregularities relating to the structure and mechanical/plumbing and electrical systems, but not provide information about hidden mould problems or contamination.

- Value fraud involves schemes in which the true value of a product or service is either much less than presented or has no value.

- Mortgage fraud can involve sophisticated plans involving several persons and sequential transactions involving one property.

- Computer-based detection systems are one of many new innovations that can help minimize mortgage fraud.

- The Registrar has the right to refuse, suspend or revoke registration based on findings of criminal activity (e.g., mortgage fraud), subject to the right of appeal to the Licence Appeal Tribunal.

- Real estate brokerages, brokers and salespersons must be familiar with all compliance requirements relating to money laundering and terrorist financing.

- Auctioneers are not licensed at a provincial level, but typically require a licence from the local municipality. Not all municipalities have such a licence.

- Three types of auctions exist: absolute, minimum bid and auction by confirmation.

- Home staging involves both interior rooms and exterior structure/landscaping.

- Regardless of the commission/fee structure selected, all brokerages must ensure that levels of service provided meet minimum regulatory requirements set out in REBBA 2002.

Web Links

Web links are included for general interest regarding selected chapter topics.

FINTRAC   Go to the Financial Transactions and Reports Analysis Centre of Canada website (*www.fintrac-canafe.gc.ca*) for detailed information regarding all compliance issues.

REALTORLink®   Members of organized real estate can access the Money Laundering Compliance Centre through the REALTORLink® website. Go to *www.realtorlink.ca*.

Strategic Thinking For Your Career

Questions are included to assist in developing your new career. No answers are provided.

1. Can you think of any local stigmas that have affected a property's value? What infamous situations have arisen in other parts of Ontario and Canada that could be viewed as stigmas that directly affected property values?

2. Have there been grow houses discovered in your local community and how is that information recorded for future reference?

3. Have I taken sufficient steps to ensure that my personal information is adequately fraud proofed?

4. Are there real estate brokerages in the local area who offer auction services to the buying and selling public?

5. Should I add home staging skills to my list of services provided to sellers?

Chapter Mini-Review

Solutions are located in the Appendix.

1. The most prudent approach regarding stigmas is to disclose their existence to potential buyers.

    ◯ True   ◯ False

2. High moisture content, saturated attic insulation and wall staining are three of several indications that the home was used as a grow operation.

    ◯ True   ◯ False

3. A home inspection will not assist in detecting whether or not a home has been previous used for a grow operation.

    ◯ True   ◯ False

4. Failure to disclose known information to a prospective buyer that the home was previously used as a grow house could result in disciplinary proceedings against a registrant.

    ◯ True   ◯ False

5. Phishing is a type of value fraud associated with the inflating of the selling price in order to obtain financing.

    ◯ True   ◯ False

6. A borrower who falsifies information on a credit application represents one type of mortgage fraud.

    ◯ True   ◯ False

7. A registrant found guilty of fraudulent activity could be subject to disciplinary action by the Real Estate Council of Ontario (e.g., a fine), but would not lose his or her registration for such activity.

    ◯ True   ◯ False

8. A suspicious transaction is best described as a financial transaction for which there are reasonable grounds to suspect that it is related to the commission of a money laundering offence.

    ◯ True   ◯ False

9. Real estate brokerages are required to retain selected forms to comply with FINTRAC requirements, two of which are *Receipt of Funds Record* and *Suspicious Transaction Report*.

    ◯ True   ◯ False

10. An auctioneer is not allowed to auction real estate in the usual course of carrying out his or her function as an auctioneer.

    ◯ True   ◯ False

11. An absolute auction is an auction with a minimum reserve bid set by the seller.

○ True   ○ False

12. Enhancing curb appeal is part of the overall home staging process.

○ True   ○ False

13. A key objective in home staging is to personalize the property, so that the buyer feels more comfortable when viewing the home.

○ True   ○ False

Active Learning Exercises

Solutions are located in the Appendix.

▣ Exercise 1   Multiple Choice

1.1 A stigmatized property:

   a. Will typically increase in value due to the stigma.

   b. Usually reflects real risk to the buyer, as opposed to perceived risk.

   c. Can remain as such for many years, particularly given widespread media coverage and associated notoriety.

   d. Cannot be remedied.

1.2 Which of the following might be a possible indication that a buyer or tenant may intend on using the property for an illegal purpose?

   a. Buying without properly viewing the property.

   b. Displaying a particular interest in privacy associated with the home.

   c. Wanting immediate possession.

   d. All of the above.

1.3 Identity fraud:

   a. Is often referred to as a *boost and flip*.

   b. Only refers to electronic scams perpetrated on the Internet.

   c. Is only possible if the innocent party has credit cards.

   d. Is also known as identity theft.

1.4 Which of the following is correct?

   a. Asking for photo identification from unknown persons is not an effective means of minimizing fraud.

   b. Registrants, according to REBBA 2002, must not only avoid misrepresentation, but also take steps to prevent fraud.

   c. Automated detection systems for mortgage fraud are used by the government, but not by private enterprises.

   d. The Registrar has the right to revoke a registration without any right of appeal by the registrant.

1.5   A compliance regime generally refers to:

a.   Various procedures involved in setting up an auction.

b.   Requirements set out in REBBA 2002 regarding compliance with the Code of Ethics.

c.   Rules, procedures and related activities that real estate brokerages must adhere to in order to be in compliance with FINTRAC requirements.

d.   Rules, procedures and related activities that apply to real estate brokerages regarding FINTRAC requirements, but not to real estate salespersons.

1.6   An auction by confirmation:

a.   Provides that the seller can establish a minimum acceptable bid.

b.   Permits the seller to reject any final high bid price.

c.   Does not provide for any restrictions or limitations on the final selling price.

d.   Provides that the seller must confirm that he or she wants to auction the property two days before the scheduled auction date.

1.7   Which of the following is a correct statement?

a.   One of the goals of home staging is to shorten the length of time required to sell a property.

b.   Repair of broken items is not normally part of the home staging process.

c.   A real estate brokerage cannot charge both a flat fee and a commission to a seller when marketing that seller's property.

d.   Home staging is a regulated business in Ontario.

■ Exercise 2   Matching

Match the words in the left column with the appropriate descriptions in the right column (not all descriptions are used).

____ Grow House	a. Ask for Photo Identification
____ Stigmatized Property	b. Auction
____ Internet Scam	c. Burn or Shred Discarded Personal Information
____ Unknown Person	d. Flat Listing Fee
____ Boost and Flip	e. Patched Holes in Subfloors
____ Personal Fraud Proofing	f. Mortgage Fraud
____ Preview/Marketing Period	g. Phishing
____ Curb Appeal	h. Perception of Risk
	i. Home Inspection
	j. Home Staging

SECTION II

CURRENT TRENDS AND ISSUES IN RESIDENTIAL REAL ESTATE

CHAPTER 8

Environmental Concerns And Related Topics

Introduction

Environmental legislation has become an increasingly focal issue in the listing and selling of real estate. Most land use regulations involving environmental matters fall to the provinces. The goal of this legislation is to prevent environmental damage and ensure that the environment is protected for future generations. Registrants require awareness of environmental initiatives in order to properly assist buyers and sellers, particularly when drafting agreements of purchase and sale.

Part of this awareness involves knowledge of environmental hazards (or potential hazards) that can be encountered in the marketplace. In this chapter, six hazards are described including asbestos, electromagnetic fields, lead, mould, radon and urea formaldehyde foam insulation. Each of these should be considered as distinct topics for discussion. In some instances, the hazard has been firmly established and defined as a dangerous substance (e.g., lead). In others, debate remains and risk is best described as a matter of personal judgement (e.g., electromagnet fields). This chapter then focuses on requirements associated with underground storage tanks and updating/removal procedures.

The chapter concludes with a broad discussion of green building and its impact on the environment, and notable energy efficiency programs impacting housing, including EnerGuide and ENERGY STAR®. Both programs are administered by the Office of Energy Efficiency (Natural Resources Canada).

Learning Outcomes

At the conclusion of this chapter, students will be able to:

- Outline various provincial regulatory requirements that impact the listing and selling of real estate, over and above those that fall to the Ministry of the Environment.
- Describe selected clauses that apply in regard to environmental compliance when drafting an agreement of purchase and sale.
- Identify and discuss six environmental hazards including asbestos, electromagnetic fields, lead, mould, radon and urea formaldehyde foam insulation and explain varying risks associated with each.
- Outline regulatory requirements regarding underground fuel storage tanks and draft appropriate clauses given various circumstances involving such tanks.
- Describe the importance of green building as it relates to house construction techniques that promote energy efficiency.
- Briefly outline the primary features of the EnerGuide program as it relates to equipment and HVAC systems and houses.
- Briefly outline the primary features of the ENERGY STAR® program.

REAL ESTATE AND THE ENVIRONMENT

Environmental issues increasingly impact real estate registrants in the listing, marketing and selling process. Federal and provincial governments share the legislative responsibility for protecting the environment and real estate considerations are primary. Each has developed environmental management legislation and administrative processes to fulfill respective mandates. In Ontario, the Ministry of the Environment is the primary ministry focused on environmental matters, but many other ministries are also involved.

Since this can result in overlap and duplication, the two governments often agree to co-ordinate their efforts and, as such, the Canadian Council of Ministers of the Environment was established to further this inter-jurisdictional co-operation. In 1990, the Council adopted a statement that called for a commitment by each government to act while respecting the jurisdiction of other governments, recognize each other's strengths and capabilities, co-operate in a spirit of partnership, and provide timely notification and appropriate consultation where one jurisdiction's legislation, policies or programs affect those of another jurisdiction.

WEB LINKS
Canadian Council of Ministers of the Environment   Go to the Council's website (*www.ccme.ca*) for detailed information about the Council and its mandate.

Regulatory Requirements

Environmental legislation has become an increasingly important factor in the listing and selling of real estate. Most land use regulations involving environmental matters fall to the provinces. The goal of provincial legislation can be broadly described as preventing environment damage and ensuring that the environment is protected for future generations. This goal is attained through various measures including public participation in environmental decision-making, procedures to assess impact of developments on the environment and controls/regulatory requirements concerning such developments. All provincial ministries are generally mandated to further sound environmental planning and investigate matters concerning pollution, waste management and waste disposal.

Environmental considerations in real estate transactions are continuously expanding and the unfolding regulatory framework is increasingly complex. Environmental responsibilities typically fall to the Ministry of the Environment, the local conservation authority for activities near or on water and the Ministry of Natural Resources and Forestry, most notably for alterations to waterfront property that involve publicly owned lands pursuant to the *Public Lands Act*. However, various exceptions exist as noted in other courses and chapters in this pre-registration course.

- The Ontario Building Code, administered by the local municipality, regulates installation of septic tanks. This function was previously performed by the Ministry of the Environment, but moved to local municipalities as part of a general government restructuring.
- The Technical Standards and Safety Authority (reporting to the Ministry of Consumer Services) oversees gasoline handling and underground storage tanks.
- Selected farm-related matters fall to the Ministry of Agriculture, Food and Rural Affairs, for example, administration of the *Farming and Food Production Protection Act* concerning normal farm practices that can involve such factors as odour, dust and flies and can impact surrounding areas, most notably residential developments.

- The Ministry of the Environment oversees the *Ontario Water Resource Act* and other legislation concerning standards for water wells. Local public health authorities typically provide bacteriological testing of wells.
- Regulatory considerations relating to activities near and on water developments has caused confusion. Government authorities are continuing to simplify review and approval processes given overlapping authorities; e.g., Ministry of Natural Resources and Forestry (activity involving public lands under water bodies; e.g., building of a dock), Parks Canada (federal authority over federally-operated canals), Ministry of Fisheries and Oceans (fish habitat protection under the *Fisheries Act*), conservation authorities (administration of regulated areas in watersheds) and municipal authorities issuing various permits for building construction.

The long-term objective is a one stop or one window approach and selected merging of responsibilities has occurred. For example, the local conservation authority can be responsible for reviews under the *Fisheries Act* (federal), depending on whether an agreement has been reached with the appropriate federal ministry. Registrants are advised to contact local authorities concerning project review processes and necessary approvals until a fully integrated approach becomes a reality.

Risks in Listing/Selling

Duties and responsibilities of real estate professionals do not normally extend into the complex world of environmental legislation, or an understanding of the intricacies of environmental laws and technical complexities of environmental problems. At the same time, an awareness of potential hazards and a general knowledge of key environmental provisions legislated to combat them is beneficial in everyday real estate negotiations with consumers.

Four recommended steps are outlined to minimize risk concerning environmental issues:

- Be well informed (keep updated, learn about the issues and watch for environmental matters affecting the local market area);
- Ensure honesty/fairness in negotiations (inquire, investigate, verify and disclose);
- Draft accurate agreements/contracts; and
- Seek expert advice when necessary.

DRAFTING CLAUSES

Buyers may seek either a representation by the seller concerning various environmental issues or an appropriate condition. No single wording in an agreement/contract can address all environmental situations. However, seven considerations are primary when drafting such clauses:

- Compliance with appropriate laws, regulations and other related requirements;
- No hazardous conditions or substances exist;
- No limitations or restrictions exist affecting the use of the property;
- No pending litigation, outstanding department/ministry orders, investigations, charges or prosecutions;
- No prior use as waste disposal site;
- All applicable licences in force; and
- Documents, records and reports will be provided on request.

SCENARIO	CLAUSE
Condition Regarding Environmental Compliance A buyer is submitting an offer and wants to ensure that all environmental laws and regulations are being complied with.	**ENV–1** **Condition—All Environmental Laws Complied With** *This Offer is conditional upon the Buyer determining, at the Buyer's own expense, that: all environmental laws and regulations have been complied with, no hazardous conditions or substances exist on the land, no limitations or restrictions affecting the continued use of the property exist, other than those specifically provided for herein, no pending litigation respecting Environmental matters, no outstanding Ministry of Environment Orders, investigation, charges or prosecutions respecting Environmental matters exist, there has been no prior use as a waste disposal site, and all applicable licenses are in force. The Seller agrees to provide to the Buyer upon request, all documents, records, and reports relating to environmental matters in possession of the Seller. The Seller further authorizes (insert appropriate Ministry), to release to the Buyer, the Buyer's Agent or Solicitor, any and all information that may be on record in the Ministry office with respect to the said property.* *Unless the Buyer gives notice in writing delivered to the Seller personally or in accordance with any other provisions for the delivery of notice in this Agreement of Purchase and Sale or any Schedule thereto not later than _____ p.m. on the _____ day of _____, 20____, that the preceding condition has been fulfilled, this Offer shall become null and void and the deposit shall be returned to the Buyer in full without deduction. This condition is included for the benefit of the Buyer and may be waived at the Buyer's sole option by notice in writing to the Seller as aforesaid within the time period stated herein.*
Environmentally Protected Zone A buyer is contemplating buying a property near a river and wants to ensure that no part of the property lies within an environmentally protected zone or flood plain.	**ENV–4** **Condition—Environmentally Protected Zone, Flood Plain, Hazard Land** *This Offer is conditional upon the Buyer determining, at the Buyer's own expense, that no portion of the property has been designated as hazard land, flood plain, or an environmentally protected zone. Unless the Buyer gives notice in writing delivered to the Seller personally or in accordance with any other provisions for the delivery of notice in this Agreement of Purchase and Sale or any Schedule thereto not later than _____ p.m. on the _____ day of _____, 20___, that this condition has been fulfilled, this Offer shall become null and void and the deposit shall be returned to the Buyer in full without deduction. This condition is included for the benefit of the Buyer and may be waived at the Buyer's sole option by notice in writing to the Seller as aforesaid within the time period stated herein.*

Hazards

Environmental issues and, more specifically, environmental hazards are significant factors in real estate transactions. Registrants must ensure accurate information is provided and due care is taken in directing consumers to seek expert advice. Fortunately, specialists are available to assist; e.g., environmental auditors and environmental lawyers.

No easy method exists to categorize significant hazards. In some instances, hazardous conditions have not gained widespread public awareness or condemnation, consequently, real estate salespeople are challenged with everyday marketplace negotiations compounded by vagueness and ambiguity.

Environmental hazards are not restricted to commercial and industrial users. Various hazardous products are usual to the average household and caution is advised. Hazardous waste depots are provided in most urban areas for dropping off such items as automotive spray paints, glues, cement, paint strippers, enamel or oil-based paints, latex and water-based paints, stains, finishes, insecticides, herbicides, rat and mouse poisons, thinners, turpentine, unused medicines, nail polish remover, wood preservatives and rust removers. Hazardous products should not be disposed of as ordinary garbage or poured down drains.

Considerable literature is available at the federal, provincial and municipal levels to provide guidance on such matters. See the next topic *Environmental Hazards* for a detailed discussion of selected hazards impacting real estate registrants.

Environmental Assessment

An environmental assessment is broadly defined as a systematic and comprehensive process involving the identification, analysis and evaluation of the environmental effects of proposed projects. Provincial ministries/departments typically work in concert with professional organizations and suppliers of environmental services to develop common assessment procedures. The overall goal is to establish and ensure effective, rational and compatible processes for assessment throughout a given jurisdictional area.

AUDIT

Buyers may require an environmental audit to assess overall environmental condition prior to purchase, as hazards and contamination can represent a significant risk. Lenders contemplating financing of such acquisitions will also normally seek similar assurances. While audits are typically associated with industrial and commercial lands, their use can be relevant to a wide range of property types and related circumstances. Environmental audits are broadly grouped under three levels of analysis, referred to as phases:

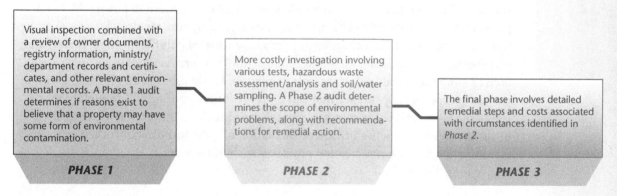

Visual inspection combined with a review of owner documents, registry information, ministry/department records and certificates, and other relevant environmental records. A Phase 1 audit determines if reasons exist to believe that a property may have some form of environmental contamination.

PHASE 1

More costly investigation involving various tests, hazardous waste assessment/analysis and soil/water sampling. A Phase 2 audit determines the scope of environmental problems, along with recommendations for remedial action.

PHASE 2

The final phase involves detailed remedial steps and costs associated with circumstances identified in *Phase 2*.

PHASE 3

ENVIRONMENTAL HAZARDS

Environmental hazards are a growing concern in residential sales. *The Real Estate Transaction—General* and previous chapters have addressed legislative controls concerning everything from underground oil tanks to wells and septic systems. However, environmental issues are more extensive, particularly regarding potential hazards.

Most consumers associate land contamination and hazardous waste with commercial properties, but difficulties can also arise in residential properties. Selected environmental concerns are highlighted, along with a description of potential risks based on current research.

Asbestos

Asbestos, a mineral fibre located in rock, is found in a variety of products including household and building supplies. Asbestos was widely used in construction from the early 1900s until the 1970s and is best known for its strengthening characteristics, thermal and acoustical insulation qualities, and fire retardant capabilities. The product is most frequently encountered in roofing materials, wall and pipe coverings, floor tiles, appliances, ceilings, patching compounds, textured paints, and door gaskets of stoves, furnaces and ovens.

Chrysotile makes up about 90% of world asbestos production and trade. In Canada, chrysotile is the only type of asbestos mined. Canada accounts for about 20 percent of world chrysotile asbestos production and exports more than half a million tonnes of asbestos products (worth more than $300 million) to 60 countries every year. The chrysotile industry employs some 2,500 people, mainly in a 100-km strip in Quebec's Eastern Townships extending from the town of Asbestos (site of the western world's largest known deposit) to East Broughton in the east. The industry also accounts for approximately 6,500 indirect jobs, the vast majority of which are in rural communities depending on a prosperous chrysotile asbestos industry.

Since 1979, Canada has been the champion of the controlled-use approach to asbestos. This approach is based on risk assessment and prohibits specific uses, such as asbestos-spraying, where workers cannot be protected. Several countries have supported Canada's position and the International Labour Organization and the World Health Organization have either adopted or supported this approach.

CLASSIFICATION

Asbestos is classified as friable and non-friable, and is described as follows.

Friable   Material that is easily crumbled, pulverized or reduced to powder by hand pressure. Friable material can be disrupted during renovation, repairs, cleaning or related activities. Asbestos is most commonly seen in the form of a fluffy, spray-on material for fireproofing and insulating walls and ceilings. Another form is the fibrous grey paper used to wrap pipes and boilers for heat insulation. Lastly, asbestos can be found with a cement-like plaster appearance that was used for soundproofing and fire retardance.

Friable asbestos is dangerous as it can release fibres into the air that are not collected by furnace filters or vacuum cleaners. Inhalation of these airborne fibres can cause an accumulation in the lungs creating problems such as lung cancer or asbestosis, a degenerative lung disease.

Non-Friable   Asbestos may be found in pre-fabricated products typically containing bonding agents (e.g., painted cement sheets used around wood-burning stoves) that prevent any airborne dispersion of fibres, unless the product is physically altered through sanding, drilling or cutting. Non-friable asbestos comes in the form of wallboard (that looks like gypsum) and in exterior cladding for structures. These products only release hazardous fibres when broken or altered.

DETECTION/MEASUREMENT

Health studies indicate that asbestos fibre, once airborne, can become a serious health threat. Provincial responses to the detection and measurement of asbestos vary. Many provinces have classified asbestos as a hazardous product and passed strict regulations governing its removal and disposal. Asbestos testing and removal of asbestos-containing material is a specialized area of environmental management and should be conducted by suitably qualified environmental experts.

RENOVATION WORK

Most difficulties in real estate arise from renovations undertaken in older buildings (usually pre-1980 structures). If alterations are contemplated, try to determine if the material contains asbestos. A qualified asbestos inspector should make the determination, however, failing this approach, plumbing, building and heating contractors can often make a reasonable judgement. As a last resort, laboratory analysis is necessary.

An experienced contractor trained in the removal of asbestos is best. Asbestos analysis may be required to determine if asbestos in a friable condition is present within an on-site facility. If asbestos is confirmed in a friable condition, removal should be accomplished under a plan developed by an asbestos abatement specialist and any removal in compliance with the plan should be verified.

Asbestos in itself is not hazardous and is only a health risk when airborne. Given proper building maintenance and avoidance of unwarranted asbestos removal, the problem need not be exaggerated. However, friable forms of asbestos; e.g., crumbling insulation around plumbing pipes, can pose a real danger. Stringent guidelines exist for the removal of such material.

Asbestos: What to Look For in Older Buildings   FOCUS

The use of asbestos in buildings has been banned in most provinces. In fact, many suppliers ceased using the product in 1973, coinciding with the ban on all spray applications during that same year.

Real estate registrants may encounter this substance in various residential and commercial properties built prior to that date. Friable asbestos is the most dangerous. Here are a few items to look for:

- Insulated water pipes that are deteriorating (asbestos insulating materials for water pipes appeared in 1920 to the early 1970s).

- Ceiling or wall materials that are crumbling due to water damage.

- Old stove, oven and furnace door gaskets.

- Homes built between 1930 and the mid-1950s may have insulation manufactured with asbestos.

- Dated fluffy sprayed-on materials may contain asbestos.

- Older homes (pre-1980) may have asbestos and should be more closely inspected (recommend a home inspection).

Persons contemplating renovation work may have problems with the removal of asbestos. Registrants should be prepared to generally discuss the issue of friable and non-friable asbestos with consumers.

Electromagnetic Fields (EMFs)

Over the years, many studies on electric and magnetic fields and their effect on humans have been completed worldwide. Some studies have shown certain biological responses. Some have indicated a possible association between electromagnetic fields and human health effects, while others have not. The worldwide scientific community has not reached a definitive conclusion on this topic.

While power utilities are sensitive to public concerns regarding possible health effects from electric and magnetic fields, at present, no conclusive scientific evidence exists to justify modification of existing practices or facilities for the generation, transmission and distribution of electricity. At the same time, exposure remains an issue.

Recommended exposure limits to prevent acute health effects have been put forth by an international committee of experts. The recommended exposure limit is 5 kV/m and 1 Gauss for 24-hour exposure of the general public. Registrants should contact the local power utility and public health authority for additional information regarding current research studies.

 WEB LINKS

Hydro One   Information concerning power utilities and related materials, including electromagnetic fields can be obtained from Hydro One. The website is *www.hydroone.ca*.

NATURE OF ELECTRIC AND MAGNETIC FIELDS

Fields found near any device that transmits, distributes or uses electricity are often referred to as extremely low frequencies (ELFs). ELF fields are at the low frequency end of the electromagnetic spectrum. Electric fields are measured in units of kilovolts per metre (kV/m) and are related to the voltage on the conductor, whereas magnetic fields, measured in milliGauss (mG) or microTesla (uT) are produced by the flow of current in the conductor.

Electric fields are produced by an appliance that is plugged into an electrical outlet regardless of whether or not the appliance is operating. Magnetic fields are produced only when the appliance is operating, that is, when current is flowing. Electric fields do not easily penetrate most materials and are usually shielded or reduced by buildings and other obstacles. Magnetic fields, however, penetrate most materials quite readily. Both electric and magnetic fields decrease in strength very rapidly as distance from the source increases.

A Matter of Personal Judgement	CAUTION

Electromagnetic fields surrounding power lines typically decrease with distance from such lines. EMFs are best categorized as a concern, as opposed to a hazard, given that studies linking EMFs with personal health hazard have been inconclusive.

Significant controversy now exists regarding degree of risk posed by such exposure. Individuals need to personally assess risk when making decisions about properties near high voltage lines, green transformer boxes and electrical transmission/distribution facilities. Radio frequency radiation from broadcast and cell towers have also fallen under close scrutiny.

POWER DELIVERY SYSTEMS

To understand electromagnetic fields, registrants must appreciate the process by which electricity is delivered to a home. The objective of an electrical power delivery system is to provide an uninterrupted supply of electricity to the consumer in a safe and cost-effective manner.

For real estate registrants, the entire power delivery system is best visualized through three major elements: generation, transport and end use.

Generation	The process by which raw energy is harnessed and converted to electricity.
Transport	The process of transporting electricity from the point of generation to the ultimate point of delivery occurs in two basic steps: transmission and distribution. Electric transmission lines, which carry large blocks of electrical energy from the generating station are familiar sights and are often distinguished by towers that support the lines. A transmission line's route ends at a substation, where the energy is parcelled out into smaller blocks and routed into neighbourhoods along distribution lines. The electricity carried on transmission lines is characterized in terms of voltage and current. The flow of electricity on a transmission or distribution line can be compared to the flow of water through a pipe. The pressure driving the water is the counterpart to the voltage on the electrical line and the water's rate of flow in the pipe is the counterpart to the electric current on the line. Transmission and distribution lines operate at constant voltages and the currents on these lines fluctuate according to load demands.
End Use	Electricity used by consumers at home, school or work constitutes the last stage of the energy's journey from its point of generation. At every stage in that journey, the transportation and use of electricity produces electric and magnetic fields. These fields result from the voltages and currents applied to our power delivery systems, as well as from all end uses of electricity, including lights, kitchen appliances, electric blankets, power tools, television sets and computers.

Lead

Lead is a bluish-grey metal contained in various products; e.g., lead pipe, lead-based paint and grooved bars found in stained glass windows. Lead is listed as a designated hazardous substance under the *Occupational Health and Safety Act* and may have implications when transacting property. Lead-based products were particularly prevalent prior to 1950 and, as a result, lead is found in varying degrees throughout most regions of the country.

During the past 40 years, lead content has been dramatically diminished, if not completely removed, from a variety of products. However, lead is found practically everywhere in Canada in varying degrees of concentration. Scientists have known for a long time that prolonged exposure to substantial amounts of lead is a definite health risk. Recently, even low level exposure has been found to cause problems, particularly with the normal development of children; e.g., behavioural difficulties, ability to learn and development of the nervous system.

Real estate registrants should be particularly aware of the following.

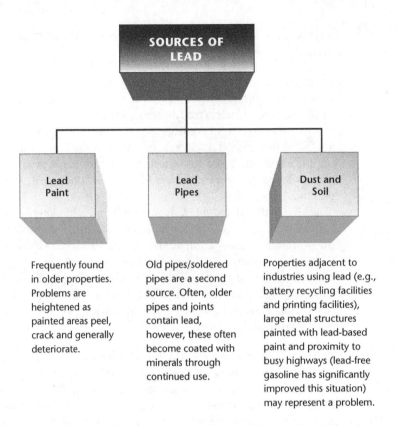

Registrants should be particularly aware of possible lead contamination in structures built before 1970, with the highest risk in pre-1950 structures. Lead dust from renovations in older homes can be a serious health danger and appropriate expert advice is required. Lead ingestion can lead to convulsions, brain damage and behavioral difficulties, particularly in younger children.

 WEB LINKS

Lead   For additional information regarding the *Occupational Health and Safety Act* and lead as a designated hazardous substance, go the Ministry of the Environment website at *www.ene.gov.on.ca*.

Mould

Mould is the growth of minute fungi, traditionally associated with decaying vegetable or animal matter, that has taken on increasing prominence in real estate. Ironically, modern construction techniques may be a significant contributing factor as building envelopes become increasingly airtight. Furnace and air-conditioning systems may only compound the matter by recirculating contaminated air. Various moulds can flourish in damp areas within buildings and research has linked various health problems to these growths including sinus infections, asthma and certain respiratory infections.

Stachybotrys atra is a particularly dangerous mould that has been associated with severe breathing difficulties, dizziness, memory loss and bleeding in the lungs. This mould produces mycotoxins and prolonged exposure to these airborne toxins can prove harmful. Fortunately, most household moulds are mild in comparison to stachybotrys atra and other related moulds (e.g., memnoniella), but nevertheless research has linked various moulds to chronic sinus infections, asthma and other ailments.

DETECTION

Moulds require water to grow and damp areas in buildings are often the culprits. Homeowners, or others responsible for building management, should watch for discolouration in building finishes and carefully inspect areas in which dampness might collect; e.g., basement storage areas and kitchen cupboards. Further, air-conditioning units and furnaces (including ducts) should be cleaned regularly and any stagnant water (e.g., in drainage pans) should be eliminated. Finished basement recreation rooms can be particularly susceptible as interior building materials may hide dampness problems entering through exterior walls. Above all, take note of any changes in personal health that may signal mould-related problems; e.g., respiratory ailments, breathing difficulties, recurring dizziness, severe headaches and/or loss of balance and extreme fatigue.

Negligent Construction   RESIDENTIAL CASE LAW

An appeal heard by the Ontario Court of Appeal has ramifications for anyone building a negligently-constructed home, be it a professional builder or an individual. The Appeal Court, in this instance, was reviewing the trial judge's decision concerning a couple who, with the assistance of a contractor and various subtrades, built a country home. They obtained a building permit from the appropriate township in 1987, but did not have a final inspection or receive an occupancy permit prior to moving into the home.

Approximately four years later, the property was listed for sale. The listing agreement described the property as well built. A buyer inspected the home, along with her father-in-law who advised her the home was well constructed. The sale was finalized using a standard residential form which included that usual entire agreement clause stating that there were no representations, warranties, collateral agreements or conditions that affect the agreement other than those stated. (Note: No warranties or other related provisions/conditions were inserted in the agreement.)

Approximately 10 months following closing, problems arose which included cracking along the centre load-bearing wall and basement dampness caused by a defective building envelope. No repairs were made and ultimately the home was infected with toxic mould rendering it uninhabitable. In ensuing litigation, the trial judge considered the home a write-off and assessed damages at $299,610 finding that the original owners had fraudulently and negligently misrepresented the home as well built. Liability was shared—75% against the owners and 25% against the township.

On appeal, the Appeal Court stated that the standard agreement of purchase and sale form used provided no warranties or guarantees. The buyer had the opportunity to inspect the property and, consequently, was bound by caveat emptor (let the buyer beware). Further, the Appeal Court could find no grounds for either fraudulent negligence or negligent misrepresentation.

However, the Court did determine that damages should be awarded for negligent construction, as the home was judged dangerous. (It is important to note that negligent construction does not arise simply from sloppy work, but rather from a situation that does or may pose a danger.) Relying on a prior Manitoba decision, the Court confirmed that a contractor (or any other person responsible for house design and construction) can be liable for negligent construction. Most notably, such responsibility by the original builder extends to subsequent buyers of buildings, as latent defects can manifest themselves at any point during the building's useful life. However, the buyer is only entitled to the reasonable cost of putting the building into a non-dangerous state. In this particular situation, the damages were reassessed to $100,657 based on repair estimates presented in the earlier 1998 trial.

Source: Mariani v. Lemstra, Court of Appeal for Ontario, Court File #C39746

continued...

COMMENTARY

In this appeal, the Judge found that although the original owners built their dream home intending to remain there for years, the practical reality is that circumstances often change, resulting in the property being sold to someone else. As such, whether the individual was a building professional or a layperson, dangers that arise from the original construction may appear at a later time and the responsibility for such matters rests with that original builder.

However, the award was reduced by approximately $200,000 as the Appeal Court found that damages were limited to direct repair costs only. Resulting mould problems and related costs were excluded as they arose from the new owner failing to take appropriate steps to promptly mitigate the situation.

Given that liability for dangerous or unsafe conditions extends well into the future, individuals (including handypersons) carrying out renovations, making additions or otherwise modifying houses must take special care. Problems could prove costly. Similarly, salespersons should be wary of structures that have undergone owner modifications. Ensure that an appropriate condition is inserted in the agreement to provide the buyer adequate opportunity to have the property fully inspected.

Radon

Radon is an invisible, odourless, tasteless gas produced by the decay of uranium that occurs naturally in the earth's crust. The gas itself is not dangerous, but becomes hazardous when it breaks down into progeny that cling to dust and soil particles. These radioactive particles also attach themselves to lung tissue when the radon gas is inhaled. Outdoors, radon is diluted, however, indoor levels of concentration can reach hazardous levels.

DETECTION/MEASUREMENT

Measurement is the only way to determine the existence and extent of radon. Radon gas is measured by picoCuries (peek-o-kur-eez) per litre (pCi/L) and radon progeny, which emit alpha, beta and gamma radiation, is measured in working levels (WL). The federal government considers any level above 0.1 or approximately 20 picoCuries of radon gas per litre to be unacceptable.

Radon escapes naturally into the air from sub-surface minerals and is not a problem at these low levels of concentration as it disperses quickly. When radon enters buildings through cracks in basement floors and walls, openings around pipes and wires, through water supplies, basement floor drains and porous building materials, the gas can build up to dangerous levels. The highest radon readings are generally found in the lowest levels of a building in winter months when doors and windows are kept closed. A significant decrease in radon typically occurs in higher levels of a building.

Indoor radon levels depend on many factors: the concentration of radon in the underlying soil, the ease with which it moves through the soil and the construction of the dwelling, which determines how the radon enters and becomes trapped within the structure. The amount of radon will vary by location across Canada. The consensus of experts is the greater the exposure to radon, the greater the risk of developing lung cancer.

Radon levels within structures can vary significantly based on the season, spaces, construction materials between rooms and levels, condition of basement (e.g., cracks and openings around pipes) and basement structure (e.g., number of vent pipes through walls and the sump pump pit). Radon is typically detected using two testing devices.

- **Charcoal Canisters**   Activated charcoal in a canister that absorbs radon is placed in a home for two days and then returned to a measuring company for analysis.

Although generally reliable, the canister method is susceptible to decay factors and the breaking down of radon, leading to reduced accuracy of measurement.

- **Alpha Track Detector**   The alpha track detector uses a plastic sheet that is sensitive to radon. Decaying radon gas in the form of radioactive emissions of alpha particles strike and damage the plastic. The measuring company counts the number of strikes (marks) on the plastic to determine the level of radon. A minimum of three months is suggested for a proper reading as opposed to the short period for charcoal canisters, hence the popularity of the charcoal method.

REMEDIAL ACTION

Health Canada estimates that less than 1 percent of Canadian homes have indoor radon levels exceeding the 20 PCi/L levels identified by the government as unacceptable. If a homeowner discovers levels between 2 PCi/L and 20 PCi/L, subsequent testing should be undertaken to accurately verify levels and take appropriate action if necessary. If the level is above 20 PCi/L, subsequent testing should still be done, along with remedial work.

Remedial action includes sealing cracks and openings within basement areas, sealing sump pump holes and service related entrance points, and covering any exposed earth such as in crawl space areas. Ventilation of basement areas and crawl space areas is also an effective means of reducing radon. Air filtering and cleaning and increased ventilation of floor/wall cavities is also important.

WEB LINKS

Radon   The Radiation Safety Institute of Canada (***www.radiationsafety.ca***) provides detailed information about radon and radon testing equipment. Firms specializing in radon testing equipment are normally located under environmental categories in the telephone directory.

Urea Formaldehyde Foam Insulation (UFFI)

Urea formaldehyde is a colourless, chemical compound found in certain resins, glues and bonding agents and, for real estate registrants, is most commonly associated with insulation. UFFI is a low density foam made from plastic resins, a foaming agent and compressed air. At time of installation, UFFI has the appearance and consistency of shaving cream. While normally identified as a white or cream-coloured substance, at least one product contains blue dye.

A controversy arose from the curing process when the product was injected into walls and other areas in residential property and formaldehyde gas was released. A product ban appeared in 1980 because of potential health concerns, after an estimated 100,000 Canadian homes were insulated, mostly between 1975 and 1979 under government incentive programs for homeowners.

A general consensus now minimizes UFFI as a health concern. However, The Canadian Real Estate Association has strongly urged its members to stay informed, not to treat UFFI as a finalized issue and maintain UFFI references in listing and sales documents and, more particularly, the agreement of purchase and sale.

R.S.O. 1990 unless seller's spouse has executed the consent hereinafter provided.

23. UFFI: Seller represents and warrants to Buyer that during the time Seller has owned the property, Seller has not caused any building on the property to be insulated with insulation containing ureaformaldehyde, and that to the best of Seller's knowledge no building on the property contains or has ever contained insulation that contains ureaformaldehyde. This warranty shall survive and not merge on the completion of this transaction, and if the building is part of a multiple unit building, this warranty shall only apply to that part of the building which is the subject of this transaction.

24. LEGAL, ACCOUNTING AND ENVIRONMENTAL ADVICE: The parties acknowledge that any information provided by the brokerage is not

DRAFTING CLAUSES

Note that the above clause relates to continuing concerns regarding urea formaldehyde foam insulation. The seller is warranting that there is no such insulation. Replacing this wording with an appropriate clause concerning testing and an inspection may be necessary. This circumstance could arise when the seller has refused to provide the warranty; i.e., a mortgagee selling under power of sale.

Three scenarios are provided to illustrate clause drafting:

SCENARIO	CLAUSE
Building Contains UFFI A buyer is submitting an offer and the seller wants to ensure that an appropriate acknowledgement is included regarding the presence of UFFI.	**UFFI–1 Acknowledgement—UFFI Present In Building** *The Seller discloses and the Buyer acknowledges that the building contains urea formaldehyde foam insulation. The Buyer accepts the property in that state and further acknowledges that the Seller does not warrant the quality or quantity of the insulation or the quality of its installation.*
Executor Unfamiliar with Structure An executor is handling an estate sale and is unaware of whether the deceased's home has been insulated with UFFI. A similar situation might involve a corporation handling a company transfer or a seller selling under power of sale.	**UFFI–2 Seller Has No Knowledge of UFFI** *The Seller has no knowledge as to whether the property has been insulated with urea formaldehyde foam insulation and specifically makes no warranty in that regard. This paragraph supersedes any other term or condition or warranty in relation to urea formaldehyde foam insulation.* **NOTE**: *Use where Seller has no personal knowledge of UFFI (i.e., a corporation handling a company transfer, Seller selling under Power of Sale, etc.). The Buyer may consider making the Offer conditional on an inspection for UFFI.*
Correction Action Taken A buyer is aware that the home was insulated with UFFI, but that the seller has taken corrective action. The buyer requests that a suitable clause be included detailing what corrective actions were taken. Typically, a schedule with supporting documentation would also be attached.	**UFFI–3 UFFI Found But Corrective Action Taken** *The Seller represents and warrants that the building was insulated with urea formaldehyde foam insulation but has undergone the following corrective actions: _____ _____. The Parties agree that this representation and warranty shall survive and not merge on completion of this transaction, but apply only to the state of the property at completion of this transaction.* **NOTE**: *Details of all corrective action should be inserted in the space provided or supporting documentation attached as a Schedule.*

Other UFFI clauses developed by the Ontario Real Estate Association address the following:

UFFI–4   *UFFI Removed From Building*

UFFI–5   *UFFI Test Performed With Negative Result*

UFFI–6   *UFFI Test Performed With Positive Result But Within Acceptable Limits*

Be Environmentally Aware **PERSPECTIVE**

Real estate registrants, actively engaged in listing, marketing and selling of property, are increasingly confronting environmental issues as legislation becomes more sophisticated and all-encompassing. While duties and responsibilities of real estate professionals do not normally extend into discussions of environmental matters, an awareness of potential hazards and a general understanding of environmental issues are beneficial in everyday real estate negotiations.

Real estate brokers and salespeople require a sensitivity to the environment, while ensuring that involvement does not extend into technical representations or the provision of expert advice. Registrants should exercise a reasonable standard of care when listing properties and answering questions. However, this standard must not approach the level of offering counsel unless individuals are suitably trained and proficient in such topics. At all times, seek expert advice when necessary.

GUIDELINES

Be Aware	Understand the general purpose and scope of environmental legislation and corresponding ministries or agencies charged with its enforcement. Provide summary information and guidance as appropriate to clients and customers, while directing enquiries to appropriate authorities.
Know About Potential Issues and Problems	Registrants should have an understanding of common hazards that might be encountered in the marketplace. Clearly, well and septic systems are key to most rural residential and recreational properties, environmental contamination and hazardous waste is primarily associated with industrial and commercial properties and environmental protection, regulated lands and flood plains are focused on properties that lie within or near watersheds. Registrants should continuously seek relevant environmental information associated with their particular areas of specialty.
Ask Relevant Questions	Take the time to fully discuss pertinent environmental issues with buyers and sellers. Use the *Seller Property Information Statement* (OREA Forms 220, 221 and 222) where applicable, as it contains a broad range of questions addressing various matters, including environmental issues.
Draft Documents Carefully	Make certain that listing agreements and associated data input sheets correctly describe the listed property. Carefully draft offers to clearly reflect the understanding of both parties to a transaction and include appropriate conditions, where necessary, to permit parties to fully investigate environmental issues.

UNDERGROUND STORAGE TANK (FUEL)

An underground oil tank is a buried or partially buried container (in direct contact with earth or backfill), which contains fuel oil to be used in appliances, such as furnaces or boilers. These tanks have fallen under close environmental scrutiny over the past few years. All such tanks must be registered with the Technical Standards and Safety Authority (TSSA) or fuel will not be delivered to the tank.

Regulatory Requirements

Regulatory controls under the *Technical Standards and Safety Act, 2001* apply to a wide range of activities including installation, testing, maintenance, repair, removal, replacement, inspection and use of appliances, equipment, components and accessories where fuel oil is to be used as a fuel. Specific requirements concerning underground tanks are highlighted given the fact that thousands of tanks were buried without any records concerning their locations. However, registrants should be aware that the legislation also addresses all aboveground fuel tanks. An aboveground tank refers to any tank that is installed at or above grade level within a building or within a secondary containment.

In regard to underground oil tanks:

- All contractors working on (i.e., repairing, installing, removing and servicing) fuel oil equipment, including underground tanks, must be registered with TSSA.
- Existing underground oil tanks must be registered. Contact TSSA for appropriate application form(s).
- Unused underground fuel tanks must be removed by a TSSA registered contractor and any contamination cleaned up.
- Underground storage tanks must be upgraded with specific leak and spill prevention equipment or removed.
- Upgrading requirements for underground tanks depend on tank age.

Leakage

Oil leakage from underground tanks can contaminate soil and groundwater, resulting in expensive environmental clean-up costs. While often difficult to detect, testing companies can usually determine if leakage has occurred.

If a leak occurs, the owner must contact a registered fuel oil contractor to help find and stop the leak and clean-up any leaked fuel oil. The owner is also required to call the Spills Action Centre of the Ministry of the Environment.

Disclosure

Problems associated with an underground fuel tank can prove costly; e.g., if a seller sells the property and conceals its presence, he/she may be open to legal action in the future. Further, if a tank leaks, cost of clean-up on the subject property, as well as adjacent properties, may fall to that owner. Salespersons should enquire of sellers about the existence of such tanks, inspect the property during the listing process, discuss the matter with the seller, contact TSSA as appropriate and disclose the existence of any such tanks to the buyer. The mere existence of an underground tank does not automatically threaten a real estate transaction, but expert advice is required and procedures must be followed.

EXAMPLE   *The Concrete Base*

Salesperson Green is currently inspecting a rental property that contains 4 residential units. During the listing process, he discovers a small raised concrete platform in the basement that was probably a base for an old furnace, long since replaced. When enquiring, Seller Smith claims no knowledge of an older oil-burning furnace, as he purchased the property approximately five years earlier and the conversion to gas had already been completed.

Prudently, Salesperson Green and the seller look around the walls for any sign of an oil pipe line. On closer inspection, they discover a protruding capped pipe in the west wall. Further investigation reveals a deteriorating vent pipe hidden under a newly constructed patio area at the rear of the property. Green advises the seller to contact the Technical Standards and Safety Authority concerning the matter. A representative of the TSSA confirms the existence of an underground tank that was subsequently removed by an approved contractor.

Upgrading/Removal

All existing underground tanks have to be registered with TSSA. Further, upgrading or removal requirements were put in place based on the age of the underground tank. These requirements were introduced to address

AGE (YEARS FROM DATE OF INSTALLATION)	DATE TO REMOVE OR UPGRADE TANK
25 and more (or unknown)	October 1, 2006
20 – 24	October 1, 2007
10 – 19	October 1, 2008
0 – 9	October 1, 2009

safety and environment concerns with underground fuel oil installations.

Other Fuel-Related Requirements	CAUTION

This topic on underground and aboveground storage tanks is focused on fuel oil storage in relation to connected appliances (e.g., a furnace). The Technical Standards and Safety Authority's scope of activities encompasses many fuel-related activities. For example, the TSSA reviews applications to install liquid fuels (gasoline, diesel), propane and natural gas facilities designed for fuelling vehicles to determine their compliance with the Act, Regulations and adopted safety codes. Farming operations, depending on the size and complexity, will have various fuel storage needs and applications that fall under the Authority.

Drafting Clauses

Clauses involving underground tanks typically focus on the fact that the tank is in compliance with statutory requirements, that a tank was located on the property but has now been removed or that such a tank exists but the seller agrees to remove it.

SCENARIO	CLAUSE
Underground Tank Complies With Statutory Requirements A buyer is submitting an offer and is aware that an underground storage tank is situated on the property.	**ENV–12** **Underground Tank—Compliance Warranty** *The Seller represents and warrants that the fuel oil tank in, on or about the property is in compliance with the requirements of the Technical Standards and Safety Act, 2002 and any Regulations thereto as amended from time to time and has been registered with the Technical Standards and Safety Authority and does not have to be removed, upgraded or replaced before October 1, 2006. Seller agrees to provide Buyer with the Registration number and all relevant documents prior to closing. This warranty shall survive and not merge upon the completion of this transaction.*
Underground Tank Removed A buyer is submitting an offer and the seller has informed the buyer that an underground tank was situated on the property, but has since been removed in accordance with the statutory requirements.	**ENV–13** **Underground Tank—Seller Has Removed** *The Buyer acknowledges that there was an underground fuel tank on the property that has been removed and the Seller agrees to provide to the Buyer at the Seller's own expense by no later than _____ p.m. on the _____ day of _____, 20____, evidence that a contractor registered under the Technical Standards and Safety Act, 2002 and any Regulations thereto as amended from time to time, has removed the said fuel oil tank, assessed the soil surrounding the underground fuel oil tank for contamination and cleaned and removed any contamination.*

SCENARIO	CLAUSE
Underground Tank Will Be Removed A buyer is submitting an offer and the seller has informed the buyer that an underground tank is situated on the property, but that such will be removed in accordance with statutory requirements at the seller's expense.	**ENV–14** Underground Tank—Seller to Remove *The Seller agrees that the Seller will, at the Seller's expense, have the underground fuel oil tank on the property removed from the property by a contractor registered under the Technical Standards and Safety Act, 2002 and any Regulations thereto as amended from time to time by no later than _____ p.m. on the _____ day of _____, 20___, and thereafter to have the soil surrounding the underground fuel oil tank assessed for contamination and any contamination cleaned and removed by a contractor registered under the Technical Standards and Safety Act, 2002 and any Regulations thereto as amended from time to time, and on or before closing to provide evidence of the said testing, cleaning and removal from the said contractor and to restore the grading and landscaping on the property to the existing or a comparable condition to which it was prior to the removal of the said fuel oil tank.*

WEB LINKS

Underground Storage Tanks   The Technical Standards & Safety Authority's website (*www.tssa.org*) provides information concerning underground storage tanks.

GREEN BUILDING AND ENERGY EFFICIENCY

Green building refers to house construction techniques that promote energy efficiencies, prudent use of resources, durability in component products and sound environmental concepts and strategies. Green building is a broad initiative rather than precisely identified by specialty fields, specific products and exact guidelines. At present, no standardized set of green building products or universally-held standards exist.

Expanded Perspective

Green building advocates originally focused on resource conservation including water-efficient appliances, faucets and fixtures, high efficiency heating and cooling systems, renewable energy systems, heat recovery systems, solar power applications, and fuel cells. However, green proponents have expanded their perspective into related areas such as non-toxic building products, solvent-free finishes and adhesives, improved indoor air quality, smart technologies, and adaptability/sustainability in housing design.

Green building now includes broader-based initiatives involving environmental, energy, resource and conservation management issues. New technologies promote energy conservation, along with lowered energy costs for both residential and commercial marketplaces. Buyers are becoming far more sensitive to energy costs as fuel prices rise. While activities involving the structural and mechanical integrity of houses (e.g., home inspections) will remain uppermost, much greater emphasis will be placed on energy efficiency audits as an integral aspect of the buying process.

ECOLOGICAL BENEFITS

Due consideration for the natural environment can result in both economic and ecological benefits; e.g., use of green roofs, retention of existing trees during construction, improved storm water runoff control and effective use of indigenous plantings to further energy conservation and minimize environmental impact.

INDOOR AIR QUALITY

Air quality within both residential and commercial structures is a growing priority. Activities typically include filtration and ventilation systems for all building areas, sealed-combustion heating systems/appliances to minimize indoor air contaminants, recycled products where feasible in construction, restricted or non-use of products impacting indoor air quality (e.g., aerosols and certain types of cleaners), air intake monitoring and the selection of environmentally-friendly, non-toxic green building materials.

WASTE RECYCLING/DIVERSION

Waste management is also key in green building. Initiatives include recycling programs for organic and inorganic materials, grey-water reclamation systems, reduced water consumption through more efficient shower heads, faucets and toilets, and use of recycled materials wherever possible.

Energy Efficiency

Various techniques can significantly reduce energy consumption. Passive methods are becoming popular; e.g., proper building orientation to maximize passive solar potential and the positive impact of appropriate shading. Structural/mechanical activities include:

- shading and glazing of windows;
- smart-window technologies;
- increased thermal resistance in all insulation;
- high furnace efficiency;
- integrated furnace/hot water heating systems;
- stationary fuel cell utilization;
- heat recovery ventilators;
- energy-efficient lighting (e.g., compact fluorescent and electronic ballasts);
- zoned heating/cooling systems and improved ductwork distribution; and
- programmable thermostats and smart technologies.

EnerGuide

EnerGuide is a program administered by the Office of Energy Efficiency pursuant to the *Energy Efficiency Act* and Energy Efficiency Regulations. These statutory provisions promote the production, purchase and use of energy-efficient products in the Canadian marketplace. The EnerGuide program currently includes EnerGuide for Equipment and HVAC, EnerGuide for Houses and EnerGuide for Vehicles. Areas of interest to registrants are highlighted.

ENERGUIDE FOR EQUIPMENT AND HVAC APPLIANCES

The EnerGuide label must be affixed to all new electrical appliances manufactured or imported into Canada. Affixing the label does not mean that the appliance is energy-efficient, but rather that it has undergone federal standards testing. The consumption level shown on the label identifies the estimated energy use for a particular appliance in relation to other appliances of similar size and type. This information provides a comparison guide only, based on pre-determined testing standards and conditions. Usage patterns, energy rates and other locational factors will impact energy consumed and savings realized.

The large number shown on the appliance label represents kilowatt hours consumed in one year. The comparative energy consumption scale illustrates where that particular product ranks in its product class against similar models.

EXAMPLE   *Analyzing Energy Efficiency*

Salesperson Smith is comparing basic versus upgraded appliances for a new condominium project. His analysis will help explain basic versus enhanced appliance packages, associated costs and energy savings estimates to potential buyers. The basic condominium appliance package has the following consumption levels (assuming $0.085 per kWh and based on label information, affixed to appliances in an unsold unit).

APPLIANCE	ENERGUIDE	RATE	ANNUAL
Refrigerator	839	.085	$71.32
Stove	735	.085	62.48
Dishwasher	654	.085	55.59
Washer	907	.085	77.10
Dryer	950	.085	80.75
TOTAL			$347.24

Labels for the more energy-efficient package, costing an additional $1,000, have a combined annual estimate of $244.32. Therefore, projected energy savings per year of $102.92 (347.32–244.32) represent a 9.7-year payback based on EnerGuide test assumptions.

Central Air Conditioning and Gas Furnaces

EnerGuide ratings for residential gas furnaces and central air conditioners are usually located on the back page of product literature, as consumers typically acquire such equipment from brochures as opposed to retail showrooms. Gas furnaces are rated using annual fuel utilization efficiency (AFUE) and air conditioners using seasonal energy efficiency ratio (SEER). Note: Air-to-air heat pumps are also rated but not discussed in this publication.

This EnerGuide program is industry-maintained and not mandated by government regulations. The Heating, Refrigeration and Air Conditioning Institute of Canada (HRAI) works in conjunction with Natural Resources Canada in ongoing program promotion and monitoring.

Room Air Conditioners

EnerGuide for room air conditioners relies on energy efficiency ratio (EER) comparisons. The EER represents energy efficiency for a particular instant and should only be used as a general guideline when comparing cooling equipment. More precisely, the EER indicates how much cooling is generated for each electricity unit consumed, given steady-state operation under laboratory conditions. The higher the EER ratio, the more energy-efficient the air conditioner.

Usage patterns, climatic conditions, energy rates and structural considerations (e.g., insulation and window efficiencies) will impact energy consumed and savings realized.

EXAMPLE   *The EER Ratio*

Landlord Smith, owner of a 12-unit residential complex, is considering installing two 5,000 BTU, louvered room air conditioners per unit. All tenants are in agreement regarding this additional service and Smith is able to offset associated capital costs through rent increases. However, tenants want to know the approximate operating expense assuming average use, as energy cost would be their responsibility.

Smith consults the EnerGuide booklet and establishes the EER for the chosen make and model, which is 463kWh.

Estimated cost per unit	= 463 x 2 (per unit) x $0.085
	= $78.71

Smith, when discussing this calculation with tenants, cautions that this amount is based on testing standards and usage pattern assumptions established by EnerGuide. He reminds them that individual costs can vary significantly (e.g., usage, which direction a room is facing and temperature preferences).

ENERGUIDE FOR HOUSES

EnerGuide For Houses is an energy rating system designed to evaluate the efficiency of existing houses according to Natural Resources Canada guidelines. EnerGuide for Houses uses software to analyze house data and produce an energy efficiency rating based on the home's estimated annual energy consumption. Homes are rated on 1–100 scale. A 0 indicates significant air leakage, limited or no insulation and high energy consumption. A home near 100 is very well insulated, properly ventilated and requires no purchased energy (e.g., a solar house). Older homes are typically in the 50–65 range, with R-2000 being above 80.

The evaluation takes into account five primary house components:

- airtightness and thermal resistance of the building envelope;
- heating system;
- domestic water supply;
- ventilation system(s); and
- permanently installed renewable energy equipment.

A standard set of default values are applied for occupancy and energy usage. The analysis assumes that four occupants are in the building 50% of the time, the temperature is set at 21°C and 225 litres of water are consumed each day.

The evaluation can be completed for new construction, as well as resale homes. In the case of new homes, a preliminary analysis is conducted based on plans with final evaluation upon home completion. An EnerGuide for Houses label is issued to the builder/ owner indicating the energy efficiency rating. Posting of the label is optional.

The Energy Efficiency Evaluation Report contains the efficiency rating, estimated annual energy consumption and costs, energy consumption by end use (e.g., space heating, lighting and appliances, and hot water), the estimated heat loss through various house components including air leakage and ventilation, basement, ceilings, exposed floors, main walls, windows or other openings, along with any recommendations for retrofits that will reduce energy use.

WEB LINKS

EnerGuide   The EnerGuide program, as well as various other energy efficiency initiatives, is handled by the Office of Energy Efficiency (Natural Resources Canada). The OEE website (*www.oee.nrcan.gc.ca*) should be accessed for current details.

ENERGY STAR®

The ENERGY STAR® symbol identifies the most energy-efficient products in the marketplace. The ENERGY STAR® program works in concert with EnerGuide labelling to not only inform consumers of the energy consumption level of selected products, but also to identify those that are the most energy-efficient. ENERGY STAR® labels are most commonly seen by consumers on residential appliances. ENERGY STAR® is administered by the Office of Energy Efficiency (Natural Resources Canada), as is the case with EnerGuide.

ENERGY STAR® FOR NEW HOMES

New homes can also qualify under ENERGY STAR® provided that they meet technical specifications set out under ENERGY STAR® and are built by an ENERGY STAR® qualified builder. At time of printing, ENERGY STAR® for New Homes is only available in Ontario and Saskatchewan.

Technical specifications include various requirements involving heating/cooling systems, ducts, windows, insulation levels in walls and ceilings, and ventilation/air leakage criteria (including the use of a recovery ventilation system (HRV)). The efficiency level of the new home is stated on the EnerGuide label, which is attached to the electrical panel once an energy evaluation is completed by a qualified ENERGY STAR® energy evaluator.

Sample EnerGuide Label   *Source: Minister of Natural Resources Canada*

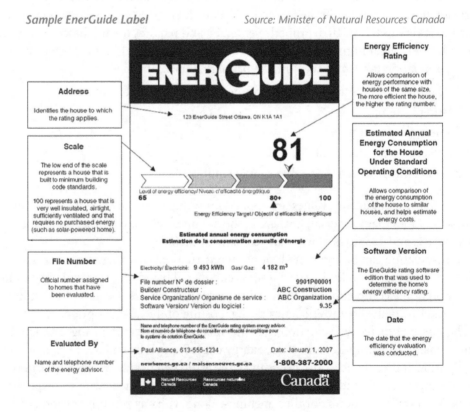

New houses are rated on a scale of 0 to 100 with most new homes receiving a 68 rating or higher. The minimum acceptable rating of an ENERGY STAR® home is 80 or higher.

ENERGY STAR® for New Homes Label
Source: Minister of Natural Resources Canada

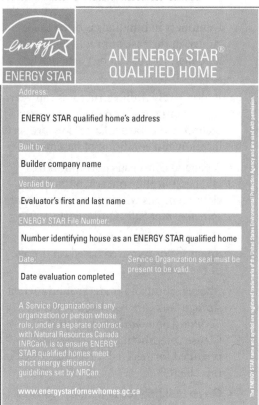

This label shows that the home is built to ENERGY STAR® for New Homes specifications and provides the homeowner with contact information for the home builder and evaluator. It can be displayed on the home's furnace or electrical box.

WEB LINKS
ENERGY STAR®
For information on Canada's ENERGY STAR® Initiative, call the toll-free publications line of Natural Resources Canada's Office of Energy Efficiency at 1-800-387-2000, or visit the web site at *http://oee.nrcan.gc.ca/residential/10759*. This site is also useful in comparing various residential energy efficiency programs including R-2000 homes.

KNOWLEDGE INTEGRATION

Notables

- Both federal and provincial govern-ments share the legislative responsibility for protecting the environment.
- Environmental responsibilities in Ontario primarily fall to the Ministry of the Environment, but other ministries and organizations are also involved.
- Registrants can minimize risk by being well informed, ensuring honesty/fairness in negotiations, drafting accurate agree-ments and seeking expert advice when necessary.
- Environmental audits can be grouped under three levels (phases) of analysis.
- Asbestos can be friable or non-friable. Health studies indicate that asbestos fibre, once airborne, can become a serious health threat.
- Hazard concerning electromagnetic fields remains a matter of personal judgement, as definitive conclusions are lacking.
- Lead is designated as a hazardous substance under the *Occupational Health and Safety Act*.

- Dampness in buildings is often the culprit in the case of mould. Finished basement rooms can be particularly susceptible.
- Radon levels within structures can vary significantly based on several factors, including the particular season, property location and condition of basement.
- A general consensus now minimizes UFFI as a health concern, but a UFFI clause remains within the *Agreement of Purchase and Sale* (OREA Form 100).
- Underground storage tanks must be upgraded or removed based on the age of the tank.
- Aboveground and underground fuel oil storage tanks are regulated under the *Technical Standards and Safety Act*. Clause constructing guidelines are provided for selected topics addressed in this chapter.
- Green building refers to house construct-ion techniques that promote energy efficiency.
- EnerGuide labels are used with equip-ment, houses and vehicles.
- ENERGY STAR® identifies highly energy efficient products, including new houses.

Web Links

Web links are included for general interest regarding selected chapter topics.

Canadian Council of Ministers of the Environment	Go to the Council's website (*www.ccme.ca*) for detailed information about the Council and its mandate.
Hydro One	Information concerning power utilities and related materials, including electromagnetic fields can be obtained from Hydro One. The website is *www.hydroone.ca*.
Lead	For additional information regarding the *Occupational Health and Safety Act* and lead as a designated hazardous substance, go the Ministry of the Environment website at *www.ene.gov.on.ca*.
Radon	The Radiation Safety Institute of Canada (*www.radiationsafety.ca*) provides detailed information about radon and radon testing equipment. Firms specializing in radon testing equipment are normally located under environmental categories in the telephone directory.
Underground Storage Tanks	The Technical Standards & Safety Authority's website (*www.tssa.org*) provides information concerning underground storage tanks.
EnerGuide	The EnerGuide program, as well as various other energy efficiency initiatives, is handled by the Office of Energy Efficiency (Natural Resources Canada). The OEE website (*www.oee.nrcan.gc.ca*) should be accessed for current details.
ENERGY STAR®	For information on Canada's ENERGY STAR® Initiative, call the toll-free publications line of Natural Resources Canada's Office of Energy Efficiency at 1-800-387-2000, or visit the web site at *http://oee.nrcan.gc.ca/residential/10759*. This site is also useful in comparing various residential energy efficiency programs, including R-2000 homes.

Strategic Thinking For Your Career

Questions are included to assist in developing your new career. No answers are provided.

1. Are there local companies that get involved in environmental audits?

2. What specific environmental hazards have been identified within the local marketplace?

3. How can I better prepare myself to discuss environmental hazards/concerns with buyers? What government publications are available from ministries and agencies discussed in this chapter?

4. Are local builders involved with the ENERGY STAR® for New Houses program administered by the Office of Energy Efficiency?

Chapter Mini-Review

Solutions are located in the Appendix.

1. All matters concerning development work on or near the water in Ontario are handled by the federal government pursuant to the *Fisheries Act*.

   ○ True   ○ False

2. A well-drafted clause relating to environmental compliance of a property should include reference to the seller agreeing to provide the buyer with applicable documents, records and reports relating to environmental matters that are in the possession of that seller.

   ○ True   ○ False

3. A Phase 2 environmental audit includes a visual inspection of the property combined with a review of available documents relating to that property.

   ○ True   ○ False

4. Friable asbestos is generally more dangerous than non-friable, as it is easily crumbled.

   ○ True   ○ False

5. The electrical power delivery system is best described using three major elements: generation, transport and end use.

   ○ True   ○ False

6. Lead contamination in residential property is limited to lead paint and lead pipes found in structures dating from the 1940's and earlier.

   ○ True   ○ False

7. Basement recreational rooms can be particularly susceptible to mould, as finished walls may hide dampness entering through exterior foundation walls.

   ○ True   ○ False

8. The concentration of radon within subsoils does not vary noticeably from one part of Canada to another.

   ○ True   ○ False

9. UFFI was used for insulation purposes in residential structures in the late 1970's, but was subsequently banned given concerns about the curing process and related health issues.

   ○ True   ○ False

10. Regulatory controls under the *Technical Standards and Safety Act* only apply to new underground storage tanks (fuel).

    ○ True   ○ False

11. The EnerGuide program applies to central air conditioning systems, but not to room air conditioners.

    ○ True   ○ False

12. ENERGY STAR® for New Houses is administered in Canada by the Office of Energy Efficiency.

    ○ True   ○ False

Active Learning Exercises

Solutions are located in the Appendix.

▣ Exercise 1   Multiple Choice

1.1   The Technical Standards and Safety Authority oversees:

    a.   The installation of docks situated on public lands.

    b.   The installation of underground storage tanks.

    c.   The installation of septic tanks.

    d.   The qualifying process for ENERGY STAR® appliances.

1.2   An environmental contractor, who is setting out remedial steps and costs associated with an environmental audit, is involved in what stage of the audit process?

    a.   Phase 1

    b.   Phase 2

    c.   Phase 3

    d.   Phase 4

1.3   Asbestos can be potentially found in older (pre-1980) structures containing which of the following?

    a.   Old stove, oven and furnace gaskets.

    b.   Older ceiling tiles.

    c.   Older insulation around plumbing pipes.

    d.   All of the above.

1.4   Which of the following is correct?

    a.   Electromagnetic fields tend to increase in strength as distance from the source increases.

    b.   Electrical fields are produced whether or not an appliance is operating.

    c.   Magnetic fields are produced whether or not an appliance is operating.

    d.   Magnetic fields do not penetrate most materials.

1.5   Radon is an invisible, odourless, tasteless gas:

    a.   That is typically produced by the decay of garbage.

    b.   That can pose a health hazard when highly concentrated in basement areas.

    c.   That can only be remediated by the continuous use of air filters.

    d.   That can only be measured by using charcoal canisters.

1.6   Which of the following is a correct statement?

    a.   Mould found in residential properties can be toxic.

    b.   The seasonal energy efficiency ratio (SEER) is a rating system to establish the energy efficiency of furnaces.

    c.   All existing underground storage tanks for fuel must be registered with the Ministry of the Environment.

    d.   ENERGY STAR® is only used to identify highly energy efficient appliances.

■ Exercise 2   Matching

Match the phrase/word in the left column with the appropriate description in the right column (not all descriptions are used).

_____ *ENERGY STAR®*	a. Call to Spills Action Centre—Ministry of the Environment
_____ *EER*	b. Hazardous Substance Under Occupational Health and Safety Act
_____ *Typical Older Homes*	c. Room Air Conditioners
_____ *Storage Tank Leak*	d. 100,000 Canadian Homes
_____ *UFFI*	e. Alpha Track Detector
_____ *Lead*	f. Normal Farm Practice
_____ *Phase 1*	g. Energy Rating of 80 or Higher
_____ *Odour, Dust and Flies*	h. Visual Inspection/Document Review
	i. Power Delivery System
	j. Energy Rating of 50–65
	k. PicoCuries

SECTION III

COMMON ERRORS AND OMISSIONS

The Residential Real Estate Transaction, as well as other pre-registration courses, outlines possible errors and omissions in the course of trading real estate. However, various topics have not yet been discussed that pose special problems to registrants. Section III contains content focusing on potential contractual difficulties when assigning offers, challenges for buyers and sellers when securing adequate insurance, special considerations concerning heritage properties and unique factors when dealing with powers of sale.

The balance of the section is directed to title-related issues, particularly involving access, fences, shore road allowances and shoreline ownership. Where applicable, drafting guidelines and explanatory notes are included to assist when preparing agreements of purchase and sale involving chapter topics.

CHAPTER 9

Contractual and Title-Related Problems

Introduction

Previous chapters have highlighted concerns about selected types of properties, but certain miscellaneous contractual and title-related issues have not been addressed. Errors and problems can arise from unexpected situations in the marketplace. Most professionals readily acknowledge that the real estate market thrives on differences...not similarities. This chapter focuses on less frequently encountered situations that nevertheless may be faced by both urban and rural registrants.

Contractual issues include assigning of offers and complexities regarding rights and liabilities in that regard. Next, in this chapter, insurance is analyzed in terms of available coverages, as well as problems that buyers can encounter when attempting to secure insurance for older properties, outdated systems and other items that insurers may not readily accept given inherent risks.

Heritage properties are discussed, along with unique considerations that impact both listing and selling of such properties. Lastly, power of sale procedures are highlighted with particular emphasis on listing essentials, marketing and drafting agreements.

The balance of the chapter details title-related matters concerning access to property, fencing issues, shore road allowances and shoreline ownership.

Learning Outcomes

At the conclusion of this chapter, students will be able to:

- Describe selected contractual issues regarding assigning offers, challenges in obtaining property insurance, use restrictions relating to heritage properties and the listing/sale of properties under power of sale.
- Identify and explain selected clauses that can be used in drafting agreements regarding these contractual issues.
- Describe title-related problems/disputes that can arise regarding access roads, access to highways, fencing and selected boundary issues.
- Identify and explain selected clauses that can be used in drafting agreements regarding these title-related concerns.
- Complete and/or critically analyze agreements that involve various errors and problems relating to contractual and title-related matters.

CONTRACTUAL ISSUES

The agreement of purchase and sale, as a preprinted form, contemplates most typical situations encountered in residential negotiations. However, circumstances can arise requiring more specialized knowledge. Four contract-related topics that can cause problems for new registrants are discussed:

- Assigning an Agreement
- Obtaining Insurance
- Heritage Property
- Power of Sale

ASSIGNING AN AGREEMENT

Assignment refers to the transfer of rights in a contract, usually in writing, to another party. The general rule of law is that all contracts are assignable with certain rare exceptions; e.g., personal service contracts are not generally assignable. The agreement of purchase and sale clearly sets out the parties to that agreement. However, circumstances can arise in which one of the parties wants to assign the contract.

Liabilities vs. Rights

As a general rule, liabilities, under a contract, cannot be assigned by the party obligated, so as to compel the other party to accept performance by an unrelated third party. However, liability can be assigned if there is express consent or an implied intention of the parties to permit the assignment. The courts may hold that such an intention was implied if the obligation does not involve a special personal qualification and if it was immaterial that the obligation was performed by someone other than the person originally liable.

Rights, as opposed to liabilities, under a contract can generally be assigned except where, for reasons of confidence between the parties or personal qualifications, such action would increase or change the obligations. For example, in a seller take-back mortgage, the court will not imply an intention to permit an assignment without the consent of that seller.

Assignment by Buyer

If a buyer contemplates the assignment of rights to a corporation or other party prior to closing, a clause in the agreement/contract can provide that the buyer has the right, at any time prior to closing, to assign the offer and be released from any further liability in regard to obligations under that agreement.

The seller should carefully consider this type of assignment as no recourse against the original buyer is possible. This clause should not be used when the agreement/contract involves a seller-take-back mortgage. In fact, the seller may wish to protect himself or herself by including a non-assignment clause, which provides that the buyer cannot either directly or indirectly assign the agreement prior to the completion date without the express written consent of the seller.

Assignment Clauses

The Ontario Real Estate Association has developed assignment clauses to address various situations found in the marketplace.

SCENARIO	CLAUSE
A buyer has purchased a property and now wishes to assign the agreement of purchase and sale (as the seller) to another party. This clause assumes that the buyer (now seller) has the right to assign the agreement.	**Assignment of Prior Agreement** *The Buyer acknowledges that the Seller has purchased the property by way of a prior accepted Agreement of Purchase and Sale, a copy of which is attached as Schedule "_____" hereto, and the Seller is assigning the Seller's rights thereunder to the Buyer. Upon acceptance of this Offer, the Seller shall give written notice of Assignment to any other parties affected by this Agreement. If the Seller is unable to complete the transaction by reason of default of the party from whom the Seller has purchased the property, the Seller shall not be liable for any damage or loss incurred by the Buyer, and this Agreement of Purchase and Sale shall become null and void and the deposit shall be returned to the Buyer in full without deduction*
A buyer has purchased a standard condominium unit and now wishes to assign the agreement of purchase and sale (as the seller) to another party. This clause assumes that the buyer (now seller) has the right to assign the agreement.	**Assignment of Prior Agreement—Condo** *The Buyer acknowledges that the Seller has purchased the property by way of a prior accepted Agreement of Purchase and Sale, a copy of which is attached as Schedule "_____" hereto, and the Seller is assigning his rights thereunder to the Buyer. Upon acceptance of this Offer, the Seller shall give written notice of Assignment to any other parties affected by this Agreement. If the Seller is unable to complete the transaction by reason of default of the party from whom he has purchased the property, the Seller shall not be liable for any damage or loss incurred by the Buyer, and this Agreement of Purchase and Sale shall become null and void and the deposit shall be returned to the Buyer in full without interest.* *The Buyer agrees to abide by all proposed or registered By-laws, Rules and Regulations applying to this property and which have been agreed to by the Seller in the prior transaction. The Buyer also acknowledges that, under the terms of this Agreement of Purchase and Sale, the price and terms agreed upon may not be the same as agreed in the prior Agreement.*
A buyer is purchasing a property and wishes to have the right to assign the agreement at his or her own option. An applicable clause is inserted in the offer.	ASSIGN–1 **Right to Assign Agreement** *The Buyer shall have the right at any time prior to closing, to assign the within Offer to any person, persons or corporation, either existing or to be incorporated, and upon delivery to the Seller of notice of such assignment, together with the assignee's covenant in favour of the Seller to be bound hereby as Buyer, the Buyer hereinbefore named shall stand released from all further liability hereunder.* **NOTE**: *Do not use when the Agreement includes a STB Charge/Mortgage.*

SCENARIO	CLAUSE
A builder has sold a home to a buyer and includes a non-assignment provision in the agreement, which includes the builder's right to grant an assignment, but only with express written consent.	**ASSIGN–2** **Right to Assign—Seller's Consent** *The Buyer covenants and agrees that the Buyer will in no way directly or indirectly assign, rent, lease, convey, list or in any way advertise for sale, sell, or otherwise transfer the Buyer's rights under this Agreement prior to completion to any other person without the express written consent of the Seller. Such consent may be granted or withheld at the Seller's sole option.*

An *Assignment of Agreement of Purchase and Sale* is provided on the following page. Cindy and Alex Lai have purchased a property at 13 Elm Street in the City of Anycity and wish to assign their rights to John and Wendy Green. Note that the purchase price of $350,000 is the total purchase price including the original Agreement of Purchase and Sale and the Assignment Agreement. While the original Agreement of Purchase and Sale would be attached as Schedule C, it has not been included in the following example.

Summary

- Rights under an agreement are generally assignable, subject to certain exceptions. Registrants should note that some agreements may include a non-assignability clause (e.g., a new home contract) or a right to assign only with seller consent.
- Liabilities are not assignable without the other party's consent. If an assignment does occur without that consent, the original buyer has continuing liability.
- Expert advice is strongly recommended for all matters concerning assignments.

Assignment Complexities   **CAUTION**

Assignments can significantly impact the client. Avoid personal involvement. Direct buyers and sellers to expert advice. Here are some examples of complexities that can arise when assigning an offer:

- HST status of a new home can be affected, if the property is not occupied as a principal residence; i.e., assigned prior to occupancy.
- The client's tax position can be impacted; i.e., profit made relating to the assignment.
- Land transfer tax implications can arise given differing sale amounts; i.e., original price vs. assigned price.
- Certain reports or services obtained concerning the property may not be assignable; e.g., home inspection reports and surveys.

OREA Ontario Real Estate Association

Form 145
for use in the Province of Ontario

Assignment of Agreement of Purchase and Sale

This Assignment of Agreement of Purchase and Sale dated this **24th** day of **July** 20**XX**

ASSIGNEE, **John W. Green and Wendy S. Green** , agrees to purchase from
(Full legal names of all Assignees)

ASSIGNOR, **Cindy M.W. Lai and Alex W. Lai** , the following
(Full legal names of all Assignors)

THE ASSIGNOR'S INTEREST IN THE REAL PROPERTY:

Address **13 Elm Street** fronting on the **South** side

of **Elm Street** in the **City of Anycity, Region of Anyregion**

and having a frontage of **52 feet** more or less by a depth of **125 feet** more or less

and legally described as **Lot 27, Plan 99 M-2894**

(the "property")
(Legal description of land including easements not described elsewhere)

PURCHASE PRICE: Dollars (CDN$) **$350,000.00**

Three Hundred and Fifty Thousand-- Dollars

DEPOSIT: Assignee submits **Upon Acceptance**
(Herewith/Upon Acceptance/as otherwise described in this Agreement)

Twenty Thousand--- Dollars (CDN$) **$20,000.00**

by negotiable cheque payable to **ABC Realty Inc.** "Deposit Holder" to be held in trust pending completion or other termination of this Assignment agreement ("Assignment") and to be credited toward the Purchase Price on completion. For the purposes of this Assignment, "Upon Acceptance" shall mean that the Assignee is required to deliver the deposit to the Deposit Holder within 24 hours of the acceptance of this Assignment agreement. The parties to this Assignment hereby acknowledge that, unless otherwise provided for in this Assignment, the Deposit Holder shall place the deposit in trust in the Deposit Holder's non-interest bearing Real Estate Trust Account and no interest shall be earned, received or paid on the deposit.

The Assignee and Assignor acknowledge that the Purchase Price noted above includes both the purchase price the Assignor is paying for the property as indicated in the Agreement of Purchase and Sale between the Assignor and the seller of the property attached hereto as Schedule C, and also includes the amount being paid by the Assignee to the Assignor as payment for the Assignment Agreement. The Assignee and Assignor agree that the funds for this transaction will be calculated and paid as set out in Schedule B attached hereto and forming part of this Agreement.

Assignee agrees to pay the balance as more particularly set out in Schedules A and B attached.

Schedules A, B (Calculation of funds for this Agreement),
C (Agreement of Purchase and Sale that is the subject of this Assignment),

attached hereto form(s) part of this Agreement.

1. **IRREVOCABILITY:** This offer shall be irrevocable by **Assignee** until **10:00** ~~a.m.~~/p.m. on the **25th**
(Assignee/Assignor)

day of **July** 20 **XX**, after which time, if not accepted, this offer shall be null and void and the deposit shall be returned to the Buyer in full without interest.

INITIALS OF ASSIGNEE(S): *JG WG*   **INITIALS OF ASSIGNOR(S):** *CL AL*

Form 145   Revised 2015   **Page 1 of 6**

2. **ASSIGNMENT:** The Assignor agrees to grant and assign to the Assignee, forthwith all the Assignor's rights, title and interest, in, under and to the Agreement of Purchase and Sale attached hereto in Schedule "C".

3. **ASSIGNEE COVENANTS:** The Assignee hereby covenants and agrees with the Assignor that forthwith upon the assignment of the Agreement of Purchase and Sale it will assume, perform, comply with and be bound by, all obligations, warranties and representations of the Assignor as contained in the Agreement of Purchase and Sale as if the Assignee had originally executed the Agreement of Purchase and Sale as buyer with the seller.

4. **ASSIGNOR COVENANTS:** The Assignor covenants and represents that:
   (a) the Assignor has the full right, power and authority to assign the prior Agreement of Purchase and Sale attached hereto as Schedule "C" (the "Agreement of Purchase and Sale") and the Assignor's interest in the property;
   (b) the Agreement of Purchase and Sale attached hereto as Schedule "C" is a full and complete copy thereof and has not been amended, supplemented, terminated or otherwise changed in any way and is in good standing and has not previously been assigned;
   (c) the Assignor will not amend the Agreement of Purchase and Sale without the Assignee's prior written consent;
   (d) after acceptance of this Assignment Agreement until the earlier of termination or completion of the Agreement of Purchase and Sale attached hereto as Schedule "C", the Assignor will not further assign the Agreement of Purchase and Sale.
   (e) neither party to the Agreement of Purchase and Sale (Schedule C) has done any act in breach of the said Agreement of Purchase and Sale or committed any omission with respect to the said Agreement of Purchase and Sale.

5. **NOTICES:** The Assignor hereby appoints the Listing Brokerage as agent for the Assignor for the purpose of giving and receiving notices pursuant to this Agreement. Where a Brokerage (Assignee's Brokerage) has entered into a representation agreement with the Assignee, the Assignee hereby appoints the Assignee's Brokerage as agent for the purpose of giving and receiving notices pursuant to this Agreement. **Where a Brokerage represents both the Assignor and the Assignee (multiple representation), the Brokerage shall not be appointed or authorized to be agent for either the Assignee or the Assignor for the purpose of giving and receiving notices.** Any notice relating hereto or provided for herein shall be in writing. In addition to any provision contained herein and in any Schedule hereto, this offer, any counter-offer, notice of acceptance thereof or any notice to be given or received pursuant to this Agreement or any Schedule hereto (any of them, **"Document"**) shall be deemed given and received when delivered personally or hand delivered to the Address for Service provided in the Acknowledgement below, or where a facsimile number or email address is provided herein, when transmitted electronically to the facsimile number or email address, respectively, in which case, the signature(s) of the party (parties) shall be deemed to be original.

FAX No.: .... **N/A** ....
(For delivery of Documents to Assignor)

FAX No.: .... **N/A** ....
(For delivery of Documents to Assignee)

Email Address: .... **N/A** ....
(For delivery of Documents to Assignor)

Email Address: .... **N/A** ....
(For delivery of Documents to Assignee)

6. **HST:** If the sale of the Property (Real Property as described above) is subject to Harmonized Sales Tax (HST), then such tax shall be
.... **included in** .... the Purchase Price. If the sale of the Property is not subject to HST, Seller agrees to certify on or before
(included in/in addition to)
closing, that the sale of the Property is not subject to HST. Any HST on chattels, if applicable, is not included in the Purchase Price.

7. **FUTURE USE:** Assignor and Assignee agree that there is no representation or warranty of any kind that the future intended use of the property by Assignee is or will be lawful except as may be specifically provided for in this Assignment.

8. **INSPECTION:** Assignee acknowledges having had the opportunity to inspect the property or the plans and documents for the property to be constructed and understands that upon acceptance of this offer there shall be a binding Assignment agreement between Assignee and Assignor.

9. **PLANNING ACT:** Provided that this Assignment shall not be effective to create or convey an interest in the property unless and until the provisions of the Planning Act RSO 1990 c. P13, as amended are complied with.

INITIALS OF ASSIGNEE(S): *JG WG*   **INITIALS OF ASSIGNOR(S):** *CL AL*

SECTION III   COMMON ERRORS AND OMISSIONS

10. **RESIDENCY:** (a) Subject to (b) below, the Assignor represents and warrants that the Assignor is not and on completion will not be a non-resident under the non-residency provisions of the Income Tax Act which representation and warranty shall survive and not merge upon the completion of this transaction and the Assignor shall deliver to the Assignee a statutory declaration that Assignor is not then a non-resident of Canada;
(b) provided that if the Assignor is a non-resident under the non-residency provisions of the Income Tax Act, the Assignee shall be credited towards the Purchase Price with the amount, if any, necessary for Assignee to pay to the Minister of National Revenue to satisfy Assignee's liability in respect of tax payable by Assignor under the non-residency provisions of the Income Tax Act by reason of this sale. Assignee shall not claim such credit if Assignor delivers on completion the prescribed certificate.

11. **ADJUSTMENTS:** Any rents, mortgage interest, realty taxes including local improvement rates and unmetered public or private utility charges and unmetered cost of fuel, as applicable, shall be apportioned and allowed to the day of completion, the day of completion itself to be apportioned to Assignee.

12. **PROPERTY ASSESSMENT:** The Assignee and Assignor hereby acknowledge that the Province of Ontario has implemented current value assessment and properties may be re-assessed on an annual basis. The Assignee and Assignor agree that no claim will be made against the Assignee and Assignor, or any Brokerage, Broker or Salesperson, for any changes in property tax as a result of a re-assessment of the property, save and except any property taxes that accrued prior to the completion of this transaction.

13. **TIME LIMITS:** Time shall in all respects be of the essence hereof provided that the time for doing or completing of any matter provided for herein may be extended or abridged by an agreement in writing signed by Assignor and Assignee or by their respective lawyers who may be specifically authorized in that regard.

14. **TENDER:** Any tender of documents or money hereunder may be made upon the Assignor or Assignee or their respective lawyers on the day set for completion. Money shall be tendered with funds drawn on a lawyer's trust account in the form of a bank draft, certified cheque or wire transfer using the Large Value Transfer System.

15. **APPROVAL OF THE AGREEMENT:** In the event that consent to this Assignment is required to be given by the seller in the Agreement of Purchase and Sale attached hereto in Schedule C, the Assignor will apply, at the sole expense of the Assignor, forthwith for the requisite consent, and if such consent is refused, then this agreement shall be null and void and the deposit monies paid hereunder shall be refunded without interest or other penalty to the Assignee.

16. **AGREE TO CO-OPERATE:** Except as otherwise expressed herein to the contrary, each of the Assignor and Assignee shall, without receiving additional consideration therefor, co-operate with and take such additional actions as may be requested by the other party, acting reasonably, in order to carry out the purpose and intent of this Assignment.

17. **DEFAULT BY SELLER:** The Assignee and Assignor acknowledge and agree that if this Assignment Agreement is not completed due to the default of the seller for the Agreement of Purchase and Sale (Schedule C) that is the subject of this Assignment, the Assignor shall not be liable for any expenses, losses or damages incurred by the Assignee and this Assignment Agreement shall become null and void and all moneys paid by the Assignee under this Assignment Agreement shall be returned to the Assignee in full without interest.

18. **LEGAL, ACCOUNTING AND ENVIRONMENTAL ADVICE:** The parties acknowledge that any information provided by the Brokerage is not legal, tax or environmental advice.

19. **CONSUMER REPORTS: The Assignee is hereby notified that a consumer report containing credit and/or personal information may be referred to in connection with this transaction.**

20. **AGREEMENT IN WRITING:** If there is conflict or discrepancy between any provision added to this Assignment (including any Schedule attached hereto) and any provision in the standard pre-set portion hereof, the added provision shall supersede the standard pre-set provision to the extent of such conflict or discrepancy. This Assignment including any Schedule attached hereto, shall constitute the entire agreement between Assignee and Assignor. There is no representation, warranty, collateral agreement or condition, which affects this Assignment other than as expressed herein. This Assignment shall be read with all changes of gender or number required by the context.

21. **TIME AND DATE:** Any reference to a time and date in this Agreement shall mean the time and date where the property is located.

INITIALS OF ASSIGNEE(S):   INITIALS OF ASSIGNOR(S):

22. SUCCESSORS AND ASSIGNS: The heirs, executors, administrators, successors and assigns of the undersigned are bound by the terms herein.

SIGNED, SEALED AND DELIVERED in the presence of: IN WITNESS whereof I have hereunto set my hand and seal:

Bruce McGowan
(Witness)

John W. Green
(Assignee)   (Seal)   DATE *July 24/xx*

Bruce McGowan
(Witness)

Wendy S. Green
(Assignee)   (Seal)   DATE *July 24/xx*

I, the Undersigned Assignor, agree to the above offer. I hereby irrevocably instruct my lawyer to pay directly to the brokerage(s) with whom I have agreed to pay commission, the unpaid balance of the commission together with applicable Harmonized Sales Tax (and any other taxes as may hereafter be applicable), from the proceeds of the sale prior to any payment to the undersigned on completion, as advised by the brokerage(s) to my lawyer.

SIGNED, SEALED AND DELIVERED in the presence of: IN WITNESS whereof I have hereunto set my hand and seal:

Anita Hill
(Witness)

Cindy M.W. Lai
(Assignor)   (Seal)   DATE *July 24/xx*

Anita Hill
(Witness)

Alex W. Lai
(Assignor)   (Seal)   DATE *July 24/xx*

CONFIRMATION OF ACCEPTANCE: Notwithstanding anything contained herein to the contrary, I confirm this Agreement with all changes both typed and written was finally accepted by all parties at *8:00* a.m./p.m. this *24th* day of *July*, 20*xx*.

Cindy M. W. Lai
(Signature of Assignor or Assignee)

IINFORMATION ON BROKERAGE(S)

Listing Brokerage ...... **ABC Realty Inc.** ...... Tel.No.(**416**) **238-4745**

123 Main Street, Anycity, Anyregion L4H 6P5   **Bruce McGowan**
(Salesperson / Broker Name)

Co-op/Buyer Brokerage ...... Tel.No.(............)

......
(Salesperson / Broker Name)

ACKNOWLEDGEMENT

I acknowledge receipt of my signed copy of this accepted Assignment Agreement and I authorize the Brokerage to forward a copy to my lawyer.

Cindy M.W. Lai
(Assignor)   DATE *July 24/xx*

Alex W. Lai
(Assignor)   DATE *July 24/xx*

Address for Service *55 West Creek Drive, Anycity*

Anyregion N5K 3L3   Tel.No.(*416*) *333-1212*

Assignor's Lawyer *James McLennon*

Address *1275 Main Street, Anycity K0J 1J3*

Email ......

(*416*) *222-1212*   (*416*) *222-2121*
Tel.No.   FAX No.

I acknowledge receipt of my signed copy of this accepted Assignment Agreement and I authorize the Brokerage to forward a copy to my lawyer.

John W. Green
(Assignee)   DATE *July 24/xx*

Wendy S. Green
(Assignee)   DATE *July 24/xx*

Address for Service *Apt. 505, 2500 Queen Street, Anycity*

Anyregion   Tel.No.(*416*) *666-1212*

Assignee's Lawyer *Wendy Kolalski*

Address *Suite 301, 275 Eastern Parkway, Anycity K0V 3C7*

Email ......

(*416*) *777-1212*   (*416*) *777-2121*
Tel.No.   FAX No.

FOR OFFICE USE ONLY   **COMMISSION TRUST AGREEMENT**

To: Co-operating Brokerage shown on the foregoing Assignment Agreement:
In consideration for the Co-operating Brokerage procuring the foregoing Assignment Agreement, I hereby declare that all moneys received or receivable by me in connection with the Transaction as contemplated in the MLS® Rules and Regulations of my Real Estate Board shall be receivable and held in trust. This agreement shall constitute a Commission Trust Agreement as defined in the MLS® Rules and shall be subject to and governed by the MLS® Rules pertaining to Commission Trust.

DATED as of the date and time of the acceptance of the foregoing Assignment Agreement.   Acknowledged by:

......
(Authorized to bind the Listing Brokerage)   (Authorized to bind the Co-operating Brokerage)

Form 145   Revised 2015   **Page 4 of 6**

SECTION III   COMMON ERRORS AND OMISSIONS

OREA Ontario Real Estate Association

Form 145
for use in the Province of Ontario

Schedule A
Assignment of Agreement of Purchase and Sale

This Schedule is attached to and forms part of the Assignment of Agreement of Purchase and Sale between:

ASSIGNEE, ... John W. Green and Wendy S. Green ...., and

ASSIGNOR, ... Cindy M.W. Lai and Alex W. Lai ....

for the purchase and sale of .... 13 Elm Street, City of Anycity, Region of Anyregion ....

.... dated the ..24th.. day of .... July ...., 20 **XX** .

BALANCE OF PAYMENT UNDER THIS ASSIGNMENT AGREEMENT: The Assignee will deliver the balance of payment for this Assignment Agreement as more particularly set out in Item 6. on Schedule B, subject to adjustments, with funds drawn on a lawyer's trust account in the form of a bank draft, certified cheque or wire transfer using the Large Value Transfer System, to the Assignor prior to completing the transaction in the Agreement of Purchase and Sale attached hereto as Schedule "C" to be held in trust without interest pending completion or other termination of the Agreement of Purchase and Sale attached hereto as Schedule "C".

This form must be initialed by all parties to the Assignment of Agreement of Purchase and Sale.

INITIALS OF ASSIGNEE(S): JG WG   **INITIALS OF ASSIGNOR(S):** CL AL

Form 145   Revised 2015   **Page 5 of 6**

OREA Ontario Real Estate Association

Form 145
for use in the Province of Ontario

Schedule B
Assignment of Agreement of Purchase and Sale

This Schedule is attached to and forms part of the Assignment of Agreement of Purchase and Sale between:

ASSIGNEE, ... John W. Green and Wendy S. Green ...., and

ASSIGNOR, ... Cindy M.W. Lai and Alex W. Lai ....

for the purchase and sale of .... 13 Elm Street, City of Anycity, Region of Anyregion ....

.... dated the .... 24th .... day of .... July ...., 20 **xx**

The Assignee and Assignor agree that the calculation of funds to be paid for this Assignment Agreement, subject to adjustments, is as set out in the following Items:

1.   Total Purchase Price including the original Agreement of Purchase and Sale and this Assignment Agreement: *↳ assignment price.* $ 350,000.00

2.   Purchase Price of original Agreement of Purchase and Sale as indicated in Schedule C: *↳ original price* $ 315,000.00

3.   Deposit(s) paid by Assignor to the seller under the original Agreement of Purchase and Sale as indicated in Schedule C, to be paid by the Assignee to the Assignor as follows: *↳ original deposit* $ 25,000.00

same *{*

① Upon acceptance of this Agreement and receipt of consent to assign from original seller, if applicable

② (Upon acceptance of this Assignment Agreement and receipt of consent to assign from original seller, if applicable)

③ (Upon final closing of original Agreement of Purchase and Sale and this Assignment Agreement)

4.   Payment by Assignee to Assignor for this Assignment Agreement: *→ profit* $ 35,000.00

5.   Deposit paid under this Assignment Agreement (in accordance with Page 1 of this Assignment Agreement):   *↳ deposit for this new agreement* $ 20,000.00

6.   Balance of the payment for this Assignment Agreement: *↳ balance* $ 15,000.00

INITIALS OF ASSIGNEE(S): *JG WG*

INITIALS OF ASSIGNOR(S): *CL AL*

Form 145   Revised 2015   **Page 6 of 6**

Assigning a Lease

A tenant may assign or sublet at will without the approval of the landlord, unless the lease stipulates otherwise or the tenancy is residential and pursuant to the *Residential Tenancies Act*. Special considerations also apply in the case of a care home under that Act. Provisions concerning residential assignments have been set out in a previous chapter.

Assuming that the lease in question is commercial with associated permission to assign, the commercial tenant may transfer all of his/her leasehold interests to a new tenant. However, unless he/she is released by the landlord, the assignor remains liable for the lease obligations to the landlord. Of course, the assignor may not remain liable if such is specifically set out in the lease terms.

SUBLETTING

If the tenant transfers something less than an entire interest, he/she sublets it. This may be either the subletting of part of the term or part of the premises. The tenant remains liable to the landlord, unless otherwise stipulated in the lease. Once again, residential subletting is subject to provisions set out in the *Residential Tenancies Act*.

Most commercial leases contain an express covenant that the tenant will not assign or sublet, or a qualified covenant that there will not be any assignment or subletting without the prior written consent of the landlord. This clause may be further qualified so that the landlord's consent will not be withheld arbitrarily. In these circumstances, the tenant can apply to a judge to obtain approval for an appropriate tenant who intends to use the premises in a reasonable manner.

Usually both the tenant and the assignee or subtenant will sign a form agreeing to be bound by the main lease and the landlord will consent to this agreement. The parties will pay the landlord's reasonable costs and legal expenses in arranging for this consent.

Mortgage Assignment   **CURIOSITY**

A mortgagee may decide to sell the mortgage to another lender by way of an assignment document. This transfer assigns the registered mortgage, as well as all rights to collect outstanding amounts due under the mortgage. The amount payable for an assignment will vary depending on how favourable the terms of the original mortgage are in comparison with market conditions at point of sale.

If the current rates are higher than the stated rate on the mortgage, then the mortgagee will probably have to discount the mortgage face value to make the offering attractive to potential assignees. The discount has the net effect of raising the overall yield. Conversely, an investor might pay additional monies to the mortgagee if the mortgage has an interest rate substantially higher than current rates.

OBTAINING INSURANCE

Clause 8 in the *Agreement of Purchase and Sale* (OREA Form 100) provides that the buyer make enquiries that the principal building may be insured against risk of fire. Historically, this clause sufficed given few problems in obtaining coverage.

These days, insurance underwriters closely scrutinize properties, particularly older homes with outdated wiring, underground oil tanks or other matters requiring remedial action. An insurance condition may be required to provide an opportunity to seek out appropriate insurance coverage. Clients may also require a stipulation in the condition regarding total premium, as costs may escalate with certain higher risk properties.

Insurance Overview

An insurance policy is an agreement in which one party (insurer) promises to pay a sum of money to another (insured) if the latter suffers a particular loss, in exchange for a premium paid by the insured. Insurance coverage for real property is two-dimensional: namely, the amount of risk covered for a particular property and the range of coverages provided. The type of coverage will vary substantially, based on the particular property and risks included.

RESIDENTIAL

Residential insurance coverage is generally grouped under owner and tenant policies. Both types are commonly packaged, that is, various coverages are included within a single policy. Most consist of four basic sections:

- **Property Insurance**   Covers what property is being insured against loss or damage, what is not insured and the types of causes of such loss or damage that will be paid under the policy. The range of coverages will vary from basic perils to more comprehensive coverages. Typically, insurance policy wordings concentrate on coverages excluded, rather than those included. A wide variety of coverage extensions are available through most insurers.

- **Liability Insurance**   Includes specified limits for liability arising out of accidents or occurrences as detailed in the policy. Liability can extend to specific personal actions liability, premises liability, tenant legal liability and selected medical payments. Once again, a wide variety of coverages are available through insurers.

- **Endorsements**   Additional coverage that is added to the insurance policy, for example, coverages relating to valuable personal articles.

- **Policy Conditions**   Various policy conditions relating to procedures concerning claims, general policy provisions and matters addressed in applicable provincial insurance legislation.

COMMERCIAL

Commercial policies are structured to provide basic coverages for property insurance and liability coverages, with additional endorsements and other policies to meet the needs of specific business activities. Specialized policies are often required. Following are a few commonly encountered business insurance coverages.

- **Boiler and Machinery Coverage**   Covers repairs and/or replacement of all major heating, ventilating and air-conditioning equipment. The premium will be directly related to the type of maintenance contract for the care of the particular item insured.

- **Errors and Omissions**   Protection for the insured if some unforeseen occurrence develops from negligence in the operation of the business.

- **Fidelity Bond**   Insures the employer against the acts of dishonest employees.

- **Loss of Income**   Covers loss of income suffered by the insured in the event of damage to the building and resulting disruption of business as a result of that damage.

- **Multi-Peril Risk**   Combination of fire and liability coverages that generally align with the basic structure of residential packaged policies. These package policies normally provide premium discounts for broader coverage features than would be the case with separate policies for fire, extended perils and liability.

SECTION III   COMMON ERRORS AND OMISSIONS

CONDOMINIUM

Insurance requirements for condominiums consist of three separate groups.

- **Condominium Corporation**   The condominium corporation requires insurance for the unit structures (excluding any improvements or betterments made by the owner) and common elements. In addition, the corporation is responsible for liability coverage, any bonding coverage required for employees and directors/officers, and director liability.

- **Unit Owner**   The unit owner should insure any improvements (built-in items, carpeting and personal belongings) and generally any risk not covered by the corporation (including the owner's liability).

- **Renter**   Renters should ensure that all personal belongings are insured and appropriate legal liability coverage is obtained.

Insurers typically provide owner policies for condominium owners structured on the same general basis as is the case for residential property. Tenant package policies are structured for both condominium tenancies as well as other rental accommodation. Real estate registrants should note that the rental agreement for a condominium may specify that the tenant provides coverage for those items owned by the landlord on the premises; e.g., appliances and carpeting.

Insurance Clauses

The Ontario Real Estate Association has developed two insurance clauses to address typical circumstances found in the marketplace.

SCENARIO	CLAUSE
Arranging Insurance A buyer has purchased a property and wants to ensure that he or she can obtain insurance by including an appropriate condition in the offer, including the seller's agreement to co-operate regarding any needed property inspection.	**INSUR–1** Condition—Arranging Insurance *This offer is conditional on the Buyer arranging insurance for the property satisfactory to the Buyer in the Buyer's sole and absolute discretion. Unless the Buyer gives notice in writing delivered to the Seller personally or in accordance with any other provisions for the delivery of notice in this Agreement of Purchase and Sale or any Schedule thereto not later than _____p.m. on the _____day of _____, 20____, that this condition is fulfilled, this offer shall be null and void and the deposit shall be returned to the Buyer in full without deduction. The Seller agrees to co-operate in providing access to the property, if necessary, for any inspection of the property required for the fulfillment of this condition. This condition is included for the benefit of the Buyer and may be waived at the Buyer's sole option by notice in writing to the Seller as aforesaid within the time period stated herein.* **NOTE:** Due to the nature of this clause, a short time frame should be chosen for this condition.

SCENARIO	CLAUSE
Arranging Insurance—Not to Exceed Specified Cost	**INSUR–2** **Condition—Arranging Insurance—Cost Not to Exceed**
A buyer has purchased a property and wants to ensure that he or she can obtain specific insurance coverages, which must not exceed a specified amount. This clause, as with the previous, includes the seller's agreement to co-operate regarding any needed property inspection.	*This offer is conditional upon the Buyer arranging insurance on the property for the following named perils: _____, at a yearly cost not to exceed _____, excluding applicable taxes. Unless the Buyer gives notice in writing delivered to the Seller personally or in accordance with any other provisions for the delivery of notice in this Agreement of Purchase and Sale or any Schedule thereto not later than _____ p.m. on the _____ day of _____, 20____, that this condition is fulfilled, this Offer shall be null and void and the deposit shall be returned to the Buyer in full without deduction. The Seller agrees to co-operate in providing access to the property, if necessary, for any inspection of the property required for the fulfillment of this condition. This condition is included for the benefit of the Buyer and may be waived at the Buyer's sole option by notice in writing to the Seller as aforesaid within the time period stated herein.*

HERITAGE PROPERTY

Registrants may encounter buildings designated as heritage property. This status can restrict internal/external changes to designated structures and increase renovation costs.

HERITAGE PROPERTY TIME LINE

1967   Ontario Heritage Foundation created as provincial centennial project. Various Ontario communities developed local museums or undertook restorations.

1974   The *Ontario Heritage Act* was passed giving municipalities specific powers for building preservation and protection of archaeological resources.

1992   Minister's Advisory Committee on new heritage legislation released a working paper.

1996   Bill 20 (amendments to land use planning legislation) made selected changes to the *Ontario Heritage Act*.

2001   The *Ontario Heritage Amendment Act, 2005*

- New powers to both province and municipalities to stop demolition of heritage sites.

- Expanded ability to identify and designate provincial heritage sites.

- Expanded, clarified guidelines and standards regarding heritage properties.

SECTION III   COMMON ERRORS AND OMISSIONS

Insurance has become an important consideration in the real estate transaction. Insurers may refuse to insure certain types of property, require substantially larger premiums or deductibles to take on certain risks, and/or demand that certain outdated or defective materials or equipment be replaced prior to providing the coverage. Registrants must be aware of important factors influencing insurers' decisions and associated underwriting policies. The impact of a refusal on the real estate transaction is immediate when mortgage financing is involved. Lending institutions will not advance funds at closing without proof of insurance to protect the lender's interests.

Insurance company policies will vary, but the following offer a range of circumstances that may pose problems in obtaining insurance:

Age of Structure	If the structure is more than 25 years old, the insuring company will want more details on the roof, heating, plumbing and electrical systems. Based on these findings, the insurer may require corrective measures or refuse to provide coverage.
Heritage Home	Special considerations come into play with heritage homes, not only from an age perspective, but also from the fact that damage replacement must either replicate or be of like quality. In some instances, insurers may require a separate endorsement on the policy to cover this portion of the risk. Added premiums typically apply.
Woodstove or Similar Appliance	If the home has a woodstove, the insurer will want assurances that the appliance has been installed correctly; does it meet Ontario Building Code and Ontario Fire Code requirements and is it vented properly?
Underground Fuel Tank	If the home has an underground fuel tank, it must meet current standards as set out by the Technical Standards and Safety Authority (as discussed in a previous chapter on environmental concerns).
Wiring	An insurer may refuse to insure a property that has a 60-amp service, knob and tube wiring, or aluminum wiring (installed in houses during the late 1960's and early 1970's).

Buyers and sellers should be aware of other issues that come into play when determining insurability and/or premiums charged:

Municipal Services	Is the property connected to water and sewer? If not, what are the age/condition of the well and septic (including support documentation)?
Fire Station/Fire Hydrant	What is the distance to the nearest fire station (in the case of a rural property) that would respond in the event of a fire or what is the proximity of the nearest fire hydrant with urban properties?
Property Location	Is the property in a floodplain or area that is prone to some form of natural disaster?
Claims Experience/ Cancellations	What claims has the buyer made against a home insurance policy in the past and has that individual ever had a policy refused or cancelled?

Background Information

The provincial government has over the years established official measures to record, celebrate and preserve Ontario's history, with particular emphasis on the preservation of structures. Interest in heritage property can be traced to the early 19th century. The first legislation, an Act of Parliament in 1817, provided for a monument to General Sir Isaac Brock at Queenston Heights. Public interest in conservation has increased steadily over the years. Hundreds of architectural, historical and museum societies have been founded.

Following the Second World War, in response to escalating development, heritage preservation grew extensively, particularly in regard to architectural, archaeological and natural heritage conservation.

In 1974, the *Ontario Heritage Act* was passed. The Act gave municipalities specific powers for the preservation and protection of archaeological resources. In June 1992, a Minister's Advisory Committee on new heritage legislation released its working paper, with a limited number of amendments made in 1996. However, the most significant changes came about on April 28, 2005 with the *Ontario Heritage Amendment Act*. These amendments provided greater municipal and provincial powers to protect heritage sites.

Real Estate Perspective

Heritage preservation and conservation, while viewed as a public good, can directly affect property and real estate activity. Large blocks of property are set aside by various levels of government and designated as culturally and/or historically important. Such activity can, at times, result in property owners being deprived of their natural rights.

Real estate registrants may encounter buildings or other archaeological resources designated under the *Ontario Heritage Act*. This designation can impact intended uses for a property and affect the ability to make both internal and external changes/renovations to structures so designated. Sellers contemplating listing and selling heritage buildings, whether individually designated or situated within a heritage conservation district, may face lengthy discussions with municipal authorities.

WEB LINKS

Heritage Property   This topic contains summary information as an introductory guide to registrants. Those involved with heritage properties should access the Ministry of Tourism, Culture and Sport website at *www.mtc.gov.on.ca/en/heritage/heritage.shtml* and also contact the local municipality.

CLAUSE IN AGREEMENT

The following clause highlights that the property is or may be designated as a heritage property.

SCENARIO	CLAUSE
Designating a Heritage Property The seller, owner of a heritage property, wants to ensure that the buyer understands that the property is designated as Heritage Property. A condition in the offer would be appropriate should the buyer wish to investigate the implications of this designation.	**HERIT–1** **Ontario Heritage Act Designation** *The parties hereto acknowledge that the subject property is/may be designated as a Heritage Property and is subject to the provisions of the Ontario Heritage Act, 1974. The Buyer acknowledges that the Seller has made this disclosure. The Buyer accepts the property with this designation and agrees to continue with this transaction.*

Ontario Heritage Trust

The Ontario Heritage Trust (formerly called the Ontario Heritage Foundation) is actively involved in protecting and promoting Ontario's heritage. The Trust offers various programs to aid in the restoration of heritage properties, as well as the protection of natural properties including marine and archaeological sites.

The Ontario Heritage Trust, as an agency of the Ministry of Culture, has various heritage assets, including heritage buildings, natural heritage sites, registered archaeological sites and conservation easement properties. As well, the Trust currently has over 21,000 catalogued cultural artifacts, more than 11,000 archival documents and approximately 1,190 provincial historical plaques.

MUNICIPAL HERITAGE COMMITTEES

Section 28 of the Act provides that the council of a municipality can establish a municipal heritage committee made up of five or more people. The committee assists and advises council on local heritage matters, including the carrying out of the heritage conservation program within the specific municipality.

WEB LINKS

Community Heritage Ontario   Community Heritage Ontario is the umbrella organization for heritage committees. Go to **http://communityheritageontario.ca** for detailed information. All committees within the province are listed on the Ministry Tourism, Culture and Sport website at **www.mtc.gov.on.ca**.

CONSERVATION REVIEW BOARD

The Conservation Review Board has a mandate to conduct hearings and make recommendations regarding heritage matters. In practice, its primary activity involves hearing objections to heritage designation and making recommendations to municipal councils on such matters. The board does not have decision-making powers and fulfills an advisory capacity only.

Key Statutory Provisions

Two parts of the *Ontario Heritage Act* have particular relevance to registrants.

HISTORIC OR ARCHITECTURAL VALUE

Part IV—Conservation of Property of Cultural Heritage Value or Interest establishes procedures for designating individual properties (real property and all buildings and structures thereon). While this text understandably focuses on structures, the reader is reminded that designation can also apply to landscapes, trees, parks and archeological sites.

Notice procedures and methods of addressing objections to such designations, along with appeal processes, are detailed in the Act. As a general guideline, registrants should be aware of the following:

- **Alterations**   Designated property cannot be altered when the alteration is likely to affect the reason for the designation.
- **Written Consent**   Alterations are only permitted if the owner applies to the council and receives written consent.
- **Demolition**   Demolition of any building or structure on the property requires similar consent. Brokers and salespersons should inquire whether or not a property has been designated at point of listing.

Local municipalities are now empowered (given changes made under the *Ontario Heritage Amendment Act, 2005*) to prohibit demolition or removal of property designated under the Act, or attach terms and conditions relating to such activity. Prior to such changes, the council only had the power to delay the demolition of a structure. As a general statement, both demolition controls and procedures for designation have been significantly strengthened with the passage of the 2005 legislation.

HERITAGE CONSERVATION DISTRICTS

Part V—Heritage Conservation Districts sets out procedures for designating one or more areas as heritage conservation districts and can incorporate such changes into the official plan. As with Part IV, procedures are detailed concerning notice periods, methods of addressing objectives and appeal processes.

Registrants should note that amendments under the *Ontario Heritage Amendment Act, 2005* provide that municipalities can now undertake studies regarding potential designation of a heritage conservation district and require that no demolitions occur during any such study for a period of one year. Further, district designation by-laws are now to be registered on the title of properties within a particular district.

Heritage Easement Agreements

Registrants will occasionally encounter heritage easements that are voluntarily entered into with property owners to ensure that heritage properties are protected over the long term. For example, municipalities may require such an agreement as a condition when funding the restoration of a structure. More often, the incentive to enter into such an agreement involves tax relief. The *Municipal Act, 2001* provides that municipalities can adopt a tax relief program to permit relief ranging from 10% to 40% of taxes levied on an eligible property (or portion thereof).

 WEB LINKS

Heritage Property Tax Relief   Go to the Ministry of Tourism, Culture and Sport website (*www.mtc.gov.on.ca/en/heritage/heritage_tax_relief.shtml*) for detailed information on tax relief measures associated with heritage easements, including information regarding heritage designation, associate tax relief eligibility and tax relief calculations.

| *Current Information Is A Must* | CAUTION |

Registrants should exercise caution in all matters involving heritage properties. Contact the local municipality for current information and listings of currently designated properties, conservation districts or current areas of study for potential designation.

Make certain that this topic is addressed in any listing presentation involving an older property of historic value. The *Seller Property Information Statement* (OREA Form 220) contains a specific question in that regard:

(b) Is the property connected to municipal sewer? (If not, Schedule 222 to be completed.)				
17. Are there any current or pending Heritage restrictions for the property or the area?				

 ## POWER OF SALE

Newly registered salespeople may encounter properties under power of sale in the marketplace. Two power of sale approaches can be taken as set out in the *Mortgages Act*:

 **SECTION III**   COMMON ERRORS AND OMISSIONS

contractual power of sale pursuant to an appropriate clause contained in the mortgage document and statutory power of sale under the *Mortgages Act*, if no clause is included.

Power of sale is a legal right of the mortgagee to force the sale of a property without judicial proceedings should default occur. Power of sale is the most frequently used method by which a mortgagee remedies a default by a mortgagor. Power of sale can often be the fairest, most inexpensive method to deal with an unpleasant financial circumstance:

- Power of sale allows the mortgagee to retrieve only what he/she is entitled to and no more.
- If a surplus occurs, then the owner/mortgagor will benefit.

The power of sale does involve certain complexities, particularly the gaining of possession and the obligation of the mortgagee to obtain the best possible value.

Listing/Selling Procedure

A notice of sale must be provided to the mortgagor, together with subsequent encumbrancers and others having an interest in the property. A prescribed notice under the *Mortgages Act* (Form 1, Notice of Sale under Mortgage) can be sent 15 days following default. The notice can be sent by registered mail or delivered by personal service.

If a contractual power of sale is undertaken, the mortgagor has 35 days to remedy this situation. If the power of sale is statutory, the time period is 45 days. No action can be taken by the mortgagee within the 35 or 45-day redemption periods.

If the time limit has expired and the default is not corrected, the mortgagee can proceed to sell the property.

CERTIFICATE OF POWER OF SALE

The steps required to effect a power of sale have been judicially determined and statutorily preserved. A *Certificate of Power of Sale* (OREA Form 262) has been developed by the Ontario Real Estate Association to verify certain matters in the listing of property under power of sale action (see the *Appendix* for a copy of OREA Form 262). A signed copy of this form should be filed with the listing authority in the listing brokerage's office for future reference.

OREA Ontario Real Estate Association   **Certificate of Power of Sale**

Form 262
for use in the Province of Ontario

I, ...,

do hereby warrant that by reason of default under a .... charge/mortgage
(first, second, third, etc.)

which I hold on ....
(description of property)

....

dated the .... day of ...., 20............... and registered

as number ....

I now have the power and authority under the provisions of my mortgage and the Mortgages Act of Ontario to list for sale the property known municipally

---

CLAUSE IN AGREEMENT

The wording of power of sale clauses in agreements of purchase and sale vary in the marketplace. A recommended clause developed by the Ontario Real Estate Association is illustrated. Each situation is unique and should be carefully analyzed prior to drafting an agreement of purchase and sale. Mortgagees may have their own specific clauses concerning power of sale.

SCENARIO	CLAUSE
Power of Sale Clause Required The seller, a mortgagee having the legal right to force the sale of a property, wants an appropriate clause inserted. This particular mortgagee does not have a specific clause for that purpose and agrees to include the OREA clause.	**MORT/POS–1** **Power of Sale (General Provision)** *It is further understood that on the date of acceptance of this Offer there is default under the terms of the Charge/Mortgage which entitles the Seller to exercise the Power of Sale. The only evidence of the default which the Buyer may require shall be a statutory declaration by the Seller setting forth the facts entitling the Seller to sell under the Power of Sale, including the particulars of the notice of exercising the Power of Sale, the names of the persons upon whom service of the notice has been effected, and declaring that default under the Charge/Mortgage entitling the Seller to exercise the Power of Sale has continued up to and including the date of acceptance of this Offer and to the time of closing. The Buyer understands and agrees that the Chargor/Mortgagor has the right to redeem the property up to the time of waiver or expiration of all rights of termination or fulfillment of all conditions and this Agreement is subject to that right. In the event of redemption by the Chargor/Mortgagor, this Agreement shall be null and void and any deposit monies paid will be refunded in full without deduction.* *Where a court of competent jurisdiction prevents the completion of the within sale by an interim, interlocutory or permanent injunction or otherwise, then the Seller (Chargee/Mortgagee) is not obliged to complete the said transaction and the Agreement shall be terminated and the deposit shall be returned to the Buyer in full without deduction. In no event shall the Seller be responsible for any costs, expenses, loss or damages incurred or suffered by the Buyer and the Seller shall not have any further liability to the Buyer whatsoever.* *Notwithstanding other provisions of this Agreement, the Seller shall not be required either on or before closing to discharge its own Charge/Mortgage or any existing Charges/Mortgages, liens or other encumbrances subsequent in priority to the Seller's Charge/Mortgage, which may be registered against the Property.* *The Buyer also acknowledges that the Seller makes no representation and/or warranties with respect to the state of repair of the premises, inclusions of chattels or fixtures, or ownership of fixtures or appliances, and the Buyer agrees to accept the property "as is". Chattels and fixtures on the premises may or may not be included with the premises but the Seller shall not be obliged to remove any chattels or fixtures. All the provisions of the Mortgages Act shall supersede any part of this Agreement which may be in variance thereof or in conflict therewith.* **NOTE:** Most Chargee(s)/Mortgagee(s) have their own specific clauses concerning Power of Sale. Each situation should be carefully analyzed prior to the drafting of an Agreement of Purchase and Sale.

SECTION III   COMMON ERRORS AND OMISSIONS

MARKETING THE POWER OF SALE PROPERTY

The mortgagee, when marketing property under power of sale, must ensure that the property is actively promoted to the public in order to obtain fair market value. Although no statutory requirement exists for a formal appraisal, a prudent mortgagee will attempt to avoid the possibility of litigation by obtaining at least two appraisals.

Caution is the operative word for anyone involved in power of sale properties. While this remedy for default often appears as the fairest means of dealing with an unfortunate financial circumstance, practical considerations must not be overlooked:

- conduct an appraisal to establish value;
- ensure reasonable time for marketing purposes;
- provide the widest possible coverage in marketing; and
- make certain the sale is an arm's length transaction.

Onus Rests With The Mortgagee

RESIDENTIAL CASE LAW

While various disputes concerning powers of sale have led to litigation, one case provides insight into the Court's perception of a mortgagee's duties when a power of sale is undertaken.

The agricultural property in question was a rough, hilly piece of land that, according to experts, had the reasonable probability of being re-zoned as a golf course. The buyer had contemplated developing the land, but prematurely fell into default on the mortgage. During successive months, he was unable to remedy the situation. In June, the appropriate notice was served. The property was subsequently listed in mid-December pursuant to this power of sale action and sold during the same month.

Without delving into all the facts of the case, the Judge's remarks regarding power of sale procedures provide insight for all real estate registrants. The Judge's concerns focused on several key issues. First, an appraisal had not been obtained on the property prior to selling it. Next, the brief number of days between the listing and sale date came under close scrutiny. The Judge first commented on the fact that some advertisements prepared by the real estate registrant probably did not appear until after the sale. The effectiveness of such marketing and the short time period was further restricted by the Christmas holidays. The Judge termed such urgency as undue haste. A further statement makes the point:

> [The mortgagee] had waited over two years to be paid and suddenly felt the necessity of selling it over the Christmas period.

According to the Judge, the offering of a property during the holiday season would hamper marketing, as few would be interested in purchasing raw land during that period. Also, this vacant agricultural land was not the type of property that would typically attract a wide range of buyers and any marketing activities should have taken that fact into account. As a final point, the Judge expressed concerns that the salesperson involved was more concerned with selling the property as quickly as possible rather than aspiring to obtain its true value.

The written judgment confirmed that a mortgagee must take reasonable precautions. The mortgagee failed in that regard, given the lack of an appraisal to establish highest and best use and associated value, together with an insufficient time period to market the property. Had these things been done, the court might have considered the final selling price to be reasonable. As a result, when determining the deficiency in value, the Judge used the actual selling price as a base and added 15% premium to that value based on expert testimony, with damages recovered by the mortgagor.

SELLER SELLING UNDER POWER OF SALE

The *Seller Selling Under Power of Sale* (OREA Form 106) is designed for use in conjunction with the *Agreement of Purchase and Sale* (Form 100) to confirm that the seller is entitled to sell the property, that a default of the particular mortgage has occurred, that the mortgagor has a right to redeem and that the seller is selling the property as is and without any guarantee as to the inclusion of any chattels or fixtures. Signatures of both buyer and seller are required.

- Clause 1 of the Seller Selling Under Power of Sale form recites the provisions under which the seller is entitled to sell the property.
- Clause 2 recites that a default has occurred under the terms of the particular mortgage, what evidence of default the buyer may require from the seller and that the mortgagor has a right to redeem the subject property until the time of waiver or expiration of all rights of termination and a firm and binding agreement of purchase and sale exists.
- Clause 3 recites that the seller is selling the property as is and without any guarantee as to the transferability or condition of any chattels or fixtures, which the seller is not obliged to remove. Provisions of the *Mortgages Act* supersede and override any part of the agreement that might conflict with that legislation.

OREA Ontario Real Estate Association

Form 106
for use in the Province of Ontario

Seller Selling Under Power of Sale
To Be Used in Conjunction with OREA Form 100

Attached to and forming part of Agreement of Purchase and Sale between ....

and .... dated the ....day of

...., 20......................

1. It is understood that the Seller is selling as mortgagee under a Power of Sale contained in a ....
   (insert 1st, 2nd, 3rd, etc.)

   mortgage made to the Seller, dated the .... day of ...., 20.................... and registered

   as number ....

2. It is further understood that on the date of acceptance of this offer there is default under the terms of the mortgage which entitles the Seller to exercise the Power of Sale. The only evidence of the default that the Buyer may require shall be a statutory declaration by the Seller setting forth the facts entitling the Seller to sell under the Power of Sale, including the particulars of the notice of exercising the Power of Sale, the names of the persons upon whom service of the notice has been effected, and declaring that default under the mortgage entitling the Seller to exercise the Power of Sale has continued up to and including the date of acceptance of this offer and to the time of closing. The Buyer understands and agrees that the mortgagor has the right to redeem the property up to the time of waiver or expiration of all rights of termination or fulfilment of all conditions, and this Agreement is subject to that right. In the event of redemption by the mortgagor, this Agreement shall be null and void and any deposit monies paid will be refunded without interest.

3. The Buyer also acknowledges that the Seller makes no representations and/or warranties with respect to state of repair of the premises, inclusions of chattels or fixtures, or ownership of fixtures or appliances, and the Buyer agrees to accept the property as is and must satisfy himself/herself with respect to any of the matters provided for in the attached agreement ordinarily warranted by the Seller. Chattels and fixtures on the premises may or may not be included with the premises but the Seller shall not be obliged to remove any chattels or fixtures. All the provisions of the Mortgages Act shall supersede any part of this Agreement which may be in variance thereof or in conflict therewith.

SIGNED, SEALED AND DELIVERED in the presence of: IN WITNESS whereof I have hereunto set my hand and seal:

.... ● DATE ....
(Witness)   (Buyer)   (Seal)

TITLE-RELATED PROBLEMS/DISPUTES

Most residential transactions involve registered subdivision plans and relatively straightforward title issues. However, registrants can encounter complex situations requiring close scrutiny and appropriate caution.

SECTION III   COMMON ERRORS AND OMISSIONS

Land, Structures and Real Estate Trading emphasized ownership rights, limitations, boundaries and easements. This chapter expands on those topics with particular emphasis regarding common access and ownership disputes, most notably involving rural/recreational properties. Five title-related topics that can cause problems for new registrants are discussed:

| Road Access | Highway Access | Fences | Shore Road Allowances | Shoreline Ownership |

ROAD ACCESS

Access arrangements can prove challenging. Optimally, the property is served by a year-round publicly-maintained road. However, seasonal publicly-maintained roads limit access in sparsely settled areas during winter months, thereby affecting property use. Contact the local municipality if any doubt exists concerning current status.

Rural/recreational registrants may also encounter private access roads. These privately deeded or undeeded rights-of-way are reason for valid concern. Descriptions, maintenance agreements and specific rights may be vague or non-existent. Further, even if a written description exists, the physical road location may differ.

Public highways also are worthy of note. Special government requirements and restrictions can apply to property adjacent to highways, including controlled-access highways, secondary highways and other public roads.

Other situations involving unopened road allowances, access across Crown lands (typically referred to as an MNR (Ministry of Natural Resources and Forestry) road) and trespass roads (publicly funded roads over private lands) go beyond the scope of this introductory course.

Road Access Act

The *Road Access Act*, enacted in 1978, gave new meaning to implied grants and the right-of-way by necessity. Such a right-of-way involves the indispensable or imperative requirement to have access to otherwise landlocked property. In the case of a cottage, a right of access to the property might be across a farm field that is subsequently barricaded by the farm owner. Since the right of access is implied, the servient tenement (the owner of the farm) cannot arbitrarily frustrate that right, otherwise he/she might fall under the provisions of the *Road Access Act*.

Under this Act, an access road is essentially a road that has not been dedicated and accepted by the municipality, but nevertheless constitutes a thoroughfare by a motor vehicle to one or more parcels of land. Such roads can only be closed by a judge's order or the specific written instructions of all persons affected. However, they can be temporarily closed for repair purposes or once per calendar year for a 24-hour period.

The Act is designed to stave off sudden actions by an owner to the detriment of other parties currently using the access route. The courts are empowered to evaluate the necessity of such a barricade, the existence of alternative access points or other remedies. In fact, the court is authorized to fine the individual or order that person to remove the barrier or other obstacle.

REAL ESTATE PERSPECTIVE

Real estate registrants should be aware that precedent cases involving this statute are somewhat limited. Further, the *Road Access Act* cannot be viewed as an immediate solution to all forms of vague access situations or erratic actions by either user or owner. Access problems rate as highly as fence line disputes in terms of frustration and legal complexities. There is no substitute for accurate descriptions of rights-of-way and properly registered easements on title. The existence of other possible access routes to a landlocked property (e.g., water access or shore road allowance) can have a direct bearing on a decision about a barricaded access route.

The issue of road access is anything but straightforward. Registrants may encounter a wide range of possibilities including publicly maintained year-round or seasonal-only roads, unopened road allowances, trespass roads and privately deeded or undeeded rights-of-way. In northern areas, registrants may also encounter roads constructed on Crown lands by the Ministry of Natural Resources and Forestry. Brokers and salespersons are cautioned regarding such matters. Make certain that access situations are fully investigated and that appropriate clauses are included in offers.

Building Permit and Insurance   CAUTION

Registrants should be aware that a deeded or undeeded access road can cause problems beyond legal considerations. Fire insurance companies may be reluctant to provide coverage where access is not available during winter months. Further, the municipality may impose various restrictions on the issuance of a building permit for a new structure or an addition. As with other matters concerning private roads, seek legal advice and consult directly with the municipality.

EXAMPLE   *Private Access Road*

Owner Smith owns a waterfront cottage and has travelled across a neighbour's land for the past several years to access his recreational property. When Smith originally purchased the property, he relied on the following description of an easement contained within the deed:

> *Together with such access across Lot 10 (the neighbour's property) for all times as required for the peaceful enjoyment of the said lands.*

Originally, Smith's cottage was used solely as a retreat and access to the property was made with a four-wheel drive all-terrain vehicle ideally suited to his neighbour's land. Smith now plans on dramatically improving the access route. His retirement plans include converting the cottage to a year-round home.

Smith approaches the neighbour and is prepared to pay for any costs to upgrade the trail to a proper road. The neighbour refuses, stating that the access for all times implies the existing arrangement. Smith argues that the upgraded road is required for the peaceful enjoyment of the land. Legal action to resolve the problem appears inevitable. The ultimate resolution of this matter falls to legal considerations that go beyond the scope of this text.

ACCESS CLAUSES

The Ontario Real Estate Association provides eight clauses to address various access situations ranging from obtaining a right-of-way to acknowledgement of water access only. One of these clauses relates to highway access *(ACC–3 Condition—Road Access to Public Highways)* and is discussed later in the chapter.

SECTION III   COMMON ERRORS AND OMISSIONS

SCENARIO	CLAUSE
Buyer is Seeking Right-of-Way A buyer is submitting an offer on a backlot cottage, but is seeking a right-of-way to the water from an adjacent lakefront cottage owner.	**ACC–1** Condition—Obtaining Right-of-way *This Offer is conditional upon the Buyer obtaining an Agreement to create an easement with (name of persons), for the purpose of* (insert specific use), *located and more particularly described as (outline planned location). Unless the Buyer gives notice in writing delivered to the Seller personally or in accordance with any other provisions for the delivery of notice in this Agreement of Purchase and Sale or any Schedule thereto not later than _____ p.m. on the _____ day of _____, 20____, that this condition is fulfilled, this Offer shall become null and void and the deposit shall be returned to the Buyer in full without deduction. This condition is included for the benefit of the Buyer and may be waived at the Buyer's sole option by notice in writing to the Seller as aforesaid within the time period stated herein.* **NOTE**: This condition must be used with caution, as further approvals will be required for the right-of-way to be legal; i.e., Committee of Adjustment.
Buyer Wants to Confirm Public Road A buyer is submitting an offer on a cottage, but is concerned that the access road is in fact a public road and maintained throughout the year.	**ACC–2** Condition—Road Access by Open Public Road *This Offer is conditional upon the Buyer determining, at the Buyer's own expense, that access by automobile to the property is by a public road which is maintained at public expense throughout the year. Unless the Buyer gives notice in writing delivered to the Seller personally or in accordance with any other provisions for the delivery of notice in this Agreement of Purchase and Sale or any Schedule thereto not later than _____ p.m. on the _____ day of _____, 20____, that this condition has been fulfilled, this Offer shall become null and void and the deposit shall be returned to the Buyer in full without deduction. This condition is included for the benefit of the Buyer and may be waived at the Buyer's sole option by notice in writing to the Seller as aforesaid within the time period stated herein.*

Seller Provides Written Assurance
 	
A buyer is concerned about road access. The seller agrees to include a *represents and warrants* clause regarding the road in question.
	ACC–4 Road Access—Alternatives
	
	The Seller represents and warrants, to the best of the Seller's knowledge and belief, that the property fronts on [choose appropriate statement]
	
	    (a) a road which is maintained on a year round basis at public expense;
	        OR
	    (b) a road which is maintained on a seasonal basis at public expense;
	        OR
	    (c) a road which is not maintained at public expense.
	
	The Parties agree that this representation and warranty shall survive and not merge on completion of this transaction, but apply only to the state of the property existing at completion of this transaction.

SCENARIO	CLUSE
Buyer Acknowledges That Road is not Publicly Maintained A buyer is submitting an offer involving a rural property that has private road access only. The seller, to avoid any possible confusion, wants a clause in the offer acknowledging this fact and also confirming the current annual cost.	**ACC–5** **Road Access—Privately Maintained Road** *The Buyer acknowledges that the private road accessing the said property is maintained by the* [insert appropriate local cottage association or other relevant group], *at an annual cost of $_____ for each property.*
Buyer Acknowledges Unregistered Easement A buyer is submitting an offer involving a remote property that has an unregistered easement. He is familiar with the general area and is aware that several properties gain access by this same easement. The following clause is inserted in the offer following advice from his solicitor on the matter.	**ACC–6** **Road Access—Unregistered Easement (Trespass Access)** *The Buyer acknowledges that the* [road/path/lane], *to the said property may be an unregistered easement. The Seller shall provide to the Buyer, on or before completion, a statutory declaration or declarations establishing that the existing* [road/path/lane], *has been used by the Seller and/or predecessors in title to gain access to the said property for a period of _____ years.* **NOTE**: In situations involving unregistered easements, legal advice should be sought.
Buyer Acknowledges Water Access Only A buyer is submitting an offer on a remote property that is only accessible by water.	**ACC–7** **Water Access** *The Buyer acknowledges that the property is only accessible by water.* **NOTE**: In water access situations (for example, island properties), the buyer would also typically want to confirm vehicle parking facilities at the shore.
Buyer Acknowledges Fluctuating Water Levels A buyer is confirming that he/she understands the water levels in the area where the property is located may fluctuate and may make access to the property from the water, or to the water from the property, difficult and/or not possible.	**ACC–8** **Water Access—Fluctuating Water Levels** *The Buyer acknowledges that the water levels in the area where the property is situated may fluctuate between a low and high water level and may be extremely low or extremely high from time to time. Therefore, access to the property through means of water and/or access to the water from the property may be difficult or not available. The Buyer agrees that no claim will be made against the Seller, or any Brokerage, Broker or Salesperson, respecting the levels of the water including without limitation matters of access whether to the property by water or from the property to the water.*

SECTION III   COMMON ERRORS AND OMISSIONS

HIGHWAY ACCESS

A highway can be broadly described as a public passage designed or intended for use by vehicular traffic. Statutory requirements, pursuant to the *Public Transportation and Highway Improvement Act* administered by the Ministry of Transportation, impact the use of abutting or adjacent lands in relation to highways, including controlled-access highways, secondary highways and other roads as described in the Act.

Real Estate Perspective

Registrants should possess a general understanding of limitations that may be imposed concerning property adjacent to or abutting highways and that fall within prescribed distances. For purposes of the Act, a highway is expansively defined as including:

> *...any common and public highway, street, avenue, parkway, driveway, square, place, bridge, viaduct, trestle or any other structure incidental thereto, any part of which is intended for or used by the general public for the passage of vehicles and includes the area between the lateral property lines thereof.*

A permit issued by the Minister is required for various activities near a highway designated as the King's highway; e.g., placing, erecting or altering buildings, fences, gasoline pumps or other structures; the placing of trees, shrubs or hedges; the displaying of signs, notices or advertising devices; the use of land for various purposes that cause individuals to congregate in large number such as a theatre or fairground; the displaying, selling or offering for sale of goods or merchandise; and the construction or use of any private road, entrance way, gate or other structure as a means of access to the highway.

Part II of the *Highway Improvement Act* relates to highways that are designated as controlled-access highways and includes more stringent requirements; i.e., greater minimum distances for activities already outlined above. A King's highway can be designated as a secondary highway (Part III) in which case the regulations that apply to a King's highway will also apply with necessary modifications as set out in the Act. County roads (Part VII of the Act) fall under the jurisdiction and control of the county and are subject to applicable rights and powers granted to municipalities under the *Planning Act*. Further the county may prohibit or regulate matters concerning the placing, erecting or altering of any gas pump, the displaying of signs and notices, and the construction or alteration of any private road, entrance way, gate or other structure or facility that permits access to a road as defined in the Act.

Registrants should also be aware that developers involved with land development proposals may require a Public Transportation and Highway Improvement Act Permit. This permit can involve either a building and land use permit when a structure is being constructed within a highway corridor control area (the control area varies by type of structure being built), or an encroachment permit when work must be completed within the highway right-of-way. The Ministry of Transportation may also dictate conditions of approval that apply to a site plan or draft plan of subdivision proposal.

HIGHWAY ACCESS CLAUSE

SCENARIO	CLAUSE
Buyer Seeking Confirmation of Public Highway Access A buyer is acquiring a vacant lot abutting a highway and wants to ensure that access to the lot has been approved.	**ACC–3 Condition—Road Access to Public Highways** *This Offer is conditional upon the Buyer determining, at the Buyer's own expense, that all vehicular entrances to and exits from the property onto public highways have been approved under the Public Transportation and Highways Improvement Act or any predecessor thereof. Unless the Buyer gives notice in writing delivered to the Seller personally or in accordance with any other provisions for the delivery of notice in this Agreement of Purchase and Sale or any Schedule thereto not later than ____ p.m. on the _____ day of _____, 20___, that his condition has been fulfilled, this Offer shall become null and void and the deposit shall be returned to the Buyer in full without deduction. This condition is included for the benefit of the Buyer and may be waived at the Buyer's sole option by notice in writing to the Seller as aforesaid within the time period stated herein.*

FENCES

Next to access, fences undoubtedly are the second most common dispute between neighbours. The *Line Fences Act* provides that a landowner may build a fence to mark his or her property boundary and is entitled to construct that fence on the property line. The Act provides a method for municipalities to settle disputes solely regarding line fences. In other words, the fence must be on the property line. Interestingly, if a property owner builds a fence within his/her property (i.e., three inches inside), this Act does not apply.

Further, the Act does not address disputes regarding boundary line location. An up-to-date survey normally resolves most matters. If not, such disputes are a civil matter requiring legal resolution. Municipalities also establish fence by-laws which differ from one locale to another, but typically set out height, construction material and overall design criteria.

Line Fences Act

A fence is generally described as any barrier enclosing or bordering a property. The purpose of the *Line Fences Act* is to provide a procedure for the resolution of line fence disputes between the owners of adjoining properties. The council of each municipality appoints a number of fence-viewers to carry out the provisions of this Act. Fence viewers are paid remuneration based on an hourly or daily rate, or a rate based on each attendance regarding a specific matter. Fence viewers may address disputes involving fences within a municipality and fences on the boundary between municipalities, or between a municipality and an unorganized territory that does not have municipal organization; i.e., portions of Northern Ontario.

FENCE CONSTRUCTION

An owner is permitted to construct and maintain a fence to mark the boundary between his/her land and adjacent lands. In the case of new construction or restoration/ maintenance, the owner may request that the municipality assist in arbitrating what costs should be incurred by each owner affected by the existing or proposed fence. The fence viewer(s) will examine the lands and, in some instances, hear evidence or examine testimony of the owners or their witnesses under oath.

An award is made that specifies the location of the fence, the designation of one-half the fence that will be maintained by each owner (or such arrangement as appears appropriate), the description of materials to be used in the construction, restoration or maintenance activity, the date of completion and the costs of the proceedings to be paid by each owner.

If by-laws pursuant to the *Municipal Act* have been passed in regard to the height and other regulations regarding fences, the description in the award must conform with such requirements. An owner dissatisfied with the award may appeal to a referee whose decision is final. Remedies are available under the *Line Fences Act* should an owner not comply with the award. Individuals involved in line fence issues and disputes should fully review the Act and seek legal advice.

Municipal Fence By-Laws

Individual municipalities may have detailed procedures relating to division (line) fences (i.e., fences dividing one property from another), including a prescribed method to arrive at an agreement with neighbours regarding fence construction, methods to use in sharing costs and mediation/arbitration procedures should a dispute arise.

Further, such by-laws set out height requirements for division fences, fences around pools and temporary fencing requirements. The by-law will also typically outline acceptable construction standards, permissible types of materials to be used and special considerations (e.g., fencing heights in front areas of property and requirements relating to corner lots given line-of-sight specifications for traffic purposes). Registrants seeking additional information should contact the local municipality.

SHORE ROAD ALLOWANCES

Shore road allowances were established in various parts of Ontario adjacent to navigable rivers and shores of lakes. Cottage buyers may be unaware of their existence as many remain unopened, but nevertheless legally exist.

The initial laying out of road allowances in Ontario included the establishment of shore road allowances that were 66' in width adjacent to navigable rivers and the shores of lakes. Such roads, although infrequently opened, were intended to provide access for commercial and public passage. The fact that such allowances have never been opened in no way limits the original conveyance nor obstructs the right of use by the public. A typical reference plan is illustrated on a subsequent page, detailing two recreational lots adjacent to a secondary highway with a 66' shore road allowance abutting the waterfront.

Townships surveyed prior to 1850 (primarily eastern and southwestern Ontario) do not contain these road allowances. Following that date, most property near water was surveyed in a manner to create public roads at the water's edge. The existence of a shore road allowance will normally appear in the deed, with the following wording:

...save and except that portion of land consisting of a sixty-six foot shoreline road allowance.

Encroachments

The real issue for cottage owners is the fact that waterfront lots may have boathouses, docks or cottages (or a portion thereof) constructed on the shore road allowance and therefore are built on land not owned by the seller. As such, a survey prepared by an Ontario land surveyor is critical when seriously considering the purchase of a recreational, shoreline property.

Closings

While municipalities are empowered under the *Municipal Act* to effect closings of shore road allowances and resolve title issues (e.g., encroachments on Crown land), objections filed from the Ministry of Natural Resources and Forestry (MNR) have directly impacted such decisions, given the MNR mandate to protect public lands and associated natural habitat in and around watercourses within the province.

Accordingly, the MNR has established certain guidelines and will generally encourage municipalities to retain shoreline where the lands contribute to the preservation of fish and wildlife habitat. Any person contemplating an application for a shore road allowance closing should seek expert advice regarding the matter. All costs regarding the acquisition of shore road closings are normally borne by the applicant. Policies, procedures and costs concerning shore road allowance closings vary from time to time. Real estate registrants should contact the local municipality and the Ministry of Natural Resources and Forestry for current requirements.

EXAMPLE   *Shore Road Closing*

Owner Smith contacted the Regional Municipality of Lake District concerning the closing of a shoreline road allowance that lies between his cottage lot and Big Lake. Following is a list of the procedures set out by the municipality:

- Get written agreement from all abutting owners.
- Obtain an application from the municipality and submit it to the municipal council.
- The application is reviewed and circulated to various ministries and most particularly, the Ministry of Natural Resources and Forestry.
- The municipality notifies the public through advertisements and posted notices.
- If no objections, a by-law is enacted and sent to the appropriate Ministry.
- A reference plan is required, prepared at the owner's expense.
- The municipality prepares legal documentation, assesses costs and registers the deed. All costs regarding the acquisition of the shore road allowance are borne by Smith. These costs will include legal, survey, administration and advertising/ notice expenses, and the purchase price established by the municipality.

SECTION III   COMMON ERRORS AND OMISSIONS

Addressing Unique Circumstances

Owners attempting to acquire shore road allowances should be aware of certain circumstances that can befall applicants.

- **Non-Conforming Status**   In some instances, cottages may fall under non-conforming status due to the age of the structure. The acquisition of a shore road allowance may disrupt the non-conforming status and invoke current zoning requirements that necessitate other unanticipated changes; e.g., structural modifications to meet current setback requirements, adherence to a site plan agreement and well/septic changes to align with present environmental regulations.

- **Cost of Individual Applications**   Application costs can be substantial, depending on the property involved, cost of a survey, purchase price and negotiations with the municipality. Individual owners might consider a group application involving several adjacent owners.

- **Diminished Frontage Acquired**   In some instances, the frontage being acquired (shoreline measurement) may be less than the existing frontage measurement for the lot; i.e., a wedge-shaped lot with the lesser measurement on the lake side of the property. This can affect future compliance with zoning regulations.

- **Fish Habitat Considerations**   The Ministry of Natural Resources and Forestry has a mandate to protect fish habitats. Certain areas of shoreline may involve complicated negotiations and consequently affect timing, application and related costs, and the amount of land that will be conveyed.

WEB LINKS

Shore Road Allowance/Closing   Registrants should investigate such road allowances within their trading area. Inquire as to current policies of the local municipality and the Ministry of Natural Resources and Forestry (***www.mnr.gov.on.ca***). Local cottage associations may be able to provide background information and helpful guidelines.

Shore Road Allowance

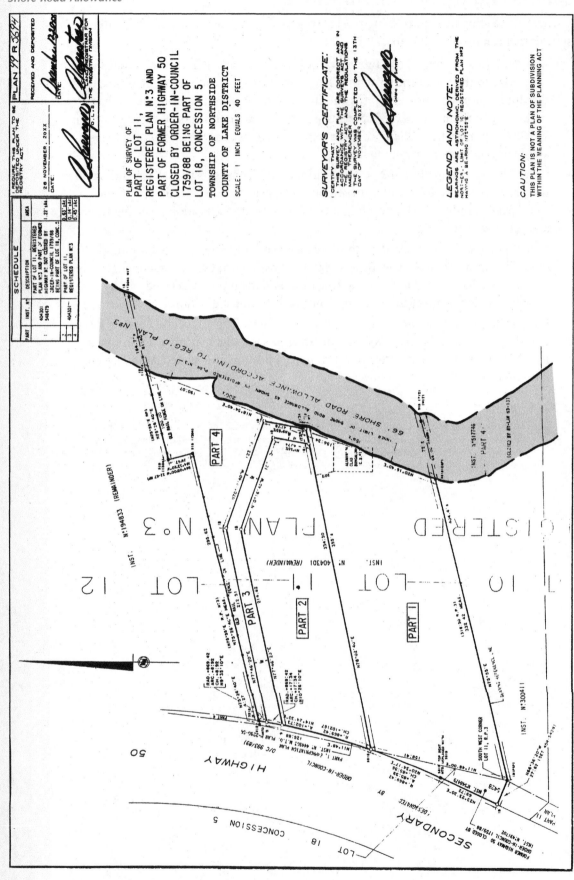

The Ontario Real Estate Association provides the following clauses when dealing with Shore Road Allowances.

SCENARIO	CLAUSE

Shore Road Allowance
 	
A buyer is submitting an offer on a cottage but is uncertain regarding the exact shoreline frontage, whether a road allowance exists that interferes with access to the frontage and any other unregistered rights or easements that exist.
	SHORE–1 **Condition—Water Frontage— Shore Road Allowance—Unregistered Easements**
	
	This Offer is conditional upon the Buyer determining at the Buyer's own expense that:
	
	  (1) the property being purchased has at least [insert appropriate frontage dimension], [metres/feet], *of frontage on* [name of lake or river];
	
	  (2) no road allowance, open or unopened, or other public or private lands exist which will interfere with the right of the Buyer to use and enjoy the said water frontage; and
	
	  (3) that there are no unregistered rights or easements.
	
	Unless the Buyer gives notice in writing delivered to the Seller personally or in accordance with any other provisions for the delivery of notice in this Agreement of Purchase and Sale or any Schedule thereto not later than _____ p.m. on the _____ day of _____, 20____, that these conditions have been fulfilled, this offer shall become null and void and the deposit shall be returned to the Buyer in full without deduction. These conditions are included for the benefit of the Buyer and may be waived at the Buyer's sole option by notice in writing to the Seller as aforesaid within the time period stated herein.

Shore Road Allowance A buyer is aware of the shore road allowance and acknowledges this fact when submitting an offer.	**SHORE–2** **Shore Road Allowance—Acknowledgement** *The Buyer acknowledges that the original shore road allowance is not closed and consequently is not part of the property being sold under this Agreement of Purchase and Sale.*
Shore Road Allowance A buyer is aware of the shore road allowance and acknowledges this fact when submitting an offer. Furthermore, some structure (e.g., a dock, boathouse or the cottage itself) is encroaching on the unowned shore road allowance.	**SHORE–3** **Shore Road Allowance—With Encroachments** *The Buyer acknowledges that the original shore road allowance is not closed and consequently is not part of the property being sold under this Agreement of Purchase and Sale, and that the improvements apparently on the said property may encroach on said unowned shore road allowance.*

SHORELINE OWNERSHIP

Ministry of Natural Resources and Forestry (MNR) policies can impact owners of shoreline property in Ontario. Over the years, many property owners have inadvertently encroached on Crown land when they improved cottages and lakefront homes. The MNR has obtained new surveys for many of these shorelines and, should owners be encroaching on Crown land, these owners are approached to either purchase or lease the Crown land affected.

Property rights associated with waterfront can be complex. Unique rights and responsibilities are involved as such properties border ungranted Crown lands. According to the MNR, approximately 87% of Ontario's land base, including land under navigable waters, is owned by the Crown (Province of Ontario). All Crown lands are managed by the Ministry under the authority of the *Public Lands Act*. The beds of navigable waterbodies are usually Crown land and, therefore, are also managed by the MNR under the *Beds of Navigable Waters Act*. Selected portions of underwater Crown land is owned by the federal government; e.g., canals and harbours. A small percentage is held through private ownership.

Owners of land bordering the shore of a navigable lake may have certain rights. Riparian rights are associated with access to the water, as opposed to ownership of the bed of the lake or river, and can include rights associated with the:

- access to and from the water from their own lands;
- natural flow and quality of water, subject to the same rights of riparian neighbours;
- increased ownership through natural accretion processes;
- navigation in the navigable waters, along with those of the general public;
- right to control trespass originating from the water;
- right to drain one's property;
- right to take water without interrupting the same rights of riparian neighbours; and
- right to protect the bank or shoreline from erosion (with approval), but not to interfere with the rights of adjacent riparian ownership.

Real Estate Perspective

Filled land and related alterations at the shoreline can result in delayed or cancelled sales until legal title is obtained by either the purchase or lease of such land. Owners of shoreline properties should determine if the shoreline has been altered; i.e., if the property occupies the lake bed. If the property is within a registered plan of subdivision, the survey measurements can be confirmed by measuring from the rear boundary to the water's edge. If the property is described on an individual survey, the owner should check side lot line measurements in relation to the plan. If the distance is greater than that shown on the plan of survey, fill may have been added.

The MNR will assist owners in determining if riparian rights have been affected by past shoreline improvements or alterations. Owners may make application to buy or lease lake bed property presently occupied. The purchase price or rental rate for Crown land is based on its market value. MNR assumes that the public is entitled to a fair and reasonable return when public lands are being utilized for individual benefit.

SECTION III   COMMON ERRORS AND OMISSIONS

KNOWLEDGE INTEGRATION

Notables

- Rights under an agreement are generally assignable subject to some exceptions, but liabilities are not without the consent of the other party.

- A residential tenant may assign or sublet in accordance with the *Residential Tenancies Act*.

- Provisions in a residential insurance policy can be grouped under four headings: property insurance, liability insurance, endorsements and conditions.

- Buyers contemplating the purchase of older residential properties containing outdated systems may experience difficulties and/or added premiums when arranging insurance.

- Internal/external changes to structures designated under the *Heritage Act* are typically restricted.

- Two power of sale approaches are available pursuant to the *Mortgages Act*: contractual and statutory.

- A mortgagee must ensure that property is actively promoted in the marketplace in order to obtain fair market value.

- Access arrangements, particularly in rural areas, can result in problems and possible litigation.

- Exercise caution regarding seasonal publicly-maintained roads, private access roads and accessibility or related limitations for properties adjacent to highways and secondary roads.

- Access to highways, as defined under the *Public Transportation and Highway Improvement Act*, requires an appropriate permit issued by the Ministry of Transportation.

- The *Line Fences Act* only applies to disputes involving fences located on the boundary line.

- Municipalities establish fence by-laws to control fence construction and appearance, including height.

- Be aware that properties abutting navigable waterways may be subject to shore road allowances.

- Alterations to shorelines can result in sale delays and cancellations.

Web Links

Web links are included for general interest regarding selected chapter topics.

Heritage Property   This topic contains summary information as an introductory guide to registrants. Those involved with heritage properties should access the Ministry of Tourism, Culture and Sport website at *www.mtc.gov.on.ca/en/heritage/heritage.shtml* and also contact the local municipality.

Community Heritage Ontario   Community Heritage Ontario is the umbrella organization for heritage committees. Go to *http://communityheritageontario.ca* for detailed information. All committees within the province are listed on the Ministry Tourism, Culture and Sport website at *www.mtc.gov.on.ca.*

Heritage Property Tax Relief   Go to the Ministry of Tourism, Culture and Sport website (*www.mtc.gov.on.ca/en/ heritage/heritage_tax_relief.shtml*) for detailed information on tax relief measures associated with heritage easements, including information regarding heritage designation, associate tax relief eligibility and tax relief calculations.

Shore Road Allowance/Closing   Registrants should investigate such road allowances within their trading area. Inquire as to current policies of the local municipality and the Ministry of Natural Resources and Forestry (*www.mnr.gov.on.ca*). Local cottage associations may be able to provide background information and helpful guidelines.

Strategic Thinking For Your Career

Questions are included to assist in developing your new career. No answers are provided.

1. What experience have salespeople had in the local area with buyers obtaining home insurance coverage? Have coverages been rejected or significantly higher premiums charged and, if so, for what reasons?

2. Are there areas in my marketplace that have been designated as Heritage Conservation Districts and what information is available locally about designated structures?

3. What provisions are included regarding fence by-law(s) for municipalities in my local trading area?

4. Do shore road allowances exist in the local marketplace and how do municipalities and the Ministry of Natural Resources and Forestry deal with closures or other matters relating to these allowances?

SECTION III

COMMON ERRORS AND OMISSIONS

Chapter Mini-Review

Solutions are located in the Appendix.

1. Assignments of agreements are relatively straightforward, as no tax implications can arise.

   ○ True   ○ False

2. Liabilities regarding an agreement are generally not assignable, unless consent is given.

   ○ True   ○ False

3. When drafting a clause concerning house insurance, the seller's agreement to provide access for an inspection is normally necessary.

   ○ True   ○ False

4. A heritage easement agreement signed between an owner and the local municipality may result in tax relief for that owner.

   ○ True   ○ False

5. When listing a power of sale property, the signed Certificate of Power of Sale must be attached to the agreement of purchase and sale.

   ○ True   ○ False

6. The OREA form titled *Seller Selling Under Power of Sale* confirms, among other things, that the seller is entitled to sell the property.

   ○ True   ○ False

7. A private access road is essentially one that has not been dedicated and accepted by a municipality, but still constitutes a thoroughfare to one or more parcels of land.

   ○ True   ○ False

8. A permit is required when erecting or altering buildings near a highway, but not the placing of shrubs or trees.

   ○ True   ○ False

9. Line fence disputes between neighbours are typically resolved through intervention by a by-law enforcement officer pursuant to the Ontario Building Code.

   ○ True   ○ False

10. The decision as to whether or not to close a shore road allowance may involve fish habitat considerations.

    ○ True   ○ False

11. Shore road allowances are adjacent to all navigable rivers and lakes in Ontario.

    ○ True   ○ False

12. Owners attempting to acquire shoreline road allowances may encounter significant application and related fees.

    ○ True   ○ False

Active Learning Exercises

Solutions are located in the Appendix.

◼ Exercise 1   Matching

Match the phrase/word in the right column with the appropriate description in the left column (not all phrases/words are used).

____	Notice of Sale Under Mortgage	a. Mortgagor in Possession
____	Statutory Power of Sale	b. Potential Tax Relief
____	Clause 3, OREA Form 106	c. 15-day period
____	Heritage Easement Agreement	d. 35-day period
____	Located on Flood Plain	e. Spouse
____	Boathouse on Public Land	f. No Power of Sale Clause in Mortgage
		g. Property Being Sold 'As Is'
		h. Insurance Risk
		i. Encroachment

■ Exercise 2   Multiple Part Question

2.1   The *Line Fences Act*:

    a.   Establishes height requirements for fences around swimming pools.

    b.   Provides a method for resolving disputes between an owner's land and adjacent lands.

    c.   Applies to rural areas only.

    d.   Establishes line-of-sight specifications for corner lot properties.

2.2   A shore road allowance, as found in some areas of Ontario,:

    a.   Is one hundred feet in width, unless otherwise specified.

    b.   Is only available for acquisition if the road allowance abuts natural habitat areas.

    c.   Was intended to provide access for commercial and public passage.

    d.   Is most commonly found in eastern Ontario townships.

2.3   A private access road:

    a.   Must be closed for a 48-hour period during each calendar year for purposes of repairs.

    b.   Includes publicly-funded roads that are either seasonally or year-round maintained.

    c.   Must be fenced, including a gate, in order to maintain its legal status.

    d.   None of the above.

2.4   Which of the following statements is correct?

    a.   Distance to a fire station may affect the rate charged for home insurance.

    b.   The *Ontario Heritage Act* applies to residential property, but not commercial.

    c.   A non-assignability clause must be inserted in a new home agreement of purchase and sale.

    d.   Insurance underwriters issue coverage for homes with underground storage tanks, regardless of age.

2.5   Local municipalities:

    a.   May establish committees to assist council regarding heritage buildings.

    b.   Create procedural rules regarding any alteration that is likely to impact the reason for designating a property as a heritage structure.

    c.   May pass by-laws establishing a conservation district.

    d.   All of the above.

2.6   Based on OREA clause wordings regarding power of sale, identify the correct statement from the following:

    a.   The buyer acknowledges that the mortgagor has the right to redeem the property up to the point of waiver or expiration of specific rights.

    b.   The mortgagee, as seller, provides limited warranties with respect to the state of repair of the property.

    c.   Chattels and fixtures located on the real property are included in the purchase price.

    d.   In the event of a redemption by the mortgagor, any deposit paid by the buyer to the mortgagee is forfeited.

■ **Exercise 3**   **Selecting the Appropriate Clause**

3.1   The buyer wants to sign the offer, but may elect to have his daughter, who is now travelling in Europe, take title on closing.

    Clause # (or) Title

3.2   The buyer wants assurance, when buying a new rural home, that the driveway providing access to an adjacent county road has received necessary approvals.

    Clause # (or) Title

3.3   The home has been identified under provincial legislation which protects structures of historical importance and the seller wants the buyer's acknowledgement of this fact.

    Clause # (or) Title

3.4   The seller wants the buyer to acknowledge that the road leading to the cottage is not publicly maintained.

    Clause # (or) Title

3.5   A neighbour mentions to the potential buyer that the listed property at one time had an oil furnace and associated buried tank. The buyer wants assurances from both insurance and environmental considerations that the tank is no longer there.

    Clause # (or) Title

SECTION III   COMMON ERRORS AND OMISSIONS

■ Exercise 4   The Cottage on Big Cedar Lake

NOTE: This is a consolidation question that requires knowledge from this chapter, previous chapters and offer drafting guidelines set out in *The Real Estate Transaction—General*.

James Freidman, a new salesperson with XYZ Real Estate Ltd., has drafted an offer for himself and Jessie MacIntyre to purchase the lakefront home owned by Patricia Marilyn Wong located on Big Cedar Lake near Anycity. The property, listed by ABC Realty Inc., is accessible by a long, winding road that may or may not be maintained year-round. He and Jessie want assurances that the road has year-round access and require a warranty regarding the well and sewage system. The buyers will be assuming an existing first mortgage due in three years subject to the lender's approval and the seller is taking back a second mortgage amortized over 25 years. The listing states that the STB must be subject to a credit report.

Critically analyze what James has prepared on the following pages, outlining errors, omissions or clause wording problems from both the buyers' and sellers' perspectives.

OREA Ontario Real Estate Association

Agreement of Purchase and Sale

Form 100
for use in the Province of Ontario

This Agreement of Purchase and Sale dated this ...... **2nd** ... day of .... **May** .... 20 **XX** ......

BUYER, ... **James E. Freidman and Jessie C. MacIntyre** ...., agrees to purchase from
(Full legal names of all Buyers)

SELLER, ... **Patricia Marilyn Wong** ...., the following
(Full legal names of all Sellers)

REAL PROPERTY:

Address .... **26 Lakeside Drive** ....

fronting on the .... **West** .... side of .... **Lakeside Drive** ....

in the .... **Township of Westside, County of Lake District** ....

and having a frontage of .... **55 feet** .... more or less by a depth of .... **121 feet** .... more or less

and legally described as .... **Part Lot 2, Concession IV, more particularly described as Part 3,**

Reference Plan 99R-1981 subject to a registered easement .... (the "property")
(Legal description of land including easements not described elsewhere)

PURCHASE PRICE: Dollars (CDN$) **$224,000.00**

.... **Two Hundred and Twenty-Four Thousand**-- Dollars

DEPOSIT: Buyer submits .... **Upon Acceptance** ....
(Herewith/Upon Acceptance/as otherwise described in this Agreement)

.... **Fifteen Thousand**-- Dollars (CDN$) **$15,000.00**

by negotiable cheque payable to .... **ABC Realty Inc.** .... "Deposit Holder" to be held
in trust pending completion or other termination of this Agreement and to be credited toward the Purchase Price on completion. For the purposes of this
Agreement, "Upon Acceptance" shall mean that the Buyer is required to deliver the deposit to the Deposit Holder within 24 hours of the acceptance of
this Agreement. The parties to this Agreement hereby acknowledge that, unless otherwise provided for in this Agreement, the Deposit Holder shall place
the deposit in trust in the Deposit Holder's non-interest bearing Real Estate Trust Account and no interest shall be earned, received or paid on the deposit.

Buyer agrees to pay the balance as more particularly set out in Schedule A attached.

SCHEDULE(S) A ....**attached hereto form(s) part of this Agreement.**

1.   **IRREVOCABILITY:** This offer shall be irrevocable by .... **Buyer** .... until **11:59** ~~a.m.~~/p.m. on the .... **4th** ....
(Seller/Buyer)

     day of .... **May** .... 20 **XX** ...., after which time, if not accepted, this offer shall be null and void and the deposit
shall be returned to the Buyer in full without interest.

2.   **COMPLETION DATE:** This Agreement shall be completed by no later than 6:00 p.m. on the .... **2nd** .... day of .... **July** ....

   20 **XX** ...... Upon completion, vacant possession of the property shall be given to the Buyer unless otherwise provided for in this Agreement.

INITIALS OF BUYER(S): (*JF JM*)   **INITIALS OF SELLER(S):** ( )

Form 100   Revised 2015   **Page 1 of 6**

SECTION III   COMMON ERRORS AND OMISSIONS

Exercise 4   Agreement of Purchase and Sale (Big Cedar Lake Cottage)—Page 2 of 6

3. NOTICES: The Seller hereby appoints the Listing Brokerage as agent for the Seller for the purpose of giving and receiving notices pursuant to this Agreement. Where a Brokerage (Buyer's Brokerage) has entered into a representation agreement with the Buyer, the Buyer hereby appoints the Buyer's Brokerage as agent for the purpose of giving and receiving notices pursuant to this Agreement. **Where a Brokerage represents both the Seller and the Buyer (multiple representation), the Brokerage shall not be appointed or authorized to be agent for either the Buyer or the Seller for the purpose of giving and receiving notices.** Any notice relating hereto or provided for herein shall be in writing. In addition to any provision contained herein and in any Schedule hereto, this offer, any counter-offer, notice of acceptance thereof or any notice to be given or received pursuant to this Agreement or any Schedule hereto (any of them, "Document") shall be deemed given and received when delivered personally or hand delivered to the Address for Service provided in the Acknowledgement below, or where a facsimile number or email address is provided herein, when transmitted electronically to that facsimile number or email address, respectively, in which case, the signature(s) of the party (parties) shall be deemed to be original.

FAX No.: .... 905-555-2121 ....
(For delivery of Documents to Seller)

FAX No.: .... 905-444-2121 ....
(For delivery of Documents to Buyer)

Email Address: .... admin@abcrealty.com ....
(For delivery of Documents to Seller)

Email Address: .... notices@xyzrealestate.com ....
(For delivery of Documents to Buyer)

4. CHATTELS INCLUDED: All window coverings and furniture in the main cottage and guest cabin, two outboard motors, rowboat and lawn mower, reverse osmosis purification system in kitchen

Unless otherwise stated in this Agreement or any Schedule hereto, Seller agrees to convey all fixtures and chattels included in the Purchase Price free from all liens, encumbrances or claims affecting the said fixtures and chattels.

5. FIXTURES EXCLUDED: None

6. RENTAL ITEMS (Including Lease, Lease to Own): The following equipment is rented and **not** included in the Purchase Price. The Buyer agrees to assume the rental contract(s), if assumable:

Hot Water Tank and Water Softener $53.85 quarterly plus applicable taxes

The Buyer agrees to co-operate and execute such documentation as may be required to facilitate such assumption.

7. HST: If the sale of the Property (Real Property as described above) is subject to Harmonized Sales Tax (HST), then such tax shall be .... included in .... the Purchase Price. If the sale of the Property is not subject to HST, Seller agrees to certify on or before
(included in/in addition to)
closing, that the sale of the Property is not subject to HST. Any HST on chattels, if applicable, is not included in the Purchase Price.

INITIALS OF BUYER(S): (JF JM)

INITIALS OF SELLER(S): ( )

Form 100   Revised 2015   **Page 2 of 6**

8. **TITLE SEARCH:** Buyer shall be allowed until 6:00 p.m. on the ...**5th**... day of ....**June**......................., 20...**XX**...., (Requisition Date) to examine the title to the Property at Buyer's own expense and until the earlier of: (i) thirty days from the later of the Requisition Date or the date on which the conditions in this Agreement are fulfilled or otherwise waived or; (ii) five days prior to completion, to satisfy Buyer that there are no outstanding

work orders or deficiency notices affecting the Property, and that its present use (..................**single family residential**....................) may be lawfully continued and that the principal building may be insured against risk of fire. Seller hereby consents to the municipality or other governmental agencies releasing to Buyer details of all outstanding work orders and deficiency notices affecting the property, and Seller agrees to execute and deliver such further authorizations in this regard as Buyer may reasonably require.

9. **FUTURE USE:** Seller and Buyer agree that there is no representation or warranty of any kind that the future intended use of the property by Buyer is or will be lawful except as may be specifically provided for in this Agreement.

10. **TITLE:** Provided that the title to the property is good and free from all registered restrictions, charges, liens, and encumbrances except as otherwise specifically provided in this Agreement and save and except for (a) any registered restrictions or covenants that run with the land providing that such are complied with; (b) any registered municipal agreements and registered agreements with publicly regulated utilities providing such have been complied with, or security has been posted to ensure compliance and completion, as evidenced by a letter from the relevant municipality or regulated utility; (c) any minor easements for the supply of domestic utility or telephone services to the property or adjacent properties; and (d) any easements for drainage, storm or sanitary sewers, public utility lines, telephone lines, cable television lines or other services which do not materially affect the use of the property. If within the specified times referred to in paragraph 8 any valid objection to title or to any outstanding work order or deficiency notice, or to the fact the said present use may not lawfully be continued, or that the principal building may not be insured against risk of fire is made in writing to Seller and which Seller is unable or unwilling to remove, remedy or satisfy or obtain insurance save and except against risk of fire (Title Insurance) in favour of the Buyer and any mortgagee, (with all related costs at the expense of the Seller), and which Buyer will not waive, this Agreement notwithstanding any intermediate acts or negotiations in respect of such objections, shall be at an end and all monies paid shall be returned without interest or deduction and Seller, Listing Brokerage and Co-operating Brokerage shall not be liable for any costs or damages. Save as to any valid objection so made by such day and except for any objection going to the root of the title, Buyer shall be conclusively deemed to have accepted Seller's title to the property.

11. **CLOSING ARRANGEMENTS:** Where each of the Seller and Buyer retain a lawyer to complete the Agreement of Purchase and Sale of the property, and where the transaction will be completed by electronic registration pursuant to Part III of the Land Registration Reform Act, R.S.O. 1990, Chapter L4 and the Electronic Registration Act, S.O. 1991, Chapter 44, and any amendments thereto, the Seller and Buyer acknowledge and agree that the exchange of closing funds, non-registrable documents and other items (the "Requisite Deliveries") and the release thereof to the Seller and Buyer will (a) not occur at the same time as the registration of the transfer/deed (and any other documents intended to be registered in connection with the completion of this transaction) and (b) be subject to conditions whereby the lawyer(s) receiving any of the Requisite Deliveries will be required to hold same in trust and not release same except in accordance with the terms of a document registration agreement between the said lawyers. The Seller and Buyer irrevocably instruct the said lawyers to be bound by the document registration agreement which is recommended from time to time by the Law Society of Upper Canada. Unless otherwise agreed to by the lawyers, such exchange of the Requisite Deliveries will occur in the applicable Land Titles Office or such other location agreeable to both lawyers.

12. **DOCUMENTS AND DISCHARGE:** Buyer shall not call for the production of any title deed, abstract, survey or other evidence of title to the property except such as are in the possession or control of Seller. If requested by Buyer, Seller will deliver any sketch or survey of the property within Seller's control to Buyer as soon as possible and prior to the Requisition Date. If a discharge of any Charge/Mortgage held by a corporation incorporated pursuant to the Trust And Loan Companies Act (Canada), Chartered Bank, Trust Company, Credit Union, Caisse Populaire or Insurance Company and which is not to be assumed by Buyer on completion, is not available in registrable form on completion, Buyer agrees to accept Seller's lawyer's personal undertaking to obtain, out of the closing funds, a discharge in registrable form and to register same, or cause same to be registered, on title within a reasonable period of time after completion, provided that on or before completion Seller shall provide to Buyer a mortgage statement prepared by the mortgagee setting out the balance required to obtain the discharge, and, where a real-time electronic cleared funds transfer system is not being used, a direction executed by Seller directing payment to the mortgagee of the amount required to obtain the discharge out of the balance due on completion.

13. **INSPECTION:** Buyer acknowledges having had the opportunity to inspect the Property and understands that upon acceptance of this offer there shall be a binding agreement of purchase and sale between Buyer and Seller. **The Buyer acknowledges having the opportunity to include a requirement for a property inspection report in this Agreement and agrees that except as may be specifically provided for in this Agreement, the Buyer will not be obtaining a property inspection or property inspection report regarding the Property.**

14. **INSURANCE:** All buildings on the property and all other things being purchased shall be and remain until completion at the risk of Seller. Pending completion, Seller shall hold all insurance policies, if any, and the proceeds thereof in trust for the parties as their interests may appear and in the event of substantial damage, Buyer may either terminate this Agreement and have all monies paid returned without interest or deduction or else take the proceeds of any insurance and complete the purchase. No insurance shall be transferred on completion. If Seller is taking back a Charge/Mortgage, or Buyer is assuming a Charge/Mortgage, Buyer shall supply Seller with reasonable evidence of adequate insurance to protect Seller's or other mortgagee's interest on completion.

INITIALS OF BUYER(S): (*JF JM*)   INITIALS OF SELLER(S): (   )

Form 100 Revised 2015 **Page 3 of 6**

SECTION III COMMON ERRORS AND OMISSIONS

Exercise 4   Agreement of Purchase and Sale (Big Cedar Lake Cottage)—Page 4 of 6

15. **PLANNING ACT:** This Agreement shall be effective to create an interest in the property only if Seller complies with the subdivision control provisions of the Planning Act by completion and Seller covenants to proceed diligently at Seller's expense to obtain any necessary consent by completion.

16. **DOCUMENT PREPARATION:** The Transfer/Deed shall, save for the Land Transfer Tax Affidavit, be prepared in registrable form at the expense of Seller, and any Charge/Mortgage to be given back by the Buyer to Seller at the expense of the Buyer. If requested by Buyer, Seller covenants that the Transfer/Deed to be delivered on completion shall contain the statements contemplated by Section 50(22) of the Planning Act, R.S.O.1990.

17. **RESIDENCY:** (a) Subject to (b) below, the Seller represents and warrants that the Seller is not and on completion will not be a non-resident under the non-residency provisions of the Income Tax Act which representation and warranty shall survive and not merge upon the completion of this transaction and the Seller shall deliver to the Buyer a statutory declaration that Seller is not then a non-resident of Canada; (b) provided that if the Seller is a non-resident under the non-residency provisions of the Income Tax Act, the Buyer shall be credited towards the Purchase Price with the amount, if any, necessary for Buyer to pay to the Minister of National Revenue to satisfy Buyer's liability in respect of tax payable by Seller under the non-residency provisions of the Income Tax Act by reason of this sale. Buyer shall not claim such credit if Seller delivers on completion the prescribed certificate.

18. **ADJUSTMENTS:** Any rents, mortgage interest, realty taxes including local improvement rates and unmetered public or private utility charges and unmetered cost of fuel, as applicable, shall be apportioned and allowed to the day of completion, the day of completion itself to be apportioned to Buyer.

19. **PROPERTY ASSESSMENT:** The Buyer and Seller hereby acknowledge that the Province of Ontario has implemented current value assessment and properties may be re-assessed on an annual basis. The Buyer and Seller agree that no claim will be made against the Buyer or Seller, or any Brokerage, Broker or Salesperson, for any changes in property tax as a result of a re-assessment of the property, save and except any property taxes that accrued prior to the completion of this transaction.

20. **TIME LIMITS:** Time shall in all respects be of the essence hereof provided that the time for doing or completing of any matter provided for herein may be extended or abridged by an agreement in writing signed by Seller and Buyer or by their respective lawyers who may be specifically authorized in that regard.

21. **TENDER:** Any tender of documents or money hereunder may be made upon Seller or Buyer or their respective lawyers on the day set for completion. Money shall be tendered with funds drawn on a lawyer's trust account in the form of a bank draft, certified cheque or wire transfer using the Large Value Transfer System.

22. **FAMILY LAW ACT:** Seller warrants that spousal consent is not necessary to this transaction under the provisions of the Family Law Act, R.S.O.1990 unless Seller's spouse has executed the consent hereinafter provided.

23. **UFFI:** Seller represents and warrants to Buyer that during the time Seller has owned the property, Seller has not caused any building on the property to be insulated with insulation containing ureaformaldehyde, and that to the best of Seller's knowledge no building on the property contains or has ever contained insulation that contains ureaformaldehyde. This warranty shall survive and not merge on the completion of this transaction, and if the building is part of a multiple unit building, this warranty shall only apply to that part of the building which is the subject of this transaction.

24. **LEGAL, ACCOUNTING AND ENVIRONMENTAL ADVICE:** The parties acknowledge that any information provided by the brokerage is not legal, tax or environmental advice.

25. **CONSUMER REPORTS: The Buyer is hereby notified that a consumer report containing credit and/or personal information may be referred to in connection with this transaction.**

26. **AGREEMENT IN WRITING:** If there is conflict or discrepancy between any provision added to this Agreement (including any Schedule attached hereto) and any provision in the standard pre-set portion hereof, the added provision shall supersede the standard pre-set provision to the extent of such conflict or discrepancy. This Agreement including any Schedule attached hereto, shall constitute the entire Agreement between Buyer and Seller. There is no representation, warranty, collateral agreement or condition, which affects this Agreement other than as expressed herein. For the purposes of this Agreement, Seller means vendor and Buyer means purchaser. This Agreement shall be read with all changes of gender or number required by the context.

27. **TIME AND DATE:** Any reference to a time and date in this Agreement shall mean the time and date where the property is located.

INITIALS OF BUYER(S): (*JF JM*)   **INITIALS OF SELLER(S):** ( )

Form 100   Revised 2015   **Page 4 of 6**

28. SUCCESSORS AND ASSIGNS: The heirs, executors, administrators, successors and assigns of the undersigned are bound by the terms herein.

SIGNED, SEALED AND DELIVERED in the presence of: IN WITNESS whereof I have hereunto set my hand and seal:

W. Westoner ....   *James Freidman* ....   ● ....   DATE *May 2/xx* ....
(Witness)   (Buyer)   (Seal)

W. Westoner ....   *Jessie MacIntyre* ....   ● ....   DATE *May 2/xx* ....
(Witness)   (Buyer)   (Seal)

I, the Undersigned Seller, agree to the above offer. I hereby irrevocably instruct my lawyer to pay directly to the brokerage(s) with whom I have agreed to pay commission, the unpaid balance of the commission together with applicable Harmonized Sales Tax (and any other taxes as may hereafter be applicable), from the proceeds of the sale prior to any payment to the undersigned on completion, as advised by the brokerage(s) to my lawyer.

SIGNED, SEALED AND DELIVERED in the presence of: IN WITNESS whereof I have hereunto set my hand and seal:

....   ● ....   DATE ....
(Witness)   (Seller)   (Seal)

....   ● ....   DATE ....
(Witness)   (Seller)   (Seal)

SPOUSAL CONSENT: The Undersigned Spouse of the Seller hereby consents to the disposition evidenced herein pursuant to the provisions of the Family Law Act, R.S.O.1990, and hereby agrees with the Buyer that he/she will execute all necessary or incidental documents to give full force and effect to the sale evidenced herein.

....   ● ....   DATE ....
(Witness)   (Spouse)   (Seal)

CONFIRMATION OF ACCEPTANCE: Notwithstanding anything contained herein to the contrary, I confirm this Agreement with all changes both typed and written was finally accepted by all parties at .... a.m./p.m. this .... day of.., 20...........

....
(Signature of Seller or Buyer)

INFORMATION ON BROKERAGE(S)		
Listing Brokerage .... ABC Realty Inc.	Tel.No.(905)	555-1212
123 Main Street, Anycity, Anyregion N1S 4T8 Albert Lee		
(Salesperson / Broker Name)		
Co-op/Buyer Brokerage .... XYZ Real Estate Ltd.	Tel.No.(905)	444-1212
44 South Street, Anycity, Anyregion K2L 4S1 W. Westoner		
(Salesperson / Broker Name)		

ACKNOWLEDGEMENT

I acknowledge receipt of my signed copy of this accepted Agreement of Purchase and Sale and I authorize the Brokerage to forward a copy to my lawyer.   I acknowledge receipt of my signed copy of this accepted Agreement of Purchase and Sale and I authorize the Brokerage to forward a copy to my lawyer.

.... DATE .... DATE ....
(Seller)   (Buyer)

.... DATE .... DATE ....
(Seller)   (Buyer)
Address for Service ....   Address for Service ....

.... Tel.No.(..........)..................   .... Tel.No.(..........)..................

Seller's Lawyer ....   Buyer's Lawyer ....

Address ....   Address ....

Email ....   Email ....

(..........)..................... (..........)..................   (..........)..................... (..........)..................
Tel.No.   FAX No.   Tel.No.   FAX No.

FOR OFFICE USE ONLY	**COMMISSION TRUST AGREEMENT**

To: Co-operating Brokerage shown on the foregoing Agreement of Purchase and Sale:
In consideration for the Co-operating Brokerage procuring the foregoing Agreement of Purchase and Sale, I hereby declare that all moneys received or receivable by me in connection with the Transaction as contemplated in the MLS® Rules and Regulations of my Real Estate Board shall be receivable and held in trust. This agreement shall constitute a Commission Trust Agreement as defined in the MLS® Rules and shall be subject to and governed by the MLS® Rules pertaining to Commission Trust.

DATED as of the date and time of the acceptance of the foregoing Agreement of Purchase and Sale.   Acknowledged by:

....
(Authorized to bind the Listing Brokerage)   (Authorized to bind the Co-operating Brokerage)

Form 100   Revised 2015   **Page 5 of 6**

SECTION III   COMMON ERRORS AND OMISSIONS

Exercise 4   Agreement of Purchase and Sale (Big Cedar Lake Cottage)—Page 6 of 6

Form 100
for use in the Province of Ontario

Schedule A
Agreement of Purchase and Sale

This Schedule is attached to and forms part of the Agreement of Purchase and Sale between:

BUYER, ... James E. Freidman and Jessie C. MacIntyre ...., and

SELLER, ... Patricia Marilyn Wong ....

for the purchase and sale of .... 26 Lakeshore Drive, Township of Westside, County of Lake District

.... dated the ..2nd.. day of .... May ...., 20..xx..

Buyer agrees to pay the balance as follows:

The Buyer agrees to pay a further sum of Thirty-Five Thousand Dollars ($35,000.00), subject to adjustments, to the Seller on completion of this transaction, with funds drawn on a lawyer's trust account in the form of a bank draft, certified cheque, or wire transfer using the Large Value Transfer System.

The Buyer agrees to assume the existing first charge/mortgage held by Anycity Financial for approximately One Hundred and Ten Thousand Dollars ($110,000.00), bearing interest at the rate of 5.0% per annum, calculated semi-annually not in advance, repayable in blended bi-weekly payments of Three Hundred and Thirteen Dollars and Twenty-Six Cents ($313.26), including both principal and interest, and due on the 19th day of October, 20xx.

The Seller agrees to take back a second charge/mortgage in the amount of Seventy-Four Thousand Dollars ($74,000.00), bearing interest at the rate of 5.75% per annum, calculated semi-annually not in advance, repayable in blended monthly payments of Four Hundred and Fifty-Two Dollars and Sixty-Two Cents ($452.62), including both principal and interest, and to run of term of five years from the date of completion of this transaction. This charge/mortgage shall contain a clause permitting the chargor/mortgagor, when not in default, the privilege of prepaying all or part of the principal sum on any payment date or dates without notice or bonus.

The Seller represents and warrants, to the best of the Seller's knowledge and belief, that:
 ♦ The property fronts on a road that is maintained on a year-round basis at public expense.
 ♦ The sewage system has been and will be in good working order on closing.
 ♦ The well provides adequate and potable water supply, and the pump and related equipment are in good working order.

The Seller acknowledges that James Freidman is a registered real estate salesperson.

This form must be initialed by all parties to the Agreement of Purchase and Sale.

INITIALS OF BUYER(S): (*JF JM*)   **INITIALS OF SELLER(S):** (xx)

Form 100   Revised 2015   **Page 6 of 6**

■ Exercise 5   Offer and Counter Offer

NOTE: This is a consolidation question that requires knowledge from this chapter, previous chapters and offer drafting guidelines set out in *The Real Estate Transaction—General*.

Edith Catherine Park and Roger Thomas Park have inspected the residential property at 79 Western Avenue in Anycity, Regional Municipality of Anyregion. A copy of the MLS® listing is provided below.

Draft an offer for the Parks through XYZ Real Estate Limited, as a buyer agent, with an offer date of June 1, 20xx. The Parks are willing to offer $285,000, with a deposit of $10,000. This offer should be conditional on arranging a new first mortgage for $240,000 and a home inspection. The mortgage interest rate is to be for no more than 6%, due in three years, with a 25-year amortization and based on monthly payments.

The buyers will increase the deposit by $5,000 upon removal of the conditions. The closing date will be August 31, 20xx. The irrevocable date is June 3, 20xx. Notices can be faxed and emailed to both listing and selling brokerages.

The sellers counter with $295,000 on June 3rd, allowing another day for the buyers to consider the counter offer. The sellers want the option to postpone the closing date by 30 days on 40 days notice. The buyers agree to all terms on June 4th. Using the forms supplied, draft the initial offer and counter offer (amend original offer) with all necessary signatures, including acknowledgements. Insert fictitious details as required.

$299,500	79 WESTERN AVENUE	MLS #: 308891
District: D	Legal: Plan 1828, Pt. Lots 19 & 20	Status: Active
Listing Date: 02/02/xx	Postal Code: N1B 3C7	

Typ	2 Stry Freehold	**Survey**	Yes	**Lot**	39.37 ft. x 123.66 ft.	
Sq. Ft.	1370	**Hydro**	100/Breaker	**Rental Equip.**	HWT, WSFTR	
Rooms	6	**UFFI**	No	**Possession**	60 days	
Bedrooms	3	**Parking**	Single Paved Drive, Single Detached Garage	**Cross Street**	James	
Baths	2.0			**Bsmt**	Full, Partially Finished— Walls Only	
Age	80	**Water**	Municipal			
Taxes	$2,479/20xx	**Sewer**	Municipal	**Heat**	Forced Air	
Assessment:	$191,400	**Fuel**	Natural Gas	**Exterior**	Vinyl/Brick, Shingles Replaced, October, 20xx	
Zone	R1					
Easement	None					

Kitchen	Eat in 2.44 x 3.35m	**L/R**	3.27 x 3.23m	**D/R**	3.30 x 2.90m
MRB	4.41 x 3.90m	**BR1**	3.35 x 3.05m	**BR2**	3.15 x 3.12m

Mortgage   Treat as Clear

Other Comments
Fully fenced rear yard, home approx. 80 years old, includes above ground pool and accessories (heater, cleaning equipment and cover). Home well maintained. Upgraded ceramic floor in kitchen.

Owners	Jeannette E. Strauss and Neil B. Strauss	**Occupancy**	Owner
Listing Office	ABC Realty Inc. 555-1212	**Commission C/B**	2.5 **Sign** Yes
Listing Salesperson	Andre Zakhary 555-1919	**Appointments**	Call LB

SECTION III   COMMON ERRORS AND OMISSIONS

Exercise 5   Agreement of Purchase and Sale (79 Western Avenue)—Page 1 of 6

OREA Ontario Real Estate Association   **Agreement of Purchase and Sale**

Form 100
for use in the Province of Ontario

This Agreement of Purchase and Sale dated this .... day of .... 20...........

BUYER, ..., agrees to purchase from
(Full legal names of all Buyers)

SELLER, ..., the following
(Full legal names of all Sellers)

REAL PROPERTY:

Address ....

fronting on the .... side of ....

in the ....

and having a frontage of .... more or less by a depth of .... more or less

and legally described as ....

.... (the "property")
(Legal description of land including easements not described elsewhere)

PURCHASE PRICE: Dollars (CDN$) ....

.... Dollars

DEPOSIT: Buyer submits ....
(Herewith/Upon Acceptance/as otherwise described in this Agreement)

.... Dollars (CDN$) ....

by negotiable cheque payable to .... "Deposit Holder" to be held
in trust pending completion or other termination of this Agreement and to be credited toward the Purchase Price on completion. For the purposes of this
Agreement, "Upon Acceptance" shall mean that the Buyer is required to deliver the deposit to the Deposit Holder within 24 hours of the acceptance of
this Agreement. The parties to this Agreement hereby acknowledge that, unless otherwise provided for in this Agreement, the Deposit Holder shall place
the deposit in trust in the Deposit Holder's non-interest bearing Real Estate Trust Account and no interest shall be earned, received or paid on the deposit.

Buyer agrees to pay the balance as more particularly set out in Schedule A attached.

SCHEDULE(S) A..**attached hereto form(s) part of this Agreement.**

1.   **IRREVOCABILITY:** This offer shall be irrevocable by .... until .... a.m./p.m. on the ....
(Seller/Buyer)

day of .... 20 ...., after which time, if not accepted, this offer shall be null and void and the deposit
shall be returned to the Buyer in full without interest.

2.   **COMPLETION DATE:** This Agreement shall be completed by no later than 6:00 p.m. on the .... day of ....

20 .... Upon completion, vacant possession of the property shall be given to the Buyer unless otherwise provided for in this Agreement.

INITIALS OF BUYER(S): ⬭   **INITIALS OF SELLER(S):** ⬭

3. **NOTICES:** The Seller hereby appoints the Listing Brokerage as agent for the Seller for the purpose of giving and receiving notices pursuant to this Agreement. Where a Brokerage (Buyer's Brokerage) has entered into a representation agreement with the Buyer, the Buyer hereby appoints the Buyer's Brokerage as agent for the purpose of giving and receiving notices pursuant to this Agreement. **Where a Brokerage represents both the Seller and the Buyer (multiple representation), the Brokerage shall not be appointed or authorized to be agent for either the Buyer or the Seller for the purpose of giving and receiving notices.** Any notice relating hereto or provided for herein shall be in writing. In addition to any provision contained herein and in any Schedule hereto, this offer, any counter-offer, notice of acceptance thereof or any notice to be given or received pursuant to this Agreement or any Schedule hereto (any of them, "Document") shall be deemed given and received when delivered personally or hand delivered to the Address for Service provided in the Acknowledgement below, or where a facsimile number or email address is provided herein, when transmitted electronically to that facsimile number or email address, respectively, in which case, the signature(s) of the party (parties) shall be deemed to be original.

FAX No.: ....   FAX No.: ....
(For delivery of Documents to Seller)   (For delivery of Documents to Buyer)

Email Address: ....   Email Address: ....
(For delivery of Documents to Seller)   (For delivery of Documents to Buyer)

4. **CHATTELS INCLUDED:**...

....

....

....

....

Unless otherwise stated in this Agreement or any Schedule hereto, Seller agrees to convey all fixtures and chattels included in the Purchase Price free from all liens, encumbrances or claims affecting the said fixtures and chattels.

5. **FIXTURES EXCLUDED:**...

....

....

....

....

6. **RENTAL ITEMS (Including Lease, Lease to Own):** The following equipment is rented and **not** included in the Purchase Price. The Buyer agrees to assume the rental contract(s), if assumable:

....

....

....

The Buyer agrees to co-operate and execute such documentation as may be required to facilitate such assumption.

7. **HST:** If the sale of the Property (Real Property as described above) is subject to Harmonized Sales Tax (HST), then such tax shall be

.... the Purchase Price. If the sale of the Property is not subject to HST, Seller agrees to certify on or before
(included in/in addition to)
closing, that the sale of the Property is not subject to HST. Any HST on chattels, if applicable, is not included in the Purchase Price.

INITIALS OF BUYER(S): (   )   INITIALS OF SELLER(S): (   )

SECTION III   COMMON ERRORS AND OMISSIONS

Exercise 5   Agreement of Purchase and Sale (79 Western Avenue)—Page 3 of 6

8. **TITLE SEARCH:** Buyer shall be allowed until 6:00 p.m. on the .... day of ...., 20..........., (Requisition Date) to examine the title to the Property at Buyer's own expense and until the earlier of: (i) thirty days from the later of the Requisition Date or the date on which the conditions in this Agreement are fulfilled or otherwise waived or; (ii) five days prior to completion, to satisfy Buyer that there are no outstanding

    work orders or deficiency notices affecting the Property, and that its present use (...) may be lawfully continued and that the principal building may be insured against risk of fire. Seller hereby consents to the municipality or other governmental agencies releasing to Buyer details of all outstanding work orders and deficiency notices affecting the property, and Seller agrees to execute and deliver such further authorizations in this regard as Buyer may reasonably require.

9. **FUTURE USE:** Seller and Buyer agree that there is no representation or warranty of any kind that the future intended use of the property by Buyer is or will be lawful except as may be specifically provided for in this Agreement.

10. **TITLE:** Provided that the title to the property is good and free from all registered restrictions, charges, liens, and encumbrances except as otherwise specifically provided in this Agreement and save and except for (a) any registered restrictions or covenants that run with the land providing that such are complied with; (b) any registered municipal agreements and registered agreements with publicly regulated utilities providing such have been complied with, or security has been posted to ensure compliance and completion, as evidenced by a letter from the relevant municipality or regulated utility; (c) any minor easements for the supply of domestic utility or telephone services to the property or adjacent properties; and (d) any easements for drainage, storm or sanitary sewers, public utility lines, telephone lines, cable television lines or other services which do not materially affect the use of the property. If within the specified times referred to in paragraph 8 any valid objection to title or to any outstanding work order or deficiency notice, or to the fact the said present use may not lawfully be continued, or that the principal building may not be insured against risk of fire is made in writing to Seller and which Seller is unable or unwilling to remove, remedy or satisfy or obtain insurance save and except against risk of fire (Title Insurance) in favour of the Buyer and any mortgagee, (with all related costs at the expense of the Seller), and which Buyer will not waive, this Agreement notwithstanding any intermediate acts or negotiations in respect of such objections, shall be at an end and all monies paid shall be returned without interest or deduction and Seller, Listing Brokerage and Co-operating Brokerage shall not be liable for any costs or damages. Save as to any valid objection so made by such day and except for any objection going to the root of the title, Buyer shall be conclusively deemed to have accepted Seller's title to the property.

11. **CLOSING ARRANGEMENTS:** Where each of the Seller and Buyer retain a lawyer to complete the Agreement of Purchase and Sale of the property, and where the transaction will be completed by electronic registration pursuant to Part III of the Land Registration Reform Act, R.S.O. 1990, Chapter L4 and the Electronic Registration Act, S.O. 1991, Chapter 44, and any amendments thereto, the Seller and Buyer acknowledge and agree that the exchange of closing funds, non-registrable documents and other items (the "Requisite Deliveries") and the release thereof to the Seller and Buyer will (a) not occur at the same time as the registration of the transfer/deed (and any other documents intended to be registered in connection with the completion of this transaction) and (b) be subject to conditions whereby the lawyer(s) receiving any of the Requisite Deliveries will be required to hold same in trust and not release same except in accordance with the terms of a document registration agreement between the said lawyers. The Seller and Buyer irrevocably instruct the said lawyers to be bound by the document registration agreement which is recommended from time to time by the Law Society of Upper Canada. Unless otherwise agreed to by the lawyers, such exchange of the Requisite Deliveries will occur in the applicable Land Titles Office or such other location agreeable to both lawyers.

12. **DOCUMENTS AND DISCHARGE:** Buyer shall not call for the production of any title deed, abstract, survey or other evidence of title to the property except such as are in the possession or control of Seller. If requested by Buyer, Seller will deliver any sketch or survey of the property within Seller's control to Buyer as soon as possible and prior to the Requisition Date. If a discharge of any Charge/Mortgage held by a corporation incorporated pursuant to the Trust And Loan Companies Act (Canada), Chartered Bank, Trust Company, Credit Union, Caisse Populaire or Insurance Company and which is not to be assumed by Buyer on completion, is not available in registrable form on completion, Buyer agrees to accept Seller's lawyer's personal undertaking to obtain, out of the closing funds, a discharge in registrable form and to register same, or cause same to be registered, on title within a reasonable period of time after completion, provided that on or before completion Seller shall provide to Buyer a mortgage statement prepared by the mortgagee setting out the balance required to obtain the discharge, and, where a real-time electronic cleared funds transfer system is not being used, a direction executed by Seller directing payment to the mortgagee of the amount required to obtain the discharge out of the balance due on completion.

13. **INSPECTION:** Buyer acknowledges having had the opportunity to inspect the Property and understands that upon acceptance of this offer there shall be a binding agreement of purchase and sale between Buyer and Seller. **The Buyer acknowledges having the opportunity to include a requirement for a property inspection report in this Agreement and agrees that except as may be specifically provided for in this Agreement, the Buyer will not be obtaining a property inspection or property inspection report regarding the Property.**

14. **INSURANCE:** All buildings on the property and all other things being purchased shall be and remain until completion at the risk of Seller. Pending completion, Seller shall hold all insurance policies, if any, and the proceeds thereof in trust for the parties as their interests may appear and in the event of substantial damage, Buyer may either terminate this Agreement and have all monies paid returned without interest or deduction or else take the proceeds of any insurance and complete the purchase. No insurance shall be transferred on completion. If Seller is taking back a Charge/ Mortgage, or Buyer is assuming a Charge/Mortgage, Buyer shall supply Seller with reasonable evidence of adequate insurance to protect Seller's or other mortgagee's interest on completion.

INITIALS OF BUYER(S): ( )   INITIALS OF SELLER(S): ( )

Form 100   Revised 2015   **Page 3 of 6**

15. PLANNING ACT: This Agreement shall be effective to create an interest in the property only if Seller complies with the subdivision control provisions of the Planning Act by completion and Seller covenants to proceed diligently at Seller's expense to obtain any necessary consent by completion.

16. DOCUMENT PREPARATION: The Transfer/Deed shall, save for the Land Transfer Tax Affidavit, be prepared in registrable form at the expense of Seller, and any Charge/Mortgage to be given back by the Buyer to Seller at the expense of the Buyer. If requested by Buyer, Seller covenants that the Transfer/Deed to be delivered on completion shall contain the statements contemplated by Section 50(22) of the Planning Act, R.S.O.1990.

17. RESIDENCY: (a) Subject to (b) below, the Seller represents and warrants that the Seller is not and on completion will not be a non-resident under the non-residency provisions of the Income Tax Act which representation and warranty shall survive and not merge upon the completion of this transaction and the Seller shall deliver to the Buyer a statutory declaration that Seller is not then a non-resident of Canada; (b) provided that if the Seller is a non-resident under the non-residency provisions of the Income Tax Act, the Buyer shall be credited towards the Purchase Price with the amount, if any, necessary for Buyer to pay to the Minister of National Revenue to satisfy Buyer's liability in respect of tax payable by Seller under the non-residency provisions of the Income Tax Act by reason of this sale. Buyer shall not claim such credit if Seller delivers on completion the prescribed certificate.

18. ADJUSTMENTS: Any rents, mortgage interest, realty taxes including local improvement rates and unmetered public or private utility charges and unmetered cost of fuel, as applicable, shall be apportioned and allowed to the day of completion, the day of completion itself to be apportioned to Buyer.

19. PROPERTY ASSESSMENT: The Buyer and Seller hereby acknowledge that the Province of Ontario has implemented current value assessment and properties may be re-assessed on an annual basis. The Buyer and Seller agree that no claim will be made against the Buyer or Seller, or any Brokerage, Broker or Salesperson, for any changes in property tax as a result of a re-assessment of the property, save and except any property taxes that accrued prior to the completion of this transaction.

20. TIME LIMITS: Time shall in all respects be of the essence hereof provided that the time for doing or completing of any matter provided for herein may be extended or abridged by an agreement in writing signed by Seller and Buyer or by their respective lawyers who may be specifically authorized in that regard.

21. TENDER: Any tender of documents or money hereunder may be made upon Seller or Buyer or their respective lawyers on the day set for completion. Money shall be tendered with funds drawn on a lawyer's trust account in the form of a bank draft, certified cheque or wire transfer using the Large Value Transfer System.

22. FAMILY LAW ACT: Seller warrants that spousal consent is not necessary to this transaction under the provisions of the Family Law Act, R.S.O.1990 unless Seller's spouse has executed the consent hereinafter provided.

23. UFFI: Seller represents and warrants to Buyer that during the time Seller has owned the property, Seller has not caused any building on the property to be insulated with insulation containing ureaformaldehyde, and that to the best of Seller's knowledge no building on the property contains or has ever contained insulation that contains ureaformaldehyde. This warranty shall survive and not merge on the completion of this transaction, and if the building is part of a multiple unit building, this warranty shall only apply to that part of the building which is the subject of this transaction.

24. LEGAL, ACCOUNTING AND ENVIRONMENTAL ADVICE: The parties acknowledge that any information provided by the brokerage is not legal, tax or environmental advice.

25. CONSUMER REPORTS: The Buyer is hereby notified that a consumer report containing credit and/or personal information may be referred to in connection with this transaction.

26. AGREEMENT IN WRITING: If there is conflict or discrepancy between any provision added to this Agreement (including any Schedule attached hereto) and any provision in the standard pre-set portion hereof, the added provision shall supersede the standard pre-set provision to the extent of such conflict or discrepancy. This Agreement including any Schedule attached hereto, shall constitute the entire Agreement between Buyer and Seller. There is no representation, warranty, collateral agreement or condition, which affects this Agreement other than as expressed herein. For the purposes of this Agreement, Seller means vendor and Buyer means purchaser. This Agreement shall be read with all changes of gender or number required by the context.

27. TIME AND DATE: Any reference to a time and date in this Agreement shall mean the time and date where the property is located.

INITIALS OF BUYER(S): ⬭   INITIALS OF SELLER(S): ⬭

Form 100   Revised 2015   Page 4 of 6

SECTION III   COMMON ERRORS AND OMISSIONS

Exercise 5   *Agreement of Purchase and Sale (79 Western Avenue)—Page 5 of 6*

28. SUCCESSORS AND ASSIGNS: The heirs, executors, administrators, successors and assigns of the undersigned are bound by the terms herein.

SIGNED, SEALED AND DELIVERED in the presence of: IN WITNESS whereof I have hereunto set my hand and seal:

....   ⬤   DATE ....
(Witness)   (Buyer)   (Seal)

....   ⬤   DATE ....
(Witness)   (Buyer)   (Seal)

I, the Undersigned Seller, agree to the above offer. I hereby irrevocably instruct my lawyer to pay directly to the brokerage(s) with whom I have agreed to pay commission, the unpaid balance of the commission together with applicable Harmonized Sales Tax (and any other taxes as may hereafter be applicable), from the proceeds of the sale prior to any payment to the undersigned on completion, as advised by the brokerage(s) to my lawyer.

SIGNED, SEALED AND DELIVERED in the presence of: IN WITNESS whereof I have hereunto set my hand and seal:

....   ⬤   DATE ....
(Witness)   (Seller)   (Seal)

....   ⬤   DATE ....
(Witness)   (Seller)   (Seal)

SPOUSAL CONSENT: The Undersigned Spouse of the Seller hereby consents to the disposition evidenced herein pursuant to the provisions of the Family Law Act, R.S.O.1990, and hereby agrees with the Buyer that he/she will execute all necessary or incidental documents to give full force and effect to the sale evidenced herein.

....   ⬤   DATE ....
(Witness)   (Spouse)   (Seal)

CONFIRMATION OF ACCEPTANCE: Notwithstanding anything contained herein to the contrary, I confirm this Agreement with all changes both typed and written was finally accepted by all parties at .... a.m./p.m. this .... day of.., 20...........

....
(Signature of Seller or Buyer)

INFORMATION ON BROKERAGE(S)

Listing Brokerage .... Tel.No.(...............)...............................

....
(Salesperson / Broker Name)

Co-op/Buyer Brokerage .... Tel.No.(...............)...............................

....
(Salesperson / Broker Name)

ACKNOWLEDGEMENT

I acknowledge receipt of my signed copy of this accepted Agreement of Purchase and Sale and I authorize the Brokerage to forward a copy to my lawyer.	I acknowledge receipt of my signed copy of this accepted Agreement of Purchase and Sale and I authorize the Brokerage to forward a copy to my lawyer.
.... DATE .... (Seller)	.... DATE .... (Buyer)
.... DATE .... (Seller)	.... DATE .... (Buyer)
Address for Service	Address for Service ....
.... Tel.No.(...........)................	.... Tel.No.(...........)................
Seller's Lawyer	Buyer's Lawyer ....
Address	Address ....
Email	Email ....
(...........)................... (...........)................... Tel.No. FAX No.	(...........)................... (...........)................... Tel.No. FAX No.

FOR OFFICE USE ONLY   **COMMISSION TRUST AGREEMENT**

To: Co-operating Brokerage shown on the foregoing Agreement of Purchase and Sale:
In consideration for the Co-operating Brokerage procuring the foregoing Agreement of Purchase and Sale, I hereby declare that all moneys received or receivable by me in connection with the Transaction as contemplated in the MLS® Rules and Regulations of my Real Estate Board shall be receivable and held in trust. This agreement shall constitute a Commission Trust Agreement as defined in the MLS® Rules and shall be subject to and governed by the MLS® Rules pertaining to Commission Trust.

DATED as of the date and time of the acceptance of the foregoing Agreement of Purchase and Sale.   Acknowledged by:

....
(Authorized to bind the Listing Brokerage)   (Authorized to bind the Co-operating Brokerage)

Form 100   Revised 2015   **Page 5 of 6**

OREA Ontario Real Estate Association

Form 100
for use in the Province of Ontario

Schedule A
Agreement of Purchase and Sale

This Schedule is attached to and forms part of the Agreement of Purchase and Sale between:

BUYER, ..., and

SELLER, ...

for the purchase and sale of ....

.... dated the .... day of ...., 20................

Buyer agrees to pay the balance as follows:

This form must be initialed by all parties to the Agreement of Purchase and Sale.

INITIALS OF BUYER(S): ⬭   INITIALS OF SELLER(S): ⬭

Form 100   Revised 2015   **Page 6 of 6**

SECTION IV

PREPARING FOR YOUR NEW CAREER

Today's real estate marketplace provides tremendous opportunities for those seeking to commit the time and energy required in this new career. The road to success in real estate sales is not easy, but hard work can pay real dividends for those committed to a properly designed plan.

Well-run sales careers, just as with well-run businesses, develop by formulating a workable plan, establishing priorities, implementing proper budgeting, ensuring efficient time management, pursuing new technologies to increase competitive edge, and continuously updating skills and knowledge to provide premier services to clients and customers.

That process begins the very first day that you begin your new career with a brokerage. Section 4 includes a final chapter to help guide you in establishing a solid foundation. This tutorial-based chapter provides step-by-step tips and guidelines for your new endeavour. *Chapter 10: Getting Started* focuses on those immediate issues faced during the first few weeks as a salesperson in a brokerage, including required documentation, what to bring, understanding brokerage policies/procedures, handling office dynamics, implementing effective prospecting techniques to network in your community and preparing for those personal firsts: that first conversation with a client or customer, showing the first house and drafting the first agreement of purchase and sale.

CHAPTER 10

Getting Started

Introduction

The first few weeks in a real estate brokerage are often full of challenges. For many, this is the first time of having to face setting up an office, organizing promotional materials, getting ready to work with buyers and sellers, putting an action plan in place and getting accustomed to unfamiliar surroundings.

Career options and expectations, along with fundamentals of the brokerage/salesperson relationship, including commission splits, were discussed in the initial pre-registration program (*Real Estate as a Professional Career*). Chapter 10 expands on these topics by giving practical ideas to effectively start your new career. This tutorial is more than a discussion of procedures, it delves into the human dimension of real estate brokerages including how to establish and build meaningful relationships with the broker of record (or manager), administrative staff, and other real estate brokers and salespersons.

Important guidelines are provided regarding networking in the community through effective use of spheres of influence, opportunity calling, conducting open houses, canvassing *For Sale By Owners* and expired listings, and cold calling. The chapter concludes with a detailed discussion of how to handle important career firsts, time planning and lastly a discussion of income/expense expectations, including examples of initial and ongoing expenses.

Learning Outcomes

At the conclusion of this chapter, students will be able to:

- Outline how discipline, planning, time management, image/promotion and attitude are key to getting started in real estate sales.
- Describe four ways to prepare for your first week in real estate sales, including the use of a career checklist regarding what to bring to the brokerage and important questions to ask.
- Identify and discuss various documentation, including benefits, deductions (including taxation) and related matters that must be addressed when starting at a real estate brokerage.
- Discuss various effective ways to handle office dynamics, including building a relationship with the broker of record or manager.
- Identify four ways to effectively network in the community, with particular reference to focusing efforts on spheres of influence, opportunity calling, *For Sale By Owners*, expired listings and cold calling.
- Describe the requirements of Canada's Anti-Spam Legislation as it relates to a registrant's advertising and marketing.
- Discuss methods to prepare for career firsts, including the first conversations with customers and clients, asking the right questions, the first showing, asking for the decision and preparing the first offer.
- Identify time planning and key prospecting activities during the first two weeks.
- Discuss income expectations and expense estimates, including initial and ongoing expenses.

A DIFFERENT MINDSET

Real estate sales demands your full time attention. Don't be misled, as some are, by the seeming lack of structure in your new found career. Set the tone immediately by starting every business day *early* regardless of whether you are coming into the brokerage, meeting prospects or working from a home office. Here's five tips to help develop a career mindset.

- **Discipline**   Discipline is everything and time is a valuable commodity that cannot be wasted. Always be looking for ways to improve productivity and get more done in less time. Learn how to be effective, don't just concentrate on being efficient. While a software program can churn out thousands of letters nothing replaces face-to-face contact. Scheduled time canvassing specific streets can prove extremely rewarding, cost effective and lucrative.

- **Planning**   Have a plan and work the plan. It doesn't have to be extensive. Some people memorize it, while others may have only a few sheets of paper. Regardless of its sophistication, a plan sets the framework for success. Real estate sales is no different than any other endeavour. Be specific about your goals, action plans, budget considerations, marketing strategy and much more. Some mistakenly believe that successful salespeople are creative, disorganized people. Usually, the reverse is true. Those who make a real impact in the marketplace are disciplined, diligent and organized professionals who know what they want and go out there to get it.

- **Time Management**   Be careful how you handle this new found opportunity. Don't let the job take over. The pros understand that balance is essential. Unfortunately, many fall into a 24 hours a day, seven days a week career trap. It's easy to do because everything about your endeavour is performance oriented: *If you don't make sales, you don't get commission cheques.* At the same time, remember that opportunity is everywhere and your job is to capitalize on it. Whether dropping your son off at hockey camp or your daughter to ballet, business can arise in some of the most unexpected places. The best motto: *Always be prepared.*

- **Image/Promotion**   Dress for work each day as if you are going to meet a client and project a professional image in everything you do. Your image building doesn't start and stop at the brokerage office. It's with you all the time. Your role as a salesperson is an integral part of what you are. Successful salespeople are always selling. It may not be obvious, but they understand the rules of the game: meet lots of people, generate a loyal clientele and constantly service those valued clients and customers.

- **Attitude**   Maintain a positive attitude. Don't let frustrations, delays and disappointments overshadow the much-anticipated highs and successes that inevitably arrive. Make a conscious effort to learn from every mistake—there will be many. Develop a mindset built on purpose and persistence. Turn every experience into a positive learning event.

PREPARING FOR THE FIRST WEEK

Preparation for your first week should begin several weeks earlier. For most new sales-people, the time between completing *The Residential* or *Commercial Real Estate Transaction* examination and obtaining RECO registration can seem endless, but it provides ample time to plan your strategy. *Remember, you cannot, in any way, be involved with the trading of real estate or related activities until registered.*

Be productive. Remember, the time required for processing a salesperson's application is necessary to ensure that every individual meets stringent requirements set out in the *Real Estate and Business Brokers Act, 2002*. Keep in mind that the approval process is not simply reviewing the application, but can involve a search of police databases, a record of offences, a record of judgments or other consumer reports that may be requested, obtained and reviewed in relation to the application.

STEP 1: Use Waiting Time Productively

Don't let those valuable days waste away while waiting for the RECO registration to arrive. Here's some suggestions. Keep in mind that brokerages may offer various training programs and associated activities to help with your preparation. Check with the broker of record or manager.

Conduct Market Research	Find out as much as you can about the local market, including trends, prices, recent changes and new developments.
Attend Training Courses	Why not consider taking one or more sales training courses? Timely topics include prospecting, listing presentations, qualifying buyers, handling objections and negotiating skills.
Conduct Sign Surveys	Do visual sign surveys for *For Sale by Owners* and brokerage signage in your market area every few days. Time spent driving around neighbourhoods not only helps sharpen your knowledge of *who's doing what* but also familiarizes you with streets, local changes and new construction.
Build a Database	Start populating an electronic database with friends, acquaintances, and business contacts. Customer relations management is the best avenue. See your broker of record or manager for guidance.
Develop a Listing Presentation	Develop the key points and artwork for your listing presentation. *The Real Estate Transaction—General* provided guidance on developing listing presentations.
Shop for Supplies	Prospective registrants should find out what supplies are provided by the brokerage. Further guidance is provided later in this chapter.
Build a Business Plan	Get your business plan developed and establish priorities. It's much better to set out the basics and then refine your plan once you begin listing and selling real estate.
Be Inquisitive	Learn as much as you can from others in the business. It's difficult to expand your horizons without asking lots of questions, talking with successful representatives and immersing yourself in how the brokerage operates.

STEP 2: Understand Your Contractual Obligations

Brokerages typically require a written contract. Most registrants are in possession of this form prior to actually joining. Carefully review all requirements. How you prepare depends in part on whether you are an employee or an independent contractor, as contractors must administer their own affairs much more so than those under an employment agreement.

REMINDER: All salespeople are viewed as employees under the *Real Estate and Business Brokers Act, 2002*, but how they are dealt with by the brokerage for taxation and related purposes will vary depending on whether an employment contract or an independent contractor agreement is signed.

THE EMPLOYED SALESPERSON

A salesperson hired under an employment agreement provides and/or pays for certain items. The *Brokerage/Salesperson Employment Agreement* (OREA Form 600) is used for illustration and discussion purposes only. Analysis is limited to selected terms, as rights/obligations in employment agreements will vary by brokerage. Check with the broker of record or manager.

SALESPERSON RESPONSIBILITIES

Salesperson responsibilities are set out under Clause 3 of the illustrated form. Most notably, the salesperson must become a member of a particular real estate board (assuming that the brokerage is a member of organized real estate) and associated fees, dues and assessments must be paid to the brokerage as required. The salesperson is also responsible for registration/renewal and associated fees required by the Real Estate Council of Ontario, including insurance coverage.

The salesperson must provide a suitable automobile, keep it insured according to brokerage requirements and submit proof to the brokerage upon request. Employed salespeople are also generally responsible for all personal expenses relating to travel, meals and lodging, unless otherwise provided for in the agreement.

The salesperson must also conduct himself or herself in accordance with all brokerage policies and procedures, regulatory requirements set out in the *Real Estate and Business Brokers Act, 2002* and any other requirements associated being a member of organized real estate (if applicable).

BROKERAGE RESPONSIBILITIES

The brokerage is required to supply the salesperson with office and secretarial facilities in line with the brokerage office policy manual. The brokerage must advise, counsel, instruct and assist the salesperson in the performance of the salesperson's duties.

A copy of the *Brokerage/Salesperson Employment Agreement* (OREA Form 600) is reprinted for reference purposes. Certain brokerage and salesperson responsibilities are highlighted for emphasis.

OREA Form 600   *Brokerage/Salesperson Employment Agreement, Page 1 of 1*

OREA Ontario Real Estate Association   **Brokerage/Salesperson Employment**
Agreement

Form 600
for use in the Province of Ontario

This Employment Agreement made this .... day of.., 20...........................
BETWEEN:
BROKERAGE: ....
AND:
SALESPERSON: ....

For the purposes of this Agreement, Salesperson includes a Broker registered under the Real Estate and Business Brokers Act, 2002.

WHEREAS the Brokerage is registered as a Brokerage and the Salesperson is registered pursuant to the Real Estate and Business Brokers Act, 2002, ("the Act");
AND WHEREAS the Brokerage wishes to employ the Salesperson on the terms and conditions contained in this Agreement;
NOW THEREFORE the Brokerage and the Salesperson agree to the employment of the Salesperson by the Brokerage in consideration of the following mutual terms, conditions and covenants of this Agreement:

1. The Brokerage:
    a) Shall supply the Salesperson with office and secretarial facilities in accordance with the Brokerage's office policies and practices in that regard;
    b) Shall advise, counsel, instruct, and assist the Salesperson in the performance of the Salesperson's duties;
    c) Shall loan, by way of advances on account of anticipated commissions, such periodic amounts as may be established from time to time by the Brokerage, it being understood and agreed that such amount(s) so advanced shall constitute a debt due and owing to the Brokerage without notice or demand;
    d) Hereby declares that any monies received or receivable on account of commission by the Brokerage from any trade in real estate conducted on behalf of the Brokerage by the Salesperson, shall be held by the Brokerage in trust and the Brokerage shall disburse in a timely fashion, directly from the Brokerage's Commission Trust Account (subject to any direction pursuant to paragraph 3(a) hereof) to the Salesperson, commission due to the Salesperson in connection with the trade, as determined in accordance with Schedule "A" hereto; (Brokerage to attach commission schedule.)
    e) Shall receive any monies on behalf of or from the Salesperson, for real estate Board and association fees, dues or assessments or for personal tax remittance, in trust and remit said monies on the Salesperson's behalf in a timely fashion by issuing a trust cheque to the Board or association or Revenue Canada for the entire amount collected on behalf of or from the Salesperson;

2. The Brokerage shall not:
    a) Pledge any portion of a Commission Trust held on behalf of the Salesperson as collateral for any loan or use said amount for any other personal or corporate reason without the express written consent of the Salesperson.

3. The Salesperson:
    a) Hereby irrevocably directs the Brokerage to deduct from any commissions payable or termination pay due and owing to the Salesperson, whether out of Commission Trust or otherwise, the amount of any indebtedness as outlined in Section 1(c) above;
    b) Shall become and remain a member in good standing of the .... Real Estate Board(s)/Association(s) and pay to the Brokerage, when required, any fees, dues or assessments required from time to time by the Board(s)/Association(s);
    c) Shall pay any registration or renewal fees imposed upon the Salesperson under any provincial legislation;
    d) Shall maintain Errors and Omissions Insurance, Consumer Deposit Insurance and Commission Protection Insurance coverage in good standing at all times;
    e) Shall supply and maintain at the Salesperson's expense, a suitable automobile and keep it insured at such limits for public liability and property damage as the brokerage may from time to time direct, and shall provide proof of such insurance to the brokerage;
    f) Shall fully and faithfully serve the Brokerage and conduct himself/herself in accordance with the Brokerage's office policies and practices, the By-laws and Code of Ethics of the Real Estate and Business Brokers Act, 2002, the Code of Ethics and Standards of Business Practice of the Canadian Real Estate Association, the by-laws, rules and regulations of the said real estate Board(s)/Association(s) and the Act.

4. The Salesperson shall not:
    a) Reduce the amount of commission on any real estate representation agreement or customer service agreement if it is contrary to the Broker's office policies and practices, without the prior written authorization of the Brokerage. If the Salesperson breaches this provision, the amount by which any such commission is reduced shall be deducted from the Salesperson's share of the commission received;
    b) Sign any document or make any representation that would be binding on the Brokerage and would be contrary to the Brokerage's office policies and practices, without the Brokerage's prior written consent.

5. The Salesperson consents to the collection, use and disclosure of personal information of the Salesperson by the Brokerage for the purpose of a transfer, sale, or financing by the Brokerage of the business, or compliance with the requirements of the Real Estate Council of Ontario, or such other use of the personal information as the Brokerage deems appropriate in connection with managing or carrying on the affairs of the business.

6. This Agreement may be terminated without notice by either party subject to the provisions of the Employment Standards Act of Ontario. Upon the termination of the Salesperson's employment, the transfer or surrender of the Salesperson's registration shall be immediately sent to the Registrar appointed pursuant to the Act. The Salesperson agrees to immediately return all keys, signs, equipment and materials supplied by the Brokerage and to surrender all listing books, certificates, or other materials in accordance with the rules and regulations of the said real estate Board(s)/Association(s).

7. The Salesperson agrees that he/she will not assign, transfer or convey, pledge or encumber this Agreement or any interests hereunder without the prior written consent of the Brokerage.

8. This Agreement and all rules and regulations hereby incorporated by reference constitute the entire Agreement between the parties and there are no oral or written conditions, warranties, promises or inducements except as referred to herein and in Schedule(s) .... attached hereto.

IN WITNESS WHEREOF the parties hereto have hereunto set their hands and seals, and in the case of a corporation, the corporate seal and the hands of duly appointed officers in that behalf:

....   ● DATE ....
(Witness)   (Signature of Salesperson)   (Seal)

....   ● DATE ....
(Witness)   (Signature of Authorized Signing Officer of Brokerage)   (Seal)

....
(Name of Brokerage)   (Title)

Form 600   Revised 2009   **Page 1 of 1**

INDEPENDENT CONTRACTOR RESPONSIBILITIES

An independent contractor essentially is contracted by a brokerage to offer services by accessing selected facilities and equipment offered by that brokerage. In return, the independent contractor agrees to pay the brokerage fees (a percentage of gross commission earned and/or a flat fee). Of course, other fees can also apply such as transaction fees, brokerage administrative fees and other charges involving transactions (e.g., listing fees and sign installation fees), as deemed by the brokerage.

Such individual is not employed by the brokerage and does not have any relationship with that brokerage other than as a self-employed independent contractor. The range of services provided will vary and are typically set out by way of a schedule to the agreement.

The commission charged for services rendered relating to any transaction is determined solely by the salesperson and belongs to the salesperson. However, both the brokerage and the salesperson acknowledge that the *Real Estate and Business Brokers Act, 2002* requires that commission be collected only by the brokerage.

Independent contractor responsibilities are precisely outlined in the agreement, but will vary from one brokerage to another. The *Independent Contractor Salesperson's Agreement* (OREA Form 601) is included for information purposes. Independent contractor responsibilities are generally covered in *Article Three—General Conditions*, including automobile and related insurance, registration and professional dues, RECO insurance and so forth. Independent contractors, under this specific agreement, must acquire all supplies needed to provide services. In doing so, such supplies must conform with brokerage specifications and standards.

BROKERAGE RESPONSIBILITIES

The primary goods and services provided by the brokerage are set out in Schedule A of the *Independent Contractor Salesperson's Agreement* (OREA Form 601), which would be altered as necessary to suit individual brokerage policies. Certain brokerage and salesperson responsibilities are highlighted for emphasis.

New salespersons will find significant variations within individual brokerage contracts regarding responsibilities. A checklist is provided (See *Step 4: Getting Ready for the Brokerage*) to help assess what *is* or *is not* supplied by the brokerage.

OREA Ontario Real Estate Association

Independent Contractor
Salesperson's Agreement

Form 601
for use in the Province of Ontario

INDEPENDENT CONTRACTOR AGREEMENT:

BETWEEN: ...., hereinafter referred to as (the "Brokerage")

AND: ...., herein referred to as (the "Salesperson")

In this Agreement, the term "Salesperson" includes a Broker registered under the Real Estate and Business Brokers Act, 2002.

WHEREAS:
A. The Brokerage is a duly registered real estate brokerage pursuant to the Real Estate and Business Brokers Act, 2002 (Ontario) (the "Act") and the regulations made pursuant thereto (the "Regulations") and owns, for the purpose thereof, all facilities and equipment required to conduct a real estate brokerage business.
B. The Salesperson is an independent contractor desiring access to such facilities and equipment for the purpose of conducting therefrom a real estate business.

NOW THEREFORE in consideration of the mutual covenants and agreements and for other good and valuable consideration as herein provided, the receipt and sufficiency of which is hereby acknowledged, the parties hereto hereby agree as follows:

ARTICLE ONE – APPOINTMENT
1.1 The Brokerage hereby retains and appoints the Salesperson as an independent contractor in accordance with this Agreement and the Salesperson hereby accepts such appointment as an independent contractor upon and subject to the terms, conditions, covenants and provisions set forth herein. The parties acknowledge that the Salesperson is a self-employed independent contractor and is not and shall not represent himself or herself to be a partner or employee of the Brokerage or to have any relationship to the Brokerage other than as a self-employed independent contractor.

ARTICLE TWO – FACILITIES
2.1 The Brokerage shall make available the services, facilities and equipment provided for in Schedule "A" attached to this Agreement.

ARTICLE THREE – GENERAL CONDITIONS
3.1 The Salesperson shall govern their conduct by the Act and Regulations and the constitution, by-laws, Code of Ethics and Standards of Business Practice of the local real estate board/association of their membership (the "Board"), and all requirements of the Real Estate Council of Ontario ("RECO") all as may be amended from time to time.
3.2 The Salesperson shall furnish their own automobile and pay all expenses thereon and shall carry liability and property damage insurance satisfactory to the Brokerage. A minimum of $ .... is required for liability insurance.
The Salesperson shall provide proof of such insurance to the Brokerage upon request.
3.3 The Salesperson shall during the Term of this Agreement:
a) maintain in good standing all registrations required by the Act and Regulations necessary to trade in real estate;
b) be a member in good standing of RECO; and
c) be a member in good standing of the Board.
3.4 The Salesperson shall maintain errors and omissions and such other insurance as RECO may require from time to time.
3.5 The Salesperson shall obtain and maintain HST registration as required by the Excise Tax Act (Canada) as amended from time to time.
3.6 The Salesperson shall not obligate the Brokerage for goods or services.
3.7 The Salesperson shall only use such real estate forms that have been approved by the Brokerage prior to their use.
3.8 The Salesperson has read and agrees to the office policy as outlined in the Brokerage's office policy manual and agree to conduct themselves accordingly and in accordance with any amendments thereto communicated to the Salesperson in writing from time to time.
3.9 The Brokerage may set-off against the Salesperson's commission or other amounts the Brokerage may owe the Salesperson or any amount due to the Brokerage from the Salesperson including without limitation payable to the Brokerage pursuant to Article Five of this Agreement.

ARTICLE FOUR – COMMISSIONS
4.1 The full amount of all gross commissions resulting from real estate transactions procured by the Salesperson and received by the Brokerage as required by the Act shall be credited to the Salesperson's account and shall remain the property of the Salesperson.

4.2 All credit balances in the Salesperson's account shall be paid by the Brokerage to the Salesperson on a .... basis, net of fees and other amounts owed to the Brokerage by the Salesperson.
4.3 The commission to be charged for any transaction shall be determined solely by the Salesperson and shall belong to the Salesperson. The parties acknowledge that the Act requires that commission be collected only by the Brokerage.

ARTICLE FIVE – FEES, EXPENSES AND COSTS
5.1 The Salesperson agrees to pay the Brokerage the Fees set out in Plan "A" or "B", as applicable, which form part of this Agreement.

ARTICLE SIX – REPRESENTATION AGREEMENTS AND CUSTOMER SERVICE AGREEMENTS
6.1 All representation agreements and customer service agreements are the property of the Brokerage according to the Act during the term of this Agreement. Upon termination of this Agreement, the Brokerage agrees to terminate any representation agreements or customer service agreements procured by the Salesperson if the seller or buyer under the agreement approves.

ARTICLE SEVEN – ADVERTISING
7.1 All advertising to be approved by the Brokerage in advance.

INITIALS OF SALESPERSON: ( )   **INITIALS OF BROKER:** ( )

Form 601   Revised 2011   **Page 1 of 4**

ARTICLE EIGHT – TERMINATION

8.1   This Agreement may be terminated by either party at any time without cause upon 24 hours written notice that may be delivered personally or by facsimile. Upon termination both parties agree to complete their obligations herein in order to complete an orderly conclusion of their relationship. The Salesperson will not have any claim on real estate transactions that have not been procured from representation agreements prior to termination, or any future commissions therefrom.

8.2   Upon termination of this Agreement, the Salesperson will return to the Brokerage all keys, listings, listing books, blueprints, signs, plans, maps, supplies and sales literature received at any time from the Brokerage. The Salesperson agrees to pay the Brokerage for the value of such items that were not returned upon termination of this Agreement.

8.3   If on termination the Salesperson is indebted to the Brokerage then until such debt has been paid, the amount outstanding from time to time shall

bear interest at the rate of .... per cent per annum calculated and payable monthly.

ARTICLE NINE – TERM

9.1   Any and all changes to this Agreement from one year to the next will be announced at a meeting of the salespeople on or about ....
each year. This Agreement will commence on the date hereof and run until the end of the current calendar year and subject to announced changes, if any, and termination as provided for herein, this Agreement will automatically renew annually (the "Term").

ARTICLE TEN – BROKERAGE'S SUPPLIES

10.1   The Salesperson shall only use supplies which conform to the Brokerage's current specifications and standards, including signs, business cards, stationery and other items used for communications or presentations to customers and prospective customers and all promotional and novelty items.

ARTICLE ELEVEN – LITIGATION, DISPUTE AND ARBITRATION

11.1   If any transaction in which the Salesperson is involved results in a dispute, arbitration, litigation or legal expense, the Salesperson shall co-operate fully with the Brokerage in the resolution or prosecution of same.

11.2   The Brokerage reserves the right to determine whether or not any litigation or dispute concerning any transaction in which the Salesperson is involved shall be prosecuted, defended or settled, or whether or not legal expense shall be incurred.

ARTICLE TWELVE – DEPOSITS

12.1   All monies, documents or property received by the Salesperson in connection with any transaction shall be delivered to the Brokerage immediately. All cheques must be made payable to the Brokerage in accordance with the Act.

ARTICLE THIRTEEN – CORRESPONDENCE

13.1   All letters received and a copy of all letters written by the Salesperson pertaining to the business of the Brokerage shall be turned over to the Brokerage for its records and shall be the property of the Brokerage. All letters are to be approved by the Brokerage before mailing.

ARTICLE FOURTEEN – INDEMNITY

14.1   The Salesperson hereby indemnifies the Brokerage against all liability, loss, damages, costs and expenses sustained, suffered or incurred by the Brokerage as a result of any breach by the Salesperson of the Salesperson's obligations under this Agreement or as a result of any claim by a third party arising out of the Salesperson's real estate business activities. This indemnity shall survive the termination of this Agreement.

ARTICLE FIFTEEN – USE AND DISTRIBUTION OF PERSONAL INFORMATION

15.1   The Salesperson consents to the collection, use and disclosure of personal information of the Salesperson by the Brokerage for the purpose of a transfer, sale, or financing by the Brokerage of the business, or compliance with the requirements of the Real Estate Council of Ontario, or such other use of the personal information as the Brokerage deems appropriate in connection with managing or carrying on the affairs of the business.

ARTICLE SIXTEEN– GENERAL AGREEMENT TERMS

16.1   Either party may waive any default of the other party under this Agreement, but, no such waiver shall affect the rights of that party in respect of any subsequent default, whether of the same or a different nature.

16.2   This Agreement which includes Schedule(s) "A", ... and Plan A or Plan B as appropriate, shall constitute the entire agreement between the parties with respect to its subject matter and supersedes all prior agreements and understandings in any way relating to that subject matter. This Agreement can only be changed by a writing signed by both parties. No remedy conferred on a party under this Agreement, or by law, shall preclude the exercise by that party of any other remedy available to it in equity or in law in respect of the same default.

16.3   This Agreement is personal to the Salesperson and no right of the Salesperson under this Agreement may be assigned without the prior written consent of the Brokerage, which consent may be arbitrarily, or unreasonably withheld. The Brokerage may, without the consent of the Salesperson, assign any of its rights under the Agreement and, following such assignment, shall be relieved of all obligations in respect of the rights so assigned. Subject to the foregoing, this Agreement shall enure to the benefit and be binding upon the parties and their respective heirs, executors, administrators, successors and permitted assigns.

16.4   The use of section headings in this Agreement is for convenience of reference only and shall not affect the interpretation of this Agreement.

16.5   All notices or other communications required or permitted under this Agreement to be given by one party to the other shall be in writing and shall be given by personal delivery (including courier), or by facsimile to the party as follows:

   a) if to the Brokerage, at Attn: ....

      Fax: (.....................)...

   b) if to the Salesperson, at Attn: ....

      Fax: (.....................)...

   Any such notice or communication shall be deemed received on the earlier of actual receipt, if delivered or on the date transmitted, if by facsimile unless received after 5:00 p.m. on a business day (i.e. a day other than a Saturday or Sunday or statutory holiday in Ontario) in which case receipt will be deemed to be on the next business day. Either party may change its address for service by giving notice thereof pursuant to the term of this Section.

16.6   Each party agrees, at the request of the other party, to do, execute and give such further and other acts, documents and assurances as may be reasonably requested in order to give full effect to this Agreement and to the transactions contemplated herein.

IN WITNESS whereof the parties have duly signed this Agreement as of the date indicated.

....	....	● DATE ....
(Witness)	(Signature of Salesperson)	(Seal)
....	....	● DATE ....
(Witness)	(Signature of Authorized Signing Officer of Brokerage)	(Seal)

Form 601   Revised 2011   **Page 2 of 4**

OREA Form 601   *Independent Contractor Salesperson's Agreement, Page 3 of 4*

OREA Ontario Real Estate Association

Form 601
for use in the Province of Ontario

Schedule "A"
Independent Contractor – Salesperson's Agreement

1. Secretarial services during normal office business hours.

2. Reception area.

3. Desk space as determined by the Brokerage.

4. Reasonable sales and administrative training, as determined by the Brokerage.

5. Use of telephone and fax facilities.

6. Standard office equipment as customarily provided in a real estate brokerage business.

7. Reasonable quantity of stationery.

8. Photocopying facility.

9. Sales Information Sheet (Trade Record) will be prepared by secretary.

10. A reasonable number of "For Sale" and "Open House" signs.

11. Multiple Listing Service processing fees and re-processing fees, where previously authorized.

12. Client and customer referral(s).

13. Listing fees, stand sign installation.

14. Courier facilities.

15. Business cards.

16. Office duty time.

17. Standard newspaper advertising program, as determined by the Brokerage. Salespersons may advertise over and above the Brokerage's program, at their own expense, provided they meet all governing provincial and local rules and regulations.

18. Brokerage to assist in all areas that are deemed essential to complete a real estate transaction if requested by the Salesperson.

19. All salespersons shall sign the inventory list.

20. Such other items and service as the Brokerage may in its sole discretion agree to provide to the Salesperson. The Brokerage has the right at any time without notice to increase or decrease said service.

21. ....

    ....

    ....

    ....

Form 601   Revised 2011   **Page 3 of 4**

PLAN "A" – FEES PAYABLE TO BROKERAGE

To compensate for administrative and operating costs incurred by the Brokerage in providing the items and services in Schedule "A" the Salesperson shall pay the Brokerage:

1A .... % of the Salesperson's net commissions on the portion of total net annual commissions not exceeding $ ....

1B .... % of the Salesperson's net commissions on the portion of total net annual commissions not exceeding $ ....

1C .... % of the Salesperson's net commissions on the portion of total net annual commissions not exceeding $ ....

1D .... % of the Salesperson's net commissions on the portion of total net annual commissions not exceeding $ ....

1E .... % of the Salesperson's net commissions on the portion of total net annual commissions not exceeding $ ....

1F .... % of the Salesperson's net commissions on the portion of total net annual commissions not exceeding $ ....

1G .... % of the Salesperson's net commissions on the portion of total net annual commissions not exceeding $ ....

Under Plan "A" plateaus will be calculated on commissions received within the contract year. Effective, on each and every anniversary date, the plateau level will start at the beginning and the Salesperson will be paid accordingly. Furthermore, in the event of any switch in plans at the Salesperson's anniversary date, they will be paid by the rules of the Plan they were on at the time the business was written.

Salesperson will be responsible to pay for:

   a)   Monthly and yearly dues and fees and other charges as charged by the Board, the Ontario Real Estate Association and the Canadian Real Estate Association;

   b)   Registration/renewal fees, monthly and yearly fees and other fees charged to the Salesperson by RECO.

Salesperson shall pay all dues and fees and miscellaneous items outstanding at the end of each calendar year and the following year's Board yearly dues by cheque on or before January 1 of the following new year.

PLAN "A" AGREEMENT

I, ... (Salesperson) hereby agree to PLAN "A".

....
(Signature of Salesperson)   (Signature of Authorized Signing Officer of Brokerage)

PLAN "B" – FEES PAYABLE TO BROKERAGE

To compensate the Brokerage for administrative and operating costs incurred by the Brokerage in providing the items and services in Schedule "A" the Salesperson shall pay the Brokerage:

1A .... % of the Salesperson's net commissions on the portion of total net annual commissions not exceeding $ ....
     The above compensation for the Brokerage applies to all transactions.

1B Plus ....

     Dollars ($ ....) desk fee per month is payable on the first day of each and every month.

     A .... interest charge per month (.................................... per annum) for late payment will be charged. The desk fee includes all the items and services as set out in Schedule "A" contained herein, except as follows:

     This plan includes .... (..) listing fees annually

     This plan includes .... (..) standard sign installations annually

Over these specific amounts, the Salesperson is responsible for, said costs and will be billed accordingly on a monthly basis. An inventory of the Salesperson's listings and sign installations will be taken prior to commencement of the contract period and shall be counted against his/her yearly maximum for that contract period.

PLAN "B" AGREEMENT

I, ... (Salesperson) hereby agree to PLAN "B".

....
(Signature of Salesperson)   (Signature of Authorized Signing Officer of Brokerage)

Form 601   Revised 2011   **Page 4 of 4**

SECTION IV   PREPARING FOR YOUR NEW CAREER

STEP 3: Assemble Needed Expertise

Salespeople need expert advice, particularly those deciding to be independent contractors. The following is by suggestion only. Individual circumstances will dictate the exact plan of action.

AUTO INSURANCE	HOME INSURANCE	ACCOUNTING	TECHNOLOGY	LEGAL
Check with your insurance broker regarding appropriate vehicle coverage for clients and customers travelling in your car.	Check with your insurance broker concerning home office coverage (if applicable). Don't forget about applicable liability coverage if clients and customers will be coming to your home office.	Obtain expert accounting advice regarding personal record keeping, allowable expenses and taxation issues. Selected taxation and benefit topics are addressed later in this chapter. Accounting advice is particularly important in the case of independent contractors.	Seek out appropriate experts for advice on computer hardware, real estate software and telecommunications equipment.	Make certain that any legal matters relating to contracts (including the employment or independent contractor agreement) are discussed with legal counsel prior to signing.

STEP 4: Get Ready for the Brokerage

In preparation for the first day, this handy checklist helps determine what you need to bring to the brokerage, what is supplied, what procedures apply and what arrangements must be made. The checklist also helps formulate questions to ask during the brokerage orientation process and provides a final check to ensure that relevant topics are addressed in that orientation.

GETTING READY CHECKLIST

Staff Services	What specific services are available during normal business hours? Who is responsible for these services?	**Hardware/ Software**	What computer equipment is available for salespeople to use within the brokerage? What hardware/software best aligns with systems currently in use in the brokerage?
Desk Space	How is desk space allocated? What fees apply (if applicable)? What equipment and supplies are provided by the brokerage for that office space?	**E-Mail**	How is e-mail communication handled in the brokerage? Do I set up a separate e-mail account or is it centrally administered by the brokerage?
Telephone	What is provided, what additional costs are incurred by salespersons and how is long distance handled (e.g., costs, procedures and access codes)?	**Internet**	What Internet access is provided to salespeople?
Pager/ Cell Phone	Does the brokerage have a pager system? Are there any special arrangements or pricing when acquiring a pager, cell phone, personal digital assistant (PDA) or similar equipment?	**Postage/ Courier**	How is postage handled regarding single or bulk mailings? What about costs when documentation has to be couriered?
Office Equipment (Photocopier, Fax, Etc.)	What office equipment is provided to salespeople? What additional costs are borne by the salesperson? How are these costs allocated; e.g., card access for photocopier, fax and so forth.	**Website/ Promotion**	What procedures do I follow to have access to the brokerage website for promotion/ advertising? Can I link a personal website to the main site and what brokerage requirements must be followed? What costs am I responsible for?
Office Supplies	What office supplies (including paper and envelopes) are supplied?		

continued

GETTING READY CHECKLIST *(continued)*

Office Access/ Security	What are normal office hours? Is a key or alternative security access (i.e., access code) required for after hours? What other security provisions must be followed (e.g., locked unattended offices and desks). What guidelines does the brokerage have regarding personal safety when listing and showing property?	**Working with Sellers**	What forms are used and procedures followed when working with sellers as clients and customers?
Office Duty (Opportunity) Time	Is office duty time allocated by the brokerage? What is the schedule and are there any specific procedures that must be followed?	**Working with Buyers**	What forms are used and procedures followed when working with buyers as clients and customers?
Multiple Listing Service®/Board Membership	What forms must be completed and what costs are involved? What processing fees apply when listing property on MLS®? What costs are borne by the brokerage or, alternatively, how are these costs and fees billed to salespeople? What about renewals?	**Listings**	How are listings processed internally within the brokerage and what assistance is provided in that regard? What approval and related procedures are in place that must be followed? What costs, such as administrative or other fees, are the salesperson's responsibility (in addition to MLS®-related fees)?
For Sale Signs/ Frames/ Installation	What does the brokerage provide in terms of *for sale* signs, sign frames, sign information boxes. What about custom signage and add-on promotion pieces? What costs are involved for sign installations?	**Agreements**	How are agreements prepared in the brokerage in readiness for presentation and possible acceptance? What software program is used? Make certain that you obtain the most up-to-date clauses.
Business Cards	Are business cards supplied? If not, what brokerage standards must be adhered to in ordering cards?	**Negotiations**	How are multiple offer situations handled? What steps are taken when processing deposits and what other circumstances and procedures should I beware of; e.g., buying and selling for my own purposes?
Advertising	What standard advertising formats are used by the brokerage, what costs apply and how are classified advertisements processed by the brokerage?	**Transactions**	How are accepted agreements of purchase and sale processed in the brokerage and what administrative or other brokerage fees (if any) apply that have not already been identified in this checklist?
Promotional Pieces	The brokerage may supply various promotional pieces or have them available for purchase. If so, what items are available; e.g., feature sheets, brochures, flyers, cards and open house signs?	**Privacy**	What is the privacy policy of the brokerage? What specific provisions apply to activities of salespeople? Is there a privacy brochure?
		Office Meetings	Are there regularly scheduled office meetings?
Forms	What forms (e.g., listings, agreements, trade record sheets and supporting forms) are provided by the brokerage and at what cost (if applicable)?	**Training**	What training is provided by the brokerage and what costs (if any) are borne by the salespeople?
		Referrals	What office procedures apply when making referrals?

STARTING AT THE BROKERAGE

Brokerages, depending on their size, may offer an information orientation either informally provided by the broker of record or manager and/or a more formal, one to four hour, group session for new salespeople. Regardless, the program is designed to acquaint the new recruit with policies and procedures, scope of duties/responsibilities, compensation/ benefit policies and basic operating practices.

The typical orientation would also include distribution of written documentation/ materials and a tour of the brokerage. As mentioned earlier, orientation program content and certain documentation will vary based on whether the brokerage uses employment or independent contractor agreements.

Orientation also provides the opportunity to convey the underlying values of the organization and its goals as they relate to salesperson conduct and productivity. A well-run orientation can be a very positive experience by:

- Answering most key questions, thereby minimizing future confusion and wasted time.
- Clarifying many aspects of the job and the realities of being successful in real estate sales.
- Minimizing tension and reducing anxieties typically associated with the challenges of a new career.
- Providing an opportunity to gain a comfort level with the brokerage and its overall operation.

First and foremost, RECO registration documents must be fully completed and forwarded. This would normally be done in advance of the orientation, but key points are included for reference purposes. At the orientation, the brokerage will provide certain materials to the new salesperson and seek written confirmation that these have been received and that the individual agrees with the policies/procedures set out. Further, forms relating to taxation and benefits will also have to be completed. General information about real estate board membership is also included, but entrance and ongoing board fees vary throughout the province.

Selected items are described for general guidance only. Additional fees can apply depending on individual circumstances and career choices made. Make certain that you are apprised of all documentation and fees at point of orientation.

STEP 1: Finalize RECO Registration

The application titled *Application for New/Reinstatement: Broker/Salesperson* must be fully completed and forwarded to RECO, along with the prescribed fee and applicable transcript from *The Residential Real Estate Transaction* or *The Commercial Real Estate Transaction*. To access the current application form, go to **www.reco.on.ca**. When applying to become registered as a salesperson or broker, you must declare in SECTION C of the application if you have any pending charges, if you have been found guilty, pleaded guilty to, or have been convicted of an offence under any law. In addition to this declaration you must provide a Canadian criminal record check from your local police or OPP detachment upon submitting your registration application to RECO.

Individuals looking to become registered as a broker or salesperson should request the record check well in advance of applying for registration since some jurisdictions are experiencing a high volume of requests and may take 8 weeks or more to process the report.

RECO PROCESSING STEPS

- Application received and name search conducted.
- Application checked for completeness and thoroughly reviewed.
- Additional searches carried out if needed; e.g., Sheriff's search for writs.
- Insurance premium invoice is issued once initial review is completed.

NOTE: Application delays are often due to errors made when completing the Application for New/Reinstatement: Broker/Salesperson. Go to *www.reco.on.ca* for a downloadable application form.

RE CO Real Estate Council of Ontario

3300 Bloor St. W.
West Tower, Suite 1200
Toronto, Ontario M8X 2X2

Tel: 416-207-4800
Toll Free: 1-800-245-6910
Fax: 416-207-4820
E-mail: registration@reco.on.ca
Website: www.reco.on.ca
MyWeb: https://myweb.reco.on.ca

REBBA 2002
Real Estate & Business Brokers Act, 2002

For office use only – Date recieved

FOR OFFICE USE ONLY	
Approved By:	Date:
Registration No.:	
Scanning Code	
NEW ☐ RST☐ CAT☐	

Form ANRBS / July 2014

Important: PRINT or TYPE all information in BLACK INK

Application for New/Reinstatement: Broker/Salesperson

All new applicants and reinstatements over 60 days must submit a current, original Canadian Criminal Record Check with this form.

SECTION A

Type of Application:

☐ New Registration

☐ New Registration - Previously/Currently
    Registered in Another Province/Territory

☐ Reinstatement of Previous Registration

Registration Category (Check One):

☐ Salesperson under the *Real Estate and Business Brokers Act, 2002*

☐ Broker under the *Real Estate and Business Brokers Act, 2002*

Last Name	Full First Name	Birth Date			Sex
		YEAR	MONTH	DAY	☐M ☐F

Middle Name	Trade Name *(See page 3 for Completion Instructions)*

Residence Address - *(If R.R.: Give Lot, Concession No. & Township) (Street Number & Name)*	Apt. or Suite	Residence Telephone No.

City	Province	Postal Code	E-mail Address	Fax No.

Address for service in Ontario *(If different from Residence Address. Must be a street address)*	Apt. or Suite	Telephone No.

City	Province	Postal Code	E-mail Address	Fax No.

SECTION B

Provide employment history for previous 2 years, including a description of any period in which you were not employed.

Name and Address of Employer (If applicable)	Description of Activity such as type of work / position / school / travel, etc	Period (previous 2 years)	
		From (yr/m/d)	To (yr/m/d)

SECTION C

Please review the Completion Instructions on Page 3, before answering YES or NO to the following questions. If you answer yes to any question and have not previously disclosed in writing, you must do so now. If you have previously disclosed this information please indicate "already on file" beneath the corresponding question. (Refer to Completion Instructions on Page 3).

1. (a) Are you a Canadian Resident who is a Canadian Citizen?   ☐ Yes ☐ No
    (b) Are you a Canadian Resident who is a Landed Immigrant? (If yes, refer to Page 3 for Completion Instructions.)   ☐ Yes ☐ No

2. Are you, or will you be, engaged or employed in any other business, occupation or profession? (If yes, refer to Page 3 for Completion Instructions.)   ☐ Yes ☐ No

3. Are you a partner, officer, director or shareholder in any other registered real estate business? (If yes, refer to Page 3 for Completion Instructions.)   ☐ Yes ☐ No

4. Are you now or have you been involved in personal bankruptcy and/or been an officer, director or majority shareholder of a corporation which has been declared bankrupt or insolvent, or is presently a party to bankruptcy or insolvency proceedings? (If yes, refer to Page 3 for Completion Instructions.)   ☐ Yes ☐ No

5. Are there any unpaid judgments and/or unpaid debts outstanding against you? (If yes, refer to Page 3 for Completion Instructions.)   ☐ Yes ☐ No

6. Have you had a registration and/or licence or professional status of any kind refused, suspended, revoked, or cancelled and/or have you been involved in any proceeding during which you resigned a registration or licence or professional status of any kind, or are there any proceedings pending? (If yes, refer to Page 3 for Completion Instructions.)   ☐ Yes ☐ No

7. Are there currently any charges pending, or have you been found guilty, pleaded guilty to, or been convicted of an offence under any law? (If yes, refer to Page 3 for Completion Instructions.)   ☐ Yes ☐ No

Important: PRINT or TYPE all information in BLACK INK
Application for New/Reinstatement: Broker/Salesperson

Page 2 of 6
Form ANRBS

SECTION D (For New Registrants Only)

The Residential Real Estate Transaction or The Commercial Real Estate Transaction course in support of this application must have been completed within 12 months of application date. Please see Page 4 for Requirements for Reinstatements.

SECTION E (For New Registrants from Other Provinces/Territories Only)

- The Interprovincial Challenge Examination transcript must be included with this application.

- Original copy of your registration and disciplinary history from the licensing body in your current or previous province/territory must be included with this application.

- Please see Page 4 for Completion Instructions - Section E

SECTION F
NOTICE & CONSENT

Any person completing and/or signing and/or submitting this form and any attachments or accompanying answers, schedules, documents, records, statements or returns, either written or oral, ("accompanying documentation") is hereby notified that the Real Estate Council of Ontario ("RECO") may verify the information on this form or the accompanying documentation, and in so doing, may request or collect additional information from, communicate with, disclose any such information to government and non government bodies (which may include trade associations, designated education organizations and providers, and past, present, and prospective employers). You are notified that any information so collected or communicated will be for purposes that include, but are not limited to:

1. Determining an applicant's eligibility for registration or continued entitlement to registration under the *Real Estate and Business Brokers Act, 2002* and its regulations and including any amendments or successor legislation ("REBBA 2002"), ensuring compliance under REBBA 2002, dealing and/or handling complaints and inquiries under REBBA 2002;

2. Purposes consistent with the Safety and Consumers Statutes Administration Act, 1996 and its regulations, RECO's purposes and obligations under the Canada Corporations Act and its regulations, RECO's Letters Patent and its corporate by-laws, and the Administrative Agreement;

3. For any other purpose consistent with the administration of REBBA 2002, consumer protection, protecting the public, and/or verification of an applicant's association or membership with trade/professional associations, registration history, including status, dates, employer's name and business address.

I understand and consent that as part of the above process, RECO may, at any time and from time to time, make inquiries and/or obtain searches of government, regulatory, discipline, or law enforcement records and databases, a record of offences, a record of judgments, financial institution records, or consumer reports. I further understand and consent that, RECO may, at any time and from time to time, during my registration cycle make additional inquiries and/or obtain additional searches of government, regulatory, discipline, or law enforcement records and databases, a record of offences, a record of judgments, financial institution records, or consumer reports.

I am aware that RECO is obligated to disclose information in accordance with law and is bound by REBBA 2002, including sections 44 and 48 of REBBA 2002 and sections 11 and 27 of the Regulation (General) under REBBA 2002.

By completing or signing or submitting this form and any of the accompanying documents, I consent to RECO verifying, requesting, collecting, communicating, disclosing, using, and maintaining such information in the manner provided above.

If you have any questions concerning the collection or disclosure or use of any information, please contact RECO.

Important: PRINT or TYPE all information in BLACK INK
Application for New/Reinstatement: Broker/Salesperson

Page 3 of 6
Form ANRBS

SECTION G			
WARNING – IT IS AN OFFENCE TO PROVIDE FALSE INFORMATION ON THIS APPLICATION			
APPLICANT'S SIGNATURE			
APPLICANT	Signature of Applicant	Registration No.	Date

CERTIFICATE OF EMPLOYER	
EMPLOYER	*I hereby certify that I have personally reviewed this application (after being completed and signed by the applicant) with the applicant and declare that the information given by the applicant is to the best of my knowledge and belief true, and request that registration be granted.*
	Registered Name of Employer / Registration No.
	Name of Authorized Signing Official (Please Print) / Signature
	Title / Date

COMPLETION INSTRUCTIONS – SECTION A
Individuals may elect to trade in real estate using just one or more of your legal given names in the correct order, a recognized short form of one of your legal given names, an anglicised version of your legal given name (an affidavit is required in support of this option) followed by your legal surname.

COMPLETION INSTRUCTIONS – SECTION C		
Question	1 (b)	If you answered yes, you must submit a copy of your Landed Immigrant Status papers, IMM1000 or a copy of your Permanent Resident cards (copy of front and back).
Question	2	If you answered yes, the information required includes:
		1. The full name of the business as well as the position held and the nature or description of the business, occupation or profession.
		2. If the other employment involves activity that falls under the definition of "trade" found in the Act, you must provide a copy of the complete job description supplied by the employer.
Question	3	If you answered yes, you must submit full particulars on a signed and dated statement.
Question	4	If you answered yes, you must submit full particulars on a signed and dated statement, along with a copy of the following documents: • Form 69: Assignment of Bankruptcy • Form 79: Statement of Assets, Liabilities • Form 65: Monthly Income & Expense Statement • Form 84: Certificate of Discharge (If applicable)
Question	5	If you answered yes, you must submit a copy of each judgment and other such documents pertaining to outstanding debts against you (example; garnishments, requirements to pay, writs of execution etc.). State the amount outstanding and repayment arrangements on a separate sheet. You must also submit full particulars regarding the circumstances that led to the matter(s) on a signed and dated statement.
Question	6	If you answered yes, you must submit full particulars on a signed and dated statement. A driver's abstract may be required in the case of a suspension.
Question	7	All new applicants and reinstatements over 60 days must submit a current, original Canadian Criminal Record Check (must be dated within 6 months of submission of application) as well as anyone that answers "yes". If "yes" is indicated individuals must also submit the full particulars on a signed and dated statement. This does not include municipal parking violations or minor Highway Traffic Act offences unless your driver's license was suspended. **This includes a charge where a conditional discharge or an absolute discharge has been granted.**

Important: PRINT or TYPE all information in BLACK INK
Application for New/Reinstatement: Broker/Salesperson

Page 4 of 6
Form ANRBS

COMPLETION INSTRUCTIONS – SECTION D

Education Requirements For Reinstatement Of First Time Salespersons

Registrants within the first two-year registration cycle under REBBA 2002 immediately prior to the termination of registration must successfully complete three additional educational courses designated by the registrar before making an application for reinstatement of registration. The courses are as follows: Real Property Law, The Commercial Real Estate Transaction or The Residential Real Estate Transaction course not completed for initial registration and one of four elective courses.

Failure to fulfill these educational requirements is a breach of Reg. 579/05, s.2(1), and your application will not be processed until the educational requirements are met.

Continuing Education Requirements for Reinstatement

As of August 1, 2013, registrants must complete one of the following options prior to submitting an application to reinstate a registration.
- Complete the new online Continuing Education Program via MYWEB, consisting of either the Residential **or** Commercial Update course, as well as two of the available online electives.

OR
- Complete the requirements of the original continuing education program, consisting of either the Residential **or** Commercial Update course, plus one CE credit for each additional month or partial month you were registered during your last registration cycle, prior to submitting an application to reinstate your registration. The Residential Update Course or Commercial Update Course must not have been declared on a prior application to RECO, and as of August 1, 2013 will only be available online via MYWEB. Your last registration cycle runs continuously from the commencement of the last renewal/reinstatement date of registration until the date the registration was terminated.

For more information regarding the continuing education requirements to apply to reinstate registration, please contact education@reco.on.ca.

COMPLETION INSTRUCTIONS – SECTION E

Requirements For New Registrants Previously/Currently Registered in Another Province/Territory

For more information on qualifying jurisdictions and the Interprovincial Challenge Examination please visit RECO's website www.reco.on.ca.

A copy of the transcript confirming successful completion of the Interprovincial Challenge Examination is required in support of this application.

An original copy of your registration history and verification of any disciplinary action, or the absence of same, received from the regulatory body in your current or previous province/territory is required in support of this application.

Applications received WITHOUT the applicable transcript and registration/disciplinary history will not be processed.

ERRORS & OMISSIONS

Failure to pay the Errors and Omissions Insurance that will be invoiced to you will be a breach of REBBA 2002 and will result in the loss of registration under REBBA 2002 and your right to trade in real estate.

REGISTRATION FEES

Payment can be made by Cheque, Bank Draft, Money Order, Visa or MasterCard made payable to the
"Real Estate Council of Ontario".

DO NOT SEND CASH BY MAIL

FEES: Broker $350 Salesperson $350

EFFECTIVE APRIL 1, 2010, SALESPERSON FEE INCREASED TO $350.

There will be an additional service charge of $35.00 for any returned cheques.

IF FURTHER ASSISTANCE IS REQUIRED, PLEASE CONTACT RECO AT 416-207-4800 OR TOLL FREE AT 1-800-245-6910

PLEASE E-MAIL (registration@reco.on.ca) OR FAX THE COMPLETED APPLICATION TO RECO.

Important: PRINT or TYPE all information in BLACK INK
Application for New/Reinstatement: Broker/Salesperson

Page 5 of 6
Form ANRBS

DECLARATION OF CONTINUING EDUCATION - REINSTATEMENT ONLY

IMPORTANT INFORMATION

- This declaration form must be submitted along with an application to renew registration. Applications received WITHOUT a properly completed and signed declaration form will not be processed.
- You must complete the Residential Update Course or the Commercial Update Course and either 18 elective CE credits from accredited providers or the new Continuing Education program available online as of August 1, 2013.
- Failure to fulfill the continuing education requirements is a breach of Regulation 579/05 and your application cannot be processed, resulting in loss of registration under the *Real Estate and Business Brokers Act, 2002*, and loss of your right to trade in real estate.

INSTRUCTIONS

1. The Residential Update Course or the Commercial Update Course must be declared by all registrants/applicants by completing the applicable section(s) below.
2. If you are declaring successful completion of the new Residential Update Course or the Commercial Update Course **PLUS** 2 electives delivered online by RECO, you must complete sections A & B.
3. If you are declaring successful completion of 18 elective credits offered under the current continuing education program, you must also declare successful completion of the Residential Update Course or the Commercial Update Course either the current course delivered by OREA, or the new online course delivered by RECO. You must then complete sections A & C.

Last name	First name	Middle name
RECO Registration No.:		OREA Student No. (OPTIONAL):

SECTION A – RESIDENTIAL UPDATE COURSE OR COMMERCIAL UPDATE COURSE COMPLETION

COMPLETION DATE:	YEAR / MONTH / DAY

SECTION B – ELECTIVE COURSES DELIVERED BY RECO

I have completed a minimum of 2 online elective courses through the new MCE Program   ☐ Yes   ☐ No

SECTION C – APPROVED CONTINUING EDUCATION COURSES

Course/Seminar Title	Name of Education Provider	Date Course / Seminar Completed (Year/Month/Day)	CREDITS
		YEAR / MONTH / DAY	
		YEAR / MONTH / DAY	
		YEAR / MONTH / DAY	
		YEAR / MONTH / DAY	
		YEAR / MONTH / DAY	
		YEAR / MONTH / DAY	
		YEAR / MONTH / DAY	
Credits carried forward from a previous reporting period (if any). *NOTE: Additional external credits reported on this renewal WILL NOT be carried forward into the new MCE Program*			
Total Credits (24 credits = Residential Update Course or Commercial Update Course 6 credits + 18 credits from external courses under previous CE program)			

DECLARATION

I declare that I have taken and completed the courses/seminars listed above and, upon request, I will furnish RECO with evidence of having taken any or all of the courses/seminars listed in this Declaration. **I also declare that I have not previously reported these courses on any Declaration.** This Declaration forms part of the Application for Renewal and is subject to all notices, consents, penalties, and other provisions contained therein or applicable to such Application by means of statutory or other legal requirements.

_____   _____
Signature   Date

PRINT

RESET

Real Estate Council of Ontario
3300 Bloor St. W., West Tower, Suite 1200
Toronto, Ontario M8X 2X2

RE CO

REBBA
Real Estate & Business Brokers Act, 2002

Tel: 416-207-4800
Toll Free: 1-800-245-6910
Fax: 416-207-4820
E-mail: registration@reco.on.ca
Website: www.reco.on.ca
MyWeb: https://myweb.reco.on.ca
Updated July 2014

Important: PRINT or TYPE all information in <u>BLACK INK</u>

CREDIT CARD PAYMENT

**PLEASE NOTE THAT INCOMPLETE CREDIT CARD PAYMENT FORMS <u>CANNOT BE PROCESSED</u>.
PLEASE ENSURE THAT ALL FIELDS ARE COMPLETED IN FULL TO ENABLE US TO PROCESS YOUR APPLICATION.**

PAYMENT INFORMATION

Name(s) of applicants	Registration number	Fee

CREDIT CARD INFORMATION

Check appropriate box: ☐ VISA ☐ MASTERCARD

Cardholder's name: _____

Card No. ☐☐☐☐-☐☐☐☐-☐☐☐☐-☐☐☐☐

Expiry Date: _____ / _____
           Month   Year

Signature: _____ Date: _____

E-mail: _____
Please note: the email address provided on this form will replace the one currently on file with the RECO (if applicable) and will be utilized as the primary email address for all future electronic communications. Should you wish to amend the address in the future you may do so by visiting My Web and making the necessary amendments.

Real Estate Council of Ontario • Tel: 416-207-4800 • Toll Free: 1-800-245-6910 • Fax: 416-207-4820 • E-mail: registration@reco.on.ca

> **EXAMPLE**   *RECO Fees*
>
> Salesperson James is finalizing his budget which includes various fees and dues when joining a local real estate brokerage. As a salesperson, James' RECO fees are as follows:
>
> | | |
> |---|---|
> | **Salesperson Registration** *(Every Two Years Based on 2016)* | $350.00 |
> | **RECO Insurance Payment** *(Annual based on 2015–2016)* | $417.00 |

STEP 2: Review the Policy Manual

The brokerage may have a formal policy manual setting out detailed procedures and practices. New salespeople should be aware that no standard policy manual exists for real estate brokerages, owing in large part to divergent operating methods throughout the province. Carefully review any such materials to ensure that they are consistent with the employment or independent contract agreement that you have, or are about to, sign.

STEP 3: Complete Necessary Records

The brokerage will require certain personal information for each new salesperson, as every brokerage must maintain up-to-date records for employees and independent contractors. Current software programs used by brokerages provide for the inclusion of extensive profiles that include personal information, registration expiry details, anniversary date of contract (employment or independent contractor) and applicable commission plan details.

BENEFITS/DEDUCTIONS

Taxation	Employed salespersons must complete a TD1X form regarding level of tax to be deducted. Every employee of a brokerage is required to file the prescribed form with the employer certifying the amount of income tax exemptions claimed. This form must be filed when he/she starts employment with a new employer or when a change in personal circumstances occurs, which affects the net claim. In the case of salaried employees, the TD1 form is used. Neither form is used with independent contractors, as they remit tax directly to the Canada Revenue Agency and brokerages do not withhold tax.
Harmonized Sales Tax (HST)	Matters concerning harmonized sales tax for employed commission salespeople are handled by the brokerage. The independent contractor is responsible for calculations and recordkeeping regarding HST payments, input tax credits and the filing of applicable tax returns. Independent contractors registered for HST purposes collect harmonized sales tax on sales of taxable goods and services. The independent contractor, as an HST registrant, may receive credit for HST paid on eligible business purchases, referred to as input tax credits, which may be claimed against HST collected that must be remitted to the Canada Revenue Agency. Independent contractors are well advised to seek expert accounting advice regarding harmonized sales tax.

Canada Pension Plan (CPP)	Employed commission salespeople who meet eligibility requirements under the Canada Pension Plan will have deductions made by the brokerage in line with current contribution requirements. Individuals meeting these requirements include:

- Individuals who are 18 years of age, but not having reached 70;
- Employed in pensionable employment during the year. Note: Real estate commission earned as an employed salesperson is considered to be pensionable income.
- Not presently receiving a Canadian retirement or disability pension.

CPP calculations for employed commission salespeople involve pro-rating calculation based on the amount of commission up to the maximum contribution set for each year.

NOTE: Deduction tables are provided for salaried employees on hourly, weekly, semi-monthly and monthly pay periods. The brokerage, as the employer, must match the contribution made by the employed commission salesperson.

Independent contractors must remit Canada Pension Plan contributions directly to the Canada Revenue Agency. Their contribution must include both employee and employer portions.

Employment Insurance (EI)	Employed commission salespeople and other employees of the brokerage pay employment insurance (EI) premiums, based on insurable earnings. A maximum contribution is set each year by the Canada Revenue Agency. The employer contribution is 1.4 times the contribution of the employed salesperson. Independent contractors are not required to make employment insurance contributions.
Other Deductions/ Fees	The brokerage, depending on the commission arrangement and internal structure, may have certain deductions from commission or other fees payable on a monthly basis. Typically, these are set out in the employment or independent contractor agreement. Such items might include desk fees, advertising levies, recoverable expenses (expenses paid by the brokerage and subsequently billed to the salesperson), listing or transaction fees and/or general administrative fees. Make certain that you clearly understand the nature of these deductions/fees and ensure that appropriate explanatory documentation is provided by the brokerage.

STEP 4: Apply for Real Estate Board Membership
(If Applicable)

Brokerages that are members of organized real estate will require completion of all membership application forms. Entrance and ongoing fees must be paid not only to the real estate board, but also to the Ontario Real Estate Association and The Canadian Real Estate Association. As board fees vary throughout the province, a hypothetical example is provided for illustration purposes.

EXAMPLE   *Board Membership*

Salesperson James has received his RECO registration and is completing necessary membership forms for the local real estate board. Two sets of fees apply: entrance fees *(one-time only)* and membership dues *(yearly)*. The total fees are as follows:

Entrance Fees		Membership Fees (Annual)	
Real Estate Board	$450	Real Estate Board—MLS® Dues	$800
Ontario Real Estate Association	$200	Ontario Real Estate Association	$510
Canadian Real Estate Association	$200	& Canadian Real Estate Association	

What Supplies Do I Need?   CURIOSITY

A salesperson's shopping list will vary based on individual circumstances, the particular market niche(s) being served and services provided by the brokerage. Here are a few suggestions:

- Tape measure (metric/imperial: minimum 25') or a digital measuring device.
- Cell phone, pager or PDA (check with brokerage for recommendations/guidance; real estate boards may have discounted rates).
- Digital camera (nothing too fancy, just small and practical with reasonable resolution for listing photos, website ads and so forth).
- Picture(s) for business card and other advertising/ promotion.
- Hanging files and folders.

- Desk organizer, pens, note pads, highlighters and binders.
- Laptop computer (with appropriate software; e.g., offer drafting, word processing and specialized real estate software (check with brokerage for recommendations and guidance concerning real estate software)). Also consider visual presentation software (e.g., PowerPoint) for listing presentation.
- Daily planner, including week/month in advance feature.
- Briefcase and/or carrying bag.

HANDLING OFFICE DYNAMICS

Start off on a positive note when first entering the brokerage. Remember, the image and attitude that you portray directly affects your relationship and ongoing communication with others.

STEP 1: Start Building a Presence as Soon as You Arrive

Your first day sets the stage for the rest of your time with that brokerage. You must believe in yourself and your abilities. Remember, people naturally gravitate to those with a positive, confident attitude. When first arriving, you are out of your comfort zone and have to make that extra effort to bridge the gap with people, to engage others and to establish professional relationships. At the same time, don't be pushy, overly aggressive or excessively confident. Maintain a positive outlook that attracts others. Attitude is everything.

Your real estate career is built on networking with others and that process begins right in the office. Networking is not a skill that is easily mastered, but it is essential both inside and outside the office. In the professional brokerage setting, networking is getting to know the people and developing trust and rapport in order to make the process of conducting business in the office smoother and more productive for all concerned. Later, networking is discussed in the broader context of developing leads and expanding your personal sphere of influence.

STEP 2: Develop a Relationship with the Broker of Record and/or Manager

The broker of record (or the manager in a larger office) wants to see you succeed and will invest the time necessary if you display the diligence, discipline and commitment to get on with your new career. Don't wait for others to direct you, take the initiative and begin demonstrating your value as an added talent within the brokerage.

Successful real estate brokerages are built on synergism. It's not what you do, but rather how you contribute to the whole. Managers look for dynamic individuals that complement the existing team. They want people that take control, work well with others and get things done.

Your job is quite simple: obtain saleable listings and successfully negotiate agreements. If the brokerage provides services or products that increase your odds of doing either, get involved. If the broker of record or manager is willing to assist, take the opportunity and learn all you can. Start good habits early—you will continuously be expanding your horizons to improve knowledge and skills.

Lastly, the broker of record or manager wants to see persistence. Nothing in sales is easy; it only looks that way when you watch a true professional at work. Do what has to be done. Not all your efforts will turn into successes. In fact, many will result in rejection, failure and disappointment. Don't dwell on the negatives. Use them as a learning tool to step over one hurdle and grasp the next opportunity.

Broker of Record Responsibilities	PERSPECTIVE

When establishing a relationship with the broker of record, remember that he or she has important responsibilities for ensuring that the brokerage complies with the Act and regulations. The broker of record must provide adequate supervision for, and deal with any lack of compliance by, employed brokers, salespersons and others within the brokerage.

A broker of record's responsibility for supervising and ensuring compliance with the Act and regulations include, but is not limited to, the following:

1. Agreements
   a. Information before agreements
   b. Contents of written agreements
   c. Copies of written agreements
   d. Seller and buyer representation agreements
   e. Agreements with customers
   f. Agreements relating to commissions
2. Disclosure before multiple representation
3. Disclosure of interest
4. Disclosure of competing offers situations
5. Maintaining proper business records
6. Maintaining brokerage's certificate of registration
7. Maintenance of trust ledger
8. Maintenance of real estate trust account
9. Maintaining duplicate of brokers' and salespersons' certificate of registration
10. Ensuring registration to trade in real estate
11. Giving written notice of termination to broker or salesperson; including copy of notice to Registrar within 5 days of termination
12. Notifying Registrar in writing within 30 days after issue or transfer of shares
13. Compliance with trust account provisions
14. Notice of changes to Registrar
15. Compliance with commission and remuneration requirements
16. Brokerage response to the Office of the Registrar if notified of a complaint

Source: For the RECOrd (Real Estate Council of Ontario, Spring 2008)

STEP 3: Build Rapport with Brokerage Staff

The orientation program just provides the basics of brokerage operations. The real inner workings are best known by administrative staff. Treat every staff member with respect and gain an appreciation for their function within the office. They too must deal with adversity, impatience, work overload—just as you do.

Time spent getting to know staff members can only return positives for your new career. Typically, staff know the pitfalls to avoid, the procedures to follow, the ways to get things done and the answers to many questions.

STEP 4: Set the Stage with Other Registrants

Establish the ground rules early when building relationships with other salespeople in the brokerage. First and foremost, develop affiliations that will bolster your positive attitude and the self discipline needed for success in this career. Don't be swayed by others who are seeking refuge in procrastination, negativity and poor work habits. Seek camaraderie with capable individuals. Stay close to those people who can help you, give you sound advice and set the proper pace. To quote an often quoted phrase about sales and success: *You can't fly with eagles, when you're working with turkeys.* Pick people who think like you. Learn from the age-old statement that *birds of a feather flock together.* Diligently look for those individuals that you want to be with and whose efforts and successes you aspire to attain.

Be wary of those who always gravitate to informal office gatherings in the reception area or coffee room. Avoid the clique that routinely meets in one salesperson's office to discuss the ills that have beset the industry or problems with management. Negativity has no place in your new career. Above all, don't get swept up in matters that don't directly relate to your goals and objectives. Let others deal with office politics, your focus is on productivity.

Lastly, don't let others set your mood regardless of errors that you will inevitably make. Remember, professionals are always learning. Your job is to advance skills based on your mistakes, not languish in them as others might want you to do. Don't dwell on errors or allow others to needlessly rekindle those memories. Your real task is to stay focused, always be learning and be proactive in advancing your career.

NETWORKING IN THE COMMUNITY

A selling career begins with building relationships in the brokerage, but the ultimate test lies in developing meaningful relationships and connections in the marketplace. Your first few weeks are critical in setting up systems that will move your career forward. While networking can be as simple as writing down a list of everyone that you know and contacting them, successful salespeople prefer a more focused plan that challenges them to develop worthwhile personal contacts on a continuing basis. Many books are written on effective networking, but most concentrate on a few key steps. The following is provided by way of suggestion only. Individual circumstances and strategies will vary.

STEP 1: Focus Your Prospecting Efforts

What are the most effective ways to network as a new salesperson? New registrants are best to focus efforts on warm contacts, not cold calls to strangers. While some people readily welcome the challenges of meeting strangers, for most, cold calling can be a difficult challenge when first building a career. Cold calling might be best left a couple of weeks until some experience and confidence is gained.

Most new registrants opt for warm contacts. The term 'warm' generally refers to contacting individuals that are known and rejection possibilities are low. The text also includes selected contacts with some individuals as being 'warm' because rejection level is relatively low; e.g., having a specific reason for contacting an unknown individual, and having information that would be of interest to that person.

SPHERE OF INFLUENCE CONTACTS

Develop a list of people that you know and make them aware that you are underway with your real estate career. These individuals are the ideal starting point, as they already know your capabilities and trust you. Remember that the product you are selling is you. Try to obtain referrals of people known by them who are contemplating buying or selling. When you approach the referred individual, you then have a reason for contacting them and have a common association with the friend or relative. These spheres of influence become the initial links into your expanding network.

OPPORTUNITY CALLING

Many events take place when homes are being listed and sold, and you can capitalize on these happenings when prospecting for new clients and customers. For example, a home sold on a particular street provides an opportunity to canvass other homes when seeking listings.

> **EXAMPLE**   *More Buyers May be Waiting*
>
> Salesperson James has just begun her new career and is networking in her community. A home has recently sold on an attractive, quiet court in suburban Anycity. Understanding opportunity calling, she immediately canvasses the twelve remaining homes on that court.
>
> Here's how she approaches the homeowners:
>
> *Good morning, I am Julia James and I work for ABC Realty Inc. A few days ago, a home sold on your street. If you are thinking of selling, now is an ideal time. When that home was being marketed, it attracted many potential buyers to this court, but only one of those buyers was successful in acquiring a property. Others are still looking and may want your property given its distinct features. I'll gladly prepare a comparative market analysis and we can discuss possible pricing. If you're interested, I will follow-up and get back to you. How is later today or tomorrow?*

Warm calling is inexpensive, productive and helpful. The 'warm' approach works in opportunity calling because you are not just introducing yourself at the door, but instead bringing information to the homeowner. Your presence on the street is a logical consequence of happenings affecting that street. Your information is beneficial to anyone contemplating selling. The cost is minimal because your canvassing efforts are focused (no expensive mailings), your purpose is clear and defined, and the level of rejection is typically very low.

OPEN HOUSES

An open house is also a warm prospecting technique. They are effective for three key reasons: potential buyers can view the listed property, the seller knows that a sincere effort is being made to sell the home and the salesperson has the opportunity to meet prospects (including the right buyer for that home).

When beginning your career and before your first listing, offer to hold open houses for others. It's a great way to meet potential prospects, assist more established representatives who perhaps don't have the time to provide open houses on all properties that they have listed and gives you the opportunity to practice communication skills.

Also, don't forget to opportunity call in the neighbourhood before the open house. Always meet the neighbours. Many times, the ultimate buyer of that property may be a person living within a short distance of the listed property, or a friend or relative of that person.

FOR SALE BY OWNERS (FSBO)

For Sale By Owners offer immediate opportunities for new salespeople, but come with certain challenges. Empathizing with the seller can turn a cold call into a warm prospect. The FSBO is usually motivated to sell, but may have had a bad experience with another registrant or simply believes that he or she can make the sale without assistance. Be prepared to handle objections. Here's a sampling:

Save the Commission	The seller wants to save the commission, but actually the buyer typically does! Buyers believe that they are paying the commission, as it is part of the purchase price. Prudent buyers always deduct the typical commission from a seller's asking price prior to any negotiations.
Right Buyer Will Find the FSBO	The seller believes that they can do it themselves, but typically they lack the marketing ability that a brokerage has to reach the widest pool of motivated buyers. Remember: The greater the buyer pool, the greater the demand. Competition for the seller's house usually translates into a better price, which can offset part or all of the commission.
No Brokerage Needed—I Can Negotiate Directly	Negotiations are difficult when buyer and seller confront one another directly. The seller may inadvertently say things that turn the buyer off. A skilled salesperson can avoid confrontation and better handle negotiations to a successful conclusion. Ironically, sellers acting on their own behalf may sell the property for less than its true worth, just as an injured person may settle for less damages than if that individual had retained a lawyer.
We'll Try it for 30 Days	Most sellers set a time line to sell the property themselves. However, they may miss the right buyer because they don't have the marketing reach of a brokerage. The ideal buyer may have already seen the home and moved on.
If I List, I'll Use a Friend	An obligation to a friend is understandable, but the seller should seek out other opinions to understand what options are available and differences in marketing strategies that can directly impact final selling price. Also, working with friends can be problematic; e.g., terminating a listing with a friend when he or she doesn't do the job. Lastly, friends may not always be totally honest about situations that need to be addressed (e.g., price reduction), as they don't want to affect the friendship.

Several Buyers Have Seen the Home	Sellers may be impressed with several showings right after the FSBO sign appears. Emphasize that this activity may involve browsers, not buyers. The skill is in finding the right motivated buyer. Potential buyers may only be using the seller's home for comparison purposes and then moving on to other properties. Often, they will complement the seller's home or express some interest, but really have no intention of buying it.
I Just Need a Lawn Sign	A lawn sign does attract some buyers to one property, but the power of a brokerage lies in attracting many buyers. Buyers call in about one property, but then look at others. More properties offered in a brokerage translates into more potential buyers. This, in turn, creates more demand for the seller and the chance of getting a better price.

Getting the Appointment

The salesperson's objective with every *For Sale By Owners* is to get a face-to-face appointment. Often, it will take several visits before rapport is established and the seller truly understands the important services that you can provide. Always have probing questions to keep the conversation going and to better understand the seller's needs?

- Why did you decide to try and sell this home yourself?
- Can you separate the qualified, motivated buyers from browsers?
- Do you have contingency plans when you are away from the house. Who will take care of requests to see the property then?
- How are you going to handle offer drafting and related paperwork?
- Has anyone pointed out the many benefits of listing your home with a brokerage and how the brokerage can attract more buyers, create demand and ultimately get the best price for your home?
- Are you flexible in terms of asking price?
- Has anyone viewed the property at this time or has anyone made an offer? What comments did they make about your home?
- What attracted you to this house when you purchased it?
- Do you have to sell this home within a specified time?
- What plans do you have once the home is sold? Can we assist in securing other property for you?
- If you decide to list, what brokerages have you already seriously considered to market the property?
- Do you know the right questions to ask brokerages in order to properly compare services and advantages/disadvantages?
- Would you spare some time for me to explain our marketing services and how we can get the best price for you?
- I have some unique services that help create demand for your home? Are you interested in hearing how these might get you a better price?

Positive persistence is the key, as most FSBO's typically insist on trying to sell for a few weeks, but ultimately a decision is necessary if the home remains unsold. When visiting, always bring something by way of marketing pieces, personal promotional items, information about the local marketplace or other materials that are of interest. Show a genuine interest. Remember, this seller (as with all motivated sellers) wants to sell the home. He or she has just chosen a different path, but ultimately they need you.

EXPIRED LISTINGS

Expired listings are also an excellent source of business and can turn from a cold call to a warm prospect. Keep in mind that you may face an initial negative reaction given the seller's lack of success in selling a home. He or she may blame the previous brokerage for not doing its job properly. Interestingly, the most significant reason for listings not selling is typically the price. Be sympathetic to the seller's opinions, but remember the number one objective is to get this home sold. You have the skills, determination and resources to get that done.

The Seller's Instructions	CAUTION

Exclusive listing agreements now contain a provision which allows the seller to either consent (or refuse to consent) to other real estate board members contacting the seller after expiration or other termination of the listing agreement to discuss listing or otherwise marketing the property. Ask your broker of record or manager for guidance in this regard before approaching any expired listings.

COLD CALLING

Cold calling is best defined as meeting an individual without a prior appointment, meeting someone who does not know you or making unsolicited phone calls in search of potential business. As mentioned previously, cold calling is a real challenge for most given negative reactions and rejection. This text recommends initialling gravitating to '*warm*' calling (making calls to known friends and acquaintances or having a specific reason to call an unknown person). However, ultimately everyone looking to expand their career beyond existing spheres of influence must seriously consider cold calling. As with prospecting methods, the manner in which you deal with the consumer is vital.

The key concern for most is rejection, particularly when cold calling by phone. Consumers routinely encounter unsolicited phone calls and many handle such calls abruptly, but this technique can be reasonably effective if handled properly. Make certain that you have a clear message as to why you are calling, be polite and end the call promptly if no interest is expressed. Don't take rejection personally. Various sales training books are available to help you in developing a phone call strategy.

The most effective cold calling is in person. Meeting the homeowner directly provides a better opportunity to describe your services, discuss relevant market trends, assess whether there is an immediate need and do appropriate follow-up. Direct, active canvassing is always best and will give you the greatest return for the effort expended. Passive, one-way communication is not nearly as effective; e.g., e-mails, newsletters (print or electronic), direct mail and promotional pieces.

A positive mental attitude is key when cold calling. Don't think of '**no**' as an outright refusal. Many other factors come into play: the prospect has had a bad day, doesn't have enough information, doesn't need your services today, but may in the future or simply doesn't have the time. Your objective is to establish an initial contact that may at some point turn into an opportunity.

Telemarketing and the National Do Not Call List   CAUTION

Cold calling for real estate leads is now under federal legislation. The law requires that telemarketers making cold calls (including real estate registrants) can only do so if registered as a subscriber to the National Do Not Call List (DNCL), including having paid applicable fees. The National DNCL became operational on September 30, 2008. Bell Canada was selected to operate this national registry service required by the Canadian Radio-Television and Telecommunications Commission (CRTC). Previously, consumers had to place '*do not call*' requests directly with each telemarketer. Now, with the National DNCL, a consumer need only register his or her number with the national database. The National Do Not Call List permits registration of land lines, cellular phones and fax machines. Consumers can register up to three different numbers. Bell Canada provides lists to telemarketers and handles consumer complaints. Online registration is available at **www.dncl.gc.ca** or call 1-866-580-DNCL (3625).

Essentially, if a consumer puts his or her name and telephone number on the National DNCL, you cannot contact them by telephone to solicit business. Certain qualifications and exceptions apply. For example, you may call a consumer who has an existing relationship with your brokerage. An existing business relationship exists if the consumer:

- Made an inquiry within the last six months, e.g., a consumer contacted the brokerage for details of properties for sale or lease or wanted to discuss the sale or lease of his or her property.

- Purchased, leased or rented a property through the brokerage in the past 18 months.

- Had a written agreement with the brokerage, e.g., a representation or customer service agreement that is still in effect or expired within the past 18 months.

Also, you may contact a consumer if he or she specifically asks to be contacted (even when registered on the National DNCL). For example, a buyer at an open house may give written permission to be contacted by signing a open house guest book, assuming that the guest book clearly indicates that such permission is being given.

Some exemptions apply, most notably contact with business consumers. Further, certain organizations are exempted from the legislation such as political parties, polling firms and registered charities. Check with your broker of record and/or manager for National DNCL brokerage policies and procedures.

CANADA'S ANTI-SPAM LEGISLATION (CASL)

Please note that the content provided below is for information purposes only. It is intended purely as an overview of Canada's anti-spam legislation (known as CASL) and how it may impact registrants. It is neither comprehensive nor intended to form legal opinion or advice. Registrants are advised to seek independent legal advice.

Canada's anti-spam legislation received Royal Assent on December 15, 2010, and became law on July 1, 2014. The full title of CASL is "*an Act to promote the efficiency and adaptability of the Canadian economy by regulating certain activities that discourage reliance on electronic means of carrying out commercial activities, and to amend the Canadian Radio-television and Telecommunications Commission Act, the Competition Act, the Personal Information Protection and Electronic Documents Act and the Telecommunications Act*" (S.C. 2010, c. 23).

Purpose of the Act
Section 3 of the legislation sets out the purpose of the Act.

3. The purpose of this Act is to promote the efficiency and adaptability of the Canadian economy by regulating commercial conduct that discourages the use of electronic means to carry out commercial activities, because that conduct

   (a) impairs the availability, reliability, efficiency and optimal use of electronic means to carry out commercial activities;

   (b) imposes additional costs on businesses and consumers;

   (c) compromises privacy and the security of confidential information; and

   (d) undermines the confidence of Canadians in the use of electronic means of communication to carry out their commercial activities in Canada and abroad.

Defining and Understanding Terms within the Act

Section 1 of the Act defines commercial activity, electronic message, and commercial electronic message (CEM) as follows:

> "commercial activity" means any particular transaction, act or conduct or any regular course of conduct that is of a commercial character, whether or not the person who carries it out does so in the expectation of profit, other than any transaction, act or conduct that is carried out for the purposes of law enforcement, public safety, the protection of Canada, the conduct of international affairs or the defence of Canada.
>
> "electronic message" means a message sent by any means of telecommunication, including a text, sound, voice or image message.
>
> "commercial electronic message" is an electronic message that, having regard to the content of the message, the hyperlinks in the message to content on a website or other database, or the contact information contained in the message, it would be reasonable to conclude has as its purpose, or one of its purposes, to encourage participation in a commercial activity, including an electronic message that
>
> (a) offers to purchase, sell, barter or lease a product, goods, a service, land or an interest or right in land;
>
> (b) offers to provide a business, investment or gaming opportunity;
>
> (c) advertises or promotes anything referred to in paragraph (a) or (b); or
>
> (d) promotes a person, including the public image of a person, as being a person who does anything referred to in any of paragraphs (a) to (c), or who intends to do so.

A CEM may be described as any electronic message that encourages participation in a commercial activity regardless of whether there is an expectation of profit. As noted, a commercial activity is broadly defined and includes, among other things, activities such as offering properties for sale, and advertising/promoting goods, a service, or a person.

An electronic address is an email account, a telephone account, an instant message account, and any other similar form. Messages sent to other users on a social media platform, such as Facebook or LinkedIn, would also qualify as sending messages to electronic addresses. CASL does not apply to:

- Twitter posts
- Facebook wall posts
- websites
- blogs

- two-way voice communication between individuals
- faxes and voice recordings sent to a telephone account (however, registrants should be mindful of the requirements of the National Do Not Call List)

Prohibitions and Requirements

Section 6 (1) of the Act prohibits the sending of CEMs unless the person to whom the message is sent has consented (either express consent or implied consent) to receiving it. Before sending a CEM to an electronic address, the sender must:

- obtain consent from the recipient
- identify himself/herself
- provide a means for the recipient to withdraw consent (i.e., an unsubscribe mechanism)

SECTION IV   PREPARING FOR YOUR NEW CAREER

Obtaining Consent

Consent can be written or implied. However, if challenged, the onus is on the sender to prove he/she has obtained consent to send the message. When requesting express consent, silence or inaction on the part of the intended recipient cannot be construed as providing consent.

Express consent must be obtained through an opt-in mechanism rather than opt-out. A pre-checked box for consent is not permitted as this would assume consent where it was not intended.

When requesting express consent, among other things, the following information must be included:

- the specific purpose must be clearly identified
- the name of the person requesting consent or, if a person is requesting consent on behalf of another person, both persons have to be identified
- contact information of the person(s) requesting consent, including a physical address and either a telephone number, email address, or website

In the case of a referral, consent from the recipient is not required provided that certain conditions are met.

- The referral must have been made by an individual who has an existing business relationship, an existing non-business relationship, a family relationship, or a personal relationship with both the sender and the recipient.
- The full name of the person making the referral and a statement that the CEM is being sent as a result of the referral must be included in the CEM.
- The CEM must contain the sender's identification information and an unsubscribe mechanism.

For more information about obtaining consent, go to the Canadian Radio-television and Telecommunications Commission (CRTC) website at **http://www.crtc.gc.ca/eng/ casl-lcap.htm.**

Consent can be implied in situations such as:

- where there has been an existing business or non-business relationship in the last two years
- the recipient of a CEM has conspicuously published his/her electronic address (e.g., on a website) or has disclosed his/her electronic address (e.g., distribution of a business card)

However, where the recipient has conspicuously published or disclosed his/her electronic address, a CEM can only be sent if:

- the content of the message relates to the recipient's role, functions, or duties in an official or business capacity, and
- the recipient, when providing a business card or publishing his/her electronic address on a website, did not state that he/she did not wish to receive CEMs at that address

Existing Business/Non-Business Relationships

The legislation includes a transitional provision that relates to consent. Where there is an existing business or non-business relationship that includes the sending of CEMs, consent is implied for a period of 36 months commencing July 1, 2014. An existing business relationship exists where two people have been doing business together within the past two years.

For registrants, this could include the purchase of a property, a listing agreement, or a buyer representation agreement. In the case of an inquiry about a registrant's services, the time limit for sending a CEM without express consent is six months from the inquiry.

Consent can be implied in non-business relationships (e.g., fellow members of an association, club, or voluntary organization). The requirement for identification information of the sender and an unsubscribe mechanism still exists.

In all cases, CEMs must contain an unsubscribe mechanism that is easy for the recipient to use. Furthermore, a recipient can terminate the consent if he/she indicates that he/she no longer wishes to receive CEMs. The transitional period can be used to obtain express consent for the receipt of CEMs where consent is currently implied. Express consent does not expire until the recipient withdraws his/her consent.

Installing Computer Programs

Section 8 of CASL applies when a computer program or application is installed on another person's computer system. A person must provide express consent before software or apps are installed on his/her electronic device. The following information must be provided to obtain express consent:

- the purpose for which the consent is being sought
- identification information of the person seeking consent
- the function and purpose of the computer program

Further disclosure of information may be required if the computer program performs additional functions, such as collecting personal information or interferes with the user's control of the computer system. For more information, go to **http://fightspam.gc.ca/eic/site/030.nsf/eng/h_00050.html**.

Penalties for Violations

Violations of any of Sections 6 to 9 of CASL could result in an administrative monetary penalty of up to $1 million for an individual and up to $10 million for a business.

Directors, officers, agents, and mandataries (i.e., people who have been given the authority to act on behalf) of a corporation can be liable if they directly authorized, assented to, acquiesced in (e.g., allowed), or participated in the commission of the violation.

The legislation is available on the Government of Canada website at **http://fightspam.gc.ca**.

STEP 2: Build Listing Sources

According to many sales representatives, successful listing practice is the key to a profitable career in real estate. Every real estate registrant uses some method of promotion to win the attention of property owners wanting to sell. Most employ a variety of methods to obtain listings. Many sources of residential listings exist, as well as a variety of reasons why people sell their properties. Often, the development of listing techniques is a matter of recognizing these reasons and developing a method of keeping in contact with owners who are contemplating a move and require real estate services. Some basic reasons to move include family, employment, financial status, neighbourhood and prestige requirements.

Experienced salespeople report a wide range of popular listing sources that can become part of your networking strategy:

- *For Sale By Owner* ads and signs.
- Former buyers.
- Neighbours of listings taken.
- Expired listings that did not sell.
- Direct mail to prime areas.
- Cold calling.
- Advertising for specific properties.
- Furniture for sale ads.

- Business transfer notices.
- Builders of custom homes.
- Social contacts and clubs.
- News items regarding marriages and business changes.
- Lawyers, estates and foreclosures.
- Mortgage and insurance companies and lending institutions.
- Legal notice column in the local newspaper.
- Personnel officers in key industries.

The above list is by no means complete. Every salesperson develops his or her own favourite forms of prospecting for listing leads and referrals.

Why are Listings So Important?	CURIOSITY

Marketable listings are key to a real estate career. Salespeople with several listings gain the benefit of other activity generated by those listings; e.g., potential buyers calling on ads and sign calls, prospects visiting open house and the distribution of *just listed* and *just sold* cards (along with opportunity knocking in the neighbourhood). Also, the salesperson generally has more control over listings than they do over buyers. As such, buyers seek out the listing salesperson. Salespeople with an inventory of saleable listings are also better assured of more steady commission income. A new salesperson should devote at least 50% of his or her time prospecting for listings when beginning a new real estate sales career.

STEP 3: Seriously Consider a Prospecting Farm

This systematic method of prospecting has been successfully used by many real estate salespeople. Farming involves the selection of a specific territory (geographic or otherwise; e.g., social) and the development of that territory by the sales representative. The farm territory need not be large. A salesperson can develop a rewarding career in residential real estate sales with a base of as few as 200 to 300 homes. Most registrants select a territory that they already know and enjoy working in. Obviously, an additional advantage is being known to at least some persons within the farming area. Regardless, the registrant must become aware of, and totally familiar with, all the political, social, physical and economic features of the entire territory.

The overall objective of farming is to become acquainted with everyone who resides within the area, make a good impression and become indelibly established in their minds as the person who offers real estate services. The accomplishment of this goal means regular communication through an organized, logical system. Mailings, novelties and institutional advertising are tools that can assist in this regard, but are only aids in the overall campaign.

Fortunately, many customer relations management (CRM) software programs are available to assist in the process. These programs can help organize your network and produce both electronic and print mailings. However, remember that there is no substitute for personal contact. Make certain that the CRM enhances your face-to-face visits and telephone calls, not replaces them.

Having the correct name of each owner in the district is critical for mailing lists and personal contact. The local taxation office is an excellent source of information. Mailers are frequently designed to pave the way for personal contact. When follow-up is done, having the mailer to refer to, and confirm that the owners did receive it, is advantageous.

The objective of general contact is to keep owners aware of what is happening in the local market; e.g., recent activity, price levels and market conditions. All homeowners are interested in the value of their home. Through personal informative meetings, a regular program of contact can be maintained with all owners in the farm territory. This is essential, not only for obtaining listings, but also for referrals and repeat business.

Farming: Getting Started   MARKET MEMO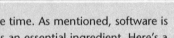

Farming can be successful if properly carried through by salespeople willing to take the time. As mentioned, software is available to assist in the process, but don't let technology take over. Personal contact is an essential ingredient. Here's a few suggestions in setting up a farming area:

- Start with a base of as few as 200 or 300 homes. Make certain that the farming areas does not exceed the number of homes that can be realistically contacted personally in a month.

- Select a known territory, one in which you will enjoy working. Proximity to the brokerage or your home is an asset, but not essential. Try to pick an area that has a reasonable annual turnover; e.g., 7% or higher which translates into 21 sales for 300 homes. A salesperson actively farming an area and well-known in that area should get 15 to 20% of all listings in an area.

- Become totally familiar with the political, social, physical and economic features of the territory.

- Establish a plan to become well-known as the sales representative in the area.

- Make regular contact with people in the territory (mailings, personal contact and newsletters). Personal contact is always best.

- Develop accurate mailing lists and customer contact cards. Be a conscientious record keeper about all contacts with people in the territory.

- Inspect every listing that is taken in your farm area and continuously maintain up-to-date statistics on sales activity in that farming area.

- Maintain a regular program of contact with all owners in the territory. Discipline is essential. Have some form of communication with every homeowner at least once a month.

- Know the amenities, shopping, transportation, schools, churches and so forth.

- When canvassing in the farm area, always be prepared with appropriate forms. Make notes of every contact with each homeowner in the farm area.

- Be positive and enthusiastic, dress for business, go out of your way to meet everyone in the farm area and door knock 2 times a year. A farm area of 700 homes will require that you knock on 28 doors per week (2 x 700 ÷ 50 weeks).

IMPORTANT: A farming area is typically geographic (e.g., a particular neighbourhood), but many variations are possible that may involve persons of a similar interest (e.g., larger social clubs and associations), an extended network arising from previous employment or some combination of all three.

STEP 4: Work Your Plan

No matter what your networking and prospecting plan is, success comes to those with discipline. Establish a goal in terms of a definite number of people that you will meet and set aside appropriate time every day to get the job done. As a new salesperson, prospecting must be Job #1. Don't linger at home or at the brokerage office. You won't find any prospects there. Start your day early and get out to meet the people.

Put your goals in writing and explain exactly how you plan to achieve them. Prospecting is essentially a numbers game. The more people that you contact, the more likely your chances of success. For example, if you plan on meeting 20 people per day, in a 5-day week, you would have introduced yourself to 100 people. Assuming a positive response of 5%, 5 of those people will result in some sale-related activity; e.g., an appointment to discuss obtaining a buyer or seller representation agreement or an opportunity to show a property. The skills that you bring to the job will determine whether or not you convert this positive response into a concrete agreement.

Take meticulous notes, preferably on your laptop computer. Secure a proper software package that allows you to track all your contacts and do follow-up via electronic and/or print mailings. Follow-up is essential whether it is a call, a handwritten note, a computer-generated mailing, a newsletter or a personal visit. Make a habit of handing out at least 10 to 20 business cards a day. Above all, be creative with your prospecting. Don't spend too much time in your car, after all no one will meet you behind the wheel. Walk the main street, wander in the mall, attend social gatherings—be visible.

EXAMPLE *Translating Effort into Reward*

Salesperson James has established a prospecting goal to meet 20 new people at day. According to his research, 1 out of every 100 contacts will result in a positive lead and that 1/3 of those leads will produce income. Average income received will be $5,500.

Contacts per Week	20 contacts/day x 5 = 100 contacts per week
Positive Leads Per Week	100 = 1 positive lead.
Positive Leads Per Year	1 x 48 (a typical working year) = 48 positive leads.
Leads Converted to Revenue	48 ÷ 3 (⅓ *of leads converted to revenue*) = 16 Occurrences
Projected Revenue	16 x $5,500 = $88,000.

If prospecting is so effective, why do many salespeople fail to realize its true potential?

No Follow-Up
Many salespersons begin with a solid prospecting plan, but then fail to maintain an organized follow-up system.

Discontinuing
Often salespersons obtain initial success from prospecting and then become focused on sales activity generated by that prospecting, only to forget what initially made them busy.

No Immediate Return
Salespersons may aggressively begin a prospecting plan, but then not obtain immediate benefit in terms of positive leads. Remember that prospecting rewards are long term and typically considerable effort is required before income is realized.

Poor Attitude
Canvassing with a poor or negative attitude can directly impact results. People want to deal with salespersons who are cheerful, enthusiastic and positive. Those with a negative attitude will not attract prospects nor will they have the stamina to keep the prospecting plan going until success is achieved.

PREPARING FOR CAREER FIRSTS

The initial days in a brokerage involve a number of *career firsts*. The first meeting with a client or customer, the first showing and the first agreement may seem daunting, but these are just part of a learning process that never ends.

The First Conversations

The new salesperson has many conversation firsts including handling incoming calls, preparing for opportunity (duty time) in the brokerage and face-to-face meetings with buyer prospects. Service is everything and proper etiquette, consideration for the prospect and willingness to meet their needs go a long way in developing your career. The following guidelines will help with your first experiences. You can then refine these as your career unfolds.

HANDLING THE INCOMING CALL

The two major objectives in handling a call are:

- Create a good first impression; and
- Arrange for a face-to-face appointment.

Use an *incoming call form* to:

- Serve as a reminder to get specific information regarding the caller; and
- Provide backup questions to gain needed information.

Develop good telephone etiquette: speak to prospects, not at them. Be forthcoming with information, involve the prospect, qualify as to needs, ask pertinent questions and above all, be helpful. The telephone call paves the way for a successful face-to-face meeting.

PREPARING FOR OPPORTUNITY (DUTY) TIME

Office time may be available to sales representatives for servicing phone calls and walk-in trade pertinent to inquiries on, and listing of, properties. The procedure for handling floor duty, assignment of times and, in fact, the existence of such times vary greatly and are wholly dependent upon brokerage policy and employment contracts between salespeople and the employing brokerage.

If duty time is offered in the brokerage, certain tips and guidelines can help.

- The immediate impression of potential clients contacting the brokerage is often dictated by the floor duty person.
- Be well informed about all listed property, have ready electronic access to needed information and be aware of all advertised property. In particular, keep the most recent print and Internet advertisements within easy reach for fast reference. Don't forget to have information on good backups to the advertised property. Remember! The caller seldom buys the advertised property. It just caught his or her interest. It's up to you to find the right property.
- Be well organized. Don't shuffle needlessly to get such things as scratch paper, a calculator, amortization schedules, area maps and your appointment book. Have the necessary paper and electronic tools ready. Don't frustrate people with '*hang on, I'll have to start up my computer.*

Some brokerages use a recording sheet completed by the sales representative to provide input about which properties are generating activity and which advertisements are effective. In some instances, the duty salesperson may provide assistance to other salespeople and co-operating brokerages. In small brokerages, for example, this can include handling calls and taking messages for fellow sales representatives.

MEETING THE PROSPECT

People buy from people they like and trust. As mentioned earlier, keep in mind that buyers are forming a first impression and may have had unsatisfactory experiences in the past.

- Demonstrate genuine interest and sincerity. Pay special attention to the image projected, overall demeanour, and verbal and body language portrayed.
- Take the time to determine whether the prospects are genuinely interested and are, in fact, qualified to buy.
- Qualify the prospects specifically concerning their needs, desires and financial capabilities.
- Review agency with them and establish the ground rules.

ASKING THE RIGHT QUESTIONS

A successful first meeting with a buyer involves asking the right questions. Qualifying is more of an art than a science. One of the most effective methods is to be totally open with the buyers. Bring them to the realization that it is a waste of everyone's time to show them properties that they cannot afford to buy or those that do not satisfy their needs. Listen carefully and look beyond responses given to questions to determine basic needs as opposed to desires, as well as underlying motivating factors. During the qualifying process, it is not uncommon to probe several times in determining actual motivations. Two of the most effective phrases to accomplish this are simply: *Why do you feel that way?* and *Are there any other reasons?*

Remember that the scope of detail will depend on whether the relationship involves a customer or a client. Of course, privacy considerations and compliance with the *Privacy Act* must be addressed when formulating questions and collecting personal information. The following is a list of items to consider when assisting the buyer. This list is not exhaustive in nature and is included for illustrative purposes only.

- General background, such as employment information, details about existing home, amount of equity (if applicable), lifestyle information, amenities and features in present home and goals.
- Physical and functional requirements such as number of bedrooms required, number of cars, preferred heating system, need for certain large rooms (e.g., dining room or family room), interests, hobbies and absolute *must have's* versus *would be nice to have.*
- Financial capabilities including discussion of GDS and TDS ratios, type of information that the lender will require, examples of common mortgage application forms used in the local area and a general estimate of price range of homes being viewed.
- The urgency of the buyer's desire to relocate will shed light on the primary motivation to seek a new home; e.g., a busy street could indicate a motivation to provide a better, safer environment for small children.
- Discussion of the buyer's experiences in the real estate market may indicate factors that the salesperson will have to overcome. For example, they may have already seen fifteen or twenty houses and have become confused or frustrated by the exercise.
- Determine whether the buyers are analytical or emotional about a purchase and respond accordingly.
- Determine whether someone else's approval will be required; e.g., another family member or a friend.

Norman Vincent Peale was probably one of the most famous believers in scripts. His scripted speeches were carefully crafted and delivered to thousands of audiences. He demonstrated impeccable word skills, perfect timing and a memorable experience for all in attendance. The real secret was that his primary speech changed very little over the years. Yes, he made adjustments, but only to make it better. As he often stated: *It's easier to change the audience than to change the speech.*

Like it or not, professional selling has a lot to do with speech writing. Some people are naturally adverse to planned (or canned) presentations, but the real truth is that successful salespeople use scripts. The best do it so well that you don't even know that it's canned. They hone their word skills by developing specific wordings for all types of situations encountered in the marketplace. For new salespeople, the scripts are initially awkward or ineffective, but gradually the power of their presentations increase when pointing out that they are the best choice to get the job done, presenting benefits of home ownership, handling objections and/or cleverly asking for a decision.

Scripts are a vital part of listing and selling, whether dealing with open house buyers, FSBO's cold calls, listing presentations or offer negotiations. Why keep trying to reinvent your message? Get a storyline together and practice to make it perfect. Most salespeople discover after a few months that they have heard most of the common questions, objections and problems. It's all a matter of developing effective scripts to address those questions, answer the objections and resolve the problems. Start out by creating a short script about yourself: who you are, why the buyer or seller should select you and what distinct services you and your brokerage provide. Next, build a short introduction that you can use when meeting people and introducing yourself. Why you are in the business, what you do better than others, what skills you have and why buyers and sellers would want to deal with you. As your career expands, develop unique scripts to handle common situations when prospecting, listing and negotiating.

The First Showing

The showing of a property is a pivotal step in the sale process. Be adequately prepared and sensitive to feedback during the showing. Various guidelines are provided to assist both with your first showing and many more.

- When setting appointments, avoid meeting the buyers at the property. There are several reasons:
    - a loss of opportunity to show the neighbourhood;
    - they may not find the property;
    - the buyers may arrive early and attempt to contact the seller directly or take a dislike to the exterior and drive away, leaving behind a frustrated seller and salesperson; and
    - it is too convenient for the buyers to simply depart without any opportunity for post qualifying.
- Make sure that all appointments are confirmed on the day of showing, both with prospective buyers and with sellers.
- Always try to prepare the seller well in advance so that he/she can spruce up the property, in addition to acting on any recommendations made at the time of listing the property.
- Try not to have the seller present unless situations arise where they are an essential source of information, or can in some way assist in the showing.
- When showing properties listed with other brokerages, make all arrangements through the listing brokerage.
- All properties should be thoroughly inspected in advance of showings to avoid unpleasant surprises. If the property has not been pre-inspected, the salesperson should openly disclose this to the buyer.

- Showing several properties in rapid succession can cause confusion. Following each showing, the buyer should be re-qualified. This may, in turn, necessitate rearranging subsequent appointments.

- Some salespeople prepare summary information regarding each property being shown and briefly introduce the buyer to these lists before the showing process.

- If there are negative attributes about a property, disclose these before the showing. The buyer is then not surprised by the drawbacks and not so easily predisposed to a negative impression. Caution is advised, however, as people's tastes differ. What the sales representative views as a drawback may not in fact appear so to others. Of course, all known material latent defects must be disclosed.

- Some believe that an ideal sequence to the order of showing properties exists, but in reality many factors can vary the approach. According to experienced salespeople, the majority of buyers purchase the location first and then the specific features within a home second. Therefore, place emphasis on the neighbourhood, amenities and general locale of the house. Secondly, discuss the layout and specific features. Plan the route taken and make certain the drive is a safe one, in a clean car.

- During the drive, discuss the amenities offered in the locale and be sensitive to the buyer's reaction. You may have selected the wrong area.

- Be patient during the showing and allow the buyer adequate time to investigate the property. Do not be afraid to leave people alone for a short period of time. Often they need that time to discuss key issues.

- If an important feature has been overlooked, mention it. Otherwise, resist any attempt at ongoing conversation, except to expand on comments made. Effective listening is a vital aspect of any showing.

- Watch the actions and expressions of the buyer.

- Try to keep the showing positive from start to end, regardless of whether the buyers like the property. Remember, both positive comments and criticisms have value in narrowing the field.

- Empathize with concerns raised. Tread carefully, be helpful and understanding. It's their decision, not yours.

- Do not be misled or dismayed by people who are critical. Often, buyers criticize what they like, as they are setting the stage for negotiations. No objections can often mean no interest. Experience will inevitably show that someone who loves everything may have great difficulty in making a decision.

- People who bring an expert friend are often insecure about their own competence. Be prepared to treat such friends as true experts and sell to them as much as to the buyer.

- Following the showing and assuming that a particular property is not the house to buy, continue the qualifying process. There is no such thing as an unsuccessful showing. By constantly re-qualifying the buyers as to required features and benefits, the right property is moving one step closer.

Asking for The First Offer

A point exists in every negotiation when the sales representative must ask for the offer. However, nothing is worse than asking for an offer before someone is ready to buy.

- Asking for the offer is not a pressure technique, but a matter of providing assurance to the buyer that what he or she thinks emotionally also has merit from a practical, objective viewpoint.
- Skilled salespeople listen and watch for signs of true interest; e.g., minor criticisms, phrases indicating acceptance, anticipated presence in the home (e.g., *We could use this room as a den*) and confirmation of a certain preference (e.g., *That's a great location for the TV*).

Many techniques are advanced in sales training materials. Following are four popular approaches to assist the buyer in arriving at a decision to make an offer:

COMPARISON

Faced with two alternatives, the buyer can make exact comparisons of benefits and features. The process then becomes not one of *Should I buy?* but rather *Which one should I buy?*

MINOR DETAILS

Often buyers can progress from minor details to major decisions. The preparation of an offer involves a number of more or less minor items; e.g., chattels, fixtures and conditions. Start there and work toward the major decision.

ADVANTAGES VS. DISADVANTAGES

This approach is often referred to as the Benjamin Franklin technique. Franklin would draw a line down the middle of a sheet of paper and list all positive arguments on one side and all negative arguments on the other. An affirmative decision would simply be based on positives outweighing negatives.

CONFIRMING ADVANTAGES

Ideal for buyers who have found the right property, but are unsure about making a decision. By summarizing major advantages and directing their attention away from minor details, things fall into proper perspective. Don't forget to summarize the benefits of home ownership and not just the features of a specific home. Home ownership can provide security, a hedge against inflation, an attractive neighbourhood and, above all, personal satisfaction.

Preparing the First Offer

The secret to professional offer drafting is practice. There are really only two choices: practice on clients and customers or do it in advance. The latter is obviously the right choice. Offer drafting is like any other skill. Don't practice on your real audience, get comfortable back-stage first. Here are some guidelines to assist:

Practice Scenarios	Have the broker of record, manager or another salesperson randomly select several listed properties and then act as fictitious buyers setting out specific terms for the offer. Draft the offers based on this information and then review as necessary to make certain all information and instructions were properly set out in the agreement.
	For added practice, list your own home including all measurements, prepare the *Seller Property Information Statement* (OREA Form 220) and then develop an offer based on a fictitious buyer. As with other scenarios, have the broker of record or manager check your work for accuracy and completeness.
Line by Line Analysis	The professional salesperson must know and understand every pre-printed line in the agreement of purchase and sale.
Explain Preprinted Clauses	Practice explaining, in your own words, what each clause means. Any of your family members can be a great audience. If they can't understand what you're saying, chances are your clients and customers won't either.
Study the Form Upside Down	That's right. Take the agreement of purchase and sale and position it on a table as if the buyer was sitting across from you. When the buyer points at a specific clause, do you know which one it is? Professionals know the forms inside out and upside down. It's a sign of skill when you can answer questions without having to refer directly to the agreement—even from across the table.
Know the Offer Software	Practice makes perfect and knowledgeable salespeople don't fumble with the computer or make unnecessary errors when preparing offers. Nothing is more embarrassing that not being able to properly work the offer drafting software, particularly when the client or customer is anxiously waiting.
Know Every Clause	Do the same thing with the clauses that will be inserted in offers, as was done with the form (or forms); i.e., complete a line by line analysis and be able to explain each one in everyday language.
Have Someone Check Every Offer	Until you are extremely confident with offer drafting, make certain that the broker of record or manager checks every offer to make certain that it is complete and accurate.

TIME PLANNING: THE FIRST TWO WEEKS

Time planning is straightforward for the new registrant, as prospecting is key. Two weeks activities are set out to help guide your activities. Obviously, timing and ability to complete these activities will depend on individual circumstances.

	WEEK ONE	**WEEK TWO**
Prospecting Activities	*Sphere of Influence* Contact 30 known individuals from your sphere of influence list and ask for business referrals. *Opportunity Calling* Meet 50 homeowners using opportunity calling techniques. *For Sale By Owners* Visit five FSBO's to practice your skills at handling objections and getting appointments to discuss your services. *Open House* Arrange with another salesperson to offer an open house near the end of Week One.	*Sphere of Influence* Contact the remaining individuals from your sphere of influence list and ask for business referrals. If less than 30 remain (i.e., 60 in total), add an appropriate number to *Opportunity Calling*. *Opportunity Calling* Meet 50 homeowners using opportunity calling techniques. *For Sale By Owners* Visit three FSBO's to practice your skills at handling objections and getting appointments to discuss your services. *Expired Listings* Visit eight expired listings to practice your skills at handling objections and getting appointments to discuss your services. *Open House(s)* Arrange for one open house near the end of Week Two. A second open house is even better, if time permits.
Other Activities	Create a *Week One* schedule in advance using your new time planner and include the following: • Any office meetings at the brokerage. • Inspection of existing inventory. • Office orientation. • Brokerage skills training or coaching provided for new salespersons. • Generally organize your office, supplies, setup of any computer equipment and so forth. • Take care of all remaining brokerage and related paperwork (as discussed earlier in the chapter). • Visit two or more open houses being offered through your brokerage. • Have lunch with one or more of the brokerage's salespeople to learn more about the business and obtain helpful guidelines for your career. • Meet with at least one lender to determine what their lending procedures are and what forms are needed. • Complete follow-up notes (or e-mails) for spheres of influence contacted. • Do follow-up on any positive leads that arose from your prospecting activities. • Assess the success of *Week One* activities and plan any adjustments for *Week Two*.	Create a *Week Two* schedule in advance and include the following: • Any office meetings at the brokerage. • Inspection of existing inventory. • Brokerage skills training or coaching provided for new salespersons. • Complete any unfinished items regarding your office, technical requirements, professional affiliations and promotional items. • Visit two or more open houses being offered through your brokerage. • Have lunch with a sales leader in the brokerage. • Do further follow-up on contacts made during Week One. • Complete follow-up notes (or e-mails) for prospects contacted during Week Two. • Do follow-up on any positive leads that arose from your prospecting activities in both Week One and Week Two. • Assess the success of *Week Two* activities and plan any adjustments for *Week Three*.

SECTION IV   PREPARING FOR YOUR NEW CAREER

What Business and Income Will You Generate?

No one has a crystal ball to predict your rewards, but clearly diligent effort improves the chances. As an example, let's assume that you have worked for two weeks and 5% of the sphere of influence and opportunity calling activities resulted in a positive lead, one out of six FSBO's or expired listings culminated in an appointment and each open house brought two positive leads.

	CONTACTS	POSITIVE LEADS
Sphere of Influence	60	3
Opportunity Calling	100	5
For Sale By Owners	8	1
Expired Listings	8	1
Open Houses	2	4

In two short weeks, you are not only fully operational, but could have 14 positive leads and an expanding network of 176 contacts (sphere of influences, opportunity calling contacts, for sale by owners and expired listings), as well as any prospect names for those who attended the open houses. More importantly, this does not include any additional leads that may have resulted from duty time or unexpected happenings.

INCOME/EXPENSE EXPECTATIONS

Income Estimate

As a final step, consider the income and expense picture. *Real Estate as a Professional Career* emphasized that predicting personal income is always a difficult task, because earning power is so dependent on individual sales ability, personal connections and market conditions. However, given the positive leads generated from our example above and by making certain assumptions about the fictitious community of Anycity, we can at least make some broad estimates:

Average Anycity Price	$250,000
Average Time to Close	60 days
Typical Commission Rate	5%
Listing or Selling Commission Earned *(assuming a 70/30 split)*	$4,375
Percentage of Positive Leads That Convert to Earned Commission	4%
Average Positive Leads Generated per Week *(see Note below)*	10

NOTE: *The time planning schedule discussed under the previous topic established 14 positive leads over two weeks (7 per week). The assumption is that 'contact to positive lead conversion' would increase over time; i.e., 20 per two week period or 10 per week.*

YEAR ONE—PROJECTED INCOME

Total Positive Leads Generated *(Based on 52 weeks)*	520
Percentage Converted to Earned Commission *(520 x .04)*	21
Listing or Selling Commission Received *($4,375 x 21)*	$91,875
Time Delay *(60 Day Delay: Time to Close— $91,875 x 10 ÷ 12)*	**$76,562**

Clearly, the figure of $76,562 is hypothetical, but the calculation does provide some basic guidance in a career filled with many unknowns.

Expense Estimate

A fictitious expense budget has also been prepared for illustration purposes. (The estimate assumes that the salesperson will join organized real estate.) Initial costs for courses do not include personal expenses. Ongoing expenses are difficult to quantify and will vary significantly based on the individual.

INITIAL EXPENSE ESTIMATE

Pre-Registration Education Courses *(Enrollment Fees Only)*		$1,820
RECO Salesperson Registration *(Every Two Years Based on 2016)*		350
RECO Insurance Payment *(Annual based on 2015–2016)*		417
Entrance Fees		
Real Estate Board (Varies by Board)	$450	
Ontario Real Estate Association	200	
Canadian Real Estate Association	200	
		850
Miscellaneous		200
TOTAL INITIAL ESTIMATE		**$3,637**

ONGOING EXPENSE ESTIMATE (YEAR ONE)

Advertising and Promotion *($225.00 per Transaction; $225 x 21)*	4,725
Professional Dues	
Real Estate Board *(MLS® Dues vary by Board)*	800
OREA and CREA	510
Professional Development	
Articling Courses	1,360
Communication Expenses *(assumes cell phone and pager)*	2,400
Auto Expenses *(leased vehicle and all operating expenses)*	15,600
Supplies *(all misc. supplies not provided by brokerage)*	1,800
Miscellaneous *(includes listing and administration fees)*	2,400
TOTAL EXPENSE ESTIMATE	**29,595**

SUMMARY

Projected Income—Year One		76,562
Expenses		
Initial Expense Estimate	3,637	
Ongoing Expense Estimate (Year One)	29,595	
Total Expenses (Year One)		33,232
NET INCOME ESTIMATE (BEFORE TAX)		**43,330**

Financial Prudence   CAUTION

Real estate income is unpredictable. Be prudent in your financial affairs. Reduce debt wherever possible and have enough cash set aside to handle a possible lack of cash flow for three to six months. Consider securing a line of credit to use as a buffer should your revenue expectations not materialize as quickly as forecasted.

Don't be lulled into a false sense of security by counting on conditional sales. Despite your best efforts, some sales will not close. Determine your future cash flow on firm sales only. Financial companies provide an option to collect commissions on firm sales before closing, but this service is not without costs. Remember, it's not what you make but what you keep.

To underscore that point even further, don't forget your tax liability. Make certain that all remittances are made in full and on time. Many inexperienced salespeople are quick to spend the commission cheque without withholding sufficient funds for the Canada Revenue Agency.

KNOWLEDGE INTEGRATION

Notables

- Real estate sales demand your full time attention.

- Be productive when waiting for your registration, but remember that you cannot in any way be involved with the trading of real estate until that registration is received.

- Carefully review and understand all agreements, the policy manual and other documentation provided by your employing brokerage.

- A handy checklist is provided to ensure that relevant topics are addressed in the brokerage orientation and can assist in deciding what to bring to the brokerage.

- New registrants should be aware of important benefits/deductions and related procedures involving taxation, Canada Pension Plan, Employment Insurance, Harmonized Sales Tax and other deductions/fees.

- Four steps are provided as guidelines to assist in handling typical office dynamics.

- Successful salespeople typically develop a formal networking plan to expand their client and customer base.

- Various networking and prospecting techniques are provided relating to sphere of influence contacts, opportunity calling, open houses, *For Sale By Owners*, expired listings and cold calling.

- Section 6 (1) of Canada's Anti-Spam Legislation prohibits the sending of commercial electronic messages (CEMs) unless the person to whom the message is sent has consented (either express consent or implied consent) to receiving it.

- Seriously consider a prospecting farm as part of your overall networking strategy.

- The initial days in a brokerage involve a number of career firsts. Use the guidelines provided for the first conversations, the first showing and the first offer.

- Make prospecting the top priority in your new career.

- A guideline is provided for time planning for the first two weeks, but the basic structure applies for many weeks.

- Income is very difficult to predict because earning power is dependent on individual sales ability, personal connections and market conditions.

- A new registrant must budget not only for ongoing expenses, but also initial costs when beginning a new career.

Strategic Thinking For Your Career

Questions are included to assist in developing your new career. No answers are provided.

1. Am I fully prepared for the first week of my new career. What specific issues do I have to address over and above those discussed in this chapter?

2. What paperwork, in addition to that discussed in this chapter, has to be completed in my particular circumstances?

3. If I am electing to be an independent contractor, is there any additional information that I require regarding remittances (e.g., CCP, income tax and HST)?

4. Are there selected skills training courses that I could take, or reference materials that I can purchase, to provide further guidance on networking, prospecting and related sales activities?

Chapter Mini-Review

Solutions are located in the Appendix.

1. Conducting a sign survey in the local community is one of several activities that can be done prior to becoming a registrant?

   ◯ True   ◯ False

2. The wording of a typical salesperson employment agreement is generally the same as those found in an independent contractor agreement.

   ◯ True   ◯ False

3. The Real Estate Council of Ontario may require a Sheriff's search for writs when reviewing a new salesperson application.

   ◯ True   ◯ False

4. Independent contractors are not normally required to make CPP contributions.

   ◯ True   ◯ False

5. A broker of record has various supervisory responsibilities regarding registrants within the brokerage, but these do not apply to independent contractors.

   ◯ True   ◯ False

6. *Do not call* legislation applies to telemarketers, but does not apply to real estate salespeople cold calling homeowners because real estate is exempted under this federal legislation.

   ◯ True   ◯ False

7. A prospecting farm can only be effective if it involves selecting a specified number of homes within a particular geographic area.

   ◯ True   ◯ False

8. One of two primary objectives of a salesperson in handling an incoming telephone call is to arrange for a face-to-face meeting.

   ◯ True   ◯ False

9. Scripting is not effective for new salespeople and is only relevant when an individual has gained considerable experience.

   ◯ True   ◯ False

10. Given the unpredictability of commission incomes, new registrants should attempt to reduce debt wherever possible, and have sufficient cash reserves for a three to six-month period.

    ◯ True   ◯ False

Active Learning Exercises

No Solutions are provided for these career preparation questions.

■ Exercise 1   Sphere of Influence

List names of friends, business and professional acquaintances, and other established contacts as a starting point for a sphere of influence database.

SPHERE OF INFLUENCE		
Name	*Address*	*Contact Information/Details*

SPHERE OF INFLUENCE		
Name	*Address*	*Contact Information/Details*

▣ Exercise 2   FSBO's and Expired Listings

List FSBO's and expired listings that you are aware of in the particular geographic area that you want to concentrate on when starting your career. Remember, this exercise is for information and tracking purposes only until such time as your registration is received.

FSBO/EXPIRED
Details/Pertinent Information

FSBO/EXPIRED
Details/Pertinent Information

■ Exercise 3   Prospecting Farm

Identify a potential geographic farm area within your local market area and determine the various things that you must do in preparation to work within this farm area (e.g., obtain names/contact information, walk the area to gain familiarity and organize your prospecting plan).

PROSPECTING FARM
Action Plan

■ Exercise 4   Expand the Checklist

The *Getting Ready for the Brokerage* checklist illustrated earlier has been reprinted with additional space. What new or follow-up questions do you now want to include based on information addressed in this chapter?

GETTING READY CHECKLIST

Staff Services	What specific services are available during normal business hours? Who is responsible for these services?	**E-Mail**	How is e-mail communication handled in the brokerage? Do I set up a separate e-mail account or is it centrally administered by the brokerage?
Desk Space	How is desk space allocated? What fees apply (if applicable)? What equipment and supplies are provided by the brokerage for that office space?	**Internet**	What Internet access is provided to salespeople?
Telephone	What is provided, what additional costs are incurred by salespersons and how is long distance handled (e.g., costs, procedures and access codes)?	**Postage/ Courier**	How is postage handled regarding single or bulk mailings? What about costs when documentation has to be couriered?
Pager/ Cell Phone	Does the brokerage have a pager system? Are there any special arrangements or pricing when acquiring a pager, cell phone, personal digital assistant (PDA) or similar equipment?	**Website/ Promotion**	What procedures do I follow to have access to the brokerage website for promotion/ advertising? Can I link a personal website to the main site and what brokerage requirements must be followed? What costs am I responsible for?
Office Equipment (Photocopier, Fax, Etc.)	What office equipment is provided to salespeople? What additional costs are borne by the salesperson? How are these costs allocated; e.g., card access for photocopier, fax and so forth.	**Office Access/ Security**	What are normal office hours? Is a key or alternative security access (i.e., access code) required for after hours? What other security provisions must be followed (e.g., locked unattended offices and desks). What guidelines does the brokerage have regarding personal safety when listing and showing property?
Office Supplies	What office supplies (including paper and envelopes) are supplied?	**Office Duty (Opportunity) Time**	Is office duty time allocated by the brokerage? What is the schedule and are there any specific procedures that must be followed?
Hardware/ Software	What computer equipment is available for salespeople to use within the brokerage? What hardware/software best aligns with systems currently in use in the brokerage?	**Multiple Listing Service®/Board Membership**	What forms must be completed and what costs are involved? What processing fees apply when listing property on MLS®? What costs are borne by the brokerage or, alternatively, how are these costs and fees billed to salespeople? What about renewals?

continued

GETTING READY CHECKLIST *(continued)*

For Sale Signs/ Frames/ Installation	What does the brokerage provide in terms of *for sale* signs, sign frames, sign information boxes. What about custom signage and add-on promotion pieces? What costs are involved for sign installations?	**Agreements**	How are agreements prepared in the brokerage in readiness for presentation and possible acceptance? What software program is used? Make certain that you obtain the most up-to-date clauses.
Business Cards	Are business cards supplied? If not, what brokerage standards must be adhered to in ordering cards?	**Negotiations**	How are multiple offer situations handled? What steps are taken when processing deposits and what other circumstances and procedures should I beware of; e.g., buying and selling for my own purposes.
Advertising	What standard advertising formats are used by the brokerage, what costs apply and how are classified advertisements processed by the brokerage?	**Transactions**	How are accepted agreements of purchase and sale processed in the brokerage and what administrative or other brokerage fees (if any) apply that have not already been identified in this checklist?
Promotional Pieces	The brokerage may supply various promotional pieces or have them available for purchase. If so, what items are available; e.g., feature sheets, brochures, flyers, cards and open house signs?	**Privacy**	What is the privacy policy of the brokerage? What specific provisions apply to activities of salespeople? Is there a privacy brochure?
Forms	What forms (e.g., listings, agreements, trade record sheets and supporting forms) are provided by the brokerage and at what cost (if applicable)?	**Office Meetings**	Are there regularly scheduled office meetings?
Working with Sellers	What forms are used and procedures followed when working with sellers as clients and customers?	**Training**	What training is provided by the brokerage and what costs (if any) are borne by the salespeople?
Working with Buyers	What forms are used and procedures followed when working with buyers as clients and customers?	**Referrals**	What office procedures apply when making referrals?
Listings	How are listings processed internally within the brokerage and what assistance is provided in that regard? What approval and related procedures are in place that must be followed? What costs, such as administrative or other fees, are the salesperson's responsibility (in addition to MLS®-related fees)?		

GETTING READY CHECKLIST—ADDITIONAL TOPICS

■ Exercise 5   Time Planning

Based on guidelines set out in this chapter, prepare a time planning schedule for the first four weeks of your career detailing both prospecting and other activities. Use this as a basic plan, and then refine and transpose it into your monthly planner upon receiving your registration.

THE FIRST FOUR WEEKS						
SUNDAY	MONDAY	TUESDAY	WEDNESDAY	THURSDAY	FRIDAY	SATURDAY

◼ Exercise 6   Budgeting

Prepare an initial budget as a general guideline only with a rough approximation of estimated income and expenses. As your career unfolds, refine these amounts as the need arises. Prudent financial management and sound budgeting are important aspects of your new career.

INCOME ESTIMATE

Average Price

Average Time to Close

Typical Commission Rate

Listing or Selling Commission Earned

Percentage of Positive Leads That Convert to Earned Commission

Average Positive Leads Generated per Week

YEAR ONE—PROJECTED INCOME

Total Positive Leads Generated

Percentage Converted to Earned Commission

Listing or Selling Commission Received

Time Delay

INITIAL EXPENSE ESTIMATE

Pre-Registration Education Courses (Enrollment Fees Only)

RECO Salesperson Registration (Every Two Years Based on 2012)

RECO Insurance Payment *(Annual based on 2011–2012—rounded)*

Entrance Fees
    Real Estate Board

    Ontario Real Estate Association

    Canadian Real Estate Association

Miscellaneous

TOTAL INITIAL ESTIMATE

ONGOING EXPENSE ESTIMATE (YEAR ONE)

Advertising and Promotion

Professional Dues

    Real Estate Board *(MLS® Dues)*

    OREA and CREA

Professional Development

    Articling Courses

Communication Expenses

Auto Expenses

Supplies

Miscellaneous

TOTAL EXPENSE ESTIMATE

SUMMARY

Projected Income—Year One

Expenses

    Initial Expense Estimate

    Ongoing Expense Estimate (Year One)

Total Expenses (Year One)

NET INCOME ESTIMATE (BEFORE TAX)

APPENDIX

THE RESIDENTIAL
REAL ESTATE TRANSACTION

APPENDIX

CONTENTS AT A GLANCE

MORTGAGE PAYMENT FACTORS

MORTGAGE PAYMENT FACTORS (per $1,000 of Loan Amount)

Weekly Payment Factors

Int. Rate	\multicolumn{5}{Amortization Period}
	5	10	15	20	25
1.00	3.943244	2.020779	1.380489	1.060742	.869211
1.25	3.967692	2.045628	1.405768	1.086459	.895367
1.50	3.992209	2.070645	1.431313	1.112538	.921982
1.75	4.016796	2.095828	1.457122	1.138977	.949052
2.00	4.041452	2.121178	1.483194	1.165774	.976572
2.25	4.066177	2.146693	1.509426	1.192925	1.004538
2.50	4.090971	2.172373	1.536117	1.220428	1.032945
2.75	4.115832	2.198216	1.562966	1.248279	1.061789
3.00	4.140761	2.224222	1.590070	1.276476	1.091063
3.25	4.165758	2.250390	1.617428	1.305015	1.120762
3.50	4.190821	2.276719	1.645038	1.333891	1.150881
3.75	4.215952	2.303208	1.672897	1.363103	1.181413
4.00	4.241149	2.329856	1.701005	1.392645	1.212352
4.25	4.266412	2.356662	1.729358	1.422515	1.243691
4.50	4.291742	2.383625	1.757955	1.452707	1.275424
4.75	4.317136	2.410745	1.786793	1.483218	1.307543
5.00	4.342596	2.438019	1.815869	1.514043	1.340042
5.25	4.368121	2.465448	1.845183	1.545178	1.372912
5.50	4.393711	2.493030	1.874731	1.576619	1.406147
5.75	4.419364	2.520764	1.904511	1.608361	1.439739
6.00	4.445082	2.548648	1.934520	1.640399	1.473680
6.25	4.470863	2.576683	1.964756	1.672729	1.507963
6.50	4.496708	2.604866	1.995217	1.705345	1.542580
6.75	4.522615	2.633197	2.025900	1.738244	1.577522
7.00	4.548585	2.661674	2.056801	1.771419	1.612781
7.25	4.574617	2.690297	2.087920	1.804867	1.648351
7.50	4.600712	2.719064	2.119252	1.838581	1.684222
7.75	4.626867	2.747974	2.150796	1.872558	1.720386
8.00	4.653084	2.777025	2.182547	1.906791	1.756836
8.25	4.679362	2.806218	2.214505	1.941276	1.793564
8.50	4.705701	2.835550	2.246666	1.976008	1.830560
8.75	4.732100	2.865020	2.279026	2.010981	1.867818
9.00	4.758559	2.894628	2.311584	2.046190	1.905329
9.25	4.785077	2.924371	2.344336	2.081630	1.943086
9.50	4.811654	2.954249	2.377280	2.117296	1.981080
9.75	4.838291	2.984260	2.410413	2.153183	2.019304
10.00	4.864986	3.014404	2.443731	2.189285	2.057750
10.25	4.891739	3.044678	2.477232	2.225598	2.096411
10.50	4.918550	3.075082	2.510913	2.262115	2.135278
10.75	4.945419	3.105614	2.544771	2.298833	2.174345
11.00	4.972345	3.136274	2.578803	2.335746	2.213604
11.25	4.999327	3.167059	2.613007	2.372849	2.253048
11.50	5.026366	3.197969	2.647379	2.410136	2.292670
11.75	5.053461	3.229002	2.681916	2.447604	2.332463
12.00	5.080613	3.260158	2.716615	2.485246	2.372420
12.25	5.107819	3.291433	2.751474	2.523058	2.412534
12.50	5.135081	3.322829	2.786490	2.561036	2.452800
12.75	5.162397	3.354342	2.821659	2.599174	2.493209

Int. Rate	\multicolumn{5}{Amortization Period}
	5	10	15	20	25
13.00	5.189768	3.385972	2.856979	2.637467	2.533757
13.25	5.217193	3.417718	2.892446	2.675911	2.574437
13.50	5.244671	3.449578	2.928059	2.714501	2.615243
13.75	5.272203	3.481550	2.963814	2.753233	2.656169
14.00	5.299788	3.513634	2.999707	2.792102	2.697209
14.25	5.327426	3.545829	3.035738	2.831104	2.738358
14.50	5.355116	3.578132	3.071901	2.870233	2.779610
14.75	5.382858	3.610543	3.108195	2.909487	2.820960
15.00	5.410651	3.643060	3.144617	2.948860	2.862404
15.25	5.438496	3.675683	3.181165	2.988348	2.903935
15.50	5.466392	3.708408	3.217834	3.027948	2.945549
15.75	5.494338	3.741237	3.254623	3.067655	2.987241
16.00	5.522335	3.774166	3.291529	3.107465	3.029007
16.25	5.550381	3.807195	3.328548	3.147374	3.070843
16.50	5.578477	3.840322	3.365680	3.187379	3.112743
16.75	5.606623	3.873546	3.402919	3.227475	3.154704
17.00	5.634817	3.906867	3.440265	3.267659	3.196722
17.25	5.663059	3.940281	3.477715	3.307927	3.238793
17.50	5.691350	3.973789	3.515265	3.348277	3.280912
17.75	5.719689	4.007389	3.552914	3.388703	3.323077
18.00	5.748075	4.041079	3.590658	3.429203	3.365284
18.25	5.776508	4.074859	3.628495	3.469774	3.407529
18.50	5.804988	4.108726	3.666424	3.510412	3.449809
18.75	5.833514	4.142681	3.704440	3.551115	3.492122
19.00	5.862087	4.176721	3.742543	3.591878	3.534462
19.25	5.890705	4.210845	3.780729	3.632699	3.576829
19.50	5.919368	4.245051	3.818996	3.673575	3.619219
19.75	5.948077	4.279340	3.857342	3.714503	3.661629
20.00	5.976830	4.313709	3.895764	3.755480	3.704057
20.25	6.005628	4.348157	3.934260	3.796504	3.746499
20.50	6.034469	4.382682	3.972829	3.837572	3.788954
20.75	6.063354	4.417285	4.011467	3.878681	3.831420
21.00	6.092283	4.451962	4.050172	3.919828	3.873893
21.25	6.121254	4.486714	4.088943	3.961011	3.916372
21.50	6.150269	4.521539	4.127777	4.002229	3.958855
21.75	6.179325	4.556436	4.166672	4.043477	4.001339
22.00	6.208423	4.591403	4.205627	4.084755	4.043823
22.25	6.237563	4.626439	4.244638	4.126059	4.086305
22.50	6.266745	4.661543	4.283704	4.167388	4.128783
22.75	6.295967	4.696714	4.322823	4.208739	4.171255
23.00	6.325229	4.731951	4.361994	4.250111	4.213720
23.25	6.354532	4.767253	4.401213	4.291502	4.256176
23.50	6.383875	4.802617	4.440480	4.332908	4.298622
23.75	6.413258	4.838044	4.479793	4.374330	4.341056
24.00	6.442679	4.873532	4.519149	4.415764	4.383477
24.25	6.472140	4.909080	4.558547	4.457210	4.425883
24.50	6.501639	4.944687	4.597985	4.498664	4.468273
24.75	6.531176	4.980351	4.637461	4.540127	4.510647

APPENDIX

MORTGAGE PAYMENT FACTORS (per $1,000 of Loan Amount)

Bi-Weekly Payment Factors

Int. Rate	Amortization Period 5	10	15	20	25
1.00	7.887244	4.041946	2.761243	2.121687	1.738588
1.25	7.936334	4.091746	2.811874	2.173178	1.790949
1.50	7.985566	4.141884	2.863038	2.225396	1.844230
1.75	8.034939	4.192359	2.914733	2.278337	1.898422
2.00	8.084452	4.243168	2.966955	2.331994	1.953518
2.25	8.134105	4.294310	3.019701	2.386364	2.009508
2.50	8.183896	4.345783	3.072968	2.441440	2.066384
2.75	8.233826	4.397587	3.126752	2.497215	2.124135
3.00	8.283894	4.449718	3.181051	2.553683	2.182751
3.25	8.334099	4.502175	3.235859	2.610839	2.242220
3.50	8.384440	4.554957	3.291174	2.668673	2.302531
3.75	8.434917	4.608062	3.346991	2.727180	2.363671
4.00	8.485530	4.661487	3.403306	2.786352	2.425628
4.25	8.536276	4.715231	3.460115	2.846180	2.488389
4.50	8.587157	4.769291	3.517414	2.906657	2.551940
4.75	8.638172	4.823667	3.575199	2.967775	2.616267
5.00	8.689319	4.878355	3.633464	3.029524	2.681357
5.25	8.740598	4.933354	3.692206	3.091897	2.747193
5.50	8.792008	4.988662	3.751419	3.154884	2.813762
5.75	8.843549	5.044277	3.811099	3.218476	2.881049
6.00	8.895220	5.100196	3.871241	3.282664	2.949037
6.25	8.947021	5.156417	3.931840	3.347438	3.017712
6.50	8.998950	5.212938	3.992890	3.412790	3.087058
6.75	9.051007	5.269757	4.054387	3.478708	3.157059
7.00	9.103192	5.326872	4.116326	3.545184	3.227698
7.25	9.155504	5.384281	4.178701	3.612207	3.298961
7.50	9.207942	5.441980	4.241507	3.679768	3.370830
7.75	9.260505	5.499968	4.304738	3.747856	3.443290
8.00	9.313193	5.558243	4.368390	3.816461	3.516325
8.25	9.366005	5.616802	4.432456	3.885572	3.589918
8.50	9.418941	5.675643	4.496930	3.955181	3.664053
8.75	9.472000	5.734763	4.561809	4.025276	3.738715
9.00	9.525180	5.794160	4.627085	4.095847	3.813887
9.25	9.578482	5.853832	4.692753	4.166883	3.889554
9.50	9.631905	5.913775	4.758807	4.238375	3.965699
9.75	9.685448	5.973989	4.825242	4.310311	4.042308
10.00	9.739110	6.034469	4.892052	4.382682	4.119365
10.25	9.792891	6.095214	4.959230	4.455478	4.196855
10.50	9.846790	6.156222	5.026772	4.528687	4.274762
10.75	9.900806	6.217489	5.094672	4.602300	4.353072
11.00	9.954939	6.279013	5.162923	4.676307	4.431771
11.25	10.009188	6.340792	5.231520	4.750697	4.510843
11.50	10.063552	6.402822	5.300456	4.825461	4.590275
11.75	10.118031	6.465103	5.369727	4.900588	4.670053
12.00	10.172624	6.527630	5.439326	4.976068	4.750162
12.25	10.227330	6.590401	5.509247	5.051892	4.830591
12.50	10.282149	6.653414	5.579484	5.128050	4.911325
12.75	10.337079	6.716667	5.650033	5.204533	4.992352

Int. Rate	Amortization Period 5	10	15	20	25
13.00	10.392121	6.780155	5.720886	5.281330	5.073659
13.25	10.447273	6.843878	5.792038	5.358432	5.155233
13.50	10.502535	6.907832	5.863483	5.435831	5.237064
13.75	10.557906	6.972015	5.935216	5.513516	5.319138
14.00	10.613385	7.036424	6.007231	5.591480	5.401445
14.25	10.668972	7.101057	6.079522	5.669712	5.483974
14.50	10.724667	7.165910	6.152083	5.748204	5.566713
14.75	10.780467	7.230981	6.224909	5.826947	5.649652
15.00	10.836373	7.296268	6.297994	5.905934	5.732780
15.25	10.892384	7.361768	6.371333	5.985155	5.816088
15.50	10.948500	7.427479	6.444919	6.064601	5.899566
15.75	11.004718	7.493397	6.518749	6.144266	5.983205
16.00	11.061040	7.559520	6.592815	6.224141	6.066994
16.25	11.117464	7.625845	6.667113	6.304219	6.150926
16.50	11.173989	7.692371	6.741637	6.384490	6.234992
16.75	11.230615	7.759094	6.816382	6.464949	6.319182
17.00	11.287342	7.826011	6.891342	6.545587	6.403490
17.25	11.344167	7.893121	6.966513	6.626397	6.487908
17.50	11.401092	7.960419	7.041889	6.707373	6.572427
17.75	11.458114	8.027905	7.117466	6.788507	6.657040
18.00	11.515233	8.095575	7.193237	6.869792	6.741741
18.25	11.572450	8.163427	7.269188	6.951222	6.826522
18.50	11.629762	8.231457	7.345344	7.032790	6.911377
18.75	11.687169	8.299665	7.421671	7.114490	6.996300
19.00	11.744671	8.368046	7.498172	7.196315	7.081284
19.25	11.802267	8.436598	7.574844	7.278260	7.166323
19.50	11.859956	8.505320	7.651682	7.360318	7.251412
19.75	11.917736	8.574208	7.728680	7.442885	7.336545
20.00	11.975610	8.643259	7.805835	7.524753	7.421716
20.25	12.033574	8.712472	7.883142	7.607118	7.506922
20.50	12.091629	8.781844	7.960596	7.689573	7.592156
20.75	12.149773	8.851372	8.038193	7.772115	7.677414
21.00	12.208066	8.921054	8.115928	7.854738	7.762691
21.25	12.266328	8.990888	8.193797	7.937436	7.847984
21.50	12.324738	9.060870	8.271797	8.020205	7.933287
21.75	12.383234	9.130999	8.349921	8.103041	8.018597
22.00	12.441816	9.201271	8.428168	8.185938	8.103910
22.25	12.500485	9.271686	8.506532	8.268892	8.189222
22.50	12.559238	9.342240	8.585009	8.351899	8.274530
22.75	12.618075	9.412930	8.663596	8.434954	8.359830
23.00	12.676996	9.483755	8.742288	8.518054	8.445119
23.25	12.736000	9.554713	8.821083	8.601194	8.530393
23.50	12.795086	9.625800	8.899975	8.684370	8.615651
23.75	12.854254	9.697014	8.978961	8.767580	8.700888
24.00	12.913502	9.768354	9.058039	8.850818	8.786102
24.25	12.972831	9.839816	9.137203	8.934082	8.871290
24.50	13.032239	9.911399	9.216451	9.017368	8.956450
24.75	13.091726	9.983100	9.295779	9.100672	9.041580

APPENDIX

MORTGAGE PAYMENT FACTORS (per $1,000 of Loan Amount)

Semi-Monthly Payment Factors

Int. Rate	\multicolumn{5}{Amortization Period}				
	5	10	15	20	25
1.00	8.544651	4.378845	2.991394	2.298530	1.883501
1.25	8.597867	4.432814	3.046258	2.354323	1.940234
1.50	8.651237	4.487149	3.101699	2.410903	1.997963
1.75	8.704760	4.541849	3.157715	2.468267	2.056681
2.00	8.758436	4.596912	3.214304	2.526408	2.116378
2.25	8.812263	4.652336	3.271460	2.585320	2.177045
2.50	8.866241	4.708119	3.329181	2.644998	2.238672
2.75	8.920369	4.764261	3.387463	2.705434	2.301247
3.00	8.974647	4.820758	3.446303	2.766622	2.364760
3.25	9.029073	4.877609	3.505695	2.828555	2.429197
3.50	9.083648	4.934811	3.565636	2.891224	2.494547
3.75	9.138371	4.992364	3.626123	2.954621	2.560796
4.00	9.193241	5.050265	3.687149	3.018739	2.627931
4.25	9.248256	5.108511	3.748711	3.083570	2.695937
4.50	9.303418	5.167101	3.810804	3.149104	2.764799
4.75	9.358724	5.226032	3.873424	3.215332	2.834503
5.00	9.414174	5.285303	3.936565	3.282245	2.905033
5.25	9.469767	5.344911	4.000222	3.349834	2.976373
5.50	9.525504	5.404854	4.064391	3.418088	3.048508
5.75	9.581382	5.465130	4.129066	3.486999	3.121420
6.00	9.637402	5.526736	4.194242	3.557556	3.195033
6.25	9.693562	5.586669	4.259913	3.626749	3.269511
6.50	9.749862	5.647929	4.326075	3.697568	3.344656
6.75	9.806302	5.709512	4.392721	3.769002	3.420511
7.00	9.862880	5.771415	4.459845	3.841040	3.497059
7.25	9.919595	5.833637	4.527443	3.913671	3.574282
7.50	9.976448	5.896175	4.595508	3.986886	3.652164
7.75	10.033437	5.959026	4.664035	4.060672	3.730686
8.00	10.090562	6.022188	4.733017	4.135019	3.809831
8.25	10.147821	6.085658	4.802449	4.209916	3.889582
8.50	10.205215	6.149343	4.872325	4.285351	3.969921
8.75	10.262742	6.213513	4.942638	4.361314	4.050831
9.00	10.320402	6.277893	5.013383	4.437793	4.132294
9.25	10.378194	6.342571	5.084553	4.514778	4.214294
9.50	10.436117	6.407544	5.156142	4.592256	4.296814
9.75	10.494170	6.472809	5.228143	4.670217	4.379836
10.00	10.552353	6.538365	5.300552	4.748649	4.463344
10.25	10.610666	6.604207	5.373361	4.827541	4.547322
10.50	10.669106	6.670335	5.446564	4.906883	4.631752
10.75	10.727674	6.736744	5.520155	4.986663	4.716620
11.00	10.786369	6.803432	5.594127	5.066869	4.801910
11.25	10.845190	6.870397	5.668474	5.147492	4.887604
11.50	10.904137	6.937635	5.743191	5.228520	4.973690
11.75	10.963208	7.005144	5.818269	5.309942	5.060150
12.00	11.022403	7.072921	5.893704	5.391748	5.146971
12.25	11.081721	7.140963	5.969489	5.473927	5.234138
12.50	11.141161	7.209267	6.045617	5.556468	5.321637
12.75	11.200723	7.277831	6.122082	5.639362	5.409453
13.00	11.260405	7.346652	6.198878	5.722597	5.497574
13.25	11.320208	7.415727	6.275999	5.806163	5.585986
13.50	11.380130	7.485053	6.353438	5.890051	5.674675
13.75	11.440171	7.554628	6.431189	5.974250	5.763629
14.00	11.500330	7.624448	6.509246	6.058751	5.852836
14.25	11.560606	7.694510	6.587603	6.143544	5.942284
14.50	11.620998	7.764812	6.666253	6.228619	6.031960
14.75	11.681506	7.835351	6.745191	6.313968	6.121853
15.00	11.742128	7.906125	6.824410	6.399580	6.211953
15.25	11.802865	7.977129	6.903905	6.485446	6.302248
15.50	11.863715	8.048362	6.983668	6.571559	6.392728
15.75	11.924678	8.119821	7.063695	6.657908	6.483382
16.00	11.985753	8.191502	7.143980	6.744485	6.574200
16.25	12.046938	8.263403	7.224516	6.831282	6.665174
16.50	12.108235	8.335522	7.305297	6.918291	6.756292
16.75	12.169640	8.407854	7.386319	7.005502	6.847548
17.00	12.231155	8.480398	7.467575	7.092909	6.938931
17.25	12.292777	8.553151	7.549060	7.180503	7.030433
17.50	12.354507	8.626109	7.630767	7.268277	7.122046
17.75	12.416344	8.699270	7.712692	7.356222	7.213761
18.00	12.478286	8.772632	7.794828	7.444333	7.305573
18.25	12.540334	8.846191	7.877171	7.532601	7.397472
18.50	12.602486	8.919944	7.959716	7.621019	7.489451
18.75	12.664741	8.993889	8.042455	7.709580	7.581505
19.00	12.727099	9.068023	8.125386	7.798279	7.673625
19.25	12.789560	9.142344	8.208501	7.887107	7.765806
19.50	12.852122	9.216848	8.291797	7.976059	7.858042
19.75	12.914784	9.291533	8.375268	8.065129	7.950326
20.00	12.977546	9.366395	8.458908	8.154309	8.042652
20.25	13.040408	9.441434	8.542714	8.243595	8.135016
20.50	13.103367	9.516644	8.626680	8.332980	8.227411
20.75	13.166425	9.592025	8.710801	8.422459	8.319833
21.00	13.229579	9.667573	8.795073	8.512026	8.412277
21.25	13.292829	9.743285	8.879491	8.601676	8.504738
21.50	13.356175	9.819160	8.964050	8.691403	8.597211
21.75	13.419616	9.895193	9.048746	8.781203	8.689692
22.00	13.483150	9.971383	9.133574	8.871070	8.782177
22.25	13.546777	10.047728	9.218530	8.960999	8.874662
22.50	13.610497	10.124223	9.303610	9.050987	8.967142
22.75	13.674309	10.200868	9.388808	9.141027	9.059615
23.00	13.738212	10.277659	9.474122	9.231116	9.152076
23.25	13.802205	10.354593	9.559547	9.321250	9.244522
23.50	13.866287	10.431669	9.645078	9.411423	9.336950
23.75	13.930458	10.508883	9.730712	9.501633	9.429357
24.00	13.994717	10.586234	9.816446	9.591875	9.521740
24.25	14.059064	10.663718	9.902273	9.682145	9.614095
24.50	14.123497	10.741333	9.988193	9.772439	9.706421
24.75	14.188016	10.819077	10.074199	9.862755	9.798714

APPENDIX

MORTGAGE PAYMENT FACTORS (per $1,000 of Loan Amount)

Monthly Payment Factors

Int. Rate	Amortization Period 5	10	15	20	25
1.00	17.092853	8.759511	5.984032	4.598017	3.767784
1.25	17.200199	8.867930	6.094097	4.709868	3.881475
1.50	17.307863	8.977093	6.205330	4.823308	3.997171
1.75	17.415843	9.086996	6.317724	4.938326	4.114856
2.00	17.524137	9.197636	6.431274	5.054912	4.234512
2.25	17.632745	9.309011	6.545972	5.173052	4.356121
2.50	17.741664	9.421115	6.661811	5.292736	4.479662
2.75	17.850895	9.533946	6.778784	5.413950	4.605115
3.00	17.960435	9.647500	6.896884	5.536680	4.732455
3.25	18.070284	9.761774	7.016102	5.660911	4.861660
3.50	18.180439	9.876762	7.136432	5.786630	4.992703
3.75	18.290900	9.992462	7.257863	5.913820	5.125560
4.00	18.401665	10.108870	7.380387	6.042465	5.260202
4.25	18.512732	10.225981	7.503996	6.172548	5.396602
4.50	18.624102	10.343792	7.628681	6.304052	5.534730
4.75	18.735771	10.462297	7.754431	6.436959	5.674556
5.00	18.847739	10.581483	7.881238	6.571250	5.816050
5.25	18.960005	10.701376	8.009091	6.706908	5.959180
5.50	19.072566	10.821941	8.137981	6.843913	6.103915
5.75	19.185423	10.943184	8.267897	6.982245	6.250221
6.00	19.298572	11.065099	8.398828	7.121884	6.398066
6.25	19.412013	11.187683	8.530764	7.262811	6.547416
6.50	19.525745	11.310931	8.663695	7.405004	6.698238
6.75	19.639766	11.434838	8.797609	7.548443	6.850496
7.00	19.754075	11.559399	8.932494	7.693106	7.004158
7.25	19.868670	11.684610	9.068341	7.838973	7.159187
7.50	19.983549	11.810465	9.205137	7.986021	7.315549
7.75	20.098712	11.936960	9.342870	8.134229	7.473210
8.00	20.214157	12.064090	9.481529	8.283575	7.632135
8.25	20.329883	12.191850	9.621103	8.434037	7.792288
8.50	20.445888	12.320234	9.761579	8.585592	7.953635
8.75	20.562170	12.449238	9.902945	8.738219	8.116142
9.00	20.678729	12.578856	10.045189	8.891895	8.279774
9.25	20.795563	12.709083	10.188298	9.046598	8.444497
9.50	20.912670	12.839914	10.332261	9.202305	8.610276
9.75	21.030049	12.971344	10.477066	9.358995	8.777079
10.00	21.147698	13.103367	10.622699	9.516644	8.944872
10.25	21.262617	13.235979	10.769149	9.675231	9.113622
10.50	21.383803	13.369173	10.916402	9.834734	9.283297
10.75	21.502255	13.502944	11.064446	9.995129	9.453864
11.00	21.620972	13.637287	11.213269	10.156396	9.625292
11.25	21.739952	13.772197	11.362858	10.318512	9.797549
11.50	21.859194	13.907667	11.513201	10.481456	9.970606
11.75	21.978696	14.043693	11.664285	10.645206	10.144431
12.00	22.098457	14.180269	11.816096	10.809741	10.318996
12.25	22.218476	14.317389	11.968624	10.975039	10.494270
12.50	22.338750	14.455048	12.121854	11.141079	10.670227
12.75	22.459278	14.593241	12.275775	11.307841	10.846838

Int. Rate	Amortization Period 5	10	15	20	25
13.00	22.580060	14.731961	12.430373	11.475304	11.024075
13.25	22.701092	14.871203	12.585637	11.643447	11.201912
13.50	22.822375	15.010961	12.741554	11.812250	11.380323
13.75	22.943906	15.151230	12.898111	11.981694	11.559282
14.00	23.065685	15.292005	13.055297	12.151759	11.738765
14.25	23.187708	15.433279	13.213098	12.322426	11.918747
14.50	23.309976	15.575047	13.371503	12.493674	12.099205
14.75	23.432486	15.717303	13.530498	12.665487	12.280116
15.00	23.555237	15.860041	13.690073	12.837844	12.461457
15.25	23.678228	16.003257	13.850215	13.010728	12.643207
15.50	23.801457	16.146944	14.010912	13.184121	12.825344
15.75	23.924922	16.291096	14.171253	13.358006	13.007848
16.00	24.048622	16.435709	14.333924	13.532364	13.190699
16.25	24.172556	16.580776	14.496215	13.707180	13.373878
16.50	24.296722	16.726291	14.659014	13.882435	13.557365
16.75	24.421119	16.872250	14.822310	14.058115	13.741144
17.00	24.545744	17.018645	14.986090	14.234202	13.925195
17.25	24.670597	17.165473	15.150344	14.410682	14.109502
17.50	24.795677	17.312727	15.315061	14.587538	14.294049
17.75	24.920981	17.460401	15.480229	14.764755	14.478820
18.00	25.046508	17.608491	15.645837	14.942319	14.663799
18.25	25.172256	17.756990	15.811874	15.120216	14.848971
18.50	25.298225	17.905892	15.978330	15.298430	15.034322
18.75	25.424413	18.055193	16.145194	15.476949	15.219837
19.00	25.550817	18.204887	16.312456	15.655759	15.405505
19.25	25.677437	18.354968	16.480104	15.834845	15.591311
19.50	25.804272	18.505431	16.648129	16.014197	15.777243
19.75	25.931319	18.656270	16.816521	16.193800	15.963289
20.00	26.058577	18.807480	16.985269	16.373642	16.149438
20.25	26.186046	18.959055	17.154364	16.553712	16.335678
20.50	26.313722	19.110990	17.323795	16.733998	16.521998
20.75	26.441605	19.263280	17.493554	16.914489	16.708389
21.00	26.569693	19.415920	17.663630	17.095172	16.894840
21.25	26.697985	19.568903	17.834015	17.276038	17.081342
21.50	26.826480	19.722225	18.004698	17.457076	17.267886
21.75	26.955175	19.875880	18.175672	17.638275	17.454462
22.00	27.084070	20.029863	18.346926	17.819625	17.641063
22.25	27.213162	20.184169	18.518453	18.001117	17.827679
22.50	27.342451	20.338793	18.690242	18.182742	18.014304
22.75	27.471935	20.493729	18.862286	18.364489	12.200930
23.00	27.601613	20.648972	19.034577	18.546351	18.387550
23.25	27.731482	20.804518	19.207105	18.728317	18.574156
23.50	27.861542	20.960361	19.379864	18.910381	18.760742
23.75	27.991791	21.116496	19.552844	19.092533	18.947302
24.00	28.122228	21.272918	19.726037	19.274765	19.133830
24.25	28.252851	21.429622	19.899437	19.457070	19.320319
24.50	28.383658	21.586603	20.073035	19.639441	19.506765
24.75	28.514649	21.743856	20.246823	19.821869	19.693162

APPENDIX

FORMS

OREA Ontario Real Estate Association **Agreement of Purchase and Sale**

Form 100
for use in the Province of Ontario

This Agreement of Purchase and Sale dated this .... day of .... 20...........

BUYER, ..., agrees to purchase from
(Full legal names of all Buyers)

SELLER, ..., the following
(Full legal names of all Sellers)

REAL PROPERTY:

Address ....

fronting on the .... side of ....

in the ....

and having a frontage of .... more or less by a depth of .... more or less

and legally described as ....

.... (the "property")
(Legal description of land including easements not described elsewhere)

PURCHASE PRICE: Dollars (CDN$) ....

.... Dollars

DEPOSIT: Buyer submits ....
(Herewith/Upon Acceptance/as otherwise described in this Agreement)

.... Dollars (CDN$) ....

by negotiable cheque payable to .... "Deposit Holder" to be held
in trust pending completion or other termination of this Agreement and to be credited toward the Purchase Price on completion. For the purposes of this
Agreement, "Upon Acceptance" shall mean that the Buyer is required to deliver the deposit to the Deposit Holder within 24 hours of the acceptance of
this Agreement. The parties to this Agreement hereby acknowledge that, unless otherwise provided for in this Agreement, the Deposit Holder shall place
the deposit in trust in the Deposit Holder's non-interest bearing Real Estate Trust Account and no interest shall be earned, received or paid on the deposit.

Buyer agrees to pay the balance as more particularly set out in Schedule A attached.

SCHEDULE(S) A...**attached hereto form(s) part of this Agreement.**

1. **IRREVOCABILITY:** This offer shall be irrevocable by .... until .... a.m./p.m. on the ....
    (Seller/Buyer)

    day of .... 20 ...., after which time, if not accepted, this offer shall be null and void and the deposit
    shall be returned to the Buyer in full without interest.

2. **COMPLETION DATE:** This Agreement shall be completed by no later than 6:00 p.m. on the .... day of ....

    20 .... Upon completion, vacant possession of the property shall be given to the Buyer unless otherwise provided for in this Agreement.

INITIALS OF BUYER(S): ⬭   INITIALS OF SELLER(S): ⬭

3. **NOTICES:** The Seller hereby appoints the Listing Brokerage as agent for the Seller for the purpose of giving and receiving notices pursuant to this Agreement. Where a Brokerage (Buyer's Brokerage) has entered into a representation agreement with the Buyer, the Buyer hereby appoints the Buyer's Brokerage as agent for the purpose of giving and receiving notices pursuant to this Agreement. **Where a Brokerage represents both the Seller and the Buyer (multiple representation), the Brokerage shall not be appointed or authorized to be agent for either the Buyer or the Seller for the purpose of giving and receiving notices.** Any notice relating hereto or provided for herein shall be in writing. In addition to any provision contained herein and in any Schedule hereto, this offer, any counter-offer, notice of acceptance thereof or any notice to be given or received pursuant to this Agreement or any Schedule hereto (any of them, "Document") shall be deemed given and received when delivered personally or hand delivered to the Address for Service provided in the Acknowledgement below, or where a facsimile number or email address is provided herein, when transmitted electronically to that facsimile number or email address, respectively, in which case, the signature(s) of the party (parties) shall be deemed to be original.

FAX No.: ....   FAX No.: ....
                        (For delivery of Documents to Seller)   (For delivery of Documents to Buyer)

Email Address: ....   Email Address: ....
                        (For delivery of Documents to Seller)   (For delivery of Documents to Buyer)

4. **CHATTELS INCLUDED:**...

....

....

....

....

Unless otherwise stated in this Agreement or any Schedule hereto, Seller agrees to convey all fixtures and chattels included in the Purchase Price free from all liens, encumbrances or claims affecting the said fixtures and chattels.

5. **FIXTURES EXCLUDED:**...

....

....

....

....

6. **RENTAL ITEMS (Including Lease, Lease to Own):** The following equipment is rented and **not** included in the Purchase Price. The Buyer agrees to assume the rental contract(s), if assumable:

....

....

....

The Buyer agrees to co-operate and execute such documentation as may be required to facilitate such assumption.

7. **HST:** If the sale of the Property (Real Property as described above) is subject to Harmonized Sales Tax (HST), then such tax shall be

.... the Purchase Price. If the sale of the Property is not subject to HST, Seller agrees to certify on or before
          (included in/in addition to)
closing, that the sale of the Property is not subject to HST. Any HST on chattels, if applicable, is not included in the Purchase Price.

INITIALS OF BUYER(S): (⬭)   INITIALS OF SELLER(S): (⬭)

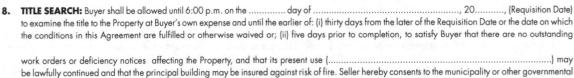
Form 100   *(continued)*   Page 3 of 6

8. **TITLE SEARCH:** Buyer shall be allowed until 6:00 p.m. on the .... day of ...., 20.........., (Requisition Date) to examine the title to the Property at Buyer's own expense and until the earlier of: (i) thirty days from the later of the Requisition Date or the date on which the conditions in this Agreement are fulfilled or otherwise waived or; (ii) five days prior to completion, to satisfy Buyer that there are no outstanding

work orders or deficiency notices affecting the Property, and that its present use (...) may be lawfully continued and that the principal building may be insured against risk of fire. Seller hereby consents to the municipality or other governmental agencies releasing to Buyer details of all outstanding work orders and deficiency notices affecting the property, and Seller agrees to execute and deliver such further authorizations in this regard as Buyer may reasonably require.

9. **FUTURE USE:** Seller and Buyer agree that there is no representation or warranty of any kind that the future intended use of the property by Buyer is or will be lawful except as may be specifically provided for in this Agreement.

10. **TITLE:** Provided that the title to the property is good and free from all registered restrictions, charges, liens, and encumbrances except as otherwise specifically provided in this Agreement and save and except for (a) any registered restrictions or covenants that run with the land providing that such are complied with; (b) any registered municipal agreements and registered agreements with publicly regulated utilities providing such have been complied with, or security has been posted to ensure compliance and completion, as evidenced by a letter from the relevant municipality or regulated utility; (c) any minor easements for the supply of domestic utility or telephone services to the property or adjacent properties; and (d) any easements for drainage, storm or sanitary sewers, public utility lines, telephone lines, cable television lines or other services which do not materially affect the use of the property. If within the specified times referred to in paragraph 8 any valid objection to title or to any outstanding work order or deficiency notice, or to the fact the said present use may not lawfully be continued, or that the principal building may not be insured against risk of fire is made in writing to Seller and which Seller is unable or unwilling to remove, remedy or satisfy or obtain insurance save and except against risk of fire (Title Insurance) in favour of the Buyer and any mortgagee, (with all related costs at the expense of the Seller), and which Buyer will not waive, this Agreement notwithstanding any intermediate acts or negotiations in respect of such objections, shall be at an end and all monies paid shall be returned without interest or deduction and Seller, Listing Brokerage and Co-operating Brokerage shall not be liable for any costs or damages. Save as to any valid objection so made by such day and except for any objection going to the root of the title, Buyer shall be conclusively deemed to have accepted Seller's title to the property.

11. **CLOSING ARRANGEMENTS:** Where each of the Seller and Buyer retain a lawyer to complete the Agreement of Purchase and Sale of the property, and where the transaction will be completed by electronic registration pursuant to Part III of the Land Registration Reform Act, R.S.O. 1990, Chapter L4 and the Electronic Registration Act, S.O. 1991, Chapter 44, and any amendments thereto, the Seller and Buyer acknowledge and agree that the exchange of closing funds, non-registrable documents and other items (the "Requisite Deliveries") and the release thereof to the Seller and Buyer will (a) not occur at the same time as the registration of the transfer/deed (and any other documents intended to be registered in connection with the completion of this transaction) and (b) be subject to conditions whereby the lawyer(s) receiving any of the Requisite Deliveries will be required to hold same in trust and not release same except in accordance with the terms of a document registration agreement between the said lawyers. The Seller and Buyer irrevocably instruct the said lawyers to be bound by the document registration agreement which is recommended from time to time by the Law Society of Upper Canada. Unless otherwise agreed to by the lawyers, such exchange of the Requisite Deliveries will occur in the applicable Land Titles Office or such other location agreeable to both lawyers.

12. **DOCUMENTS AND DISCHARGE:** Buyer shall not call for the production of any title deed, abstract, survey or other evidence of title to the property except such as are in the possession or control of Seller. If requested by Buyer, Seller will deliver any sketch or survey of the property within Seller's control to Buyer as soon as possible and prior to the Requisition Date. If a discharge of any Charge/Mortgage held by a corporation incorporated pursuant to the Trust And Loan Companies Act (Canada), Chartered Bank, Trust Company, Credit Union, Caisse Populaire or Insurance Company and which is not to be assumed by Buyer on completion, is not available in registrable form on completion, Buyer agrees to accept Seller's lawyer's personal undertaking to obtain, out of the closing funds, a discharge in registrable form and to register same, or cause same to be registered, on title within a reasonable period of time after completion, provided that on or before completion Seller shall provide to Buyer a mortgage statement prepared by the mortgagee setting out the balance required to obtain the discharge, and, where a real-time electronic cleared funds transfer system is not being used, a direction executed by Seller directing payment to the mortgagee of the amount required to obtain the discharge out of the balance due on completion.

13. **INSPECTION:** Buyer acknowledges having had the opportunity to inspect the Property and understands that upon acceptance of this offer there shall be a binding agreement of purchase and sale between Buyer and Seller. **The Buyer acknowledges having the opportunity to include a requirement for a property inspection report in this Agreement and agrees that except as may be specifically provided for in this Agreement, the Buyer will not be obtaining a property inspection or property inspection report regarding the Property.**

14. **INSURANCE:** All buildings on the property and all other things being purchased shall be and remain until completion at the risk of Seller. Pending completion, Seller shall hold all insurance policies, if any, and the proceeds thereof in trust for the parties as their interests may appear and in the event of substantial damage, Buyer may either terminate this Agreement and have all monies paid returned without interest or deduction or else take the proceeds of any insurance and complete the purchase. No insurance shall be transferred on completion. If Seller is taking back a Charge/Mortgage, or Buyer is assuming a Charge/Mortgage, Buyer shall supply Seller with reasonable evidence of adequate insurance to protect Seller's or other mortgagee's interest on completion.

INITIALS OF BUYER(S): (⬭)   INITIALS OF SELLER(S): (⬭)

Form 100   Revised 2015   **Page 3 of 6**

APPENDIX

15. PLANNING ACT: This Agreement shall be effective to create an interest in the property only if Seller complies with the subdivision control provisions of the Planning Act by completion and Seller covenants to proceed diligently at Seller's expense to obtain any necessary consent by completion.

16. DOCUMENT PREPARATION: The Transfer/Deed shall, save for the Land Transfer Tax Affidavit, be prepared in registrable form at the expense of Seller, and any Charge/Mortgage to be given back by the Buyer to Seller at the expense of the Buyer. If requested by Buyer, Seller covenants that the Transfer/Deed to be delivered on completion shall contain the statements contemplated by Section 50(22) of the Planning Act, R.S.O.1990.

17. RESIDENCY: (a) Subject to (b) below, the Seller represents and warrants that the Seller is not and on completion will not be a non-resident under the non-residency provisions of the Income Tax Act which representation and warranty shall survive and not merge upon the completion of this transaction and the Seller shall deliver to the Buyer a statutory declaration that Seller is not then a non-resident of Canada; (b) provided that if the Seller is a non-resident under the non-residency provisions of the Income Tax Act, the Buyer shall be credited towards the Purchase Price with the amount, if any, necessary for Buyer to pay to the Minister of National Revenue to satisfy Buyer's liability in respect of tax payable by Seller under the non-residency provisions of the Income Tax Act by reason of this sale. Buyer shall not claim such credit if Seller delivers on completion the prescribed certificate.

18. ADJUSTMENTS: Any rents, mortgage interest, realty taxes including local improvement rates and unmetered public or private utility charges and unmetered cost of fuel, as applicable, shall be apportioned and allowed to the day of completion, the day of completion itself to be apportioned to Buyer.

19. PROPERTY ASSESSMENT: The Buyer and Seller hereby acknowledge that the Province of Ontario has implemented current value assessment and properties may be re-assessed on an annual basis. The Buyer and Seller agree that no claim will be made against the Buyer or Seller, or any Brokerage, Broker or Salesperson, for any changes in property tax as a result of a re-assessment of the property, save and except any property taxes that accrued prior to the completion of this transaction.

20. TIME LIMITS: Time shall in all respects be of the essence hereof provided that the time for doing or completing of any matter provided for herein may be extended or abridged by an agreement in writing signed by Seller and Buyer or by their respective lawyers who may be specifically authorized in that regard.

21. TENDER: Any tender of documents or money hereunder may be made upon Seller or Buyer or their respective lawyers on the day set for completion. Money shall be tendered with funds drawn on a lawyer's trust account in the form of a bank draft, certified cheque or wire transfer using the Large Value Transfer System.

22. FAMILY LAW ACT: Seller warrants that spousal consent is not necessary to this transaction under the provisions of the Family Law Act, R.S.O.1990 unless Seller's spouse has executed the consent hereinafter provided.

23. UFFI: Seller represents and warrants to Buyer that during the time Seller has owned the property, Seller has not caused any building on the property to be insulated with insulation containing ureaformaldehyde, and that to the best of Seller's knowledge no building on the property contains or has ever contained insulation that contains ureaformaldehyde. This warranty shall survive and not merge on the completion of this transaction, and if the building is part of a multiple unit building, this warranty shall only apply to that part of the building which is the subject of this transaction.

24. LEGAL, ACCOUNTING AND ENVIRONMENTAL ADVICE: The parties acknowledge that any information provided by the brokerage is not legal, tax or environmental advice.

25. CONSUMER REPORTS: The Buyer is hereby notified that a consumer report containing credit and/or personal information may be referred to in connection with this transaction.

26. AGREEMENT IN WRITING: If there is conflict or discrepancy between any provision added to this Agreement (including any Schedule attached hereto) and any provision in the standard pre-set portion hereof, the added provision shall supersede the standard pre-set provision to the extent of such conflict or discrepancy. This Agreement including any Schedule attached hereto, shall constitute the entire Agreement between Buyer and Seller. There is no representation, warranty, collateral agreement or condition, which affects this Agreement other than as expressed herein. For the purposes of this Agreement, Seller means vendor and Buyer means purchaser. This Agreement shall be read with all changes of gender or number required by the context.

27. TIME AND DATE: Any reference to a time and date in this Agreement shall mean the time and date where the property is located.

INITIALS OF BUYER(S): ⬭   INITIALS OF SELLER(S): ⬭

Form 100   Revised 2015   **Page 4 of 6**

28. SUCCESSORS AND ASSIGNS: The heirs, executors, administrators, successors and assigns of the undersigned are bound by the terms herein.

SIGNED, SEALED AND DELIVERED in the presence of: IN WITNESS whereof I have hereunto set my hand and seal:

.... ● DATE ....
(Witness) (Buyer) (Seal)

.... ● DATE ....
(Witness) (Buyer) (Seal)

I, the Undersigned Seller, agree to the above offer. I hereby irrevocably instruct my lawyer to pay directly to the brokerage(s) with whom I have agreed to pay commission, the unpaid balance of the commission together with applicable Harmonized Sales Tax (and any other taxes as may hereafter be applicable), from the proceeds of the sale prior to any payment to the undersigned on completion, as advised by the brokerage(s) to my lawyer.

SIGNED, SEALED AND DELIVERED in the presence of: IN WITNESS whereof I have hereunto set my hand and seal:

.... ● DATE ....
(Witness) (Seller) (Seal)

.... ● DATE ....
(Witness) (Seller) (Seal)

SPOUSAL CONSENT: The Undersigned Spouse of the Seller hereby consents to the disposition evidenced herein pursuant to the provisions of the Family Law Act, R.S.O.1990, and hereby agrees with the Buyer that he/she will execute all necessary or incidental documents to give full force and effect to the sale evidenced herein.

.... ● DATE ....
(Witness) (Spouse) (Seal)

CONFIRMATION OF ACCEPTANCE: Notwithstanding anything contained herein to the contrary, I confirm this Agreement with all changes both typed and written was finally accepted by all parties at .... a.m./p.m. this .... day of.., 20...........

....
(Signature of Seller or Buyer)

INFORMATION ON BROKERAGE(S)
Listing Brokerage .... Tel.No.(...............)..
....
(Salesperson / Broker Name)
Co-op/Buyer Brokerage .... Tel.No.(...............)..
....
(Salesperson / Broker Name)

ACKNOWLEDGEMENT

I acknowledge receipt of my signed copy of this accepted Agreement of Purchase and Sale and I authorize the Brokerage to forward a copy to my lawyer.

.... DATE ....
(Seller)

.... DATE ....
(Seller)

Address for Service ....

.... Tel.No.(...........)..................

Seller's Lawyer ....

Address ....

Email ....

(...........)..................................... (...........).....................
Tel.No. FAX No.

I acknowledge receipt of my signed copy of this accepted Agreement of Purchase and Sale and I authorize the Brokerage to forward a copy to my lawyer.

.... DATE ....
(Buyer)

.... DATE ....
(Buyer)

Address for Service ....

.... Tel.No.(...........)..................

Buyer's Lawyer ....

Address ....

Email ....

(...........)..................................... (...........).....................
Tel.No. FAX No.

FOR OFFICE USE ONLY	**COMMISSION TRUST AGREEMENT**

To: Co-operating Brokerage shown on the foregoing Agreement of Purchase and Sale:
In consideration for the Co-operating Brokerage procuring the foregoing Agreement of Purchase and Sale, I hereby declare that all moneys received or receivable by me in connection with the Transaction as contemplated in the MLS® Rules and Regulations of my Real Estate Board shall be receivable and held in trust. This agreement shall constitute a Commission Trust Agreement as defined in the MLS® Rules and shall be subject to and governed by the MLS® Rules pertaining to Commission Trust.
DATED as of the date and time of the acceptance of the foregoing Agreement of Purchase and Sale. Acknowledged by:

....
(Authorized to bind the Listing Brokerage) (Authorized to bind the Co-operating Brokerage)

APPENDIX

Form 100   *(continued)*

 **Ontario Real Estate Association**

Form 100
for use in the Province of Ontario

Schedule A
Agreement of Purchase and Sale

This Schedule is attached to and forms part of the Agreement of Purchase and Sale between:

BUYER, ..., and

SELLER, ...

for the purchase and sale of ....

.... dated the .... day of ...., 20...............

Buyer agrees to pay the balance as follows:

This form must be initialed by all parties to the Agreement of Purchase and Sale.

INITIALS OF BUYER(S): ⬭   **INITIALS OF SELLER(S):** ⬭

Form 100   Revised 2015   **Page 6 of 6**

OREA Ontario Real Estate Association

Form 101
for use in the Province of Ontario

Agreement of Purchase and Sale
Condominium Resale

This Agreement of Purchase and Sale dated this .... day of .... 20..........

BUYER, ..., agrees to purchase from
(Full legal names of all Buyers)

SELLER, ..., the following
(Full legal names of all Sellers)

PROPERTY:

a unit in the condominium property known as .... No.......................
(Apartment/Townhouse/Suite/Unit)

located at ....

in the ....

being .... Condominium Plan No ....
(Legal Name of Condominium Corporation)

Unit Number .... Level No. .... Building No. .... together with ownership

or exclusive use of Parking Space(s) ...., together with ownership or exclusive use of
(Number(s), Level(s))

Locker(s) ...., together with Seller's proportionate undivided tenancy-in-common interest
(Number(s), Level(s))

in the common elements appurtenant to the Unit as described in the Declaration and Description including the exclusive right to use such other parts of the common elements appurtenant to the Unit as may be specified in the Declaration and Description: the Unit, the proportionate interest in the common elements appurtenant thereto, and the exclusive use portions of the common elements, being herein called the "Property".

PURCHASE PRICE: Dollars (CDN$) ....

.... Dollars

DEPOSIT: Buyer submits ....
(Herewith/Upon Acceptance/as otherwise described in this Agreement)

.... Dollars (CDN$) ....

by negotiable cheque payable to .... "Deposit Holder" to be held in trust pending completion or other termination of this Agreement and to be credited toward the Purchase Price on completion. For the purposes of this Agreement, "Upon Acceptance" shall mean that the Buyer is required to deliver the deposit to the Deposit Holder within 24 hours of the acceptance of this Agreement. The parties to this Agreement hereby acknowledge that, unless otherwise provided for in this Agreement, the Deposit Holder shall place the deposit in trust in the Deposit Holder's non-interest bearing Real Estate Trust Account and no interest shall be earned, received or paid on the deposit.

Buyer agrees to pay the balance as more particularly set out in Schedule A attached.

SCHEDULE(S) A..**attached hereto form(s) part of this Agreement.**

1. **IRREVOCABILITY:** This offer shall be irrevocable by .... until .... a.m./p.m. on the ....
(Seller/Buyer)

   day of .... 20 ...., after which time, if not accepted, this offer shall be null and void and the deposit shall be returned to the Buyer in full without interest.

2. **COMPLETION DATE:** This Agreement shall be completed by no later than 6:00 p.m. on the .... day of ....,

   20 .... Upon completion, vacant possession of the property shall be given to the Buyer unless otherwise provided for in this Agreement.

INITIALS OF BUYER(S): ( )   **INITIALS OF SELLER(S):** ( )

APPENDIX

3. **NOTICES:** The Seller hereby appoints the Listing Brokerage as agent for the Seller for the purpose of giving and receiving notices pursuant to this Agreement. Where a Brokerage (Buyer's Brokerage) has entered into a representation agreement with the Buyer, the Buyer hereby appoints the Buyer's Brokerage as agent for the purpose of giving and receiving notices pursuant to this Agreement. **Where a Brokerage represents both the Seller and the Buyer (multiple representation), the Brokerage shall not be appointed or authorized to be agent for either the Buyer or the Seller for the purpose of giving and receiving notices.** Any notice relating hereto or provided for herein shall be in writing. In addition to any provision contained herein and in any Schedule hereto, this offer, any counter-offer, notice of acceptance thereof or any notice to be given or received pursuant to this Agreement or any Schedule hereto (any of them, "Document") shall be deemed given and received when delivered personally or hand delivered to the Address for Service provided in the Acknowledgement below, or where a facsimile number or email address is provided herein, when transmitted electronically to that facsimile number or email address, respectively, in which case, the signature(s) of the party (parties) shall be deemed to be original.

FAX No.: ....   FAX No.: ....
(For delivery of Documents to Seller)   (For delivery of Documents to Buyer)

Email Address: ....   Email Address: ....
(For delivery of Documents to Seller)   (For delivery of Documents to Buyer)

4. **CHATTELS INCLUDED:**...
....
....
....
....

Unless otherwise stated in this Agreement or any Schedule hereto, Seller agrees to convey all fixtures and chattels included in the Purchase Price free from all liens, encumbrances or claims affecting the said fixtures and chattels.

5. **FIXTURES EXCLUDED:**...
....
....
....

6. **RENTAL ITEMS (Including Lease, Lease to Own):** The following equipment is rented and **not** included in the Purchase Price. The Buyer `agrees to assume the rental contract(s), if assumable:
....
....
....

The Buyer agrees to co-operate and execute such documentation as may be required to facilitate such assumption.

7. **COMMON EXPENSES:** Seller warrants to Buyer that the common expenses presently payable to the Condominium Corporation in respect of the

Property are approximately $ .... per month, which amount includes the following: ....
....
....

8. **PARKING AND LOCKERS:** Parking and Lockers are as described above or assigned as follows: ....
.... at an additional cost of: ....

INITIALS OF BUYER(S): ( )   INITIALS OF SELLER(S): ( )

APPENDIX

9. **HST:** If the sale of the Property (Real Property as described above) is subject to Harmonized Sales Tax (HST), then such tax shall be

.... the Purchase Price. If the sale of the Property is not subject to HST, Seller agrees to certify on or before
(included in/in addition to)
closing, that the sale of the Property is not subject to HST. Any HST on chattels, if applicable, is not included in the Purchase Price.

10. **TITLE SEARCH:** Buyer shall be allowed until 6:00 p.m. on the .... day of ...., 20......., (Requisition Date)
to examine the title to the Property at Buyer's own expense and until the earlier of: (i) thirty days from the later of the Requisition Date or the date
on which the conditions in this Agreement are fulfilled or otherwise waived or; (ii) five days prior to completion, to satisfy Buyer that there are no

outstanding work orders or deficiency notices affecting the Property, and that its present use (..)
may be lawfully continued. If within that time any valid objection to title or to any outstanding work order or deficiency notice, or to the fact the said
present use may not lawfully be continued, is made in writing to Seller and which Seller is unable or unwilling to remove, remedy or satisfy or obtain
insurance save and except against risk of fire (Title Insurance) in favour of the Buyer and any mortgagee, (with all related costs at the expense of the
Seller), and which Buyer will not waive, this Agreement notwithstanding any intermediate acts or negotiations in respect of such objections, shall be
at an end and all monies paid shall be returned without interest or deduction and Seller, Listing Brokerage and Co-operating Brokerage shall not be
liable for any costs or damages. Save as to any valid objection so made by such day and except for any objection going to the root of the title, Buyer
shall be conclusively deemed to have accepted Seller's title to the Property. Seller hereby consents to the municipality or other governmental agencies
releasing to Buyer details of all outstanding work orders and deficiency notices affecting the Property, and Seller agrees to execute and deliver such
further authorizations in this regard as Buyer may reasonably require.

11. **TITLE:** Buyer agrees to accept title to the Property subject to all rights and easements registered against title for the supply and installation of telephone
services, electricity, gas, sewers, water, television cable facilities and other related services; provided that title to the Property is otherwise good and
free from all encumbrances except: (a) as herein expressly provided; (b) any registered restrictions, conditions or covenants that run with the land
provided such have been complied with; (c) the provisions of the Condominium Act and its Regulations and the terms, conditions and provisions of
the Declaration, Description and By-laws, Occupancy Standards By-laws, including the Common Element Rules and other Rules and Regulations; and
(d) any existing municipal agreements, zoning by-laws and/or regulations and utilities or service contracts.

12. **CLOSING ARRANGEMENTS:** Where each of the Seller and Buyer retain a lawyer to complete the Agreement of Purchase and Sale of the Property,
and where the transaction will be completed by electronic registration pursuant to Part III of the Land Registration Reform Act, R.S.O. 1990, Chapter
L4 and the Electronic Registration Act, S.O. 1991, Chapter 44, and any amendments thereto, the Seller and Buyer acknowledge and agree that
the exchange of closing funds, nonregistrable documents and other items (the "Requisite Deliveries") and the release thereof to the Seller and Buyer
will (a) not occur at the same time as the registration of the transfer/deed (and any other documents intended to be registered in connection with the
completion of this transaction) and (b) be subject to conditions whereby the lawyer(s) receiving any of the Requisite Deliveries will be required to hold
same in trust and not release same except in accordance with the terms of a document registration agreement between the said lawyers. The Seller
and Buyer irrevocably instruct the said lawyers to be bound by the document registration agreement which is recommended from time to time by the
Law Society of Upper Canada. Unless otherwise agreed to by the lawyers, such exchange of the Requisite Deliveries will occur in the applicable Land
Titles Office or such other location agreeable to both lawyers.

13. **STATUS CERTIFICATE AND MANAGEMENT OF CONDOMINIUM:** Seller represents and warrants to Buyer that there are no special assessments
contemplated by the Condominium Corporation, and there are no legal actions pending by or against or contemplated by the Condominium
Corporation. The Seller consents to a request by the Buyer or the Buyer's authorized representative for a Status Certificate from the Condominium
Corporation. Buyer acknowledges that the Condominium Corporation may have entered into a Management Agreement for the management of the
condominium property.

14. **DOCUMENTS AND DISCHARGE:** Buyer shall not call for the production of any title deed, abstract, survey or other evidence of title to the Property
except such as are in the possession or control of Seller. Seller agrees to deliver to Buyer, if it is possible without incurring any costs in so doing,
copies of all current condominium documentation of the Condominium Corporation, including the Declaration, Description, By-laws, Common Element
Rules and Regulations and the most recent financial statements of the Condominium Corporation. If a discharge of any Charge/Mortgage held by a
corporation incorporated pursuant to the Trust And Loan Companies Act (Canada), Chartered Bank, Trust Company, Credit Union, Caisse Populaire
or Insurance Company and which is not to be assumed by Buyer on completion, is not available in registrable form on completion, Buyer agrees to
accept Seller's lawyer's personal undertaking to obtain, out of the closing funds, a discharge in registrable form and to register same, or cause same
to be registered, on title within a reasonableperiod of time after completion, provided that on or before completion Seller shall provide to Buyer a
mortgage statement prepared by the mortgagee setting out the balance required to obtain the discharge, and, where a real-time electronic cleared
funds transfer system is not being used, a direction executed by Seller directing payment to the mortgagee of the amount required to obtain the
discharge out of the balance due on completion.

15. **MEETINGS:** Seller represents and warrants to Buyer that at the time of the acceptance of this Offer the Seller has not received a notice convening
a special or general meeting of the Condominium Corporation respecting; (a) the termination of the government of the condominium property; (b)
any substantial alteration in or substantial addition to the common elements or the renovation thereof; OR (c) any substantial change in the assets or
liabilities of the Condominium Corporation; and Seller covenants that if Seller receives any such notice prior to the date of completion Seller shall
forthwith notify Buyer in writing and Buyer may thereupon at Buyer's option declare this Agreement to be null and void and all monies paid by Buyer
shall be refunded without interest or deduction.

INITIALS OF BUYER(S): ( )   INITIALS OF SELLER(S): ( )

APPENDIX

16. **INSPECTION:** Buyer acknowledges having had the opportunity to inspect the Property and understands that upon acceptance of this offer there shall be a binding agreement of purchase and sale between Buyer and Seller. **The Buyer acknowledges having the opportunity to include a requirement for a property inspection report in this Agreement and agrees that except as may be specifically provided for in this Agreement, the Buyer will not be obtaining a property inspection or property inspection report regarding the Property.**

17. **APPROVAL OF THE AGREEMENT:** In the event that consent to this sale is required to be given by the Condominium Corporation or the Board of Directors, the Seller will apply forthwith for the requisite consent, and if such consent is refused, then this Agreement shall be null and void and the deposit monies paid hereunder shall be refunded without interest or other penalty to the Buyer.

18. **INSURANCE:** The Unit and all other things being purchased shall be and remain at the risk of the Seller until completion. In the event of substantial damage to the Property Buyer may at Buyer's option either permit the proceeds of insurance to be used for repair of such damage in accordance with the provisions of the Insurance Trust Agreement, or terminate this Agreement and all deposit monies paid by Buyer hereunder shall be refunded without interest or deduction. If Seller is taking back a Charge/Mortgage, or Buyer is assuming a Charge/Mortgage, Buyer shall supply Seller with reasonable evidence of adequate insurance to protect Seller's or other mortgagee's interest on completion.

19. **DOCUMENT PREPARATION:** The Transfer/Deed shall, save for the Land Transfer Tax Affidavit, be prepared in registrable form at the expense of Seller, and any Charge/Mortgage to be given back by the Buyer to Seller at the expense of the Buyer.

20. **RESIDENCY:** (a) Subject to (b) below, the Seller represents and warrants that the Seller is not and on completion will not be a non-resident under the non-residency provisions of the Income Tax Act which representation and warranty shall survive and not merge upon the completion of this transaction and the Seller shall deliver to the Buyer a statutory declaration that Seller is not then a non-resident of Canada; (b) provided that if the Seller is a non-resident under the non-residency provisions of the Income Tax Act, the Buyer shall be credited towards the Purchase Price with the amount, if any, necessary for Buyer to pay to the Minister of National Revenue to satisfy Buyer's liability in respect of tax payable by Seller under the non-residency provisions of the Income Tax Act by reason of this sale. Buyer shall not claim such credit if Seller delivers on completion the prescribed certificate.

21. **ADJUSTMENTS:** Common Expenses; realty taxes, including local improvement rates; mortgage interest; rentals; unmetered public or private utilities and fuel where billed to the Unit and not the Condominium Corporation; are to be apportioned and allowed to the day of completion, the day of completion itself to be apportioned to the Buyer. There shall be no adjustment for the Seller's share of any assets or liabilities of the Condominium Corporation including any reserve or contingency fund to which Seller may have contributed prior to the date of completion.

22. **PROPERTY ASSESSMENT:** The Buyer and Seller hereby acknowledge that the Province of Ontario has implemented current value assessment and properties may be re-assessed on an annual basis. The Buyer and Seller agree that no claim will be made against the Buyer or Seller, or any Brokerage, Broker or Salesperson, for any changes in property tax as a result of a re-assessment of the Property, save and except any property taxes that accrued prior to the completion of this transaction.

23. **TIME LIMITS:** Time shall in all respects be of the essence hereof provided that the time for doing or completing of any matter provided for herein may be extended or abridged by an agreement in writing signed by Seller and Buyer or by their respective lawyers who may be specifically authorized in that regard.

24. **TENDER:** Any tender of documents or money hereunder may be made upon Seller or Buyer or their respective lawyers on the day set for completion. Money shall be tendered with funds drawn on a lawyer's trust account in the form of a bank draft, certified cheque or wire transfer using the Large Value Transfer System.

25. **FAMILY LAW ACT:** Seller warrants that spousal consent is not necessary to this transaction under the provisions of the Family Law Act, R.S.O. 1990 unless Seller's spouse has executed the consent hereinafter provided.

26. **UFFI:** Seller represents and warrants to Buyer that during the time Seller has owned the Property, Seller has not caused any building on the Property to be insulated with insulation containing ureaformaldehyde, and that to the best of Seller's knowledge no building on the Property contains or has ever contained insulation that contains ureaformaldehyde. This warranty shall survive and not merge on the completion of this transaction, and if the building is part of a multiple unit building, this warranty shall only apply to that part of the building which is the subject of this transaction.

27. **LEGAL, ACCOUNTING AND ENVIRONMENTAL ADVICE:** The parties acknowledge that any information provided by the brokerage is not legal, tax or environmental advice.

28. **CONSUMER REPORTS: The Buyer is hereby notified that a consumer report containing credit and/or personal information may be referred to in connection with this transaction.**

29. **AGREEMENT IN WRITING:** If there is conflict or discrepancy between any provision added to this Agreement (including any Schedule attached hereto) and any provision in the standard pre-set portion hereof, the added provision shall supersede the standard pre-set provision to the extent of such conflict or discrepancy. This Agreement including any Schedule attached hereto, shall constitute the entire Agreement between Buyer and Seller. There is no representation, warranty, collateral agreement or condition, which affects this Agreement other than as expressed herein. For the purposes of this Agreement, Seller means vendor and Buyer means purchaser. This Agreement shall be read with all changes of gender or number required by the context.

30. **TIME AND DATE:** Any reference to a time and date in this Agreement shall mean the time and date where the Property is located.

INITIALS OF BUYER(S): ( )   INITIALS OF SELLER(S): ( )

APPENDIX

Form 101   *(continued)*

31. SUCCESSORS AND ASSIGNS: The heirs, executors, administrators, successors and assigns of the undersigned are bound by the terms herein.

SIGNED, SEALED AND DELIVERED in the presence of: IN WITNESS whereof I have hereunto set my hand and seal:

.... ● DATE ....
(Witness)   (Buyer)   (Seal)

.... ● DATE ....
(Witness)   (Buyer)   (Seal)

I, the Undersigned Seller, agree to the above offer. I hereby irrevocably instruct my lawyer to pay directly to the brokerage(s) with whom I have agreed to pay commission, the unpaid balance of the commission together with applicable Harmonized Sales Tax (and any other taxes as may hereafter be applicable), from the proceeds of the sale prior to any payment to the undersigned on completion, as advised by the brokerage(s) to my lawyer.

SIGNED, SEALED AND DELIVERED in the presence of: IN WITNESS whereof I have hereunto set my hand and seal:

.... ● DATE ....
(Witness)   (Seller)   (Seal)

.... ● DATE ....
(Witness)   (Seller)   (Seal)

SPOUSAL CONSENT: The Undersigned Spouse of the Seller hereby consents to the disposition evidenced herein pursuant to the provisions of the Family Law Act, R.S.O.1990, and hereby agrees with the Buyer that he/she will execute all necessary or incidental documents to give full force and effect to the sale evidenced herein.

.... ● DATE ....
(Witness)   (Spouse)   (Seal)

CONFIRMATION OF ACCEPTANCE: Notwithstanding anything contained herein to the contrary, I confirm this Agreement with all changes both typed and written was finally accepted by all parties at .... a.m./p.m. this .... day of.., 20..........

....
(Signature of Seller or Buyer)

INFORMATION ON BROKERAGE(S)

Listing Brokerage .... Tel.No.(.................)....................................

....
(Salesperson / Broker Name)

Co-op/Buyer Brokerage .... Tel.No.(.................)....................................

....
(Salesperson / Broker Name)

ACKNOWLEDGEMENT

I acknowledge receipt of my signed copy of this accepted Agreement of Purchase and Sale and I authorize the Brokerage to forward a copy to my lawyer.   I acknowledge receipt of my signed copy of this accepted Agreement of Purchase and Sale and I authorize the Brokerage to forward a copy to my lawyer.

.... DATE .... DATE ....
(Seller)   (Buyer)

.... DATE .... DATE ....
(Seller)   (Buyer)
Address for Service ....   Address for Service ....

.... Tel.No.(..........)....   .... Tel.No.(..........)....

Seller's Lawyer ....   Buyer's Lawyer ....

Address ....   Address ....

Email ....   Email ....

(..........).. (..........)............   (..........).. (..........)............
        Tel.No.   FAX No.   Tel.No.   FAX No.

Property Manager: ....
(Name)   (Address)   (Tel No.,FAX No)

APPENDIX

Form 101   (continued)   Page 6 of 6

 **Ontario Real Estate Association**

Form 101
for use in the Province of Ontario

Schedule A
Agreement of Purchase and Sale –
Condominium Resale

This Schedule is attached to and forms part of the Agreement of Purchase and Sale between:

BUYER, ..., and

SELLER, ...

for the purchase and sale of ....

.... dated the .... day of ...., 20 ....

Buyer agrees to pay the balance as follows:

This form must be initialed by all parties to the Agreement of Purchase and Sale.

INITIALS OF BUYER(S):   **INITIALS OF SELLER(S):**

Form 101   Revised 2015   **Page 6 of 6**

APPENDIX

OREA Ontario Real Estate Association

Form 102
for use in the Province of Ontario

Agreement of Purchase and Sale
Co-operative Building Resale Agreement

This Agreement of Purchase and Sale dated this .... day of .... 20..............

BUYER, ..., agrees to purchase from
(Full legal names of all Buyers)

SELLER, ..., the following
(Full legal names of all Sellers)

REAL PROPERTY AND SHARES:

The exclusive right to occupy and use .... (the "Unit")

in the Co-operative Apartment Building located at: ....

in the ....

Parking Space(s) .... Locker ....(the "Property")

and .... shares (the "shares") in the Capital of .... (the "Corporation")

PURCHASE PRICE: Dollars (CDN$) ....

.... Dollars

DEPOSIT: Buyer submits ....
(Herewith/Upon Acceptance/as otherwise described in this Agreement)

.... Dollars (CDN$) ....

by negotiable cheque payable to .... "Deposit Holder" to be held in
trust pending completion or other termination of this Agreement and to be credited toward the Purchase Price on completion. For the purposes of this
Agreement, "Upon Acceptance" shall mean that the Buyer is required to deliver the deposit to the Deposit Holder within 24 hours of the acceptance of
this Agreement. The parties to this Agreement hereby acknowledge that, unless otherwise provided for in this Agreement, the Deposit Holder shall place
the deposit in trust in the Deposit Holder's non-interest bearing Real Estate Trust Account and no interest shall be earned, received or paid on the deposit

Buyer agrees to pay the balance as more particularly set out in Schedule A attached.

SCHEDULE(S) A..**attached hereto form(s) part of this Agreement.**

1.   **IRREVOCABILITY:** This offer shall be irrevocable by .... until .... a.m./p.m. on the
                                                                        (Seller/Buyer)

.... day of .... 20 ...., after which time, if not accepted, this offer shall be null and
void and the deposit shall be returned to the Buyer in full without interest.

2.   **COMPLETION DATE:** This Agreement shall be completed by no later than 6:00 p.m. on the .... day of ....

20 .... Upon completion, vacant possession of the property shall be given to the Buyer unless otherwise provided for in this Agreement.

INITIALS OF BUYER(S): ( )   **INITIALS OF SELLER(S):** ( )

Form 102   Revised 2015   **Page 1 of 6**

APPENDIX

3. **NOTICES:** The Seller hereby appoints the Listing Brokerage as agent for the Seller for the purpose of giving and receiving notices pursuant to this Agreement. Where a Brokerage (Buyer's Brokerage) has entered into a representation agreement with the Buyer, the Buyer hereby appoints the Buyer's Brokerage as agent for the purpose of giving and receiving notices pursuant to this Agreement. **Where a Brokerage represents both the Seller and the Buyer (multiple representation), the Brokerage shall not be appointed or authorized to be agent for either the Buyer or the Seller for the purpose of giving and receiving notices.** Any notice relating hereto or provided for herein shall be in writing. In addition to any provision contained herein and in any Schedule hereto, this offer, any counter-offer, notice of acceptance thereof or any notice to be given or received pursuant to this Agreement or any Schedule hereto (any of them, "Document") shall be deemed given and received when delivered personally or hand delivered to the Address for Service provided in the Acknowledgement below, or where a facsimile number or email address is provided herein, when transmitted electronically to that facsimile number or email address, respectively, in which case, the signature(s) of the party (parties) shall be deemed to be original.

FAX No.: .... FAX No.: ....
(For delivery of Documents to Seller)   (For delivery of Documents to Buyer)

Email Address: .... Email Address: ....
(For delivery of Documents to Seller)   (For delivery of Documents to Buyer)

4. **CHATTELS INCLUDED:**...

....

....

....

....

Unless otherwise stated in this Agreement or any Schedule hereto, Seller agrees to convey all fixtures and chattels included in the Purchase Price free from all liens, encumbrances or claims affecting the said fixtures and chattels.

5. **FIXTURES EXCLUDED:**..

....

....

....

6. **RENTAL ITEMS (Including Lease, Lease to Own):** The following equipment is rented and **not** included in the Purchase Price. The Buyer agrees to assume the rental contract(s), if assumable:

....

....

....

The Buyer agrees to co-operate and execute such documentation as may be required to facilitate such assumption.

7. **MAINTENANCE EXPENSES:** Seller warrants that the maintenance expenses presently payable to the Corporation in respect of the property are

approximately $ .... per month and include: ....

....

....

....

INITIALS OF BUYER(S): ( )   **INITIALS OF SELLER(S):** ( )

APPENDIX

Form 102 *(continued)*

8. **PARKING AND LOCKERS:** Parking and Lockers are as described above or assigned as follows: ....

.... at an additional cost of: ....

9. **HST:** If the sale of the Property (Real Property as described above) is subject to Harmonized Sales Tax (HST), then such tax shall be

.... the Purchase Price. If the sale of the Property is not subject to HST, Seller agrees to certify on or before
.....(included in/in addition to).....
closing, that the sale of the Property is not subject to HST. Any HST on chattels, if applicable, is not included in the Purchase Price.

10. **APPROVAL:** This Agreement is subject to Seller, at the Seller's own expense, obtaining approval of the Board of Directors of the Corporation to the sale and transfer of the Seller's shares in the capital of the Corporation to the Buyer and approval of the Buyer as shareholder and occupant of the

Unit, and if such approval is not obtained by 11:59 p.m. on the .... day of ...., 20............. this agreement shall become null and void and the Buyer's deposit shall be returned to the Buyer in full without deduction. The buyer agrees to cooperate and provide such information and documentation as may be within control of the Buyer in order to obtain said approval.

11. **TITLE SEARCH:** Buyer shall be allowed until 6:00 p.m. on the .... day of ...., 20......, (Requisition Date) to examine the Corporation's title to the Property at the Buyer's expense and until the earlier of: (i) thirty days from the later of the Requisition Date or the date on which the conditions in this Agreement are fulfilled or otherwise waived or; (ii) five days prior to completion, to satisfy the Buyer that there are

no outstanding work orders or deficiency notices affecting the Property, and that its present use (..) may be lawfully continued. If within that time any valid objection to title or to any outstanding work order or deficiency notice, or to the fact the said present use may not lawfully be continued, is made in writing to Seller and which Seller is unable or unwilling to remove, remedy or satisfy and which Buyer will not waive, this Agreement notwithstanding any intermediate acts or negotiations in respect of such objections, shall be at an end and all monies paid shall be returned without interest or deduction and Seller, Listing Brokerage and Co-operating Brokerage shall not be liable for any costs or damages. Save as to any valid objection so made by such day and except for any objection going to the root of the title, Buyer shall be conclusively deemed to have accepted Seller's title to the Property. Seller hereby consents to the municipality or other governmental agencies releasing to Buyer details of all outstanding work orders affecting the Property, and Seller agrees to execute and deliver such further authorizations in this regard as Buyer may reasonably require.

12. **CORPORATION DOCUMENTATION:** The Seller shall deliver to the Buyer on or before closing:
    (a) a certified copy of the Resolution of the Board of Directors of the Corporation approving the Buyer as a shareholder and as an occupant of the Unit;
    (b) a share certificate for the Seller's shares in the capital of the Corporation endorsed in favour of the Buyer;
    (c) a certificate or letter from the Corporation confirming:
       (i) with respect to the Property, that all charges and obligations have been paid or discharged as of the date of closing;
       (ii) with respect to the Corporation that the affairs of the Corporation are in order and that there are no legal actions pending against the Corporation or contemplated by the Corporation, that there are no special assessments contemplated by the Corporation, that there are no orders or complaints against the real property by the Building, Health or Fire Departments, that no sale of real property is contemplated, and the Building is not and never has been insulated with Urea-Formaldehyde Foam Insulation.

13. **OCCUPANCY AGREEMENT:** The Buyer agrees on or before closing to enter into an Occupancy Agreement with the Corporation and to abide by the rules and regulations of the Corporation.

14. **TITLE:** Buyer agrees to accept the Corporation's title to the Property subject to all rights and easements registered against title for the supply and installation of telephone services, electricity, gas, sewers, water, television cable facilities and other related services; provided that title to the Property is otherwise good and free from all encumbrances except: (a) as herein expressly provided; (b) any registered restrictions, conditions or covenants that run with the land provided such have been complied with; and (c) any existing municipal agreements, zoning by-laws and/or regulations and utility or service contracts.

15. **DOCUMENTS AND DISCHARGE:** Buyer shall not call for the production of any title deed, abstract, survey or other evidence of title to the Property except such as are in the possession or control of Seller. If a discharge of any Charge/Mortgage, lien or other encumbrance held by a corporation incorporated pursuant to the Trust And Loan Companies Act (Canada), Chartered Bank, Trust Company, Credit Union, Caisse Populaire or Insurance Company and which is not to be assumed by Buyer on completion, is not available in registrable form on completion, Buyer agrees to accept Seller's lawyer's personal undertaking to obtain, out of the closing funds, a discharge in registrable form and to register same, or cause same to be registered, on title within a reasonable period of time after completion, provided that on or before completion Seller shall provide to Buyer a statement prepared by the mortgagee, lienholder or encumbrancer setting out the balance required to obtain the discharge, and, where a real-time electronic cleared funds transfer system is not being used, a direction executed by Seller directing payment to the mortgagee, lienholder or encumbrancer of the amount required to obtain the discharge out of the balance due on completion.

INITIALS OF BUYER(S): ⬭   INITIALS OF SELLER(S): ⬭

APPENDIX

16. **MEETINGS:** Seller represents and warrants to Buyer that at the time of the acceptance of this Offer the Seller has not received a notice convening a special or general meeting of the Corporation respecting; (a) the termination of the government of the property; (b) the winding up or dissolution of the Corporation; (c) any substantial alteration in or substantial addition to the property or the renovation thereof; OR (d) any substantial change in the assets or liabilities of the Corporation; and Seller covenants that if the Seller receives any such notice prior to the date of completion the Seller shall forthwith notify Buyer in writing and the Buyer may thereupon at the Buyer's option declare this Agreement to be null and void and all monies paid by Buyer shall be refunded without interest or deduction.

17. **INSPECTION:** Buyer acknowledges having had the opportunity to inspect the Property and understands that upon acceptance of this offer there shall be a binding agreement of purchase and sale between Buyer and Seller. **The Buyer acknowledges having the opportunity to include a requirement for a property inspection report in this Agreement and agrees that except as may be specifically provided for in this Agreement, the Buyer will not be obtaining a property inspection or property inspection report regarding the Property.**

18. **INSURANCE:** The Unit and all other things being purchased shall be and remain at the risk of the Seller until completion. In the event of substantial damage to the real property Buyer may at the Buyer's option either permit the proceeds of insurance to be used for repair of such damage in accordance with the provisions of the Insurance Trust Agreement or other insurance arrangement, or terminate this Agreement and all deposit monies paid by Buyer hereunder shall be refunded without interest or deduction. If Seller is taking back a Charge/Mortgage, or Buyer is assuming a Charge/Mortgage, Buyer shall supply Seller with reasonable evidence of adequate insurance to protect Seller's or other mortgagee's interest on completion.

19. **RESIDENCY:** (a) Subject to (b) below, the Seller represents and warrants that the Seller is not and on completion will not be a non-resident under the non-residency provisions of the Income Tax Act which representation and warranty shall survive and not merge upon the completion of this transaction and the Seller shall deliver to the Buyer a statutory declaration that Seller is not then a non-resident of Canada;
(b) provided that if the Seller is a non-resident under the non-residency provisions of the Income Tax Act, the Buyer shall be credited towards the Purchase Price with the amount, if any, necessary for Buyer to pay to the Minister of National Revenue to satisfy Buyer's liability in respect of tax payable by Seller under the non-residency provisions of the Income Tax Act by reason of this sale.Buyer shall not claim such credit if Seller delivers on completion the prescribed certificate.

20. **ADJUSTMENTS:** Maintenance expenses and, where billed to the Unit and not the Corporation, realty taxes, including local improvement rates; mortgage interest; rentals; unmetered public or private utilities and fuel; are to be apportioned and allowed to the day of completion, the day of completion itself to be apportioned to the Buyer. There shall be no adjustment for the Seller's share of any reserve or contingency fund to which the Seller may have contributed prior to the date of completion.

21. **TIME LIMITS:** Time shall in all respects be of the essence hereof provided that the time for doing or completing of any matter provided for herein may be extended or abridged by an agreement in writing signed by Seller and Buyer or by their respective lawyers who may be specifically authorized in that regard.

22. **TENDER:** Any tender of documents or money hereunder may be made upon Seller or Buyer or their respective lawyers on the day set for completion. Money shall be tendered with funds drawn on a lawyer's trust account in the form of a bank draft, certified cheque or wire transfer using the Large Value Transfer System

23. **FAMILY LAW ACT:** Seller warrants that spousal consent is not necessary to this transaction under the provisions of the Family Law Act, R.S.O.1990 unless Seller's spouse has executed the consent hereinafter provided.

24. **LEGAL, ACCOUNTING AND ENVIRONMENTAL ADVICE:** The parties acknowledge that any information provided by the brokerage is not legal, tax or environmental advice.

25. **CONSUMER REPORTS: The Buyer is hereby notified that a consumer report containing credit and/or personal information may be referred to in connection with this transaction.**

26. **AGREEMENT IN WRITING:** If there is conflict or discrepancy between any provision added to this Agreement (including any Schedule attached hereto) and any provision in the standard pre-set portion hereof, the added provision shall supersede the standard pre-set provision to the extent of such conflict or discrepancy. This Agreement including any Schedule attached hereto, shall constitute the entire Agreement between Buyer and Seller. There is no representation, warranty, collateral agreement or condition, which affects this Agreement other than as expressed herein. For the purposes of this Agreement, Seller means vendor and Buyer means purchaser. This Agreement shall be read with all changes of gender or number required by the context.

27. **TIME AND DATE:** Any reference to a time and date in this Agreement shall mean the time and date where the property is located.

INITIALS OF BUYER(S): ⬭ **INITIALS OF SELLER(S):** ⬭

APPENDIX

Form 102   *(continued)*

28. SUCCESSORS AND ASSIGNS: The heirs, executors, administrators, successors and assigns of the undersigned are bound by the terms herein.

SIGNED, SEALED AND DELIVERED in the presence of: IN WITNESS whereof I have hereunto set my hand and seal:

....   ●   DATE ....
(Witness)   (Buyer)   (Seal)

....   ●   DATE ....
(Witness)   (Buyer)   (Seal)

I, the Undersigned Seller, agree to the above offer. I hereby irrevocably instruct my lawyer to pay directly to the brokerage(s) with whom I have agreed to pay commission, the unpaid balance of the commission together with applicable Harmonized Sales Tax (and any other taxes as may hereafter be applicable), from the proceeds of the sale prior to any payment to the undersigned on completion, as advised by the brokerage(s) to my lawyer.

SIGNED, SEALED AND DELIVERED in the presence of: IN WITNESS whereof I have hereunto set my hand and seal:

....   ●   DATE ....
(Witness)   (Seller)   (Seal)

....   ●   DATE ....
(Witness)   (Seller)   (Seal)

SPOUSAL CONSENT: The Undersigned Spouse of the Seller hereby consents to the disposition evidenced herein pursuant to the provisions of the Family Law Act, R.S.O.1990, and hereby agrees with the Buyer that he/she will execute all necessary or incidental documents to give full force and effect to the sale evidenced herein.

....   ●   DATE ....
(Witness)   (Spouse)   (Seal)

CONFIRMATION OF ACCEPTANCE: Notwithstanding anything contained herein to the contrary, I confirm this Agreement with all changes both typed and written was finally accepted by all parties at .... a.m./p.m. this .... day of..., 20..........

....
(Signature of Seller or Buyer)

INFORMATION ON BROKERAGE(S)

Listing Brokerage .... Tel.No.(................)...

....
(Salesperson / Broker Name)

Co-op/Buyer Brokerage .... Tel.No.(................)...

....
(Salesperson / Broker Name)

ACKNOWLEDGEMENT

I acknowledge receipt of my signed copy of this accepted Agreement of Purchase and Sale and I authorize the Brokerage to forward a copy to my lawyer.	I acknowledge receipt of my signed copy of this accepted Agreement of Purchase and Sale and I authorize the Brokerage to forward a copy to my lawyer.
.... DATE .... (Seller)	.... DATE .... (Buyer)
.... DATE .... (Seller)	.... DATE .... (Buyer)
Address for Service	Address for Service ....
.... Tel.No.(..........)...............	.... Tel.No.(..........)...............
Seller's Lawyer	Buyer's Lawyer ....
Address	Address ....
Email	Email ....
(..........)....................... (..........)............... Tel.No. FAX No.	(..........)....................... (..........)............... Tel.No. FAX No.

Property Manager: ....
           (Name)   (Address)   (Tel No.,FAX No.)

FOR OFFICE USE ONLY   **COMMISSION TRUST AGREEMENT**

To: Co-operating Brokerage shown on the foregoing Agreement of Purchase and Sale:
In consideration for the Co-operating Brokerage procuring the foregoing Agreement of Purchase and Sale, I hereby declare that all moneys received or receivable by me in connection with the Transaction as contemplated in the MLS® Rules and Regulations of my Real Estate Board shall be receivable and held in trust. This agreement shall constitute a Commission Trust Agreement as defined in the MLS® Rules and shall be subject to and governed by the MLS® Rules pertaining to Commission Trust.

DATED as of the date and time of the acceptance of the foregoing Agreement of Purchase and Sale.   Acknowledged by:

....
(Authorized to bind the Listing Brokerage)   (Authorized to bind the Co-operating Brokerage)

APPENDIX

Schedule A
Agreement of Purchase and Sale –
Co-operative Building Resale

Form 102
for use in the Province of Ontario

This Schedule is attached to and forms part of the Agreement of Purchase and Sale between:

BUYER, ..., and

SELLER, ...

for the purchase and sale of ....

.... dated the .... day of ...., 20...............

Buyer agrees to pay the balance as follows:

This form must be initialed by all parties to the Agreement of Purchase and Sale.

INITIALS OF BUYER(S): ⬭   INITIALS OF SELLER(S): ⬭

Form 102   Revised 2015   **Page 6 of 6**

APPENDIX

Form 106   *Seller Selling Under Power of Sale*   Page 1 of 1

OREA Ontario Real Estate Association

Form 106
for use in the Province of Ontario

Seller Selling Under Power of Sale
To Be Used in Conjunction with OREA Form 100

Attached to and forming part of Agreement of Purchase and Sale between ....

and .... dated the ....day of

...., 20.....................

1. It is understood that the Seller is selling as mortgagee under a Power of Sale contained in a ....
    (insert 1st, 2nd, 3rd, etc.)

    mortgage made to the Seller, dated the .... day of ...., 20.................... and registered

    as number ....

2. It is further understood that on the date of acceptance of this offer there is default under the terms of the mortgage which entitles the Seller to exercise the Power of Sale. The only evidence of the default that the Buyer may require shall be a statutory declaration by the Seller setting forth the facts entitling the Seller to sell under the Power of Sale, including the particulars of the notice of exercising the Power of Sale, the names of the persons upon whom service of the notice has been effected, and declaring that default under the mortgage entitling the Seller to exercise the Power of Sale has continued up to and including the date of acceptance of this offer and to the time of closing. The Buyer understands and agrees that the mortgagor has the right to redeem the property up to the time of waiver or expiration of all rights of termination or fulfilment of all conditions, and this Agreement is subject to that right. In the event of redemption by the mortgagor, this Agreement shall be null and void and any deposit monies paid will be refunded without interest.

3. The Buyer also acknowledges that the Seller makes no representations and/or warranties with respect to state of repair of the premises, inclusions of chattels or fixtures, or ownership of fixtures or appliances, and the Buyer agrees to accept the property as is and must satisfy himself/herself with respect to any of the matters provided for in the attached agreement ordinarily warranted by the Seller. Chattels and fixtures on the premises may or may not be included with the premises but the Seller shall not be obliged to remove any chattels or fixtures. All the provisions of the Mortgages Act shall supersede any part of this Agreement which may be in variance thereof or in conflict therewith.

SIGNED, SEALED AND DELIVERED in the presence of: IN WITNESS whereof I have hereunto set my hand and seal:

.... ● DATE ....
(Witness)   (Buyer)   (Seal)

.... ● DATE ....
(Witness)   (Buyer)   (Seal)

SIGNED, SEALED AND DELIVERED in the presence of: IN WITNESS whereof I have hereunto set my hand and seal:

.... ● DATE ....
(Witness)   (Seller)   (Seal)

.... ● DATE ....
(Witness)   (Seller)   (Seal)

APPENDIX

OREA Ontario Real Estate Association

Form 110
for use in the Province of Ontario

Agreement of Purchase and Sale
Mobile/Modular/Manufactured Home on Leased Premises

This Agreement of Purchase and Sale dated this .... day of .... 20.............

BUYER, ..., agrees to purchase from
(Full legal names of all Buyers)

SELLER, ..., the following
(Full legal names of all Sellers)

PROPERTY:

The .... building (the "Dwelling") more fully described as:
(Mobile/Modular/Manufactured)

Manufacturer ....

Model (if applicable) ....

Serial Number .... Year ....

Length .... Width ....

Located At: (address, lot/site number, etc.) .... (the "Land")

Name of Mobile Home Park (if applicable) ....

The parties agree that the Land on which the Dwelling is located is not the property of the Seller and is not included as part of this Agreement.

PURCHASE PRICE: Dollars (CDN$) ....

.... Dollars

DEPOSIT: Buyer submits ....
(Herewith/Upon Acceptance/as otherwise described in this Agreement)

.... Dollars (CDN$) ....

by negotiable cheque payable to .... "Deposit Holder" to be held in trust pending completion or other termination of this Agreement and to be credited toward the Purchase Price on completion. For the purposes of this Agreement, "Upon Acceptance" shall mean that the Buyer is required to deliver the deposit to the Deposit Holder within 24 hours of the acceptance of this Agreement. The parties to this Agreement hereby acknowledge that, unless otherwise provided for in this Agreement, the Deposit Holder shall place the deposit in trust in the Deposit Holder's non-interest bearing Real Estate Trust Account and no interest shall be earned, received or paid on the deposit.

Buyer agrees to pay the balance as more particularly set out in Schedule A attached.

SCHEDULE(S) A, B (Lease) .... **attached hereto form(s) part of this Agreement.**

1. **IRREVOCABILITY:** This offer shall be irrevocable by .... until .... a.m./p.m. on the

   .... day of .... 20 ...., after which time, if not accepted, this offer shall be null and void and the deposit shall be returned to the Buyer in full without interest.

INITIALS OF BUYER(S): ( )   INITIALS OF SELLER(S): ( )

Form 110   Revised 2015   **Page 1 of 6**

APPENDIX

2. COMPLETION DATE: This Agreement shall be completed by no later than 6:00 p.m. on the .... day of ....

20............. Upon completion, vacant possession of the Dwelling shall be given to the Buyer unless otherwise provided for in this Agreement.

3. NOTICES: The Seller hereby appoints the Listing Brokerage as agent for the Seller for the purpose of giving and receiving notices pursuant to this Agreement. Where a Brokerage (Buyer's Brokerage) has entered into a representation agreement with the Buyer, the Buyer hereby appoints the Buyer's Brokerage as agent for the purpose of giving and receiving notices pursuant to this Agreement. **Where a Brokerage represents both the Seller and the Buyer (multiple representation), the Brokerage shall not be appointed or authorized to be agent for either the Buyer or the Seller for the purpose of giving and receiving notices.** Any notice relating hereto or provided for herein shall be in writing. In addition to any provision contained herein and in any Schedule hereto, this offer, any counter-offer, notice of acceptance thereof or any notice to be given or received pursuant to this Agreement or any Schedule hereto (any of them, "Document") shall be deemed given and received when delivered personally or hand delivered to the Address for Service provided in the Acknowledgement below, or where a facsimile number or email address is provided herein, when transmitted electronically to that facsimile number or email address, respectively, in which case, the signature(s) of the party (parties) shall be deemed to be original.

FAX No.: ....   FAX No.: ....
        (For delivery of Documents to Seller)   (For delivery of Documents to Buyer)

Email Address: ....   Email Address: ....
        (For delivery of Documents to Seller)   (For delivery of Documents to Buyer)

4. CHATTELS INCLUDED: In addition to the Dwelling, the following are included in the Purchase Price:

....

....

....

....

Unless otherwise stated in this Agreement or any Schedule hereto, Seller agrees to convey all fixtures and chattels included in the Purchase Price free from all liens, encumbrances or claims affecting the said fixtures and chattels.

5. FIXTURES EXCLUDED: The following items are not included in the Purchase Price:

....

....

....

....

6. RENTAL ITEMS (Including Lease, Lease to Own): The following equipment is rented and **not** included in the Purchase Price. The Buyer agrees to assume the rental contract(s), if assumable:

....

....

The Buyer agrees to co-operate and execute such documentation as may be required to facilitate such assumption.

INITIALS OF BUYER(S): ( )   INITIALS OF SELLER(S): ( )

APPENDIX

7. **HST:** I If the sale of the property (Real Property as described above) is subject to Harmonized Sales Tax (HST) then such tax shall be **in addition to** the Purchase Price. If the sale of the property is not subject to HST, Seller agrees to certify on or before closing, that the sale of the property is not subject to HST. Any HST on chattels, if applicable, is not included in the Purchase Price.

8. **RULES AND REGULATIONS:** The Buyer acknowledges that the Land lease may include Rules and Regulations for the occupancy of the Land and the Buyer agrees to accept and comply with said Rules and Regulations.

9. **LEASE:** The Buyer acknowledges that Dwelling is currently situate upon the Land pursuant to a Lease as more particularly set out in Schedule B attached hereto. The Seller agrees to assign the Seller's interest in the Lease to the Buyer and the Buyer agrees to accept the assignment of the Lease. If the said Lease contains a provision requiring that the Landlord consent to the assignment of the Lease, then Seller will apply forthwith for the requisite consent, and provide a copy in writing of the consent, and if such consent is refused and the Buyer does not enter into a new lease agreement with the Landlord, then this Agreement shall be null and void at the option of the Buyer and the deposit monies shall be refunded without interest or other penalty to the Buyer. The Buyer agrees to cooperate and provide such information and documentation as may be within control of the Buyer in order to obtain said assignment of Lease.

10. **TITLE:** Provided that the title to the Dwelling is good and free from all charges, liens, and encumbrances except as otherwise specifically provided

in this Agreement. Buyer shall be allowed until 6:00 p.m. on the .... day of.., 20......., (Requisition Date) to examine the title to the Dwelling at Buyer's own expense and until thirty days from the Requisition Date or the date on which the conditions in this

Agreement are fulfilled or otherwise waived to satisfy Buyer that its present use (..) may be lawfully continued and that the Dwelling may be insured against risk of fire. Seller hereby consents to the Landlord of the Land, the municipality or other governmental agencies releasing to Buyer details of all matters affecting the Dwelling, and Seller agrees to execute and deliver such further authorizations in this regard as Buyer may reasonably require. If within the specified times referred to above any valid objection to title or to the fact the said present use may not lawfully be continued, or that the Dwelling may not be insured against risk of fire is made in writing to Seller and which Seller is unable or unwilling to remove, remedy or satisfy and which Buyer will not waive, this Agreement notwithstanding any intermediate acts or negotiations in respect of such objections, shall be at an end and all monies paid shall be returned without interest or deduction and Seller, Listing Brokerage and Co-operating Brokerage shall not be liable for any costs or damages. Save as to any valid objection so made by such day and except for any objection going to the root of the title, Buyer shall be conclusively deemed to have accepted Seller's title to the Dwelling.

11. **FUTURE USE:** Seller and Buyer agree that there is no representation or warranty of any kind that the future intended use of the Dwelling by Buyer is or will be lawful except as may be specifically provided for in this Agreement.

12. **DOCUMENTS AND DISCHARGE:** Buyer shall not call for the production of any prior Bills of Sale or other evidence of title to the Dwelling except such as are in the possession or control of Seller. If requested by Buyer, Seller will deliver any sketch or plans of the Dwelling, including informational material from the manufacturer, within Seller's control to Buyer as soon as possible and prior to the Requisition Date. If a discharge of any security interest held by a corporation incorporated pursuant to the Trust And Loan Companies Act (Canada), Chartered Bank, Trust Company, Credit Union, Caisse Populaire or Insurance Company and which is not to be assumed by Buyer on completion, is not available in registrable form on completion, Buyer agrees to accept Seller's lawyer's personal undertaking to obtain, out of the closing funds, a registrable discharge and to register same, or cause same to be registered within a reasonable period of time after completion, provided that on or before completion Seller shall provide to Buyer a statement prepared by the security interest holder setting out the balance required to obtain the discharge, and, where a real-time electronic cleared funds transfer system is not being used, a direction executed by Seller directing payment to the holder of the amount required to obtain the discharge out of the balance due on completion.

13. **INSPECTION:** Buyer acknowledges having had the opportunity to inspect the Dwelling and understands that upon acceptance of this offer there shall be a binding agreement of purchase and sale between Buyer and Seller.

INITIALS OF BUYER(S): ⬭   **INITIALS OF SELLER(S):** ⬭

APPENDIX

14. **INSURANCE:** The Dwelling and all buildings on the Land and all other things being purchased shall be and remain until completion at the risk of Seller. Pending completion, Seller shall hold all insurance policies, if any, and the proceeds thereof in trust for the parties as their interests may appear and in the event of substantial damage, Buyer may either terminate this Agreement and have all monies paid returned without interest or deduction or else take the proceeds of any insurance and complete the purchase. No insurance shall be transferred on completion. If Seller is taking back a Security Interest, or Buyer is assuming a Security Interest, Buyer shall supply Seller with reasonable evidence of adequate insurance to protect Seller's or other security holder's interest on completion.

15. **DOCUMENT PREPARATION:** The Bill of Sale shall be prepared in registrable form at the expense of Seller, and any Security Interest to be given back by the Buyer to Seller at the expense of the Buyer.

16. **RESIDENCY:** (a) Subject to (b) below, the Seller represents and warrants that the Seller is not and on completion will not be a non-resident under the non-residency provisions of the Income Tax Act which representation and warranty shall survive and not merge upon the completion of this transaction and the Seller shall deliver to the Buyer a statutory declaration that Seller is not then a non-resident of Canada;
    (b) provided that if the Seller is a non-resident under the non-residency provisions of the Income Tax Act, the Buyer shall be credited towards the Purchase Price with the amount, if any, necessary for Buyer to pay to the Minister of National Revenue to satisfy Buyer's liability in respect of tax payable by Seller under the non-residency provisions of the Income Tax Act by reason of this sale.Buyer shall not claim such credit if Seller delivers on completion the prescribed certificate.

17. **ADJUSTMENTS:** Any rents, security deposits, security interest, realty taxes including local improvement rates, unmetered public or private utility charges and unmetered cost of fuel, as applicable, shall be apportioned and allowed to the day of completion, the day of completion itself to be apportioned to Buyer.

18. **TIME LIMITS:** Time shall in all respects be of the essence hereof provided that the time for doing or completing of any matter provided for herein may be extended or abridged by an agreement in writing signed by Seller and Buyer or by their respective lawyers who may be specifically authorized in that regard.

19. **TENDER:** Any tender of documents or money hereunder may be made upon Seller or Buyer or their respective lawyers on the day set for completion.Money shall be tendered with funds drawn on a lawyer's trust account in the form of a bank draft, certified cheque or wire transfer using the Large Value Transfer System.

20. **FAMILY LAW ACT:** Seller warrants that spousal consent is not necessary to this transaction under the provisions of the Family Law Act, unless Seller's spouse has executed the consent hereinafter provided.

21. **UFFI:** Seller represents and warrants to Buyer that during the time Seller has owned the Dwelling, Seller has not caused the Dwelling or any structure on the property to be insulated with insulation containing ureaformaldehyde, and that to the best of Seller's knowledge no building on the property contains or has ever contained insulation that contains ureaformaldehyde. This warranty shall survive and not merge on the completion of this transaction.

22. **LEGAL, ACCOUNTING AND ENVIRONMENTAL ADVICE:** The parties acknowledge that any information provided by the brokerage is not legal, tax or environmental advice.

23. **CONSUMER REPORTS: The Buyer is hereby notified that a consumer report containing credit and/or personal information may be referred to in connection with this transaction.**

24. **AGREEMENT IN WRITING:** If there is conflict or discrepancy between any provision added to this Agreement (including any Schedule attached hereto) and any provision in the standard pre-set portion hereof, the added provision shall supersede the standard pre-set provision to the extent of such conflict or discrepancy. This Agreement including any Schedule attached hereto, shall constitute the entire Agreement between Buyer and Seller. There is no representation, warranty, collateral agreement or condition, which affects this Agreement other than as expressed herein. For the purposes of this Agreement, Seller means vendor and Buyer means purchaser. This Agreement shall be read with all changes of gender or number required by the context.

25. **TIME AND DATE:** Any reference to a time and date in this Agreement shall mean the time and date where the Dwelling is located.

INITIALS OF BUYER(S): ( )   INITIALS OF SELLER(S): ( )

APPENDIX

26. SUCCESSORS AND ASSIGNS: The heirs, executors, administrators, successors and assigns of the undersigned are bound by the terms herein.

SIGNED, SEALED AND DELIVERED in the presence of: IN WITNESS whereof I have hereunto set my hand and seal:

....   ●   DATE ....
(Witness)   (Buyer)   (Seal)

....   ●   DATE ....
(Witness)   (Buyer)   (Seal)

I, the Undersigned Seller, agree to the above offer. I hereby irrevocably instruct my lawyer to pay directly to the brokerage(s) with whom I have agreed to pay commission, the unpaid balance of the commission together with applicable Harmonized Sales Tax (and any other taxes as may hereafter be applicable), from the proceeds of the sale prior to any payment to the undersigned on completion, as advised by the brokerage(s) to my lawyer.

SIGNED, SEALED AND DELIVERED in the presence of: IN WITNESS whereof I have hereunto set my hand and seal:

....   ●   DATE ....
(Witness)   (Seller)   (Seal)

....   ●   DATE ....
(Witness)   (Seller)   (Seal)

SPOUSAL CONSENT: The Undersigned Spouse of the Seller hereby consents to the disposition evidenced herein pursuant to the provisions of the Family Law Act, R.S.O.1990, and hereby agrees with the Buyer that he/she will execute all necessary or incidental documents to give full force and effect to the sale evidenced herein.

....   ●   DATE ....
(Witness)   (Spouse)   (Seal)

CONFIRMATION OF ACCEPTANCE: Notwithstanding anything contained herein to the contrary, I confirm this Agreement with all changes both typed

and written was finally accepted by all parties at .... a.m./p.m. this .... day of..., 20..........

....
(Signature of Seller or Buyer)

INFORMATION ON BROKERAGE(S)

Listing Brokerage ....   Tel.No.(...............)..................................

....
(Salesperson / Broker Name)

Co-op/Buyer Brokerage ....   Tel.No.(...............)..................................

....
(Salesperson / Broker Name)

ACKNOWLEDGEMENT

I acknowledge receipt of my signed copy of this accepted Agreement of Purchase and Sale and I authorize the Brokerage to forward a copy to my lawyer.	I acknowledge receipt of my signed copy of this accepted Agreement of Purchase and Sale and I authorize the Brokerage to forward a copy to my lawyer.
.... DATE .... (Seller)	.... DATE .... (Buyer)
.... DATE .... (Seller) Address for Service	.... DATE .... (Buyer) Address for Service ....
.... Tel.No.(...........).............	.... Tel.No.(...........).............
Seller's Lawyer	Buyer's Lawyer ....
Address	Address ....
Email	Email ....
(...........)...................... (...........)............. Tel.No. FAX No.	(...........)...................... (...........)............. Tel.No. FAX No.

FOR OFFICE USE ONLY   **COMMISSION TRUST AGREEMENT**

To: Co-operating Brokerage shown on the foregoing Agreement of Purchase and Sale:
In consideration for the Co-operating Brokerage procuring the foregoing Agreement of Purchase and Sale, I hereby declare that all moneys received or receivable by me in connection with the Transaction as contemplated in the MLS® Rules and Regulations of my Real Estate Board shall be receivable and held in trust. This agreement shall constitute a Commission Trust Agreement as defined in the MLS® Rules and shall be subject to and governed by the MLS® Rules pertaining to Commission Trust.
DATED as of the date and time of the acceptance of the foregoing Agreement of Purchase and Sale.   Acknowledged by:

....
(Authorized to bind the Listing Brokerage)   (Authorized to bind the Co-operating Brokerage)

Form 110   Revised 2015   **Page 5 of 6**

Form 110   *(continued)*   Page 6 of 6

 **Ontario Real Estate Association**

Form 110
for use in the Province of Ontario

Schedule A – Agreement of Purchase and Sale
Mobile/Modular/Manufactured Home on Leased Premises

This Schedule is attached to and forms part of the Agreement of Purchase and Sale between:

BUYER, ...,and

SELLER, ...

for the purchase and sale of ....

.... dated the .... day of ...., 20..............

Buyer agrees to pay the balance as follows:

This form must be initialed by all parties to the Agreement of Purchase and Sale.

INITIALS OF BUYER(S): (⬭)   INITIALS OF SELLER(S): (⬭)

Form 110   Revised 2015   **Page 6 of 6**

APPENDIX

OREA Ontario Real Estate Association

Form 111
for use in the Province of Ontario

Agreement of Purchase and Sale - POTL
Common Elements Condominium

This Agreement of Purchase and Sale dated this .... day of .... 20...........

BUYER, ..., agrees to purchase from
(Full legal names of all Buyers)

SELLER, ..., the following
(Full legal names of all Sellers)

REAL PROPERTY (Parcel of Tied Land – POTL):

Address ....

fronting on the .... side of ....

in the ....

and having a frontage of .... more or less by a depth of .... more or less

and legally described as ....

.... (the "property")
(Legal description of land including easements not described elsewhere)

COMMON ELEMENTS CONDOMINIUM:

The property shall be deemed to include a common interest in the Condominium Corporation being..
(Legal Name of Condominium Corporation)

.... Condominium Plan No.................................... as more particularly set out on the Declaration and Description.

PURCHASE PRICE: Dollars (CDN$) ....

....Dollars

DEPOSIT: Buyer submits ....
(Herewith/Upon Acceptance/as otherwise described in this Agreement)

.... Dollars (CDN$) ....

by negotiable cheque payable to .... "Deposit Holder" to be held in trust pending completion or other termination of this Agreement and to be credited toward the Purchase Price on completion. For the purposes of this Agreement, "Upon Acceptance" shall mean that the Buyer is required to deliver the deposit to the Deposit Holder within 24 hours of the acceptance of this Agreement. The parties to this Agreement hereby acknowledge that, unless otherwise provided for in this Agreement, the Deposit Holder shall place the deposit in trust in the Deposit Holder's non-interest bearing Real Estate Trust Account and no interest shall be earned, received or paid on the deposit.
Buyer agrees to pay the balance as more particularly set out in Schedule A attached.

SCHEDULE(S) A..**attached hereto form(s) part of this Agreement.**

1. **IRREVOCABILITY:** This offer shall be irrevocable by .... until .... a.m./p.m. on the ....
(Seller/Buyer)

   day of .... 20 ...., after which time, if not accepted, this offer shall be null and void and the deposit shall be returned to the Buyer in full without interest.

INITIALS OF BUYER(S): ( )   **INITIALS OF SELLER(S):** ( )

Form 111   Revised 2015   **Page 1 of 7**

APPENDIX

2. **COMPLETION DATE:** This Agreement shall be completed by no later than 6:00 p.m. on the .... day of ....,

20 .... Upon completion, vacant possession of the property shall be given to the Buyer unless otherwise provided for in this Agreement.

3. **NOTICES:** The Seller hereby appoints the Listing Brokerage as agent for the Seller for the purpose of giving and receiving notices pursuant to this Agreement. Where a Brokerage (Buyer's Brokerage) has entered into a representation agreement with the Buyer, the Buyer hereby appoints the Buyer's Brokerage as agent for the purpose of giving and receiving notices pursuant to this Agreement. **Where a Brokerage represents both the Seller and the Buyer (multiple representation), the Brokerage shall not be appointed or authorized to be agent for either the Buyer or the Seller for the purpose of giving and receiving notices.** Any notice relating hereto or provided for herein shall be in writing. In addition to any provision contained herein and in any Schedule hereto, this offer, any counter-offer, notice of acceptance thereof or any notice to be given or received pursuant to this Agreement or any Schedule hereto (any of them, "Document") shall be deemed given and received when delivered personally or hand delivered to the Address for Service provided in the Acknowledgement below, or where a facsimile number or email address is provided herein, when transmitted electronically to that facsimile number or email address, respectively, in which case, the signature(s) of the party (parties) shall be deemed to be original.

FAX No.: ....   FAX No.: ....
(For delivery of Documents to Seller)   (For delivery of Documents to Buyer)

Email Address: ....   Email Address: ....
(For delivery of Documents to Seller)   (For delivery of Documents to Buyer)

4. **CHATTELS INCLUDED:** ....

....

....

....

....

Unless otherwise stated in this Agreement or any Schedule hereto, Seller agrees to convey all fixtures and chattels included in the Purchase Price free from all liens, encumbrances or claims affecting the said fixtures and chattels.

5. **FIXTURES EXCLUDED:** ....

....

....

....

....

6. **RENTAL ITEMS (Including Lease, Lease to Own):** The following equipment is rented and **not** included in the Purchase Price. The Buyer agrees to assume the rental contract(s), if assumable:

....

....

....

....

The Buyer agrees to co-operate and execute such documentation as may be required to facilitate such assumption.

INITIALS OF BUYER(S): ⬭   INITIALS OF SELLER(S): ⬭

APPENDIX

7. **HST:** If the sale of the Property (Real Property as described above) is subject to Harmonized Sales Tax (HST), then such tax shall be

.... the Purchase Price. If the sale of the Property is not subject to HST, Seller agrees to certify on or
　　　　　　　(included in/in addition to)
before closing, that the sale of the Property is not subject to HST. Any HST on chattels, if applicable, is not included in the Purchase Price.

8. **TITLE SEARCH:** Buyer shall be allowed until 6:00 p.m. on the .... day of ...., 20............., (Requisition Date) to examine the title to the property at Buyer's own expense and until the earlier of: (i) thirty days from the later of the Requisition Date or the date on which the conditions in this Agreement are fulfilled or otherwise waived or; (ii) five days prior to completion, to satisfy Buyer that there are no outstanding

work orders or deficiency notices affecting the property, and that its present use (..) may be lawfully continued and that the principal building may be insured against risk of fire. Seller hereby consents to the municipality or other governmental agencies releasing to Buyer details of all outstanding work orders and deficiency notices affecting the property, and Seller agrees to execute and deliver such further authorizations in this regard as Buyer may reasonably require.

9. **FUTURE USE:** Seller and Buyer agree that there is no representation or warranty of any kind that the future intended use of the property by Buyer is or will be lawful except as may be specifically provided for in this Agreement.

10. **TITLE:** Provided that the title to the property is good and free from all registered restrictions, charges, liens, and encumbrances except as otherwise specifically provided in this Agreement and save and except for (a) any registered restrictions or covenants that run with the land providing that such are complied with; (b) any registered municipal agreements and registered agreements with publicly regulated utilities providing such have been complied with, or security has been posted to ensure compliance and completion, as evidenced by a letter from the relevant municipality or regulated utility; (c) any minor easements for the supply of domestic utility or telephone services to the property or adjacent properties; and (d) any easements for drainage, storm or sanitary sewers, public utility lines, telephone lines, cable television lines or other services which do not materially affect the use of the property. If within the specified times referred to in paragraph 8 any valid objection to title or to any outstanding work order or deficiency notice, or to the fact the said present use may not lawfully be continued, or that the principal building may not be insured against risk of fire is made in writing to Seller and which Seller is unable or unwilling to remove, remedy or satisfy or obtain insurance save and except against risk of fire (Title Insurance) in favour of the Buyer and any mortgagee, (with all related costs at the expense of the Seller), and which Buyer will not waive, this Agreement notwithstanding any intermediate acts or negotiations in respect of such objections, shall be at an end and all monies paid shall be returned without interest or deduction and Seller, Listing Brokerage and Co-operating Brokerage shall not be liable for any costs or damages. Save as to any valid objection so made by such day and except for any objection going to the root of the title, Buyer shall be conclusively deemed to have accepted Seller's title to the property.

11. **CLOSING ARRANGEMENTS:** Where each of the Seller and Buyer retain a lawyer to complete the Agreement of Purchase and Sale of the property, and where the transaction will be completed by electronic registration pursuant to Part III of the Land Registration Reform Act, R.S.O. 1990, Chapter L4 and the Electronic Registration Act, S.O. 1991, Chapter 44, and any amendments thereto, the Seller and Buyer acknowledge and agree that the exchange of closing funds, non-registrable documents and other items (the "Requisite Deliveries") and the release thereof to the Seller and Buyer will (a) not occur at the same time as the registration of the transfer/deed (and any other documents intended to be registered in connection with the completion of this transaction) and (b) be subject to conditions whereby the lawyer(s) receiving any of the Requisite Deliveries will be required to hold same in trust and not release same except in accordance with the terms of a document registration agreement between the said lawyers. The Seller and Buyer irrevocably instruct the said lawyers to be bound by the document registration agreement which is recommended from time to time by the Law Society of Upper Canada. Unless otherwise agreed to by the lawyers, such exchange of the Requisite Deliveries will occur in the applicable Land Titles Office or such other location agreeable to both lawyers.

12. **DOCUMENTS AND DISCHARGE:** Buyer shall not call for the production of any title deed, abstract, survey or other evidence of title to the property except such as are in the possession or control of Seller. If requested by Buyer, Seller will deliver any sketch or survey of the property within Seller's control to Buyer as soon as possible and prior to the Requisition Date. If a discharge of any Charge/Mortgage held by a corporation incorporated pursuant to the Trust And Loan Companies Act (Canada), Chartered Bank, Trust Company, Credit Union, Caisse Populaire or Insurance Company and which is not to be assumed by Buyer on completion, is not available in registrable form on completion, Buyer agrees to accept Seller's lawyer's personal undertaking to obtain, out of the closing funds, a discharge in registrable form and to register same, or cause same to be registered, on title within a reasonable period of time after completion, provided that on or before completion Seller shall provide to Buyer a mortgage statement prepared by the mortgagee setting out the balance required to obtain the discharge, and, where a real-time electronic cleared funds transfer system is not being used, a direction executed by Seller directing payment to the mortgagee of the amount required to obtain the discharge out of the balance due on completion.

INITIALS OF BUYER(S): ⬭　　　　INITIALS OF SELLER(S): ⬭

Form 111   Revised 2015   **Page 3 of 7**

APPENDIX

Form 111   *(continued)*   Page 4 of 7

13. **INSPECTION:** Buyer acknowledges having had the opportunity to inspect the property and understands that upon acceptance of this offer there shall be a binding agreement of purchase and sale between Buyer and Seller. **The Buyer acknowledges having the opportunity to include a requirement for a property inspection report in this Agreement and agrees that except as may be specifically provided for in this Agreement, the Buyer will not be obtaining a property inspection or property inspection report regarding the property.**

14. **INSURANCE:** All buildings on the property and all other things being purchased shall be and remain until completion at the risk of Seller. Pending completion, Seller shall hold all insurance policies, if any, and the proceeds thereof in trust for the parties as their interests may appear and in the event of substantial damage, Buyer may either terminate this Agreement and have all monies paid returned without interest or deduction or else take the proceeds of any insurance and complete the purchase. No insurance shall be transferred on completion. If Seller is taking back a Charge/Mortgage, or Buyer is assuming a Charge/Mortgage, Buyer shall supply Seller with reasonable evidence of adequate insurance to protect Seller's or other mortgagee's interest on completion.

15. **PLANNING ACT:** This Agreement shall be effective to create an interest in the property only if Seller complies with the subdivision control provisions of the Planning Act by completion and Seller covenants to proceed diligently at Seller's expense to obtain any necessary consent by completion.

16. **DOCUMENT PREPARATION:** The Transfer/Deed shall, save for the Land Transfer Tax Affidavit, be prepared in registrable form at the expense of Seller, and any Charge/Mortgage to be given back by the Buyer to Seller at the expense of the Buyer. If requested by Buyer, Seller covenants that the Transfer/Deed to be delivered on completion shall contain the statements contemplated by Section 50(22) of the Planning Act, R.S.O.1990.

17. **RESIDENCY:** (a) Subject to (b) below, the Seller represents and warrants that the Seller is not and on completion will not be a non-resident under the non-residency provisions of the Income Tax Act which representation and warranty shall survive and not merge upon the completion of this transaction and the Seller shall deliver to the Buyer a statutory declaration that Seller is not then a non-resident of Canada;
(b) provided that if the Seller is a non-resident under the non-residency provisions of the Income Tax Act, the Buyer shall be credited towards the Purchase Price with the amount, if any, necessary for Buyer to pay to the Minister of National Revenue to satisfy Buyer's liability in respect of tax payable by Seller under the non-residency provisions of the Income Tax Act by reason of this sale. Buyer shall not claim such credit if Seller delivers on completion the prescribed certificate.

18. **ADJUSTMENTS:** Common Expenses; realty taxes, including local improvement rates; mortgage interest; rentals; unmetered public or private utilities and fuel where billed to the Parcel of Tied Land and not the Condominium Corporation; are to be apportioned and allowed to the day of completion, the day of completion itself to be apportioned to the Buyer. There shall be no adjustment for the Seller's share of any assets or liabilities of the Condominium Corporation including any reserve or contingency fund to which Seller may have contributed prior to the date of completion.

19. **PROPERTY ASSESSMENT:** The Buyer and Seller hereby acknowledge that the Province of Ontario has implemented current value assessment and properties may be re-assessed on an annual basis. The Buyer and Seller agree that no claim will be made against the Buyer or Seller, or any Brokerage, Broker or Salesperson, for any changes in property tax as a result of a re-assessment of the property, save and except any property taxes that accrued prior to the completion of this transaction.

20. **TIME LIMITS:** Time shall in all respects be of the essence hereof provided that the time for doing or completing of any matter provided for herein may be extended or abridged by an agreement in writing signed by Seller and Buyer or by their respective lawyers who may be specifically authorized in that regard.

21. **TENDER:** Any tender of documents or money hereunder may be made upon Seller or Buyer or their respective lawyers on the day set for completion. Money shall be tendered with funds drawn on a lawyer's trust account in the form of a bank draft, certified cheque or wire transfer using the Large Value Transfer System.

22. **FAMILY LAW ACT:** Seller warrants that spousal consent is not necessary to this transaction under the provisions of the Family Law Act, R.S.O.1990 unless Seller's spouse has executed the consent hereinafter provided.

23. **UFFI:** Seller represents and warrants to Buyer that during the time Seller has owned the property, Seller has not caused any building on the property to be insulated with insulation containing ureaformaldehyde, and that to the best of Seller's knowledge no building on the property contains or has ever contained insulation that contains ureaformaldehyde. This warranty shall survive and not merge on the completion of this transaction, and if the building is part of a multiple unit building, this warranty shall only apply to that part of the building which is the subject of this transaction.

INITIALS OF BUYER(S): (⬭)   INITIALS OF SELLER(S): (⬭)

Form 111   Revised 2015   **Page 4 of 7**

APPENDIX

24. **LEGAL, ACCOUNTING AND ENVIRONMENTAL ADVICE:** The parties acknowledge that any information provided by the brokerage is not legal, tax or environmental advice.

25. **CONSUMER REPORTS: The Buyer is hereby notified that a consumer report containing credit and/or personal information may be referred to in connection with this transaction.**

26. **AGREEMENT IN WRITING:** If there is conflict or discrepancy between any provision added to this Agreement (including any Schedule attached hereto) and any provision in the standard pre-set portion hereof, the added provision shall supersede the standard pre-set provision to the extent of such conflict or discrepancy. This Agreement including any Schedule attached hereto, shall constitute the entire Agreement between Buyer and Seller. There is no representation, warranty, collateral agreement or condition, which affects this Agreement other than as expressed herein. For the purposes of this Agreement, Seller means vendor and Buyer means purchaser. This Agreement shall be read with all changes of gender or number required by the context.

27. **TIME AND DATE:** Any reference to a time and date in this Agreement shall mean the time and date where the property is located.

28. **COMMON ELEMENTS CONDOMINIUM:**

a). **COMMON EXPENSES:** The Seller warrants to the Buyer that the common expenses presently payable to the Condominium Corporation in respect

of the Property are approximately $ .... per month, which includes the following:

....

....

....

....

b). **STATUS CERTIFICATE AND MANAGEMENT OF CONDOMINIUM:** The Seller represents and warrants to the Buyer that there are no special assessments contemplated by the Condominium Corporation, and there are no legal actions pending by or against or contemplated by the Condominium Corporation. The Seller consents to a request by the Buyer or the Buyer's authorized representative for a Status Certificate from the Condominium Corporation. Buyer acknowledges that the Condominium Corporation may have entered into a Management Agreement for the management of the condominium property.Seller agrees to deliver to Buyer, if it is possible without incurring any costs in so doing, copies of all current condominium documentation of the Condominium Corporation, including the Declaration, Description, By-laws, Common Element Rules and Regulations and the most recent financial statements of the Condominium Corporation.

c). **MEETINGS:** The Seller represents and warrants to the Buyer that at the time of the acceptance of this Offer the Seller has not received a notice convening a special or general meeting of the Condominium Corporation respecting:
(i) the termination of the government of the condominium property;
(ii) any substantial alteration in or substantial addition to the common elements or the renovation thereof; OR
(iii) any substantial change in the assets or liabilities of the Condominium Corporation; and Seller covenants that if the Seller receives any such notice prior to the date of completion Seller shall forthwith notify the Buyer in writing and Buyer may thereupon at the Buyer's option declare the Agreement null and void and all monies paid by the Buyer shall be refunded without interest or deduction.

d). **TITLE:** The Buyer agrees to accept title to the Property subject to the provisions of the Condominium Act and its Regulations and the terms, conditions and provisions of the Declaration, Description and Bylaws, Occupancy Standards Bylaws, including the Common Element Rules and other Rules and Regulations.

Condominium Property Manager: ....
                                                                                 (Name)

....
                              (Address)   (Tel No.,FAX No.)

APPENDIX

29. SUCCESSORS AND ASSIGNS: The heirs, executors, administrators, successors and assigns of the undersigned are bound by the terms herein.

SIGNED, SEALED AND DELIVERED in the presence of: IN WITNESS whereof I have hereunto set my hand and seal:

.... (Seal)   DATE ....
(Witness)   (Buyer)

.... (Seal)   DATE ....
(Witness)   (Buyer)

I, the Undersigned Seller, agree to the above offer. I hereby irrevocably instruct my lawyer to pay directly to the brokerage(s) with whom I have agreed to pay commission, the unpaid balance of the commission together with applicable Harmonized Sales Tax (and any other taxes as may hereafter be applicable), from the proceeds of the sale prior to any payment to the undersigned on completion, as advised by the brokerage(s) to my lawyer.

SIGNED, SEALED AND DELIVERED in the presence of: IN WITNESS whereof I have hereunto set my hand and seal:

.... (Seal)   DATE ....
(Witness)   (Seller)

.... (Seal)   DATE ....
(Witness)   (Seller)

SPOUSAL CONSENT: The Undersigned Spouse of the Seller hereby consents to the disposition evidenced herein pursuant to the provisions of the Family Law Act, R.S.O.1990, and hereby agrees with the Buyer that he/she will execute all necessary or incidental documents to give full force and effect to the sale evidenced herein.

.... (Seal)   DATE ....
(Witness)   (Spouse)

CONFIRMATION OF ACCEPTANCE: Notwithstanding anything contained herein to the contrary, I confirm this Agreement with all changes both typed and written was finally accepted by all parties at .... a.m./p.m. this .... day of..., 20...........

....
(Signature of Seller or Buyer)

INFORMATION ON BROKERAGE(S)

Listing Brokerage .... Tel.No.(...............).......................................
....
(Salesperson / Broker Name)

Co-op/Buyer Brokerage .... Tel.No.(...............).......................................
....
(Salesperson / Broker Name)

ACKNOWLEDGEMENT

I acknowledge receipt of my signed copy of this accepted Agreement of Purchase and Sale and I authorize the Brokerage to forward a copy to my lawyer.	I acknowledge receipt of my signed copy of this accepted Agreement of Purchase and Sale and I authorize the Brokerage to forward a copy to my lawyer.
.... DATE .... (Seller)	.... DATE .... (Buyer)
.... DATE .... (Seller)	.... DATE .... (Buyer)
Address for Service	Address for Service ....
.... Tel.No.(..........).......	.... Tel.No.(..........).......
Seller's Lawyer	Buyer's Lawyer ....
Address	Address ....
Email	Email ....
(..........)........................... (..........).... FAX No. Tel.No.	(..........)........................... (..........).... FAX No. Tel.No.

FOR OFFICE USE ONLY   **COMMISSION TRUST AGREEMENT**

To: Co-operating Brokerage shown on the foregoing Agreement of Purchase and Sale:
In consideration for the Co-operating Brokerage procuring the foregoing Agreement of Purchase and Sale, I hereby declare that all moneys received or receivable by me in connection with the Transaction as contemplated in the MLS® Rules and Regulations of my Real Estate Board shall be receivable and held in trust. This agreement shall constitute a Commission Trust Agreement as defined in the MLS® Rules and shall be subject to and governed by the MLS® Rules pertaining to Commission Trust.
DATED as of the date and time of the acceptance of the foregoing Agreement of Purchase and Sale.   Acknowledged by:

....
(Authorized to bind the Listing Brokerage)   (Authorized to bind the Co-operating Brokerage)

APPENDIX

Form 111
for use in the Province of Ontario

Schedule A
Agreement of Purchase and Sale - POTL
Common Elements Condominium

This Schedule is attached to and forms part of the Agreement of Purchase and Sale between:

BUYER, ..., and

SELLER, ...

for the purchase and sale of ....

.... dated the .... day of ...., 20...............

Buyer agrees to pay the balance as follows:

This form must be initialed by all parties to the Agreement of Purchase and Sale.

INITIALS OF BUYER(S): ( )   **INITIALS OF SELLER(S):** ( )

Form 111   Revised 2015   **Page 7 of 7**

APPENDIX

OREA Ontario Real Estate Association

Agreement of Purchase and Sale
Co-ownership Building Resale Agreement

Form 115
for use in the Province of Ontario

This Agreement of Purchase and Sale dated this...................... day of .... 20....................

BUYER,.., agrees to purchase from
(Full legal names of all Buyers)

SELLER,..., the following
(Full legal names of all Sellers)

REAL PROPERTY AND SHARES: A .... percentage in the property legally described as:

....

as tenant-in-common with all the other co-owners that are the co-owners from time to time, together with the exclusive right to occupy and

use ....(the "Unit")

in the Co-ownership Building located at:..

in the...

Parking Space(s)... Locker..(the "Property")

and...shares (the "shares") in the Capital of..(the "Corporation")

PURCHASE PRICE: Dollars (CDN$) ....

....Dollars

DEPOSIT: Buyer submits ....
(Herewith/Upon Acceptance/as otherwise described in this Agreement)

.... Dollars (CDN$)..

by negotiable cheque payable to.. .... "Deposit Holder" to be held in
trust pending completion or other termination of this Agreement and to be credited toward the Purchase Price on completion. For the purposes of this
Agreement, "Upon Acceptance" shall mean that the Buyer is required to deliver the deposit to the Deposit Holder within 24 hours of the acceptance of
this Agreement. The parties to this Agreement hereby acknowledge that, unless otherwise provided for in this Agreement, the Deposit Holder shall place
the deposit in trust in the Deposit Holder's non-interest bearing Real Estate Trust Account and no interest shall be earned, received or paid on the deposit
Buyer agrees to pay the balance as more particularly set out in Schedule A attached.

SCHEDULE(S) A...**attached hereto form(s) part of this Agreement.**

1. **IRREVOCABILITY:** This offer shall be irrevocable by .... until .... a.m./p.m. on the ....
(Seller/Buyer)

     day of .... 20 ...., after which time, if not accepted, this offer shall be null and void and the deposit shall be
     returned to the Buyer in full without interest.

2. **COMPLETION DATE:** This Agreement shall be completed by no later than 6:00 p.m. on the .... day of .... 20 ......
     Upon completion, vacant possession of the property shall be given to the Buyer unless otherwise provided for in this Agreement.

INITIALS OF BUYER(S): (⬭)   **INITIALS OF SELLER(S):** (⬭)

Form 115   Revised 2015   **Page 1 of 6**

APPENDIX

3. **NOTICES:** The Seller hereby appoints the Listing Brokerage as agent for the Seller for the purpose of giving and receiving notices pursuant to this Agreement. Where a Brokerage (Buyer's Brokerage) has entered into a representation agreement with the Buyer, the Buyer hereby appoints the Buyer's Brokerage as agent for the purpose of giving and receiving notices pursuant to this Agreement. **Where a Brokerage represents both the Seller and the Buyer (multiple representation), the Brokerage shall not be appointed or authorized to be agent for either the Buyer or the Seller for the purpose of giving and receiving notices.** Any notice relating hereto or provided for herein shall be in writing. In addition to any provision contained herein and in any Schedule hereto, this offer, any counter-offer, notice of acceptance thereof or any notice to be given or received pursuant to this Agreement or any Schedule hereto (any of them, "Document") shall be deemed given and received when delivered personally or hand delivered to the Address for Service provided in the Acknowledgement below, or where a facsimile number or email address is provided herein, when transmitted electronically to that facsimile number or email address, respectively, in which case, the signature(s) of the party (parties) shall be deemed to be original.

FAX No.: .... FAX No.: ....
(For delivery of Documents to Seller) (For delivery of Documents to Buyer)

Email Address: .... Email Address: ....
(For delivery of Documents to Seller) (For delivery of Documents to Buyer)

4. **CHATTELS INCLUDED:**...

....

....

Unless otherwise stated in this Agreement or any Schedule hereto, Seller agrees to convey all fixtures and chattels included in the Purchase Price free from all liens, encumbrances or claims affecting the said fixtures and chattels.

5. **FIXTURES EXCLUDED:**...

....

....

6. **RENTAL ITEMS (Including Lease, Lease to Own):** The following equipment is rented and **not** included in the Purchase Price. The Buyer agrees to assume the rental contract(s), if assumable:

....

....

....

The Buyer agrees to co-operate and execute such documentation as may be required to facilitate such assumption.

7. **MAINTENANCE EXPENSES:** Seller warrants that the maintenance expenses presently payable to the Corporation in respect of the property are

approximately $.. per month and include:..

....

....

8. **PARKING AND LOCKERS:** Parking and Lockers are as described above or assigned as follows:..

.... at an additional cost of:...

9. **HST:** If the sale of the Property (Real Property as described above) is subject to Harmonized Sales Tax (HST), then such tax shall be

.... the Purchase Price. If the sale of the Property is not subject to HST, Seller agrees to certify on or before
(included in/in addition to)
closing, that the sale of the Property is not subject to HST. Any HST on chattels, if applicable, is not included in the Purchase Price.

INITIALS OF BUYER(S): ( ) INITIALS OF SELLER(S): ( )

APPENDIX

Form 115　*(continued)*　　　　　　　　　　　　　　　　　　　　　　　Page 3 of 6

10. **APPROVAL:** This Agreement is subject to Seller, at the Seller's own expense, obtaining approval of the Board of Directors of the Corporation to the sale and transfer of the Seller's shares in the capital of the Corporation to the Buyer and approval of the Buyer as shareholder and occupant of the

    Unit, and if such approval is not obtained by 11:59 p.m. on the .... day of ...., 20....... this agreement shall become null and void and the Buyer's deposit shall be returned to the Buyer in full without deduction. The buyer agrees to cooperate and provide such information and documentation as may be within control of the Buyer in order to obtain said approval.

11. **TITLE SEARCH:** Buyer shall be allowed until 6:00 p.m. on the .... day of...................................., 20......, (Requisition Date) to examine the title to the Property at Buyer's own expense and until the earlier of: (i) thirty days from the later of the Requisition Date or the date on which the conditions in this Agreement are fulfilled or otherwise waived or; (ii) five days prior to completion, to satisfy Buyer that there are no outstanding

    work orders or deficiency notices affecting the Property, and that its present use (...) may be lawfully continued. If within that time any valid objection to title or to any outstanding work order or deficiency notice, or to the fact the said present use may not lawfully be continued, is made in writing to Seller and which Seller is unable or unwilling to remove, remedy or satisfy or obtain insurance save and except against risk of fire (Title Insurance) in favour of the Buyer and any mortgagee, (with all related costs at the expense of the Seller), and which Buyer will not waive, this Agreement notwithstanding any intermediate acts or negotiations in respect of such objections, shall be at an end and all monies paid shall be returned without interest or deduction and Seller, Listing Brokerage and Co-operating Brokerage shall not be liable for any costs or damages. Save as to any valid objection so made by such day and except for any objection going to the root of the title, Buyer shall be conclusively deemed to have accepted Seller's title to the Property. Seller hereby consents to the municipality or other governmental agencies releasing to Buyer details of all outstanding work orders and deficiency notices affecting the Property, and Seller agrees to execute and deliver such further authorizations in this regard as Buyer may reasonably require.

12. **CORPORATION DOCUMENTATION:** The Seller shall deliver to the Buyer on or before closing:
    (a) a certified copy of the Resolution of the Board of Directors of the Corporation approving the Buyer as a shareholder and as an occupant of the Unit;
    (b) a share certificate for the Seller's shares in the capital of the Corporation endorsed in favour of the Buyer.
    (c) a certificate or letter from the Corporation confirming:
    　　(i) with respect to the Property, that all charges and obligations have been paid or discharged as of the date of closing;
    　　(ii) with respect to the Corporation that the affairs of the Corporation are in order and that there are no legal actions pending against the Corporation or contemplated by the Corporation, that there are no special assessments contemplated by the Corporation, that there are no orders or complaints against the real property by the Building, Health or Fire Departments, and the Building is not and never has been insulated with Urea-Formaldehyde Foam Insulation.

13. **OCCUPANCY AGREEMENT:** The Buyer agrees on or before closing to enter into an Occupancy Agreement with the Corporation and to abide by the rules and regulations of the Corporation.

14. **TITLE:** The Buyer agrees to accept the title to the Property subject to all rights and easements registered against title for the supply and installation of telephone services, electricity, gas, sewers, water, television cable facilities and other related services; provided that title to the Property is otherwise good and free from all encumbrances except: (a) as herein expressly provided; (b) any registered restrictions, conditions or covenants that run with the land provided such have been complied with; and (c) any existing municipal agreements, zoning by-laws and/or regulations and utility or service contracts.

15. **DOCUMENTS AND DISCHARGE:** Buyer shall not call for the production of any title deed, abstract, survey or other evidence of title to the Property except such as are in the possession or control of Seller. If a discharge of any Charge/Mortgage, lien or other encumbrance held by a corporation incorporated pursuant to the Trust And Loan Companies Act (Canada), Chartered Bank, Trust Company, Credit Union, Caisse Populaire or Insurance Company and which is not to be assumed by Buyer on completion, is not available in registrable form on completion, Buyer agrees to accept Seller's lawyer's personal undertaking to obtain, out of the closing funds, a discharge in registrable form and to register same, or cause same to be registered, on title within a reasonable period of time after completion, provided that on or before completion Seller shall provide to Buyer a statement prepared by the mortgagee, lienholder or encumbrancer setting out the balance required to obtain the discharge, and, where a real-time electronic cleared funds transfer system is not being used, a direction executed by Seller directing payment to the mortgagee, lienholder or encumbrancer of the amount required to obtain the discharge out of the balance due on completion.

16. **MEETINGS:** Seller represents and warrants to Buyer that at the time of the acceptance of this Offer the Seller has not received a notice convening a special or general meeting of the Corporation respecting; (a) the termination of the government of the property; (b) the winding up or dissolution of the Corporation; (c) any substantial alteration in or substantial addition to the property or the renovation thereof; OR (d) any substantial change in the assets or liabilities of the Corporation; and Seller covenants that if the Seller receives any such notice prior to the date of completion the Seller shall forthwith notify Buyer in writing and the Buyer may thereupon at the Buyer's option declare this Agreement to be null and void and all monies paid by Buyer shall be refunded without interest or deduction.

INITIALS OF BUYER(S): ⬭　　　　　　　**INITIALS OF SELLER(S):** ⬭

APPENDIX

17. **INSPECTION:** Buyer acknowledges having had the opportunity to inspect the Property and understands that upon acceptance of this offer there shall be a binding agreement of purchase and sale between Buyer and Seller. **The Buyer acknowledges having the opportunity to include a requirement for a property inspection report in this Agreement and agrees that except as may be specifically provided for in this Agreement, the Buyer will not be obtaining a property inspection or property inspection report regarding the Property.**

18. **INSURANCE:** The Unit and all other things being purchased shall be and remain at the risk of the Seller until completion. In the event of substantial damage to the real property Buyer may at the Buyer's option either permit the proceeds of insurance to be used for repair of such damage in accordance with the provisions of the Insurance Trust Agreement or other insurance arrangement, or terminate this Agreement and all deposit monies paid by Buyer hereunder shall be refunded without interest or deduction. If Seller is taking back a Charge/Mortgage, or Buyer is assuming a Charge/Mortgage, Buyer shall supply Seller with reasonable evidence of adequate insurance to protect Seller's or other mortgagee's interest on completion.

19. **DOCUMENT PREPARATION:** The Transfer/Deed shall, save for the Land Transfer Tax Affidavit, be prepared in registrable form at the expense of Seller, and any Charge/Mortgage to be given back by the Buyer to Seller at the expense of the Buyer.

20. **RESIDENCY:** (a) Subject to (b) below, the Seller represents and warrants that the Seller is not and on completion will not be a non-resident under the non-residency provisions of the Income Tax Act which representation and warranty shall survive and not merge upon the completion of this transaction and the Seller shall deliver to the Buyer a statutory declaration that Seller is not then a non-resident of Canada;
(b) provided that if the Seller is a non-resident under the non-residency provisions of the Income Tax Act, the Buyer shall be credited towards the Purchase Price with the amount, if any, necessary for Buyer to pay to the Minister of National Revenue to satisfy Buyer's liability in respect of tax payable by Seller under the non-residency provisions of the Income Tax Act by reason of this sale.Buyer shall not claim such credit if Seller delivers on completion the prescribed certificate.

21. **ADJUSTMENTS:** Maintenance expenses and, where billed to the Unit and not the Corporation, realty taxes, including local improvement rates; mortgage interest; rentals; unmetered public or private utilities and fuel; are to be apportioned and allowed to the day of completion, the day of completion itself to be apportioned to the Buyer. There shall be no adjustment for the Seller's share of any reserve or contingency fund to which the Seller may have contributed prior to the date of completion.

22. **PROPERTY ASSESSMENT:** The Buyer and Seller hereby acknowledge that the Province of Ontario has implemented current value assessment and properties may be re-assessed on an annual basis. The Buyer and Seller agree that no claim will be made against the Buyer or Seller, or any Brokerage, Broker or Salesperson, for any changes in property tax as a result of a re-assessment of the Property, save and except any property taxes that accrued prior to the completion of this transaction.

23. **TIME LIMITS:** Time shall in all respects be of the essence hereof provided that the time for doing or completing of any matter provided for herein may be extended or abridged by an agreement in writing signed by Seller and Buyer or by their respective lawyers who may be specifically authorized in that regard.

24. **TENDER:** Any tender of documents or money hereunder may be made upon Seller or Buyer or their respective lawyers on the day set for completion. Money shall be tendered with funds drawn on a lawyer's trust account in the form of a bank draft, certified cheque or wire transfer using the Large Value Transfer System.

25. **FAMILY LAW ACT:** Seller warrants that spousal consent is not necessary to this transaction under the provisions of the Family Law Act, R.S.O.1990 unless Seller's spouse has executed the consent hereinafter provided.

26. **LEGAL, ACCOUNTING AND ENVIRONMENTAL ADVICE:** The parties acknowledge that any information provided by the brokerage is not legal, tax or environmental advice.

27. **CONSUMER REPORTS: The Buyer is hereby notified that a consumer report containing credit and/or personal information may be referred to in connection with this transaction.**

28. **AGREEMENT IN WRITING:** If there is conflict or discrepancy between any provision added to this Agreement (including any Schedule attached hereto) and any provision in the standard pre-set portion hereof, the added provision shall supersede the standard pre-set provision to the extent of such conflict or discrepancy. This Agreement including any Schedule attached hereto, shall constitute the entire Agreement between Buyer and Seller. There is no representation, warranty, collateral agreement or condition, which affects this Agreement other than as expressed herein. For the purposes of this Agreement, Seller means vendor and Buyer means purchaser. This Agreement shall be read with all changes of gender or number required by the context.

29. **TIME AND DATE:** Any reference to a time and date in this Agreement shall mean the time and date where the Property is located.

INITIALS OF BUYER(S): ⬭   INITIALS OF SELLER(S): ⬭

APPENDIX

30. SUCCESSORS AND ASSIGNS: The heirs, executors, administrators, successors and assigns of the undersigned are bound by the terms herein.

SIGNED, SEALED AND DELIVERED in the presence of: IN WITNESS whereof I have hereunto set my hand and seal:

.... ● DATE ....
(Witness)   (Buyer)   (Seal)

.... ● DATE ....
(Witness)   (Buyer)   (Seal)

I, the Undersigned Seller, agree to the above offer. I hereby irrevocably instruct my lawyer to pay directly to the brokerage(s) with whom I have agreed to pay commission, the unpaid balance of the commission together with applicable Harmonized Sales Tax (and any other taxes as may hereafter be applicable), from the proceeds of the sale prior to any payment to the undersigned on completion, as advised by the brokerage(s) to my lawyer.

SIGNED, SEALED AND DELIVERED in the presence of: IN WITNESS whereof I have hereunto set my hand and seal:

.... ● DATE ....
(Witness)   (Seller)   (Seal)

.... ● DATE ....
(Witness)   (Seller)   (Seal)

SPOUSAL CONSENT: The Undersigned Spouse of the Seller hereby consents to the disposition evidenced herein pursuant to the provisions of the Family Law Act, R.S.O.1990, and hereby agrees with the Buyer that he/she will execute all necessary or incidental documents to give full force and effect to the sale evidenced herein.

.... ● DATE ....
(Witness)   (Spouse)   (Seal)

CONFIRMATION OF ACCEPTANCE: Notwithstanding anything contained herein to the contrary, I confirm this Agreement with all changes both typed and written was finally accepted by all parties at .... a.m./p.m. this .... day of..., 20..........

                                                            ....
                                                            (Signature of Seller or Buyer)

INFORMATION ON BROKERAGE(S)

Listing Brokerage .... Tel.No.(.................)...............................

....
(Salesperson / Broker Name)

Co-op/Buyer Brokerage .... Tel.No.(.................)...............................

....
(Salesperson / Broker Name)

ACKNOWLEDGEMENT

I acknowledge receipt of my signed copy of this accepted Agreement of Purchase and Sale and I authorize the Brokerage to forward a copy to my lawyer.	I acknowledge receipt of my signed copy of this accepted Agreement of Purchase and Sale and I authorize the Brokerage to forward a copy to my lawyer.
.... DATE .... (Seller)	.... DATE .... (Buyer)
.... DATE .... (Seller)	.... DATE .... (Buyer)
Address for Service	Address for Service ....
.... Tel.No.(..........)...............	.... Tel.No.(..........)...............
Seller's Lawyer	Buyer's Lawyer ....
Address	Address ....
Email	Email ....
(..........)..................... (..........)........... Tel.No. FAX No.	(..........)..................... (..........)........... Tel.No. FAX No.

Property Manager: ....
                          (Name)   (Address)   (Tel No.,FAX No)

FOR OFFICE USE ONLY   **COMMISSION TRUST AGREEMENT**

To: Co-operating Brokerage shown on the foregoing Agreement of Purchase and Sale:
In consideration for the Co-operating Brokerage procuring the foregoing Agreement of Purchase and Sale, I hereby declare that all moneys received or receivable by me in connection with the Transaction as contemplated in the MLS® Rules and Regulations of my Real Estate Board shall be receivable and held in trust. This agreement shall constitute a Commission Trust Agreement as defined in the MLS® Rules and shall be subject to and governed by the MLS® Rules pertaining to Commission Trust.

DATED as of the date and time of the acceptance of the foregoing Agreement of Purchase and Sale.   Acknowledged by:

....
(Authorized to bind the Listing Brokerage)   (Authorized to bind the Co-operating Brokerage)

APPENDIX

Form 115
for use in the Province of Ontario

Schedule A
Agreement of Purchase and Sale –
Co-ownership Building Resale

This Schedule is attached to and forms part of the Agreement of Purchase and Sale between:

BUYER,..., and

SELLER,..

for the purchase and sale of ....

.... dated the .... day of ...., 20.............

Buyer agrees to pay the balance as follows:

This form must be initialed by all parties to the Agreement of Purchase and Sale.

INITIALS OF BUYER(S):   ( )   INITIALS OF SELLER(S):   ( )

Form 115   Revised 2015   **Page 6 of 6**

APPENDIX

OREA Ontario Real Estate Association

Assignment of Agreement of Purchase and Sale

Form 145
for use in the Province of Ontario

This Assignment of Agreement of Purchase and Sale dated this .... day of .... 20...........

ASSIGNEE, ..., agrees to purchase from
(Full legal names of all Assignees)

ASSIGNOR, ..., the following
(Full legal names of all Assignors)

THE ASSIGNOR'S INTEREST IN THE REAL PROPERTY:

Address .... fronting on the .... side

of .... in the ....

and having a frontage of .... more or less by a depth of .... more or less

and legally described as ....

.... (the "property")
(Legal description of land including easements not described elsewhere)

PURCHASE PRICE: Dollars (CDN$) ....

....Dollars

DEPOSIT: Assignee submits ....
(Herewith/Upon Acceptance/as otherwise described in this Agreement)

.... Dollars (CDN$) ....

by negotiable cheque payable to .... "Deposit Holder" to be held in trust pending completion or other termination of this Assignment agreement ("Assignment") and to be credited toward the Purchase Price on completion. For the purposes of this Assignment, "Upon Acceptance" shall mean that the Assignee is required to deliver the deposit to the Deposit Holder within 24 hours of the acceptance of this Assignment agreement. The parties to this Assignment hereby acknowledge that, unless otherwise provided for in this Assignment, the Deposit Holder shall place the deposit in trust in the Deposit Holder's non-interest bearing Real Estate Trust Account and no interest shall be earned, received or paid on the deposit.

The Assignee and Assignor acknowledge that the Purchase Price noted above includes both the purchase price the Assignor is paying for the property as indicated in the Agreement of Purchase and Sale between the Assignor and the seller of the property attached hereto as Schedule C, and also includes the amount being paid by the Assignee to the Assignor as payment for the Assignment Agreement. The Assignee and Assignor agree that the funds for this transaction will be calculated and paid as set out in Schedule B attached hereto and forming part of this Agreement.

Assignee agrees to pay the balance as more particularly set out in Schedules A and B attached.

**Schedules A, B (Calculation of funds for this Agreement),
C (Agreement of Purchase and Sale that is the subject of this Assignment),**

....**attached hereto form(s) part of this Agreement.**

1.   **IRREVOCABILITY:** This offer shall be irrevocable by .... until .... a.m./p.m. on the ....
(Assignee/Assignor)

     day of .... 20 ...., after which time, if not accepted, this offer shall be null and void and the deposit shall be returned to the Buyer in full without interest.

                INITIALS OF ASSIGNEE(S): (⬭)   **INITIALS OF ASSIGNOR(S):** (⬭)

Form 145   Revised 2015   **Page 1 of 6**

APPENDIX

2. **ASSIGNMENT:** The Assignor agrees to grant and assign to the Assignee, forthwith all the Assignor's rights, title and interest, in, under and to the Agreement of Purchase and Sale attached hereto in Schedule "C".

3. **ASSIGNEE COVENANTS:** The Assignee hereby covenants and agrees with the Assignor that forthwith upon the assignment of the Agreement of Purchase and Sale it will assume, perform, comply with and be bound by, all obligations, warranties and representations of the Assignor as contained in the Agreement of Purchase and Sale as if the Assignee had originally executed the Agreement of Purchase and Sale as buyer with the seller.

4. **ASSIGNOR COVENANTS:** The Assignor covenants and represents that:
   (a) the Assignor has the full right, power and authority to assign the prior Agreement of Purchase and Sale attached hereto as Schedule "C" (the "Agreement of Purchase and Sale") and the Assignor's interest in the property;
   (b) the Agreement of Purchase and Sale attached hereto as Schedule "C" is a full and complete copy thereof and has not been amended, supplemented,terminated or otherwise changed in any way and is in good standing and has not previously been assigned.
   (c) the Assignor will not amend the Agreement of Purchase and Sale without the Assignee's prior written consent;
   (d) after acceptance of this Assignment Agreement until the earlier of termination or completion of the Agreement of Purchase and Sale attached hereto as Schedule "C", the Assignor will not further assign the Agreement of Purchase and Sale.
   (e) neither party to the Agreement of Purchase and Sale (Schedule C) has done any act in breach of the said Agreement of Purchase and Sale or committed any omission with respect to the said Agreement of Purchase and Sale.

5. **NOTICES:** The Assignor hereby appoints the Listing Brokerage as agent for the Assignor for the purpose of giving and receiving notices pursuant to this Agreement. Where a Brokerage (Assignee's Brokerage) has entered into a representation agreement with the Assignee, the Assignee hereby appoints the Assignee's Brokerage as agent for the purpose of giving and receiving notices pursuant to this Agreement. **Where a Brokerage represents both the Assignor and the Assignee (multiple representation), the Brokerage shall not be appointed or authorized to be agent for either the Assignee or the Assignor for the purpose of giving and receiving notices.** Any notice relating hereto or provided for herein shall be in writing. In addition to any provision contained herein and in any Schedule hereto, this offer, any counter-offer, notice of acceptance thereof or any notice to be given or received pursuant to this Agreement or any Schedule hereto (any of them, **"Document"**) shall be deemed given and received when delivered personally or hand delivered to the Address for Service provided in the Acknowledgement below, or where a facsimile number or email address is provided herein, when transmitted electronically to the facsimile number or email address, respectively, in which case, the signature(s) of the party (parties) shall be deemed to be original.

FAX No.: ....   FAX No.: ....
                 (For delivery of Documents to Assignor)   (For delivery of Documents to Assignee)

Email Address: ....   Email Address: ....
                 (For delivery of Documents to Assignor)   (For delivery of Documents to Assignee)

6. **HST:** If the sale of the Property (Real Property as described above) is subject to Harmonized Sales Tax (HST), then such tax shall be

   .... the Purchase Price. If the sale of the Property is not subject to HST, Seller agrees to certify on or before
              (included in/in addition to)
   closing, that the sale of the Property is not subject to HST. Any HST on chattels, if applicable, is not included in the Purchase Price.

7. **FUTURE USE:** Assignor and Assignee agree that there is no representation or warranty of any kind that the future intended use of the property by Assignee is or will be lawful except as may be specifically provided for in this Assignment.

8. **INSPECTION:** Assignee acknowledges having had the opportunity to inspect the property or the plans and documents for the property to be constructed and understands that upon acceptance of this offer there shall be a binding Assignment agreement between Assignee and Assignor.

9. **PLANNING ACT:** Provided that this Assignment shall not be effective to create or convey an interest in the property unless and until the provisions of the Planning Act RSO 1990 c. P13, as amended are complied with.

INITIALS OF ASSIGNEE(S): ⬭   INITIALS OF ASSIGNOR(S): ⬭

APPENDIX

10. **RESIDENCY:** (a) Subject to (b) below, the Assignor represents and warrants that the Assignor is not and on completion will not be a non-resident under the non-residency provisions of the Income Tax Act which representation and warranty shall survive and not merge upon the completion of this transaction and the Assignor shall deliver to the Assignee a statutory declaration that Assignor is not then a non-resident of Canada; (b) provided that if the Assignor is a non-resident under the non-residency provisions of the Income Tax Act, the Assignee shall be credited towards the Purchase Price with the amount, if any, necessary for Assignee to pay to the Minister of National Revenue to satisfy Assignee's liability in respect of tax payable by Assignor under the non-residency provisions of the Income Tax Act by reason of this sale. Assignee shall not claim such credit if Assignor delivers on completion the prescribed certificate.

11. **ADJUSTMENTS:** Any rents, mortgage interest, realty taxes including local improvement rates and unmetered public or private utility charges and unmetered cost of fuel, as applicable, shall be apportioned and allowed to the day of completion, the day of completion itself to be apportioned to Assignee.

12. **PROPERTY ASSESSMENT:** The Assignee and Assignor hereby acknowledge that the Province of Ontario has implemented current value assessment and properties may be re-assessed on an annual basis. The Assignee and Assignor agree that no claim will be made against the Assignee and Assignor, or any Brokerage, Broker or Salesperson, for any changes in property tax as a result of a re-assessment of the property, save and except any property taxes that accrued prior to the completion of this transaction.

13. **TIME LIMITS:** Time shall in all respects be of the essence hereof provided that the time for doing or completing of any matter provided for herein may be extended or abridged by an agreement in writing signed by Assignor and Assignee or by their respective lawyers who may be specifically authorized in that regard.

14. **TENDER:** Any tender of documents or money hereunder may be made upon the Assignor or Assignee or their respective lawyers on the day set for completion. Money shall be tendered with funds drawn on a lawyer's trust account in the form of a bank draft, certified cheque or wire transfer using the Large Value Transfer System.

15. **APPROVAL OF THE AGREEMENT:** In the event that consent to this Assignment is required to be given by the seller in the Agreement of Purchase and Sale attached hereto in Schedule C, the Assignor will apply, at the sole expense of the Assignor, forthwith for the requisite consent, and if such consent is refused, then this agreement shall be null and void and the deposit monies paid hereunder shall be refunded without interest or other penalty to the Assignee.

16. **AGREE TO CO-OPERATE:** Except as otherwise expressed herein to the contrary, each of the Assignor and Assignee shall, without receiving additional consideration therefor, co-operate with and take such additional actions as may be requested by the other party, acting reasonably, in order to carry out the purpose and intent of this Assignment.

17. **DEFAULT BY SELLER:** The Assignee and Assignor acknowledge and agree that if this Assignment Agreement is not completed due to the default of the seller for the Agreement of Purchase and Sale (Schedule C) that is the subject of this Assignment, the Assignor shall not be liable for any expenses, losses or damages incurred by the Assignee and this Assignment Agreement shall become null and void and all moneys paid by the Assignee under this Assignment Agreement shall be returned to the Assignee in full without interest.

18. **LEGAL, ACCOUNTING AND ENVIRONMENTAL ADVICE:** The parties acknowledge that any information provided by the Brokerage is not legal, tax or environmental advice.

19. **CONSUMER REPORTS: The Assignee is hereby notified that a consumer report containing credit and/or personal information may be referred to in connection with this transaction.**

20. **AGREEMENT IN WRITING:** If there is conflict or discrepancy between any provision added to this Assignment (including any Schedule attached hereto) and any provision in the standard pre-set portion hereof, the added provision shall supersede the standard pre-set provision to the extent of such conflict or discrepancy. This Assignment including any Schedule attached hereto, shall constitute the entire agreement between Assignee and Assignor. There is no representation, warranty, collateral agreement or condition, which affects this Assignment other than as expressed herein. This Assignment shall be read with all changes of gender or number required by the context.

21. **TIME AND DATE:** Any reference to a time and date in this Agreement shall mean the time and date where the property is located.

INITIALS OF ASSIGNEE(S): ⬭   INITIALS OF ASSIGNOR(S): ⬭

APPENDIX

22. SUCCESSORS AND ASSIGNS: The heirs, executors, administrators, successors and assigns of the undersigned are bound by the terms herein.

SIGNED, SEALED AND DELIVERED in the presence of: IN WITNESS whereof I have hereunto set my hand and seal:

....   ● DATE ....
(Witness)   (Assignee)   (Seal)

....   ● DATE ....
(Witness)   (Assignee)   (Seal)

I, the Undersigned Assignor, agree to the above offer. I hereby irrevocably instruct my lawyer to pay directly to the brokerage(s) with whom I have agreed to pay commission, the unpaid balance of the commission together with applicable Harmonized Sales Tax (and any other taxes as may hereafter be applicable), from the proceeds of the sale prior to any payment to the undersigned on completion, as advised by the brokerage(s) to my lawyer.

SIGNED, SEALED AND DELIVERED in the presence of: IN WITNESS whereof I have hereunto set my hand and seal:

....   ● DATE ....
(Witness)   (Assignor)   (Seal)

....   ● DATE ....
(Witness)   (Assignor)   (Seal)

CONFIRMATION OF ACCEPTANCE: Notwithstanding anything contained herein to the contrary, I confirm this Agreement with all changes both typed

and written was finally accepted by all parties at .... a.m./p.m. this .... day of ...., 20...........

....
(Signature of Assignor or Assignee)

IINFORMATION ON BROKERAGE(S)

Listing Brokerage .... Tel.No.(..............).................................

....
(Salesperson / Broker Name)

Co-op/Buyer Brokerage .... Tel.No.(..............).................................

....
(Salesperson / Broker Name)

ACKNOWLEDGEMENT

I acknowledge receipt of my signed copy of this accepted Assignment Agreement and I authorize the Brokerage to forward a copy to my lawyer.	I acknowledge receipt of my signed copy of this accepted Assignment Agreement and I authorize the Brokerage to forward a copy to my lawyer.
.... DATE .... (Assignor)	.... DATE .... (Assignee)
.... DATE .... (Assignor)	.... DATE .... (Assignee)
Address for Service	Address for Service ....
.... Tel.No.(..........).................	.... Tel.No.(..........).................
Assignor's Lawyer	Assignee's Lawyer ....
Address	Address ....
Email	Email ....
(..........)......................... (..........)........ FAX No. Tel.No. FAX No.	(..........)......................... (..........)........ FAX No. Tel.No. FAX No.

FOR OFFICE USE ONLY   **COMMISSION TRUST AGREEMENT**

To: Co-operating Brokerage shown on the foregoing Assignment Agreement:
In consideration for the Co-operating Brokerage procuring the foregoing Assignment Agreement, I hereby declare that all moneys received or receivable by me in connection with the Transaction as contemplated in the MLS® Rules and Regulations of my Real Estate Board shall be receivable and held in trust. This agreement shall constitute a Commission Trust Agreement as defined in the MLS® Rules and shall be subject to and governed by the MLS® Rules pertaining to Commission Trust.
DATED as of the date and time of the acceptance of the foregoing Assignment Agreement.   Acknowledged by:

....
(Authorized to bind the Listing Brokerage)   (Authorized to bind the Co-operating Brokerage)

Form 145   Revised 2015   **Page 4 of 6**

APPENDIX

OREA Ontario Real Estate Association

Form 145
for use in the Province of Ontario

Schedule A
Assignment of Agreement of Purchase and Sale

This Schedule is attached to and forms part of the Assignment of Agreement of Purchase and Sale between:

ASSIGNEE,.., and

ASSIGNOR,..

for the purchase and sale of ....

.... dated the .... day of ...., 20............. .

BALANCE OF PAYMENT UNDER THIS ASSIGNMENT AGREEMENT: The Assignee will deliver the balance of payment for this Assignment Agreement as more particularly set out in Item 6. on Schedule B, subject to adjustments, with funds drawn on a lawyer's trust account in the form of a bank draft, certified cheque or wire transfer using the Large Value Transfer System, to the Assignor prior to completing the transaction in the Agreement of Purchase and Sale attached hereto as Schedule "C" to be held in trust without interest pending completion or other termination of the Agreement of Purchase and Sale attached hereto as Schedule "C".

This form must be initialed by all parties to the Assignment of Agreement of Purchase and Sale.

INITIALS OF ASSIGNEE(S):   INITIALS OF ASSIGNOR(S):

Form 145   Revised 2015   **Page 5 of 6**

APPENDIX

OREA Ontario Real Estate Association

Form 145
for use in the Province of Ontario

Schedule B
Assignment of Agreement of Purchase and Sale

This Schedule is attached to and forms part of the Assignment of Agreement of Purchase and Sale between:

ASSIGNEE,..., and

ASSIGNOR,...

for the purchase and sale of ....

.... dated the .... day of ...., 20.............

The Assignee and Assignor agree that the calculation of funds to be paid for this Assignment Agreement, subject to adjustments, is as set out in the following Items:

1.   Total Purchase Price including the original Agreement of Purchase and Sale
and this Assignment Agreement: $ _____

2.   Purchase Price of original Agreement of Purchase and Sale as indicated
in Schedule C: $ _____

3.   Deposit(s) paid by Assignor to the seller under the original Agreement of Purchase
and Sale as indicated in Schedule C, to be paid by the Assignee to the Assignor
as follows: $ _____

....

(Upon acceptance of this Assignment Agreement and receipt of consent to assign from original seller, if applicable)

(Upon final closing of original Agreement of Purchase and Sale and this Assignment Agreement)

4.   Payment by Assignee to Assignor for this Assignment Agreement: $ _____

5.   Deposit paid under this Assignment Agreement (in accordance with Page 1 of this
Assignment Agreement): $ _____

6.   Balance of the payment for this Assignment Agreement: $ _____

INITIALS OF ASSIGNEE(S): ⬭   **INITIALS OF ASSIGNOR(S):** ⬭

Form 220   *Seller Property Information Statement—Residential*   Page 1 of 3

OREA Ontario Real Estate Association   **Seller Property Information Statement**
Form 220   **Residential**
for use in the Province of Ontario

ANSWERS MUST BE COMPLETE AND ACCURATE This statement is designed in part to protect Sellers by establishing that correct information concerning the property is being provided to buyers. All of the information contained herein is provided by the Sellers to the brokerage/broker/salesperson. Any person who is in receipt of and utilizes this Statement acknowledges and agrees that **the information is being provided for information purposes only and is not a warranty as to the matters recited hereinafter even if attached to an Agreement of Purchase and Sale.** The brokerage/broker/salesperson shall not be held responsible for the accuracy of any information contained herein.

BUYERS MUST STILL MAKE THEIR OWN ENQUIRIES Buyers must still make their own enquiries notwithstanding the information contained on this statement. Each question and answer must be considered and where necessary, keeping in mind that the Sellers' knowledge of the property may be inaccurate or incomplete, additional information can be requested from the Sellers or from an independent source such as the municipality. Buyers can hire an independent inspector to examine the property to determine whether defects exist and to provide an estimate of the cost of repairing problems that have been identified. **This statement does not provide information on psychological stigmas that may be associated with a property.**

For the purposes of this Seller Property Information Statement, a "Seller" includes a landlord or a prospective landlord and a "buyer" includes a tenant, or a prospective tenant.

PROPERTY:	SELLER(S) TO **INITIAL** EACH APPLICABLE BOX		
SELLER(S):			

GENERAL: (Provide Applicable ADDITIONAL COMMENTS)	YES	NO	UNKNOWN	NOT APPLICABLE
1. I have occupied the property from.................................to.................................				
2. Does any other party have an ownership or spousal interest in the property?				
3. Is the property a condominium or a freehold property that includes an interest in a common elements condominium, (POTL)? (If yes, Schedule 221 to be completed.)				
4. Does ownership of this property require membership in an Association and payment of Association fees? If yes, specify..				
5. Is the property subject to first right of refusal, option, lease, rental agreement or other listing?				
6. Are there any encroachments, registered easements, or rights-of-way?				
7. Is there a plan of survey? Date of survey...				
8. Are there any disputes concerning the boundaries of the property?				
9. Are you aware of any non-compliance with zoning regulations?				
10. Are you aware of any pending developments, projects or rezoning applications in the neighbourhood?				
11. Are there any public projects planned for the neighbourhood? eg: road widenings, new highways, expropriations etc.				
12. Are there any restrictive covenants that run with the land?				
13. Are there any drainage restrictions?				
14. Are there any local levies or unusual taxes being charged at the present time or contemplated? If so, at what cost? .... Expiry date..				
15. Have you received any notice, claim, work order or deficiency notice affecting the property from any person or any public body?				
16. (a) Is the property connected to municipal water? (If not, Schedule 222 to be completed.)				
(b) Is the property connected to municipal sewer? (If not, Schedule 222 to be completed.)				
17. Are there any current or pending Heritage restrictions for the property or the area?				

INITIALS OF BUYER(S): ⬭

Form 220   Revised 2016   **Page 1 of 3**

Form 220   *(continued)*   Page 2 of 3

GENERAL (cont'd): (Provide Applicable ADDITIONAL COMMENTS)	YES	NO	UNKNOWN	NOT APPLICABLE
18. Are there any conditional sales contracts, leases, rental agreements or service contracts? eg: furnace, alarm system, hot water tank, propane tank, etc. Specify.. Are they assignable or will they be discharged?.................................				
19. Are there any defects in any appliances or equipment included with the property?				
20. Do you know the approximate age of the building(s)?Age.. Any additions: Age...........................				
21. Are you aware of any past or pending claims under the Tarion Warranty Corporation (formerly ONHWP)? Tarion Warranty Corporation/ONHWP Registration No...........................				
22. Will the sale of this property be subject to HST?				

ADDITIONAL COMMENTS:..

....

....

....

....

ENVIRONMENTAL: (Provide Applicable ADDITIONAL COMMENTS)	YES	NO	UNKNOWN	NOT APPLICABLE
1. Are you aware of possible environmental problems or soil contamination of any kind on the property or in the immediate area? eg: radon gas, toxic waste, underground gasoline or fuel tanks etc.				
2. Are there any existing or proposed waste dumps, disposal sites or land fills in the immediate area?				
3. Are there any hydro generating projects planned for the immediate area? eg: Wind Turbines				
4. Is the property subject to flooding?				
5. Is the property under the jurisdiction of any Conservation Authority or Commission?				
6. Are you aware of any excessive erosion, settling, slippage, sliding or other soil problems?				
7. Does the property have any abandoned or de-commissioned ☐ well ☐ septic system ☐ swimming pool ☐ foundation ☐ other, specify...				
8. **(a)** Is there a fuel oil tank on the property? If yes, complete the following: ☐ Underground. Date for required upgrading or removal.. ☐ Aboveground. Age of tank........................... Date of last inspection...........................				
(b) Does the fuel oil tank comply with the Technical Standards and Safety Authority requirements and any other requirements for fuel to be delivered?				
9. Has the use of the property ever been for the growth or manufacture of illegal substances?				

ADDITIONAL COMMENTS:..

....

....

....

....

INITIALS OF BUYER(S): ⬭

Form 220   Revised 2016   **Page 2 of 3**

APPENDIX

IMPROVEMENTS AND STRUCTURAL: (Provide Applicable ADDITIONAL COMMENTS)	YES	NO	UNKNOWN	NOT APPLICABLE
1. Are you aware of any structural problems?				
2. (a) Have you made any renovations, additions or improvements to the property?				
(b) Was a building permit obtained?				
(c) Has the final building inspection been approved or has a final occupancy permit been obtained?				
3. To the best of your knowledge have the building(s) ever contained ureaformaldehyde insulation?				
4. Is there vermiculite insulation on the property? If yes, has it been tested for asbestos?..				
5. (a) Are you aware of any deficiencies or non-compliance with the Ontario Fire Code?				
(b) Is your property equipped with operational smoke detectors?				
(c) Is the property equipped with operational carbon monoxide detectors?				
6. (a) Is the woodstove(s)/chimney(s)/fireplace(s)/insert(s) in good working order?				
(b) Has the wood energy system been **WETT** inspected? (Wood Energy Technology Transfer)				
7. Are you aware of any problems with the central air conditioning system?				
8. Are you aware of any problems with the heating system?				
9. (a) Are you aware of any moisture and/or water problems?				
(b) Are you aware of any roof leakage or unrepaired damage? Age of roof covering				
(c) Are you aware of any damage due to wind, fire, flood, insects, termites, rodents, pets or wood rot?				
(d) Have any repairs been carried out to correct any past or present problems related to (a), (b) and/or (c)? If yes, explain in additional comments below.				
10. (a) Are you aware of any problems with the electrical system? Size of service...................................				
(b) Type of wiring: ☐ copper ☐ aluminium ☐ knob-and-tube ☐ other...................................				
11. Are you aware of any problems with the plumbing system?				
12. Is there any lead, galvanized metal, cast iron or Kitec plumbing on the property?				
13. Are you aware of any problems with the swimming pool, sauna, hot tub, jet bathtub or lawn sprinkler system?				

ADDITIONAL COMMENTS: ....

....

....

....

Schedule(s) attached hereto and forming part of this Statement include:...

The Sellers state that the above information is true, based on their current actual knowledge as of the date below. Any important changes to this information known to the Sellers will be disclosed by the Sellers prior to closing. Sellers are responsible for the accuracy of all answers. Sellers further agree to indemnify and hold the Brokerage/Broker/Salesperson harmless from any liability incurred as a result of any buyer relying on this information. The Sellers hereby authorize the Brokerage to post a copy of this Seller Property Information Statement into the database(s) of the appropriate MLS® system and that a copy of this Seller Property Information Statement be delivered by their agent or representative to prospective buyers or their agents or representatives. The Sellers hereby acknowledge receipt of a true copy of this statement.

.... DATE................................   .... DATE....................................
(Signature of Seller)   (Signature of Seller)

I acknowledge that the information provided herein is not warranted and hereby acknowledge receipt of a copy of the above information including any applicable Schedule(s).

....   DATE...
(Signature of Buyer or Authorized Representative)

....   DATE...
(Signature of Buyer)

Form 220   Revised 2016   **Page 3 of 3**

APPENDIX

Seller Property Information Statement
Schedule for Condominium

Form 221
for use in the Province of Ontario

This Schedule is attached to and forms part of the Seller Property Information Statement (Form 220) for:

PROPERTY:		**SELLER(S) TO INITIAL** **EACH APPLICABLE BOX**			
SELLER(S):					

CONDOMINIUM CORPORATION: (Provide Applicable ADDITIONAL COMMENTS)	YES	NO	UNKNOWN	NOT APPLICABLE
1. **(a)** Condominium fee $..				
(b) Condominium fee includes:				
(c) Cost for amenities not included in Condominium fee $........................				
Details				
2. Are there any special assessments approved or contemplated?				
3. Have you received any written notice of lawsuit(s) pending?				
4. Have you been informed of any notices, claims, work orders or deficiency notices affecting the common elements received from any person or any public body?				
5. **(a)** Has a reserve fund study been completed? Date of Study.................				
(b) Approximate amount of reserve fund as of last notification $...............				
6. **(a)** Are there any restrictions on pets?				
(b) Are there any restrictions on renting the property?				
(c) Are there any other restrictions on the use of the property?				
7. **(a)** If any renovations, additions or improvements were made to the unit and/or common elements, was approval of the Condominium Corporation obtained?				
(b) Is approval of any prospective buyer required by the Condominium Corporation?				
(c) Are any other approvals required by the Condominium Corporation or Property Manager? If yes, specify:				
(d) Name of Property Management Company				
8. Are there any pending rule or by-law amendments which may alter or restrict the uses of the property?				
9. Is the Condominium registered?				
10. Parking: Number of Spaces .... ☐ Owned ☐ Exclusive Use ☐ Leased or Licensed Parking space number(s)...				
11. Locker:.. ☐ Owned ☐ Exclusive Use Locker number(s)...				
12. **(a)** Amenities: ☐ Pool ☐ Sauna ☐ Exercise ☐ Room ☐ Meeting/Party Room ☐ Boat Docking ☐ Guest Parking ☐ Other......................................				
(b) Are you aware of any problems with any of the common element amenities? If yes, specify:				

ADDITIONAL COMMENTS:...
....
....

INITIALS OF BUYER(S): ⬭

Form 221   Revised 2014   **Page 1 of 1**

APPENDIX

OREA Ontario Real Estate Association   **Certificate of Power of Sale**

Form 262
for use in the Province of Ontario

I, ...,

do hereby warrant that by reason of default under a .... charge/mortgage
                                                          (first, second, third, etc.)

which I hold on ....
                                              (description of property)

....

dated the .... day of ...., 20.............. and registered

as number ....

I now have the power and authority under the provisions of my mortgage and the Mortgages Act of Ontario to list for sale the property known municipally

as: ....
                                            (address of property)

....

SIGNED, SEALED AND DELIVERED in the presence of: IN WITNESS whereof I have hereunto set my hand and seal:

....   ● DATE ....
(Witness)   (Mortgagee or Authorized Representative)   (Seal)

                                                 Form 262   Revised 2011   **Page 1 of 1**

OREA Ontario Real Estate Association

Residential Information Checklist

Form 820
for use in the province of Ontario

PROPERTY:				
DATE:				

GENERAL: (Provide Applicable ADDITIONAL COMMENTS)	YES	NO	UNKNOWN	NOT APPLICABLE
1. I have occupied the property from.....................to......................				
2. Does any other party have an ownership or spousal interest in the property?				
3. Is the property a condominium or a freehold property that includes an interest in a common elements condominium, (POTL)? (If yes, Schedule 821 to be completed.)				
4. Does ownership of this property require membership in an Association and payment of Association fees? If yes, specify..				
5. Is the property subject to first right of refusal, option, lease, rental agreement or other listing?				
6. Are there any encroachments, registered easements, or rights-of-way?				
7. Is there a plan of survey? Date of survey..............................				
8. Are there any disputes concerning the boundaries of the property?				
9. Are you aware of any non-compliance with zoning regulations?				
10. Are you aware of any pending developments, projects or rezoning applications in the neighbourhood?				
11. Are there any public projects planned for the neighbourhood? eg: road widenings, new highways, expropriations etc.				
12. Are there any restrictive covenants that run with the land?				
13. Are there any drainage restrictions?				
14. Are there any local levies or unusual taxes being charged at the present time or contemplated? If so, at what cost? .... Expiry date........................				
15. Have you received any notice, claim, work order or deficiency notice affecting the property from any person or any public body?				

GENERAL (CONT'D): (Provide Applicable ADDITIONAL COMMENTS)	YES	NO	UNKNOWN	NOT APPLICABLE
16. **a)** Is the property connected to municipal water? (If not, Schedule 822 to be completed.)				
b) Is the property connected to municipal sewer? (If not, Schedule 822 to be completed.)				
17. Are there any current or pending Heritage restrictions for the property or the area?				
18. Are there any conditional sales contracts, leases, rental agreements or service contracts? eg: furnace, alarm system, hot water tank, propane tank, etc. Specify... Are they assignable or will they be discharged?..				
19. Are there any defects in any appliances or equipment included with the property?				
20. Do you know the approximate age of the building(s)? Age............................... Any additions: Age...				
21. Are you aware of any past or pending claims under the Tarion Warranty Corporation (formerly ONHWP)? Tarion Warranty Corporation/ONHWP Registration No..................................				
22. Will the sale of this property be subject to HST?				

ADDITIONAL COMMENTS: ....

....

....

....

....

....

ENVIRONMENTAL: (Provide Applicable ADDITIONAL COMMENTS)	YES	NO	UNKNOWN	NOT APPLICABLE
1. Are you aware of possible environmental problems or soil contamination of any kind on the property or in the immediate area? eg: radon gas, toxic waste, underground gasoline or fuel tanks etc.				
2. Are there any existing or proposed waste dumps, disposal sites or land fills in the immediate area??				
3. Are there any hydro generating projects planned for the immediate area? eg: Wind Turbines				

APPENDIX

ENVIRONMENTAL (CONT'D): (Provide Applicable ADDITIONAL COMMENTS)	YES	NO	UNKNOWN	NOT APPLICABLE
4. Is the property subject to flooding?				
5. Is the property under the jurisdiction of any Conservation Authority or Commission?				
6. Are you aware of any excessive erosion, settling, slippage, sliding or other soil problems?				
7. Does the property have any abandoned or de-commissioned ☐ well ☐ septic system ☐ swimming pool ☐ foundation ☐ other, specify...				
8. **a)** Is there a fuel oil tank on the property? If yes, complete the following: ☐ Underground. Date for required upgrading or removal.. . ☐ Aboveground. Age of tank.......................... Date of last inspection..........................				
b) Does the fuel oil tank comply with the Technical Standards and Safety Authority requirements and any other requirements for fuel to be delivered?				
9. Has the use of the property ever been for the growth or manufacture of illegal substances?				

ADDITIONAL COMMENTS: ....

....

....

....

....

....

IMPROVEMENTS AND STRUCTURAL: (Provide Applicable ADDITIONAL COMMENTS)	YES	NO	UNKNOWN	NOT APPLICABLE
1. Are you aware of any structural problems?				
2. **a)** Have you made any renovations, additions or improvements to the property?				
b) Was a building permit obtained?				
c) Has the final building inspection been approved or has a final occupancy permit been obtained?				
3. To the best of your knowledge have the building(s) ever contained ureaformaldehyde insulation?				
4. Is there vermiculite insulation on the property? If yes, has it been tested for asbestos?..				

IMPROVEMENTS AND STRUCTURAL (CONT'D): (Provide Applicable ADDITIONAL COMMENTS)	YES	NO	UNKNOWN	NOT APPLICABLE
5. **a)** Are you aware of any deficiencies or non-compliance with the Ontario Fire Code?				
b) Is your property equipped with operational smoke detectors?				
c) Is the property equipped with operational carbon monoxide detectors?				
6. **a)** Is the woodstove(s)/chimney(s)/fireplace(s)/insert(s) in good working order?				
b) Has the wood energy system been **WETT** inspected? (Wood Energy Technology Transfer)				
7. Are you aware of any problems with the central air conditioning system?				
8. Are you aware of any problems with the heating system?				
9. **a)** Are you aware of any moisture and/or water problems?				
b) Are you aware of any roof leakage or unrepaired damage? Age of roof covering				
c) Are you aware of any damage due to wind, fire, flood, insects, termites, rodents, pets or wood rot?				
d) Have any repairs been carried out to correct any past or present problems related to (a), (b) and/or (c)? If yes, explain in additional comments below..				
10. **a)** Are you aware of any problems with the electrical system? Size of service....................................				
b) Type of wiring: ☐ copper ☐ aluminium ☐ knob-and-tube ☐ other...				
11. Are you aware of any problems with the plumbing system?				
12. Is there any lead, galvanized metal, cast iron or Kitec plumbing on the property?				
13. Are you aware of any problems with the swimming pool, sauna, hot tub, jet bathtub or lawn sprinkler system?				

ADDITIONAL COMMENTS: ....

....

....

....

....

....

Schedule(s) attached hereto and forming part of this Statement include: ....

Form 820   Revised 2016   **Page 4 of 4**

 **Ontario Real Estate Association**

Residential Information Checklist
Condominium

Form 821
for use in the Province of Ontario

Schedule is attached to and forms part of the Residential Information Checklist (Form #820) for:

PROPERTY:

DATE:

CONDOMINIUM CORPORATION: (Provide Applicable ADDITIONAL COMMENTS)	YES	NO	UNKNOWN	NOT APPLICABLE
1. **a)** Condominium fee $..				
b) Condominium fee includes:				
c) Cost for amenities not included in Condominium fee $				
Details				
2. Are there any special assessments approved or contemplated?				
3. Have you received any written notice of lawsuit(s) pending?				
4. Have you been informed of any notices, claims, work orders or deficiency notices affecting the common elements received from any person or any public body?				
5. **a)** Has a reserve fund study been completed? Date of Study				
b) Approximate amount of reserve fund as of last notification $...........				
6. **a)** Are there any restrictions on pets?				
b) Are there any restrictions on renting the property?				
c) Are there any other restrictions on the use of the property?				
7. **a)** If any renovations, additions or improvements were made to the unit and/or common elements, was approval of the Condominium Corporation obtained?				
b) Is approval of any prospective buyer required by the Condominium Corporation?				
c) Are any other approvals required by the Condominium Corporation or Property Manager? If yes, specify:				
d) Name of Property Management Company				
8. Are there any pending rule or by-law amendments which may alter or restrict the uses of the property?				
9. Is the Condominium registered?				
10. Parking: Number of Spaces .... ☐ Owned ☐ Exclusive Use ☐ Leased or Licensed Parking space number(s)...				
11. Locker:.. ☐ Owned ☐ Exclusive Use Locker number(s)				
12. **a)** Amenities: ☐ Pool ☐ Sauna ☐ Exercise Room ☐ Meeting/Party Room ☐ Boat Docking ☐ Guest Parking ☐ Other..................................				
b) Are you aware of any problems with any of the common element amenities? If yes, specify:				

ADDITIONAL COMMENTS: ....
....
....
....

APPENDIX

Form 822   *Residential Information Checklist—Water Supply, Waste Disposal, Access, Shoreline, Utilities*   Page 1 of 1

Residential Information Checklist
Water Supply, Waste Disposal,
Access, Shoreline, Utilities

Form 822
for use in the Province of Ontario

This Schedule is attached to and forms part of the Residential Information Checklist (Form #820) for:

PROPERTY:
DATE:

WATER SUPPLY AND WASTE DISPOSAL: (Provide Applicable ADDITIONAL COMMENTS)	YES	NO	UNKNOWN	NOT APPLICABLE
1. **a)** What is your water source? ☐ Municipal ☐ Drilled ☐ Bored ☐ Dug ☐ Cistern ☐ Lake ☐ Community ☐ Shared ☐ Other				
b) If your water source is Community/Shared, is there a transferrable written agreement?				
c) Are you aware of any problem re: quantity of water? (If yes, explain below)				
d) Are you aware of any problems re: quality of water? (If yes, explain below)				
e) Do you have any water treatment devices?				
f) Is your water system operable year round? Heated lines? ☐ Yes ☐ No				
g) Date and result of most recent water test..				
h) Are any documents available for the well? If yes, specify				
i) Does the property have any abandoned well(s)?				
2. **a)** What kind of sewage disposal system services the property? ☐ Municipal ☐ Septic tank with tile bed ☐ Holding tank ☐ Other (Explain below)				
b) Are you aware of any problems with the sewage system? Date septic/holding tank last pumped.................................. Age of system				
c) What documentation for the sewage system is available? ☐ Use Permit ☐ Location Sketch ☐ Maintenance Records ☐ Inspection Certificate ☐ Other				
3. Are all the well(s), water line(s) and waste disposal system(s) within the boundaries of the subject property?				

ACCESS, SHORELINE, UTILITIES: (Provide Applicable ADDITIONAL COMMENTS)	YES	NO	UNKNOWN	NOT APPLICABLE
1. **a)** Is property access by municipal road? If yes; ☐ Open all year ☐ Seasonally open				
b) Is the property serviced by a private road? Cost $.......................... per year.				
2. If your access is across private property, access is: ☐ Right of way ☐ Deeded ☐ Other .... Cost $.......................... per year.				
3. **a)** If water access only, access is: ☐ Deeded ☐ Leased ☐ Other (Explain below)				
b) Water access cost of: Parking $.......................... Dock $.......................... per year.				
4. **a)** Is the original Shore Road Allowance owned?				
b) Are there any pending applications for shoreline improvement?				
c) Are there any disputes concerning the shoreline or improvements on the shoreline?				
d) Are there any structures or docks on the original Shore Road Allowance?				
e) Is the original Road Allowance included in the lot size?				
5. Does the boundary of the property extend beyond the water line? If yes, explain below.				
6. **a)** Is hydro available to the property?				
b) Is the owner responsible for the installation, replacement/maintenance of any utility poles/equipment?				

ADDITIONAL COMMENTS: ....
....
....
....

Form 822   New 2015   **Page 1 of 1**

OREA Ontario Real Estate Association

Green Information Checklist
Residential

Form 824
for use in the Province of Ontario

PROPERTY:
DATE:

ENERGY RATING / CERTIFICATE
(Check all that apply, certificate required)

	Rate / Certificate	Date
☐ EnerGuide	....	.... / .... / ....
☐ R-2000	....	.... / .... / ....
☐ LEED (Certified, Silver, Gold, Platinum)	....	.... / .... / ....
☐ Energy Star	....	.... / .... / ....
☐ BOMA Go Green	....	.... / .... / ....
☐ Green Globes	....	.... / .... / ....
☐ Green Standard	....	.... / .... / ....
☐ Other:...	....	.... / .... / ....

APPLIANCES AND COMPONENTS INCLUDED
(The Energy/Guide Label does not indicate an Energy Star Rated Efficient Appliance)

☐ Energy Star-rated Dishwasher   ☐ Energy Star-rated Room Air Conditioner
☐ Energy Star-rated Refrigerator   ☐ Energy Star-rated Dehumidifier
☐ Energy Star-rated Microwave   ☐ Energy Star-rated Clothes Washer
☐ Energy Star-rated Stove/Oven   ☐ Energy Star-rated Clothes Dryer
☐ Energy Star-rated Freezer   ☐ Clothesline Internal/External (where permitted)

☐ Other: ....

ENERGY SOURCE

☐ Electric On-The-Grid   ☐ Solar Photovoltaic System
☐ Electric Partial-Grid   ☐ Wind Turbine
☐ Electric Off-The-Grid   ☐ FIT (Ontario Power Authority program)
        ☐ micro FIT (Ontario Power Authority program)

☐ Other: ....

LIGHTING

☐ Automatic control system for lighting   ☐ Solar powered walkway or outdoor lighting area
☐ Natural day lighting   ☐ Solar / Sun tubes(s)
☐ Skylights   ☐ Compact Fluorescent Lighting
        ☐ LED Lighting

☐ Other: ....

VENTILATION (specify quantity where appropriate)

☐ Ventilation System
☐ Whole House Fan
☐ Heat Recovery Ventilator

___ No. of Ceiling Fan(s)
☐ HEPA Air Filtration Unit
☐ Natural Ventilation System
☐ Solar Attic Fan

☐ Other: ....

SPACE COOLING & HEATING

☐ Geothermal Heat Pump
☐ Heat Pump, Energy Star Rated
☐ Passive cooling & heating
☐ Cooling - Evaporative cooling (swamp cooler)
☐ Cooling - High SEER air conditioner (13 or higher)
☐ Overhangs above south-facing windows
☐ Heating - 90% or higher energy efficiency furnace

☐ Heating - 90% or higher energy efficiency boiler
☐ Heating - Active solar heating
☐ Heating - Baseboard hot water heat
☐ Heating - Radiant floor heating
☐ Heating - Solar water heating
☐ HVAC zones
☐ Programmable Thermostats
☐ Heat Recovery Ventilator

☐ Other: ....

WATER CONSERVATION (specify quantity where appropriate)

☐ On Demand Hot Water Heater
☐ Hot Water Heat Recovery
___ No. of Low Flush Toilet(s)
___ No. of Dual Flush Toilet(s)
☐ Waterless Urinals
___ No. of Low Flow Faucets

___ No. of Infrared No-Touch Faucets
___ No. of Low Flow Shower Heads
☐ Solar Heated Hot Water
☐ Grey Water Recovery System
☐ Rainwater Collection and Purification System
☐ Hot Water Recirculation Pump
☐ Solar Pool Heating Collectors

☐ Other: ....

INSULATION

Basement

☐ R-Value:____ (Minimum R13) (Higher Number = Better Insulation Value)

    ☐ Cellulose - Post Consumer Recycled Content
    ☐ Formaldehyde-Free Insulation
    ☐ Natural Fibre
    ☐ Structural Insulated Panels

Ceiling and Attic

☐ R-Value:____ (Minimum R38) (Higher Number = Better Insulation Value)

    ☐ Cellulose - Post Consumer Recycled Content
    ☐ Formaldehyde-Free Insulation
    ☐ Natural Fibre
    ☐ Soy Based Spray Foam
    ☐ Spray Foam
    ☐ Hatch To Attic Space (weather stripped and insulated)

Floors

☐ R-Value:____(Higher Number = Better Insulation Value)

    ☐ Cellulose - Post Consumer Recycled Content
    ☐ Foam Board
    ☐ Sub-Floor Modular Insulated Panel
    ☐ Cork Board
    ☐ Rigid Board Insulation

APPENDIX

Walls

☐ R-Value:____ (Minimum R11) (Higher Number = Better Insulation Value)
    ☐ Cellulose - Post Consumer Recycled Content
    ☐ Formaldehyde-Free Insulation
    ☐ Natural Fibre
    ☐ Cork Board
    ☐ Rigid Board Insulation
    ☐ Soy Based Spray Foam
    ☐ Spray Foam
    ☐ Structural Insulated Panels (SIPs)
    ☐ Thermal Mass Construction

☐ Other : ....

ROOF

☐ Reflective Roof Coating
☐ Green Roof - Vegetation/Garden
☐ Living Roof
☐ Metal Roofing - Recycled Content

☐ Reflective Roofing - Energy Star
☐ Radiant Roof Barriers
☐ EPDM   ☐ TPO
☐ Insulated Protective Membrane
☐ Solar Shingles

☐ Other: ....

WINDOWS & DOORS

☐ Energy Star Windows, Climate Zone _B_
☐ Energy-efficient Window Coatings
☐ Window Frames Highest Insulation

☐ Energy Star Doors, Climate Zone _B_
☐ Low-E Window Coating
☐ Spectrally Selective Glass
☐ Space Filling Foam

☐ Other: ....

FINISHES

☐ Flooring Alternatives:
    ☐ Locally Sourced
    ☐ Bamboo Flooring
    ☐ Cork Flooring
☐ Recycled Content Countertops

☐ Salvaged Wood Flooring
☐ Green Carpet
☐ Marmoleum
☐ Refaced Cupboards
☐ Low VOC Paint (Green Seal Certified Product)
☐ Organic Based Clay (Used as an alternative to paint)

☐ Other: ....

BUILDING MATERIALS AND TECHNIQUES

☐ Advanced Framing Techniques
☐ Building Material Reuse/Exchange
☐ Cement Board Siding
☐ House/Building Wraps - Radiant System
☐ Natural Fibre Insulation
    (Recycled Blue Jean Material or Other Recycled Natural Content)
☐ Recycled Building Materials
☐ Recycled Content Dry Wall

☐ Sustainable Harvested Certified Wood
☐ High-Ash Content Concrete Flooring
☐ Insulating Concrete Forms
☐ Straw Bale Construction
☐ Earthen Built/Rammed Earth
☐ Straw Bale Construction
☐ Adobe
☐ Reclaimed Metal Construction

☐ Other: ....

RECYCLING

☐ Built In Recycling (storage)
☐ Built In Composting Centre (green storage)

☐ Outdoor Recycling Storage
☐ Composting Box

APPENDIX

Form 824   *(continued)*

LANDSCAPING

☐ Bioswale for storm water
☐ Composite & plastic decking material-recycled content
☐ Composite & plastic fencing material-recycled content
☐ Restore and enhance natural vegetation & native plants
☐ Integrated pest management (NON CHEMICAL)

☐ Mulch - locally produced "green waste"
☐ Natural water / drainage features
☐ Permeable Paving Stones
☐ Rain Garden Feature for Run Off
☐ Rainwater Barrel Collection

☐ Other: ....

SURROUNDING ENVIRONMENT & MISC.

☐ Cover for wildlife
☐ Curb side recycling
☐ Parks and public lands within 2 kilometres

☐ Deciduous Shade Trees
☐ Recycling facilities within 2 kilometres
☐ Public transportation designated stop within 500 metres

☐ Other: ....

ORIENTATION AND SITE PLACEMENT

☐ Earth bermed

☐ Passive solar design

☐ Other: ....

ADDITIONAL COMMENTS:

....

....

....

....

....

....

....

....

....

....

....

....

....

Schedule(s) attached hereto and forming part of this Statement include: ....

APPENDIX

OREA Ontario Real Estate Association

Agreement to Lease
Residential

Form 400
for use in the Province of Ontario

This Agreement to Lease dated this .... day of.., 20................

TENANT (Lessee), ...
(Full legal names of all Tenants)

LANDLORD (Lessor), ...
(Full legal name of Landlord)

ADDRESS OF LANDLORD ....
(Legal address for the purpose of receiving notices)

The Tenant hereby offers to lease from the Landlord the premises as described herein on the terms and subject to the conditions as set out in this Agreement.

1. **PREMISES:** Having inspected the premises and provided the present tenant vacates, I/we, the Tenant hereby offer to lease, premises known as:

    ....

2. **TERM OF LEASE:** The lease shall be for a term of .... commencing ....

3. **RENT:** The Tenant will pay to the said Landlord monthly and every month during the said term of the lease the sum of ....

    .... Canadian Dollars (CDN$...................................),
    payable in advance on the first day of each and every month during the currency of the said term. First and last months' rent to be paid in advance upon completion or date of occupancy, whichever comes first.

4. **DEPOSIT AND PREPAID RENT:** The Tenant delivers..
    (Herewith/Upon acceptance/as otherwise described in this Agreement)

    by negotiable cheque payable to.. "Deposit Holder"

    in the amount of..

    Canadian Dollars (CDN$.......................................) as a deposit to be held in trust as security for the faithful performance by the Tenant of all

    terms, covenants and conditions of the Agreement and to be applied by the Landlord against the .... and ....
    month's rent. If the Agreement is not accepted, the deposit is to be returned to the Tenant without interest or deduction.

    For the purposes of this Agreement, "Upon Acceptance" shall mean that the Tenant is required to deliver the deposit to the Deposit Holder within 24 hours of the acceptance of this Agreement. The parties to this Agreement hereby acknowledge that, unless otherwise provided for in this Agreement, the Deposit Holder shall place the deposit in trust in the Deposit Holder's non-interest bearing Real Estate Trust Account and no interest shall be earned, received or paid on the deposit.

5. **USE:** The Tenant and Landlord agree that unless otherwise agreed to herein, only the Tenant named above and any person named in a Rental Application completed prior to this Agreement will occupy the premises.

    Premises to be used only for:..

    ....

    ....

    ....

6. **SERVICES AND COSTS:** The cost of the following services applicable to the premises shall be paid as follows:

	LANDLORD	TENANT		LANDLORD	TENANT
Gas	☐	☐	Cable TV	☐	☐
Oil	☐	☐	Condominium/Cooperative fees	☐	☐
Electricity	☐	☐	Garbage Removal	☐	☐
Hot water heater rental	☐	☐	Other:	☐	☐
Water and Sewerage Charges	☐	☐	Other:	☐	☐

    The Landlord will pay the property taxes, but if the Tenant is assessed as a Separate School Supporter, Tenant will pay to the Landlord a sum sufficient to cover the excess of the Separate School Tax over the Public School Tax, if any, for a full calendar year, said sum to be estimated on the tax rate for the current year, and to be payable in equal monthly installments in addition to the above mentioned rental, provided however, that the full amount shall become due and be payable on demand on the Tenant.

INITIALS OF TENANT(S): ( )   INITIALS OF LANDLORD(S): ( )

APPENDIX

7. **PARKING:** ....
    ....
    ....

8. **ADDITIONAL TERMS:** ....
    ....
    ....
    ....

9. **SCHEDULES:** The schedules attached hereto shall form an integral part of this Agreement to Lease and consist of: **Schedule(s) A** ....
    ....

10. **IRREVOCABILITY:** This offer shall be irrevocable by .... until .... a.m./p.m. on the ....
    (Landlord/Tenant)

    day of..,20.....................after which time if not accepted, this Agreement shall be null and
    void and all monies paid thereon shall be returned to the Tenant without interest or deduction.

11. **NOTICES:** The Landlord hereby appoints the Listing Brokerage as agent for the Landlord for the purpose of giving and receiving notices pursuant to this Agreement. Where a Brokerage (Tenant's Brokerage) has entered into a representation agreement with the Tenant, the Tenant hereby appoints the Tenant's Brokerage as agent for the purpose of giving and receiving notices pursuant to this Agreement. **Where a Brokerage represents both the Landlord and the Tenant (multiple representation), the Brokerage shall not be appointed or authorized to be agent for either the Tenant or the Landlord for the purpose of giving and receiving notices.** Any notice relating hereto or provided for herein shall be in writing. In addition to any provision contained herein and in any Schedule hereto, this offer, any counter-offer, notice of acceptance thereof or any notice to be given or received pursuant to this Agreement or any Schedule hereto (any of them, "Document") shall be deemed given and received when delivered personally or hand delivered to the Address for Service provided in the Acknowledgement below, or where a facsimile number or email address is provided herein, when transmitted electronically to that facsimile number or email address, respectively, in which case, the signature(s) of the party (parties) shall be deemed to be original.

    FAX No.: .... FAX No.: ....
    (For delivery of Documents to Landlord)   (For delivery of Documents to Tenant)

    Email Address: .... Email Address: ....
    (For delivery of Documents to Landlord)   (For delivery of Documents to Tenant)

12. **EXECUTION OF LEASE:** Lease shall be drawn by the Landlord on the Landlord's standard form of lease, and shall include the provisions as contained herein and in any attached schedule, and shall be executed by both parties before possession of the premises is given. The Landlord shall provide the tenant with information relating to the rights and responsibilities of the Tenant and information on the role of the Landlord and Tenant Board and how to contact the Board. (Information For New Tenants as made available by the Landlord and Tenant Board and available at www.ltb.gov.on.ca)

13. **ACCESS:** The Landlord shall have the right, at reasonable times to enter and show the demised premises to prospective tenants, purchasers or others. The Landlord or anyone on the Landlord's behalf shall also have the right, at reasonable times, to enter and inspect the demised premises.

14. **INSURANCE:** The Tenant agrees to obtain and keep in full force and effect during the entire period of the tenancy and any renewal thereof, at the Tenant's sole cost and expense, fire and property damage and public liability insurance in an amount equal to that which a reasonably prudent Tenant would consider adequate. The Tenant agrees to provide the Landlord, upon demand at any time, proof that said insurance is in full force and effect and to notify the Landlord in writing in the event that such insurance is cancelled or otherwise terminated.

15. **RESIDENCY:** The Landlord shall forthwith notify the Tenant in writing in the event the Landlord is, at the time of entering into this Agreement, or, becomes during the term of the tenancy, a non-resident of Canada as defined under the Income Tax Act, RSC 1985, c.1 (ITA) as amended from time to time, and in such event the Landlord and Tenant agree to comply with the tax withholding provisions of the ITA.

16. **USE AND DISTRIBUTION OF PERSONAL INFORMATION:** The Tenant consents to the collection, use and disclosure of the Tenant's personal information by the Landlord and/or agent of the Landlord, from time to time, for the purpose of determining the creditworthiness of the Tenant for the leasing, selling or financing of the premises or the real property, or making such other use of the personal information as the Landlord and/or agent of the Landlord deems appropriate.

17. **CONFLICT OR DISCREPANCY:** If there is any conflict or discrepancy between any provision added to this Agreement (including any Schedule attached hereto) and any provision in the standard pre-set portion hereof, the added provision shall supersede the standard pre-set provision to the extent of such conflict or discrepancy. This Agreement, including any Schedule attached hereto, shall constitute the entire Agreement between Landlord and Tenant. There is no representation, warranty, collateral agreement or condition, which affects this Agreement other than as expressed herein. This Agreement shall be read with all changes of gender or number required by the context.

18. **CONSUMER REPORTS: The Tenant is hereby notified that a consumer report containing credit and/or personal information may be referred to in connection with this transaction.**

INITIALS OF TENANT(S): ( )   INITIALS OF LANDLORD(S): ( )

APPENDIX

Form 400   *(continued)*

19. BINDING AGREEMENT: This Agreement and acceptance thereof shall constitute a binding agreement by the parties to enter into the Lease of the Premises and to abide by the terms and conditions herein contained.

SIGNED, SEALED AND DELIVERED in the presence of: IN WITNESS whereof I have hereunto set my hand and seal:

....   ● DATE ....
(Witness)   (Tenant or Authorized Representative)   (Seal)

....   ● DATE ....
(Witness)   (Tenant or Authorized Representative)   (Seal)

....   ● DATE ....
(Witness)   (Guarantor)   (Seal)

We/I the Landlord hereby accept the above offer, and agree that the commission together with applicable HST (and any other tax as may hereafter be applicable) may be deducted from the deposit and further agree to pay any remaining balance of commission forthwith.

SIGNED, SEALED AND DELIVERED in the presence of: IN WITNESS whereof I have hereunto set my hand and seal:

....   ● DATE ....
(Witness)   (Landlord or Authorized Representative)   (Seal)

....   ● DATE ....
(Witness)   (Landlord or Authorized Representative)   (Seal)

CONFIRMATION OF ACCEPTANCE: Notwithstanding anything contained herein to the contrary, I confirm this Agreement with all changes both typed and written was

finally acceptance by all parties at .... a.m./p.m. this .... day of ...., 20.......... ....
(Signature of Landlord or Tenant)

INFORMATION ON BROKERAGE(S)

Listing Brokerage .... Tel.No.(...............)...............................

....
(Salesperson / Broker Name)

Co-op/Buyer Brokerage .... Tel.No.(...............)...............................

....
(Salesperson / Broker Name)

ACKNOWLEDGEMENT

I acknowledge receipt of my signed copy of this accepted Agreement of Lease and I authorize the Brokerage to forward a copy to my lawyer.	I acknowledge receipt of my signed copy of this accepted Agreement of Lease and I authorize the Brokerage to forward a copy to my lawyer.
.... DATE .... (Landlord)	.... DATE .... (Tenant)
.... DATE .... (Landlord) Address for Service	.... DATE .... (Tenant) Address for Service ....
.... Tel.No.(...........).....................	.... Tel.No.(...........).....................
Landlord's Lawyer	Tenant's Lawyer ....
Address	Address ....
Email	Email ....
(...........)..................... (...........)..................... Tel.No. FAX No.	(...........)..................... (...........)..................... Tel.No. FAX No.

FOR OFFICE USE ONLY   **COMMISSION TRUST AGREEMENT**

To: Co-operating Brokerage shown on the foregoing Agreement to Lease:
In consideration for the Co-operating Brokerage procuring the foregoing Agreement to Lease, I hereby declare that all moneys received or receivable by me in connection with the Transaction as contemplated in the MLS Rules and Regulations of my Real Estate Board shall be receivable and held in trust. This agreement shall constitute a Commission Trust Agreement as defined in the MLS Rules and shall be subject to and governed by the MLS Rules pertaining to Commission Trust.

DATED as of the date and time of the acceptance of the foregoing Agreement to Lease.   Acknowledged by:

....
(Authorized to bind the Listing Brokerage)   (Authorized to bind the Co-operating Brokerage)

Form 400   Revised 2015   **Page 3 of 4**

Form 400   *(continued)*

OREA Ontario Real Estate Association

Form 400
for use in the Province of Ontario

Schedule A
Agreement to Lease - Residential

This Schedule is attached to and forms part of the Agreement to Lease between:

TENANT (Lessee), ..., and

LANDLORD (Lessor), ...

for the lease of ....

.... dated the .... day of ...., 20..............

This form must be initialled by all parties to the Agreement to Lease.

INITIALS OF TENANT(S):   INITIALS OF LANDLORD(S):

Form 400   Revised 2015   **Page 4 of 4**

APPENDIX

Rental Application
Residential

Form 410
for use in the Province of Ontario

I/We hereby make application to rent ....

from the .... day of .... 20........... at a monthly rental of $...

to become due and payable in advance on the .... day of each and every month during my tenancy.

1. Name .... Date of birth .... SIN No. (Optional) ....

     Drivers License No .... Occupation ....

2. Name .... Date of birth .... SIN No. (Optional).............................

     Drivers License No .... Occupation ....

3. Other Occupants: Name .... Relationship .... Age ....

                     Name .... Relationship .... Age ....

                     Name .... Relationship .... Age ....

     Do you have any pets? .... If so, describe ....

     Why are you vacating your present place of residence? ....

LAST TWO PLACES OF RESIDENCE

Address ....   Address ....

....

From .... To ....   From .... To ....

Name of Landlord ....   Name of Landlord ....

Telephone: (.............).......................................   Telephone: (.............).......................................

PRESENT EMPLOYMENT   **PRIOR EMPLOYMENT**

Employer ....   I...

Business address ....   I...

Business telephone ....   I...

Position held ....   I...

Length of employment ....   I...

Name of supervisor ....   I...

Current salary range: Monthly $ ....

                                                       Form 410   Revised 2009   **Page 1 of 2**

APPENDIX

SPOUSE'S PRESENT EMPLOYMENT   **PRIOR EMPLOYMENT**

Employer ....   I...

Business address ....   I...

Business telephone ....   I...

Position held ....   I...

Length of employment ....   I...

Name of supervisor ....   I...

Current salary range: Monthly $ ....

Name of Bank .... Branch .... Address ....

Chequing Account # ....   Savings Account # ....

FINANCIAL OBLIGATIONS

Payments to .... Amount: $ ....

Payments to .... Amount: $ ....

PERSONAL REFERENCES

Name .... Address ....

Telephone: (..........)................ Length of Acquaintance .... Occupation ....

Name .... Address ....

Telephone: (..........)................ Length of Acquaintance................ Occupation ....

AUTOMOBILE(S)

Make .... Model .... Year .... Licence No ....

Make .... Model .... Year .... Licence No ....

The Applicant consents to the collection, use and disclosure of the Applicant's personal information by the Landlord and/or agent of the Landlord, from time to time, for the purpose of determining the creditworthiness of the Applicant for the leasing, selling or financing of the premises or the real property, or making such other use of the personal information as the Landlord and/or agent of the Landlord deems appropriate.

The Applicant represents that all statements made above are true and correct. **The Applicant is hereby notified that a consumer report containing credit and/or personal information may be referred to in connection with this rental.** The Applicant authorizes the verification of the information contained in this application and information obtained from personal references. This application is not a Rental or Lease Agreement. In the event that this application is not accepted, any deposit submitted by the Applicant shall be returned.

....
Signature of Applicant   Date   Signature of Applicant   Date

Telephone: (..........).................................   Telephone: (..........).................................

APPENDIX

 **Ontario Real Estate Association**

Form 600
for use in the Province of Ontario

Brokerage/Salesperson Employment
Agreement

This Employment Agreement made this .... day of.. , 20..........................
BETWEEN:
BROKERAGE: ....
AND:
SALESPERSON: ....

For the purposes of this Agreement, Salesperson includes a Broker registered under the Real Estate and Business Brokers Act, 2002.

WHEREAS the Brokerage is registered as a Brokerage and the Salesperson is registered pursuant to the Real Estate and Business Brokers Act, 2002, ("the Act");
AND WHEREAS the Brokerage wishes to employ the Salesperson on the terms and conditions contained in this Agreement;
NOW THEREFORE the Brokerage and the Salesperson agree to the employment of the Salesperson by the Brokerage in consideration of the following mutual terms, conditions and covenants of this Agreement:

1. The Brokerage:
    a) Shall supply the Salesperson with office and secretarial facilities in accordance with the Brokerage's office policies and practices in that regard;
    b) Shall advise, counsel, instruct, and assist the Salesperson in the performance of the Salesperson's duties;
    c) Shall loan, by way of advances on account of anticipated commissions, such periodic amounts as may be established from time to time by the Brokerage, it being understood and agreed that such amount(s) so advanced shall constitute a debt due and owing to the Brokerage without notice or demand;
    d) Hereby declares that any monies received or receivable on account of commission by the Brokerage from any trade in real estate conducted on behalf of the Brokerage by the Salesperson, shall be held by the Brokerage in trust and the Brokerage shall disburse in a timely fashion, directly from the Brokerage's Commission Trust Account (subject to any direction pursuant to paragraph 3(a) hereof) to the Salesperson, commission due to the Salesperson in connection with the trade, as determined in accordance with Schedule "A" hereto; (Brokerage to attach commission schedule.)
    e) Shall receive any monies on behalf of or from the Salesperson, for real estate Board and association fees, dues or assessments or for personal tax remittance, in trust and remit said monies on the Salesperson's behalf in a timely fashion by issuing a trust cheque to the Board or association or Revenue Canada for the entire amount collected on behalf of or from the Salesperson;

2. The Brokerage shall not:
    a) Pledge any portion of a Commission Trust held on behalf of the Salesperson as collateral for any loan or use said amount for any other personal or corporate reason without the express written consent of the Salesperson.

3. The Salesperson:
    a) Hereby irrevocably directs the Brokerage to deduct from any commissions payable or termination pay due and owing to the Salesperson, whether out of Commission Trust or otherwise, the amount of any indebtedness as outlined in Section 1(c) above;
    b) Shall become and remain a member in good standing of the .... Real Estate Board(s)/Association(s) and pay to the Brokerage, when required, any fees, dues or assessments required from time to time by the Board(s)/Association(s);
    c) Shall pay any registration or renewal fees imposed upon the Salesperson under any provincial legislation;
    d) Shall maintain Errors and Omissions Insurance, Consumer Deposit Insurance and Commission Protection Insurance coverage in good standing at all times;
    e) Shall supply and maintain at the Salesperson's expense, a suitable automobile and keep it insured at such limits for public liability and property damage as the brokerage may from time to time direct, and shall provide proof of such insurance to the brokerage;
    f) Shall fully and faithfully serve the Brokerage and conduct himself/herself in accordance with the Brokerage's office policies and practices, the By-laws and Code of Ethics of the Real Estate and Business Brokers Act, 2002, the Code of Ethics and Standards of Business Practice of the Canadian Real Estate Association, the by-laws, rules and regulations of the said real estate Board(s)/Association(s) and the Act.

4. The Salesperson shall not:
    a) Reduce the amount of commission on any real estate representation agreement or customer service agreement if it is contrary to the Broker's office policies and practices, without the prior written authorization of the Brokerage. If the Salesperson breaches this provision, the amount by which any such commission is reduced shall be deducted from the Salesperson's share of the commission received;
    b) Sign any document or make any representation that would be binding on the Brokerage and would be contrary to the Brokerage's office policies and practices, without the Brokerage's prior written consent.

5. The Salesperson consents to the collection, use and disclosure of personal information of the Salesperson by the Brokerage for the purpose of a transfer, sale, or financing by the Brokerage of the business, or compliance with the requirements of the Real Estate Council of Ontario, or such other use of the personal information as the Brokerage deems appropriate in connection with managing or carrying on the affairs of the business.

6. This Agreement may be terminated without notice by either party subject to the provisions of the Employment Standards Act of Ontario. Upon the termination of the Salesperson's employment, the transfer or surrender of the Salesperson's registration shall be immediately sent to the Registrar appointed pursuant to the Act. The Salesperson agrees to immediately return all keys, signs, equipment and materials supplied by the Brokerage and to surrender all listing books, certificates, or other materials in accordance with the rules and regulations of the said real estate Board(s)/Association(s).

7. The Salesperson agrees that he/she will not assign, transfer or convey, pledge or encumber this Agreement or any interests hereunder without the prior written consent of the Brokerage.

8. This Agreement and all rules and regulations hereby incorporated by reference constitute the entire Agreement between the parties and there are no oral or written conditions, warranties, promises or inducements except as referred to herein and in Schedule(s) .... attached hereto.

IN WITNESS WHEREOF the parties hereto have hereunto set their hands and seals, and in the case of a corporation, the corporate seal and the hands of duly appointed officers in that behalf:

....   ● DATE ....
(Witness)   (Signature of Salesperson)   (Seal)

....   ● DATE ....
(Witness)   (Signature of Authorized Signing Officer of Brokerage) (Seal)

....
(Name of Brokerage)   (Title)

Form 600   Revised 2009   **Page 1 of 1**

OREA Ontario Real Estate Association

Independent Contractor
Salesperson's Agreement

Form 601
for use in the Province of Ontario

INDEPENDENT CONTRACTOR AGREEMENT:

BETWEEN: ...., hereinafter referred to as (the "Brokerage")

AND: ...., herein referred to as (the "Salesperson")

In this Agreement, the term "Salesperson" includes a Broker registered under the Real Estate and Business Brokers Act, 2002.

WHEREAS:

A. The Brokerage is a duly registered real estate brokerage pursuant to the Real Estate and Business Brokers Act, 2002 (Ontario) (the "Act") and the regulations made pursuant thereto (the "Regulations") and owns, for the purpose thereof, all facilities and equipment required to conduct a real estate brokerage business.

B. The Salesperson is an independent contractor desiring access to such facilities and equipment for the purpose of conducting therefrom a real estate business.

NOW THEREFORE in consideration of the mutual covenants and agreements and for other good and valuable consideration as herein provided, the receipt and sufficiency of which is hereby acknowledged, the parties hereto hereby agree as follows:

ARTICLE ONE – APPOINTMENT

1.1 The Brokerage hereby retains and appoints the Salesperson as an independent contractor in accordance with this Agreement and the Salesperson hereby accepts such appointment as an independent contractor upon and subject to the terms, conditions, covenants and provisions set forth herein. The parties acknowledge that the Salesperson is a self-employed independent contractor and is not and shall not represent himself or herself to be a partner or employee of the Brokerage or to have any relationship to the Brokerage other than as a self-employed independent contractor.

ARTICLE TWO – FACILITIES

2.1 The Brokerage shall make available the services, facilities and equipment provided for in Schedule "A" attached to this Agreement.

ARTICLE THREE – GENERAL CONDITIONS

3.1 The Salesperson shall govern their conduct by the Act and Regulations and the constitution, by-laws, Code of Ethics and Standards of Business Practice of the local real estate board/association of their membership (the "Board"), and all requirements of the Real Estate Council of Ontario ("RECO") as may be amended from time to time.

3.2 The Salesperson shall furnish their own automobile and pay all expenses thereon and shall carry liability and property damage insurance

satisfactory to the Brokerage. A minimum of $ .... is required for liability insurance.
The Salesperson shall provide proof of such insurance to the Brokerage upon request.

3.3 The Salesperson shall during the Term of this Agreement:
a) maintain in good standing all registrations required by the Act and Regulations necessary to trade in real estate;
b) be a member in good standing of RECO; and
c) be a member in good standing of the Board.

3.4 The Salesperson shall maintain errors and omissions and such other insurance as RECO may require from time to time.

3.5 The Salesperson shall obtain and maintain HST registration as required by the Excise Tax Act (Canada) as amended from time to time.

3.6 The Salesperson shall not obligate the Brokerage for goods or services.

3.7 The Salesperson shall only use such real estate forms that have been approved by the Brokerage prior to their use.

3.8 The Salesperson has read and agrees to the office policy as outlined in the Brokerage's office policy manual and agree to conduct themselves accordingly and in accordance with any amendments thereto communicated to the Salesperson in writing from time to time.

3.9 The Brokerage may set-off against the Salesperson's commission or other amounts the Brokerage may owe the Salesperson or any amount due to the Brokerage from the Salesperson including without limitation payable to the Brokerage pursuant to Article Five of this Agreement.

ARTICLE FOUR – COMMISSIONS

4.1 The full amount of all gross commissions resulting from real estate transactions procured by the Salesperson and received by the Brokerage as required by the Act shall be credited to the Salesperson's account and shall remain the property of the Salesperson.

4.2 All credit balances in the Salesperson's account shall be paid by the Brokerage to the Salesperson on a .... basis, net of fees and other amounts owed to the Brokerage by the Salesperson.

4.3 The commission to be charged for any transaction shall be determined solely by the Salesperson and shall belong to the Salesperson. The parties acknowledge that the Act requires that commission be collected only by the Brokerage.

ARTICLE FIVE – FEES, EXPENSES AND COSTS

5.1 The Salesperson agrees to pay the Brokerage the Fees set out in Plan "A" or "B", as applicable, which form part of this Agreement.

ARTICLE SIX – REPRESENTATION AGREEMENTS AND CUSTOMER SERVICE AGREEMENTS

6.1 All representation agreements and customer service agreements are the property of the Brokerage according to the Act during the term of this Agreement. Upon termination of this Agreement, the Brokerage agrees to terminate any representation agreements or customer service agreements procured by the Salesperson if the seller or buyer under the agreement approves.

ARTICLE SEVEN – ADVERTISING

7.1 All advertising to be approved by the Brokerage in advance.

INITIALS OF SALESPERSON: ⬭   **INITIALS OF BROKER:** ⬭

Form 601   Revised 2011   **Page 1 of 4**

ARTICLE EIGHT – TERMINATION

8.1 This Agreement may be terminated by either party at any time without cause upon 24 hours written notice that may be delivered personally or by facsimile. Upon termination both parties agree to complete their obligations herein in order to complete an orderly conclusion of their relationship. The Salesperson will not have any claim on real estate transactions that have not been procured from representation agreements prior to termination, or any future commissions therefrom.

8.2 Upon termination of this Agreement, the Salesperson will return to the Brokerage all keys, listings, listing books, blueprints, signs, plans, maps, supplies and sales literature received at any time from the Brokerage. The Salesperson agrees to pay the Brokerage for the value of such items that were not returned upon termination of this Agreement.

8.3 If on termination the Salesperson is indebted to the Brokerage then until such debt has been paid, the amount outstanding from time to time shall

bear interest at the rate of .... per cent per annum calculated and payable monthly.

ARTICLE NINE – TERM

9.1 Any and all changes to this Agreement from one year to the next will be announced at a meeting of the salespeople on or about ....
each year. This Agreement will commence on the date hereof and run until the end of the current calendar year and subject to announced changes, if any, and termination as provided for herein, this Agreement will automatically renew annually (the "Term").

ARTICLE TEN – BROKERAGE'S SUPPLIES

10.1 The Salesperson shall only use supplies which conform to the Brokerage's current specifications and standards, including signs, business cards, stationery and other items used for communications or presentations to customers and prospective customers and all promotional and novelty items.

ARTICLE ELEVEN – LITIGATION, DISPUTE AND ARBITRATION

11.1 If any transaction in which the Salesperson is involved results in a dispute, arbitration, litigation or legal expense, the Salesperson shall co-operate fully with the Brokerage in the resolution or prosecution of same.

11.2 The Brokerage reserves the right to determine whether or not any litigation or dispute concerning any transaction in which the Salesperson is involved shall be prosecuted, defended or settled, or whether or not legal expense shall be incurred.

ARTICLE TWELVE – DEPOSITS

12.1 All monies, documents or property received by the Salesperson in connection with any transaction shall be delivered to the Brokerage immediately. All cheques must be made payable to the Brokerage in accordance with the Act.

ARTICLE THIRTEEN – CORRESPONDENCE

13.1 All letters received and a copy of all letters written by the Salesperson pertaining to the business of the Brokerage shall be turned over to the Brokerage for its records and shall be the property of the Brokerage. All letters are to be approved by the Brokerage before mailing.

ARTICLE FOURTEEN – INDEMNITY

14.1 The Salesperson hereby indemnifies the Brokerage against all liability, loss, damages, costs and expenses sustained, suffered or incurred by the Brokerage as a result of any breach by the Salesperson of the Salesperson's obligations under this Agreement or as a result of any claim by a third party arising out of the Salesperson's real estate business activities. This indemnity shall survive the termination of this Agreement.

ARTICLE FIFTEEN – USE AND DISTRIBUTION OF PERSONAL INFORMATION

15.1 The Salesperson consents to the collection, use and disclosure of personal information of the Salesperson by the Brokerage for the purpose of a transfer, sale, or financing by the Brokerage of the business, or compliance with the requirements of the Real Estate Council of Ontario, or such other use of the personal information as the Brokerage deems appropriate in connection with managing or carrying on the affairs of the business.

ARTICLE SIXTEEN– GENERAL AGREEMENT TERMS

16.1 Either party may waive any default of the other party under this Agreement, but, no such waiver shall affect the rights of that party in respect of any subsequent default, whether of the same or a different nature.

16.2 This Agreement which includes Schedule(s) "A", ... and Plan A or Plan B as appropriate, shall constitute the entire agreement between the parties with respect to its subject matter and supersedes all prior agreements and understandings in any way relating to that subject matter. This Agreement can only be changed by a writing signed by both parties. No remedy conferred on a party under this Agreement, or by law, shall preclude the exercise by that party of any other remedy available to it in equity or in law in respect of the same default.

16.3 This Agreement is personal to the Salesperson and no right of the Salesperson under this Agreement may be assigned without the prior written consent of the Brokerage, which consent may be arbitrarily, or unreasonably withheld. The Brokerage may, without the consent of the Salesperson, assign any of its rights under the Agreement and, following such assignment, shall be relieved of all obligations in respect of the rights so assigned. Subject to the foregoing, this Agreement shall enure to the benefit and be binding upon the parties and their respective heirs, executors, administrators, successors and permitted assigns.

16.4 The use of section headings in this Agreement is for convenience of reference only and shall not affect the interpretation of this Agreement.

16.5 All notices or other communications required or permitted under this Agreement to be given by one party to the other shall be in writing and shall be given by personal delivery (including courier), or by facsimile to the party as follows:

a) if to the Brokerage, at Attn: ....

Fax: (......................)...

b) if to the Salesperson, at Attn: ....

Fax: (......................)...

Any such notice or communication shall be deemed received on the earlier of actual receipt, if delivered or on the date transmitted, if by facsimile unless received after 5:00 p.m. on a business day (i.e. a day other than a Saturday or Sunday or statutory holiday in Ontario) in which case receipt will be deemed to be on the next business day. Either party may change its address for service by giving notice thereof pursuant to the term of this Section.

16.6 Each party agrees, at the request of the other party, to do, execute and give such further and other acts, documents and assurances as may be reasonably requested in order to give full effect to this Agreement and to the transactions contemplated herein.

IN WITNESS whereof the parties have duly signed this Agreement as of the date indicated.

....   ● DATE ....
(Witness)   (Signature of Salesperson)   (Seal)

....   ● DATE ....
(Witness)   (Signature of Authorized Signing Officer of Brokerage)   (Seal)

Schedule "A"
Independent Contractor – Salesperson's Agreement

Form 601
for use in the Province of Ontario

1. Secretarial services during normal office business hours.

2. Reception area.

3. Desk space as determined by the Brokerage.

4. Reasonable sales and administrative training, as determined by the Brokerage.

5. Use of telephone and fax facilities.

6. Standard office equipment as customarily provided in a real estate brokerage business.

7. Reasonable quantity of stationery.

8. Photocopying facility.

9. Sales Information Sheet (Trade Record) will be prepared by secretary.

10. A reasonable number of "For Sale" and "Open House" signs.

11. Multiple Listing Service processing fees and re-processing fees, where previously authorized.

12. Client and customer referral(s).

13. Listing fees, stand sign installation.

14. Courier facilities.

15. Business cards.

16. Office duty time.

17. Standard newspaper advertising program, as determined by the Brokerage. Salespersons may advertise over and above the Brokerage's program, at their own expense, provided they meet all governing provincial and local rules and regulations.

18. Brokerage to assist in all areas that are deemed essential to complete a real estate transaction if requested by the Salesperson.

19. All salespersons shall sign the inventory list.

20. Such other items and service as the Brokerage may in its sole discretion agree to provide to the Salesperson. The Brokerage has the right at any time without notice to increase or decrease said service.

21. ....

....

....

....

APPENDIX

Form 601 *(continued)*   Page 4 of 4

PLAN "A" – FEES PAYABLE TO BROKERAGE

To compensate for administrative and operating costs incurred by the Brokerage in providing the items and services in Schedule "A" the Salesperson shall pay the Brokerage:

1A .... % of the Salesperson's net commissions on the portion of total net annual commissions not exceeding $ ....

1B .... % of the Salesperson's net commissions on the portion of total net annual commissions not exceeding $ ....

1C .... % of the Salesperson's net commissions on the portion of total net annual commissions not exceeding $ ....

1D .... % of the Salesperson's net commissions on the portion of total net annual commissions not exceeding $ ....

1E .... % of the Salesperson's net commissions on the portion of total net annual commissions not exceeding $ ....

1F .... % of the Salesperson's net commissions on the portion of total net annual commissions not exceeding $ ....

1G .... % of the Salesperson's net commissions on the portion of total net annual commissions not exceeding $ ....

Under Plan "A" plateaus will be calculated on commissions received within the contract year. Effective, on each and every anniversary date, the plateau level will start at the beginning and the Salesperson will be paid accordingly. Furthermore, in the event of any switch in plans at the Salesperson's anniversary date, they will be paid by the rules of the Plan they were on at the time the business was written.

Salesperson will be responsible to pay for:
a)   Monthly and yearly dues and fees and other charges as charged by the Board, the Ontario Real Estate Association and the Canadian Real Estate Association;
b)   Registration/renewal fees, monthly and yearly fees and other fees charged to the Salesperson by RECO.

Salesperson shall pay all dues and fees and miscellaneous items outstanding at the end of each calendar year and the following year's Board yearly dues by cheque on or before January 1 of the following new year.

PLAN "A" AGREEMENT

I, ... (Salesperson) hereby agree to PLAN "A".

....
(Signature of Salesperson)   (Signature of Authorized Signing Officer of Brokerage)

PLAN "B" – FEES PAYABLE TO BROKERAGE

To compensate the Brokerage for administrative and operating costs incurred by the Brokerage in providing the items and services in Schedule "A" the Salesperson shall pay the Brokerage:

1A .... % of the Salesperson's net commissions on the portion of total net annual commissions not exceeding $ ....
The above compensation for the Brokerage applies to all transactions.

1B Plus ....

Dollars ($ ....) desk fee per month is payable on the first day of each and every month.

A .... interest charge per month (.... per annum) for late payment will be charged.
The desk fee includes all the items and services as set out in Schedule "A" contained herein, except as follows:

This plan includes .... (..) listing fees annually

This plan includes .... (..) standard sign installations annually

Over these specific amounts, the Salesperson is responsible for, said costs and will be billed accordingly on a monthly basis. An inventory of the Salesperson's listings and sign installations will be taken prior to commencement of the contract period and shall be counted against his/her yearly maximum for that contract period.

PLAN "B" AGREEMENT

I, ... (Salesperson) hereby agree to PLAN "B".

....
(Signature of Salesperson)   (Signature of Authorized Signing Officer of Brokerage)

Form 601   Revised 2011   **Page 4 of 4**

APPENDIX

Individual Identification Information Record

Form 630
for use in the Province of Ontario

NOTE: An Individual Identification Information Record is required by the *Proceeds of Crime (Money Laundering) and Terrorist Financing Act*. This Record must be completed by the REALTOR® member whenever they act in respect to the purchase or sale of real estate.

It is recommended that the Individual Identification Information Record be completed:

    (i)   for a buyer when the offer is submitted and/or a deposit made, and

    (ii)   for a seller when the seller accepts the offer.

Transaction Property Address:...

....

....

Sales Representative/Broker Name:...

Date:...

A. Verification of Individual

NOTE: This section must be completed for clients that are individuals or unrepresented individuals who are not clients, but are parties to the transaction (e.g. unrepresented buyer or seller). Where an unrepresented individual refuses to provide identification after reasonable efforts are made to verify that identification, a REALTOR® member must keep a record of that refusal and consider sending a Suspicious Transaction Report to FINTRAC if there are reasonable grounds to suspect that the transaction involves property from the proceeds of crime, or terrorist activity. Where you are using an agent or mandatary to verify an individual, see procedure described in CREA's FINTRAC Compliance manual.

1. **Full legal name of individual:** ....

2. **Address:**...

....

....

....

3. **Date of Birth:** ....

4. **Nature of Principal Business or Occupation:** ....

5. **Type of Identification Document*:**...
                              (must view the original, see below for list of acceptable documents)

6. **Document Identifier Number:** ....

7. **Issuing Jurisdiction:** ....
                     (insert name of the applicable Province, Territory, Foreign Jurisdiction or "Federal Government of Canada")

8. **Document Expiry Date:** ....
                              (must be valid and not expired)

*Acceptable identification documents: birth certificate, driver's licence, provincial health insurance card (not acceptable if from Ontario, Nova Scotia, Manitoba or Prince Edward Island), passport, record of landing, permanent resident card, old age security card, a certificate of Indian status, or SIN card (although SIN numbers are not to be included on any report sent to FINTRAC). Other acceptable identification documents: provincial or territorial identification card issued by the Insurance Corporation of British Columbia, Alberta Registries, Saskatchewan Government Insurance, the Department of Service Nova Scotia and Municipal Relations, the Department of Transportation and Infrastructure Renewal of the Province of Prince Edward Island, Service New Brunswick, the Department of Government Services and Lands of the Province of Newfoundland and Labrador, the Department of Transportation of the Northwest Territories or the Department of Community Government and Transportation of the Territory of Nunavut. If identification document is from a foreign jurisdiction, it must be equivalent to one of the above identification documents.

 **Ontario Real Estate Association**

Individual Identification Information Record

Form 630
for use in the Province of Ontario

B. Verification of Third Parties *(if applicable)*

NOTE: Complete this section of the form when a client or unrepresented individual is acting on behalf of a third party. Where you cannot determine if there is a third party, but there are reasonable grounds to suspect the individual is acting on behalf of a third party, you must keep a record of that fact.

1. **Name of third party:** ....

2. **Address:** ....

   ....

   ....

   ....

3. **Date of Birth:** ....

4. **Nature of Principal Business or Occupation:** ....

5. **Incorporation number and place of issue** *(if applicable)***:** ....

6. **Relationship between third party and client:** ....

   ....

   ....

   ....

 2 of 4

APPENDIX

 **Ontario Real Estate Association**

Form 630
for use in the Province of Ontario

Individual Identification Information Record

Only complete Sections C and D for your clients.

C. Client Risk *(ask your Compliance Officer if this section is applicable)*

Determine the level of risk of a money laundering or terrorist financing offence for this client by determining the appropriate cluster of client in your policies and procedures manual this client falls into and checking one of the checkboxes below:

Low Risk

☐ Canadian Citizen or Resident Physically Present

☐ Canadian Citizen or Resident Not Physically Present

☐ Canadian Citizen or Resident – High Crime Area – No Other Higher Risk Factors Evident

☐ Foreign Citizen or Resident that does not Operate in a High Risk Country (physically present or not)

☐ Other, explain:

Medium Risk

☐ Explain:

High Risk

☐ Foreign Citizen or Resident that operates in a High Risk Country (physically present or not)

☐ Other, explain:

If you determined that the client's risk was high, tell your brokerage's Compliance Officer. They will want to consider this when conducting the overall brokerage risk assessment, which occurs every two years. It will also be relevant in completing Section D below. Note that your brokerage may have developed other clusters not listed above. If no cluster is appropriate, the agent will need to provide a risk assessment of the client, and explain their assessment, in the relevant space above.

APPENDIX

 **Ontario Real Estate Association**

Form 630
for use in the Province of Ontario

Individual Identification
Information Record

D. Business Relationship
(ask your Compliance Officer when this section is applicable if you don't know)

D.1. Purpose and Intended Nature of the Business Relationship

Check the appropriate boxes.

Acting as an agent for the purchase or sale of:

☐ Residential property   ☐ Residential property for income purposes

☐ Commercial property   ☐ Land for Commercial Use

☐ Other, please specify:. . . . .

D.2. Measures Taken to Monitor Business Relationship and Keep Client Information Up-To-Date

D.2.1. Ask the Client if their name, address or principal business or occupation has changed and if it has include the updated information on page one.

D.2.2 Keep all relevant correspondence with the client on file in order to maintain a record of the information you have used to monitor the business relationship with the client. Optional - if you have taken measures beyond simply keeping correspondence on file, specify them here:

D.2.3. If the client is high risk you must conduct enhanced measures to monitor the brokerage's business relationship and keep their client information up to date. Optional - consult your Compliance Officer and document what enhanced measures you have applied:

D.3 Suspicious Transactions

Don't forget, if you see something suspicious during the transaction report it to your Compliance Officer. Consult your policies and procedures manual for more information.

APPENDIX

OREA Ontario Real Estate Association

Form 631
for use in the Province of Ontario

Corporation/Entity Identification Information Record

NOTE: A Corporation/Entity Identification Information Record is required by the *Proceeds of Crime (Money Laundering) and Terrorist Financing Act*. This Record must be completed by the REALTOR® member whenever they act in respect to the purchase or sale of real estate.

It is recommended that the Corporation/Entity Identification Information Record be completed:

    (i)   for a buyer when the offer is submitted and/or a deposit made, and

    (ii)   for a seller when the seller accepts the offer.

Transaction Property Address: ....

....

....

Sales Representative/Broker Name: ....

Date: ....

A.1. Verification of Corporation

1. Name of corporation: ....

2. Corporate Address: ....

....

....

3. Nature of Principal Business: ....

4. Name of Directors: As set out in certificate of corporate status or other record confirming corporation's existence.

....

....

5. Type and Source of Verification Record:

Must confirm existence of the corporation (e.g., certificate of corporate status, published annual report, government notice of assessment). If record is in paper format, a copy must be kept. If record is an electronic version, a record of the corporation's registration number and type and source of record (e.g., Corporations Canada website) must be kept.

....

....

6. Registration number of corporation: ....

7. Copy of corporate record showing authority to bind corporation regarding transaction:

(e.g., certificate of incumbency, articles of incorporation, by-laws setting out officers duly authorized to sign on behalf of corporation)

....

....

APPENDIX

 **Ontario Real Estate Association**

Form 631
for use in the Province of Ontario

Corporation/Entity Identification Information Record

A.2. Verification of Other Entity *(if applicable)*

1. **Name of other entity:** ....

2. **Address:** ....

   ....

   ....

3. **Nature of Principal Business:** ....

4. **Type of Verification Record:** Must confirm existence of other entity (e.g., partnership agreement, articles of association).

   ....

5. **Source of Record:** ....

   Record may be paper or an electronic version. If record is in paper format, a copy must be kept. If record is an electronic version, a record of the entity's registration number and type and source of record must be kept.

6. **Registration number:** ....

B. Verification of Third Parties *(if applicable)*

NOTE: Complete this section of the form when a client is acting on behalf of a third party. Where you cannot determine if there is a third party, but there are reasonable grounds to suspect the client is acting on behalf of a third party, you must keep a record of that fact.

1. **Name of other entity:** ....

2. **Address:** ....

   ....

   ....

3. **Date of Birth:** ....

4. **Nature of Principal Business or Occupation:** ....

   ....

5. **Incorporation number and place of issue** *(if applicable)***:** ....

   ....

6. **Relationship between third party and client:** ....

   ....

   ....

 This document has been prepared by The Canadian Real Estate Association to assist members in complying with requirements of Canada's *Proceeds of Crime (Money Laundering) and Terrorist Financing Regulations*. © 2014-2015.   **2** of 4

APPENDIX

 **Ontario Real Estate Association**

Form 631
for use in the Province of Ontario

Corporation/Entity Identification Information Record

Only complete Sections C and D for your clients.

C. Client Risk *(ask your Compliance Officer if this section is applicable)*

Determine the level of risk of a money laundering or terrorist financing offence for this client by determining the appropriate cluster of client in your policies and procedures manual this client falls into and checking one of the checkboxes below:

Low Risk

☐ Canadian Corporation or Entity

☐ Foreign Corporation or Entity that does not operate in a High Risk Country

☐ Other, explain:

Medium Risk

☐ Explain:

High Risk

☐ Foreign Corporation or Entity that operates in a High Risk Country

☐ Other, explain:

If you determined that the client's risk was high, tell your brokerage's Compliance Officer. They will want to consider this when conducting the overall brokerage risk assessment, which occurs every two years. It will also be relevant in completing Section D below. Note that your brokerage may have developed other clusters not listed above. If no cluster is appropriate, the agent will need to provide a risk assessment of the client, and explain their assessment, in the relevant space above.

 3 of 4

APPENDIX

 **Corporation/Entity Identification Information Record**

Form 631
for use in the Province of Ontario

D. Business Relationship
(ask your Compliance Officer when this section is applicable if you don't know)

D.1. Purpose and Intended Nature of the Business Relationship

Check the appropriate boxes.

Acting as an agent for the purchase or sale of:

☐ Land for Commercial Use

☐ Commercial property

☐ Other, please specify:. . . . .

D.2. Measures Taken to Monitor Business Relationship and Keep Client Information Up-To-Date

D.2.1. If the client is a corporation, ask if its name and address and name of its directors have changed and if they have include the updated information on page one. If the client is an entity other than a corporation, ask if its name, address and principal place of business has changed and if they have include the updated information on page one.

D.2.2 Keep all relevant correspondence with the client on file in order to maintain a record of the information you have used to monitor the business relationship with the client. Optional - if you have taken measures beyond simply keeping correspondence on file, specify them here:

D.2.3. If the client is high risk you must conduct enhanced measures to monitor the brokerage's business relationship and keep their client information up to date. Optional - consult your Compliance Officer and document what enhanced measures you have applied:

D.3 Suspicious Transactions

Don't forget, if you see something suspicious during the transaction report it to your Compliance Officer. Consult your policies and procedures manual for more information.

 This document has been prepared by The Canadian Real Estate Association to assist members in complying with requirements of Canada's *Proceeds of Crime (Money Laundering) and Terrorist Financing Regulations*. © 2014-2015.

OREA Ontario Real Estate Association

Identification Mandatary/ Agent Agreement

Form 632
for use in the Province of Ontario

BETWEEN:
REAL ESTATE BROKER: _____ , having its principal office at _____ (the "**Broker**");

_____

_____

_____

and
IDENTIFICATION AGENT: _____ , having its principal office at _____

_____

_____

_____

The parties agree to the terms and conditions set out in this agreement as of _____, 20___ (the "**Effective Date**").

1. Purpose

This agreement constitutes a written agreement as required by Section 64.1 of the Regulations under the Proceeds of Crime (Money Laundering) and Terrorist Financing Act.

2. Services

(a) On request, the Agent will provide the Broker with the identification services described in Schedule A in respect of an individual and/or the identification services described in Schedule B in respect of a corporation or other entity (the "**Services**"). The Broker will make available to the Agent all reasonable information required to enable the Agent to perform the Services.

(b) The Broker will compensate the Agent as follows: _____

3. Approvals and Authority

The Agent will obtain Broker's prior written approval for all Services it performs on the Broker's behalf.

4. Termination

Either party may terminate this agreement at any time on written notice to the other, provided that the Agent is required to complete any Services requested at the time of termination, and the Broker is required to pay for such Services.

5. Indemnification

The Agent will indemnify the Broker against any claims, liability, costs and reasonable expenses arising directly from the Agent's negligent acts or omissions in the performance of the Services.

6. Confidentiality

The Agent acknowledges that any information received from the Broker and/or the individuals from whom the Agent may obtain information under this Agreement is proprietary and confidential, and constitutes "personal information" within the meaning of the *Personal Information Protection and Electronic Documents Act* (PIPEDA) (collectively, "Confidential Information"). The Agent will not reveal to any third party any information provided by the Broker, except as required by the Regulations or as necessary to perform the Services, either during or subsequent to the term of this Agreement, and will at all times comply with the provisions of PIPEDA or any applicable provincial privacy legislation as well as any privacy policies of the Broker. Upon termination of this Agreement, the Agent will return to the Broker all Confidential Information in the possession of the Agent.

7. Regulatory Compliance

The parties acknowledge that the Broker is subject to a number of regulatory regimes, including regulations and regulatory requirements, decisions, rulings and guidelines issued by the Financial Transactions and Reports Analysis Centre of Canada ("FINTRAC"). The Agent will provide its reasonable assistance to the Broker in order to facilitate the Broker's compliance with FINTRAC requirements.

The Agent will abide by the policies and procedures designated by Broker and lawfully issued by Broker in accordance with the *Proceeds of Crime (Money Laundering) and Terrorist Financing Act*, regulations and regulatory requirements, decisions, rulings and guidelines issued by FINTRAC.

1
of 4

APPENDIX

 **Ontario Real Estate Association**

Form 632
for use in the Province of Ontario

Identification Mandatary/ Agent Agreement

8. Non-Assignable

This Agreement is not assignable by either party without mutual consent, which consent will not be unreasonably withheld.

9. Audit

The Agent grants to the Broker the right, at all reasonable times, to examine and audit all records in its possession or under its control which directly pertain to the Services provided to the Broker under this Agreement or as otherwise may be required under the Regulations.

10. Applicable Law

This Agreement will be construed in accordance with the laws of the [Insert name of Province/Territory]
_____ and the laws of Canada applicable therein.

11. Severability

The obligations and agreements of the Broker and Agent under this Agreement will be treated as separate and severable.

12. Complete Agreement

This Agreement, including the attached Schedules, constitutes the entire Agreement between the Broker and the Agent. The terms cannot be changed, except by an instrument in writing signed by the parties.

The Agent's authority to act on behalf of the Broker is limited to the rights, duties and responsibilities set out in this Agreement.

IN WITNESS WHEREOF the parties have executed this agreement the _____ day of _____, 20____ .

BROKER

Per: _____

Title: Authorized Signing Officer

Date: _____

_____

_____

_____

_____

_____

_____

AGENT

Per: _____

Title: Authorized Signing Officer

Date: _____

_____

_____

_____

_____

_____

_____

APPENDIX

 **Ontario Real Estate Association**

Identification Mandatary/ Agent Agreement

Form 632
for use in the Province of Ontario

Schedule A - Services with respect to individuals

1. Agent will take the necessary steps to verify and provide the following information to the Broker when dealing with an individual:

(a) Full legal name of individual: _____

(b) Address: _____

_____

(c) Date of Birth: _____

(d) Nature of Principal Business or Occupation: _____

(e) Type of Identification Document (e.g. drivers permit, passport, or government issued ID)[1]

_____

(Note: provide photocopy of Identification Document)

(f) Document Identifier Number: _____

(g) Issuing Jurisdiction: _____

(h) Document Expiry: _____

2. Agent will take necessary steps to verify whether or not the individual is acting on behalf of a third party and provide the following information to the Broker:

(a) Is Client acting on behalf of a third party?

Yes ☐   No ☐   Reasonable suspicion[2] ☐

(b) Name of third party: _____

(c) Address: _____

(d) Date of Birth: _____

(e) Nature of Principal Business or Occupation: _____

(f) Incorporation number and place of issue (if applicable): _____

(g) Relationship between third party and client: _____

_____

_____

_____

_____

_____

_____

_____

_____

[1] List of Acceptable Identification Documents is subject to change at the sole discretion of the Broker upon notice to agent. The following may apply: birth certificate, driver's licence, provincial health insurance card (not acceptable if from Ontario, Manitoba, Nova Scotia or Prince Edward Island), passport, record of landing, permanent resident card, old age security card, a certificate of Indian status, or SIN card (although SIN numbers are not to be included on any report sent to FINTRAC). Other acceptable identification documents: provincial or territorial identification card issued by the Insurance Corporation of British Columbia, Alberta Registries, Saskatchewan Government Insurance, the Department of Service Nova Scotia and Municipal Relations, the Department of Transportation and Infrastructure Renewal of the Province of Prince Edward Island, Service New Brunswick, the Department of Government Services and Lands of the Province of Newfoundland and Labrador, the Department of Transportation of the Northwest Territories or the Department of Community Government and Transportation of the Territory of Nunavut. If identification document is from a foreign jurisdiction, it must be equivalent to one of the above identification documents.
[2] Reasonable suspicion would arise when circumstances indicate the possibility of a third party but the individual will not confirm.

APPENDIX

OREA Ontario Real Estate Association

Form 632
for use in the Province of Ontario

Identification Mandatory/ Agent Agreement

Schedule B - Services in respect of corporations/other entities

Corporation

1. Agent will take the necessary steps to verify and provide the following information to the Broker when dealing with a corporation (with a copy of the actual record, where indicated):

(a) Name of corporation: _____

(b) Corporate address: _____

_____

(c) Nature of Principal Business: _____

(d) Names of Directors[3]: _____

(e) Copy of record confirming existence of corporation: _____

(i) Type of verification record[4]: _____

(ii) Source of verification record[5]: _____

(f) Registration number of corporation: _____

(g) Copy of corporate record showing authority to bind corporation regarding transaction[6]:

_____

Other entity (e.g., partnership)

2. Agent will take the necessary steps to verify and provide the following information to the Broker when dealing with an entity (with a copy of the actual record, where indicated):

(a) Name of entity: _____

(b) Entity address: _____

_____

(c) Nature of Principal Business: _____

(d) Copy of record confirming existence of entity: _____

(i) Type of verification record[7]: _____

(ii) Source of verification record[8]: _____

(e) Registration number of entity: _____

3. Agent will take the necessary steps to verify whether or not the corporation or entity is acting on behalf of a third party.

(a) Is Client acting on behalf of a third party?

Yes ☐   No ☐   Reasonable suspicion[9] ☐

(b) Name of third party: _____

(c) Address: _____

_____

(d) Date of Birth: _____

(e) Nature of Principal Business or Occupation: _____

(f) Incorporation number and place of issue (if applicable): _____

(g) Relationship between third party and client: _____

---

[3] As set out in certificate of corporate status or other record confirming corporation's existence.

[4] For example, certificate of corporate status, published annual report, government notice of assessment.

[5] If record is in paper format, a copy must be sent by the Agent to the Broker. If the record is an electronic version, a record of the corporation's registration number and type and source of record (e.g., Corporations Canada website) must be indicated above.

[6] For example, certificate of incumbency, articles of incorporation, by-laws setting out officers duly authorized to sign on behalf of corporation. A copy must be sent by the Agent to the Broker.

[7] For example, partnership agreement, articles of association.

[8] If record is in paper format, a copy must be sent by the Agent to the Broker. If the record is an electronic version, a record of the entity's registration number and type and source of record must be indicated above.

[9] Reasonable suspicion would arise when circumstances indicate the possibility of a third party but the entity's representative will not confirm.

REALTOR

4
of 4

OREA Ontario Real Estate Association   **Consent Agreement**

Form 633
for use in the Province of Ontario

_____
[date]

VIA _____
[means of communication]

_____
[address]
_____
_____

Attention: _____
[name of lawyer or representative]

Dear Sir or Madam:

Re: Identification Information Record - _____
[details of transaction (e.g., address)]

Real estate agents/brokers are subject to the *Proceeds of Crime (Money Laundering) and Terrorist Financing Act* and its associated Regulations. As such, we are required to confirm the existence of, and ascertain the name and address of, every corporation or other entity (e.g., partnership) on whose behalf we conduct a transaction, as well as the names of its directors. We are also required to confirm that the person entering into the transaction on behalf of the corporation has the power to bind the corporation regarding the transaction. We therefore request your assistance in completing our Identification Information Record

with respect to the above-noted transaction for_____
[name of corporation]

We enclose a form which lists the information we are required to include in our records. Please complete the form, attach the requested documents and return the materials to

_____ at _____
[name]   [refer to mailing address or email address]

We also enclose a consent from _____ to the release
of this information.   [name of corporation]

We are required to confirm the existence of _____
[name of corporation]

and complete the information record within 30 days of the closing of this transaction or, where the corporation is the buyer, within 30 days of the deposit being made. We would

therefore appreciate receiving the documents listed above no later than_____
[date]

If you have any questions please do not hesitate to contact us.

Yours very truly,

APPENDIX

 **OREA** Ontario Real Estate Association   **Consent Agreement**

Form 633
for use in the Province of Ontario

Information Form Respecting Corporations/Other Entities

If you act for a corporation

1. Please provide the following information:

(a) Name of corporation:	
(b) Corporate address:	
(c) Nature of Principal Business:	
(d) Names of Directors:	

2. Please provide the following records:

(a) Copy of a corporate record showing authority to bind corporation regarding transaction[1]

(b) Copy of record confirming existence of corporation[2]:

(c) If the records are in paper format, please enclose a copy with this form. In the event that you provide an electronic version of a record which is publically accessible, please provide the following information:

i.	Registration number of corporation:	
ii.	Type of verification record[3]:	
iii.	Source of verification record[4]:	

---

[1] For example, certificate of incumbency, articles of incorporation or by-laws setting out the officers duly authorized to sign on behalf of corporation.

[2] For example, certificate of corporate status or other record confirming corporation's existence.

[3] For example, certificate of corporate status, published annual report, government notice of assessment.

[4] For example, Corporations Canada website.

2
of 5

 **Consent Agreement**

Form 633
for use in the Province of Ontario

If you act for an entity other than a corporation (e.g., partnership)

1. Please provide the following information:

(a) Name of entity:	
(b) Entity address:	
(c) Nature of Principal Business:	

2. Please provide the following records:

(a) Copy of record confirming existence of entity[5]:

If the record is in paper format, please enclose a copy with this form. In the event that you provide an electronic version of a record which is publically accessible, please provide the following information:

i.	Registration number of entity:	
ii.	Type of verification record:	
iii.	Source of verification record:	

Whether you act for a corporation or an entity other than a corporation

Please indicate whether or not the corporation or entity is acting on behalf of a third party with respect to this real estate transaction.

(a) Is corporation or entity acting on behalf of a third party?

Yes		No		Reasonable suspicion[6]	

---

[5] For example, partnership agreement, articles of association.
[6] Reasonable suspicion would arise when circumstances indicate the possibility of a third party but the entity's representative will not confirm.

APPENDIX

OREA Ontario Real Estate Association   **Consent Agreement**

Form 633
for use in the Province of Ontario

(b) Name of third party:	
(c) Address:	
(d) Date of Birth:	
(e) Nature of Principal Business or Occupation:	
(f) Incorporation number and place of issue (if applicable):	
(g) Relationship between third party and corporation or entity:	

APPENDIX

Form 633
for use in the Province of Ontario

Consent

I, _____ as a duly authorized representative of _____ ,
        [name of individual]   *[name of corporation]*

hereby authorize _____ to release and communicate to _____
                        [lawyer]   *[name]*

the corporation information set out in the attached Information Form Respecting Corporations/Other Entities

for the sole purpose of enabling _____ to comply with his/her obligations
                                            [name]

under the *Proceeds of Crime (Money Laundering) and Terrorist Financing Act* and its associated Regulations.

Name in print:	
Signature:	
Date:	

Form 635   *Receipt of Funds Record*   Page 1 of 1

OREA **Ontario Real Estate Association**   **Receipt of Funds Record**

Form 635
for use in the Province of Ontario

NOTE: A Receipt of Funds record is required by the *Proceeds of Crime (Money Laundering) and Terrorist Financing Act* for every amount of funds that a REALTOR® member receives in the course of a single purchase or sale real estate transaction.
A REALTOR® does NOT have to complete a Receipt of Funds Record if:
   (i)   the funds are received from a financial entity or a public body that is buying or selling; or,
   (ii) a Large Cash Transaction Record must be completed; or,
   (iii) the deposit does not go into the trust account of a licensed practitioner. In other words, if the deposit goes directly into the account of a builder, lawyer or notary, or developer, a Receipt of Funds Record does not have to be completed by a member acting as the buyers' agent.

When this Record is completed, it is the responsibility of the broker to ensure that a record is kept for five years from the date it was created.
   (i)   When a REALTOR® member completes a Receipt of Funds Record, they must also complete an Identification Information Record at the same time, unless the Identification Information Record was completed prior to the receipt of funds.
   (ii) When both the buyer and seller are represented, it is the agent of the buyer who is required to complete and retain a Receipt of Funds Record in respect of the deposit made, regardless of who retains the deposit.

Transaction Property Address: ....

....

....

Sales Representative/Broker Name: ....

Date: ....

1. **Amount of Funds Received:** .... **Currency:** ....

   ☐ **Cheque** ☐ **Certified Cheque** ☐ **Cash** ☐ **Bank Draft**

   ☐ **Other, explain:** ....

(a) **If cash, indicate method of receipt** *(in person, mail, courier, other (explain))* ....

(b) **If cheque, indicate: Number of account:** ....

   Financial Institution: .... **Name of account holder:** ....

2. **Date of receipt of funds:** ....

3. **Account where funds were deposited** *(eg. Broker's trust account)*: ....

Where there are two agents involved in a transaction and the funds are deposited in the listing agent's account the buyer's agent is responsible for completing the receipt of funds record. However, the buyer's agent is not required to include the number and type of the listing agent's account or the name of the person or entity that is the holder of that account if, after taking reasonable measures, they are unable to do so. Further, if dealing with trust accounts, although the buyer's agent must indicate that the funds were deposited into the listing agent's trust account, the buyer's agent would not be required to include the number of the trust account or the name or entity that holds the trust account.

Note that if multiple accounts are affected, information on all accounts affected needs to be recorded. For example, assuming the buyer's agent transfers funds from their account into the listing agent's account, both accounts are affected by the transaction and therefore both numbers are to be recorded on the Receipt of Funds Record. However, the features noted in the previous paragraph with respect to the listing agent's accounts still apply.

   Indicate type of account where deposit has been made: ☐ **Trust** ☐ **Other**

   Number of account: .... **Name of account holder:** ....

4. **Purpose of funds (e.g., deposit for purchase):** ....

5. **Other details concerning receipt of funds:** ....

....

1 of 1

APPENDIX

 **Ontario Real Estate Association**   **Risk Assessment Form**

Form 639
for use in the Province of Ontario

Part 1 The purpose of this form is to assist you in assessing and documenting the threats and vulnerabilities to money laundering and terrorist financing to which your brokerage may be exposed as required by law. This form must be completed at least once every two years and kept on file for five years.

Date: ....

Office: ....

Completed By: ....

Broker Verification: ....
　　　　　　　　　　　　　　(Signature)　　　　　　　　　　　　　　　　　　(Date)

Part 2 The following checklist provides examples to facilitate your risk assessment. It should not be considered an exhaustive list. You can customize this checklist if you feel that this is appropriate in order to properly assess your brokerage's risks related to money laundering and terrorist financing.

	Frequently	Occasionally	Seldom	Never	N/A	Don't Know
Identify whether your Brokerage provides any of the following services:						
Do you offer services that make it difficult to fully identify clients?						
Do you offer electronic funds payment services?						
Do you offer funds transfers? (domestic and international)						
Identify whether you deal with clients or provide products or services in the following geographic locations:						
Are client properties located in a high-crime rate area?						
Do you or your clients operate or undertake activities in the following countries:						
• Any country subject to sanctions, embargoes or similar measures issued by, for example, the United Nations ("UN"). In some circumstances, sanctions or measures similar to those issued by bodies such as the UN, but which may not be universally recognized. (Please see URL information #1 and #2 on page 3)						
• Any country identified as financial secrecy havens or jurisdictions. (Please see URL information #3 and #4 on page 3)						
• Any country identified by the Financial Action Task Force (FATF) As non-cooperative in the fight against money laundering or subject to an FATF statement? You can consult the current Non-Cooperative Countries and Territories listed on the FATF's Website. (Please see URL information #5 on page 3)						
• Any country identified by credible sources 　- As lacking appropriate money laundering laws and regulations 　- As providing funding or support for terrorist activities? 　- As having significant levels of corruption, or other criminal activity? (Please see URL information #5-8 on page 3)						

 This document has been prepared by The Canadian Real Estate Association to assist members in complying with requirements of Canada's *Proceeds of Crime (Money Laundering) and Terrorist Financing Regulations.* © 2014-2015.

 1 of 4

APPENDIX

OREA Ontario Real Estate Association   **Risk Assessment Form**

Form 639
for use in the Province of Ontario

Identify whether any of the following applies to individual clients:	Frequently	Occasionally	Seldom	Never	N/A	Don't Know
Have you dealt with successive transactions of the same property in a short period of time?						
Do your clients operate a "cash business"?						
Do your clients conduct transactions involving multiple cash deposits?						
Do your clients' businesses generate large amounts of cash for certain transactions that are not normally cash intensive?						
Does your client use intermediate vehicles (such as corporations, trusts, foundations, partnerships) or other structures that do not seem usual for their business or seem very complex and unnecessary?						
Are your clients foreign residents, do you have clients that are foreign residents?						
Have any clients been identified as having engaged in activity that is consistent with the indicators identified for Suspicious Transactions? (Please see URL information #9 on page 3)						
Are 3rd party vehicles (i.e. trusts) used to obscure the true owner of the transaction?						
Are your clients intermediaries?						
Do your clients use unsupervised intermediaries?						
Do you deal with assignments of a legally binding contract?						

Identify whether any of the following applies to Corporate or business clients:	Frequently	Occasionally	Seldom	Never	N/A	Don't Know
Is the client an unregistered charity or other unregulated "not for profit" organization (especially one operating on a "cross-border" basis)?						
Does the client's structure or nature of its business or relationship make it difficult to identify the true owners or controllers?						
Are 3rd party vehicles (i.e. trusts) used to obscure the true owner of the transaction?						
Are your clients intermediaries?						
Do your clients use unsupervised intermediaries?						
Do you deal with assignments of a legally binding contract?						

2 of 4

APPENDIX

 **Risk Assessment Form**

Form 639
for use in the Province of Ontario

	Frequently	Occasionally	Seldom	Never	N/A	Don't Know
Identify whether any of the following apply to your business practices:						
Do you rely on a salesperson for such obligations as client identification?						
Does client identification take place other than face-to-face?						
Is your client base primarily repeat business?						
Is your client base primarily referral business?						
Is your client base primarily new business?						

1) UN:
http://www.un.org/sc/committees/index.shtml
http://www.un.org/Docs/sc/unsc_resolutions.html

2) Canada:
http://www.international.gc.ca/trade/sanctions-en.asp

3) OECD:
http://www.oecd.org/countries/monaco/listofunco-operativetaxhavens.htm

4) International Money Laundering Information Network:
http://www.imolin.org/imolin/finhaeng.html#Map.%20%20Majlor%20Financial%20Havens

5) FATF:
http://www.fatf-gafi.org/topics/high-riskandnon-cooperativejurisdictions/

6) MONEYVAL:
http://www.coe.int/t/dghl/monitoring/moneyval/

7) IMF:
http://www.imf.org/external/country/index.htm

8) IMoLIN:
http://www.imolin.org/imolin/amlid/index.jspx?lf_id=

9) FINTRAC Guideline 2 - Suspicious Transactions:
http://www.fintrac.gc.ca/publications/guide/Guide2/2-eng.asp#s8-9

APPENDIX

 **Risk Assessment Form**

Ontario Real Estate
Association

Form 639
for use in the Province of Ontario

Part 3 Based on all of your responses in Part 2, and any other factor that you think may be relevant, rank
your brokerage's overall risk of a money laundering offence or a terrorist financing offence and explain
how you arrived at this rationale in the space below.

**For greater clarity, if you are completing this form as part of a mandatory two year review, you
are required to explain the rationale used to determine your brokerage's risk level during this
review even if your risk level has not changed.**

Attach additional pages if necessary.

Brokerage Overall Risk Level:	☐ Low	☐ Medium	☐ High

Explanation:

Part 4 **Risk Mitigation Strategy**

You are required to develop written *Proceeds of Crime (Money Laundering) and Terrorist Financing Act*
compliance policies and procedures. CREA has prepared an Office Compliance Manual to use as a
reference tool to help you get started. It is available on REALTOR Link®. If you incorporate the Office
Compliance Manual into your compliance policies and procedures, you must tailor it to reflect the
nature, size and complexity of your operations.

If you determined in Part 3 that your brokerage overall risk level is high, you must consult and apply
the section of your compliance policies and procedures relating to mitigating high risks. This means
if the overall risk level is high, your Compliance Manual must specifically address any areas that
place your brokerage at high risk for money laundering and terrorist financing by explaining how your
brokerage will mitigate these risks.

CLAUSES

RESIDENTIAL AND COMMERCIAL CLAUSES

Introduction

The Ontario Real Estate Association can best fulfil its responsibility and role in organized real estate by ensuring that all persons engaged in real estate brokerage business, either as brokers or salespersons, have an opportunity to be properly trained and well informed, and thereby better serve the public in a professional manner. To this end, this series of clauses is provided to complement the growing list of educational programs, reference materials, standard forms, and video instruction available to the general membership.

General Disclaimer and Caution to User

The Ontario Real Estate Association has developed these clauses for the use of its members in drafting Agreements of Purchase and Sale. The clauses which are contained herein are provided solely for the purpose of guidance and do not in any way constitute required wording.

Take note that every real estate transaction is unique and the Ontario Real Estate Association does not warrant and is not responsible in any way for the adequacy, sufficiency, applicability, accuracy or suitability of any of the clauses or provisions hereinafter set out. Further, the Ontario Real Estate Association assumes no liability for the utilization of any of the clauses or provisions hereinafter set out.

The real estate professional is encouraged to seek expert advice in the drafting of agreements.

Important Instructions To Users

(a) Typed Supersedes Printed: Any clauses added to the body of the Offer will supersede any information in the pre-printed form. Therefore, care must be taken with any inclusions.

(b) Conditions versus Warranties/Representations: The decision to utilize a condition, warranty, or other representation will depend largely on circumstances. The vast majority of clauses are presented in "condition" format. However, various warranty examples have been included. The reader should note that most warranties included in the handbook are made "to the best knowledge and belief," survive the closing, and do not extend beyond completion of the transaction. Many variations exist in the marketplace and caution is advised when using warranties and representations. A limited number of such clauses has been included for information purposes only.

(c) Alternative Wordings: In select instances, alternative wordings are provided for the same general topic area (i.e., road access to a recreational property might address rights-of-way, unregistered easements, public road access, privately maintained road, etc.). Users should carefully read all possibilities and revise as required to meet individual circumstances.

(d) Capitalized Words: The first letter of selected words has been capitalized for emphasis only (i.e., Buyer, Seller, Agreement of Purchase and Sale, Lease) and should not be viewed as a required format.

(e) Use of Pronouns: This text should be read with all changes of gender and number as the reader may feel are required.

TABLE OF CONTENTS

APPENDIX

APPENDIX

APPENDIX

APPENDIX

APPENDIX

APPENDIX

APPENDIX

APPENDIX

ACCESS

This Offer is conditional upon the Buyer obtaining an Agreement to create an easement with (name of persons), for the purpose of (insert specific use), located and more particularly described as (outline planned location). Unless the Buyer gives notice in writing delivered to the Seller personally or in accordance with any other provisions for the delivery of notice in this Agreement of Purchase and Sale or any Schedule thereto not later than _____ p.m. on the day of _____, 20_____, that this condition is fulfilled, this Offer shall become null and void and the deposit shall be returned to the Buyer in full without deduction. This condition is included for the benefit of the Buyer and may be waived at the Buyer's sole option by notice in writing to the Seller as aforesaid within the time period stated herein.

NOTE: This condition must be used with caution, as further approvals will be required for the right-of-way to be legal (i.e., Committee of Adjustments).

ACC–1

Condition—Obtaining Right-of-way

This Offer is conditional upon the Buyer determining, at the Buyer's own expense, that access by automobile to the property is by a public road which is maintained at public expense throughout the year. Unless the Buyer gives notice in writing delivered to the Seller personally or in accordance with any other provisions for the delivery of notice in this Agreement of Purchase and Sale or any Schedule thereto not later than _____ p.m. on the _____ day of _____, 20_____, that this condition has been fulfilled, this Offer shall become null and void and the deposit shall be returned to the Buyer in full without deduction. This condition is included for the benefit of the Buyer and may be waived at the Buyer's sole option by notice in writing to the Seller as aforesaid within the time period stated herein.

ACC–2

Condition—Road Access by Open Public Road

This Offer is conditional upon the Buyer determining, at the Buyer's own expense, that all vehicular entrances to and exits from the property onto public highways have been approved under the Public Transportation and Highways Improvement Act or any predecessor thereof. Unless the Buyer gives notice in writing delivered to the Seller personally or in accordance with any other provisions for the delivery of notice in this Agreement of Purchase and Sale or any Schedule thereto not later than _____ p.m. on the _____ day of _____, 20_____, that his condition has been fulfilled, this Offer shall become null and void and the deposit shall be returned to the Buyer in full without deduction. This condition is included for the benefit of the Buyer and may be waived at the Buyer's sole option by notice in writing to the Seller as aforesaid within the time period stated herein.

ACC–3

Condition—Road Access to Public Highways

The Seller represents and warrants, to the best of the Seller's knowledge and belief, that the property fronts on: [choose appropriate statement]

    (a) a road which is maintained on a year round basis at public expense; OR
                    OR
    (b) a road which is maintained on a seasonal basis at public expense; OR
                    OR
    (c) a road which is not maintained at public expense.

The Parties agree that this representation and warranty shall survive and not merge on completion of this transaction, but apply only to the state of the property existing at completion of this transaction.

ACC–4

Road Access—Alternatives

The Buyer acknowledges that the private road accessing the said property is maintained by the [insert appropriate local cottage association or other relevant group], at an annual cost of $_____ for each property.

ACC–5

Road Access—Privately Maintained Road

APPENDIX

ACC–6

Road Access—Unregistered Easement (Trespass Access)

The Buyer acknowledges that the [road/path/lane], to the said property may be an unregistered easement. The Seller shall provide to the Buyer, on or before completion, a statutory declaration or declarations establishing that the existing [road/path/lane], has been used by the Seller and/or predecessors in title to gain access to the said property for a period of _____ years.

NOTE: In situations involving unregistered easements, legal advice should be sought.

ACC–7

Water Access

The Buyer acknowledges that the property is only accessible by water.

ACC–8

Water Access— Fluctuating Water Levels

The Buyer acknowledges that the water levels in the area where the property is situated may fluctuate between a low and high water level and may be extremely low or extremely high from time to time. Therefore, access to the property through means of water and/or access to the water from the property may be difficult or not available. The Buyer agrees that no claim will be made against the Seller, or any Brokerage, Broker or Salesperson, respecting the levels of the water including without limitation matters of access whether to the property by water or from the property to the water.

ASSIGNMENT OF AGREEMENT

ASSIGN–1

Right to Assign Agreement

The Buyer shall have the right at any time prior to closing, to assign the within Offer to any person, persons or corporation, either existing or to be incorporated, and upon delivery to the Seller of notice of such assignment, together with the assignee's covenant in favour of the Seller to be bound hereby as Buyer, the Buyer hereinbefore named shall stand released from all further liability hereunder.

NOTE: Do not use when the Agreement includes a STB Charge/Mortgage.

ASSIGN–2

Right to Assign— Seller's Consent

The Buyer covenants and agrees that the Buyer will in no way directly or indirectly assign, rent, lease, convey, list or in any way advertise for sale, sell, or otherwise transfer the Buyer's rights under this Agreement prior to completion to any other person or entity without the express written consent of the Seller. Such consent may be granted or withheld at the Seller's sole option.

ASSOCIATION FEES

ASSOC–1

Association Fees on Title

The Buyer acknowledges that there are agreements, restrictions and covenants registered on the title pertaining to an association and that there is an association fee payable in respect thereof. The Seller warrants that the said fee payable to the association in respect of the property is approximately $ _____ per _____ [year/month] and includes but is not limited to_____.
The Buyer agrees to accept the title subject to the said agreements, restrictions and covenants and assume payment of the association fee, to be adjusted as of completion.

APPENDIX

BUILDINGS/CONSTRUCTION

This Offer is conditional upon the Buyer determining, at the Buyer's own expense, that a building permit for the structure indicated on Schedule "_____" attached hereto is available with respect to the property. Unless the Buyer gives notice in writing to the Seller personally or in accordance with any other provisions for the delivery of notice in this Agreement of Purchase and Sale or any Schedule thereto not later than _____ p.m. on the _____ day of _____, 20_____ , that this condition has been fulfilled, this Offer shall become null and void and the deposit shall be returned to the Buyer in full without deduction. This condition is included for the benefit of the Buyer and may be waived at the Buyer's sole option by notice in writing to the Seller as aforesaid within the time period stated herein.

BUILD/CONST–1

Condition—Obtaining
Building Permit

CHATTELS/EQUIPMENT/FIXTURES

This offer is conditional upon the Buyer reviewing the terms of any rental agreements, rental contracts, lease contracts or lease to own agreements ("Rental Agreements") with respect to the rental items not included in the purchase price but to be assumed by the Buyer and finding such terms to be satisfactory to the Buyer in the Buyer's sole and absolute discretion. The Seller will provide copies of such rental agreements within _____ days of acceptance of this offer. Unless the Buyer gives notice in writing to the Seller personally or in accordance with any other provisions for delivery of notice in this Agreement of Purchase and Sale or any Schedule thereto not later than 5 p.m. on the _____ day of _____, 20_____, that this condition is fulfilled, this offer shall be null and void and the deposit shall be returned to the Buyer in full without deduction. This condition is included for the sole benefit of the Buyer and may be waived at the Buyer's sole option by notice in writing to the Seller as aforesaid within the time period stated herein.

CHATT–1

Condition—
Rental Contracts

The Seller represents and warrants that the chattels and fixtures as included in this Agreement of Purchase and Sale will be in good working order and free from all liens and encumbrances on completion. The Parties agree that this representation and warranty shall survive and not merge on completion of this transaction, but apply only to the state of the property at completion of this transaction.

CHATT–2

Chattels and Fixtures—
Good Working Order

The Buyer acknowledges that there is no express or implied warranty by the Seller on the chattels included in this Agreement of Purchase and Sale.

CHATT–3

Chattels—No Warranty

The Seller warrants that all the mechanical, electrical, heating, ventilation, air conditioning systems, air compressors, elevators, conveyor systems, sprinkler systems, boilers, and all other equipment on the real property shall be in good working order on completion. The Parties agree that this warranty shall survive and not merge on completion of this transaction, but apply only to those circumstances existing at the completion of this transaction.

CHATT–4

Equipment—
Good Working Order

The Seller agrees to give the Buyer the first right to negotiate for the purchase of any equipment to be sold by the Seller upon a price to be mutually agreed upon. In the event that the parties cannot agree to a price at least _____ days prior to the date of completion, then said first right shall become null and void.

CHATT–5

Equipment—
Purchase of Additional

APPENDIX

CHATT–6

Equipment—Removal

The Seller agrees to remove, at the expense of the Seller, any machinery or equipment, including mountings protruding from walls and floors, and to repair any damage caused by said removal.

....

CHATT–7

Lighting Fixtures

All lighting fixtures on the premises are included in the purchase price and are to be in good working order on completion.

....

CHATT–8

Rental Items

The following equipment is rented and not included in the Purchase Price. The Buyer agrees to assume the rental contract(s) if assumable: _____ [item] having a payment of $ _____, _____[monthly, quarterly, etc.].

NOTE: A variety of items may be rentals, e.g. hot water tank, air conditioner, water softener, furnace, furnace burner, etc. Care must be taken to ensure all rentals are documented.

COMPLETION DATE

COMP–1

Change of Completion Date by Buyer

Notwithstanding the completion date set out in this Offer, the Buyer may _____ [advance/postpone] the completion date of the transaction by not more than _____ days, by giving written notice of the amended completion date to the Seller or the Seller's Solicitor at least _____ days in advance of the earlier of the completion date set out herein and the amended completion date.

....

COMP–2

Change of Completion Date by Seller

Notwithstanding the completion date set out in this Offer, the Seller may _____ [advance/postpone] the completion date of the transaction by not more than _____ days, by giving written notice of the amended completion date to the Buyer or the Buyer's Solicitor at least _____ days in advance of the earlier of the completion date set out herein and the amended completion date.

....

COMP–3

Change of Completion Date—Mutual Agreement

Notwithstanding the completion date set out in this Agreement, the Buyer and Seller may, by mutual agreement in writing, advance or extend the date of completion of this transaction.

....

COMP–4

Change of Completion Date—Probate Trustee

The Buyer and Seller agree that the Seller, upon giving a minimum of _____ days written notice to the Buyer (excluding, Saturday, Sunday or Statutory Holidays), may unilaterally extend the date set for completion, one or more times, not to exceed _____ days in total, for the purpose of obtaining a Certificate of Appointment of Estate Trustee.

APPENDIX

CONDOMINIUM

This offer is conditional upon the Buyer's lawyer reviewing the Status Certificate and Attachments and finding the Status Certificate and Attachments satisfactory in the Buyer's Lawyer's sole and absolute discretion. The _____ [Buyer/Seller] agrees to request at the _____ [Buyer's/Seller's] expense, the Status Certificate and attachments within _____ days of acceptance of this Offer. Unless the Buyer gives notice in writing to the Seller personally or in accordance with any other provisions for the delivery of notice in this Agreement of Purchase and Sale or any Schedule thereto not later than 5 p.m. on the _____ day of _____, 20____, that this condition is fulfilled, this Offer shall be null and void and the deposit shall be returned to the Buyer in full without deduction.

This condition is included for the benefit of the Buyer and may be waived at the Buyer's sole option by notice in writing to the Seller as aforesaid within the time period stated herein.

CONDO–1

Condition—
Review of Condominium
Documents—
By Specific Date

This offer is conditional upon the Buyer's lawyer reviewing the Status Certificate and Attachments and finding the Status Certificate and Attachments satisfactory in the Buyer's Lawyer's sole and absolute discretion. The _____ [Buyer/Seller] agrees to request at the _____ [Buyer's/Seller's] expense, the Status Certificate and attachments within _____ days after acceptance of this Offer. Unless the Buyer gives notice in writing to the Seller personally or in accordance with any other provisions for the delivery of notice in this Agreement of Purchase and Sale or any Schedule thereto not later than 5 p.m. on the fifth day (excluding Saturdays, Sundays and Statutory Holidays) following receipt by the Buyer of the Status Certificate and attachments, that this condition is fulfilled, this Offer shall be null and void and the deposit shall be returned to the Buyer in full without deduction. This condition is included for the benefit of the Buyer and may be waived at the Buyer's sole option by notice in writing to the Seller as aforesaid within the time period stated herein.

CONDO–2

Condition—
Review of Condominium
Documents—
Within ____ Days

The Seller represents and warrants that, with respect to the unit, the Condominium Act, Declaration, Bylaws and Rules of the Condominium Corporation have been complied with, and that no improvements, additions, alterations or repairs that require the consent of the Condominium Corporation have been carried out in the said unit, the exclusive use areas or the common elements, unless the required consent has been obtained from the Condominium Corporation. This warranty shall survive and not merge on the completion of this transaction.

CONDO–3

Alterations By Owner

The Buyer covenants and agrees that no alterations will be made to the unit during the term of interim occupancy. Upon completion of the transaction, the Buyer agrees to abide by the Bylaws and Rules relating to alterations and changes within the unit.

CONDO–4

Alterations/Changes to Unit
During Interim Occupancy

The Buyer hereby covenants with the Seller and with the Condominium Corporation that the Buyer, members of the household, and guests, will comply with the Condominium Act, the Declaration, the Bylaws and all Rules and Regulations, in using the unit and the common elements, and will be subject to the same duties imposed by the above as those applicable to other individual unit owners.

CONDO–5

Compliance by Buyers,
Guests and Family Members

The Buyer acknowledges that any default in payment of occupancy fees shall be deemed to be a default under the terms and conditions of the Agreement of Purchase and Sale, and subject to the remedies provided herein for the Seller.

CONDO–6

Default by New Buyers
During Interim Occupancy

APPENDIX

CONDO-7

Occupancy by Buyer Prior to Completion of Construction

The Buyer acknowledges that the unit being acquired is currently under construction. The Buyer shall take occupancy of the unit provided that the interior of the unit has been substantially completed, notwithstanding that the common areas have not been substantially finished. The Seller agrees to complete same in a good and workmanlike manner in a reasonable period of time. The Buyer further acknowledges that failure to complete either the unit or the common areas by the occupancy date in no way relieves the Buyer from completing the transaction.

CONDO-8

Occupancy by Buyer Prior to Completion—Payment of Occupancy Fee

The Buyer shall be entitled to occupy the property from the _____ day of _____, 20_____, until the date of completion at a monthly fee hereinafter referred to as an occupancy fee. The occupancy fee shall be calculated based on the proportionate share of the common expenses, the estimated realty taxes, and mortgage interest as detailed herein (or designated as Schedule "_____" attached to and forming part of this Agreement). Said occupancy fee shall be due and payable on a monthly basis, in advance, commencing on the 1st day of each month following the date of occupancy. Partial charges prior to the 1st day of the initial month shall be pro-rated accordingly. The Buyer further agrees to provide the Seller with post-dated cheques to cover the occupancy cost for a period of twelve months, or such period to be established by the Seller whichever is the lesser.

CONDO-9

Permission to Access Unit

The Buyer agrees to allow the Seller access to the unit for the purpose of inspection, maintenance, or completion of uncompleted work for a period of six (6) months following the date of completion, provided that reasonable notice is given to the Buyer. Any subsequent access shall be pursuant to the Bylaws, Rules and Regulations as established by the Board of Directors of the Condominium Corporation.

CONDO-10

Tenant to Occupy Property

The Buyer agrees to abide by the Declaration, Bylaws, Rules and Regulations of the Condominium Corporation and, if the property is to be rented, the Buyer agrees to inform all tenants of the Rules and Regulations and receive written acknowledgement of the tenants regarding their willingness to abide by same within the rental document. It is clearly understood that all rental agreements shall conform with the Rules and Regulations as passed from time to time by the Board of Directors of the Condominium Corporation.

APPENDIX

DEPOSITS/PAYMENTS

The Buyer agrees to pay a further sum of _____ ($ _____), subject to adjustments, to the Seller on completion of this transaction, with funds drawn on a lawyer's trust account in the form of a bank draft, certified cheque or wire transfer using the Large Value Transfer System.

DEP/PAY–1

A Further Sum of

....

The Buyer agrees to pay the balance of the purchase price, subject to adjustments, to the Seller on completion of this transaction, with funds drawn on a lawyer's trust account in the form of a bank draft, certified cheque or wire transfer using the Large Value Transfer System.

DEP/PAY–2

Balance of Purchase Price

....

The Buyer agrees to pay a further sum of _____ ($ _____), to _____, by negotiable cheque, not later than _____ p.m. on the _____ day of _____, 20_____, as a supplementary deposit to be held in trust in the same manner as the initial deposit pending completion or other termination of this Agreement. This amount is to be credited towards the purchase price on completion of this transaction.

DEP/PAY–3

Deposit Increase—Additional Payment

....

The Buyer agrees to pay the following supplementary deposits in the amounts stated not later than: [List Appropriate Times, Dates and Amounts] to _____, by negotiable cheque, to be held in trust pending completion or other termination of this Agreement. Such payments are to be credited towards the purchase price on completion of this transaction.

DEP/PAY–4

Deposit Increase—Multiple Payments

....

The Buyer agrees to pay a further sum of _____ ($ _____), to _____, by negotiable cheque, at the time of notification of fulfilment or removal of the condition pertaining to _____, as an additional deposit to be held in trust pending completion or other termination of this Agreement. This amount is to be credited towards the purchase price on completion of this transaction.

DEP/PAY–5

Deposit Increase—On Removal of Condition(s)

....

The parties to this Agreement hereby acknowledge that the Deposit Holder shall place the deposit in trust in the Deposit Holder's interest bearing real estate trust account, which earns interest at _____, and the Deposit Holder shall pay any interest it earns or receives on the deposit to _____ at the same rate of interest the Deposit Holder earns or receives on the Deposit Holder's real estate trust account.

NOTE: The Listing Brokerage is required to have Social Insurance Number(s) before paying interest on deposits.

DEP/PAY–6

Deposit Interest—Payment of All Interest Earned

....

The parties to this Agreement hereby acknowledge and agree that the Deposit Holder shall place the deposit in the Deposit Holder's interest bearing real estate trust account, which earns interest at _____, and the Deposit Holder shall pay interest at a rate of _____ on the deposit to _____. The parties to this Agreement hereby acknowledge and agree that the Deposit Holder shall be entitled to retain the difference between the interest earned on the deposit and the agreed rate of interest payable.

DEP/PAY–7

Deposit Interest—Payment of Interest at a Rate Less Than Earned

DEP/PAY–8

Deposit Interest—Payment of Interest Earned Provided Minimum Amount Earned

The parties to this Agreement hereby acknowledge and agree that the Deposit Holder shall place the deposit in the Deposit Holder's interest bearing real estate trust account, which earns interest at _____, and the Deposit Holder shall pay any interest it earns or receives on the deposit to _____, provided the amount of the interest that the Deposit Holder earns or receives on the deposit is equal to or greater than _____. The parties to this Agreement hereby acknowledge and agree that the Deposit Holder shall be entitled to retain any interest earned or retained on the deposit, which is less than _____.

DEP/PAY–9

Deposit Interest—Term Deposit Bearing Interest

The parties to this Agreement hereby acknowledge that the Deposit Holder shall place all deposit monies in an interest bearing security with any accrued interest on the deposit to be paid to the Buyer as soon as possible after completion or other termination of this Agreement. The deposit holder will immediately inform the person depositing the trust money as to the interest rate received on the deposit. In the event that the closing date is advanced or the transaction is terminated, the party receiving the interest agrees to accept the short-term rate for deposits withdrawn before maturity.

DEVELOPMENT/SEVERANCE/SUBDIVISION

NOTE: The sale of large parcels of land and vacant land can be subject to capital gains and/or HST. This can depend upon present and future use, who is selling, and who is buying. Expert advice should be sought.

DEV–1

Condition—Services— Hydro/Telephone

This Offer is conditional upon the Buyer determining, at the Buyer's own expense, that the provision of service by hydro and telephone to the said property shall not exceed a cost of _____ ($ _____). Unless the Buyer gives notice in writing delivered to the Seller personally or in accordance with any other provisions for the delivery of notice in this Agreement of Purchase and Sale or any Schedule thereto not later than _____ p.m. on the _____ day of _____, 20_____, that this condition is fulfilled, this Offer shall become null and void and the deposit shall be returned to the Buyer in full without deduction. This condition is included for the benefit of the Buyer and may be waived at the Buyer's sole option by notice in writing to the Seller as aforesaid within the time period stated herein.

DEV–2

Condition—Severance— Seller Undertakes Expense and Completion

This Offer is conditional upon the Buyer obtaining, at the Seller's expense, a consent to sever the property as follows: (provide description of proposed severance). Unless the Buyer gives notice in writing delivered to the Seller personally or in accordance with any other provisions for the delivery of notice in this Agreement of Purchase and Sale or any Schedule thereto not later than _____ p.m. on the _____ day of _____, 20_____, that this condition is fulfilled, this Offer shall become null and void and the deposit shall be returned to the Buyer in full without deduction. The Seller agrees to sign any requisite documents required for the above condition and do all things reasonably necessary in support of the satisfaction of the condition.

The Seller understands and acknowledges that the Seller shall be responsible for satisfying any conditions imposed for approval of the severance, and if such conditions give the Seller options in the manner of compliance, the Buyer shall determine which option will be selected. The Seller shall obtain a reference plan prepared by an Ontario Land Surveyor suitable for registration purposes in the Land Registry Office in which the said property is located.

NOTE: Additional wording may be inserted concerning the extension of the completion date if the severance is not completed and limits of cost relating to obtaining said severance.

This Offer is conditional upon the Buyer determining, at the Buyer's own expense, the cost of constructing roads, installing necessary services, and generally ascertaining if the terrain will permit development at a reasonable price. Unless the Buyer gives notice in writing delivered to the Seller personally or in accordance with any other provisions for the delivery of notice in this Agreement of Purchase and Sale or any Schedule thereto not later than _____ p.m. on the _____ day of _____, 20_____, that this condition is fulfilled, this Offer shall become null and void and the deposit shall be returned to the Buyer in full without deduction. This condition is included for the benefit of the Buyer and may be waived at the Buyer's sole option by notice in writing to the Seller as aforesaid within the time period stated herein.

DEV–3

Condition—Suitability for Roads/Services

....

The Seller acknowledges that it is the intention of the Buyer to develop and/or renovate and resell the property.

DEV–4

Intention of Buyer to Develop

....

The Seller warrants that the lands are not subject to a Site Plan Development Agreement.

DEV–5

No Site Plan Development Agreement

....

The Seller acknowledges that the Buyer is acquiring the property for development, and the purchase price is calculated on the basis of _____ ($_____) per acre. In the event of a discrepancy in area, the purchase price will be adjusted accordingly at time of completion.

NOTE: Survey or other acceptable confirmation of exact acreage is required.

DEV–6

Price Based Upon Acreage

....

The Seller agrees to co-operate with the Buyer in the application for and registration of any plan or plans of subdivision on the said property and the Seller agrees to execute any requisite documents for the application and registration of any plan of subdivision, provided that the Buyer pay all costs for the application, requirements for approval and registration of the plan of subdivision.

DEV–7

Seller Consents to Subdivide

....

The Seller shall be permitted the right to remain upon and continue the Seller's use of the real property, free of any payment of rent for a period of _____ after the date of completion, provided that the Seller agrees to vacate the property at the end of the period and provided that the Seller shall, during the period, maintain the lands and buildings in good repair and not permit waste upon the property. The Seller shall pay taxes, insurance and utilities during this period. The Buyer shall have free access to the lands during this period and reasonable access to the buildings. The Seller shall be permitted to remove all personal property from the said property either during this period or upon vacating the property. These provisions, where applicable, shall not lapse or merge on completion of this transaction.

DEV–8

Seller Permitted to Remain on Property

....

The Seller warrants that municipal services to the subject property include _____ and _____ are available for use by the Buyer, Buyer to pay any usual connection charges.

DEV–9

Services—Warranty

APPENDIX

DOCKS/BOATHOUSES

DOCKS-1

**Condition—Docks/
Boathouses (Including
Reference to Conservation
and/or Canal Authorities)**

This Offer is conditional upon the Buyer determining, at the Buyer's own expense, that the [boathouse, dock, pier, etc.], used in conjunction with the property, and passing to the Buyer on completion, [has/have] received all necessary approvals and permits from the Ministry of Natural Resources, the Federal Government under the *Navigable Waters Protection Act*, Canada, from [insert appropriate conservation or canal authority as required], and from all other relevant authorities. Unless the Buyer gives notice in writing delivered to the Seller personally or in accordance with any other provisions for the delivery of notice in this Agreement of Purchase and Sale or any Schedule thereto not later than _____ p.m. on the _____ day of _____, 20_____, that this condition has been fulfilled, this Offer shall become null and void and the deposit shall be returned to the Buyer in full without deduction. This condition is included for the benefit of the Buyer and may be waived at the Buyer's sole option by notice in writing to the Seller as aforesaid within the time period stated herein.

DOCKS-2

**Docks/Boathouses—
Warranty (Including
Reference to Conservation
and/or Canal Authorities)**

The Seller represents and warrants to the best of his knowledge and belief that the [boathouse, dock, pier, etc.], used in conjunction with the property, and passing to the Buyer on completion, [has/have] received all necessary approvals and permits from the Ministry of Natural Resources, the Federal Government under the *Navigable Waters Protection Act*, Canada, from [insert appropriate conservation or canal authority as required], and from all other relevant authorities. The Parties agree that these representations and warranties shall survive and not merge on completion of this transaction, but apply only to those circumstances existing at completion of this transaction.

ELECTRONIC

ELEC-1

Electronic Signature

The parties hereto consent and agree to the use of electronic signature pursuant to the *Electronic Commerce Act 2000*, S.O. 2000, c17 as amended from time to time with respect to this Agreement and any other documents respecting this transaction.

ENVIRONMENTAL

This Offer is conditional upon the Buyer determining, at the Buyer's own expense that all environmental laws and regulations have been complied with, no hazardous conditions or substances exist on the land, no limitations or restrictions affecting the continued use of the property exist, other than those specifically provided for herein, no pending litigation respecting Environmental matters, no outstanding Ministry of Environment Orders, investigation, charges or prosecutions respecting Environmental matters exist, there has been no prior use as a waste disposal site, and all applicable licences are in force. The Seller agrees to provide to the Buyer upon request, all documents, records, and reports relating to environmental matters in possession of the Seller. The Seller further authorizes (insert appropriate Ministry), to release to the Buyer, the Buyer's Representative or Solicitor, any and all information that may be on record in the Ministry office with respect to the said property.

Unless the Buyer gives notice in writing delivered to the Seller personally or in accordance with any other provisions for the delivery of notice in this Agreement of Purchase and Sale or any Schedule thereto not later than _____ p.m. on the _____ day of _____, 20_____, that the preceding condition has been fulfilled, this Offer shall become null and void and the deposit shall be returned to the Buyer in full without deduction. This condition is included for the benefit of the Buyer and may be waived at the Buyer's sole option by notice in writing to the Seller as aforesaid within the time period stated herein.

ENV-1

Condition—All Environmental Laws Complied With

....

This Offer is conditional upon the Buyer determining, at the Buyer's own expense, that the property does not contain a habitat or critical habitat as defined in the *Species at Risk Act*, SC 2002, C29, nor a habitat as defined in the *Endangered Species Act*, 2007 S.O. 2007, C6. Unless the Buyer gives notice in writing delivered to the Seller personally or in accordance with any other provisions for the delivery of notice in this Agreement of Purchase and Sale or any Schedule thereto not later than _____ p.m. on the _____ day of _____, 20_____, that this condition has been fulfilled, this Offer shall become null and void and the deposit shall be returned to the Buyer in full without deduction. This condition is included for the benefit of the Buyer and may be waived at the Buyer's sole option by notice in writing to the Seller as aforesaid within the time period stated herein.

ENV-2

Condition— Endangered Species

....

This Offer is conditional upon the approval of the terms hereof by the Buyer's Solicitor. Unless the Buyer gives notice in writing delivered to the Seller personally or in accordance with any other provisions for the delivery of notice in this Agreement of Purchase and Sale or any Schedule thereto not later than _____ p.m. on the _____ day of _____, 20_____, that this condition is fulfilled, this Offer shall be null and void and the deposit shall be returned to the Buyer in full without deduction. This condition is included for the benefit of the Buyer and may be waived at the Buyer's sole option by notice in writing to the Seller as aforesaid within the time period stated herein. The Buyer and Seller hereby acknowledge that enactments and proposed enactments by the Federal, Provincial and Municipal Governments may have an impact on the use of land. The Buyer and Seller hereby acknowledge that the foregoing condition is inserted specifically to allow the Buyer to obtain legal advice as to the potential impact of Federal, Provincial and Municipal laws and enactments and Regulations made thereto that may affect the subject property, presently or in the immediate future. The Buyer and Seller further acknowledge that such opinions fall outside the qualifications and ability of the Brokerage and accordingly, the Buyer and Seller hereby agree that they shall hold harmless and indemnify the Brokerage from any claims, actions or causes of action that may be the result of such Legislation or future enactments.

ENV-3

Condition— Environmental Legislation— Lawyer's Approval and Acknowledgement

APPENDIX

ENV-4

Condition—
Environmentally Protected
Zone, Flood Plain, Hazard
Land

This Offer is conditional upon the Buyer determining, at the Buyer's own expense, that no portion of the property has been designated as hazard land, flood plain, or an environmentally protected zone. Unless the Buyer gives notice in writing delivered to the Seller personally or in accordance with any other provisions for the delivery of notice in this Agreement of Purchase and Sale or any Schedule thereto not later than _____ p.m. on the _____ day of _____, 20____, that this condition has been fulfilled, this Offer shall become null and void and the deposit shall be returned to the Buyer in full without deduction. This condition is included for the benefit of the Buyer and may be waived at the Buyer's sole option by notice in writing to the Seller as aforesaid within the time period stated herein.

ENV-5

Condition—
Oil Tank—Aboveground or
Underground

This Agreement is conditional upon the Buyer obtaining a report from a fuel oil distributor registered under the Technical Standards and Safety Act, 2002, and any Regulations thereto as amended from time to time stating the tank system in, on or about the property is in a safe operating condition and complies with the requirements of the *Technical Standards and Safety Act, 2002*, and any Regulations thereto as amended from time to time. Seller agrees to allow access to the property by the fuel oil distributor for purpose of obtaining a report. Unless the Buyer gives notice in writing delivered to the Seller personally or in accordance with any other provisions for the delivery of notice in this Agreement of Purchase and Sale or any Schedule thereto not later than _____ p.m. on the _____ day of _____, 20____, that this condition has been fulfilled, this Offer shall be null and void and the deposit shall be returned to the Buyer in full without deduction. This condition is included for the benefit of the Buyer and may be waived at the Buyer's sole option by notice in writing to the Seller as aforesaid within the time period stated herein.

ENV-6

Agricultural Activities
Acknowledgement

The Buyer acknowledges that the property lies within, partially within, adjacent to or within two kilometres of an area zoned, used or identified for agricultural and food production activities and that such activities occur in the area. These activities may include intensive operations that cause discomfort and inconveniences that involve, but not limited to dust, noise, flies, light, odour, smoke, traffic, vibration, operating of machinery during any 24 hour period, storage and utilization of manure and the application by spraying or otherwise of chemical fertilizers, soil amendments, herbicides and pesticides. One or more of these inconveniences have protection in Ontario under the *Farming and Food Production Protection Act*.

ENV-7

Endangered Species—
Acknowledgement

The Buyer acknowledges that the property may contain a habitat or critical habitat as defined in the *Species at Risk Act*, SC 2002, C29, and/or a habitat as defined in the *Endangered Species Act*, 2007 S.O. 2007, C6.

ENV-8

Environmental Issues—
Release of Documents from
Appropriate Ministries

The Seller authorizes the [insert appropriate Ministry], to release to the Buyer, or the Buyer's Representative or Solicitor, any and all information that may be on record in the Ministry's office with respect to the said property.

APPENDIX

The Seller represents and warrants to the best of the Seller's knowledge and belief that during the period of his ownership of the property, that all environmental laws and regulations have been complied with, no hazardous conditions or substances exist on the land, no limitations or restrictions affecting the continued use of the property exist, other than those specifically provided for herein, no pending litigation respecting Environmental matters, no outstanding Ministry of Environment Orders, investigations, charges or prosecutions regarding Environmental matters exist, there has been no prior use as a waste disposal site, and all applicable licences are in force. The Seller agrees to provide to the Buyer upon request, all documents, records, and reports relating to environmental matters that are in the possession of the Seller. The Seller further authorizes [insert appropriate Ministry], to release to the Buyer, the Buyer's Agent or Solicitor, any and all information that may be on record in the Ministry office with respect to the said property.

The Parties agree that this representation and warranty shall form an integral part of this Agreement and survive the completion of this transaction, but apply only to circumstances existing at completion of this transaction.

ENV-9

Environmental Warranty— All Laws Complied With

The Buyer acknowledges that the use of the property and buildings and structures thereon may have been for the growth or manufacture of illegal substances and acknowledges that the Seller makes no representations and/or warranties with respect to the state of repair of the premises and the Buyer accepts the property and the buildings and structures thereon in their present state and in an "as is" condition.

ENV-10

Growth or Manufacture of Illegal Substances— Acknowledgment

The Seller represents and warrants that during the time the Seller has owned the property, the use of the property and the buildings and structures thereon has not been for the growth or manufacture of any illegal substances, and that to the best of the Seller's knowledge and belief, the use of the property and the buildings and structures thereon has never been for the growth or manufacture of illegal substances. This warranty shall survive and not merge on the completion of this transaction.

ENV-11

No Growth or Manufacture of Illegal Substances— Warranty

The Seller represents and warrants that the fuel oil tank in, on or about the property is in compliance with the requirements of the *Technical Standards and Safety Act, 2002*, and any Regulations thereto as amended from time to time and has been registered with the Technical Standards and Safety Authority. Seller agrees to provide Buyer with the Registration number and all relevant documents prior to closing. This warranty shall survive and not merge upon the completion of this transaction.

ENV-12

Underground Tank— Compliance Warranty

The Buyer acknowledges that there was an underground fuel tank on the property that has been removed and the Seller agrees to provide to the Buyer at the Seller's own expense by no later than _____ p.m. on the _____ day of _____, 20_____, evidence that a contractor registered under the *Technical Standards and Safety Act, 2002*, and any Regulations thereto as amended from time to time, has removed the said fuel oil tank, assessed the soil surrounding the underground fuel oil tank for contamination and cleaned and removed any contamination.

ENV-13

Underground Tank—Seller Has Removed

The Seller agrees that the Seller will, at the Seller's expense, have the underground fuel oil tank on the property removed from the property by a contractor registered under the *Technical Standards and Safety Act, 2002*, and any Regulations thereto as amended from time to time by no later than _____ p.m. on the _____ day of _____, 20_____, and thereafter to have the soil surrounding the underground fuel oil tank assessed for contamination and any contamination cleaned and removed by a contractor registered under the *Technical Standards and Safety Act, 2002*, and any Regulations thereto as amended from time to time, and on or before closing to provide evidence of the said testing, cleaning and removal from the said contractor and to restore the grading and landscaping on the property to the existing or a comparable condition to which it was prior to the removal of the said fuel oil tank.

ENV-14

Underground Tank—Seller to Remove

APPENDIX

FRANCHISE

FRANCH–1

Condition—Buyer to Approve Documentation

This offer is conditional upon the Buyer reviewing the terms of any agreements, contracts, between the Seller and _____("Franchisor") with respect to the purchase of the business and finding such terms to be satisfactory to the Buyer in the Buyer's sole and absolute discretion. The Seller will provide copies of such Franchise Agreement within _____ days of acceptance of this offer. Unless the Buyer gives notice in writing to the Seller personally or in accordance with any other provisions for delivery of notice in this Agreement of Purchase and Sale or any Schedule thereto not later than 5 p.m. on the _____ day of _____, 20_____, that this condition is fulfilled, this offer shall be null and void and the deposit shall be returned to the Buyer in full without deduction. This condition is included for the sole benefit of the Buyer and may be waived at the Buyer's sole option by notice in writing to the Seller as aforesaid within the time period stated herein.

FRANCH–2

Condition—Buyer to be Approved

This offer is conditional upon the Buyer being approved by _____("Franchisor") with respect to the purchase of the business and the assumption of any agreements or contracts between the Seller and the Franchisor. Unless the Buyer gives notice in writing to the Seller personally or in accordance with any other provisions for delivery of notice in this Agreement of Purchase and Sale or any Schedule thereto not later than 5 p.m. on the _____ day of _____, 20_____, that this condition is fulfilled, this offer shall be null and void and the deposit shall be returned to the Buyer in full without deduction.

FUEL TANK

FUEL–1

Acknowledgement— Adjustment Clause

The Seller and Buyer agree that there shall be no adjustment on completion for the unmetered cost of fuel.

GREEN ENERGY

GREEN–1

Condition—MicroFIT Contract

This offer is conditional upon the Buyer reviewing all requisite documentation relating to the Seller's MicroFIT contract with the Ontario Power Authority and determining the terms of the contract are satisfactory to the Buyer in the Buyer's sole and absolute discretion. Unless the Buyer gives notice in writing delivered to the Seller personally or in accordance with any other provisions for the delivery of notice in this Agreement of Purchase and Sale or any Schedule thereto not later than _____ p.m. on the _____ day of _____, 20_____, that this condition is fulfilled, this offer shall become null and void and the deposit shall be returned to the Buyer in full without deduction. This condition is included for the benefit of the Buyer and may be waived at the Buyer's sole option by notice in writing to the Seller as aforesaid within the time period stated herein.

The Seller agrees to provide the Buyer with a copy of the requisite documentation within _____ days of the acceptance of this offer.

GREEN–2

Acknowledgement— MicroFIT Contract

The Buyer acknowledges the Buyer has reviewed all requisite documents relating to the Seller's MicroFIT contract with the Ontario Power Authority and understands the Buyer must take the necessary steps to obtain the assignment of the contract to the Buyer, and understands that failure to obtain the required assignment will result in termination of the MicroFIT contract.

APPENDIX

The Buyer acknowledges that any decommissioning of the renewable energy facility will require that all governmental, legislative and contractual requirements must be complied with at the expense of the property owner, and may include, without limitation, the requirements that the facility must be dismantled and removed, the site and any lands and water negatively affected by the facility must be restored to and left in a safe and clean condition.

GREEN-3
Decommissioning
Renewable Energy Facility

....

The Buyer acknowledges and accepts that the subject property is located in an area where renewable energy producing equipment is proposed or already in operation, including, but not limited to Wind Turbines and Solar Energy Collectors.

GREEN-4
Renewable Energy Projects

....

The Seller represents and warrants to the Buyer that to the best of the Seller's knowledge and belief there are no wind turbine(s) installed or proposed to be installed within _____ of the boundaries of the subject property. The parties agree that this representation and warranty shall survive and not merge on completion of this transaction.

GREEN-5
Wind Turbines—Warranty

CAUTION: The topic of Green Energy and Renewable Energy can be very complicated and Members must be prepared to create specific clauses to deal with unique circumstances, as required.

NOTE: Members should also be aware that Renewable Energy installations can affect the insurability of a property and clauses may be required to verify the insurability of a property and the costs of insurance.

HERITAGE

The parties hereto acknowledge that the subject property is/may be designated as a Heritage Property and is subject to the provisions of the *Ontario Heritage Act, 1974*. The Buyer acknowledges that the Seller has made this disclosure. The Buyer accepts the property with this designation and agrees to continue with this transaction.

HERIT-1
Ontario Heritage Act
Designation

HST

NOTE 1: HST is applicable to new properties, substantially renovated properties, properties where input tax credits have been claimed.

NOTE 2: The sale of large parcels of land and vacant land can be subject to capital gains and/or HST. This can depend upon present and future use, who is selling, and who is buying. EXPERT ADVICE SHOULD BE SOUGHT.

The Buyer shall deliver to the Seller on closing:

HST-1
HST Buyer is Registrant
(Commercial Component)

1. a statutory declaration that the Buyer is a registrant within the meaning of Part IX of the *Excise Tax Act of Canada* (the "Act") and that the Buyer's registration is in full force and effect;

2. reasonable evidence of the Buyer's registration under the Act; and

3. an undertaking by the Buyer to remit any tax eligible under the Act in respect of this transaction and to indemnify the Seller against all loss, costs and damages resulting from the Buyer's failure to do so.

INSPECTION OF PROPERTY

INSP–1

**Condition—
Inspection of Property by a
Home Inspector—
General Inspection**

This Offer is conditional upon the inspection of the subject property by a home inspector at the Buyer's own expense, and the obtaining of a report satisfactory to the Buyer in the Buyer's sole and absolute discretion. Unless the Buyer gives notice in writing delivered to the Seller personally or in accordance with any other provisions for the delivery of notice in this Agreement of Purchase and Sale or any Schedule thereto not later than _____ p.m. on the _____ day of _____, 20_____, that this condition is fulfilled, this Offer shall be null and void and the deposit shall be returned to the Buyer in full without deduction. The Seller agrees to co-operate in providing access to the property for the purpose of this inspection. This condition is included for the benefit of the Buyer and may be waived at the Buyer's sole option by notice in writing to the Seller as aforesaid within the time period stated herein.

INSP–2

**Condition—Inspection of
Property by a Home
Inspector—General
Inspection—Condo**

This Offer is conditional upon the inspection of the unit and common elements by a home inspector at the Buyer's own expense and the obtaining of a report satisfactory to the Buyer in the Buyer's sole and absolute discretion. Unless the Buyer gives notice in writing delivered to the Seller personally or in accordance with any other provisions for the delivery of notice in this Agreement of Purchase and Sale or any Schedule thereto not later than _____ p.m. on the _____ day of _____, 20_____, that this condition is fulfilled, this Offer shall be null and void and the deposit shall be returned to the Buyer in full without deduction. The Seller agrees to co-operate in providing access to the unit for the purpose of this inspection. This condition is included for the benefit of the Buyer and may be waived at the Buyer's sole option by notice in writing to the Seller as aforesaid within the time period stated herein.

INSP–3

**Condition—
Inspection of Property—
Limited Inspection**

This Offer is conditional upon the Buyer, at the Buyer's own expense, having the relevant building(s) inspected by a bona fide home inspection firm to determine that the building(s) are in sound structural and mechanical condition and that the electrical system is safe and adequate, and that, in the written opinion of the home inspection firm, all deficiencies can be remedied at a cost not greater than _____ ($ _____). Unless the Buyer gives notice in writing delivered to the Seller personally or in accordance with any other provisions for the delivery of notice in this Agreement of Purchase and Sale or any Schedule thereto not later than _____ p.m. on the _____ day of _____ 20_____, that this condition is fulfilled, this Offer shall be null and void and the deposit shall be returned to the Buyer in full without deduction. The Seller agrees to co-operate in providing access to the property for the purpose of this inspection. The Seller agrees this condition is included for the benefit of the Buyer and may be waived at the Buyer's sole option by notice in writing to the Seller as aforesaid within the time period stated herein.

INSP–4

**Condition—
Inspection of Property—
Seller Allowed to Remedy**

This Offer is conditional upon the inspection of the subject property by a home inspector at the Buyer's own expense and the obtaining of a report satisfactory to the Buyer or, if not satisfactory to the Buyer, a report revealing deficiencies in the property which the Seller is willing and able to remedy. Unless the Buyer gives notice in writing delivered to the Seller personally or in accordance with any other provisions for the delivery of notice in this Agreement of Purchase and Sale or any Schedule thereto not later than _____ p.m. on the _____ day of _____, 20_____, that this condition is fulfilled, this Offer shall be null and void and the deposit shall be returned to the Buyer in full without deduction. The Seller agrees to co-operate in providing access to the property for the purpose of this inspection. This condition is included for the benefit of the Buyer and may be waived at the Buyer's sole option by notice in writing to the Seller as aforesaid within the time period stated herein.

APPENDIX

This Offer is conditional upon the inspection of the subject unit by a home inspector at the Buyer's own expense and the obtaining of a report satisfactory to the Buyer or, if not satisfactory to the Buyer, a report revealing deficiencies in the unit which the Seller is willing and able to remedy. Unless the Buyer gives notice in writing to the Seller personally or in accordance with any other provisions for the delivery of notice in this Agreement of Purchase and Sale or any Schedule thereto not later than _____ p.m. on the _____ day of _____, 20_____, that this condition is fulfilled, this Offer shall be null and void and the deposit shall be returned to the Buyer in full without deduction. The Seller agrees this condition is included for the benefit of the Buyer and may be waived at the Buyer's sole option by notice in writing to the Seller as aforesaid within the time period stated herein.

INSP–5

Condition—
Inspection—Seller Allowed
to Remedy—Condo

This Offer is conditional upon the Buyer or the Buyer's appointed representative inspecting the subject property for termites and obtaining a report satisfactory to the Buyer at the Buyer's own expense. Unless the Buyer gives notice in writing delivered to the Seller personally or in accordance with any other provisions for the delivery of notice in this Agreement of Purchase and Sale or any Schedule thereto not later than _____ p.m. on the _____ day of _____, 20_____, that this condition is fulfilled, this Offer shall be null and void and the deposit shall be returned to the Buyer in full without deduction. The Seller agrees to co-operate in providing access to the property for the purpose of this inspection. This condition is included for the benefit of the Buyer and may be waived at the Buyer's sole option by notice in writing to the Seller as aforesaid within the time period stated herein.

INSP–6

Condition—
Inspection of Property—
Termites

This Offer is conditional upon the inspection of the subject property by _____ and the obtaining of a report satisfactory to the Buyer at the Buyer's own expense. Unless the Buyer gives notice in writing delivered to the Seller personally or in accordance with any other provisions for the delivery of notice in this Agreement of Purchase and Sale or any Schedule thereto not later than _____ p.m. on the _____ day of _____, 20_____, that this condition is fulfilled, this Offer shall be null and void and the deposit shall be returned to the Buyer in full without deduction. The Seller agrees to co-operate in providing access to the property for the purpose of this inspection. This condition is included for the benefit of the Buyer and may be waived at the Buyer's sole option by notice in writing to the Seller as aforesaid within the time period stated herein.

INSP–7

Condition—
Inspection of Property—
Third Party

This Offer is conditional upon the inspection of the unit and common elements by _____ and the obtaining of a report satisfactory to the Buyer at the Buyer's own expense. Unless the Buyer gives notice in writing delivered to the Seller personally or in accordance with any other provisions for the delivery of notice in this Agreement of Purchase and Sale or any Schedule thereto not later than _____ p.m. on the _____ day of _____, 20_____, that this condition is fulfilled, this Offer shall be null and void and the deposit shall be returned to the Buyer in full without deduction. The Seller agrees to cooperate in providing access to the unit for the purpose of this inspection. This condition is included for the benefit of the Buyer and may be waived at the Buyer's sole option by notice in writing to the Seller as aforesaid within the time period stated herein.

INSP–8

Condition—
Inspection of Property
by a Third Party—Condo

APPENDIX

INSP-9

Condition— Retrofit Inspection of Property Fire—General Inspection

This Offer is conditional upon the inspection of the subject property at the Buyer's own expense, and the obtaining of a report satisfactory to the Buyer in the Buyer's sole and absolute discretion respecting retrofitting pursuant to and in compliance with the *Fire Protection and Prevention Act, 1997*, and its regulations as amended from time to time. Unless the Buyer gives notice in writing delivered to the Seller personally or in accordance with any other provisions for the delivery of notice in this Agreement of Purchase and Sale or any Schedule thereto not later than _____ p.m. on the _____ day of _____, 20_____, that this condition is fulfilled, this Offer shall be null and void and the deposit shall be returned to the Buyer in full without deduction. The Seller agrees to co-operate in providing access to the property for the purpose of this inspection. This condition is included for the benefit of the Buyer and may be waived at the Buyer's sole option by notice in writing to the Seller as aforesaid within the time period stated herein.

INSP-10

Condition— Retrofit Inspection of Property Electricity— General Inspection

This Offer is conditional upon the inspection of the subject property at the Buyer's own expense, and the obtaining of a report satisfactory to the Buyer in the Buyer's sole and absolute discretion respecting retrofitting pursuant to and in compliance with the *Electricity Act, 1998*, and its regulations as amended from time to time. Unless the Buyer gives notice in writing delivered to the Seller personally or in accordance with any other provisions for the delivery of notice in this Agreement of Purchase and Sale or any Schedule thereto not later than _____ p.m. on the _____ day of _____, 20_____, that this condition is fulfilled, this Offer shall be null and void and the deposit shall be returned to the Buyer in full without deduction. The Seller agrees to co-operate in providing access to the property for the purpose of this inspection. This condition is included for the benefit of the Buyer and may be waived at the Buyer's sole option by notice in writing to the Seller as aforesaid within the time period stated herein.

NOTE: Both conditions, INSP–9 and INSP–10, are required to be fulfilled for a Retrofit Certificate of Compliance.

INSP-11

Condition— WETT Inspection

This offer is conditional upon the Buyer obtaining at the Buyer's expense a Wood Energy Technology Transfer (WETT) inspection, and obtaining a report satisfactory to the Buyer in the Buyer's sole and absolute discretion. Unless the Buyer gives notice in writing delivered to the Seller personally or in accordance with any other provisions for the delivery of notice in this Agreement of Purchase and Sale or any Schedule thereto not later than _____ p.m. on the _____ day of _____, 20_____ , that this condition is fulfilled, this offer shall be null and void and the deposit shall be returned to the Buyer in full without deduction. The Seller agrees to co-operate in providing access to the property for the purpose of this inspection. This condition is included for the benefit of the Buyer and may be waived at the Buyer's sole option by notice in writing to the Seller as aforesaid within the time period stated herein.

INSP-12

Delivery of Report

In the event the foregoing condition is not fulfilled or waived by the Buyer, the Buyer agrees to provide the Seller with a true copy of the Inspection Report and all estimates related thereto prior to the return of the deposit herein.

INSP-13

Inspection of Systems

Upon acceptance of this Offer, the Buyer shall be allowed to enter the premises, from time to time, after permission from the Seller, for the purpose of obtaining information about heating and electrical systems, maintenance, and any other related utility service for the building.

APPENDIX

The Buyer shall have the right to inspect the property prior to completion for the purpose of inspection for _____
_____
[e.g., financing, insurance, estimate(s) from contractor(s) etc.] to a maximum of _____ time(s), at a mutually agreed upon time(s). The Seller agrees to provide access to the property for the purpose of the inspection(s).

INSP-14

Right of Inspection Prior to Completion

. . . .

The Buyer shall have the right to inspect the property one further time prior to completion, at a mutually agreed upon time, provided that written notice is given to the Seller. The Seller agrees to provide access to the property for the purpose of this inspection.

INSP-15

Right of Re-inspection Prior to Completion

. . . .

The Seller(s) acknowledge(s) and consent(s) to a third party taking photographs/videos of the property as required for the purpose of an inspection with respect to the above.

NOTE: This clause may be added to an inspection condition (e.g., appraisal, home inspection, when there is an expectation that photos/videos will be taken by the third party).

INSP-16

Seller's Consent for Photos/Videos

INSURANCE

This offer is conditional on the Buyer arranging insurance for the property satisfactory to the Buyer in the Buyer's sole and absolute discretion. Unless the Buyer gives notice in writing delivered to the Seller personally or in accordance with any other provisions for the delivery of notice in this Agreement of Purchase and Sale or any Schedule thereto not later than _____ p.m. on the _____ day of _____, 20_____, that this condition is fulfilled, this offer shall be null and void and the deposit shall be returned to the Buyer in full without deduction. The Seller agrees to co-operate in providing access to the property, if necessary, for any inspection of the property required for the fulfillment of this condition. This condition is included for the benefit of the Buyer and may be waived at the Buyer's sole option by notice in writing to the Seller as aforesaid within the time period stated herein.

NOTE: Due to the nature of this clause, a short time frame should be chosen for this condition.

INSUR-1

Condition— Arranging Insurance

. . . .

This offer is conditional upon the Buyer arranging insurance on the property for the following named perils: _____ at a yearly cost not to exceed _____, excluding applicable taxes. Unless the Buyer gives notice in writing delivered to the Seller personally or in accordance with any other provisions for the delivery of notice in this Agreement of Purchase and Sale or any Schedule thereto not later than _____ p.m. on the _____ day of _____, 20_____, that this condition is fulfilled, this Offer shall be null and void and the deposit shall be returned to the Buyer in full without deduction. The Seller agrees to co-operate in providing access to the property, if necessary, for any inspection of the property required for the fulfillment of this condition. This condition is included for the benefit of the Buyer and may be waived at the Buyer's sole option by notice in writing to the Seller as aforesaid within the time period stated herein.

INSUR-2

Condition— Arranging Insurance— Cost Not to Exceed

KITEC/PLUMBING

KIT–1

Seller Warrants and Represents—No Kitec Plumbing on Property

The Seller represents and warrants to the Buyer that during the time the Seller owned the property, the Seller has not installed in any building on the property Kitec plumbing, any fittings for Kitec plumbing nor any Kitec Plumbing Systems ("Kitec") and that to the best of the undersigned's knowledge, no building on the property contains or has ever contained Kitec. This representation and warranty shall survive and not merge on the completion of the above transaction, and if the building is part of a multiple unit building, this warranty shall only apply to the part of the building, which is subject to this transaction.

KIT–2

Buyer Acknowledges—Kitec Plumbing on Property

The Buyer acknowledges that the property and buildings and structures has had installed therein or thereon Kitec plumbing, fittings for Kitec plumbing or Kitec Plumbing Systems ("Kitec") and acknowledges that the Seller makes no representations and/or warranties with respect to the state of repair of the premises respecting the said Kitec and the Buyer accepts the property and the buildings and structures thereon in their present state and in an "as is" condition.

LANDLEASE

LAND/LSE–1

Condition— Landlease— Landlord's Approval

This Offer is conditional upon the Landlord consenting to the assignment of the landlease to the Buyer. Unless the Buyer gives notice in writing delivered to the Seller personally or in accordance with any other provisions for the delivery of notice in this Agreement of Purchase and Sale or any Schedule thereto not later than _____ p.m. on the _____ day of _____, 20_____, that this condition has been fulfilled, this Offer shall become null and void and the deposit shall be returned to the Buyer in full without deduction. The Buyer hereby agrees to proceed immediately to make an application and provide such material as may be required by the Landlord for approval of the Buyer as Tenant.

NOTE: This clause is a true Condition Precedent and neither a Seller nor a Buyer is entitled to waive this condition.

LAND/LSE–2

Landlease— Buyer to Assume

The Seller agrees to assign, and the Buyer agrees to assume, the existing landlease on the property, with [insert name of Tenant], a copy of which is attached as Schedule "_____".

NOTE: See also LAND/LSE–3 Option to Purchase and LAND/LSE–1 Condition—Landlease—Landlord's Approval.

LAND/LSE–3

Landlease— Option to Purchase

During the currency of this landlease, the Buyer shall have the option of purchasing the land for a sum of _____ ($ _____), which is not included in the above purchase price.

NOTE: See also LAND/LSE–2 Buyer to Assume and LAND/LSE–1 Condition—Landlease—Landlord's Approval.

LAWYER'S APPROVAL

This Offer is conditional upon the approval of the terms hereof by the Buyer's Solicitor. Unless the Buyer gives notice in writing delivered to the Seller personally or in accordance with any other provisions for the delivery of notice in this Agreement of Purchase and Sale or any Schedule thereto not later than _____ p.m. on the _____ day of _____, 20_____, that this condition is fulfilled, this Offer shall be null and void and the deposit shall be returned to the Buyer in full without deduction. This condition is included for the benefit of Buyer and may be waived at the Buyer's sole option by notice in writing to the Seller as aforesaid within the time period stated herein.

LAW–1

Condition—
Lawyer's Approval—Buyer

....

This Offer is conditional upon the approval of the terms hereof by the Seller's Solicitor. Unless the Seller gives notice in writing delivered to the Buyer or to the Buyer's address as hereinafter indicated personally or in accordance with any other provisions for the delivery of notice in this Agreement of Purchase and Sale or any Schedule thereto not later than _____ p.m. on the _____ day of _____, 20_____, that this condition is fulfilled, this Offer shall be null and void and the deposit shall be returned to the Buyer in full without deduction. This condition is included for the benefit of Seller and may be waived at the Seller's sole option by notice in writing to the Buyer as aforesaid within the time period stated herein.

LAW–2

Condition—
Lawyer's Approval—Seller

....

The Parties to this Agreement acknowledge that the real estate Broker(s) so named in this Agreement has recommended that the Parties obtain independent professional advice prior to signing this document. The Parties further acknowledge that no information provided by such real estate Broker(s) is to be construed as legal, tax or environmental advice.

LAW–3

Legal, Accounting or
Environmental Advice

LEASE APPROVAL

Upon acceptance of this Offer, the Seller agrees to provide the Buyer with copies of all leases on the property. Upon review by the Buyer, if the terms of said leases are unacceptable to the Buyer, in the Buyer's sole and absolute discretion, the Buyer shall have the right to terminate this Agreement by notice in writing delivered to the Seller personally or in accordance with any other provisions for the delivery of notice in this Agreement of Purchase and Sale or any Schedule thereto not later than _____ p.m. on the _____ day of _____, 20_____, and the deposit shall be returned to the Buyer in full without deduction.

LEASE/APP–1

Condition—Buyer's Right
to Review Leases
(Condition Subsequent)

APPENDIX

LEASE/APP–2

Condition—Inspection of
Leases and Real Property
(Condition Subsequent)

This Agreement is conditional upon the Buyer inspecting and approving the real property, the Leases (or Offers to Lease if no Leases are available), and improvements. Unless the Buyer notifies the Seller in writing delivered to the Seller personally or in accordance with any other provisions for the delivery of notice in this Agreement of Purchase and Sale or any Schedule thereto not later than _____ p.m. on the _____ day of _____, 20_____, that the Buyer is not satisfied with any of the above inspections, the Buyer shall be deemed to have waived this condition and this Agreement shall remain valid and binding.

The Seller agrees to:

a) Supply the Buyer not later than _____ p.m. on the _____ day of _____, 20_____, with all Leases and/or Offers to Lease which are in force at the time of acceptance of this Offer and a set of "as built" building plans for the development of the site (if such are in its possession);

b) Allow the Buyer, its agents and employees, to inspect the land and improvements at mutually convenient time or times; and

c) Authorize all governmental and other authorities having jurisdiction over the real property to release to the Buyer all information such authorities have on file respecting the property.

Should the Buyer hire agents, the cost and responsibility of such work shall be for the account of the Buyer. The Buyer covenants and agrees to restore the property forthwith after inspection to its pre-existing physical condition prior to the time of the first such inspection.

If the Buyer is not satisfied with the results of the Buyer's inspection, the Buyer shall so notify the Seller, who may elect to remedy such results. If the Seller does not remedy such results to the satisfaction of the Buyer, the Buyer may terminate this Agreement by notice in writing delivered to the Seller personally or in accordance with any other provisions for the delivery of notice in this Agreement of Purchase and Sale or any Schedule thereto not later than _____ p.m. on the _____ day of _____, 20_____, and the deposit shall be returned to the Buyer in full without deduction.

The Buyer agrees to treat the results of such inspections in a strictly confidential manner and not to disclose the results to a third party except where required by law. There shall be no compulsory requirement to disclose the result to the Seller.

LEASE/COMMERCIAL

This Offer is conditional upon the approval of the terms hereof by the Landlord's Board of Directors. Unless the Landlord gives notice in writing delivered to the Tenant personally or in accordance with any other provisions for the delivery of notice in this Agreement to Lease or any Schedule thereto not later than _____ p.m. on the _____ day of _____, 20_____, that this condition is fulfilled, this Offer shall be null and void and the deposit shall be returned to the Tenant in full without deduction.

NOTE: This Clause is a true condition precedent and neither Landlord nor Tenant is entitled to waive this condition.

LEASE/COMM–1

Condition—
Approval from Board of
Directors—Landlord

....

This Offer is conditional upon the approval of the terms hereof by the Tenant's Board of Directors. Unless the Tenant gives notice in writing delivered to the Landlord personally or in accordance with any other provisions for the delivery of notice in this Agreement to Lease or any Schedule thereto not later than _____ p.m. on the _____ day of _____, 20_____, that this condition is fulfilled, this Offer shall be null and void and the deposit shall be returned to the Tenant in full without deduction.

NOTE: This Clause is a true condition precedent and neither Landlord nor Tenant is entitled to waive this condition.

LEASE/COMM–2

Condition—
Approval from Board of
Directors—Tenant

....

The Landlord shall have until not later than _____ p.m. on the _____ day of _____, 20_____, to verify that the financial covenant of the Tenant is satisfactory to the Landlord. If the Tenant's covenant is not acceptable to the Landlord, the Landlord may terminate this Agreement by notice in writing delivered to the Tenant personally or in accordance with any other provisions for the delivery of notice in this Agreement to Lease or any Schedule thereto within the time period stated above and the Tenant's deposit shall be returned in full without deduction.

LEASE/COMM–3

Condition—Financial
Covenant of Tenant
(Condition Subsequent)

....

This Offer is conditional upon the approval of the terms hereof by the Landlord's Solicitor. Unless the Landlord gives notice in writing delivered to the Tenant personally or in accordance with any other provisions for the delivery of notice in this Agreement to Lease or any Schedule thereto not later than _____ p.m. on the _____ day of _____, 20_____, that this condition is fulfilled, this Offer shall be null and void and the deposit shall be returned to the Tenant in full without deduction. This condition is included for the benefit of the Landlord and may be waived at the Landlord's sole option by notice in writing to the Tenant as aforesaid within the time period stated herein.

LEASE/COMM–4

Condition—
Lawyer's Approval—
Landlord

....

This Offer is conditional upon the approval of the terms hereof by the Tenant's Solicitor. Unless the Tenant gives notice in writing delivered to the Landlord personally or in accordance with any other provisions for the delivery of notice in this Agreement to Lease or any Schedule thereto not later than _____ p.m. on the _____ day of _____, 20_____, that this condition is fulfilled, this Offer shall be null and void and the deposit shall be returned to the Tenant in full without deduction. This condition is included for the benefit of the Tenant and may be waived at the Tenant's sole option by notice in writing to the Landlord as aforesaid within the time period stated herein.

LEASE/COMM–5

Condition—
Lawyer's Approval—Tenant

APPENDIX

LEASE/COMM-6

**Condition—
Occupancy Permit
(Condition Subsequent)**

The Tenant shall obtain an occupancy permit from the relevant municipality prior to taking occupancy. If the Tenant gives notice in writing delivered to the Landlord personally or in accordance with any other provisions for the delivery of notice in this Agreement to Lease or any Schedule thereto not later than _____ p.m. on the _____ day of_____, 20_____, that an occupancy permit is not obtainable prior to the date set for occupancy, this Agreement, and the Lease, if signed, shall be terminated and the Tenant's deposit shall be returned in full without deduction. The Landlord agrees to provide the Tenant with all of the plans and drawings required for said permit, at the Landlord's expense.

LEASE/COMM-7

**Condition—Zoning
Satisfaction (Condition
Subsequent))**

The Tenant shall have until not later than _____ p.m. on the _____ day of _____, 20_____, to satisfy itself that the property is zoned in final and binding form under the relevant zoning bylaws and official plan to permit it to develop or use the property for the purpose of _____. If the Tenant is not so satisfied at the Tenant's sole and arbitrary discretion, the Tenant may terminate this Agreement by notice in writing delivered to the Landlord personally or in accordance with any other provisions for the delivery of notice in this Agreement to Lease or any Schedule thereto within the time period stated above and the deposit shall be returned to the Tenant in full without deduction.

LEASE/COMM-8

Agreement to Sign Lease

Prior to the Tenant taking possession of the demised premises, the parties shall execute the Lease in the form attached hereto, as Schedule "_____" of the Agreement to Lease.

LEASE/COMM-9

**Alterations and
Improvements**

The Tenant may make any necessary alterations and improvements to said premises, at the Tenant's own expense, subject to the Landlord's written consent, and such consent shall not be unreasonably withheld. The Tenant may, however, make any necessary minor internal improvements to said premises, at the Tenant's own expense, without the Landlord's consent and in compliance with all applicable governmental bylaws and codes governing the use of the demised premises.

LEASE/COMM-10

Arbitration

All disputes or differences arising in regard to the contract shall be settled by arbitration in accordance with the *Arbitration Act of Ontario, 1991*, or any subsequent legislation in effect at the date of commencement of such arbitration.

NOTE: Care must be taken not to create a conflict with this clause and clauses providing for settlement of disputes or differences by alternate means.

LEASE/COMM-11

Area Defined

The Landlord and Tenant agree that the rentable area of the leased premises is about _____ square feet, with the actual area to be adjusted accordingly, should the actual measurement differ. The area shall be measured by using the current Building Owners and Managers Association Standards.

LEASE/COMM-12

Area Measurement

The Landlord and the Tenant agree that, should the actual square footage differ from the area stated herein, the annual rental rate shall be adjusted to reflect the actual square footage of the demised premises.

LEASE/COMM-13

Assign or Sub-lease

The Lease shall contain a clause permitting the Tenant to assign or sub-lease the demised premises, in whole or part, at any time or times, with consent of the Landlord, and such consent shall not be unreasonably withheld or delayed. Provided that consent as aforesaid shall be required if the Tenant is a corporation and there has been a change of control in the corporation, notwithstanding, the Tenant shall remain on covenant.

APPENDIX

The Tenant shall have the right to assign its interests under this Lease to a limited company, partnership, or person. The Tenant agrees to send written notice to the Landlord of its intention to assign to the Landlord and obtain the Landlord's written approval prior to any assignment. Such approval shall not be arbitrarily or unreasonably withheld or delayed.

LEASE/COMM-14

Assignment—
Approval by Landlord

It is understood and agreed between the Parties that the Tenant may assign the Lease to an individual, company, partnership or joint venture in which it has a financial interest without consent of the Landlord, provided that the Tenant shall not be relieved of any liability under this Agreement.

LEASE/COMM-15

Assignment Without Approval

The Tenant's use of the premises is to comply with all requirements of the municipal zoning bylaws, the requirements of the Ministry of the Environment and the rules and regulations of the *Environmental Protection Act* and any amendments thereto.

The Tenant agrees to indemnify and hold harmless the Landlord from and against any claims, demands, losses, costs, damages, actions, suits or proceedings which may be brought or commenced by anyone or any group including any environmental agency or group as a result of the Tenant's use of the premises or any breach by the Tenant of any rules, bylaws, and regulations.

The Tenant warrants that no noxious or environmentally unfriendly chemicals or products shall be allowed to enter the drains throughout the lease term, and upon vacating the premises, no such chemicals or products shall be left on the premises.

LEASE/COMM-16

Chemicals—
Compliance with Regulations

The Tenant covenants to comply with all applicable governmental bylaws and codes governing the use of the demised premises.

LEASE/COMM-17

Compliance with By-laws and Codes

The Tenant hereby covenants and agrees that the contents, terms and conditions of this Agreement and the Lease to be executed shall be kept strictly confidential. It is understood that the Tenant will not, without written permission of the Landlord, discuss or reveal the terms of this Agreement with other Parties including, but not limited to other tenants, prospective tenants, real estate agents, suppliers or customers, save and except for the legal and financial advisors of the Tenant.

LEASE/COMM-18

Confidentiality

The Landlord may require that all mechanical, electrical, roofing and structural work to be done with respect to the leased premises, by the Tenant at any time, be carried out by the Landlord's contractors and employees at the Tenant's costs, such costs to be competitive with the prices obtained by the Tenant from its contractors.

LEASE/COMM-19

Contractors to be Used

At any time after the _____ day of _____, 20_____, should the Landlord undertake to proceed with full or partial demolition of the building, then upon_____ full calendar months written notice from the Landlord to the Tenant, of the Landlord's undertaking to demolish, the Tenant agrees to vacate the premises, and surrender the unexpired portion of the term, at the expiry of the above notice period. Upon surrender of the premises, the Landlord shall pay to the Tenant by way of compensation for improvements an amount standing in the same proportion to the cost to the Tenant of leasehold improvements made by the Tenant pursuant to the provisions of the Lease or with the consent of the Landlord as the unexpired portion of the term stands to the period of time from the Tenant's payment of such cost to the end of the unexpired portion of the term.

LEASE/COMM-20

Demolition Clause

APPENDIX

LEASE/COMM–21

Early Occupancy— Gross Rent Free

It is understood and agreed that, provided a formal lease has been executed by both the Landlord and the Tenant, and upon Tenant providing evidence of Tenant's insurance satisfactory to the Landlord, the Tenant shall be granted possession of the demised premises on the _____ day of _____, 20_____, gross rent free to the Lease Commencement Date, in order to prepare the premises for the operation of its business, provided that, during the said rent-free period, the Tenant shall comply with all the terms and conditions of the lease.

NOTE: This Clause should be used in conjunction with an Insurance Clause specifically outlining insurance requirements.

LEASE/COMM–22

Early Occupancy— Net Rent Free

It is understood and agreed that, provided a formal lease has been executed by both the Landlord and the Tenant, and upon Tenant providing evidence of Tenant's insurance satisfactory to the Landlord, the Tenant shall be granted possession of the demised premises on the _____ day of _____, 20_____, net rent free to the Lease Commencement Date, in order to prepare the premises for the operation of its business, provided that, during the said rent-free period, the Tenant shall comply with all the terms and conditions of the lease, and be responsible for the Tenant's proportionate share of all expenses of the property, save and except for payment of minimum rent.

LEASE/COMM–23

Electrical and Mechanical Equipment in Good Working Order

The Landlord warrants that all mechanical, heating, ventilating, air conditioning equipment (HVAC), and electrical equipment will be in good working order, normal wear and tear excepted, on or before the occupancy date set herein.

LEASE/COMM–24

Entire Agreement

It is understood and agreed that the contract resulting from the acceptance of this Offer shall be as expressly set out herein and in the schedules attached hereto and, except as expressly set out herein and in the attached schedules hereto, there are no collateral or other representations, warranties, conditions or agreements between the Landlord and Tenant, and none shall be implied.

LEASE/COMM–25

Escalation Clause for Property Taxes

The Tenant shall pay its proportionate share of any increase in property taxes and local improvement levies over the base year of 20_____.

LEASE/COMM–26

First Right of Refusal on Vacant Space—Lease

The Tenant shall have the first right of refusal on adjacent space if and when such space becomes available. In the event that the Landlord receives an Offer which it finds acceptable, it shall so notify the Tenant in writing, and the Tenant shall have 72 hours to match the Offer, by notice in writing delivered to the Landlord, failing which the Tenant shall have lost its first right of refusal. For purposes herein, adjacent space shall be deemed to be space on the first floor above, the first floor below, and/or adjoining space on the same floor as the subject unit.

The Landlord covenants and agrees with the Tenant that, during the term of the lease or any renewal thereof, the Landlord will give the Tenant three (3) business days to submit an Offer upon the same terms and conditions as any bona fide Offer to purchase the leased property that the Landlord has received and is willing to accept, and any Lease executed by the Landlord and Tenant shall include this first right of refusal. The Landlord shall give the Tenant written notice of such bona fide Offer and a copy of such Offer to the Tenant. In the event that the Tenant submits to the Landlord, within the time period described above, a written and signed Offer to purchase the property upon the same terms and conditions as the Offer initially received by the Landlord, the Landlord shall accept the Offer submitted by the Tenant. In the event that the Tenant fails to deliver to the Landlord, within the time limit described above, a written and signed Offer to purchase the property on the same terms and conditions as the initial Offer, the Landlord shall be at liberty to sell the property to the Buyer who submitted the initial Offer. Should the Tenant exercise the said first right of refusal, the Landlord agrees to pay the Agents so named in this Agreement, (or their successor companies) a fee of _____.

LEASE/COMM–27

First Right of Refusal to Purchase

It is agreed that the lease arising from this Offer shall be based on a rental rate which includes the Landlord paying realty taxes, outside maintenance, building insurance, heat, hydro and water rates that pertain to the subject leased premises.

LEASE/COMM–28

Gross Lease

It is understood and agreed that any lease arising from this Offer shall be based on a rental rate which shall include the Tenant's proportionate share of realty taxes, outside maintenance, building insurance, heat, hydro, water rates, and management fees, if any. All inclusions have a base year of 20_____, and are subject to yearly adjustments according to actual increases. Such increases above the base year shall be paid proportionately by the Tenant.

LEASE/COMM–29

Gross Lease with Escalations

The Tenant acknowledges that HST will be collectable by the Landlord on the rent paid and on common area expenses as defined herein.

LEASE/COMM–30

HST—Lease

The obligations created by the Tenant so named herein shall be jointly and severally assumed by the guarantor, whose name is identified at the end of this Agreement, and the guarantor agrees to be bound by the terms herein. In the enforcement of its rights under this guarantee, the Landlord may proceed against the guarantor as if the guarantor were named as Tenant under this Lease.

LEASE/COMM–31

Guarantor

The Lease shall contain a clause requiring the Tenant to obtain insurance, at the expense of the Tenant, as required by the Landlord and which may include insurance on the property and operations of the Tenant, including insurance for fire and such additional perils as are normally insured against, liability insurance, boiler and machinery insurance, plate glass insurance and any other insurance as may be reasonably required by the Landlord.

LEASE/COMM–32

Insurance— Tenant to Obtain

The Tenant shall have the option to cancel the Lease at any time during the Lease, provided that the Tenant gives the Landlord at least _____ days written notice of the Tenant's intention to cancel, and provided that the Tenant is not in default at the time of giving of such notice, or at the time of termination itself. The payment for this option shall be a cancellation fee of _____, payable at the time of giving notice of intention to cancel.

LEASE/COMM–33

Lease Cancellation Privilege

APPENDIX

LEASE/COMM-34

Lease Form

Attached hereto as Schedule "_____" is a copy of the Landlord's standard Lease form, which the Landlord will alter to reflect the business terms defined herein, and the Tenant agrees to sign same subject to minor adjustments as negotiated between the Landlord's and the Tenant's Solicitors, both acting reasonably. In the event of a difference or contradiction between this Offer and the standard Lease form, the terms of the Lease as so negotiated shall prevail, save for manifest error.

LEASE/COMM-35

Net Lease

The rent is to be on an absolutely net basis to the Landlord, and the Tenant agrees to pay as additional rent, its proportionate share of the cost of operation and maintenance for the site, to include but not limited to water, heat, hydro, administrative costs, garbage disposal, realty taxes, outside maintenance and building insurance, (except for structural repairs and items of a capital nature) including all costs of maintaining, repairing, replacing, upkeep, servicing and including, without limiting the generality of the foregoing, other costs and expenses which are defined in the Landlord's lease. These common area costs are currently estimated to be $ _____ per square foot per year, and will be adjusted annually according to actual costs. At the end of the calendar year the Landlord will itemize the common area costs, should the Tenant so request.

LEASE/COMM-36

Option to Purchase

In consideration of the sum of _____ ($ _____) paid by the Tenant to the Landlord, the receipt of which is hereby acknowledged, and in consideration of the terms and conditions herein recited, the Landlord gives to the Tenant an option irrevocable within the time limit herein for acceptance, to purchase, free and clear of all encumbrances, the lands and premises situated at _____ in the _____ of _____ in the _____ of _____. The option shall be open for acceptance by notice in writing delivered to the Landlord not later than _____ p.m. on the _____ day of _____, 20_____. The terms of the purchase shall be the following: _____.

LEASE/COMM-37

Option to Renew—Appraisal

Provided that the Tenant is not in default under the terms of the lease, the Tenant shall have the option to renew said Lease for a further term of _____ (_____) years, on the same terms and conditions, save and except for a further renewal, and the rental rate, which shall be the then current rent for similar location, and on similar lease terms at the time of renewal, provided that the Tenant advises the Landlord in writing _____ (_____) months prior to the end of the term that the Tenant wishes to exercise the Tenant's option to renew. If the Landlord and Tenant do not agree by one month prior to the end of the term on the rental rate for the renewal term, the matter shall be determined by appraisal. The cost of these appraisals shall be shared equally by Landlord and Tenant. Either the Landlord or the Tenant (the "Notifying Party") may by notice (the "First Notice") to the other (the "Other Party") designate an appraiser. The Other Party may within 10 days following the giving of the First Notice designate a second appraiser by notice (the "Second Notice") to the Notifying Party, failing which the first appraiser shall be the sole appraiser. Within 10 days following the giving of the Second Notice (if given), the two appraisers shall appoint a third appraiser, failing which either party may apply to a judge of the Ontario Court (General Division) as persona designata to appoint the third appraiser. The sole appraiser, or if there are three appraisers, the three appraisers, independently of each other, shall proceed to determine the fair market rental rate for the renewal term. If there is a sole appraiser, the rate determined by the sole appraiser shall be the rate for the renewal term. If there are three appraisers, the two rental rates determined by the appraisers which are closest to each other in amount shall be averaged, or, if the highest and lowest rate differ from the other rate by the same amount, all three rates shall be averaged, and the average rate shall be the rate for the renewal term. Any appraiser appointed pursuant hereto shall be a person with the qualifications and experience requisite to appraise property of the type and location of the demised premises.

APPENDIX

Provided that the Tenant is not at any time in default of any covenants within the lease, the Tenant shall be entitled to renew this lease for additional term(s) of _____ (_____) year(s) _____ (_____) month(s) (each) on written notice to the Landlord given not less than _____ months prior to the expiry of the current term at a rental rate to be negotiated. In the event the Landlord and Tenant cannot agree on the fixed minimum rent at least two months prior to expiry of the current lease, the fixed minimum rent for the renewal period shall be determined by arbitration in accordance with the Arbitration Act or any successor or replacement act.

LEASE/COMM-38

Option to Renew—Arbitration

. . . .

The Landlord will provide the Tenant with a minimum of _____ (_____) parking spaces, included in the rent, during the term of the Lease, and the Tenant and the customers, representatives and agents of the Tenant shall have the sole and exclusive right to use these parking spaces set out in Schedule "_____" attached.

LEASE/COMM-39

Parking

. . . .

It is understood and agreed that the Tenant may utilize the existing partitions in the demised premises and may re-locate such partitions and build additional partitions, as required by the Tenant.

LEASE/COMM-40

Partitions

. . . .

The Tenant may build additional partitions, as required, subject to approval by the Landlord, provided that such approval shall not be unreasonably withheld.

LEASE/COMM-41

Partitions with Approval

. . . .

The Tenant's proportionate share of such common area shall be defined as the Tenant's area defined herein, divided by the total rentable area, expressed as a percentage. For purposes herein, the rentable area is defined as _____ and the Tenant's area shall be defined as _____.

LEASE/COMM-42

Proportionate Share

. . . .

Notwithstanding the Lease Commencement Date, the Tenant shall not be obliged to pay minimum rent during the first _____ month(s) of the term, provided, however, that the Tenant shall be responsible to pay for all additional rent from the Lease Commencement Date.

LEASE/COMM-43

Rent Free Period

. . . .

The rent paid by the Tenant to the Landlord shall be _____ per annum, paid 1/12 monthly in advance. This rate shall be on a _____ basis to the Landlord.

NOTE: For use when the Clause is not included in the pre-printed Agreement to Lease.

LEASE/COMM-44

Rental Amount

. . . .

The Tenant may, at the Tenant's own expense, subject to the written approval of the Landlord, install any fittings, fixtures, and partitions that may be necessary for the operation of the Tenant's business, from time to time during the lease term, provided that upon termination of the lease term or renewal thereof, the Tenant shall, at the option of the Landlord, restore the premises to its original condition, at no cost to the Landlord.

LEASE/COMM-45

Restoring Premises to Original Condition

. . . .

The Lease shall contain a clause providing that the Tenant shall have full access at all times from _____ for the purpose of shipping and receiving.

LEASE/COMM-46

Shipping and Receiving Access

APPENDIX

LEASE/COMM–47

Signs

The Tenant may install in, upon, or about the said premises any signs and advertising material which shall remain the property of the Tenant, which the Tenant may remove upon the expiration of the Lease, provided that all damage caused is repaired and the premises left in good repair. All signs and location(s) are to be approved beforehand in writing by the Landlord (such consent not to be unreasonably withheld) and must conform with all applicable governmental bylaws and codes.

LEASE/COMM–48

Space Layout Sketch

The Tenant shall provide the Landlord, within three (3) days of acceptance of this Offer, a layout sketch showing the area that the Landlord is to improve for the Tenant.

LEASE/COMM–49

Structural Penetration

It is agreed and understood that no openings may be made in the floors, walls and roof of the demised premises without the prior written consent of the Landlord. Should the Landlord consent to such work, it shall be done and maintained in a professional manner, at the sole cost of the Tenant.

LEASE/COMM–50

Use of Common Areas

It is understood and agreed that the Tenant shall have the right to use, in common with all others entitled thereto, the common areas of the property, including lobbies, hallways, common rooms, entrances, driveways, parking lots and common lands appurtenant to the building containing the demised premises, and the Tenant covenants that the Tenant will not obstruct these common areas.

LEASE/COMM–51

Work by Landlord

As an inducement for the Tenant to enter into a Lease contract with the Landlord, the Landlord covenants that it will carry out the following work prior to the Tenant taking possession, at no cost to the Tenant: [insert as needed].

LEASE/COMM–52

Workmanlike Manner

Any work carried out by the Landlord, or the Tenant, their employees, agents or contractors shall be done in a workmanlike and professional manner and in compliance with all applicable governmental bylaws and codes governing the use of the demised premises.

LEASE/RESIDENTIAL

NOTE: For the purpose of these clauses "Tenant" and "Landlord" have been used. Tenant = Lessee and Landlord = Lessor. Either term may be used.

NOTE: In all cases please refer to the *Residential Tenancies Act*.

NOTE: It is not lawful for a Landlord to "demand" post-dated cheques for rent as a requirement when leasing residential premises.

This Offer to Lease is conditional upon the Landlord satisfying the Landlord concerning the personal and/or credit worthiness of the Tenant. The Tenant hereby consents to having the Landlord conduct or cause to be conducted a personal and/or credit investigation in respect to the Tenant. Unless the Landlord gives notice in writing delivered to the Tenant personally or in accordance with any other provisions for the delivery of notice in this Agreement to Lease or any Schedule thereto not later than _____p.m. on the _____ day of _____, 20_____, that this condition is fulfilled, this Offer shall be null and void and the deposit shall be returned to the Tenant in full without deduction. This condition is included for the benefit of the Landlord and may be waived at the Landlord's sole option by notice in writing to the Tenant as aforesaid within the time period stated herein.

NOTE: To comply with the *Consumer Reporting Act,* if the Landlord refuses to grant a lease due to information contained in a Consumer Report, the Landlord must give Notice that:

A) Refusal was due to information received from a consumer reporting agency or other person; and

B) Upon written request of the Tenant (within 60 days of notice) the Landlord is obligated to inform the Tenant of the nature and source of the information.

LEASE/RES–1
Condition—Credit Check

- -

Tenant and Landlord agree that an accepted Agreement to Lease shall form a completed lease and no other lease will be signed between the Parties.

NOTE: If using this clause, delete the reference to a lease being drawn from the Agreement to Lease.

LEASE/RES–2
Agreement to Lease Only/
No Lease to be Signed

- -

Landlord shall provide alterations and improvements as detailed on Schedule "_____" attached hereto, at the Landlord's own expense, in a good and workmanlike manner prior to the commencement of the lease.

LEASE/RES–3
Alterations/Improvements

- -

The following appliances belonging to the Landlord are to remain on the premises for the Tenant's use: (include itemized list with description: make, model, and serial number).

LEASE/RES–4
Appliances Included

- -

Landlord represents and warrants that the appliances as listed in this Agreement to Lease will be in good working order at the commencement of the lease term. Tenant agrees to maintain said appliances in a state of ordinary cleanliness at the Tenant's cost.

LEASE/RES–5
Appliances and Landlord/
Tenant Responsibilities

- -

Tenant agrees that any chattels left on the rented premises, and not specifically mentioned herein, may remain and be stored on the premises at no cost to, and shall remain at the risk of, the Landlord.

LEASE/RES–6
Chattels Left by Owner

- -

Landlord agrees to have the carpets professionally cleaned prior to the commencement of the lease at the Landlord's cost, and Tenant shall have the carpets professionally cleaned at end of lease term at Tenant's cost.

LEASE/RES–7
Cleaning of Carpets

APPENDIX

LEASE/RES-8

Condo By-law Compliance

Tenant shall comply with all the Bylaws of the Condominium Corporation.

....

LEASE/RES-9

Consent to Decorate

Tenant agrees not to make any decorating changes to the premises without the express written consent of the Landlord or his authorized agent.

....

LEASE/RES-10

Increase in Rent

Tenant agrees that an increase of _____ % will be in effect on the second year of this lease, in accordance with the guidelines established under the applicable rent review legislation.

NOTE: The increase inserted must not take the rent above the legal maximum.

....

LEASE/RES-11

Maintenance of Grounds

The Tenant shall keep the lawns in good condition and shall not injure or remove the shade trees, shrubbery, hedges or any other tree or plant which may be in, upon or about the premises, and shall keep the sidewalks in front and at the sides of the premises free of snow and ice.

....

LEASE/RES-12

Maintenance of Swimming Pool

Tenant agrees to provide general maintenance for the swimming pool located on the premises, including cleaning, use of chemicals, opening and winterizing of pool. The Landlord shall be responsible for the upkeep of the equipment, including both chattels and fixtures associated with the operation of the pool.

NOTE: The Landlord may wish to reserve the right to open and/or winterize the pool.

....

LEASE/RES-13

Option to Purchase

In consideration of the sum of _____ ($_____) paid by the Tenant to the Landlord, the receipt of which is hereby acknowledged, and in consideration of the terms and conditions herein recited, the Landlord gives to the Tenant an option irrevocable within the time limit herein for acceptance, to purchase, free and clear of all encumbrances, the lands and premises situated at _____ in the _____ of_____ in the _____ of _____. The option shall be open for acceptance by notice in writing delivered to the Landlord not later than _____ p.m. on the _____ day of _____, 20_____. The terms of the purchase shall be the following: _____.

....

LEASE/RES-14

Permission to Sublet— Subject to Landlord's Approval

Landlord shall permit Tenant to sublet during the lease term, subject to approval of the Landlord, which shall not be unreasonably withheld.

....

LEASE/RES-15

Pets

Tenant agrees to be responsible for any repair or replacement cost due to the presence of any pets on the premises. Tenant further agrees that if pets are kept on the premises, Tenant shall, at lease termination, have the carpets professionally cleaned and make any repairs that may be necessary to restore any damages caused by pets.

....

LEASE/RES-16

Renewal Options

Tenant, if not in default hereunder, shall have the option, by written notice, given to the Landlord at least _____ days before the end of the lease term, to renew the lease for a further year term on the following terms and conditions: [Itemize tenancy particulars as agreed by the Parties.].

APPENDIX

The Tenant agrees to allow the Landlord or his agent to show the property at all reasonable hours to prospective Buyers or Tenants, after giving the Tenant at least twenty four (24) hours written notice of such showing, and to allow the Landlord to affix a For Sale or For Rent sign on the property.

LEASE/RES–17

Showing of Rental Property

Landlord shall pay real estate taxes, [condominium fees and parking *if applicable*] and maintain fire insurance on the premises. Tenant acknowledges the Landlord's fire insurance on the premises provides no coverage on Tenant's personal property.

LEASE/RES–18

Taxes/Fire Insurance

Tenant agrees to pay the cost of all utilities required on the premises during the term of the lease and any extension thereof, including but not limited to electricity, water, sewer and gas or other fuel. Tenant further agrees to provide proof to the Landlord on or before the date of possession that the services have been transferred to the Tenant's name.

LEASE/RES–19

Tenant Pays Utilities

The Landlord covenants and agrees with the Tenant that, during the term of the lease or any renewal thereof, the Landlord will give the Tenant three (3) business days to submit an Offer upon the same terms and conditions as any bona fide Offer to purchase the leased property that the Landlord has received and is willing to accept, and any Lease executed by the Landlord and Tenant shall include this first right of refusal.

The Landlord shall give the Tenant written notice of such bona fide Offer and a copy of such Offer to the Tenant. In the event that the Tenant submits to the Landlord, within the time period described above, a written and signed Offer to purchase the property upon the same terms and conditions as the Offer initially received by the Landlord, the Landlord shall accept the Offer submitted by the Tenant. In the event that the Tenant fails to deliver to the Landlord, within the time limit described above, a written and signed Offer to purchase the property on the same terms and conditions as the initial Offer, the Landlord shall be at liberty to sell the property to the Buyer who submitted the initial Offer. Should the Tenant exercise the said first right of refusal, the Landlord agrees to pay the Agents so named in this Agreement, (or their successor companies) a fee of _____.

LEASE/RES–20

Tenant's First Right of Refusal

MAINTENANCE

The Seller agrees to leave the premises, including the floors, in a clean and broom swept condition.

MAINT–1

Cleaning

The Seller agrees to repair at the expense of the Seller, prior to the date of completion, any openings or holes in walls, floors, ceilings or window areas resulting from the removal of equipment, as requested after discussion with the Buyer and more particularly as hereinafter set out: _____ _____ [list where] and permit the Buyer the right to inspect the premises to ensure that said repairs have been completed.

MAINT–2

Equipment—Seller to Repair Damage on Removal

The Seller agrees to clean, repair or replace any damaged floor covering in the sections of the building as indicated by the Buyer and more particularly as hereinafter set out: _____ _____ [list where] and permit the Buyer the right to inspect the premises to ensure that said cleaning, repairing or replacing has been completed.

MAINT–3

Floors

APPENDIX

MORTGAGES

MORT–1

**Condition—
Approval to Assume
Existing Mortgage
(Condition Precedent)**

The Buyer agrees to assume the existing _____ Charge/Mortgage held by _____ for approximately _____ , ($_____), bearing interest at the rate of _____ % per annum, calculated semi-annually not in advance, repayable in blended monthly payments of _____ ($ _____), including both principal and interest, and due on the _____ day of _____, 20_____. This Offer is conditional upon the Buyer obtaining the approval of the Chargee/Mortgagee to assume the existing Charge/Mortgage. Unless the Buyer gives notice in writing delivered to the Seller personally or in accordance with any other provisions for the delivery of notice in this Agreement of Purchase and Sale or any Schedule thereto not later than _____ p.m. on the _____ day of _____, 20_____, that this condition is fulfilled, this Offer shall be null and void and the deposit shall be returned to the Buyer in full without deduction. The Buyer hereby agrees to proceed immediately to make an application and provide such material as may be required by the Chargee/Mortgagee for approval of the Buyer as the Chargor/Mortgagor.

NOTE: This clause is a true Condition Precedent and neither a Seller nor a Buyer is entitled to waive this condition.

MORT–2

**Condition—
Arranging a New Mortgage**

This Offer is conditional upon the Buyer arranging, at the Buyer's own expense, a new _____ Charge/Mortgage for not less than _____ ($ _____), bearing interest at a rate of not more than ___ % per annum, calculated semi-annually not in advance, repayable in blended monthly payments of about _____ ($ _____), including principal and interest, and to run for a term of not less than _____ years from the date of completion of this transaction. Unless the Buyer gives notice in writing delivered to the Seller personally or in accordance with any other provisions for the delivery of notice in this Agreement of Purchase and Sale or any Schedule thereto not later than _____ p.m. on the _____ day of _____, 20_____, that this condition is fulfilled, this Offer shall be null and void and the deposit shall be returned to the Buyer in full without deduction. This condition is included for the benefit of the Buyer and may be waived at the Buyer's sole option by notice in writing to the Seller as aforesaid within the time period stated herein.

NOTE 1: A waiver for the Buyer is included unless the Charge/Mortgage is to be arranged with specific Chargee/Mortgagee (i.e., if it is to be arranged through the Seller's Chargee/ Mortgagee then so state in the description and DO NOT provide a waiver, otherwise the Seller could suffer a substantial monetary penalty to discharge an existing Charge/Mortgage) – or see **MORT-11** below).

NOTE 2: If a Seller Take Back Charge/Mortgage is also being arranged, include **MORT-15** with **MORT-14** to prevent an Oklahoma offer (otherwise the property could be over financed to the detriment of the Seller's security).

NOTE 3: In the event a Finder's Fee is received from a lending institution or Mortgage Broker, it is wise to include an acknowledgement such as the following:

> *"The Seller acknowledges that the agent will receive a Finder's Fee of $_____ in connection with the arranging of financing for the Buyer".*

MORT–3

**Condition—
Arranging a New Mortgage
as Percentage of Purchase
Price**

This Offer is conditional upon the Buyer arranging, at the Buyer's own expense, a new _____ Charge/Mortgage for not less than _____ % of the purchase price, bearing interest at a rate of not more than _____ % per annum, calculated semi-annually not in advance, repayable in equal blended monthly payments, amortized over a period of not less than _____ years and to run for a term of not less than _____ years from the date of completion of this transaction. Unless the Buyer gives notice in writing delivered to the Seller personally or in accordance with any other provisions for the delivery of notice in this Agreement of Purchase and Sale or any Schedule thereto not later than _____ p.m. on the _____ day of _____, 20 _____, that this condition is fulfilled, this Offer shall be null and void and the deposit shall be returned to the Buyer in full without deduction. This condition is included for the benefit of the Buyer and may be waived at the Buyer's sole option by notice in writing to the Seller as aforesaid within the time period stated herein.

This Offer is conditional upon the Buyer arranging, at the Buyer's own expense, a new _____ Charge/Mortgage satisfactory to the Buyer in the Buyer's sole and absolute discretion. Unless the Buyer gives notice in writing delivered to the Seller personally or in accordance with any other provisions for the delivery of notice in this Agreement of Purchase and Sale or any Schedule thereto not later than _____ p.m. on the _____ day of _____, 20_____, that this condition is fulfilled, this Offer shall be null and void and the deposit shall be returned to the Buyer in full without deduction. This condition is included for the benefit of the Buyer and may be waived at the Buyer's sole option by notice in writing to the Seller as aforesaid within the time period stated herein.

NOTE: Sellers should be aware that this condition does not contain any specific terms of the proposed financing Buyers wish to arrange and thus provides Buyers with more latitude in declining financing.

Buyers using this clause should be advised they have an obligation to make a "good faith" effort to arrange the necessary financing, and should not use this clause inappropriately as a means to cancel the transaction.

MORT–4

Condition—
Arranging New Mortgage Satisfactory to Buyer

The Buyer may terminate this Agreement through written notice delivered to the Seller personally or in accordance with any other provisions for the delivery of notice in this Agreement of Purchase and Sale or any Schedule thereto not later than _____ p.m. on the _____ day of _____, 20_____, if a new first Charge/Mortgage cannot be arranged by the Buyer, at the Buyer's expense. This Charge/Mortgage is to be for a sum of not less than _____ ($ _____) bearing interest at a rate of not more than _____% per annum, calculated semi-annually, not in advance, repayable in blended monthly payments of about _____, ($ _____), including both principal and interest, and to run for a term of not less than _____ year(s) from the date of completion of this transaction. Upon receipt of the above notice, this Agreement shall be null and void and the deposit shall be returned to the Buyer in full without deduction. If no such notice is received within the above time limit, then this term of contract shall be deemed waived by the Buyer and this Agreement shall remain valid and binding whether or not such Charge/Mortgage has been arranged.

MORT–5

Condition—
Arranging New Mortgage (Condition Subsequent)

This Offer is conditional upon the Seller being satisfied concerning the personal and/or credit worthiness of the Buyer. Unless the Seller gives notice in writing to the Buyer personally or in accordance with any other provisions for the delivery of notice in this Agreement of Purchase and Sale or any Schedule thereto not later than _____ p.m. on the _____ day of _____, 20_____, that this condition is fulfilled, this Offer shall be null and void and the deposit shall be returned to the Buyer in full without deduction. This condition is included for the benefit of the Seller and may be waived at the Seller's sole option by notice in writing to the Buyer as aforesaid within the time period stated herein.

MORT–6

Condition—Credit Check

This Offer is conditional upon the Seller being satisfied that the cost to discharge the _____ Charge(s)/Mortgage(s) shall not exceed the sum of _____, ($_____). Unless the Seller gives notice in writing delivered to the Buyer personally or in accordance with any other provisions for the delivery of notice in this Agreement of Purchase and Sale or any Schedule thereto not later than _____ p.m. on the _____ day of _____, 20_____, that this condition is fulfilled, this Offer shall be null and void and the deposit shall be returned to the Buyer in full without deduction. This condition is included for the benefit of the Seller and may be waived at the Seller's sole option by notice in writing to the Buyer as aforesaid within the time period stated herein.

NOTE: Most discharges are covered in the printed Agreement.

MORT–7

Condition—
Discharge of Mortgage(s)—
Cost

APPENDIX

MORT-8

Condition—
Overleveraged Property

The Seller hereby acknowledges that the real property is subject to registered encumbrances that may, given the Seller's obligation to pay commissions and other related closing costs, exceed the available proceeds of sale from this transaction. This Offer shall, therefore, be conditional upon the Seller obtaining the written approval of all Chargees/Mortgagees and other registered encumbrancers as to the final acceptance of this Offer and their agreement to discharge their encumbrances without payment in the aggregate of more than the available proceeds from this transaction. Unless the Seller gives notice in writing delivered to the Buyer personally or in accordance with any other provisions for the delivery of notice in this Agreement of Purchase and Sale or any Schedule thereto not later than _____ p.m. on the _____ day of _____, 20_____, that this condition is fulfilled, this Offer shall be null and void and the deposit shall be returned to the Buyer in full without deduction. This condition is included for the benefit of the Seller and may be waived at the Seller's sole option by notice in writing to the Buyer as aforesaid within the time period stated herein.

MORT-9

Condition—
Paydown of Existing
Mortgage by Seller

The Seller agrees to pay the existing _____ Chargee/Mortgagee the sum required to reduce the interest rate by _____% for the term of _____ year(s) of this Charge/Mortgage. This Offer is conditional upon the Seller being satisfied that the cost to reduce the interest rate to _____% shall not exceed the sum of _____ ($ _____). Unless the Seller gives notice in writing delivered to the Buyer personally or in accordance with any other provisions for the delivery of notice in this Agreement of Purchase and Sale or any Schedule thereto not later than _____ p.m. on the _____ day of _____, 20_____, that this condition is fulfilled, this Offer shall be null and void and the deposit shall be returned to the Buyer in full without deduction. This condition is included for the benefit of the Seller and may be waived at the Seller's sole option by notice in writing to the Buyer as aforesaid within the time period stated herein.

MORT-10

Condition—
Sale of Mortgage by Seller

This Offer is conditional upon the Seller obtaining at the Seller's own expense, a commitment for the sale of the aforementioned _____Charge/Mortgage [for an amount of not less than _____($_____)] OR [at a discount of not more than _____% of the amount of said Charge/Mortgage]. Unless the Seller gives notice in writing delivered to the Buyer personally or in accordance with any other provisions for the delivery of notice in this Agreement of Purchase and Sale or any Schedule thereto not later than _____ p.m. on the _____ day of _____, 20_____, that this condition is fulfilled, this Offer shall be null and void and the deposit shall be returned to the Buyer in full without deduction. This condition is included for the benefit of the Seller and may be waived at the Seller's sole option by notice in writing to the Buyer as aforesaid within the time period stated herein.

MORT-11

Discharge of Existing
Mortgage—Buyer to Pay
Prepayment Charges

If the Charge/Mortgage being arranged by the Buyer is not obtained through the existing Chargee/Mortgagee, _____, the Buyer will pay to the Seller, in addition to the purchase price, all prepayment and bonus charges which the existing Chargee/Mortgagee lawfully charges the Seller.

MORT-12

Discharge of Existing
Mortgage—Seller to Pay
Prepayment Charges

The Seller acknowledges that there may be a penalty to discharge the existing Charge/Mortgage and agrees to pay any costs, expenses or penalties incurred in discharging the existing Charge/Mortgage.

APPENDIX

The Buyer agrees to assume the existing _____ Charge/Mortgage held by _____ for approximately _____ ($_____), bearing interest at the rate of _____ % per annum, calculated semi-annually not in advance, repayable in blended monthly payments of _____ ($_____), including both principal and interest, and due on the _____ day of _____, 20_____.

NOTE: The personal covenant of the original Chargor/Mortgagor still applies following the assumption of the Charge/Mortgage by the Buyer.

> **MORT–13**
>
> Existing Mortgage—Buyer to Assume (No Approval)

The Seller agrees to take back a _____ Charge/Mortgage in the amount of _____ ($_____), bearing interest at the rate of _____% per annum, calculated semi-annually not in advance, repayable in blended monthly payments of _____ ($_____), including both principal and interest, and to run for a term of _____ years from the date of completion of this transaction. (See Prepayment Privileges, Clauses **MORT–23**, **MORT–24**, **MORT–25** & **MORT–26**.)

NOTE: Without a prepayment privilege, the borrower does not have any automatic right to early discharge of the Charge/Mortgage or prepayment of principal.

> **MORT–14**
>
> Seller Take Back Mortgage

In the event that the first mortgage arranged by the Buyer has a principal amount in excess of _____ ($_____), the principal amount of the second mortgage will be reduced by the excess amount, with a corresponding reduction in the payment for the second mortgage. The Buyer agrees to provide the Seller or the Seller's lawyer with a confirmation of the principal amount of the first mortgage to be registered.

NOTE: To be used with MORT–14 when the offer is conditional on arranging a prior mortgage.

> **MORT–15**
>
> Seller Take Back Mortgage—Second Mortgage Clause to Prevent Overfinancing (Oklahoma)

The Seller agrees to take back a _____ Charge/Mortgage [for the balance of the Purchase price] OR [in the amount of _____ ($_____)] bearing interest at the rate of _____% per annum, repayable interest only _____ [state payment interval; e.g., monthly, quarterly, etc.] and maturing on the _____ day of _____, 20___. (See Prepayment Privileges, Clauses **MORT–23**, **MORT–24**, **MORT–25** & **MORT–26**.)

NOTE: Without a prepayment privilege, the borrower does not have any automatic right to early discharge of the Charge/Mortgage or prepayment of principal.

> **MORT–16**
>
> Seller Take Back Mortgage—Simple Interest Only

The Buyer acknowledges that the Charge/Mortgage being taken back by the Seller may be sold. The Buyer agrees to co-operate fully with the Seller in connection with the sale of this Charge/Mortgage, and shall provide such personal and financial information, together with such documents as the Assignee of the Charge/Mortgage may reasonably require, forthwith upon request by the Seller, in order that the sale of the Charge/Mortgage may be completed.

> **MORT–17**
>
> Seller Take Back—To Be Sold By Seller Prior to Closing (Buyer to Co-operate)

The Buyer warrants that the down payment stated in this transaction shall be at least _____ % of the purchase price and does not incur any payment obligations or indebtedness.

> **MORT–18**
>
> Seller Take Back—Source of Downpayment

The Buyer shall deliver to the Chargee/Mortgagee on the closing of this transaction, and on each anniversary of the closing, a series of post-dated cheques to cover all Charge/Mortgage payments due during the next twelve months.

> **MORT–19**
>
> Term—Post Dated Cheque Requirement

APPENDIX

MORT–20

Term—Postponement–1

This Charge/Mortgage shall contain a clause permitting the renewal or replacement of the existing first Charge/Mortgage at any time, provided that any increase in the principal amount of the new first Charge/ Mortgage over the amount of principal owing under the first Charge/Mortgage at the time of renewal or replacement shall be applied in reduction of the principal amount of this Charge/Mortgage; and the Chargee/Mortgagee hereunder shall execute and deliver to the Chargor/ Mortgagor such postponement agreement, Charge/Mortgage Statement, or other documents as the new first Chargee/Mortgagee may reasonably require, forthwith upon request.

NOTE: If Charge/Mortgage being arranged is a third, etc., change clause to read: "replacement of the first and/or second Charge(s)/Mortgage(s)" and "principal owing under the first and/or second Charge(s)/Mortgage(s)".

MORT–21

Term—Postponement–2

The Chargor/Mortgagor shall have the privilege of renewing or replacing the existing first Charge/ Mortgage at any time provided that any increase in the principal of the new first Charge/Mortgage over the amount of principal owing under the first Charge/Mortgage at the time of renewal or replacement shall be applied without penalty in reduction of the principal amount of this Charge/ Mortgage and the Chargee/Mortgagee will execute and deliver to the Chargor/Mortgagor a postponement agreement in favour of the new first Chargee/Mortgagee.

MORT–22

Term—Postponement–3

The Chargee/Mortgagee will execute and deliver to the Chargor/Mortgagor a postponement agreement in favour of the new first Chargee/Mortgagee, provided that such replacement Charge/ Mortgage shall not bear interest in excess of _____% per annum and if such financing is for an amount greater than the outstanding principal balance of the existing first Charge/Mortgage at the date of registration of the new first Charge/Mortgage, such increase shall be paid towards the reduction of the principal balance outstanding on this Charge/Mortgage.

MORT–23

Term—Prepayment—
Fully Open

This Charge/Mortgage shall contain a clause permitting the Chargor/Mortgagor, when not in default, the privilege of prepaying all or part of the principal sum outstanding at any time or times without notice or bonus.

MORT–24

Term—Prepayment—Open
in Accordance with Principal
Amounts Falling Due

This Charge/Mortgage shall contain a clause permitting the Chargor/Mortgagor, when not in default, the privilege of prepaying all or part of the principal sum on any payment date or dates without notice or bonus, provided that any partial prepayment shall equal the sum of the principal amounts of the payment(s) next falling due under the Charge/Mortgage.

MORT–25

Term—Prepayment—
Open on Anniversary Date

This Charge/Mortgage shall contain a clause permitting the Chargor/Mortgagor, when not in default, the privilege of prepaying on each anniversary date a sum not to exceed _____% of the original principal amount, without notice or bonus.

MORT–26

Term—Prepayment—
Subject to Bonus

This Charge/Mortgage shall contain a clause permitting the Chargor/Mortgagor, when not in default, the privilege of prepaying on any payment date a sum not to exceed _____% of the original principal amount, subject to a bonus of _____ month's interest on the amount of principal being repaid.

MORT–27

Term—Renewal—
Same Terms Except for
Further Renewal

This Charge/Mortgage shall contain a clause permitting the Chargor/Mortgagor, when not in default, the privilege of renewing this Charge/Mortgage on its maturity, for a further term of _____ year(s) on the same terms and conditions save and except for the right to any further renewal.

APPENDIX

This Charge/Mortgage shall contain a clause permitting the Chargor/Mortgagor, when not in default, the privilege of renewing this Charge/Mortgage upon its maturity, for a further term of _____ year(s) at the rate of interest charged by _____, on the date thirty days preceding the maturity date of the Charge/Mortgage, to credit worthy borrowers for _____ year Charge/Mortgage loans, and otherwise on the same terms and conditions save and except for the right of a further renewal.

MORT–28

Term—Renewal—
At Current Rate of Interest

This Charge/Mortgage shall contain a clause providing that the Chargor/Mortgagor shall have the right to alter or demolish any or all of the existing buildings now on the property without such activity constituting waste under the terms of this Charge/Mortgage, provided that such alteration or demolition shall comply with all applicable bylaws, building codes or other applicable laws or regulations.

MORT–29

Term—Right to Demolish

This Charge/Mortgage shall contain a clause providing that if the Chargor/Mortgagor sells, assigns, or otherwise transfers title to the property or places a Charge/Mortgage on the property without the express consent of the Chargee/Mortgagee then, at the sole option of the Chargee/Mortgagee, all monies secured thereby shall become due and payable immediately, together with interest accrued to the date thereof.

MORT–30

Term—Transfer/
Acceleration Provision—
At Option of Mortgagee

MORTGAGES/DEVELOPMENT

This Charge/Mortgage shall contain a clause permitting the dedication of all roads and other lands required by municipal and provincial authorities on any proposed plan or plans of sub-division and providing for a discharge of such lands, as may be required for such purposes, from the Charge/Mortgage, without additional payment by the Chargor/Mortgagor other than the normal legal costs of the Chargee/Mortgagee.

MORT/DEV–1

Mortgagee's Consent—
Dedication of Road

This Charge/Mortgage shall contain a clause requiring the Chargee/Mortgagee to postpone the Charge/ Mortgage in favour of the granting of any easements to municipal or other governmental authorities or Public Utilities Commission or Corporation, required for the supply and/or installation of gas, telephone, electricity, water, sewer, railroad, or other similar services, without additional payment by the Chargor/ Mortgagor other than the normal legal costs of the Chargee/ Mortgagee.

MORT/DEV–2

Mortgagee's Consent—
Granting of Easements

This Charge/Mortgage shall contain a clause permitting the Chargor/Mortgagor to apply to register the lands, or any part or parts, under the Land Titles System, and the Chargee/Mortgagee agrees to execute any and all documents required by the Chargor/Mortgagor with respect thereto, provided that the Chargor/Mortgagor pay all costs of said registration.

MORT/DEV–3

Mortgagee's Consent—
Registration in Land Titles

This Charge/Mortgage shall contain a clause requiring the Chargee/Mortgagee, upon written notice, to execute applications and all other documents required for the Chargor/Mortgagor to change the Official Plan, if necessary, and to re-zone the lands to a zoning suitable to the Chargor/ Mortgagor, or to amend any bylaws, and to support such application or applications for re-zoning or amending of bylaws and to co-operate with the Chargor/Mortgagor in all reasonable respects, provided that the Chargor/Mortgagor pay all costs of said re-zoning.

MORT/DEV–4

Mortgagee's Consent—
Re-zoning

APPENDIX

MORT/DEV-5

Mortgagee's Consent—
Subdivide

This Charge/Mortgage shall contain a clause permitting the Chargor/Mortgagor to register a plan or plans of sub-division on the Charged/Mortgaged lands and the Chargee/Mortgagee agrees to cooperate with the Chargor/Mortgagor and execute any required documents for the application and registration of any plan of sub-division, provided that the Chargor/Mortgagor pay all costs for the application, requirements for approval and registration of the plan of sub-division.

MORTGAGES/POWER OF SALE

MORT/POS-1

Power of Sale (General
Provision)

It is further understood that on the date of acceptance of this Offer there is default under the terms of the Charge/Mortgage which entitles the Seller to exercise the Power of Sale. The only evidence of the default which the Buyer may require shall be a statutory declaration by the Seller setting forth the facts entitling the Seller to sell under the Power of Sale, including the particulars of the notice of exercising the Power of Sale, the names of the persons upon whom service of the notice has been effected, and declaring that default under the Charge/Mortgage entitling the Seller to exercise the Power of Sale has continued up to and including the date of acceptance of this Offer and to the time of closing. The Buyer understands and agrees that the Chargor/Mortgagor has the right to redeem the property up to the time of waiver or expiration of all rights of termination or fulfillment of all conditions and this Agreement is subject to that right. In the event of redemption by the Chargor/Mortgagor, this Agreement shall be null and void and any deposit monies paid will be refunded in full without deduction.

Where a court of competent jurisdiction prevents the completion of the within sale by an interim, interlocutory or permanent injunction or otherwise, then the Seller (Chargee/Mortgagee) is not obliged to complete the said transaction and the Agreement shall be terminated and the deposit shall be returned to the Buyer in full without deduction. In no event shall the Seller be responsible for any costs, expenses, loss or damages incurred or suffered by the Buyer and the Seller shall not have any further liability to the Buyer whatsoever.

Notwithstanding other provisions of this Agreement, the Seller shall not be required either on or before closing to discharge its own Charge/Mortgage or any existing Charges/Mortgages, liens or other encumbrances subsequent in priority to the Seller's Charge/Mortgage, which may be registered against the Property.

The Buyer also acknowledges that the Seller makes no representation and/or warranties with respect to the state of repair of the premises, inclusions of chattels or fixtures, or ownership of fixtures or appliances, and the Buyer agrees to accept the property "as is". Chattels and fixtures on the premises may or may not be included with the premises but the Seller shall not be obliged to remove any chattels or fixtures. All the provisions of the *Mortgages Act* shall supersede any part of this Agreement which may be in variance thereof or in conflict therewith.

NOTE: Most Chargee(s)/Mortgagee(s) have their own specific clauses concerning Power of Sale. Each situation should be carefully analyzed prior to the drafting of an Agreement of Purchase and Sale.

NEW HOMES

NEW-1

Builder Registered

The Seller represents and warrants, to the best of the Seller's knowledge and belief, that the said home and its builder are both registered under the Ontario New Home Warranty Program. The Parties agree that this representation and warranty shall form an integral part of this Agreement and survive the completion of this transaction. Documents attesting to these registrations are attached as Schedule "_____" and form part of this Agreement of Purchase and Sale.

APPENDIX

The Seller agrees to complete the house, the (itemize any other structures), and grounds in a good and workmanlike manner, in accordance with all the specifications outlined in Schedule "_____" attached hereto and forming part of this Agreement of Purchase and Sale.

NEW-2
Completion of Construction

The Buyer and the Seller acknowledge and agree that the HST payable in connection with the purchase and sale transaction contemplated by this Agreement of Purchase and Sale is included in the purchase price subject to the provisions hereinafter set out.

NEW-3
HST—New Homes

Notwithstanding that the purchase price payable by the Buyer includes HST, the Buyer hereby assigns and transfers to the Seller all of the Buyer's rights, title and interest in any rebates, refunds or credits available, including Federal Sales Tax rebates and HST rebates to which the Buyer is entitled in connection with the payment of HST payable on the transfer to the Buyer of ownership or possession of the property. The Buyer further appoints and authorizes the Seller or the Seller's agents to be the Buyer's authorized representative and attorney for the purposes of applying for and collecting such tax rebates. The Buyer agrees to execute, at no cost to the Seller, any and all documents required to give effect to this provision.

The Buyer represents and warrants to the Seller that the Buyer shall personally occupy the property or cause one or more of the Buyer's relations to occupy the property as the Buyer's or the Buyer's relation's primary place of residence upon completion and agrees to deliver to the Seller on closing a Statutory Declaration in the Seller's form in which the Buyer declares that the property being purchased by the Buyer is for use as the Buyer's or the Buyer's relation's primary place of residence and will be so occupied forthwith upon completion.

In the event that the Buyer breaches the warranty or any of the provisions referred to above which results in the Buyer being ineligible or the Seller being unable to obtain the rebates referred to herein then the Buyer shall pay to the Seller forthwith an amount equal to the amount which the Buyer would have been eligible to obtain were it not for such breach or failure to carry out the Buyer's obligations.

NOTE: Definition of Relation as set out in the *Excise Tax Act*.

> *Relation*—A relation means an individual related to you by blood, marriage, common-law partnership, or adoption within the meaning of the *Income Tax Act*. "Blood relation" is limited to parents, children, or other descendants or siblings. "Marriage relation" includes your spouse or a person who is connected to your spouse by blood or adoption. A relation includes a common-law partner, a former spouse or a former common-law partner.

NOTE: In Ontario, Tarion requires that when a new home is sold, the Agreement must include the standard Tarion form of Addendum, exactly as published by Tarion and complete the form without any revisions or deletions. The required Addendum (Schedule) is statutorily deemed to be part of the Agreement of Purchase and Sale. To obtain the Tarion forms, go to the Tarion website at **http://www.tarion.com/Pages/default.aspx**.

NEW-4
Link to TARION Schedules

PARKING

The Seller agrees to remove all equipment, storage containers and any other materials, including refuse and debris, from the property and to leave the parking area in a clean and vacant condition.

PARK-1
Parking Area

APPENDIX

RENT/SALE OF PROPERTY

NOTE: The following rental clauses have been developed for the sale of small rental properties (e.g., duplexes and triplexes etc.). For large multi-unit complexes special conditions will apply and expert assistance should be sought.

NOTE: Since rental properties fall within the definition of a "business" in the *Real Estate and Business Brokers Act*, the appropriate financial statements or Form 503 must be delivered to the Buyer.

RENT–1

Adjustment of Purchase Price Due to Shortfall in Rental Income

The Parties agree that if the actual rent, including any planned increases as declared in this Agreement, is less than the rent warranted, including any planned increases by the Seller, then the Parties agree that the Seller shall pay the Buyer as liquidated damages, the amount of the difference times a factor of _____, as either an adjustment on the purchase price of the property or as a separate payment at the sole discretion of the Buyer.

NOTE: The factor is negotiable between the Parties, but is often based on the ratio between the overall purchase price and gross rent (gross rental multiplier).

RENT–2

Confidentiality of Disclosed Rental Information

The Buyer will hold in strict confidence any knowledge about the rent review situations of the property, financial documents, leases, and such other records of the property which the Buyer obtains from this Agreement or any other source, subject only to the use of such information in order to obtain professional advice and in the application or appeal process concerning rent review.

RENT–3

Increase of Rent with Notices Prior to Completion of Sale

The Seller shall, at the earliest legally permitted time to completion, give notices of rent increases, at the statutory rate or as otherwise agreed between the Buyer and the Seller, and provide the Buyer with proof of proper service thereof.

RENT–4

No Rent Increases Pending Completion of Sale

Pending completion, the Seller shall not give any notices of rent increases.

RENT–5

Notices to Tenants of New Owner

Upon completion, the Seller shall provide the Buyer with a notice to all tenants advising them of the new owner and requiring all future rents to be paid as the Buyer directs. The Seller will pay to the Buyer any rent paid to the Seller in error or in violation of the direction for a period of _____ months following completion, after which period the Seller may refuse to accept rent from tenants or return it to them.

NOTE: Lawyers for parties will treat rent deposits and interest thereon as part of the adjustment process.

The Seller represents and warrants, to the best of the Seller's knowledge and belief, that the current actual rents are:

Unit	Current Rent	Last Increase (Date/Amount)

RENT–6
Rent—No Warranty Re
Legality of Rents

The Parties agree that this representation and warranty shall survive and not merge on completion of this transaction, but apply only to those circumstances existing at completion of this transaction. The Parties also agree that the warranty given is as to actual rents only, and does not extend to the legality of the rents.

NOTE: Additional categories may be used to expand tenancy information: Apartment #, Tenant Name, Type of Tenancy, Expiry Date, Rent Due Date, Prepaid Rent, and Tenancy Particulars (Items included in Rent).

NOTE: The actual lease documents should be attached as a Schedule to the Agreement. If too many documents, consider making Offer conditional upon inspection of tenancy agreement.

The Seller represents and warrants, to the best of the Seller's knowledge and belief that, during the period of the Seller's ownership, the property has been rented in accordance with Landlord and Tenant legislation and that any rent increase has been effected in accordance with relevant rent review legislation. The Parties agree that this representation and warranty shall survive and not merge on completion of this transaction, but apply only to those circumstances existing at completion of this transaction.

RENT–7
Rent—
General Warranty by Seller

The Seller represents and warrants, to the best of the Seller's knowledge and belief, that there are no disputes between the Seller as landlord and any tenant as to the state of repair of the leased premises, the payment of rents, contravention of applicable rent review legislation for residential tenancies, or other material items concerning the tenants' lease agreements other than as specifically set out in this Agreement of Purchase and Sale. The Parties agree that these representations and warranties shall survive and not merge on completion of this transaction, but apply only to those circumstances existing at completion of this transaction.

RENT–8
Rent—Seller Warranty
Regarding Disputes

Unless otherwise agreed between the Buyer and the Seller, the Seller shall not renegotiate any leases after this Agreement becomes unconditional.

RENT–9
Seller Not to Renegotiate
Leases Prior to Completion
without Buyer Instruction

The Seller shall make reasonable attempts to renegotiate leases with current tenants [for terms not to exceed _____ years] as agreed between the Buyer and Seller.

RENT–10
Seller to Renegotiate
Leases

APPENDIX

RENT REVIEW

RENT/REV–1

Rent Review Application Pending—Buyer to Pay/Buyer to Control

The Parties agree that the Seller will allow the pending rent review application, and any appeal thereof, to be continued in the Seller's name, in the control of the Buyer and at the expense of the Buyer including the payment of any liability for costs in the Divisional Court or a higher court. Provided further, that if an appeal is brought to, or defended in, the Divisional Court or a higher court the Buyer shall provide the Seller's Solicitor with the amount of _____ ($ _____), at each level of court to which the appeal is taken, to a maximum amount of _____ ($ _____), to be held in trust as security for the Seller's liability for costs.

NOTE: Buyers using this clause should seek legal advice as to potential amounts involved.

RENT/REV–2

Rent Review Application Pending—Seller to Pay/Buyer to Control

The Parties agree that the Seller will co-operate with the Buyer in completing all pending rent review applications and appeals thereof which shall be at the expense of the Seller up to a maximum of _____ ($ _____), until the completion of any appeal whether to the Landlord and Tenant Board or to the Divisional Court, provided further that such application and appeals shall be in the control of the Buyer throughout.

NOTE: Buyers and Sellers using this clause should seek legal advice as to potential amounts involved.

RENT/REV–3

Rent Review Application— Seller to Provide Financial Information and Documentation Necessary for Rent Review Application

The Seller shall provide the Buyer with any and all financial information and/or documents in the Seller's possession and control, which the Buyer requires to effect or defend any rent review application or appeal.

NOTE: See confidentiality clause RENT–2.

REPRESENTATIONS/WARRANTIES

NOTE 1: Various warranty clauses are provided. Care must be taken to ensure that the correct wording is utilized to reflect the agreement of the parties.

NOTE 2: When drafting these clauses, you may wish to provide a specific time limit for the Buyer to notify the Seller. (See Warranties – Specific Time Period)

REP/WARR–1

Seller Not Liable

The Buyer acknowledges the Buyer has been informed of the following possible latent defect(s) in the property: _____. The Buyer further acknowledges it is the Buyer's sole responsibility to complete their own due diligence concerning this defect, for example, obtaining a report concerning this defect, and the Buyer releases the Seller of all liability for current and future damages resulting from this possible defect.

NOTE: This clause should be used only when a specific defect is identified and disclosed and should not be used by the Seller as a general "as is" clause.

REP/WARR–2

Seller Representations— General

The Seller represents and warrants that on completion: _____ [e.g., There is no known damage to the basement, roof, or elsewhere caused by water seepage or flooding]. The Parties agree that these representations and warranties shall survive and not merge on completion of this transaction, but apply only to the state of the property at completion of this transaction.

The Seller represents and warrants that on completion: _____
[e.g., There is no known damage to the basement, roof, or elsewhere caused by water seepage or flooding]. The Parties agree that these representations and warranties shall survive and not merge on completion of this transaction, but apply only to the state of the property at completion of this transaction. The Buyer, at the Buyer's sole option, may terminate this Agreement at any time prior to completion in the event any of the representations and warranties contained herein are incorrect, and the deposit shall be returned to the Buyer in full without deduction.

REP/WARR-3

**Seller Representations—
Termination Remedy**

. . . .

The Parties agree that the representations and warranties stated herein shall survive and not merge on completion, but shall expire at _____ p.m. on the _____ day of _____, 20_____, and be of no further force and effect unless the Buyer, prior to such expiry, has given written notice of a claim under the warranty to the Seller.

REP/WARR-4

**Warranties—
Specific Time Period**

. . . .

The Parties agree that the representations and warranties stated herein shall survive and not merge on completion of this transaction.

REP/WARR-5

**Warranties—
Survive Completion**

. . . .

The Parties agree that the representations and warranties stated herein shall survive and not merge on completion of this transaction, but apply only to the state of the property at completion of this transaction.

REP/WARR-6

**Warranties—Survive
Completion—Limited to
Current Transaction**

SALE OF BUYER'S PROPERTY

This Offer is conditional upon the sale of the Buyer's property known as _____.
Unless the Buyer gives notice in writing delivered to the Seller personally or in accordance with any other provisions for the delivery of notice in this Agreement of Purchase and Sale or any Schedule thereto not later than _____ p.m. on the _____ day of _____, 20_____, that this condition is fulfilled, this Offer shall be null and void and the deposit shall be returned to the Buyer in full without deduction. This condition is included for the benefit of the Buyer and may be waived at the Buyer's sole option by notice in writing to the Seller as aforesaid within the time period stated herein.

SBP-1

**Condition—
Buyer's Property**

. . . .

This Offer is conditional upon the Buyer receiving notification of the removal of all conditions in an existing Agreement of Purchase and Sale for the property known as _____.
Unless the Buyer gives notice in writing delivered to the Seller personally or in accordance with any other provisions for the delivery of notice in this Agreement of Purchase and Sale or any Schedule thereto not later than _____ p.m. on the _____ day of _____, 20_____, that this condition is fulfilled, this Offer shall be null and void and the deposit shall be returned to the Buyer in full without deduction. This condition is included for the benefit of the Buyer and may be waived at the Buyer's sole option by notice in writing to the Seller as aforesaid within the time period stated herein.

SBP-2

**Condition—
Removal of All Conditions—
Buyer's Property**

SBP-3

**Condition—
Seller's Release from
Previous Agreement**

This Offer is conditional upon the Seller obtaining a release from a prior Agreement of Purchase and Sale. Unless the Seller gives notice in writing delivered to the Buyer personally or in accordance with any other provisions for the delivery of notice in this Agreement of Purchase and Sale or any Schedule thereto not later than _____ p.m. on the _____ day of _____, 20_____ , that this condition is fulfilled, this Offer shall be null and void and the deposit shall be returned to the Buyer in full without deduction.

NOTE: This clause is a true Condition Precedent and neither a Seller nor a Buyer is entitled to waive this condition.

SBP-4

**Escape Clause—
Buyer's Property**

Provided further that the Seller may continue to offer the property for sale and, in the event the Seller receives another Offer satisfactory to the Seller, the Seller may so notify the Buyer in writing by delivery to the Buyer personally or in accordance with any other provisions for the delivery of notice in this Agreement of Purchase and Sale or any Schedule thereto. The Buyer shall have _____ hours from the giving of such notice to waive this condition by notice in writing delivered to the Seller personally or in accordance with any other provisions for the delivery of notice in this Agreement of Purchase and Sale or any Schedule thereto, failing which this Offer shall be null and void, and the Buyer's deposit shall be returned in full without deduction.

NOTE: The Escape Clause only requires the removal of one specific condition.

SBP-5

**Escape Clause—
Notices Re: Multiple
Representation**

If the Listing Brokerage represents both the Seller and the Buyer in this transaction in multiple representation, the Brokerage is not authorized to receive the Notice to Remove Condition on behalf of the Buyer and the Brokerage is not authorized to receive the Notice of Waiver of Condition on behalf of the Seller. Said notices will be delivered by the Brokerage either to the parties to the transaction, the address of the parties, the lawyers representing the parties, or transmitted to the fax number or email address designated by the parties other than the Brokerage's fax number or email address.

NOTE: This clause to be used with escape clause only.

SBP-6

**Escape Clause—
Removal of All Conditions**

Provided further that the Seller may continue to offer the property for sale and, in the event the Seller receives another Offer satisfactory to the Seller, the Seller may so notify the Buyer personally or in accordance with any other provisions for the delivery of notice in this Agreement of Purchase and Sale or any Schedule thereto. The Buyer shall have _____ hours from the giving of such notice to waive any and all conditions by notice in writing delivered to the Seller personally or in accordance with any other provisions for the delivery of notice in this Agreement of Purchase and Sale or any Schedule thereto, failing which this Offer shall be null and void and the deposit shall be returned to the Buyer in full without deduction.

APPENDIX

SEWER/WATER

NOTE: Sale of Property with a well and/or septic system involves specific knowledge of the system. (e.g., There is a difference in a well's performance depending on many variables, e.g., the amount of available water, the delivery capacity of the well system, the amount of water that can be delivered over a certain period of time, and seasonable variables. The type of well, drilled, bored, or dug can also affect performance). Expert advice should be sought.

This Offer is conditional upon the Buyer determining, at the Buyer's own expense, that:

(1) all sewage systems serving the property are wholly within the setback requirements of the said property and have received all required Certificates of Installation and Approval pursuant to the *Environmental Protection Act*;

(2) all sewage systems serving the property have been constructed in accordance with the said Certificates of Installation and Approval;

(3) all sewage systems serving the property have received all required use permits under the said Act or any other legislation; and further, that on inspection, the septic bed is in good working order.

The Buyer shall be allowed to retain at the Buyer's own expense, a professional in the septic business to make an examination of the septic system.

Seller agrees to allow access to the property for the purposes of a septic inspection and agrees to allow the Buyer to request information as outlined above from the appropriate authorities having jurisdiction.

Unless the Buyer gives notice in writing delivered to the Seller personally or in accordance with any other provisions for the delivery of notice in this Agreement of Purchase and Sale or any Schedule thereto not later than _____ p.m. on the _____ day of _____, 20_____, that these conditions have been fulfilled, this Offer shall become null and void and the deposit shall be returned to the Buyer in full without deduction. These conditions are included for the benefit of the Buyer and may be waived at the Buyer's sole option by notice in writing to the Seller as aforesaid within the time period stated herein.

NOTE: SEWER/WATER-1 does not speak to the working order of the Septic System and, therefore, should be used in conjunction with SEWER/WATER-4.

| SEWER/WATER-1 |
| Condition—
Sewage Systems—
Approvals |

This Offer is conditional upon the Buyer determining, at the Buyer's own expense, that:

(1) there is an adequate water supply to meet the Buyer's household needs;

(2) the pump and all related equipment serving the property are in proper operating condition; and

(3) the Buyer can obtain a Bacteriological Analysis of Drinking Water from the authority having jurisdiction indicating that there is no significant evidence of bacterial contamination.

Unless the Buyer gives notice in writing delivered to the Seller personally or in accordance with any other provisions for the delivery of notice in this Agreement of Purchase and Sale or any Schedule thereto not later than _____ p.m. on the _____ day of _____, 20_____, that these conditions have been fulfilled, this Offer shall become null and void and the deposit shall be returned to the Buyer in full without deduction. These conditions are included for the benefit of the Buyer and may be waived at the Buyer's sole option by notice in writing to the Seller as aforesaid within the time period stated herein. The Seller agrees to allow access to the subject property to the Buyer or the Buyer's agent for the purpose of satisfying this condition.

| SEWER/WATER-2 |
| Condition—
Water Supply—
All Well Types |

APPENDIX

SEWER/WATER-3

Sewage Systems—
Approvals—Warranty

The Seller represents and warrants, to the best of the Seller's knowledge and belief, that:

(1) all sewage systems serving the property are wholly within the setback requirements of the said property, and have received all required Certificates of Installation and Approval pursuant to the *Environmental Protection Act*;

(2) all sewage systems serving the property have been constructed in accordance with the said Certificates of Installation and Approval;

(3) all sewage systems serving the property have received all required Use permits under the said Act or any other legislation; and further, all sewage systems serving the property have been maintained in good working order during the Seller's occupancy and will be in good working order on closing.

Further, the Seller agrees to provide any and all documentation relating to the sewage system, within the Seller's possession, or which may be made available to the Seller by the appropriate authorities, and given to the Buyer prior to the last date set for examining title. The Parties agree that these representations and warranties shall survive and not merge on completion of this transaction, but apply only to the state of the property existing at the completion of this transaction.

SEWER/WATER-4

Sewage System—
Good Working Order—
Warranty

The Seller represents and warrants, to the best of the Seller's knowledge and belief, that, during the Seller's occupancy of the building, the sewage system has been and will be in good working order on closing. The Parties agree that this representation and warranty shall survive and not merge on completion of this transaction, but apply only to the state of the property existing at completion of this transaction.

SEWER/WATER-5

Water Supply—
All Well Types—Warranty

The Seller represents and warrants, to the best of the Seller's knowledge and belief, that, during the Seller's occupancy of the property, the pump and all related equipment serving the said property have performed adequately, and will be in good working order on closing and are currently capable of delivering not less than _____ gallons per minute (GPM) on the continuous basis of not less than _____ hours. The Parties agree that this representation and warranty shall survive and not merge on completion of this transaction, but apply only to the state of the property at completion of this transaction.

NOTE: If the Seller does not know the current status of the well, the Seller should be advised to verify through a professional well inspection as the current water supply can vary from the original well record. The supply of water is contingent on many variables, e.g. the actual amount of water in the well, the capacity of the well system to deliver the water and over what length of time will the GPM be sustained.

APPENDIX

SHORE ROAD ALLOWANCES

This Offer is conditional upon the Buyer determining at the Buyer's own expense that:

(1) the property being purchased has at least [insert appropriate frontage dimension], [metres/feet], of frontage on [name of lake or river];

(2) no road allowance, open or unopened, or other public or private lands exist which will interfere with the right of the Buyer to use and enjoy the said water frontage; and

(3) that there are no unregistered rights or easements.

Unless the Buyer gives notice in writing delivered to the Seller personally or in accordance with any other provisions for the delivery of notice in this Agreement of Purchase and Sale or any Schedule thereto not later than _____ p.m. on the _____ day of _____, 20_____, that these conditions have been fulfilled, this offer shall become null and void and the deposit shall be returned to the Buyer in full without deduction. These conditions are included for the benefit of the Buyer and may be waived at the Buyer's sole option by notice in writing to the Seller as aforesaid within the time period stated herein.

SHORE–1

Condition—
Water Frontage—
Shore Road Allowance—
Unregistered Easements

. . . .

The Buyer acknowledges that the original shore road allowance is not closed and consequently is not part of the property being sold under this Agreement of Purchase and Sale.

SHORE–2

Shore Road Allowance—
Acknowledgement

. . . .

The Buyer acknowledges that the original shore road allowance is not closed and consequently is not part of the property being sold under this Agreement of Purchase and Sale, and that the improvements apparently on the said property may encroach on said unowned shore road allowance.

SHORE–3

Shore Road Allowance—
With Encroachments

SOIL TEST

This Offer is conditional upon the Buyer obtaining at the Buyer's own expense, soil tests verifying the land is satisfactory to the Buyer, in the Buyer's sole and absolute discretion, for the construction of a _____ on the land. Unless the Buyer gives notice in writing delivered to the Seller personally or in accordance with any other provisions for the delivery of notice in this Agreement of Purchase and Sale or any Schedule thereto not later than _____ p.m. on the _____ day of _____, 20_____, that this condition is fulfilled, this Offer shall be null and void and the deposit shall be returned to the Buyer in full without deduction. The Seller agrees to co-operate in providing access to the land for the purpose of the soil tests. This condition is included for the benefit of the Buyer and may be waived at the Buyer's sole option by notice in writing to the Seller as aforesaid within the time period stated herein. If the Buyer fails to provide a notice of fulfilment of the condition or fails to waive the condition as provided above, the Buyer agrees to reasonably restore any alterations to the condition of the property caused by the soil tests.

SOIL–1

Condition—
Satisfactory Soil Test

. . . .

The Seller agrees to grant the Buyer and the Buyer's authorized agent the right to enter the property for the purpose of surveying and conducting soil tests prior to the completion of this transaction. Such permission does not extend to any alteration of the lands, servicing work, removal of trees, soil, or any other activity which would alter the current state of the property.

SOIL–2

Preliminary Work—
Access to Property

SPIS

SPIS–1

**Condition—
Buyer's Acceptance of SPIS**

This Offer is conditional upon the Buyer receiving a Seller Property Information Statement completed by the Seller and the Buyer accepting the information on the form as satisfactory in the Buyer's sole and absolute discretion. Unless the Buyer gives notice in writing delivered to the Seller personally or in accordance with any other provisions for the delivery of notice in this Agreement of Purchase and Sale or any Schedule thereto not later than _____ p.m. on the _____ day of _____, 20_____, that this condition is fulfilled, this offer shall be null and void and the deposit shall be returned to the Buyer in full without deduction. This condition is included for the benefit of the Buyer and may be waived at the Buyer's sole option by notice in writing to the Seller as aforesaid within the time period stated herein.

The Seller hereby agrees to deliver to the Buyer upon acceptance of this Agreement a Seller Property Information Statement for the property with complete and accurate answers, to the best of the Seller's knowledge and belief, to the questions contained therein.

SPIS–2

**SPIS—
Buyer's Acknowledgement**

The Buyer acknowledges that the Buyer has received a completed Seller Property Information Statement from the Seller and has had an opportunity to read the information provided by the Seller on the Seller Property Information Statement prior to submitting this offer.

SURVEYS

NOTE 1: See Form 100, Clause—Documents and Discharge.

NOTE 2: Buyer should acknowledge, in the Offer, any known easements. See Form 100, Clause—Title.

NOTE 3: Allow adequate time and ensure deadline is prior to end of requisition period. Alternatively, the requirement for a survey could be "within days after waiver of all conditions (and prior to end of requisition period)".

NOTE 4: Do not use the phrase "up-to-date". This expression is subject to different interpretation by individual Buyers, Sellers and their respective Solicitors.

SURVEY–1

**Buyer Acknowledges
Possible Survey
Requirement**

The Buyer acknowledges that a new survey may be required for purposes of financing and also to satisfy the requirements of the Buyer's Solicitor, and agrees to obtain said survey at the Buyer's expense.

SURVEY–2

**Seller to Provide Existing
Survey with Declaration**

The Seller agrees to provide, at the Seller's own expense, not later than _____ p.m. on the _____ day of _____, 20_____, an existing survey of said property showing the current location of all structures, buildings, fences, improvements, easements, rights-of-way, and encroachments affecting said property. The Seller will further deliver, on completion, a declaration confirming that there have been no additions to the structures, buildings, fences, and improvements on the property since the date of this survey.

SURVEY–3

**Seller to Provide
New Survey**

The Seller agrees to provide, at the Seller's own expense, not later than _____ p.m. on the _____ day of _____, 20_____, a new survey of said property showing the current location of all structures, buildings, fences, improvements, easements, rights-of-way, and encroachments affecting said property.

APPENDIX

The Seller agrees to provide, at the expense of the Seller, a survey of the property, completed by an Ontario Land Surveyor, showing the current location of all buildings, structures, additions, fences, improvements, easements, rights-of-way and encroachments affecting the property. The Seller also agrees to supply all building plans, mechanical drawings, and any other plans, and all warranties and service manuals, if available, applicable to any equipment or chattels included in the purchase price.

SURVEY–4

Survey, Building Plans, Mechanical Drawings, Warranties

SWIMMING POOL

The Seller represents and warrants to the best of the Seller's knowledge and belief that the swimming pool, its equipment, and the fencing of the said pool, comply with all applicable bylaws, regulations, and legislation. The Parties agree that this representation and warranty shall survive and not merge on completion of this transaction, but apply only to the state of the property existing at completion of this transaction.

SWIM–1

By-Law Compliance

The Seller represents and warrants that the swimming pool and equipment are now, and on the completion date shall be, in good working order. The Parties agree that this representation and warranty shall survive and not merge on completion of this transaction, but apply only to the state of the property existing at completion of this transaction.

SWIM–2

Good Working Order— Warranty

The Seller agrees to winterize the swimming pool and equipment prior to completion, and shall provide a written undertaking on completion that the Seller shall be responsible for any costs or expenses incurred by the Buyer if the swimming pool and equipment are not properly winterized, provided only that the Buyer gives written notice of any claim to the Seller not later than _____ p.m. on the _____ day of _____, 20_____, failing which the Seller accepts no responsibility for costs.

SWIM–3

Winterization

TAX/PROPERTY

The Buyer understands and acknowledges that the Buyer is taking title to the real property knowing that the Seller's tax rate is based on a calculation of a property class that will not apply to the Buyer on completion. The Buyer further acknowledges that the Buyer will have to make application to qualify for the Farmland Class tax rate defined under the *Assessment Act of Ontario*, Regulation 282, 1998, Ontario Fair Assessment System and if the property does not qualify for the Farmland Class tax rate, the Buyer's property tax rate may be substantially higher than the Seller's.

TAX–1

Farm Tax—Buyer's Acknowledgement

The Seller warrants that the lands are free and clear of any local improvement charges and will be free and clear of local improvement charges on completion and that Seller has not received any notification of future local improvement charges for the property. If local improvement charges are not paid as of completion, they will be adjusted as a benefit to the Buyer on completion.

TAX–2

Local Improvement Charges

APPENDIX

TAX–3

Tax Holdback—
Completion of Building
Increases Assessment

The Buyer and Seller acknowledge that the property taxes have not been finally assessed prior to completion of the building(s) on the property. The Buyer and Seller agree that the Seller's solicitor shall hold back the amount of $ _____ for the payment of property taxes for the period prior to completion of this transaction. The Buyer or the Buyer's solicitor shall forthwith after notification by the municipality notify the Seller's solicitor of the amount of finally assessed property taxes. The Seller's solicitor shall immediately after notification pay the hold back or the amount thereof necessary to be paid in payment of the taxes accruing or owing prior to date of completion. If there has been no notification to the Seller's solicitor as aforesaid within three years after the completion of this transaction, the Seller's solicitor may release the holdback to the Seller. The Seller's solicitor shall supply a personal undertaking on completion to the Buyer to evidence the foregoing.

NOTE: This clause applies to the resale of nearly new construction, where the initial assessment was based only on land value.

TENANCY/ASSUMPTION

TEN–1

Assume Single Tenancy—
No Lease

The Seller represents and warrants that the _____ [property, basement, or _____ floor apartment] is occupied by _____ as a monthly tenant at the rate of _____ ($ _____) per month, payable on the _____ day of each month. The Parties agree that this representation and warranty shall survive and not merge on completion of this transaction, but apply only to those circumstances at completion of this transaction.

. . . .

TEN–2

Assume Single Tenancy—
With Lease

The _____ [property, basement, or _____ floor apartment] is occupied by _____ pursuant to a lease expiring on the _____ day of _____, 20_____. The Seller represents and warrants that the copy of the said lease attached hereto as Appendix _____ is a true and complete copy of the said lease. The Parties agree that this representation and warranty shall survive and not merge on completion of this transaction, but apply only to those circumstances existing at completion of this transaction.

. . . .

TEN–3

Assumption of Tenancies—
Multiple Units

Buyer agrees to assume the existing tenancies, as set out in the attached Schedule "_____", which the Seller warrants are the only tenancies affecting the property.

NOTE: Schedule should itemize categories such as: Apartment #, Tenant Name, Tenancy, Expiry Date, Rent Due Date, Prepaid Rent, and Tenancy Particulars (Items included in Rent).

NOTE: The actual lease documents should be attached as a Schedule to the Agreement. If too many documents, consider making Offer conditional upon inspection of tenancy agreement.

TITLE

The Buyer acknowledges that it has no legal or equitable interest in the Property as a result of entering into this Agreement until such time as the Buyer has completed the transaction. The Buyer covenants and agrees that the Buyer shall not cause or permit the registration of this Agreement or any memorandum or any notice (including a certificate of pending litigation or caution) thereof or with respect thereto at any time at the Land Registry Office or the Land Titles Office for _____ or in any other office of public record. If the Buyer shall be in breach of this covenant, the Seller shall, in addition to all other rights and remedies in law or in equity, be entitled to:

a) Cancel this Agreement and retain the deposit and any earned interest, free of all claims by the Buyer; and

b) A decree of order restraining or removing such registration and the Buyer shall not plead in defence thereto that there would be an adequate remedy at law, it being recognized and agreed that the injury and damage resulting from such breach would be impossible to measure monetarily.

In case of any such registration, the Buyer, on behalf of the Buyer and the Buyer's successors and assigns and on behalf of anyone claiming under the Buyer, hereby irrevocably appoints, nominates and constitutes the Seller as the Buyer's true and lawful attorney for the Buyer and in the Buyer's name and on the Buyer's behalf to execute all documents, releases, agreements and things as may be necessary or desirable to ensure that title to the Property is free of all claims of the Buyer.

TITLE–1
Agreement Not To Be Registered

....

The Seller hereby declares to the Buyer, and the Buyer acknowledges, understands, and accepts that this property is subject to certain reservations of the Crown, specifically but not limited to the fact that the [describe specific limitations and reservations] have been reserved.

TITLE–2
Crown Restrictions

....

The Buyer agrees to accept title to the property subject to an easement in favour of _____ _____.

TITLE–3
Easement— Acknowledgement

....

The Seller acknowledges and agrees that the Buyer has entered into this Agreement as Trustee for an unnamed Principal (the "Principal") and that upon the Buyer delivering written notice to the Seller of the name of the Principal, the Seller will complete the transaction with the Principal as if the Principal had been the party who originally signed the Agreement, and the Buyer who signed the Agreement shall have no personal liability for the Agreement.

TITLE–4
In Trust for Undisclosed Principal

....

The Seller agrees that the Buyer shall have the right to apply to register the lands or any part or parts under the Land Titles System, and Seller agrees to execute all documents required by the Buyer with respect thereto, provided that the Buyer pay all costs of said application and registration.

TITLE–5
Seller's Consent for Registration in Land Titles

APPENDIX

UFFI

UFFI–1

Acknowledgement—UFFI Present in Building

The Seller discloses and the Buyer acknowledges that the building contains urea formaldehyde foam insulation. The Buyer accepts the property in that state and further acknowledges that the Seller does not warrant the quality or quantity of the insulation or the quality of its installation.

UFFI–2

Seller has No Knowledge of UFFI

The Seller has no knowledge as to whether the property has been insulated with urea formaldehyde foam insulation and specifically makes no warranty in that regard. This paragraph supersedes any other term or condition or warranty in relation to urea formaldehyde foam insulation.

NOTE: Use where Seller has no personal knowledge of UFFI (i.e. a corporation handling a company transfer, Seller selling under Power of Sale, etc.). The Buyer may consider making the Offer conditional on an inspection for UFFI.

UFFI–3

UFFI Found But Corrective Action Taken

The Seller represents and warrants that the building was insulated with urea formaldehyde foam insulation but has undergone the following corrective actions: _____ _____. The Parties agree that this representation and warranty shall survive and not merge on completion of this transaction, but apply only to the state of the property at completion of this transaction.

NOTE: Details of all corrective action should be inserted in the space provided or supporting documentation attached as a Schedule.

UFFI–4

UFFI Removed from Building

The Seller represents and warrants that, although urea formaldehyde foam insulation (UFFI) was installed in the building, such UFFI was removed in _____, _____, by _____ , and the Seller further warrants that, to the best of his knowledge, no UFFI has been installed in the building since such removal. The Parties agree that this representation and warranty shall survive and not merge on completion of this transaction, but apply only to the state of the property at completion of this transaction. As evidence of the removal, the Seller attaches the following documents as Schedule "_____" which shall form part of this Agreement of Purchase and Sale.

UFFI–5

UFFI Test Performed with Negative Result

The Seller represents and warrants that the building was tested for the presence of urea formaldehyde foam insulation (UFFI) on the _____ day of _____, 20_____, by _____, and the result of such testing indicated that no UFFI was present in the building, and on the basis of such results the Seller provides this warranty. This clause applies only to UFFI and does not, in any way, include the testing of urea formaldehyde emissions from sources other than UFFI. The Parties agree that this representation and warranty shall survive and not merge on completion of this transaction, but apply only to the state of the property at completion of this transaction. As evidence of such testing, the Seller attaches the following documents as Schedule "_____" which shall form part of this Agreement of Purchase and Sale: _____ _____ [itemize documents].

UFFI–6

UFFI Test Performed with Positive Result But Within Acceptable Limits

The Seller acknowledges that the building contains urea formaldehyde foam insulation (UFFI) and was tested for the presence of emissions from UFFI on the _____ day of _____, 20_____, by _____, and the results of such testing indicated that emission from UFFI are within the acceptable limits and no further actions have been taken. As evidence of such testing, the Seller attaches the following documents as Schedule "_____" which shall form part of this Agreement of Purchase and Sale: _____ _____.

VACANT POSSESSION/NOTICES

The Buyer hereby authorizes and directs the Seller, and the Seller agrees, when this Agreement becomes unconditional, to give to the tenant(s) the requisite notices under the *Residential Tenancies Act*, requiring vacant possession of the property for use by the Buyer or the Buyer's immediate family, effective as of the _____ day of _____, 20_____, and the seller agrees to deliver copies of the requisite notices to the Buyer immediately after service of the notices upon the tenant. The Buyer and the Seller hereby agree in the event that the tenant fails to vacate the property prior to completion of the transaction, the Buyer agrees to assume the existing tenant upon completion of this transaction. Upon vacant possession being provided to the Buyer, the Buyer or the Buyer's immediate family agrees to take possession of and occupy the property forthwith thereafter. The Buyer agrees to provide the Seller with a written indemnity on completion, indemnifying the Seller from all actions, causes of action, claims and demands of any kind whatsoever, that may occur in the event that the Buyer does not take possession of and occupy the property as aforesaid.

NOTE: Due to the current state of Landlord and Tenant Law, the Seller will not be able to "guarantee" vacant possession on completion if a tenant refuses to vacate.

> **VAC–1**
>
> Vacant Possession/Notices

VERMICULITE

This Offer is conditional upon the Buyer testing the subject property for the presence of asbestos within the vermiculite insulation located upon property at the Buyer's own expense, and the obtaining of a report, respecting the said test satisfactory to the Buyer in the Buyer's sole and absolute discretion. Unless the Buyer gives notice in writing delivered to the Seller personally or in accordance with any other provisions for the delivery of notice in this Agreement of Purchase and Sale or any Schedule thereto not later than _____ p.m. on the _____ day of _____, 20_____, that this condition is fulfilled, this Offer shall be null and void and the deposit shall be returned to the Buyer in full without deduction. The Seller agrees to co-operate in providing access to the property for the purpose of this inspection. This condition is included for the benefit of the Buyer and may be waived at the Buyer's sole option by notice in writing to the Seller as aforesaid within the time period stated herein.

> **VER–1**
>
> Condition—
> Testing of Property for
> Vermiculite

The Seller has no knowledge as to whether the property has been insulated with insulation containing vermiculite and specifically makes no warranty in that regard. This paragraph supersedes any other term or condition or warranty in relation to vermiculite insulation.

> **VER–2**
>
> No Knowledge of
> Vermiculite

The Seller represents and warrants that the building was tested for the presence of asbestos within the vermiculite insulation located upon the property on the _____ day of _____, 20_____, by _____, and the result of such testing indicated that no asbestos was present in the vermiculite insulation in the building, and on the basis of such results the Seller provides this warranty. This clause applies only to vermiculite insulation and does not, in any way, include the testing of the presence of asbestos from sources other than the vermiculite insulation. The Parties agree that this representation and warranty shall survive and not merge on completion of this transaction, but apply only to the state of the property at completion of this transaction. As evidence of such testing, the Seller attaches the following documents as Schedule "_____" which shall form part of this Agreement of Purchase and Sale:

_____.

> **VER–3**
>
> Vermiculite—Asbestos Test
> Performed With Negative
> Result

APPENDIX

VER–4

Vermiculite Corrective Action

The Seller represents and warrants that the building was insulated with vermiculite insulation but has undergone the following corrective actions: _____. The Parties agree that this representation and warranty shall survive and not merge on completion of this transaction, but apply only to the state of the property at completion of this transaction.

NOTE: Details of all corrective action should be inserted in the space provided or supporting documentation attached as a Schedule.

VER–5

Vermiculite Removed from the Building

The Seller represents and warrants that, although vermiculite insulation was installed in the building, such vermiculite insulation was removed in _____, _____, by _____, and the Seller further warrants that, to the best of his knowledge, no vermiculite insulation has been installed in the building since such removal. The Parties agree that this representation and warranty shall survive and not merge on completion of this transaction, but apply only to the state of the property at completion of this transaction. As evidence of the removal, the Seller attaches the following documents as Schedule "_____" which shall form part of this Agreement of Purchase and Sale.

VER–6

Vermiculite Warranty

The Seller represents and warrants to the Buyer that during the time the Seller has owned the property, Seller has not caused any building on the property to be insulated with insulation containing vermiculite, and to the best of the Seller's knowledge no building on the property contains or has ever contained insulation containing vermiculite. This warranty shall survive and not merge on the completion of this transaction, and if the building is part of a multiple unit building, this warranty shall only apply to that part of the building which is the subject of this transaction.

ZONING

ZONING–1

Condition— Re-zoning/Minor Variance

This Offer is conditional upon the [Buyer/Seller] obtaining at the [Buyer's/Seller's] expense, a [re-zoning/minor variance], to allow for [specify exact variance/use] for said property. Both Buyer and Seller agree to proceed in a diligent manner to acquire the [re-zoning/minor variance]. Unless the [Buyer/Seller] gives notice in writing delivered to the [Seller/Buyer] not later than _____ p.m. on the _____ day of _____, 20___, that this condition is fulfilled, this Offer shall become null and void and the deposit shall be returned to the Buyer in full without deduction.

NOTE: If the Buyer wishes to retain the right to purchase the property, even though the rezoning or minor variance is not approved, then a "Waiver" should be included.

ZONING–2

Condition— Re-zoning with Seller's Consent

This Offer is conditional upon the Buyer obtaining at the Buyer's expense, a re-zoning of the property to permit _____ for the said property. Both Buyer and Seller agree to proceed in a diligent manner to obtain the re-zoning. Unless the Buyer gives notice in writing delivered to the Seller personally or in accordance with any other provisions for the delivery of notice in this Agreement of Purchase and Sale or any Schedule thereto not later than _____ p.m. on the _____ day of _____, 20_____, that this condition has been fulfilled, this Offer shall become null and void and the deposit shall be returned to the Buyer in full without deduction. This condition is included for the benefit of the Buyer and may be waived at the Buyer's sole option by notice in writing to the Seller as aforesaid within the time period stated herein.

The Seller agrees, upon written notice, to execute applications and all other documents required for the Buyer to change the official plan, if necessary, and to re-zone the lands to a zoning suitable to the Buyer, or to amend any bylaws, and to support such application or applications for re-zoning or amending of bylaws, and to co-operate with the Buyer, in all reasonable respects, provided that the Buyer pay all costs of said re-zoning.

APPENDIX

The Buyer shall have until not later than _____ p.m. on the _____ day of _____, 20_____, to satisfy the Buyer that the property is zoned in final and binding form under the relevant zoning bylaws and official plan to permit it to develop or use the property for the purpose of _____. If the Buyer is not so satisfied at the Buyer's sole and arbitrary discretion, the Buyer may terminate this Agreement by notice in writing delivered to the Seller personally or in accordance with any other provisions for the delivery of notice in this Agreement of Purchase and Sale or any Schedule thereto prior to the expiry of such period and the deposit shall be returned to the Buyer in full without deduction.

ZONING–3

Condition—
Zoning Satisfaction
(Condition Subsequent)

The Seller represents and warrants, to the best of his knowledge and belief, that:

(1) the buildings now located on the property are located wholly on the property and comply with all zoning and building bylaws; and

(2) the driveways serving the property are located wholly within the limits of the property, and entrance relating to such driveways have been approved by the appropriate road authority.

The Parties agree that these representations and warranties shall survive and not merge on completion of this transaction, but apply only to the state of the property existing at completion of this transaction.

ZONING–4

Location of
Buildings/Driveways

The Buyer acknowledges that the municipality where the property is situated may have a bylaw that restricts or limits the owner's right to rent out property and the buyer agrees to purchase the property subject to that restriction or limitation.

ZONING–5

Restriction—Short Term
Accommodation

The Seller warrants that the lands are zoned as _____ under bylaw _____ for the municipality of _____.

ZONING–6

Zoning—Warranty

APPENDIX

SOLUTIONS

CHAPTER 1
RESIDENTIAL HOUSING

Chapter Mini-Review

CH1 **MR**

1. For zoning purposes, a detached dwelling is best described as a building consisting of one dwelling unit.

    True   False

   A detached dwelling should be clearly differentiated from other housing configurations in which more than one dwelling unit is located within a building structure; e.g., a semi-detached, link home or townhouse.

2. The blank space for present use in the *Title Search* clause (Clause 8) in the *Agreement of Purchase and Sale* (OREA Form 100) must be filled out when drafting an agreement.

    True   **False**

   The blank space need not be completed, as the preprinted wording provides that the current use may be lawfully continued, unless otherwise stated.

3. Zoning provisions concerning home-based businesses will typically set out restrictions as to signage and number of non-resident employees.

    True   False

   The scope of such restrictions will vary by municipality.

4. The term *built form* refers to the design, appearance and configuration of existing structures within a community.

    True   False

   Built form is a significant consideration when addressing intensification in existing Ontario communities.

5. A private amenity in a gated community is typically a recreational facility or clubhouse that is not part of the common amenities within a gated community, and is operated as a separate business.

    True   False

   A golf course in a gated community might be an example of a private amenity with additional fees for residents to join the club and obtain ongoing golf privileges.

6. Flex-housing is a term introduced by the Ontario Building Code to describe new requirements that now apply to new residential construction.

    True   **False**

   Flex-housing is a term introduced by Canada Mortgage and Housing Corporation that emphasizes flexibility in housing to changing family and generational needs.

7. The *Residential Tenancies Act* includes provisions relating to care homes; i.e., various retirement residences offering accommodation and care to mature adults and seniors.

    True   False

   The Act applies to most retirement residences providing accommodation and care.

APPENDIX

8. A life lease community is a condominium project that provides the opportunity for mature adults to occupy a unit for the life of that individual (or individuals in the case of a couple).

  True   ✔ **False**

A life lease community, as described in this text, is not a condominium and is not governed under the *Condominium Act*.

9. The owner of a land lease community must allow real estate brokerages to place for sale or for rent signs on the listed home within that community.

  True   ✔ **False**

The landlord can prohibit signs from being placed on homes within the land lease community, but must provide an alternative (i.e., bulletin board in a prominent place).

10. Co-ownership places ownership and control directly in the hands of the tenant in common owners.

 True   False

Co-ownership involves property ownership directly by two more tenants in common.

Active Learning Exercises

▦ Exercise 1   Multiple Choice

1.1   A linked dwelling is best described as a:

a. Dwelling consisting of one dwelling unit.

Incorrect. This best describes a detached dwelling.

b. **Dwelling connected below grade by a concrete wall.**

✔ *CORRECT.* Height/thickness of the linking wall are typically set out in the municipal zoning by-law.

c. Dwelling that is attached by a party wall.

Incorrect. A dwelling attached by a party wall is a semi-detached dwelling.

d. Dwelling that is one of three or four separate dwelling units divided horizontally or vertically.

Incorrect. This statement best describes a triplex or a fourplex.

APPENDIX

1.2 Which of the following is a correct statement regarding home-based businesses?

a. Signage restrictions are rarely imposed on these businesses.

Incorrect. Signage restrictions are commonly imposed on home-based businesses by municipalities.

b. No business deductions are available for taxation purposes involving home-based businesses.

Incorrect. Business deductions are available for valid expenses; e.g., occupancy expense.

c. **Special rules may apply for health professionals operating a home-based office.**

✓ *CORRECT.* Special provisions may involve signage, separate entrance and parking. Reminder: Such special provisions are at the discretion of individual municipalities.

d. Business licenses are required for all home-based businesses.

Incorrect. Business licenses may be required for certain businesses, but not all businesses. Check with the municipality.

1.3 Gated communities:

a. Are found only in United States.

Incorrect. Gated communities are found in many countries, including Canada.

b. Are restricted to land lease communities in Ontario.

Incorrect. No such restriction applies in Ontario, although many gated communities are found on land lease property.

c. Must have security personnel at the entrance.

Incorrect. No such requirement exists, but larger gated communities typically opt for this arrangement. Smaller ones may use pass cards.

d. **Have not been widely accepted in Ontario at this time.**

✓ *CORRECT.* Gated communities are not commonly found in Ontario.

1.4 Which of the following statements is correct?

a. **A unique agreement of purchase and sale has been developed for modular or manufactured homes in land lease communities.**

✓ *CORRECT.* See *Agreement of Purchase and Sale— Mobile/Modular/Manufactured Home on Leased Premises* in this chapter.

b. Life lease communities are governed by the *Residential Tenancies Act.*

Incorrect. The *Residential Tenancies Act* does not address life lease communities, but does include provisions concerning land lease communities.

c. For legislative purposes, requirements for a land lease home are different than those for a mobile home.

Incorrect. The *Residential Tenancies Act* uses the terms land lease community and mobile home park interchangeably.

d. Tarion warranty coverage applies to residential dwellings in life lease communities.

Incorrect. Tarion warranty coverage does not apply.

APPENDIX

1.5 In a land lease community:

a. The landlord cannot include a right of first refusal in a tenancy agreement.

Incorrect. Landlords may include such a provision, subject to other requirements in the *Residential Tenancies Act.*

b. **Can include a right of first refusal, but such a right is subject to additional requirements under the Act.**

 CORRECT. The landlord can have a right of first refusal subject to a time limit to exercise that right.

c. Must include a right of first refusal in all tenancy agreements.

Incorrect. No such requirement exists, but if such a right is included it must meet other regulatory requirements.

d. A landlord must act for the tenant in selling his or her home.

Incorrect. The landlord *may*, NOT *must*, act for a tenant.

1.6 Which of the following is a correct statement?

a. The *Agreement of Purchase and Sale—Co-operative Building Resale* provides that both a share is sold and an occupancy agreement is created or assigned.

 CORRECT. The sale of an interest in a co-operative addresses both ownership and occupancy.

b. Modular homes are not largely constructed in a controlled environment, as is the case with manufactured homes.

Incorrect. Both modular and manufactured homes are largely constructed in a controlled environment.

c. *Places to Grow* legislation primarily promotes expansion of existing municipal boundaries.

Incorrect. Places to Grow legislation focuses on intensification within existing urban environments.

d. Section 9 of the Building Code focuses on building requirements for large, multi-story buildings.

Incorrect. Section 9 focuses on smaller residential structures with three stories or less.

■ Exercise 2   Matching

g.	Street Townhouse	Two or More Attached Dwellings Divided Vertically
c.	Intensification	Expanded Use of Existing Land and Services
k.	Built Form	Height, Shape and Appearance of Existing Buildings
a.	Retirement Residence	Private Pay Mature Adult Accommodation
b.	Factory-Built Housing	Modular Home
i.	Co-ownership	Tenants in Common
h.	Timeshare	Fractional Interest Based on Time Intervals
f.	Life Lease	Right to Occupy for Occupant's Life

No Match: d., e. and j.

■ Exercise 3   Offer Drafting
The completed agreement is shown on the following pages.

APPENDIX

OREA Ontario Real Estate Association

Agreement of Purchase and Sale
Co-operative Building Resale Agreement

Form 102
for use in the Province of Ontario

This Agreement of Purchase and Sale dated this ....**1st**........ day of ....**June**........................ 20..**XX**....

BUYER, ...**Vincent A. Rogato**.., agrees to purchase from
(Full legal names of all Buyers)

SELLER, ...**Sharon W. Wingate**.., the following
(Full legal names of all Sellers)

REAL PROPERTY AND SHARES:

The exclusive right to occupy and use ....**Suite 205**........................ (the "Unit")

in the Co-operative Apartment Building located at: ....**3397 West Shore Blvd.**........

in the ....**City of Anycity, Region of Anyregion**........................

Parking Space(s) ....**B05**........ Locker ....**A27**........(the "Property")

and ....**87**........ shares (the "shares") in the Capital of ....**3397 West Shore Blvd. Inc.**........ (the "Corporation")

PURCHASE PRICE: Dollars (CDN$) ....**$238,900.00**........

........**Two-Hundred and Thirty-Eight Thousand Nine Hundred**-- Dollars

DEPOSIT: Buyer submits ....**Upon Acceptance**........................
(Herewith/Upon Acceptance/as otherwise described in this Agreement)

........**Twelve Thousand**-- Dollars (CDN$) ....**$12,000.00**........

by negotiable cheque payable to ....**ABC Realty Inc.**........................ "Deposit Holder" to be held in trust pending completion or other termination of this Agreement and to be credited toward the Purchase Price on completion. For the purposes of this Agreement, "Upon Acceptance" shall mean that the Buyer is required to deliver the deposit to the Deposit Holder within 24 hours of the acceptance of this Agreement. The parties to this Agreement hereby acknowledge that, unless otherwise provided for in this Agreement, the Deposit Holder shall place the deposit in trust in the Deposit Holder's non-interest bearing Real Estate Trust Account and no interest shall be earned, received or paid on the deposit

Buyer agrees to pay the balance as more particularly set out in Schedule A attached.

SCHEDULE(S) A........................**attached hereto form(s) part of this Agreement.**

1.   **IRREVOCABILITY:** This offer shall be irrevocable by ....**Buyer**........................ until ....**6:00**........ a.m./p.m. on the
(Seller/Buyer)

........**2nd**........ day of ....**June**........................ 20 ..**XX**...., after which time, if not accepted, this offer shall be null and void and the deposit shall be returned to the Buyer in full without interest.

2.   **COMPLETION DATE:** This Agreement shall be completed by no later than 6:00 p.m. on the ..**20th**.. day of ....**August**........

20 ..**XX**...... Upon completion, vacant possession of the property shall be given to the Buyer unless otherwise provided for in this Agreement.

INITIALS OF BUYER(S): (*VR*)   **INITIALS OF SELLER(S):** (*SW*)

Form 102   Revised 2015   **Page 1 of 6**

3. **NOTICES:** The Seller hereby appoints the Listing Brokerage as agent for the Seller for the purpose of giving and receiving notices pursuant to this Agreement. Where a Brokerage (Buyer's Brokerage) has entered into a representation agreement with the Buyer, the Buyer hereby appoints the Buyer's Brokerage as agent for the purpose of giving and receiving notices pursuant to this Agreement. **Where a Brokerage represents both the Seller and the Buyer (multiple representation), the Brokerage shall not be appointed or authorized to be agent for either the Buyer or the Seller for the purpose of giving and receiving notices.** Any notice relating hereto or provided for herein shall be in writing. In addition to any provision contained herein and in any Schedule hereto, this offer, any counter-offer, notice of acceptance thereof or any notice to be given or received pursuant to this Agreement or any Schedule hereto (any of them, "Document") shall be deemed given and received when delivered personally or hand delivered to the Address for Service provided in the Acknowledgement below, or where a facsimile number or email address is provided herein, when transmitted electronically to that facsimile number or email address, respectively, in which case, the signature(s) of the party (parties) shall be deemed to be original.

FAX No.: ....   FAX No.: ....
(For delivery of Documents to Seller)   (For delivery of Documents to Buyer)

Email Address: ....   Email Address: ....
(For delivery of Documents to Seller)   (For delivery of Documents to Buyer)

4. **CHATTELS INCLUDED:** Acme Model R320 refrigerator, Acme Model S500 stove, Acme Model D200 dishwasher, and Acme Model S550 stacking washer/dryer.

....

....

....

Unless otherwise stated in this Agreement or any Schedule hereto, Seller agrees to convey all fixtures and chattels included in the Purchase Price free from all liens, encumbrances or claims affecting the said fixtures and chattels.

5. **FIXTURES EXCLUDED:** Dining room light fixture.

....

....

....

6. **RENTAL ITEMS (Including Lease, Lease to Own):** The following equipment is rented and **not** included in the Purchase Price. The Buyer agrees to assume the rental contract(s), if assumable:

N/A

....

....

The Buyer agrees to co-operate and execute such documentation as may be required to facilitate such assumption.

7. **MAINTENANCE EXPENSES:** Seller warrants that the maintenance expenses presently payable to the Corporation in respect of the property are

approximately $ ....625.00............ per month and include: ...property taxes, building insurance, heat, hydro, water

....

....

INITIALS OF BUYER(S): (*VR*)   **INITIALS OF SELLER(S):** (*SW*)

Form 102   Revised 2015   **Page 2 of 6**

8. **PARKING AND LOCKERS:** Parking and Lockers are as described above or assigned as follows: ......N/A.........................

.... at an additional cost of: ....

9. **HST:** If the sale of the Property (Real Property as described above) is subject to Harmonized Sales Tax (HST), then such tax shall be

...............**included in**.................... the Purchase Price. If the sale of the Property is not subject to HST, Seller agrees to certify on or before
<u>(included in/in addition to)</u>

closing, that the sale of the Property is not subject to HST. Any HST on chattels, if applicable, is not included in the Purchase Price.

10. **APPROVAL:** This Agreement is subject to Seller, at the Seller's own expense, obtaining approval of the Board of Directors of the Corporation to the sale and transfer of the Seller's shares in the capital of the Corporation to the Buyer and approval of the Buyer as shareholder and occupant of the

Unit, and if such approval is not obtained by 11:59 p.m. on the ...15th.. day of ....June................, 20XX........ this agreement shall become null and void and the Buyer's deposit shall be returned to the Buyer in full without deduction. The buyer agrees to cooperate and provide such information and documentation as may be within control of the Buyer in order to obtain said approval.

11. **TITLE SEARCH:** Buyer shall be allowed until 6:00 p.m. on the ...20th.. day of ....July..................., 20XX.., (Requisition Date) to examine the Corporation's title to the Property at the Buyer's expense and until the earlier of: (i) thirty days from the later of the Requisition Date or the date on which the conditions in this Agreement are fulfilled or otherwise waived or; (ii) five days prior to completion, to satisfy the Buyer that there are

no outstanding work orders or deficiency notices affecting the Property, and that its present use (.....**single family residential**........) may be lawfully continued. If within that time any valid objection to title or to any outstanding work order or deficiency notice, or to the fact the said present use may not lawfully be continued, is made in writing to Seller and which Seller is unable or unwilling to remove, remedy or satisfy and which Buyer will not waive, this Agreement notwithstanding any intermediate acts or negotiations in respect of such objections, shall be at an end and all monies paid shall be returned without interest or deduction and Seller, Listing Brokerage and Co-operating Brokerage shall not be liable for any costs or damages. Save as to any valid objection so made by such day and except for any objection going to the root of the title, Buyer shall be conclusively deemed to have accepted Seller's title to the Property. Seller hereby consents to the municipality or other governmental agencies releasing to Buyer details of all outstanding work orders affecting the Property, and Seller agrees to execute and deliver such further authorizations in this regard as Buyer may reasonably require.

12. **CORPORATION DOCUMENTATION:** The Seller shall deliver to the Buyer on or before closing:
   (a) a certified copy of the Resolution of the Board of Directors of the Corporation approving the Buyer as a shareholder and as an occupant of the Unit;
   (b) a share certificate for the Seller's shares in the capital of the Corporation endorsed in favour of the Buyer;
   (c) a certificate or letter from the Corporation confirming:
      (i) with respect to the Property, that all charges and obligations have been paid or discharged as of the date of closing;
      (ii) with respect to the Corporation that the affairs of the Corporation are in order and that there are no legal actions pending against the Corporation or contemplated by the Corporation, that there are no special assessments contemplated by the Corporation, that there are no orders or complaints against the real property by the Building, Health or Fire Departments, that no sale of real property is contemplated, and the Building is not and never has been insulated with Urea-Formaldehyde Foam Insulation.

13. **OCCUPANCY AGREEMENT:** The Buyer agrees on or before closing to enter into an Occupancy Agreement with the Corporation and to abide by the rules and regulations of the Corporation.

14. **TITLE:** Buyer agrees to accept the Corporation's title to the Property subject to all rights and easements registered against title for the supply and installation of telephone services, electricity, gas, sewers, water, television cable facilities and other related services; provided that title to the Property is otherwise good and free from all encumbrances except: (a) as herein expressly provided; (b) any registered restrictions, conditions or covenants that run with the land provided such have been complied with; and (c) any existing municipal agreements, zoning by-laws and/or regulations and utility or service contracts.

15. **DOCUMENTS AND DISCHARGE:** Buyer shall not call for the production of any title deed, abstract, survey or other evidence of title to the Property except such as are in the possession or control of Seller. If a discharge of any Charge/Mortgage, lien or other encumbrance held by a corporation incorporated pursuant to the Trust And Loan Companies Act (Canada), Chartered Bank, Trust Company, Credit Union, Caisse Populaire or Insurance Company and which is not to be assumed by Buyer on completion, is not available in registrable form on completion, Buyer agrees to accept Seller's lawyer's personal undertaking to obtain, out of the closing funds, a discharge in registrable form and to register same, or cause same to be registered, on title within a reasonable period of time after completion, provided that on or before completion Seller shall provide to Buyer a statement prepared by the mortgagee, lienholder or encumbrancer setting out the balance required to obtain the discharge, and, where a real-time electronic cleared funds transfer system is not being used, a direction executed by Seller directing payment to the mortgagee, lienholder or encumbrancer of the amount required to obtain the discharge out of the balance due on completion.

INITIALS OF BUYER(S): (*VR*)   INITIALS OF SELLER(S): (*SW*)

Form 102   Revised 2015   **Page 3 of 6**

16. **MEETINGS:** Seller represents and warrants to Buyer that at the time of the acceptance of this Offer the Seller has not received a notice convening a special or general meeting of the Corporation respecting; (a) the termination of the government of the property; (b) the winding up or dissolution of the Corporation; (c) any substantial alteration in or substantial addition to the property or the renovation thereof; OR (d) any substantial change in the assets or liabilities of the Corporation; and Seller covenants that if the Seller receives any such notice prior to the date of completion the Seller shall forthwith notify Buyer in writing and the Buyer may thereupon at the Buyer's option declare this Agreement to be null and void and all monies paid by Buyer shall be refunded without interest or deduction.

17. **INSPECTION:** Buyer acknowledges having had the opportunity to inspect the Property and understands that upon acceptance of this offer there shall be a binding agreement of purchase and sale between Buyer and Seller. **The Buyer acknowledges having the opportunity to include a requirement for a property inspection report in this Agreement and agrees that except as may be specifically provided for in this Agreement, the Buyer will not be obtaining a property inspection or property inspection report regarding the Property.**

18. **INSURANCE:** The Unit and all other things being purchased shall be and remain at the risk of the Seller until completion. In the event of substantial damage to the real property Buyer may at the Buyer's option either permit the proceeds of insurance to be used for repair of such damage in accordance with the provisions of the Insurance Trust Agreement or other insurance arrangement, or terminate this Agreement and all deposit monies paid by Buyer hereunder shall be refunded without interest or deduction. If Seller is taking back a Charge/Mortgage, or Buyer is assuming a Charge/Mortgage, Buyer shall supply Seller with reasonable evidence of adequate insurance to protect Seller's or other mortgagee's interest on completion.

19. **RESIDENCY:** (a) Subject to (b) below, the Seller represents and warrants that the Seller is not and on completion will not be a non-resident under the non-residency provisions of the Income Tax Act which representation and warranty shall survive and not merge upon the completion of this transaction and the Seller shall deliver to the Buyer a statutory declaration that Seller is not then a non-resident of Canada;
(b) provided that if the Seller is a non-resident under the non-residency provisions of the Income Tax Act, the Buyer shall be credited towards the Purchase Price with the amount, if any, necessary for Buyer to pay to the Minister of National Revenue to satisfy Buyer's liability in respect of tax payable by Seller under the non-residency provisions of the Income Tax Act by reason of this sale. Buyer shall not claim such credit if Seller delivers on completion the prescribed certificate.

20. **ADJUSTMENTS:** Maintenance expenses and, where billed to the Unit and not the Corporation, realty taxes, including local improvement rates; mortgage interest; rentals; unmetered public or private utilities and fuel; are to be apportioned and allowed to the day of completion, the day of completion itself to be apportioned to the Buyer. There shall be no adjustment for the Seller's share of any reserve or contingency fund to which the Seller may have contributed prior to the date of completion.

21. **TIME LIMITS:** Time shall in all respects be of the essence hereof provided that the time for doing or completing of any matter provided for herein may be extended or abridged by an agreement in writing signed by Seller and Buyer or by their respective lawyers who may be specifically authorized in that regard.

22. **TENDER:** Any tender of documents or money hereunder may be made upon Seller or Buyer or their respective lawyers on the day set for completion. Money shall be tendered with funds drawn on a lawyer's trust account in the form of a bank draft, certified cheque or wire transfer using the Large Value Transfer System

23. **FAMILY LAW ACT:** Seller warrants that spousal consent is not necessary to this transaction under the provisions of the Family Law Act, R.S.O.1990 unless Seller's spouse has executed the consent hereinafter provided.

24. **LEGAL, ACCOUNTING AND ENVIRONMENTAL ADVICE:** The parties acknowledge that any information provided by the brokerage is not legal, tax or environmental advice.

25. **CONSUMER REPORTS: The Buyer is hereby notified that a consumer report containing credit and/or personal information may be referred to in connection with this transaction.**

26. **AGREEMENT IN WRITING:** If there is conflict or discrepancy between any provision added to this Agreement (including any Schedule attached hereto) and any provision in the standard pre-set portion hereof, the added provision shall supersede the standard pre-set provision to the extent of such conflict or discrepancy. This Agreement including any Schedule attached hereto, shall constitute the entire Agreement between Buyer and Seller. There is no representation, warranty, collateral agreement or condition, which affects this Agreement other than as expressed herein. For the purposes of this Agreement, Seller means vendor and Buyer means purchaser. This Agreement shall be read with all changes of gender or number required by the context.

27. **TIME AND DATE:** Any reference to a time and date in this Agreement shall mean the time and date where the property is located.

INITIALS OF BUYER(S): (*VR*)   INITIALS OF SELLER(S): (*SW*)

APPENDIX

28. SUCCESSORS AND ASSIGNS: The heirs, executors, administrators, successors and assigns of the undersigned are bound by the terms herein.

SIGNED, SEALED AND DELIVERED in the presence of: IN WITNESS whereof I have hereunto set my hand and seal:

Anthony Movis
(Witness)

Vincent A. Rogato
(Buyer) (Seal) DATE _June 1/xx_

(Witness)

(Buyer) (Seal) DATE

I, the Undersigned Seller, agree to the above offer. I hereby irrevocably instruct my lawyer to pay directly to the brokerage(s) with whom I have agreed to pay commission, the unpaid balance of the commission together with applicable Harmonized Sales Tax (and any other taxes as may hereafter be applicable), from the proceeds of the sale prior to any payment to the undersigned on completion, as advised by the brokerage(s) to my lawyer.

SIGNED, SEALED AND DELIVERED in the presence of: IN WITNESS whereof I have hereunto set my hand and seal:

Albert Lee
(Witness)

Sharon W. Wingate
(Seller) (Seal) DATE _June 2/xx_

(Witness)

(Seller) (Seal) DATE

SPOUSAL CONSENT: The Undersigned Spouse of the Seller hereby consents to the disposition evidenced herein pursuant to the provisions of the Family Law Act, R.S.O.1990, and hereby agrees with the Buyer that he/she will execute all necessary or incidental documents to give full force and effect to the sale evidenced herein.

(Witness)

(Spouse) (Seal) DATE

CONFIRMATION OF ACCEPTANCE: Notwithstanding anything contained herein to the contrary, I confirm this Agreement with all changes both typed and written was finally accepted by all parties at _3:00_ a.m./p.m. this _2nd_ day of _June_ , 20 _xx_ .

Sharon W. Wingate
(Signature of Seller or Buyer)

INFORMATION ON BROKERAGE(S)

Listing Brokerage ...... **ABC Realty Inc.** ...... Tel.No.(_416_) _555-1212_

123 Main Street, Anycity, Anyregion L4H 6P5 **Albert Lee**
(Salesperson / Broker Name)

Co-op/Buyer Brokerage ...... **XYZ Real Estate Ltd.** ...... Tel.No.(_416_) _666-1212_

29 Maple Drive, Anycity, Anyregion L2J 7K6 **Anthony Movis**
(Salesperson / Broker Name)

ACKNOWLEDGEMENT

I acknowledge receipt of my signed copy of this accepted Agreement of Purchase and Sale and I authorize the Brokerage to forward a copy to my lawyer.

Sharon W. Wingate DATE _June 2/xx_
(Seller)

DATE
(Seller)

Address for Service _3397 West Shore Blvd., #205_

Anycity N8B 2C3 Tel.No.(_416_) _777-1212_

Seller's Lawyer _Cindy Jones and Associates_

Address _565 Pine Street, Anycity RK4 8L9_

Email

(_416_) _666-5544_ (_416_) _666-5454_
Tel.No. FAX No.

I acknowledge receipt of my signed copy of this accepted Agreement of Purchase and Sale and I authorize the Brokerage to forward a copy to my lawyer.

Vincent A. Rogato DATE _June 2/xx_
(Buyer)

DATE
(Buyer)

Address for Service _1321 Summerlin Court, Anycity B6L 7J9_

Tel.No.(_416_) _888-1212_

Buyer's Lawyer _George Roberts and Associates_

Address _15 Concession Street, Anycity B5D 3P9_

Email

(_416_) _777-5353_ (_416_) _777-5454_
Tel.No. FAX No.

Property Manager: **Anycity Property Management 30 Welland Drive, Anycity, ON K0N 1P0 416-999-1212 / 416-999-2121**
(Name) (Address) (Tel No.,FAX No.)

FOR OFFICE USE ONLY **COMMISSION TRUST AGREEMENT**

To: Co-operating Brokerage shown on the foregoing Agreement of Purchase and Sale:
In consideration for the Co-operating Brokerage procuring the foregoing Agreement of Purchase and Sale, I hereby declare that all moneys received or receivable by me in connection with the Transaction as contemplated in the MLS® Rules and Regulations of my Real Estate Board shall be receivable and held in trust. This agreement shall constitute a Commission Trust Agreement as defined in the MLS® Rules and shall be subject to and governed by the MLS® Rules pertaining to Commission Trust.

DATED as of the date and time of the acceptance of the foregoing Agreement of Purchase and Sale. Acknowledged by:

Albert Lee
(Authorized to bind the Listing Brokerage)

Anthony Movis
(Authorized to bind the Co-operating Brokerage)

Form 102 Revised 2015 **Page 5 of 6**

APPENDIX

OREA Ontario Real Estate Association

Form 102
for use in the Province of Ontario

Schedule A
**Agreement of Purchase and Sale –
Co-operative Building Resale**

This Schedule is attached to and forms part of the Agreement of Purchase and Sale between:

BUYER, ... Vincent A. Rogato ...., and

SELLER, ... Sharon W. Wingate ....

for the purchase and sale of .... Suite 205, 3397 West Shore Blvd., Anycity, Anyregion ....

.... dated the .... 1st .. day of .... June ...., 20. XX ....

Buyer agrees to pay the balance as follows:

The Buyer agrees to pay a further sum of Two Hundred and Twenty-Six Thousand, Nine Hundred Dollars ($226,900.00), subject to adjustments, to the Seller on completion of this transaction, with funds drawn on a lawyer's trust account in the form of a bank draft, certified cheque, or wire transfer using the Large Value Transfer System.

This Offer is conditional upon the inspection of the subject property by a home inspector at the Buyer's own expense, and the obtaining of a report satisfactory to the Buyer in the Buyer's sole and absolute discretion. Unless the Buyer gives notice in writing delivered to the Seller personally or in accordance with any other provisions for the delivery of notice in this Agreement of Purchase and Sale or any Schedule attached thereto not later than 6:00 p.m. on the 12th day of June, 20xx, that this condition is fulfilled, this Offer shall be null and void and the deposit shall be returned to the Buyer in full without deduction. The Seller agrees to co-operate in providing access to the property for the purpose of this inspection. This condition is included for the benefit of the Buyer and may be waived at the Buyer's sole option by notice in writing to the Seller as aforesaid within the time period stated herein.

This form must be initialed by all parties to the Agreement of Purchase and Sale.

INITIALS OF BUYER(S): (VR)   **INITIALS OF SELLER(S):** (SW)

Form 102   Revised 2015   **Page 6 of 6**

CHAPTER 2
RESIDENTIAL CONDOMINIUM

Chapter Mini-Review

1. When seeking approval for a condominium, an application (including a draft plan) is typically delivered to the local municipality, who in turn circulates the materials to persons and public agencies having an interest in the application.

    True   False

   The word *'typically'* is included in this question, as situations can arise where a municipality does not have the authority. The application would be handled by the Ministry of Municipal Affairs and Housing.

2. If a high-rise residential condominium is constructed that falls under Part 9 of the Ontario Building Code, the developer must comply with design and site review requirements of the Tarion Warranty Corporation.

    True   **False**

   High-rise construction falls under Sec. 3 of the Ontario Building Code. Section 9 relates to housing and small structures.

3. The declaration sets out the proportionate amount for each unit in order to determine each unit's contribution to common expenses.

    True   False

   The exact method used to arrive at the proportionate share may vary. This calculation is commonly based on unit square footage in relation to total unit square footage, but alternate methods can be used.

4. The declarant must hold a freehold interest in the land in order for a condominium corporation to be formed pursuant to the *Condominium Act*.

    True   **False**

   The declarant can hold either a freehold or a leasehold interest in the land.

5. The directors of a condominium corporation must adhere to a standard of care in carrying out their functions, unless otherwise instructed by the management company that handles day-to-day affairs of the corporation.

    True   **False**

   Directors must adhere to a standard of care despite any instruction to the contrary.

6. Rules cannot be made, amended or repealed by the board of directors without holding a general meeting of owners.

    True   **False**

   Rules are effective in 30 days, if no meeting of unit owners is requisitioned.

7. Ownership interests in a vacant land condominium are based on the size of individual land units.

    True   False

   As such, larger land unit owners have a larger proportionate ownership interest.

APPENDIX

Chapter Mini-Review (continued)

8. A unit owner, who owns a separately-titled parking space, may be permitted to sell the space to another owner at fair market value depending on provisions set out in the declaration, by-laws and/or rules.

    True   ◯ False

   This is a true statement as the sale would be subject to provisions set out in the declaration, by-laws and/or rules.

9. A common element condominium is generally referred to as a standard condominium pursuant to the *Condominium Act*.

   ◯ True   **False**

   A standard condominium is the original type of condominium, which remains the most prevalent in the province. Other types, such as the common elements condominium, were introduced during the past decade.

10. In the *Condominium Resale Agreement* (OREA Form 101), the preprinted wording provides that the agreement is subject to the buyer's approval of the status certificate within the title search requisition period.

    ◯ True   **False**

    The preprinted wording only refers to consent by the seller to request the certificate. An appropriate condition should be inserted regarding buyer approval.

11. Use restrictions in condominium documentation are always detailed in the rules, as opposed to the by-laws or the declaration.

    ◯ True   **False**

    Use restrictions can appear in any or all of these documents.

12. If repair costs exceed monies available in the reserve fund, a special assessment may be levied against unit owners to meet such expenses.

     True   ◯ False

    A special assessment would be needed to make up the shortfall.

Active Learning Exercises

■ Exercise 1   Common Expenses

	YEARLY	MONTHLY
Unit Common Expenses		
$2,871,500 x .002758 (0.2758%)	$7,919.60	$659.97
Parking Spaces (Separately Titled)		
2,871,500 x .000196 (0.0196%)	562.81	46.90
2,871,500 x .000179 (0.0179%)	514.00	42.83
Total		**$749.70**

APPENDIX

■ **Exercise 2   Condominium Facts**

2.1 The board of directors is obligated to terminate the condominium when substantial damage occurs to a condominium (exceeding 25% of the replacement cost of buildings and other structures).

  Correct    Not Correct

Reason: The corporation is only obligated to terminate the condominium if, after appropriate notice to owners, a meeting of the owners is requisitioned and 80% of unit owners consent to the termination. Otherwise, necessary repairs must be made.

2.2 A minimum of 10% of the budgeted amount for common expense contributions must be held in the reserve fund at all times.

  Correct    Not Correct

Reason: The initial reserve fund must be the greater of sufficient money to handle repairs and replacements based on life expectancies and replacements costs, or 10% of the budgeted amount for common expense contributions. When the first reserve fund study is completed and thereafter, study specifics determine what funds must be in reserve for ongoing repairs and replacements.

2.3 A phased condominium can make sound economic sense, particularly with larger condominium projects.

  Correct    Not Correct

Reason: The phased condominium permits the successive development of condominium projects in which additional common elements and units are added under a single condominium corporation. This process avoids duplication (e.g., several boards of directors) and promotes cost efficiencies (e.g., bulk buying of utilities).

2.4 In the *Agreement of Purchase and Sale—Condominium Resale* (OREA Form 101), the seller only represents and warrants that there are no special assessments, but does not make any other representations/warranties concerning the condominium corporation.

  Correct    Not Correct

Reason: The seller also represents and warrants that he/she has not received a notice convening a special meeting regarding condominium termination, substantial alterations/additions to the common elements or any substantial change in corporation assets/liabilities.

2.5 A seller could obtain a status certificate to assist in the listing process and make such document available to the buyer. The buyer would then not need to request a status certificate when making an offer.

○ Correct    Not Correct

Reason: The seller may elect to request a certificate at time of listing. This would assist in the listing process and also provide valuable information for the buyer when viewing the property and making an offer. However, currency of certificate information must be considered. For example, significant developments could well take place between the date of listing and offer date; e.g., a special assessment, increase in common expense payments or judgments filed against the corporation.

Interestingly, some lawyers require when a status certificate is obtained at point of offer that another be requested immediately before closing, particularly in the case of extended closing dates.

APPENDIX

2.6 If a status certificate is not issued by a condominium corporation when requested by a buyer, a certificate is deemed to be provided stating certain facts regarding common expenses.

☑ **Correct**　　　　　　○ **Not Correct**

Reason: The deemed certificate states that no default in common expenses has taken place, no increase in common expenses has occurred since the date of the current year's budget and no levies have been assessed against the unit.

■ Exercise 3　Form Comparison

CLAUSE	WORDING DIFFERENCE
Real Property Description	Legal descriptions of freehold properties include a lot and plan number, along with lot dimensions. Condominiums are described by Unit, Level and Condominium Plan numbers including a reference to ownership/exclusive use of parking and/or storage, along with tenancy in common interest in the common elements.
Clause 7	Monthly maintenance fee and what the fee includes.
Clause 8	Parking and lockers.
Clauses 11	Buyer to accept property title subject to the *Condominium Act*, declaration, description, by-laws and rules/regulations.
Clause 13	Financial health of the condominium corporation and authority to request a status certificate.
Clause 14	Production of condominium documentation pertaining to the condominium corporation.
Clause 15	Seller warrant regarding no scheduled special or general meeting regarding governance changes, alterations or additions to common elements, or changes in assets/liabilities.
Clause 17	Agreement approval by the condominium corporation, if applicable.
Clause 18	Reference to unit and insurance trust agreement.
Clause 21	Includes an adjustment for common expenses.

The condominium form also has a space for information on the property manager (Page 5 following Acknowledgements). Also note that the clause found in the *Agreement of Purchase and Sale* (OREA Form 100), relating to compliance with subdivision control, has understandably been deleted.

■ Exercise 4　Analyzing the Condominium Resale Agreement

Chattels	Description of appliances should be more specific.
Additional Parking Space	Further information required regarding cost and length of assignment.

APPENDIX

Irrevocability	Counter offer changes incorrectly prepared. Buyer not changed to seller.
Completion Date	No such date exists.
Initialling	Raymond Ng's initials are missing.
Spousal Consent	Natalie Sharma's signature is required. See exercise details.
Confirmation of Acceptance	Dated after irrevocable date.
Mortgage Assumption	Typically, a condition would be required. Most conventional mortgages include a provision that any assumption must be approved by the mortgagee.
Seller Take Back	STB poorly drafted from both buyer and seller perspectives. 1. Buyer not provided any flexibility regarding prepayment. 2. Seller not provided ability to complete credit check. 3. No postponement clause included (first mortgage expires before second—see exercise details).
Offer Math	Deposit + Further Sum + Mortgage Assumption + STB does not add up to $285,000. Further sum amount is incorrect, both on original offer and signback. Should have been $17,000 increased to $24,000.
Status Certificate	The offer should have been conditional on a review of the status certificate for the protection of the buyer.

■ Exercise 5   SPIS—Unit 4, 17 Manor Hill Road

SECTION	LINE	CONCERN	BRIEF EXPLANATION/ACTION PLAN
SPIS Form 220			
General	10	Additional Townhouses	What location? When is construction scheduled? Impact on unit; e.g., what does partially obstructed mean? See additional comments on SPIS.
	12	Restrictive Covenants	Not Completed. Any significant restrictions that impact unit.
	13	Drainage Restrictions	Any significant restrictions that impact unit.
	14	Local Levies/Other Taxes	Unknown. Further information required. Check with tax department.
	15	Claims	As above (Item #14).
	18	Appliances	Identify appliances. Rental or conditional sales contracts? Assumable? How much to discharge? Verify source documents.
	22	HST Status Unknown	Confirm with accountant.

APPENDIX

SECTION	LINE	CONCERN	BRIEF EXPLANATION/ACTION PLAN
Improvements and Structural	1	Leaking Windows	See additional comments. Is there an installation warranty? Should be checked.
	2	Renovations	See additional comments. Owner altered pass-through and added a small rear deck. Was condo approval received? Is there a possible structural problem? No building permit was issued. Verify status.
	10	Type of Wiring	Unknown. Buyer will want to verify.

SPIS Form 221—Condominium Schedule

Condominium Corporation	1	Condominium Fee	Require more detail on which utilities are included.
	2	Special Assessment	Seller answers as *no,* but special assessment may be pending due to windows. Status certificate will also furnish additional details.
	5	Reserve Fund	Check reserve fund amount and determine if Reserve Fund Study has been made, as it could affect monthly common expense fees.
	6	By-Law Amendments	See additional comments. No pet by-law being considered. Check current status. Rentals restricted to minimum six month duration. Could impact scope of potential buyers.
	7	Approval	No approval for pass through or small rear deck. Does satellite dish require board approval?

CH2 EX5

■ Exercise 6   The Partially-Completed Offer

CH2 EX6

The fully completed offer is shown on the following pages.

APPENDIX

OREA Ontario Real Estate Association

Agreement of Purchase and Sale
Condominium Resale

Form 101
for use in the Province of Ontario

This Agreement of Purchase and Sale dated this ...... **8th** ...... day of .... **September** .... 20 **XX**

BUYER, ... **Barbara Lopez** ...., agrees to purchase from
(Full legal names of all Buyers)

SELLER, ... **Victoria Anne Cooper and Joseph Alan Cooper** ...., the following
(Full legal names of all Sellers)

PROPERTY:
a unit in the condominium property known as .... **Townhouse** .... No...... **7**
(Apartment/Townhouse/Suite/Unit)

located at .... **394 Highland Road** ....

in the .... **City of Anycity, Regional Municipality of Anyregion** ....

being .... **Anyregion** .... Condominium Plan No .... **210** ....
(Legal Name of Condominium Corporation)

Unit Number ...... **7** ...... Level No. ...... **1** ...... Building No. ...... **1** ...... together with ownership

or exclusive use of Parking Space(s) .... **16 and 17**   **Level A** ...., together with ownership or exclusive use of
(Number(s), Level(s))

Locker(s) ...... **N/A** ......, together with Seller's proportionate undivided tenancy-in-common interest
(Number(s), Level(s))

in the common elements appurtenant to the Unit as described in the Declaration and Description including the exclusive right to use such other parts of the common elements appurtenant to the Unit as may be specified in the Declaration and Description: the Unit, the proportionate interest in the common elements appurtenant thereto, and the exclusive use portions of the common elements, being herein called the "Property".   *BL* **$215,000.00** *VC JC*

PURCHASE PRICE: *BL*   *VC JC*   Dollars (CDN$) ...... ~~$200,000.00~~ ......
     Fifteen Thousand
Two Hundred and ~~Nine Thousand~~ -- Dollars

DEPOSIT: Buyer submits .... **Upon Acceptance** ....
(Herewith/Upon Acceptance/as otherwise described in this Agreement)

  Five Thousand -- Dollars (CDN$) ...... **$5,000.00** ......

by negotiable cheque payable to .... **ABC Realty Inc.** .... "Deposit Holder" to be held
in trust pending completion or other termination of this Agreement and to be credited toward the Purchase Price on completion. For the purposes of this Agreement, "Upon Acceptance" shall mean that the Buyer is required to deliver the deposit to the Deposit Holder within 24 hours of the acceptance of this Agreement. The parties to this Agreement hereby acknowledge that, unless otherwise provided for in this Agreement, the Deposit Holder shall place the deposit in trust in the Deposit Holder's non-interest bearing Real Estate Trust Account and no interest shall be earned, received or paid on the deposit.

Buyer agrees to pay the balance as more particularly set out in Schedule A attached.

SCHEDULE(S) A .... **attached hereto form(s) part of this Agreement.**
                      BL **Seller** *VC JC*   *BL VC JC* **10th**

1.   **IRREVOCABILITY:** This offer shall be irrevocable by .... ~~**Buyer**~~ .... until ...... **5:00** ...... ~~a.m.~~/p.m. on the **9th**
(Seller/Buyer)

day of .... **September** .... 20 **XX** ......, after which time, if not accepted, this offer shall be null and void and the deposit shall be returned to the Buyer in full without interest.

2.   **COMPLETION DATE:** This Agreement shall be completed by no later than 6:00 p.m. on the ...... **1st** ...... day of .... **December** ....,

20 **XX** .... Upon completion, vacant possession of the property shall be given to the Buyer unless otherwise provided for in this Agreement.

INITIALS OF BUYER(S): (*BL*)   **INITIALS OF SELLER(S):** (*VC JC*)

Form 101   Revised 2015   **Page 1 of 6**

3. **NOTICES:** The Seller hereby appoints the Listing Brokerage as agent for the Seller for the purpose of giving and receiving notices pursuant to this Agreement. Where a Brokerage (Buyer's Brokerage) has entered into a representation agreement with the Buyer, the Buyer hereby appoints the Buyer's Brokerage as agent for the purpose of giving and receiving notices pursuant to this Agreement. **Where a Brokerage represents both the Seller and the Buyer (multiple representation), the Brokerage shall not be appointed or authorized to be agent for either the Buyer or the Seller for the purpose of giving and receiving notices.** Any notice relating hereto or provided for herein shall be in writing. In addition to any provision contained herein and in any Schedule hereto, this offer, any counter-offer, notice of acceptance thereof or any notice to be given or received pursuant to this Agreement or any Schedule hereto (any of them, "Document") shall be deemed given and received when delivered personally or hand delivered to the Address for Service provided in the Acknowledgement below, or where a facsimile number or email address is provided herein, when transmitted electronically to that facsimile number or email address, respectively, in which case, the signature(s) of the party (parties) shall be deemed to be original.

FAX No.: ....   FAX No.: ....
(For delivery of Documents to Seller)   (For delivery of Documents to Buyer)

Email Address: ....   Email Address: ....
(For delivery of Documents to Seller)   (For delivery of Documents to Buyer)

4. **CHATTELS INCLUDED:** Sun Glamour patio set including four chairs, table, and umbrella; mirror located in foyer; and broadloom in living room, dining room, family room, and three bedrooms

Unless otherwise stated in this Agreement or any Schedule hereto, Seller agrees to convey all fixtures and chattels included in the Purchase Price free from all liens, encumbrances or claims affecting the said fixtures and chattels.

5. **FIXTURES EXCLUDED:** Dining room chandelier

6. **RENTAL ITEMS (Including Lease, Lease to Own):** The following equipment is rented and **not** included in the Purchase Price. The Buyer ` agrees to assume the rental contract(s), if assumable:

Hot water tank and water softener @ $51.20 per month (plus applicable taxes)

The Buyer agrees to co-operate and execute such documentation as may be required to facilitate such assumption.

7. **COMMON EXPENSES:** Seller warrants to Buyer that the common expenses presently payable to the Condominium Corporation in respect of the Property are approximately $ 189.05 per month, which amount includes the following: Water charges, lawn and road maintenance, garbage pickup, and insurance (common elements)

8. **PARKING AND LOCKERS:** Parking and Lockers are as described above or assigned as follows: N/A
.... at an additional cost of: ....

INITIALS OF BUYER(S): (*BL*)   INITIALS OF SELLER(S): (*VC JC*)

Form 101   Revised 2015   **Page 2 of 6**

APPENDIX

9. **HST:** If the sale of the Property (Real Property as described above) is subject to Harmonized Sales Tax (HST), then such tax shall be
..............**included in**.............. the Purchase Price. If the sale of the Property is not subject to HST, Seller agrees to certify on or before
(included in/in addition to)
closing, that the sale of the Property is not subject to HST. Any HST on chattels, if applicable, is not included in the Purchase Price.

10. **TITLE SEARCH:** Buyer shall be allowed until 6:00 p.m. on the ..**30th**.. day of ....**October**.............., 20.**XX**., (Requisition Date)
to examine the title to the Property at Buyer's own expense and until the earlier of: (i) thirty days from the later of the Requisition Date or the date
on which the conditions in this Agreement are fulfilled or otherwise waived or; (ii) five days prior to completion, to satisfy Buyer that there are no

outstanding work orders or deficiency notices affecting the Property, and that its present use (..............**single family residential**..............)
may be lawfully continued. If within that time any valid objection to title or to any outstanding work order or deficiency notice, or to the fact the said
present use may not lawfully be continued, is made in writing to Seller and which Seller is unable or unwilling to remove, remedy or satisfy or obtain
insurance save and except against risk of fire (Title Insurance) in favour of the Buyer and any mortgagee, (with all related costs at the expense of the
Seller), and which Buyer will not waive, this Agreement notwithstanding any intermediate acts or negotiations in respect of such objections, shall be
at an end and all monies paid shall be returned without interest or deduction and Seller, Listing Brokerage and Co-operating Brokerage shall not be
liable for any costs or damages. Save as to any valid objection so made by such day and except for any objection going to the root of the title, Buyer
shall be conclusively deemed to have accepted Seller's title to the Property. Seller hereby consents to the municipality or other governmental agencies
releasing to Buyer details of all outstanding work orders and deficiency notices affecting the Property, and Seller agrees to execute and deliver such
further authorizations in this regard as Buyer may reasonably require.

11. **TITLE:** Buyer agrees to accept title to the Property subject to all rights and easements registered against title for the supply and installation of telephone
services, electricity, gas, sewers, water, television cable facilities and other related services; provided that title to the Property is otherwise good and
free from all encumbrances except: (a) as herein expressly provided; (b) any registered restrictions, conditions or covenants that run with the land
provided such have been complied with; (c) the provisions of the Condominium Act and its Regulations and the terms, conditions and provisions of
the Declaration, Description and By-laws, Occupancy Standards By-laws, including the Common Element Rules and other Rules and Regulations; and
(d) any existing municipal agreements, zoning by-laws and/or regulations and utilities or service contracts.

12. **CLOSING ARRANGEMENTS:** Where each of the Seller and Buyer retain a lawyer to complete the Agreement of Purchase and Sale of the Property,
and where the transaction will be completed by electronic registration pursuant to Part III of the Land Registration Reform Act, R.S.O. 1990, Chapter
L4 and the Electronic Registration Act, S.O. 1991, Chapter 44, and any amendments thereto, the Seller and Buyer acknowledge and agree that
the exchange of closing funds, nonregistrable documents and other items (the "Requisite Deliveries") and the release thereof to the Seller and Buyer
will (a) not occur at the same time as the registration of the transfer/deed (and any other documents intended to be registered in connection with the
completion of this transaction) and (b) be subject to conditions whereby the lawyer(s) receiving any of the Requisite Deliveries will be required to hold
same in trust and not release same except in accordance with the terms of a document registration agreement between the said lawyers. The Seller
and Buyer irrevocably instruct the said lawyers to be bound by the document registration agreement which is recommended from time to time by the
Law Society of Upper Canada. Unless otherwise agreed to by the lawyers, such exchange of the Requisite Deliveries will occur in the applicable Land
Titles Office or such other location agreeable to both lawyers.

13. **STATUS CERTIFICATE AND MANAGEMENT OF CONDOMINIUM:** Seller represents and warrants to Buyer that there are no special assessments
contemplated by the Condominium Corporation, and there are no legal actions pending by or against or contemplated by the Condominium
Corporation. The Seller consents to a request by the Buyer or the Buyer's authorized representative for a Status Certificate from the Condominium
Corporation. Buyer acknowledges that the Condominium Corporation may have entered into a Management Agreement for the management of the
condominium property.

14. **DOCUMENTS AND DISCHARGE:** Buyer shall not call for the production of any title deed, abstract, survey or other evidence of title to the Property
except such as are in the possession or control of Seller. Seller agrees to deliver to Buyer, if it is possible without incurring any costs in so doing,
copies of all current condominium documentation of the Condominium Corporation, including the Declaration, Description, By-laws, Common Element
Rules and Regulations and the most recent financial statements of the Condominium Corporation. If a discharge of any Charge/Mortgage held by a
corporation incorporated pursuant to the Trust And Loan Companies Act (Canada), Chartered Bank, Trust Company, Credit Union, Caisse Populaire
or Insurance Company and which is not to be assumed by Buyer on completion, is not available in registrable form on completion, Buyer agrees to
accept Seller's lawyer's personal undertaking to obtain, out of the closing funds, a discharge in registrable form and to register same, or cause same
to be registered, on title within a reasonableperiod of time after completion, provided that on or before completion Seller shall provide to Buyer a
mortgage statement prepared by the mortgagee setting out the balance required to obtain the discharge, and, where a real-time electronic cleared
funds transfer system is not being used, a direction executed by Seller directing payment to the mortgagee of the amount required to obtain the
discharge out of the balance due on completion.

15. **MEETINGS:** Seller represents and warrants to Buyer that at the time of the acceptance of this Offer the Seller has not received a notice convening
a special or general meeting of the Condominium Corporation respecting; (a) the termination of the government of the condominium property; (b)
any substantial alteration in or substantial addition to the common elements or the renovation thereof; OR (c) any substantial change in the assets or
liabilities of the Condominium Corporation; and Seller covenants that if Seller receives any such notice prior to the date of completion Seller shall
forthwith notify Buyer in writing and Buyer may thereupon at Buyer's option declare this Agreement to be null and void and all monies paid by Buyer
shall be refunded without interest or deduction.

INITIALS OF BUYER(S): (*BL*)   INITIALS OF SELLER(S): (*VC JC*)

APPENDIX

16. **INSPECTION:** Buyer acknowledges having had the opportunity to inspect the Property and understands that upon acceptance of this offer there shall be a binding agreement of purchase and sale between Buyer and Seller. **The Buyer acknowledges having the opportunity to include a requirement for a property inspection report in this Agreement and agrees that except as may be specifically provided for in this Agreement, the Buyer will not be obtaining a property inspection or property inspection report regarding the Property.**

17. **APPROVAL OF THE AGREEMENT:** In the event that consent to this sale is required to be given by the Condominium Corporation or the Board of Directors, the Seller will apply forthwith for the requisite consent, and if such consent is refused, then this Agreement shall be null and void and the deposit monies paid hereunder shall be refunded without interest or other penalty to the Buyer.

18. **INSURANCE:** The Unit and all other things being purchased shall be and remain at the risk of the Seller until completion. In the event of substantial damage to the Property Buyer may at Buyer's option either permit the proceeds of insurance to be used for repair of such damage in accordance with the provisions of the Insurance Trust Agreement, or terminate this Agreement and all deposit monies paid by Buyer hereunder shall be refunded without interest or deduction. If Seller is taking back a Charge/Mortgage, or Buyer is assuming a Charge/Mortgage, Buyer shall supply Seller with reasonable evidence of adequate insurance to protect Seller's or other mortgagee's interest on completion.

19. **DOCUMENT PREPARATION:** The Transfer/Deed shall, save for the Land Transfer Tax Affidavit, be prepared in registrable form at the expense of Seller, and any Charge/Mortgage to be given back by the Buyer to Seller at the expense of the Buyer.

20. **RESIDENCY:** (a) Subject to (b) below, the Seller represents and warrants that the Seller is not and on completion will not be a non-resident under the non-residency provisions of the Income Tax Act which representation and warranty shall survive and not merge upon the completion of this transaction and the Seller shall deliver to the Buyer a statutory declaration that Seller is not then a non-resident of Canada; (b) provided that if the Seller is a non-resident under the non-residency provisions of the Income Tax Act, the Buyer shall be credited towards the Purchase Price with the amount, if any, necessary for Buyer to pay to the Minister of National Revenue to satisfy Buyer's liability in respect of tax payable by Seller under the non-residency provisions of the Income Tax Act by reason of this sale. Buyer shall not claim such credit if Seller delivers on completion the prescribed certificate.

21. **ADJUSTMENTS:** Common Expenses; realty taxes, including local improvement rates; mortgage interest; rentals; unmetered public or private utilities and fuel where billed to the Unit and not the Condominium Corporation; are to be apportioned and allowed to the day of completion, the day of completion itself to be apportioned to the Buyer. There shall be no adjustment for the Seller's share of any assets or liabilities of the Condominium Corporation including any reserve or contingency fund to which Seller may have contributed prior to the date of completion.

22. **PROPERTY ASSESSMENT:** The Buyer and Seller hereby acknowledge that the Province of Ontario has implemented current value assessment and properties may be re-assessed on an annual basis. The Buyer and Seller agree that no claim will be made against the Buyer or Seller, or any Brokerage, Broker or Salesperson, for any changes in property tax as a result of a re-assessment of the Property, save and except any property taxes that accrued prior to the completion of this transaction.

23. **TIME LIMITS:** Time shall in all respects be of the essence hereof provided that the time for doing or completing of any matter provided for herein may be extended or abridged by an agreement in writing signed by Seller and Buyer or by their respective lawyers who may be specifically authorized in that regard.

24. **TENDER:** Any tender of documents or money hereunder may be made upon Seller or Buyer or their respective lawyers on the day set for completion. Money shall be tendered with funds drawn on a lawyer's trust account in the form of a bank draft, certified cheque or wire transfer using the Large Value Transfer System.

25. **FAMILY LAW ACT:** Seller warrants that spousal consent is not necessary to this transaction under the provisions of the Family Law Act, R.S.O. 1990 unless Seller's spouse has executed the consent hereinafter provided.

26. **UFFI:** Seller represents and warrants to Buyer that during the time Seller has owned the Property, Seller has not caused any building on the Property to be insulated with insulation containing ureaformaldehyde, and that to the best of Seller's knowledge no building on the Property contains or has ever contained insulation that contains ureaformaldehyde. This warranty shall survive and not merge on the completion of this transaction, and if the building is part of a multiple unit building, this warranty shall only apply to that part of the building which is the subject of this transaction.

27. **LEGAL, ACCOUNTING AND ENVIRONMENTAL ADVICE:** The parties acknowledge that any information provided by the brokerage is not legal, tax or environmental advice.

28. **CONSUMER REPORTS: The Buyer is hereby notified that a consumer report containing credit and/or personal information may be referred to in connection with this transaction.**

29. **AGREEMENT IN WRITING:** If there is conflict or discrepancy between any provision added to this Agreement (including any Schedule attached hereto) and any provision in the standard pre-set portion hereof, the added provision shall supersede the standard pre-set provision to the extent of such conflict or discrepancy. This Agreement including any Schedule attached hereto, shall constitute the entire Agreement between Buyer and Seller. There is no representation, warranty, collateral agreement or condition, which affects this Agreement other than as expressed herein. For the purposes of this Agreement, Seller means vendor and Buyer means purchaser. This Agreement shall be read with all changes of gender or number required by the context.

30. **TIME AND DATE:** Any reference to a time and date in this Agreement shall mean the time and date where the Property is located.

INITIALS OF BUYER(S): *BL*   **INITIALS OF SELLER(S):** *VC JC*

APPENDIX

31. SUCCESSORS AND ASSIGNS: The heirs, executors, administrators, successors and assigns of the undersigned are bound by the terms herein.

SIGNED, SEALED AND DELIVERED in the presence of: IN WITNESS whereof I have hereunto set my hand and seal:

Albert Lee ....
(Witness)

Barbara Lopez .... ⬤ DATE *Sept. 8/xx*
(Buyer)   (Seal)

....
(Witness)

.... ⬤ DATE ....
(Buyer)   (Seal)

I, the Undersigned Seller, agree to the above offer. I hereby irrevocably instruct my lawyer to pay directly to the brokerage(s) with whom I have agreed to pay commission, the unpaid balance of the commission together with applicable Harmonized Sales Tax (and any other taxes as may hereafter be applicable), from the proceeds of the sale prior to any payment to the undersigned on completion, as advised by the brokerage(s) to my lawyer.

SIGNED, SEALED AND DELIVERED in the presence of: IN WITNESS whereof I have hereunto set my hand and seal:

Patricia Johnston ....
(Witness)

Victoria Cooper .... ⬤ DATE *Sept. 9/xx*
(Seller)   (Seal)

Patricia Johnston ....
(Witness)

Joseph Cooper .... ⬤ DATE *Sept. 9/xx*
(Seller)   (Seal)

SPOUSAL CONSENT: The Undersigned Spouse of the Seller hereby consents to the disposition evidenced herein pursuant to the provisions of the Family Law Act, R.S.O.1990, and hereby agrees with the Buyer that he/she will execute all necessary or incidental documents to give full force and effect to the sale evidenced herein.

....
(Witness)

.... ⬤ DATE ....
(Spouse)   (Seal)

CONFIRMATION OF ACCEPTANCE: Notwithstanding anything contained herein to the contrary, I confirm this Agreement with all changes both typed and written was finally accepted by all parties at ....*10:30*.... a.m./~~p.m.~~ this ......*10th*...... day of.................*September*................., 20..*XX*....

....*Barbara Lopez*.................
(Signature of Seller or Buyer)

INFORMATION ON BROKERAGE(S)

Listing Brokerage .... **ABC Realty Inc.**   Tel.No.(**705**) **555-1212**

     123 Main Street, Anycity, Anyregion L4H 6P5   **Albert Lee**
                               (Salesperson / Broker Name)

Co-op/Buyer Brokerage .... Tel.No.(................)

....
(Salesperson / Broker Name)

ACKNOWLEDGEMENT

I acknowledge receipt of my signed copy of this accepted Agreement of Purchase and Sale and I authorize the Brokerage to forward a copy to my lawyer.	I acknowledge receipt of my signed copy of this accepted Agreement of Purchase and Sale and I authorize the Brokerage to forward a copy to my lawyer.
Victoria Cooper .... DATE *Sept. 10/xx* (Seller)	*Barbara Lopez* .... DATE *Sept. 10/xx* (Buyer)
Joseph Cooper .... DATE *Sept. 10/xx* (Seller)	.... DATE .... (Buyer)
Address for Service *Unit 7, 394 Highland Road*	Address for Service *32 Dinsdale Crescent, Anycity K9B 3V5*
Anycity L2P 1J0 Tel.No.(*705*) *666-1212*	.... Tel.No.(..........)
Seller's Lawyer *Mr. James Ogilvie*	Buyer's Lawyer *Anderson, Hayward and Jones*
Address *291 Centre Street, Anycity K3C 1B2*	Address *Suite 200, Centennial Plaza, Anycity K3C 2C7*
Email	Email ....
(*705*) *666-1212* (*705*) *666-2121* Tel.No. FAX No.	(*705*) *444-1212* (*705*) *444-2121* Tel.No. FAX No.

Property Manager: **Anycity Property Management**   **30 Welland Drive, Anycity K0N 1P0**   **705-999-1212 705-999-2121**
                (Name)   (Address)   (Tel No.,FAX No)

FOR OFFICE USE ONLY   **COMMISSION TRUST AGREEMENT**

To: Co-operating Brokerage shown on the foregoing Agreement of Purchase and Sale:
In consideration for the Co-operating Brokerage procuring the foregoing Agreement of Purchase and Sale, I hereby declare that all moneys received or receivable by me in connection with the Transaction as contemplated in the MLS® Rules and Regulations of my Real Estate Board shall be receivable and held in trust. This agreement shall constitute a Commission Trust Agreement as defined in the MLS® Rules and shall be subject to and governed by the MLS® Rules pertaining to Commission Trust.

DATED as of the date and time of the acceptance of the foregoing Agreement of Purchase and Sale.   Acknowledged by:

....
(Authorized to bind the Listing Brokerage)   (Authorized to bind the Co-operating Brokerage)

   Form 101   Revised 2015   **Page 5 of 6**

APPENDIX

OREA Ontario Real Estate Association

Form 101
for use in the Province of Ontario

Schedule A
Agreement of Purchase and Sale –
Condominium Resale

This Schedule is attached to and forms part of the Agreement of Purchase and Sale between:

BUYER, ... Barbara Lopez ...., and

SELLER, ... Victoria Anne Cooper and Joseph Alan Cooper ....

for the purchase and sale of .. Unit 7, 394 Highland Road, City of Anycity, Regional Municipality of Anyregion ..

.... dated the ..... 8th .... day of .... September ...., 20 .xx ....

Buyer agrees to pay the balance as follows:

~~Ten~~ *BL* *VC JC*   ($210,000.00)   *BL* *VC JC*

The Buyer agrees to pay a further sum of Two Hundred and ~~Four~~ Thousand Dollars (~~$204,000.00~~), subject to adjustments, to the Seller on completion of this transaction, with funds drawn on a lawyer's trust account in the form of a bank draft, certified cheque, or wire transfer using the Large Value Transfer System.

This offer is conditional upon:

(1) The Buyer arranging, at the Buyer's own expense, a new first charge/mortgage for not less than One Hundred and Eighty Thousand Dollars ($180,000.00), bearing interest at a rate of not more than 5.5% per annum, calculated semi-annually not in advance, repayable in blended bi-weekly payments of about Five Hundred and Six Dollars and Forty-Eight Cents ($506.48), including principal and interest, and to run for a term of not less than two years from the date of completion of this transaction.

(2) The inspection of the subject property by a home inspector at the Buyer's own expense, and the obtaining of a report satisfactory to the Buyer in the Buyer's sole and absolute discretion. The Seller agrees to co-operate in providing access to the property for the purpose of this inspection.

(3) The Buyer's solicitor reviewing the following condominium corporation's documentation: A Status Certificate and attachments, and finding all of the foregoing satisfactory in the Buyer's solicitor's sole and absolute discretion. The Buyer agrees to request at the Buyer's expense the Status Certificate and attachments within two days of acceptance of this offer.

Unless the Buyer gives notice in writing delivered to the Seller personally or in accordance with any other provisions for the delivery of notice in this Agreement of Purchase and Sale or any Schedule thereto not later than 11:59 p.m. on the 30th day of September, 20xx, that these conditions are fulfilled, this Offer shall be null and void and the deposit shall be returned to the Buyer in full without deduction. These conditions are included for the benefit of the Buyer and may be waived at the Buyer's sole option by notice in writing to the Seller as aforesaid within the time period stated herein.

The Buyer shall have the right to inspect the property one further time prior to completion, at a mutually agreed upon time, provided that written notice is given to the Seller. The Seller agrees to provide access to the property for the purpose of this inspection.

This form must be initialed by all parties to the Agreement of Purchase and Sale.

INITIALS OF BUYER(S): (*BL*)   INITIALS OF SELLER(S): (*VC JC*)

Form 101   Revised 2015   **Page 6 of 6**

CHAPTER 3
RESIDENTIAL LEASING

Chapter Mini-Review

1. A fixed term tenancy is best described as a tenancy with a fixed period, but indefinite length; that is, the tenancy automatically renews itself unless notice is provided to the contrary.

   ○ True   **False**

   This statement describes a periodic tenancy, not a fixed term tenancy.

2. Predominant use is an important consideration in establishing if a tenancy is residential or commercial.

    True   ○ False

   Predominant use is an important consideration, but other factors can come into play, particularly when assessing a hybrid situation involving both residential and commercial usage.

3. A legally enforceable lease only requires that the parties to the lease are identified by full legal names and the leased premises is sufficiently described to be readily identifiable.

   ○ True   **False**

   The two requirements are required for an enforceable lease, but other elements are also required such as consideration and start/end dates.

4. A tenant may register his/her leasehold interest at the land registration office.

    True   ○ False

   A leasehold interest, as with other interests relating to real estate, can be registered (within the land registry system), to provide a written record of the tenant's interests.

5. A preprinted blank lease must be attached to the *Agreement to Lease—Residential* (OREA Form 400) in order to make the agreement legally enforceable.

   ○ True   **False**

   Attaching the blank lease to the Agreement to Lease—Residential is strongly recommended, but not mandatory.

6. Adjudication is used by the Landlord and Tenant Board to resolve all disputes between landlords and tenants.

   ○ True   **False**

   The Landlord and Tenant Board use mediation, as well as adjudication, to resolve landlord/tenant disputes.

7. According to the *Residential Tenancies Act*, the former tenant is not liable to the landlord for any obligations under the lease following an assignment of that lease to another party.

   ○ True   **False**

   Both the assignee and the former tenant are liable to the landlord for their respective periods; i.e., the former tenant for the period up to the assignment and the assignee for the period following the assignment.

8. A *no pet* provision in a residential lease is void, subject to certain exceptions, most notably a lease involving a residential condominium in which pet restrictions are properly documented and enforced.

    True   ○ False

   A condominium's declaration, by-laws and rules may contain enforceable no pet provisions.

APPENDIX

9. A landlord must provide written 24-hour notice when planning to carry out repairs or do work in a rental unit.

    True   ◯ False

   Entry for repair purposes is permitted with a 24-hour notice period.

10. A residential landlord must give 60 days written notice of any increase in rent.

    ◯ True   **False**

    The correct notice period for a rent increase is 90 days.

11. The *Residential Tenancies Act* provides that a landlord may make application to terminate a residential tenancy before the end of the term if a tenant has substantially interfered with the reasonable enjoyment of other tenants.

     True   ◯ False

    The Act contains various reasons for termination by the landlord including if the tenant has substantially interfered with the reasonable enjoyment of other tenants.

12. Any residential landlord may give notice of termination to an existing tenant(s) at the end of a term if he or she has accepted an offer to sell the property.

    ◯ True   **False**

    This provision only applies to residential complexes containing no more than three residential units.

Active Learning Exercises

■ Exercise 1   Multiple Choice

1.1 An agreement to lease is technically referred to as:

a. An agreement of purchase and sale.

Incorrect. An agreement of purchase and sale involves the sale of property, not rentals.

b. **An agreement for lease without settled form of lease.**

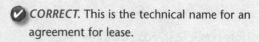 **CORRECT.** This is the technical name for an agreement for lease.

c. An agreement for lease subject to formal lease signing.

Incorrect. This form name is not used in the marketplace.

d. An agreement to lease with lease affixed.

Incorrect. This form name is not used in the marketplace.

APPENDIX

1.2 Which of the following is NOT an exemption under the *Residential Tenancies Act*? **This question requires that the *incorrect* option be identified.**

a. Living accommodation for the travelling or vacationing public.

This option is correct. Living accommodation for the travelling or vacationing public is exempt under the Act.

b. Living accommodation provided for rehabilitative or therapeutic services.

This option is correct. Living accommodation provided for rehabilitative or therapeutic services is exempt under the Act.

c. Premises occupied by an individual for business or agricultural purposes, with living accommodation attached for that person.

This option is correct. Premises occupied by an individual for business or agricultural purposes with living accommodation attached for that person, is exempt under the Act.

d. **Living accommodation provided to a landlord's spouse, parent or child on a daily or weekly basis.**

THIS IS THE INCORRECT OPTION. Living accommodation provided to a landlord's spouse, parent or child on a daily or weekly basis is not exempt under the Act.

1.3 If possession of a rental unit is required by the landlord:

a. The landlord must give 120 days notice to the tenant.

Incorrect. The notice period is 60 days.

b. Such possession must be for a minimum term of one year.

Incorrect. A minimum term is not set out in the *Residential Tenancies Act.*

c. **Such possession can only be obtained at the end of the term.**

CORRECT. Possession by the landlord can only be obtained at the end of the tenancy term.

d. The landlord can only gain possession if the property has more than three residential units.

Incorrect. The landlord can only gain possession if the property has *no more than* three residential units.

1.4 Termination by a tenant:

a. Requires 60 days notice, if tenancy is monthly.

Incorrect. This statement is correct, but a more appropriate answer option is provided.

b. Must be made in writing.

Incorrect. This statement is correct, but a more appropriate answer option is provided.

c. Is only possible in accordance with the *Residential Tenancies Act.*

Incorrect. This statement is correct, but a more suitable answer option is provided.

d. **All of the above.**

CORRECT. All of the above answer options are correct statements.

APPENDIX

1.5 Which of the following statements is correct?

a. Seasonal or temporary accommodation is exempt under the *Residential Tenancies Act.*

CORRECT. This is one of several exemptions provided under the Act.

b. Members of the Landlord and Tenant Board are appointed by the Court.

Incorrect. Members of the Landlord and Tenant Board are appointed by the provincial government.

c. The rent control guideline published annually must be 2% or higher.

Incorrect. The rent control guideline published annually varies and represents the percentage change from year to year in the Consumer Price Index (Ontario).

d. Salespersons are exempted from entry requirements and associated notice periods set out in the *Residential Tenancies Act.*

Incorrect. A brokerage (including employed brokers and salespersons) is viewed as an agent of the landlord and is subject to the same requirements as the landlord in carrying out various duties for that landlord.

1.6 When a tenant is subletting a residential unit, he or she:

a. He/She must pay reasonable out-of-pocket expenses to the landlord relating to the sublet.

CORRECT. Out-of-pocket expenses are the tenant's responsibility.

b. He/she no longer liable under the original tenancy agreement.

Incorrect. The tenant remains liable for breaches arising during the subtenancy period.

c. The landlord can arbitrarily withhold consent to the sublet.

Incorrect. Consent cannot be unreasonably withheld.

d. The landlord cannot make application to terminate the subtenancy due to the subtenant damaging the unit.

Incorrect. The landlord can make application to the Landlord and Tenant Board.

1.7 A landlord may make application to terminate a tenancy before the end of the term if:

a. Possession is required by the landlord.

Incorrect. This situation relates to termination at the end of the term.

b. The property is being sold.

Incorrect. This situation relates to termination at the end of the term.

c. Too many persons are occupying the rental unit in contravention of local by-laws.

CORRECT. Overcrowding can result in termination before the end of the term.

d. Demolition or extensive renovations are being undertaken.

Incorrect. This situation relates to termination at the end of the term.

APPENDIX

1.8 Which of the following is a correct statement?

a. A landlord can require that a tenant provide post-dated rent cheques.

Incorrect. A landlord cannot require post-dated cheques from a tenant.

b. A landlord must pay 4% annual interest on tenants' rent deposits.

Incorrect. The interest rate is calculated based on changes in the Consumer Price Index (Ontario).

c. A landlord is required to collect a rent deposit.

Incorrect. No such requirement exists, but if a rent deposit is collected, it must be done in accordance with provisions in the Act.

d. **The maximum rent deposit is one month's rent.**

✅ *CORRECT.* The rent deposit can be less than one month's rent, but cannot exceed one month's rent.

CH3 EX2

■ Exercise 2   Rent Calculations

2.1 Current Annual Rent: ($1,125 + 1,250) x 12 = $28,500.00

Permitted Increase: [(1,125 x .029) x 12] + [(1,250 x .029) x 12] =   826.50

Maximum Projected Annual Lawful Rent   **$29,326.50**

2.2 November 20xx.

2.3 Year One: $875 x .024 = $21.00

Year Two: ($875 + $21.00) x .027 = $24.19

2.4 The landlord may establish the rent based on market conditions. Rent guidelines do not apply to new tenants occupying a residential rental unit.

CH3 EX3

■ Exercise 3   Residential Tenancies Act

3.1 Caution is advised. Abandonment can be complex. First, the unit is not deemed abandoned if the tenant is paying the rent. Second, substantial evidence should precede taking any action. Assurances must be obtained that the tenant has truly left the premises and will not be returning. Salespersons should make further enquiries of the landlord and seek guidance from the broker of record or manager.

3.2 The tenant is not correct regarding the *no pet* provision. First, if the rental unit is a condominium, a *no pet* provision within the condominium documentation can be enforced against the tenant. Second, while the *no pet* provision generally applies, a landlord can take action to remove an animal if that animal causes substantial interference, causes a serious allergic reaction or is inherently dangerous.

3.3 The salesperson is not correct. A third possibility should be noted. The landlord may consent to the assignment, but then subsequently refuse a specific assignee.

3.4 The landlord is not correct. Twenty-four hour written notice is required.

APPENDIX

3.5   The tenant is not correct. Other increases are possible. For example, the landlord may apply to the Landlord and Tenant Board for an additional increase relating to capital expenditures.

■ Exercise 4   Drafting an Agreement to Lease—Residential

The completed agreement is shown on the following pages.

APPENDIX

OREA Ontario Real Estate Association

Agreement to Lease
Residential

Form 400
for use in the Province of Ontario

This Agreement to Lease dated this .... **25th** .... day of .... **August** .... , 20.**xx**.........

TENANT (Lessee), ... **Barbara Ellen Forsyth and Raymond Steven Forsyth** ....
(Full legal names of all Tenants)

LANDLORD (Lessor), ... **Mario Galletta** ....
(Full legal name of Landlord)

ADDRESS OF LANDLORD .... **39 Elizabeth Crescent, Anycity K7E 8O7** ....
(Legal address for the purpose of receiving notices)

The Tenant hereby offers to lease from the Landlord the premises as described herein on the terms and subject to the conditions as set out in this Agreement.

1. **PREMISES:** Having inspected the premises and provided the present tenant vacates, I/we, the Tenant hereby offer to lease, premises known as:
   10 Roxway Drive, Anycity (Legal Description: Lot 10, Plan M-2983, City of Anycity)

2. **TERM OF LEASE:** The lease shall be for a term of .... **Two Years** .... commencing .... **October 1, 20xx**

3. **RENT:** The Tenant will pay to the said Landlord monthly and every month during the said term of the lease the sum of .... *BF RF* *MG*
   Two Thousand Six Hundred and Fifty   *BF RF* *MG*   *BF RF* **$2,650.00** *MG*
   ~~Two Thousand Three Hundred~~ --- Canadian Dollars (CDN$......~~2,300.00~~......),
   payable in advance on the first day of each and every month during the currency of the said term. First and last months' rent to be paid in advance upon completion or date of occupancy, whichever comes first.

4. **DEPOSIT AND PREPAID RENT:** The Tenant delivers......... **Upon Acceptance** ....
   (Herewith/Upon acceptance/as otherwise described in this Agreement)

   by negotiable cheque payable to......... **ABC Realty Inc.** .... "Deposit Holder"
   Five Thousand Three Hundred   *BF RF* *MG*
   in the amount of.........~~Four Thousand Six Hundred~~ ---
   BF RF **5,300.00** *MG*
   Canadian Dollars (CDN$.........~~4,600.00~~.........) as a deposit to be held in trust as security for the faithful performance by the Tenant of all

   terms, covenants and conditions of the Agreement and to be applied by the Landlord against the .... **first** .... and .... **last** ....
   month's rent. If the Agreement is not accepted, the deposit is to be returned to the Tenant without interest or deduction.

   For the purposes of this Agreement, "Upon Acceptance" shall mean that the Tenant is required to deliver the deposit to the Deposit Holder within 24 hours of the acceptance of this Agreement. The parties to this Agreement hereby acknowledge that, unless otherwise provided for in this Agreement, the Deposit Holder shall place the deposit in trust in the Deposit Holder's non-interest bearing Real Estate Trust Account and no interest shall be earned, received or paid on the deposit.

5. **USE:** The Tenant and Landlord agree that unless otherwise agreed to herein, only the Tenant named above and any person named in a Rental Application completed prior to this Agreement will occupy the premises.

   Premises to be used only for:......... **single family residential**

6. **SERVICES AND COSTS:** The cost of the following services applicable to the premises shall be paid as follows:

	LANDLORD	TENANT		LANDLORD	TENANT
Gas	☐	☑	Cable TV	☐	☑
Oil	☐	☐	Condominium/Cooperative fees	☐	☐
Electricity	☐	☑	Garbage Removal	☐	☐
Hot water heater rental	☐	☑	Other: **Security System**	☐	☑
Water and Sewerage Charges	☑	☐	Other:	☐	☐

The Landlord will pay the property taxes, but if the Tenant is assessed as a Separate School Supporter, Tenant will pay to the Landlord a sum sufficient to cover the excess of the Separate School Tax over the Public School Tax, if any, for a full calendar year, said sum to be estimated on the tax rate for the current year, and to be payable in equal monthly installments in addition to the above mentioned rental, provided however, that the full amount shall become due and be payable on demand on the Tenant.

INITIALS OF TENANT(S): (*BF RF*)   INITIALS OF LANDLORD(S): (*MG*)

Form 400   Revised 2015   **Page 1 of 4**

7. **PARKING:** Paved parking and single-car garage

8. **ADDITIONAL TERMS:** All existing drapery rods and window coverings in the kitchen, dining room, living room and three bedrooms. The following appliances are inlcuded: WestRange stove and refrigerator, Fountain Delux dishwasher, Durability Plus washer and dryer, and EasyLight gas barbecue. Tenant and Landlord agree that an accepted Agreement to Lease shall form a completed lease and no other lease will be signed between the Parties.

9. **SCHEDULES:** The schedules attached hereto shall form an integral part of this Agreement to Lease and consist of: **Schedule(s) A** None

10. **IRREVOCABILITY:** This offer shall be irrevocable by *BF RF* **Landlord** *MG* ~~Tenant~~ until 11:59 ~~a.m.~~/p.m. on the *BF RF* **27th** *MG* ~~26th~~
(Landlord/Tenant)
day of August ,20 XX after which time if not accepted, this Agreement shall be null and void and all monies paid thereon shall be returned to the Tenant without interest or deduction.

11. **NOTICES:** The Landlord hereby appoints the Listing Brokerage as agent for the Landlord for the purpose of giving and receiving notices pursuant to this Agreement. Where a Brokerage (Tenant's Brokerage) has entered into a representation agreement with the Tenant, the Tenant hereby appoints the Tenant's Brokerage as agent for the purpose of giving and receiving notices pursuant to this Agreement. **Where a Brokerage represents both the Landlord and the Tenant (multiple representation), the Brokerage shall not be appointed or authorized to be agent for either the Tenant or the Landlord for the purpose of giving and receiving notices.** Any notice relating hereto or provided for herein shall be in writing. In addition to any provision contained herein and in any Schedule hereto, this offer, any counter-offer, notice of acceptance thereof or any notice to be given or received pursuant to this Agreement or any Schedule hereto (any of them, "Document") shall be deemed given and received when delivered personally or hand delivered to the Address for Service provided in the Acknowledgement below, or where a facsimile number or email address is provided herein, when transmitted electronically to that facsimile number or email address, respectively, in which case, the signature(s) of the party (parties) shall be deemed to be original.

FAX No.: 905-555-2121   FAX No.:
(For delivery of Documents to Landlord)   (For delivery of Documents to Tenant)

Email Address: admin@abcrealty.com   Email Address:
(For delivery of Documents to Landlord)   (For delivery of Documents to Tenant)
BF RF   MG

12. **EXECUTION OF LEASE:** ~~Lease shall be drawn by the Landlord on the Landlord's standard form of lease, and shall include the provisions as contained herein and in any attached schedule, and shall be executed by both parties before possession of the premises is given.~~ The Landlord shall provide the tenant with information relating to the rights and responsibilities of the Tenant and information on the role of the Landlord and Tenant Board and how to contact the Board. (Information For New Tenants as made available by the Landlord and Tenant Board and available at www.ltb.gov.on.ca)

13. **ACCESS:** The Landlord shall have the right, at reasonable times to enter and show the demised premises to prospective tenants, purchasers or others. The Landlord or anyone on the Landlord's behalf shall also have the right, at reasonable times, to enter and inspect the demised premises.

14. **INSURANCE:** The Tenant agrees to obtain and keep in full force and effect during the entire period of the tenancy and any renewal thereof, at the Tenant's sole cost and expense, fire and property damage and public liability insurance in an amount equal to that which a reasonably prudent Tenant would consider adequate. The Tenant agrees to provide the Landlord, upon demand at any time, proof that said insurance is in full force and effect and to notify the Landlord in writing in the event that such insurance is cancelled or otherwise terminated.

15. **RESIDENCY:** The Landlord shall forthwith notify the Tenant in writing in the event the Landlord is, at the time of entering into this Agreement, or, becomes during the term of the tenancy, a non-resident of Canada as defined under the Income Tax Act, RSC 1985, c.1 (ITA) as amended from time to time, and in such event the Landlord and Tenant agree to comply with the tax withholding provisions of the ITA.

16. **USE AND DISTRIBUTION OF PERSONAL INFORMATION:** The Tenant consents to the collection, use and disclosure of the Tenant's personal information by the Landlord and/or agent of the Landlord, from time to time, for the purpose of determining the creditworthiness of the Tenant for the leasing, selling or financing of the premises or the real property, or making such other use of the personal information as the Landlord and/or agent of the Landlord deems appropriate.

17. **CONFLICT OR DISCREPANCY:** If there is any conflict or discrepancy between any provision added to this Agreement (including any Schedule attached hereto) and any provision in the standard pre-set portion hereof, the added provision shall supersede the standard pre-set provision to the extent of such conflict or discrepancy. This Agreement, including any Schedule attached hereto, shall constitute the entire Agreement between Landlord and Tenant. There is no representation, warranty, collateral agreement or condition, which affects this Agreement other than as expressed herein. This Agreement shall be read with all changes of gender or number required by the context.

18. **CONSUMER REPORTS:** The Tenant is hereby notified that a consumer report containing credit and/or personal information may be referred to in connection with this transaction.

INITIALS OF TENANT(S): (*BF RF*)   **INITIALS OF LANDLORD(S):** (*MG*)

19. BINDING AGREEMENT: This Agreement and acceptance thereof shall constitute a binding agreement by the parties to enter into the Lease of the Premises and to abide by the terms and conditions herein contained.

SIGNED, SEALED AND DELIVERED in the presence of: IN WITNESS whereof I have hereunto set my hand and seal:

Albert Lee	*Barbara Forsyth*	(Seal)	DATE *Aug. 25/xx*
(Witness)	(Tenant or Authorized Representative)		
Albert Lee	*Ray Forsyth*	(Seal)	DATE *Aug. 25/xx*
(Witness)	(Tenant or Authorized Representative)		
(Witness)	(Guarantor)	(Seal)	DATE

We/I the Landlord hereby accept the above offer, and agree that the commission together with applicable HST (and any other tax as may hereafter be applicable) may be deducted from the deposit and further agree to pay any remaining balance of commission forthwith.

SIGNED, SEALED AND DELIVERED in the presence of: IN WITNESS whereof I have hereunto set my hand and seal:

Albert Lee	*Mario Galletta*	(Seal)	DATE *Aug. 26/xx*
(Witness)	(Landlord or Authorized Representative)		
(Witness)	(Landlord or Authorized Representative)	(Seal)	DATE

CONFIRMATION OF ACCEPTANCE: Notwithstanding anything contained herein to the contrary, I confirm this Agreement with all changes both typed and written was finally acceptance by all parties at *3:30* ~~a.m.~~/p.m. this *27th* day of *August*, 20 *XX*   *Ray Forsyth*
(Signature of Landlord or Tenant)

INFORMATION ON BROKERAGE(S)

Listing Brokerage ABC Realty Inc.   Tel.No.(905) 555-1212
   123 Main Street, Anycity, Anyregion L4H 6P5   Albert Lee
                                                    (Salesperson / Broker Name)

Co-op/Buyer Brokerage .... Tel.No.(...............)

....
                                                    (Salesperson / Broker Name)

ACKNOWLEDGEMENT

I acknowledge receipt of my signed copy of this accepted Agreement of Lease and I authorize the Brokerage to forward a copy to my lawyer.

Mario Galletta	DATE *Aug. 27/xx*
(Landlord)	
	DATE
(Landlord)	

Address for Service *39 Elizabeth Cres. Anycity*
K7E 8C7   Tel.No.(*905*) *444-1212*

Landlord's Lawyer *G. Myers c/o Myers and Smallwood*

Address *15 Melrose Blvd., Anycity R9C 3T4*

Email ....

(*905*) *333-1212*   (*905*) *333-2121*
    Tel.No.   FAX No.

I acknowledge receipt of my signed copy of this accepted Agreement of Lease and I authorize the Brokerage to forward a copy to my lawyer.

Barbara Forsyth	DATE *Aug. 27/xx*
(Tenant)	
Ray Forsyth	DATE *Aug. 27/xx*
(Tenant)	

Address for Service *Apt. 207, 32 Standwood Cres., Anycity*
K87 8B3   Tel.No.(*905*) *666-1212*

Tenant's Lawyer *Ms. A. Willman c/o Bartlett, Winslow & Phillip*

Address *385 Vanier Drive, Anycity K97 3C7*

Email ....

(*905*) *777-1212*   (*905*) *777-2121*
    Tel.No.   FAX No.

FOR OFFICE USE ONLY   **COMMISSION TRUST AGREEMENT**

To: Co-operating Brokerage shown on the foregoing Agreement to Lease:
In consideration for the Co-operating Brokerage procuring the foregoing Agreement to Lease, I hereby declare that all moneys received or receivable by me in connection with the Transaction as contemplated in the MLS Rules and Regulations of my Real Estate Board shall be receivable and held in trust. This agreement shall constitute a Commission Trust Agreement as defined in the MLS Rules and shall be subject to and governed by the MLS Rules pertaining to Commission Trust.

DATED as of the date and time of the acceptance of the foregoing Agreement to Lease.   Acknowledged by:

....
(Authorized to bind the Listing Brokerage)   (Authorized to bind the Co-operating Brokerage)

Form 400   Revised 2015   **Page 3 of 4**

CHAPTER 4
COTTAGE PROPERTY

CH4 MR

Chapter Mini-Review

1. A low pitch on a cottage roof can pose problems during thawing periods following winter months.

    True   ◯ False

   Low pitch roofs are particularly vulnerable to ice damming.

2. Cottage owners, when winterizing existing cottages, must follow mandatory procedures set by the municipality regarding amount of insulation.

   ◯ True   **False**

   Municipalities do not have mandatory procedures regarding winterizing and significant variations are found in the recreational marketplace.

3. A buyer wishing to have a prospective cottage inspected must use the services of a home inspector.

   ◯ True   **False**

   Buyers can perform the inspection themselves or use any third party; e.g., a person knowledgeable about cottages, a home inspector or another person of their choice.

4. Chlorine disinfecting is used following construction of a new well to remove bacteria that may reside in the water and well equipment during the installation process.

    True   ◯ False

   Chlorine disinfecting is also used when well repairs are undertaken. Some owners may use chlorine in an attempt to resolve a contamination issue in an existing well, as identified when a bacteriological test was conducted. While shocking a well with chlorine will remove the immediate contamination problem, it does not address the underlying problem (e.g., ground water seeping into the well).

5. Cottage owners must use a raised absorption bed according to requirements set out in the Ontario Building Code.

   ◯ True   **False**

   A raised absorption bed is not a requirement for all cottages, but may be required given terrain and/or soil conditions.

6. The *Public Lands Act* is administered by the Ministry of the Environment.

   ◯ True   **False**

   The *Public Lands Act* is administered by the Ministry of Natural Resources and Forestry.

APPENDIX

Chapter Mini-Review (continued)

7. The Ministry responsible for aquatic plant control varies based on whether the cottage owner is using chemicals or mechanical means.

 True   False

At present, chemicals are overseen by the Ministry of the Environment, with mechanical falling to the Ministry of Natural Resources and Forestry.

8. Shore road allowances are found on inland lakes throughout Ontario.

○ True   False

Shore road allowances are not found in townships surveyed prior to 1850 (primarily eastern and southwestern Ontario).

9. A public road allowance set out by the original Crown surveyors remains open, unless it has not been used for the last 50 years.

○ True   False

A public road allowance remains open, unless officially closed by municipal decree.

10. A cottage building lot that falls within an environmentally-sensitive area may be subject to more stringent zoning requirements than other properties within that particular municipality.

 True   False

Cottage property falling within environmentally-sensitive areas may have more restrictive conditions regarding such things as setbacks and location of structures.

11. The cost of obtaining hydro service in a recreational area is in part dependent on the cottage's distance from an existing primary line.

 True   False

Hydro One will supply 30 metres of secondary line from the last pole on a dedicated, accepted road allowance. Beyond that, the owner will be responsible for additional costs.

APPENDIX

Active Learning Exercises

▣ Exercise 1   Multiple Choice

1.1   The Ontario Building Code:

a.   Applies to new year-round cottages, but not new seasonal cottages.

Incorrect. The Ontario Building Code applies to all new cottage structures.

b.   Sets out requirements regarding aquatic plant control.

Incorrect. Aquatic plant control is overseen by the Ministry of Natural Resources and Forestry.

c.   **Regulates the installation of septic tanks.**

✔ *CORRECT.* The Ontario Building Code covers installation of septic tanks.

d.   Regulates requirements regarding hydro and telephone services provided in recreational areas.

Incorrect. The Ontario Building Code is not involved with the provision of these services.

1.2   A raised absorption bed:

a.   Can only be used in new cottage installations and not with older cottages.

Incorrect. Raised absorption beds can be used in both situations.

b.   Must be used in all new cottage installations.

Incorrect. A raised absorption bed is used when the need arises.

c.   **Uses imported soil and approved filter sand.**

✔ *CORRECT.* By using special soil and filtering sand, the total area of the absorption bed can be reduced.

d.   Cannot be used in rocky areas.

Incorrect. Raised absorption beds can be effective in such areas.

1.3   The construction of a boathouse on an Ontario inland lake:

a.   Is prohibited as it could affect fish habitat.

Incorrect. Boathouses are not prohibited, but fish habitat is a consideration in obtaining a permit.

b.   Is not subject to local zoning provisions.

Incorrect. The construction of a boathouse is subject to local zoning provisions.

c.   Cannot be built on lands falling under the *Public Lands Act.*

Incorrect. The Ministry of Natural Resources and Forestry administers the *Public Lands Act.* The Ministry will permit a boathouse subject to necessary approvals and a permit.

d.   **Can be subject to obtaining a work permit from the Ministry of Natural Resources and Forestry.**

✔ *CORRECT.* Whether or not a work permit is required depends on the size of the boathouse.

APPENDIX

CH4   EX1

1.4 Which of the following is correct?

a. A two-storey boathouse is prohibited on Ontario inland lakes.

Incorrect. Two-storey boathouses may be permitted, depending on circumstances including Ministry of Natural Resources and Forestry approval.

b. **Cottage buyers should enquire about the access road to the prospective cottage to ensure that it aligns with their expectations.**

✅*CORRECT.* Road access to cottages is a key consideration in the buyer process.

c. Inadequate footings are rarely the cause of structural movement in older cottages.

Incorrect. Inadequate footings are a significant source of structural movement problems in cottages.

d. Acid rain has not been a problem in Ontario's cottage areas.

Incorrect. Acid rain remains a problem and is continuously monitored by the Ministry of the Environment.

1.5 A zoning provision relating to a boat dock may:

a. Detail location of the dock in relation to the side lot line.

Incorrect. This is a correct statement, but a more appropriate answer option is available.

b. Limit the distance that the dock projects into the waterway.

Incorrect. This is a correct statement, but a more appropriate answer option is available.

c. Restrict the size of a land-based sundeck or other structure joined to the dock.

Incorrect. This is a correct statement, but a more appropriate answer option is available..

d. **All of the above.**

✅*CORRECT.* All of the above answer options are correct.

1.6 Which of the following is a correct statement?

a. **A vaulted ceiling in an older cottage may prove difficult to properly insulate.**

✅*CORRECT.* A vaulted ceiling may prove challenging and expensive to properly insulate and refinish.

b. One bacteriological test every three or four years is sufficient for cottage wells.

Incorrect. Initially, two or three tests (spaced two or three weeks apart) should be taken with follow up testing either once or twice a year.

c. If hydro service is provided to a seasonal cottage, then telephone service is assured.

Incorrect. The telephone company will make an independent assessment of the situation. Telephone service is not assured, but the existence of hydro service is a positive factor in the decision process.

d. Seasonal cottage owners do not receive municipal garbage pickup and must deliver garbage to a central landfill.

Incorrect. Whether or not garbage pickup is available will depend on procedures within the applicable municipality. Typically, distance and use of a private road are key determining factors in not receiving garbage pickup.

APPENDIX

■ **Exercise 2   Mini-Scenarios**   `CH4` `EX2`

2.1   The most likely cause would involve an inadequate footing. The footing may have been installed on weak soil and was of insufficient size or depth.

2.2   The cottage may have little or no insulation in the crawl space below the main level living areas. Additionally, the new owner will have to consider ventilation issues in that crawl space.

2.3   Possible questions include: who owns the road? what costs are involved (e.g., access and/or maintenance fees)?, and is there a registered and permanent right to use that road?

2.4   He should approach the local municipality for additional information. Municipal approval is required and the owner must bring the road up to acceptable standards or provide financial and other assurances that the municipality will be paid if it undertakes to do the work.

2.5   The salesperson should advise the buyer client to contact an insurance professional about fire insurance, as distance from the fire hall or the possibility of no fire department service could impact whether or not insurance would be available and at what cost. The salesperson should also recommend including an appropriate condition if an offer is being drafted to buy the cottage.

APPENDIX

CHAPTER 5
VACANT LAND

Chapter Mini-Review

1. An important consideration in buying vacant land is to determine whether any easements or other restrictions impact the property.

    True   False

   In addition to easements and other restrictions, access to the land is also a key consideration.

2. Vacant rural land is typically sold based on the square footage of the land.

    True   **False**

   Vacant rural land is rarely sold based on square footage. Square footage is used in some instances when transacting commercial land.

3. Costs relating to the severance of a property are normally the responsibility of the seller, not the buyer.

    True   False

   The seller is typically responsible for severance costs. See Clause DEV-2 for a typical wording.

4. An owner can readily make significant design changes to a residential structure during construction without the need for further municipal approval relating to the building permit.

    True   **False**

   Significant changes in design would probably require municipal approval.

5. The Managed Forest Tax Incentive Program only applies to wooded land situated in Northern Ontario.

    True   **False**

   The Management Forest Tax Incentive Program applies throughout Ontario.

6. Only very large farm corporations can be viewed as viable farms.

    True   **False**

   Smaller, medium-sized and large farms can be viable. The key to viability is not size, but rather good management and the ability to generate a reasonable return.

7. A farm specializing in fruit is best described as a special purpose farm.

    True   False

   Other examples would include tobacco and vegetable farms.

8. The *Nutrient Management Act* is focused on various environmental considerations involving farms, including the storage and handling of commercial fertilizers.

   True   False

   This Act also addresses proper record keeping, qualifications for farmers and establishing minimum distance requirements regarding fertilizer application to land.

APPENDIX

Active Learning Exercises

▣ Exercise 1   Multiple Choice

1.1 A farm that produces soybean only is best described as a:

a. Cash crop farm.	✔ *CORRECT.* Other cash crop operations might include grain, wheat and corn.
b. Viable farm.	*Incorrect.* Viability relates to sound management, not a particular farming activity.
c. Livestock farm.	*Incorrect.* A livestock farm involves the raising of animals.
d. Farm corporation.	*Incorrect.* A soybean farming operation may or may not be a farm corporation.

1.2 Which of the following is a correct statement regarding important factors to consider when buying vacant land?

a. Buyers need not be concerned about access or easement considerations, as these rarely impact the purchase of vacant land.	*Incorrect.* Access and easements are key factors to consider when buying vacant land.
b. An offer cannot be accepted by the seller until a land severance for the land in question is finalized.	*Incorrect.* An offer can be accepted pending final severance approval.
c. Regulatory agencies, such as a conservation authority, can directly impact land use.	✔ *CORRECT.* Conservation authorities can impact land usage and building construction within regulated areas.
d. The municipality reviews a building permit application from a zoning perspective only.	*Incorrect.* Building permit applications are reviewed from zoning, architectural/structural and mechanical perspectives.

1.3 The Managed Forest Tax Incentive Program:

a. States that the buyer need not be approved, provided that the seller has previously been approved.	*Incorrect.* The buyer must make application and be approved.
b. Is overseen by the Municipal Property Assessment Corporation.	*Incorrect.* The Ministry of Natural Resources and Forestry oversees the program.
c. Applies only to forested areas of less than 10 acres.	*Incorrect.* The program applies to forested areas of *more than* 10 acres.
d. Requires that a Managed Forest Plan be prepared.	✔ *CORRECT.* This plan is typically developed from a long term perspective; e.g., 20 years.

CH5 **EX1**   **1.4**   Which of the following statements is correct?

a. A major trend in farming is the increasing number of family farms.

Incorrect. The reverse is true. Family farms are decreasing in number.

b. Availability/installation cost of services is rarely a consideration when considering the purchase of rural land.

Incorrect. Both availability and installation cost of services are important considerations, particularly in the case of remote land.

c. **The *Nutrient Management Act* introduced new standards for land-applied materials containing nutrients; e.g., fertilizers.**

✔ *CORRECT.* The Act came into effect in 2002 and addresses many regulatory requirements involving land-applied materials containing nutrients.

d. The *Nutrient Management Act* applies only to special purpose farms.

Incorrect. This Act applies to most farming operations including special purpose, livestock and cash crop farms.

1.5   The *Farming and Food Production Protection Act*:

a. States that an individual cannot build a rural residence in close proximity to an operating farm.

Incorrect. The Act makes no reference to such a restriction.

b. **Provides legislative protection for operating farms from restrictive municipal by-laws concerning normal farm practices.**

✔ *CORRECT.* The Act seeks to protect farmers from by-laws and related complaints provided that farming activities fall within the definition of a normal farm practice.

c. Protects farmers from complaints regarding all types of farming disturbances.

Incorrect. The Act only provides protection for normal farm practices, as defined under the Act.

d. Protects rural residential owners from disturbances caused by farmers relating to odour, dust, flies, light, smoke, noise and vibrations.

Incorrect. The protection involves the farmer causing such disturbances as part of normal farm practices, not the adjacent rural residential owner.

Exercise 2   Matching

j.	*Frontage*	*Abuts a Public Street or Highway*
e.	*Secondary Line*	*Hydro One Networks Inc.*
c.	*Managed Forest Tax Incentive Program*	*Not Less Than Four Hectares*
g.	*Disturbance*	*Odour, Dust and Flies*
i.	*Building Location*	*Setback from Public Road*
h.	*Vacant Land—Ongoing Costs*	*Taxes, Fencing and Liability Insurance*
b.	*Landowner Report*	*Prepared by Seller*

Not Used: a., d. and f.

Exercise 3   The Agreement of Purchase and Sale

The completed agreement is shown on the following pages.

APPENDIX

OREA Ontario Real Estate Association   **Agreement of Purchase and Sale**

Form 100
for use in the Province of Ontario

This Agreement of Purchase and Sale dated this .... **12th** .... day of .... **August** .... 20.. **XX** ....

BUYER, ... **James B. Witnell** ...., agrees to purchase from
(Full legal names of all Buyers)

SELLER, ... **Mary V. Goldman** ...., the following
(Full legal names of all Sellers)

REAL PROPERTY:

Address .... **3477 West Concession Road** ....

fronting on the .... **North** .... side of .... **West Concession Road** ....

in the .... **Township of Anytownship, Regional Municipality of Anyregion** ....

and having a frontage of .... **300 feet** .... more or less by a depth of .... **435 feet** .... more or less

and legally described as ..... **Part of Lot 10, Plan 270, more particularly described as Part 2 on**

Reference Plan 99R2320 .... (the "property")
(Legal description of land including easements not described elsewhere)

                                                                            JW **$143,500.00** *MG*
PURCHASE PRICE: *JW MG*   Dollars (CDN$) ..... ~~$135,000.00~~
    One Hundred and Forty-Three Thousand Five Hundred
    ~~One Hundred and Thirty Five Thousand~~ -- Dollars

DEPOSIT: Buyer submits .... **Upon Acceptance** ....
(Herewith/Upon Acceptance/as otherwise described in this Agreement)

...... **Ten Thousand**-- Dollars (CDN$) ..... **$10,000.00** ....

by negotiable cheque payable to .... **ABC Realty Inc.** .... "Deposit Holder" to be held
in trust pending completion or other termination of this Agreement and to be credited toward the Purchase Price on completion. For the purposes of this
Agreement, "Upon Acceptance" shall mean that the Buyer is required to deliver the deposit to the Deposit Holder within 24 hours of the acceptance of
this Agreement. The parties to this Agreement hereby acknowledge that, unless otherwise provided for in this Agreement, the Deposit Holder shall place
the deposit in trust in the Deposit Holder's non-interest bearing Real Estate Trust Account and no interest shall be earned, received or paid on the deposit.

Buyer agrees to pay the balance as more particularly set out in Schedule A attached.

SCHEDULE(S) A .... **and B** .... **attached hereto form(s) part of this Agreement.**
                                    JW **Seller** *MG*   *JW* **14th** *MG*
1.   **IRREVOCABILITY:** This offer shall be irrevocable by .... ~~Buyer~~ .... until .. **8:00** .. ~~a.m.~~/p.m. on the .. ~~13th~~ ..
                                    (Seller/Buyer)

     day of .... **August** .... 20 .. **XX** .., after which time, if not accepted, this offer shall be null and void and the deposit
     shall be returned to the Buyer in full without interest.

2.   **COMPLETION DATE:** This Agreement shall be completed by no later than 6:00 p.m. on the .. **20th** .. day of .... **October** ....

     20 .. **XX** ...... Upon completion, vacant possession of the property shall be given to the Buyer unless otherwise provided for in this Agreement.

INITIALS OF BUYER(S): (*JW*)   **INITIALS OF SELLER(S):** (*MG*)

APPENDIX

3. **NOTICES:** The Seller hereby appoints the Listing Brokerage as agent for the Seller for the purpose of giving and receiving notices pursuant to this Agreement. Where a Brokerage (Buyer's Brokerage) has entered into a representation agreement with the Buyer, the Buyer hereby appoints the Buyer's Brokerage as agent for the purpose of giving and receiving notices pursuant to this Agreement. **Where a Brokerage represents both the Seller and the Buyer (multiple representation), the Brokerage shall not be appointed or authorized to be agent for either the Buyer or the Seller for the purpose of giving and receiving notices.** Any notice relating hereto or provided for herein shall be in writing. In addition to any provision contained herein and in any Schedule hereto, this offer, any counter-offer, notice of acceptance thereof or any notice to be given or received pursuant to this Agreement or any Schedule hereto (any of them, "Document") shall be deemed given and received when delivered personally or hand delivered to the Address for Service provided in the Acknowledgement below, or where a facsimile number or email address is provided herein, when transmitted electronically to that facsimile number or email address, respectively, in which case, the signature(s) of the party (parties) shall be deemed to be original.

FAX No.: ....   FAX No.: ....

(For delivery of Documents to Seller)   (For delivery of Documents to Buyer)

Email Address: ....   Email Address: ....

(For delivery of Documents to Seller)   (For delivery of Documents to Buyer)

4. **CHATTELS INCLUDED:** N/A
....

....

....

Unless otherwise stated in this Agreement or any Schedule hereto, Seller agrees to convey all fixtures and chattels included in the Purchase Price free from all liens, encumbrances or claims affecting the said fixtures and chattels.

5. **FIXTURES EXCLUDED:** N/A
....

....

....

....

6. **RENTAL ITEMS (Including Lease, Lease to Own):** The following equipment is rented and **not** included in the Purchase Price. The Buyer agrees to assume the rental contract(s), if assumable:

N/A
....

....

The Buyer agrees to co-operate and execute such documentation as may be required to facilitate such assumption.

7. **HST:** If the sale of the Property (Real Property as described above) is subject to Harmonized Sales Tax (HST), then such tax shall be

.... in addition to .... the Purchase Price. If the sale of the Property is not subject to HST, Seller agrees to certify on or before

(included in/in addition to)

closing, that the sale of the Property is not subject to HST. Any HST on chattels, if applicable, is not included in the Purchase Price.

INITIALS OF BUYER(S): *(JW)*   INITIALS OF SELLER(S): *(MG)*

Form 100   Revised 2015   **Page 2 of 6**

APPENDIX

8. **TITLE SEARCH:** Buyer shall be allowed until 6:00 p.m. on the .....30th.... day of ....September................., 20.XX...., (Requisition Date) to examine the title to the Property at Buyer's own expense and until the earlier of: (i) thirty days from the later of the Requisition Date or the date on which the conditions in this Agreement are fulfilled or otherwise waived or; (ii) five days prior to completion, to satisfy Buyer that there are no outstanding

work orders or deficiency notices affecting the Property, and that its present use (..........residential vacant land................................) may be lawfully continued and that the principal building may be insured against risk of fire. Seller hereby consents to the municipality or other governmental agencies releasing to Buyer details of all outstanding work orders and deficiency notices affecting the property, and Seller agrees to execute and deliver such further authorizations in this regard as Buyer may reasonably require.

9. **FUTURE USE:** Seller and Buyer agree that there is no representation or warranty of any kind that the future intended use of the property by Buyer is or will be lawful except as may be specifically provided for in this Agreement.

10. **TITLE:** Provided that the title to the property is good and free from all registered restrictions, charges, liens, and encumbrances except as otherwise specifically provided in this Agreement and save and except for (a) any registered restrictions or covenants that run with the land providing that such are complied with; (b) any registered municipal agreements and registered agreements with publicly regulated utilities providing such have been complied with, or security has been posted to ensure compliance and completion, as evidenced by a letter from the relevant municipality or regulated utility; (c) any minor easements for the supply of domestic utility or telephone services to the property or adjacent properties; and (d) any easements for drainage, storm or sanitary sewers, public utility lines, telephone lines, cable television lines or other services which do not materially affect the use of the property. If within the specified times referred to in paragraph 8 any valid objection to title or to any outstanding work order or deficiency notice, or to the fact the said present use may not lawfully be continued, or that the principal building may not be insured against risk of fire is made in writing to Seller and which Seller is unable or unwilling to remove, remedy or satisfy or obtain insurance save and except against risk of fire (Title Insurance) in favour of the Buyer and any mortgagee, (with all related costs at the expense of the Seller), and which Buyer will not waive, this Agreement notwithstanding any intermediate acts or negotiations in respect of such objections, shall be at an end and all monies paid shall be returned without interest or deduction and Seller, Listing Brokerage and Co-operating Brokerage shall not be liable for any costs or damages. Save as to any valid objection so made by such day and except for any objection going to the root of the title, Buyer shall be conclusively deemed to have accepted Seller's title to the property.

11. **CLOSING ARRANGEMENTS:** Where each of the Seller and Buyer retain a lawyer to complete the Agreement of Purchase and Sale of the property, and where the transaction will be completed by electronic registration pursuant to Part III of the Land Registration Reform Act, R.S.O. 1990, Chapter L4 and the Electronic Registration Act, S.O. 1991, Chapter 44, and any amendments thereto, the Seller and Buyer acknowledge and agree that the exchange of closing funds, non-registrable documents and other items (the "Requisite Deliveries") and the release thereof to the Seller and Buyer will (a) not occur at the same time as the registration of the transfer/deed (and any other documents intended to be registered in connection with the completion of this transaction) and (b) be subject to conditions whereby the lawyer(s) receiving any of the Requisite Deliveries will be required to hold same in trust and not release same except in accordance with the terms of a document registration agreement between the said lawyers. The Seller and Buyer irrevocably instruct the said lawyers to be bound by the document registration agreement which is recommended from time to time by the Law Society of Upper Canada. Unless otherwise agreed to by the lawyers, such exchange of the Requisite Deliveries will occur in the applicable Land Titles Office or such other location agreeable to both lawyers.

12. **DOCUMENTS AND DISCHARGE:** Buyer shall not call for the production of any title deed, abstract, survey or other evidence of title to the property except such as are in the possession or control of Seller. If requested by Buyer, Seller will deliver any sketch or survey of the property within Seller's control to Buyer as soon as possible and prior to the Requisition Date. If a discharge of any Charge/Mortgage held by a corporation incorporated pursuant to the Trust And Loan Companies Act (Canada), Chartered Bank, Trust Company, Credit Union, Caisse Populaire or Insurance Company and which is not to be assumed by Buyer on completion, is not available in registrable form on completion, Buyer agrees to accept Seller's lawyer's personal undertaking to obtain, out of the closing funds, a discharge in registrable form and to register same, or cause same to be registered, on title within a reasonable period of time after completion, provided that on or before completion Seller shall provide to Buyer a mortgage statement prepared by the mortgagee setting out the balance required to obtain the discharge, and, where a real-time electronic cleared funds transfer system is not being used, a direction executed by Seller directing payment to the mortgagee of the amount required to obtain the discharge out of the balance due on completion.

13. **INSPECTION:** Buyer acknowledges having had the opportunity to inspect the Property and understands that upon acceptance of this offer there shall be a binding agreement of purchase and sale between Buyer and Seller. **The Buyer acknowledges having the opportunity to include a requirement for a property inspection report in this Agreement and agrees that except as may be specifically provided for in this Agreement, the Buyer will not be obtaining a property inspection or property inspection report regarding the Property.**

14. **INSURANCE:** All buildings on the property and all other things being purchased shall be and remain until completion at the risk of Seller. Pending completion, Seller shall hold all insurance policies, if any, and the proceeds thereof in trust for the parties as their interests may appear and in the event of substantial damage, Buyer may either terminate this Agreement and have all monies paid returned without interest or deduction or else take the proceeds of any insurance and complete the purchase. No insurance shall be transferred on completion. If Seller is taking back a Charge/Mortgage, or Buyer is assuming a Charge/Mortgage, Buyer shall supply Seller with reasonable evidence of adequate insurance to protect Seller's or other mortgagee's interest on completion.

INITIALS OF BUYER(S): (*JW*)   INITIALS OF SELLER(S): (*MG*)

Form 100   Revised 2015   **Page 3 of 6**

15. **PLANNING ACT:** This Agreement shall be effective to create an interest in the property only if Seller complies with the subdivision control provisions of the Planning Act by completion and Seller covenants to proceed diligently at Seller's expense to obtain any necessary consent by completion.

16. **DOCUMENT PREPARATION:** The Transfer/Deed shall, save for the Land Transfer Tax Affidavit, be prepared in registrable form at the expense of Seller, and any Charge/Mortgage to be given back by the Buyer to Seller at the expense of the Buyer. If requested by Buyer, Seller covenants that the Transfer/Deed to be delivered on completion shall contain the statements contemplated by Section 50(22) of the Planning Act, R.S.O.1990.

17. **RESIDENCY:** (a) Subject to (b) below, the Seller represents and warrants that the Seller is not and on completion will not be a non-resident under the non-residency provisions of the Income Tax Act which representation and warranty shall survive and not merge upon the completion of this transaction and the Seller shall deliver to the Buyer a statutory declaration that Seller is not then a non-resident of Canada; (b) provided that if the Seller is a non-resident under the non-residency provisions of the Income Tax Act, the Buyer shall be credited towards the Purchase Price with the amount, if any, necessary for Buyer to pay to the Minister of National Revenue to satisfy Buyer's liability in respect of tax payable by Seller under the non-residency provisions of the Income Tax Act by reason of this sale. Buyer shall not claim such credit if Seller delivers on completion the prescribed certificate.

18. **ADJUSTMENTS:** Any rents, mortgage interest, realty taxes including local improvement rates and unmetered public or private utility charges and unmetered cost of fuel, as applicable, shall be apportioned and allowed to the day of completion, the day of completion itself to be apportioned to Buyer.

19. **PROPERTY ASSESSMENT:** The Buyer and Seller hereby acknowledge that the Province of Ontario has implemented current value assessment and properties may be re-assessed on an annual basis. The Buyer and Seller agree that no claim will be made against the Buyer or Seller, or any Brokerage, Broker or Salesperson, for any changes in property tax as a result of a re-assessment of the property, save and except any property taxes that accrued prior to the completion of this transaction.

20. **TIME LIMITS:** Time shall in all respects be of the essence hereof provided that the time for doing or completing of any matter provided for herein may be extended or abridged by an agreement in writing signed by Seller and Buyer or by their respective lawyers who may be specifically authorized in that regard.

21. **TENDER:** Any tender of documents or money hereunder may be made upon Seller or Buyer or their respective lawyers on the day set for completion. Money shall be tendered with funds drawn on a lawyer's trust account in the form of a bank draft, certified cheque or wire transfer using the Large Value Transfer System.

22. **FAMILY LAW ACT:** Seller warrants that spousal consent is not necessary to this transaction under the provisions of the Family Law Act, R.S.O.1990 unless Seller's spouse has executed the consent hereinafter provided.

23. **UFFI:** Seller represents and warrants to Buyer that during the time Seller has owned the property, Seller has not caused any building on the property to be insulated with insulation containing ureaformaldehyde, and that to the best of Seller's knowledge no building on the property contains or has ever contained insulation that contains ureaformaldehyde. This warranty shall survive and not merge on the completion of this transaction, and if the building is part of a multiple unit building, this warranty shall only apply to that part of the building which is the subject of this transaction.

24. **LEGAL, ACCOUNTING AND ENVIRONMENTAL ADVICE:** The parties acknowledge that any information provided by the brokerage is not legal, tax or environmental advice.

25. **CONSUMER REPORTS: The Buyer is hereby notified that a consumer report containing credit and/or personal information may be referred to in connection with this transaction.**

26. **AGREEMENT IN WRITING:** If there is conflict or discrepancy between any provision added to this Agreement (including any Schedule attached hereto) and any provision in the standard pre-set portion hereof, the added provision shall supersede the standard pre-set provision to the extent of such conflict or discrepancy. This Agreement including any Schedule attached hereto, shall constitute the entire Agreement between Buyer and Seller. There is no representation, warranty, collateral agreement or condition, which affects this Agreement other than as expressed herein. For the purposes of this Agreement, Seller means vendor and Buyer means purchaser. This Agreement shall be read with all changes of gender or number required by the context.

27. **TIME AND DATE:** Any reference to a time and date in this Agreement shall mean the time and date where the property is located.

INITIALS OF BUYER(S): (*JW*)   **INITIALS OF SELLER(S):** (*MG*)

APPENDIX

28. SUCCESSORS AND ASSIGNS: The heirs, executors, administrators, successors and assigns of the undersigned are bound by the terms herein.

SIGNED, SEALED AND DELIVERED in the presence of: IN WITNESS whereof I have hereunto set my hand and seal:

Mark Nayak
(Witness)

James B. Witnell   ● (Seal)   DATE *Aug. 12/xx*
(Buyer)

_____
(Witness)

_____   ● (Seal)   DATE _____
(Buyer)

I, the Undersigned Seller, agree to the above offer. I hereby irrevocably instruct my lawyer to pay directly to the brokerage(s) with whom I have agreed to pay commission, the unpaid balance of the commission together with applicable Harmonized Sales Tax (and any other taxes as may hereafter be applicable), from the proceeds of the sale prior to any payment to the undersigned on completion, as advised by the brokerage(s) to my lawyer.

SIGNED, SEALED AND DELIVERED in the presence of: IN WITNESS whereof I have hereunto set my hand and seal:

Patricia Johnston
(Witness)

Mary V. Goldman   ● (Seal)   DATE *Aug. 13/xx*
(Seller)

_____
(Witness)

_____   ● (Seal)   DATE _____
(Seller)

SPOUSAL CONSENT: The Undersigned Spouse of the Seller hereby consents to the disposition evidenced herein pursuant to the provisions of the Family Law Act, R.S.O.1990, and hereby agrees with the Buyer that he/she will execute all necessary or incidental documents to give full force and effect to the sale evidenced herein.

_____   ● (Seal)   DATE _____
(Witness)   (Spouse)

CONFIRMATION OF ACCEPTANCE: Notwithstanding anything contained herein to the contrary, I confirm this Agreement with all changes both typed and written was finally accepted by all parties at *6:00* a.m./p.m. this *14th* day of *August*, 20*XX*.

James B. Witnell
(Signature of Seller or Buyer)

INFORMATION ON BROKERAGE(S)

Listing Brokerage ...... ABC Realty Inc. ...... Tel.No.(416) 555-1212
123 Main Street, Anycity, Anyregion L4H 6P6   Patricia Johnston
(Salesperson / Broker Name)

Co-op/Buyer Brokerage ...... XYZ Real Estate Limited ...... Tel.No.(416) 666-1212
25 Maple Drive, Anycity, Anyregion L2J 7P6   Mark Nayak
(Salesperson / Broker Name)

ACKNOWLEDGEMENT

I acknowledge receipt of my signed copy of this accepted Agreement of Purchase and Sale and I authorize the Brokerage to forward a copy to my lawyer.

Mary V. Goldman   DATE *Aug. 14/xx*
(Seller)

_____   DATE _____
(Seller)
Address for Service *375 Parkdale Road, Anycity*
K7T 6R6 .... Tel.No.(*416*) *333-1212*
Seller's Lawyer *Hoddson Law Associates*
Address *355 Bishop Boulevard, Anycity K1R 3B5*
Email _____
(*416*) *222-1212* (*416*) *222-2121*
Tel.No.   FAX No.

I acknowledge receipt of my signed copy of this accepted Agreement of Purchase and Sale and I authorize the Brokerage to forward a copy to my lawyer.

James B. Witnell   DATE *Aug. 14/xx*
(Buyer)

_____   DATE _____
(Buyer)
Address for Service *50 King Street, Suite 511, Anycity*
K9O 3J5 .... Tel.No.(*416*) *777-1212*
Buyer's Lawyer *Stewart Millard and Stoltz*
Address *291 Westside Drive, Anycity K9C 4B2*
Email _____
(*416*) *888-1212* (*416*) *888-2121*
Tel.No.   FAX No.

FOR OFFICE USE ONLY   **COMMISSION TRUST AGREEMENT**

To: Co-operating Brokerage shown on the foregoing Agreement of Purchase and Sale:
In consideration for the Co-operating Brokerage procuring the foregoing Agreement of Purchase and Sale, I hereby declare that all moneys received or receivable by me in connection with the Transaction as contemplated in the MLS® Rules and Regulations of my Real Estate Board shall be receivable and held in trust. This agreement shall constitute a Commission Trust Agreement as defined in the MLS® Rules and shall be subject to and governed by the MLS® Rules pertaining to Commission Trust.

DATED as of the date and time of the acceptance of the foregoing Agreement of Purchase and Sale.   Acknowledged by:

Patricia Johnston   *Mark Nayak*
(Authorized to bind the Listing Brokerage)   (Authorized to bind the Co-operating Brokerage)

Form 100   Revised 2015   **Page 5 of 6**

APPENDIX

OREA Ontario Real Estate Association

Form 100
for use in the Province of Ontario

Schedule A
Agreement of Purchase and Sale

This Schedule is attached to and forms part of the Agreement of Purchase and Sale between:

BUYER, ... James B. Witnell ...., and

SELLER, ... Mary V. Goldman ....

for the purchase and sale of .... 3477 West Concession Road, Township of Anytownship, Regional

.... Municipality of Anyregion .... dated the 12th day of .... August ...., 20 **XX**

Buyer agrees to pay the balance as follows: *JW   MG*

JW   The Buyer agrees to pay a further sum of <s>One Hundred and Twenty-Five Thousand Dollars</s>
MG   (<s>$125,000.00</s>) **$133,500.00** , subject to adjustments, to the Seller on completion of this transaction, with funds

One Hundred and Thirty-Three Thousand, Five Hundred Dollars
drawn on a lawyer's trust account in the form of a bank draft, certified cheque, or wire transfer using
the Large Value Transfer System.

This Offer is conditional upon the Buyer satisfying himself, at the Buyer's expense, that a building
permit for the structure indicated on Schedule "B" attached hereto is available with respect to the
property. Unless the Buyer gives notice in writing to the Seller personally or in accordance with any
other provisions for the delivery of notice in this Agreement of Purchase and Sale or any Schedule
thereto not later than 6:00 p.m. on the 15th day of September, 20xx, that this condition is fulfilled,
this Offer shall become null and void and the deposit shall be returned to the Buyer in full without
deduction. This condition is included for the benefit of the Buyer and may be waived at the Buyer's
sole option by notice in writing to the Seller as aforesaid within the time period stated herein.

This Offer is conditional upon the Buyer determining, at the Buyer's own expense, that the provision
of service by hydro and telephone to the said property shall not exceed a cost of Two Thousand
Dollars ($2,000.00). Unless the Buyer gives notice in writing delivered to the Seller personally or in
accordance with any other provisions for the delivery of notice in this Agreement of Purchase and
Sale or any Schedule thereto not later than 6:00 p.m. on the 15th day of September, 20xx, that this
condition is fulfilled, this Offer shall become null and void and the deposit shall be returned to the
Buyer in full without deduction. This condition is included for the benefit of the Buyer and may be
waived at the Buyer's sole option by notice in writing to the Seller as aforesaid within the time
period stated herein.

The Seller agrees to provide, at the Seller's own expense, not later than 6:00 p.m. on the 15th day
of September, 20xx, a new survey of said property showing the current location of all fences,
improvements, easements, rights-of-way, and encroachments affecting the said property.

This form must be initialed by all parties to the Agreement of Purchase and Sale.

INITIALS OF BUYER(S): (*JW*)   INITIALS OF SELLER(S): (*MG*)

APPENDIX

CHAPTER 6
NEW HOMES

Chapter Mini-Review

1. All salespersons selling new homes for a builder are exempt from registration under the *Real Estate and Business Brokers Act, 2002*.

    True   **False**

   Builders may employ salaried staff to handle sales activity involving their owned new home inventory.

2. Real estate brokerages may be contracted by a new home builder to provide only specific services when marketing and selling new homes.

    True   ◯ False

   The specific services to be provided are subject to negotiations between the parties. In providing such services, the real estate brokerage must fully comply with all requirements set out in REBBA 2002.

3. A building permit application typically contains other support documentation, such as architectural drawings and a detailed site plan.

    True   ◯ False

   Exact documentation can vary by municipality depending on requirements set out in the municipal by-laws.

4. Construction standards for homes is covered under Part 3 of the Ontario Building Code.

    True   **False**

   Construction standards for homes is covered under Part 9 of the Ontario Building Code.

5. Homes enrolled in the new home warranty program must, among other things, be in compliance with the Ontario Building Code.

    True   ◯ False

   New homes must comply with the Ontario Building Code, as well as other requirements set out by the not-for-profit corporation administering the program.

6. The new home warranty program is administered by the Ontario government.

   ◯ True   **False**

   The new home warranty program is administered by the not-for-profit Tarion Warranty Corporation.

7. Under Tarion warranty coverages, all defects in workmanship are warrantied for a seven-year period.

   ◯ True   **False**

   The warranty specifically regarding defects in workmanship and materials is for a one-year period.

8. Every agreement for a new home (including a condominium) provides the buyer with a right to terminate if closing delay occurs.

   ◯ True   **False**

   A builder, for example, may delay a closing up to five days without giving notice, but the buyer has no right to terminate under this circumstance.

9. An ownership change concerning a resale home does not disrupt remaining warranty coverage, subject to when that home was initially enrolled with the Tarion Warranty Corporation.

 True   False

The new home warranty remains for the duration of the warranty period beginning from initial date of enrollment.

10. The Certificate of Completion and Possession is completed at the same time as the Pre-Delivery Inspection.

 True   False

The CCP marks the official date of possession when the warranty coverage starts and the Pre-Delivery Inspection provides the buyer with the opportunity to describe various uncompleted, missing or damaged items as of that official date.

11. Construction performance guidelines assist homeowners in understanding how disputed items will be resolved.

 True   False

The guidelines are built on historical claims data.

12. In Ontario, an owner of a property is able to, for a given period of time, holdback 15% of the value of the services or materials that are supplied to an improvement under a contract with that owner.

 True   **False**

The *Construction Lien Act* provides for a 10% holdback. The Act encompasses contracts with an owner that are related to an improvement to or on land; e.g., landscaping, renovating a house, installing a new bathroom, repairing a roof, constructing an addition, demolishing a garage, etc.

Active Learning Exercises

◼ Exercise 1   Scenarios

1.1 Seasonal homes or homes built for temporary occupancy are excluded from warranty coverage (provided they meet certain specifications; e.g., not built on permanent foundation or not insulated sufficiently for year-round living). The builder could construct this new structure and not require registration. A claim would not be considered by the Tarion Warranty Corporation.

1.2 The casement windows would be covered by the two-year warranty regarding defects in materials and work, including caulking windows and doors so that the building envelope prevents water penetration. As for the book shelves, defects in materials, design and work supplied or installed by the homeowner/buyer are not covered.

1.3 Yes, Khan is covered for the subsequent damage discovered after the issuance of the Certificate of Completion and Possession. While pre-delivery inspection provides an opportunity to identify defects, this in no way infringes on general warranty provisions concerning undetected defects, provided they occur within coverage time limits.

APPENDIX

1.4   McCrae and the buyer can change a critical date by mutual agreement in writing (see *Section 4: Changing Critical Dates—By Mutual Agreement*).

1.5   In most instances, the defects themselves are covered, but not secondary damage. The repair to the flashing would be covered. In all probability, the resulting staining would also fall under the new home warranty. However, the damage to the chest of drawers is secondary damage. The homeowner would have to rely on his or her home insurance. Coverage for the loss would depend on insurance policy wording.

1.6   No. Coverage excludes commercial or residential buildings undergoing renovation. More specifically, the exclusion relates to any homes that have been lived in, built on existing footings or foundations, or constructed in converted buildings.

1.7   The damage appears to come from a main water line breakage. The warranty program might not cover the damage. The issue centres on the exact location of the rupture. If municipal services are at fault, Jones may have to pursue the city and/or file a claim under his home insurance policy. If the Tarion Warranty Corporation is involved (i.e., the rupture involved lines installed by the builder or a subcontractor within the property's boundary beyond the junction to the city services), the extent of warranty will depend on what is judged primary and secondary damage. Remember that while the primary cause is covered, family room carpets, baseboards and drywall might be viewed as secondary and not covered. The property owner might have to rely on his/her homeowner's insurance to cover the secondary damage.

1.8   A strike is one of several events defined in the Tarion Freehold Form as an unavoidable delay (see *Section 12: Definitions*). If an unavoidable delay occurs, the builder may extend the firm closing date based on procedures set out in *Section 5: Extending Dates—Due to Unavoidable Delay*.

APPENDIX

◼ Exercise 2   New Home Warranty and the Resale Property

Confirm details regarding the original purchase; e.g., builder, Tarion warranty enrolment number and possession date.

- Discuss the partially finished basement.
- Discuss basement improvements not covered by the new home warranty.
- Was building permit issued for basement finishing work; i.e., framing, plumbing and electrical?
- Is work in compliance with the Ontario Building Code?
- Are the Lams contemplating a secondary unit on the lower level?
- Has the work in any way affected the structural integrity of the residence?
- Has any claim been filed by the Lams concerning possible basement dampness and wall cracks leading to the basement window? If so, what is the current status? As a further possibility, was the basement window part of the original structure or added by Mr. Lam?
- If no claim has been filed, the property appears to fall within the two-year time coverage period. Seller should fully investigate with the Tarion Warranty Corporation.

APPENDIX

CHAPTER 7
STIGMATIZED PROPERTY, GROW OPERATIONS AND OTHER TOPICAL ISSUES

Chapter Mini-Review

1. The most prudent approach regarding stigmas is to disclose their existence to potential buyers.

    True   ◯ False

   If a registrant made the conscious decision to not inform a buyer of a known stigma, the court would undoubtedly side with the innocent consumer who could not make an informed decision given the lack of material information about the property.

2. High moisture content, saturated attic insulation and wall staining are three of several indications that the home was used as a grow operation.

    True   ◯ False

   Other indications include rusting of furnace and chimneys/flues, service line alterations and repairs/painting to high areas where holes were cut through walls and floors.

3. A home inspection will not assist in detecting whether or not a home has been previous used for a grow operation.

   ◯ True   **False**

   A home inspection can identify structural, mechanical, plumbing and electrical system issues that may have resulted from a grow operation, but a home inspection will not uncover such matters as chemical contamination and other health risks, such as hidden mould.

4. Failure to disclose known information to a prospective buyer that the home was previously used as a grow house could result in disciplinary proceedings against a registrant.

    True   False

   Such information would be undoubtedly viewed as material information. The non-disclosure of such information is in violation of the Code of Ethics.

5. Phishing is a type of value fraud associated with the inflating of the selling price in order to obtain financing.

   ◯ True   **False**

   Phishing relates to identity fraud and scams intended to deceive Internet users into divulging personal information.

6. A borrower who falsifies information on a credit application represents one type of mortgage fraud.

    True   ◯ False

   This type of activity is not directly related to financial gain, but nevertheless is done to advance personal interests.

7. A registrant found guilty of fraudulent activity could be subject to disciplinary action by the Real Estate Council of Ontario (e.g., a fine), but would not lose his or her registration for such activity.

    True   **False**

   Two decisions are cited in this chapter involving loss of registration due to fraudulent activity.

APPENDIX

8. A suspicious transaction is best described as a financial transaction for which there are reasonable grounds to suspect that it is related to the commission of a money laundering offence.

 True   False

Chapter materials include various 'reasonable grounds' upon which to suspect money laundering or related activities.

9. Real estate brokerages are required to retain selected forms to comply with FINTRAC requirements, two of which are *Receipt of Funds Record* and *Suspicious Transaction Report*.

 True   False

The remaining forms are *Large Cash Transaction Report, Individual Identification Information Record, Corporation/Entity Identification Information Record* and a *Self-Assessed Risk Management Report* (completed every two years).

10. An auctioneer is not allowed to auction real estate in the usual course of carrying out his or her function as an auctioneer.

 True   **False**

A specific exemption is included in REBBA 2002 allowing auctioneers to sell real estate as part of their overall duties; e.g., the auctioning of an estate that includes a home, automobile and all furnishings.

11. An absolute auction is an auction with a minimum reserve bid set by the seller.

 True   **False**

An absolute auction is an auction with no minimum reserve bid.

12. Enhancing curb appeal is part of the overall home staging process.

 True   False

Staging involves both interior and exterior (curb appeal) processes to prepare the home for sale.

13. A key objective in home staging is to personalize the property, so that the buyer feels more comfortable when viewing the home.

 True   **False**

On the contrary, a key objective is to depersonalize the property and minimize the seller's personal touches (e.g., family photos).

APPENDIX

Active Learning Exercises

■ Exercise 1   Multiple Choice

1.1 A stigmatized property:

a. Will typically increase in value due to the stigma.

Incorrect. Value typically decreases due to the stigma.

b. Usually reflects real risk to the buyer, as opposed to perceived risk.

Incorrect. Stigmatized property typically involve perceived risk.

c. **Can remain as such for many years, particularly given widespread media coverage and associated notoriety.**

CORRECT. The stigma can remain for many years if widely known.

d. Cannot be remedied.

Incorrect. In some instances, the stigma can be remedied through remodelling or changing the civic address.

1.2 Which of the following might be a possible indication that a buyer or tenant may intend on using the property for an illegal purpose?

a. Buying without properly viewing the property.

Incorrect. While this is a possible indication, a more suitable answer option is available.

b. Displaying a particular interest in privacy associated with the home.

Incorrect. While this is a possible indication, a more suitable answer option is available.

c. Wanting immediate possession.

Incorrect. While this is a possible indication, a more suitable answer option is available.

d. **All of the above.**

CORRECT. All of the above answer options are correct.

1.3 Identity fraud:

a. Is often referred to as a *boost and flip*.

Incorrect. The boost and flip is associated with mortgage fraud (value fraud).

b. Only refers to electronic scams perpetrated on the Internet.

Incorrect. Identity fraud involves all types of fraud relating to stolen identification information, not just scams involving the Internet.

c. Is only possible if the innocent party has credit cards.

Incorrect. While a great deal of identify fraud involves credit cards, fraudsters can also use social insurance numbers and banking information to commit fraud.

d. **Is also known as identity theft.**

CORRECT. Identity fraud and identity theft are generally viewed as analogous terms.

APPENDIX

1.4 Which of the following is correct?

a. Asking for photo identification from unknown persons is not an effective means of minimizing fraud.

Incorrect. Seeking such confirmation is an important step in minimizing fraud.

b. **Registrants, according to REBBA 2002, must not only avoid misrepresentation, but also take steps to prevent fraud.**

✔ *CORRECT.* Section 38 of the Code of Ethics includes a specific requirement regarding registrants preventing fraud.

c. Automated detection systems for mortgage fraud are used by the government, but not by private enterprises.

Incorrect. Automated detection systems are now used widely by lenders, insurers and other mortgage service providers.

d. The Registrar has the right to revoke a registration without any right of appeal by the registrant.

Incorrect. Registration revocation is subject to appeal to the Licence Appeal Tribunal.

1.5 A compliance regime generally refers to:

a. Various procedures involved in setting up an auction.

Incorrect. The term *compliance regime* does not directly relate to auctions.

b. Requirements set out in REBBA 2002 regarding compliance with the Code of Ethics.

Incorrect. This terminology is not used in relation to REBBA 2002.

c. **Rules, procedures and related activities that real estate brokerages must adhere to in order to be in compliance with FINTRAC requirements.**

✔ *CORRECT.* A compliance regime must be established by every real estate brokerage.

d. Rules, procedures and related activities that apply to real estate brokerages regarding FINTRAC requirements, but not to real estate salespersons.

Incorrect. FINTRAC compliance applies to real estate brokerages, brokers and salespersons.

1.6 An auction by confirmation:

a. Provides that the seller can establish a minimum acceptable bid.

Incorrect. This best describes a minimum bid auction.

b. **Permits the seller to reject any final high bid price.**

✔ *CORRECT.* The seller is provided the right to reject any final high bid price.

c. Does not provide for any restrictions or limitations on the final selling price.

Incorrect. This best describes an absolute auction.

d. Provides that the seller must confirm that he or she wants to auction the property two days before the scheduled auction date.

Incorrect. No such requirement exists in typical auctions offered in Ontario.

APPENDIX

1.7 Which of the following is a correct statement?

a. One of the goals of home staging is to shorten the length of time required to sell a property.

✓ *CORRECT.* The other goal is to get the most money possible for the seller by attracting more motivated buyers.

b. Repair of broken items is not normally part of the home staging process.

Incorrect. Repairs are a normal part of the home staging process.

c. A real estate brokerage cannot charge both a flat fee and a commission to a seller when marketing that seller's property.

Incorrect. A real estate brokerage can charge a flat fee, a percentage of the sale price or a combination of both.

d. Home staging is a regulated business in Ontario.

Incorrect. Home stagers are not regulated in Ontario.

■ Exercise 2   Matching

e.	Grow House	Patched Holes in Subfloors
h.	Stigmatized Property	Perception of Risk
g.	Internet Scam	Phishing
a.	Unknown Person	Ask for Photo Identification
f.	Boost and Flip	Mortgage Fraud
c.	Personal Fraud Proofing	Burn or Shred Discarded Personal Information
b.	Preview/Marketing Period	Auction
j.	Curb Appeal	Home Staging

No Match: d. and i.

APPENDIX

CHAPTER 8
ENVIRONMENTAL CONCERNS AND RELATED TOPICS

Chapter Mini-Review

1. All matters concerning development work on or near the water in Ontario are handled by the federal government pursuant to the *Fisheries Act.*

    True   **False**

   Development work on or near the water can involve both federal and provincial ministries. The Ministry of Natural Resources and Forestry is typically involved as it has jurisdiction for public lands under water bodies.

2. A well-drafted clause relating to environmental compliance of a property should include reference to the seller agreeing to provide the buyer with applicable documents, records and reports relating to environmental matters that are in the possession of that seller.

    True   ◯ False

   This is one of several requirements that should be detailed in a properly-drafted clause regarding environmental compliance.

3. A Phase 2 environmental audit includes a visual inspection of the property combined with a review of available documents relating to that property.

   ◯ True   **False**

   This best describes a Phase 1 audit. A Phase 2 audit is a more costly investigation involving various sampling and testing procedures.

4. Friable asbestos is generally more dangerous than non-friable, as it is easily crumbled.

    True   ◯ False

   Friable is generally more dangerous as it can easily become airborne when disturbed. Once airborne, asbestos fibre can become a serious health risk when entering the lungs.

5. The electrical power delivery system is best described using three major elements: generation, transport and end use.

    True   ◯ False

   The objective of this three-part delivery system is to deliver electricity in a safe and cost-effective manner.

6. Lead contamination in residential property is limited to lead paint and lead pipes found in structures dating from the 1940's and earlier.

   ◯ True   **False**

   Lead was still widely used in the 1950's and was not largely eliminated in residential structures until after 1970.

7. Basement recreational rooms can be particularly susceptible to mould, as finished walls may hide dampness entering through exterior foundation walls.

    True   ◯ False

   Finished basement areas are particularly vulnerable to mould, but any damp area within a structure should be closely analyzed.

APPENDIX

8. The concentration of radon within subsoils does not vary noticeably from one part of Canada to another.

 True   ✓ False

Radon concentrations can vary significantly based on topography and underlying rock composition.

9. UFFI was used for insulation purposes in residential structures in the late 1970's, but was subsequently banned given concerns about the curing process and related health issues.

✓ True   ○ False

The product was banned, but a general consensus now minimizes UFFI as a health hazard.

10. Regulatory controls under the *Technical Standards and Safety Act* only apply to new underground storage tanks (fuel).

○ True   ✓ False

Regulatory controls apply both to existing and new underground storage tanks (fuel).

11. The EnerGuide program applies to central air conditioning systems, but not to room air conditioners.

 True   ✓ False

The EnerGuide program applies to both.

12. ENERGY STAR® for New Houses is administered in Canada by the Office of Energy Efficiency.

✓ True   ○ False

The Office of Energy Efficiency is an operating division within Natural Resources Canada which oversees various energy efficiency programs.

APPENDIX

Active Learning Exercises

■ Exercise 1   Multiple Choice

1.1 The Technical Standards and Safety Authority oversees:

a. The installation of docks situated on public lands.

> *Incorrect.* Dock installation is most directly overseen by the Ministry of Natural Resources and Forestry.

b. **The installation of underground storage tanks.**

> ✔ *CORRECT.* The installation of underground storage tanks is overseen by the Technical Standards and Safety Authority.

c. The installation of septic tanks.

> *Incorrect.* The Building Code covers installation of septic tanks.

d. The qualifying process for ENERGY STAR® appliances.

> *Incorrect.* The ENERGY STAR® program is a federal initiative overseen by the Office of Energy Efficiency (Natural Resources Canada).

1.2 An environmental contractor, who is setting out remedial steps and costs associated with an environmental audit, is involved in what stage of the audit process?

a. Phase 1

> *Incorrect.* The Phase 1 level is a visual inspection combined with document review.

b. Phase 2

> *Incorrect.* The Phase 2 level involves testing, sampling and analysis.

c. **Phase 3**

> ✔ *CORRECT.* The Phase 3 level involves detailed remedial steps and costs associated with circumstances found in Phase 2.

d. Phase 4

> *Incorrect.* A Phase 4 level does not exist.

1.3 Asbestos can be potentially found in older (pre-1980) structures containing which of the following?:

a. Old stove, oven and furnace gaskets.

> *Incorrect.* Asbestos can be found in older gaskets, but a more appropriate answer option is available.

b. Older ceiling tiles.

> *Incorrect.* Asbestos can be found in older ceiling tiles, but a more appropriate answer option is available.

c. Older insulation around plumbing pipes.

> *Incorrect.* Asbestos can be found in older insulation around plumbing pipes, but a more appropriate answer option is available.

d. **All of the above.**

> ✔ *CORRECT.* All of the above answer options are correct.

CH8   EX1   **1.4** Which of the following is correct?

a. Electromagnetic fields tend to increase in strength as distance from the source increases.

Incorrect. These fields decrease in strength as distance from the source increases.

b. **Electrical fields are produced whether or not an appliance is operating.**

✓ *CORRECT.* Electrical fields are produced whether or not an appliance is operating.

c. Magnetic fields are produced whether or not an appliance is operating.

Incorrect. Magnetic fields are only produced when an appliance is operating.

d. Magnetic fields do not penetrate most materials.

Incorrect. Magnetic fields penetrate most materials.

1.5 Radon is an invisible, odourless, tasteless gas:

a. That is typically produced by the decay of garbage.

Incorrect. Radon is produced by the decay of uranium.

b. **That can pose a health hazard when highly concentrated in basement areas.**

✓ *CORRECT.* Radon can pose a health risk if present in high concentration levels.

c. That can only be remediated by the continuous use of air filters.

Incorrect. Various forms of remedial action are possible, one of which is air filtering.

d. That can only be measured by using charcoal canisters.

Incorrect. Two testing devices are typically used to detect radon, the other being an alpha track detector.

1.6 Which of the following is a correct statement?

a. **Mould found in residential properties can be toxic.**

✓ *CORRECT.* Mould found in residential properties can be toxic but, fortunately, most are not.

b. The seasonal energy efficiency ratio (SEER) is a rating system to establish the energy efficiency of furnaces.

Incorrect. SEER is a rating system involving air conditioners, not furnaces.

c. All existing underground storage tanks for fuel must be registered with the Ministry of the Environment.

Incorrect. All existing underground storage tanks must be registered with the Technical Standards and Safety Authority.

d. ENERGY STAR® is only used to identify highly energy efficient appliances.

Incorrect. ENERGY STAR® is also used for other purposes; e.g., new houses.

APPENDIX

▣ Exercise 2   Matching

g.	*ENERGY STAR®*	*Energy Rating of 80 or Higher*
c.	*EER*	*Room Air Conditioners*
j.	*Typical Older Home*	*Energy Rating of 50–65*
a.	*Storage Tank Leak*	*Call to Spills Action Centre—Ministry of the Environment*
d.	*UFFI*	*100,000 Canadian Homes*
b.	*Lead*	*Hazardous Substance Under Occupational Health and Safety Act*
h.	*Phase 1*	*Visual Inspection/Document Review*
f.	*Odour, Dust and Flies*	*Normal Farm Practice*

No Match: i. and k.

APPENDIX

CHAPTER 9
CONTRACTUAL AND
TITLE-RELATED PROBLEMS

Chapter Mini-Review

1. Assignments of agreements are relatively straightforward, as no tax implications can arise.

   ○ True    **False**

   Tax implications include HST status on a new home, taxable profit made from assignment and land transfer tax implications.

2. Liabilities regarding an agreement are generally not assignable, unless consent is given.

    **True**   ○ False

   As a general rule, liabilities under a contract cannot be assigned by the party obligated, but such could occur if express consent was given.

3. When drafting a clause concerning house insurance, the seller's agreement to provide access for an inspection is normally necessary.

   ✔ **True**   ○ False

   An inspection by the insurer may be necessary in order to obtain coverage.

4. A heritage easement agreement signed between an owner and the local municipality may result in tax relief for that owner.

    **True**   ○ False

   Tax relief can vary between 10% and 40% on eligible properties.

5. When listing a power of sale property, the signed Certificate of Power of Sale must be attached to the agreement of purchase and sale.

   ○ True    **False**

   A certificate of power of sale is not attached to an offer, but is rather filed with the listing authority in the listing brokerage's office.

6. The OREA form titled *Seller Selling Under Power of Sale* confirms, among other things, that the seller is entitled to sell the property.

    **True**   ○ False

   This form is intended to be used in conjunction with the *Agreement of Purchase and Sale* (OREA Form 100).

7. A private access road is essentially one that has not been dedicated and accepted by a municipality, but still constitutes a thoroughfare to one or more parcels of land.

   ✔ **True**   ○ False

   Such roads can only be closed by a judge's order or the specific instructions of all persons affected by such closing.

8. A permit is required when erecting or altering buildings near a highway, but not the placing of shrubs or trees.

   ○ True    **False**

   A permit is required for shrubs or trees, as well as various other activities including placing of signs, notices or advertising devices.

APPENDIX

9. Line fence disputes between neighbours are typically resolved through intervention by a by-law enforcement officer pursuant to the Ontario Building Code.

 True **False**

Line fence disputes are typically settled by a fence viewer under the *Line Fences Act*. In some instances, municipalities may have established a by-law to address such matters including mediation/ arbitration should a dispute arise.

10. The decision as to whether or not to close a shore road allowance may involve fish habitat considerations.

 True False

The Ministry of Natural Resources and Forestry has a mandate to protect public lands and natural habitat and may intervene in such a closing if the fish habitat is being potentially jeopardized.

11. Shore road allowances are adjacent to all navigable rivers and lakes in Ontario.

 True **False**

Townships in Ontario surveyed prior to 1850 do not include shore road allowances.

12. Owners attempting to acquire shoreline road allowances may encounter significant application and related fees.

 True False

Costs, including a survey, can be significant depending on the shoreline involved in the negotiations.

Active Learning Exercises

■ Exercise 1   Matching

c.	Notice of Sale under Mortgage	15-Day Period
f.	Statutory Power of Sale	No Power of Sale Clause in Mortgage
g.	Clause 3, OREA Form 106	Property is Being Sold "As Is"
b.	Heritage Easement Agreement	Potential Tax Relief
h.	Located on Flood Plain	Insurance Risk
i.	Boathouse on Public Land	Encroachment

No Match: a., d. and e.

APPENDIX

■ **Exercise 2   Multiple Part Question**

2.1   The *Line Fences Act*:

a.   Establishes height requirements for fences around swimming pools.

Incorrect. Height requirements for pools are established by a municipal fence by-law.

b.   **Provides a method for resolving disputes between an owner's land and adjacent lands.**

✔ *CORRECT.* Disputes are handled by a fence viewer.

c.   Applies to rural areas only.

Incorrect. The *Line Fences Act* applies throughout the province, although municipalities may have passed by-laws to address disputes.

d.   Establishes line-of-sight specifications for corner lot properties.

Incorrect. Line-of-sight specifications are established under a municipal fence by-law.

2.2   A shore road allowance, as found in some areas of Ontario:

a.   Is one hundred feet in width, unless otherwise specified.

Incorrect. The typical shore road allowance is 66 feet in width, unless otherwise specified.

b.   Is only available for acquisition if the road allowance abuts natural habitat areas.

Incorrect. Acquisition will prove difficult if shore allowance abuts natural habitat area, as such areas are protected by the Ministry of Natural Resources and Forestry.

c.   **Was intended to provide access for commercial and public passage.**

✔ *CORRECT.* Shore road allowances were originally intended for commercial and public passage.

d.   Is most commonly found in eastern Ontario townships.

Incorrect. Townships in eastern Ontario were surveyed prior to 1850 and do not contain these road allowances.

2.3   A private access road:

a.   Must be closed for a 48-hour period during each calendar year for purposes of repairs.

Incorrect. Access roads can remain open year round.

b.   Includes publicly-funded roads that are either seasonally or year-round maintained.

Incorrect. Private access roads are not publicly maintained.

c.   Must be fenced, including a gate, in order to maintain its legal status.

Incorrect. No such requirement exists.

d.   **None of the above.**

✔ *CORRECT.* None of the above answer options are correct.

APPENDIX

2.4 Which of the following statements is correct?

a. Distance to a fire station may affect the rate charged for home insurance.

✔ *CORRECT.* Insurance rates for rural areas are typically adjusted upwards as distance to a fire station increases.

b. The *Ontario Heritage Act* applies to residential property, but not commercial.

Incorrect. The *Ontario Heritage Act* applies to both residential and commercial property.

c. A non-assignability clause must be inserted in a new home agreement of purchase and sale.

Incorrect. Non-assignability clauses are commonly found in new home agreements, but are not required.

d. Insurance underwriters issue coverage for homes with underground storage tanks, regardless of age.

Incorrect. Older underground storage tanks must be replaced in accordance with requirements overseen by the Technical Standards and Safety Authority.

2.5 Local municipalities:

a. May establish committees to assist council regarding heritage buildings.

Incorrect. While committees do assist on local heritage matters, a more appropriate answer option is available.

b. Create procedural rules regarding any alteration that is likely to impact the reason for designating a property as a heritage structure.

Incorrect. While municipalities can create procedural rules, a more appropriate answer option is available.

c. May pass by-laws establishing a conservation district.

Incorrect. While municipalities may pass by-laws establishing a conservation district, a more appropriate answer option is available.

d. All of the above.

✔ *CORRECT.* All of the above answer options are correct.

2.6 Based on OREA clause wordings regarding power of sale, identify the correct statement from the following:

a. The buyer acknowledges that the mortgagor has the right to redeem the property up to the point of waiver or expiration of specific rights.

✔ *CORRECT.* The mortgagor does have this right.

b. The mortgagee, as seller, provides limited warranties with respect to the state of repair of the property.

Incorrect. No such warranties are provided.

c. Chattels and fixtures located on the real property are included in the purchase price.

Incorrect. The seller makes no representations about chattels and fixtures located on the real property.

d. In the event of a redemption by the mortgagor, any deposit paid by the buyer to the mortgagee is forfeited.

Incorrect. Any deposit paid will be refunded if the mortgagor redeems the property.

APPENDIX

Exercise 3   Selecting the Appropriate Clause

3.1 **ASSIGN–3**   Right to Assign Agreement

3.2 **ACC–3**   Condition—Road Access to Public Highways

3.3 **HERIT–1**   Ontario Heritage Act Designation

3.4 **ACC-5**   Road Access—Privately Maintained Road

3.5 **ENV-13**   Underground Tank—Seller Has Removed.

Exercise 4   The Cottage on Big Cedar Lake

This consolidation question involves knowledge gained in this chapter, previous chapters and topics covered in *The Real Estate Transaction—General*. Notable errors, omissions and clause wording problems include:

Buyer's Perspective

Address	There is a discrepancy between the address on page 1 and on Schedule A.
Legal Description	Includes subject to easement. Clarification needed; e.g., does this refer to road access, shoreline road allowance or a utility easement?
Pay a Further Sum	Should read as $25,000, not $35,000 ($224000 – ($15,000 + 110,000 + 74,000)).
STB Payment	Should read as $462.52, not $452.62
Postponement	First mortgage expires before second. Postponement clause required.
Warranty/ Representations	Full wording is missing; e.g., representation and warranty survives closing, etc. A condition would be more appropriate. Warranty places significant legal burden on the seller, particularly regarding the well and septic system. A condition appears more appropriate under the circumstances.
Disclosure	Disclosure must be made in advance of offer presentation. See OREA Form 160, *Registrant's Disclosure of Interest—Acquisition of Property*.
Chattels Included	Lacks sufficient detail.
Mortgage Assumptions	Condition regarding lender approval is missing.

Seller's Perspective

STB	LTV is 82% ($184,000/224,000). Credit check is advisable.
STB	Fully open mortgage may cause record keeping difficulties for the seller. A more reasonable approach would involve payments in accordance with principal amounts falling due.

APPENDIX

▣ Exercise 5   Offer and Counter Offer

Drafting Notes

Students will note that chattel and rental item descriptions are limited. This frequently occurs given limited space on listing forms. However, in a real-life situation, additional details can be obtained from the listing salesperson and/or from an inspection of the property prior to drafting the offer.

Given age of home (and possibly related structures such as the fence), the representation/ warranty clause for the pool includes not only reference to equipment working order but also by-law compliance.

The completed form is illustrated on the following pages.

OREA Ontario Real Estate Association

Agreement of Purchase and Sale

Form 100
for use in the Province of Ontario

This Agreement of Purchase and Sale dated this **1st** day of **June** 20 **XX**

BUYER, **Edith Catherine Park and Roger Thomas Park** , agrees to purchase from
(Full legal names of all Buyers)

SELLER, **Jeannette E. Strauss and Neil B. Strauss** , the following
(Full legal names of all Sellers)

REAL PROPERTY:

Address **79 Western Avenue**

fronting on the **North** side of **Western Avenue**

in the **City of Anycity, Regional Municipality of Anyregion**

and having a frontage of **39.37 feet** more or less by a depth of **123.66 feet** more or less

and legally described as **Pt. Lots 19 & 20, Registered Plan 1828**

(the "property")
(Legal description of land including easements not described elsewhere)

EP RP   **$295,000.00**   *JS NS*

PURCHASE PRICE: *EP RP*   *JS NS*   Dollars (CDN$) ~~**$285,000.00**~~
Two Hundred and Ninety-Five Thousand

~~Two Hundred and Eighty-Five Thousand~~-- Dollars

DEPOSIT: Buyer submits **Upon Acceptance**
(Herewith/Upon Acceptance/as otherwise described in this Agreement)

Ten Thousand--- Dollars (CDN$) **$10,000.00**

by negotiable cheque payable to **ABC Realty Inc.** "Deposit Holder" to be held
in trust pending completion or other termination of this Agreement and to be credited toward the Purchase Price on completion. For the purposes of this
Agreement, "Upon Acceptance" shall mean that the Buyer is required to deliver the deposit to the Deposit Holder within 24 hours of the acceptance of
this Agreement. The parties to this Agreement hereby acknowledge that, unless otherwise provided for in this Agreement, the Deposit Holder shall place
the deposit in trust in the Deposit Holder's non-interest bearing Real Estate Trust Account and no interest shall be earned, received or paid on the deposit.

Buyer agrees to pay the balance as more particularly set out in Schedule A attached.

SCHEDULE(S) A **attached hereto form(s) part of this Agreement.**

                          EP RP   **Seller** *JS NS*   *EP RP* **4th** *JS NS*

1. **IRREVOCABILITY:** This offer shall be irrevocable by ~~**Buyer**~~ until **11:59** ~~a.m.~~/p.m. on the ~~**3rd**~~
(Seller/Buyer)

day of **June** 20 **XX**, after which time, if not accepted, this offer shall be null and void and the deposit
shall be returned to the Buyer in full without interest.

2. **COMPLETION DATE:** This Agreement shall be completed by no later than 6:00 p.m. on the **31st** day of **August**

20 **XX** Upon completion, vacant possession of the property shall be given to the Buyer unless otherwise provided for in this Agreement.

INITIALS OF BUYER(S): (*EP RP*)   **INITIALS OF SELLER(S):** (*JS NS*)

Form 100   Revised 2015   **Page 1 of 6**

APPENDIX

3. **NOTICES:** The Seller hereby appoints the Listing Brokerage as agent for the Seller for the purpose of giving and receiving notices pursuant to this Agreement. Where a Brokerage (Buyer's Brokerage) has entered into a representation agreement with the Buyer, the Buyer hereby appoints the Buyer's Brokerage as agent for the purpose of giving and receiving notices pursuant to this Agreement. **Where a Brokerage represents both the Seller and the Buyer (multiple representation), the Brokerage shall not be appointed or authorized to be agent for either the Buyer or the Seller for the purpose of giving and receiving notices.** Any notice relating hereto or provided for herein shall be in writing. In addition to any provision contained herein and in any Schedule hereto, this offer, any counter-offer, notice of acceptance thereof or any notice to be given or received pursuant to this Agreement or any Schedule hereto (any of them, "Document") shall be deemed given and received when delivered personally or hand delivered to the Address for Service provided in the Acknowledgement below, or where a facsimile number or email address is provided herein, when transmitted electronically to that facsimile number or email address, respectively, in which case, the signature(s) of the party (parties) shall be deemed to be original.

FAX No.: ......416-555-2121...... (For delivery of Documents to Seller)   FAX No.: ......416-444-2121...... (For delivery of Documents to Buyer)

Email Address: ...admin@abcrealty.com... (For delivery of Documents to Seller)   Email Address: ...notices@xyzrealestate.com... (For delivery of Documents to Buyer)

4. **CHATTELS INCLUDED:** Above ground pool and accessories, including heater, cleaning equipment, and cover.

Unless otherwise stated in this Agreement or any Schedule hereto, Seller agrees to convey all fixtures and chattels included in the Purchase Price free from all liens, encumbrances or claims affecting the said fixtures and chattels.

5. **FIXTURES EXCLUDED:** None

6. **RENTAL ITEMS (Including Lease, Lease to Own):** The following equipment is rented and **not** included in the Purchase Price. The Buyer agrees to assume the rental contract(s), if assumable:

Hot water tank and water softener at $48 per month (plus applicable taxes)

The Buyer agrees to co-operate and execute such documentation as may be required to facilitate such assumption.

7. **HST:** If the sale of the Property (Real Property as described above) is subject to Harmonized Sales Tax (HST), then such tax shall be ......included in...... the Purchase Price. If the sale of the Property is not subject to HST, Seller agrees to certify on or before (included in/in addition to)
closing, that the sale of the Property is not subject to HST. Any HST on chattels, if applicable, is not included in the Purchase Price.

INITIALS OF BUYER(S): *EP RP*   INITIALS OF SELLER(S): *JS NS*

Form 100   Revised 2015   **Page 2 of 6**

8. **TITLE SEARCH:** Buyer shall be allowed until 6:00 p.m. on the ....10th.... day of ....July................, 20..XX.., (Requisition Date) to examine the title to the Property at Buyer's own expense and until the earlier of: (i) thirty days from the later of the Requisition Date or the date on which the conditions in this Agreement are fulfilled or otherwise waived or; (ii) five days prior to completion, to satisfy Buyer that there are no outstanding

   work orders or deficiency notices affecting the Property, and that its present use (..............single family residential..............) may be lawfully continued and that the principal building may be insured against risk of fire. Seller hereby consents to the municipality or other governmental agencies releasing to Buyer details of all outstanding work orders and deficiency notices affecting the property, and Seller agrees to execute and deliver such further authorizations in this regard as Buyer may reasonably require.

9. **FUTURE USE:** Seller and Buyer agree that there is no representation or warranty of any kind that the future intended use of the property by Buyer is or will be lawful except as may be specifically provided for in this Agreement.

10. **TITLE:** Provided that the title to the property is good and free from all registered restrictions, charges, liens, and encumbrances except as otherwise specifically provided in this Agreement and save and except for (a) any registered restrictions or covenants that run with the land providing that such are complied with; (b) any registered municipal agreements and registered agreements with publicly regulated utilities providing such have been complied with, or security has been posted to ensure compliance and completion, as evidenced by a letter from the relevant municipality or regulated utility; (c) any minor easements for the supply of domestic utility or telephone services to the property or adjacent properties; and (d) any easements for drainage, storm or sanitary sewers, public utility lines, telephone lines, cable television lines or other services which do not materially affect the use of the property. If within the specified times referred to in paragraph 8 any valid objection to title or to any outstanding work order or deficiency notice, or to the fact that said present use may not lawfully be continued, or that the principal building may not be insured against risk of fire is made in writing to Seller and which Seller is unable or unwilling to remove, remedy or satisfy or obtain insurance save and except against risk of fire (Title Insurance) in favour of the Buyer and any mortgagee, (with all related costs at the expense of the Seller), and which Buyer will not waive, this Agreement notwithstanding any intermediate acts or negotiations in respect of such objections, shall be at an end and all monies paid shall be returned without interest or deduction and Seller, Listing Brokerage and Co-operating Brokerage shall not be liable for any costs or damages. Save as to any valid objection so made by such day and except for any objection going to the root of the title, Buyer shall be conclusively deemed to have accepted Seller's title to the property.

11. **CLOSING ARRANGEMENTS:** Where each of the Seller and Buyer retain a lawyer to complete the Agreement of Purchase and Sale of the property, and where the transaction will be completed by electronic registration pursuant to Part III of the Land Registration Reform Act, R.S.O. 1990, Chapter L4 and the Electronic Registration Act, S.O. 1991, Chapter 44, and any amendments thereto, the Seller and Buyer acknowledge and agree that the exchange of closing funds, non-registrable documents and other items (the "Requisite Deliveries") and the release thereof to the Seller and Buyer will (a) not occur at the same time as the registration of the transfer/deed (and any other documents intended to be registered in connection with the completion of this transaction) and (b) be subject to conditions whereby the lawyer(s) receiving any of the Requisite Deliveries will be required to hold same in trust and not release same except in accordance with the terms of a document registration agreement between the said lawyers. The Seller and Buyer irrevocably instruct the said lawyers to be bound by the document registration agreement which is recommended from time to time by the Law Society of Upper Canada. Unless otherwise agreed to by the lawyers, such exchange of the Requisite Deliveries will occur in the applicable Land Titles Office or such other location agreeable to both lawyers.

12. **DOCUMENTS AND DISCHARGE:** Buyer shall not call for the production of any title deed, abstract, survey or other evidence of title to the property except such as are in the possession or control of Seller. If requested by Buyer, Seller will deliver any sketch or survey of the property within Seller's control to Buyer as soon as possible and prior to the Requisition Date. If a discharge of any Charge/Mortgage held by a corporation incorporated pursuant to the Trust And Loan Companies Act (Canada), Chartered Bank, Trust Company, Credit Union, Caisse Populaire or Insurance Company and which is not to be assumed by Buyer on completion, is not available in registrable form on completion, Buyer agrees to accept Seller's lawyer's personal undertaking to obtain, out of the closing funds, a discharge in registrable form and to register same, or cause same to be registered, on title within a reasonable period of time after completion, provided that on or before completion Seller shall provide to Buyer a mortgage statement prepared by the mortgagee setting out the balance required to obtain the discharge, and, where a real-time electronic cleared funds transfer system is not being used, a direction executed by Seller directing payment to the mortgagee of the amount required to obtain the discharge out of the balance due on completion.

13. **INSPECTION:** Buyer acknowledges having had the opportunity to inspect the Property and understands that upon acceptance of this offer there shall be a binding agreement of purchase and sale between Buyer and Seller. **The Buyer acknowledges having the opportunity to include a requirement for a property inspection report in this Agreement and agrees that except as may be specifically provided for in this Agreement, the Buyer will not be obtaining a property inspection or property inspection report regarding the Property.**

14. **INSURANCE:** All buildings on the property and all other things being purchased shall be and remain until completion at the risk of Seller. Pending completion, Seller shall hold all insurance policies, if any, and the proceeds thereof in trust for the parties as their interests may appear and in the event of substantial damage, Buyer may either terminate this Agreement and have all monies paid returned without interest or deduction or else take the proceeds of any insurance and complete the purchase. No insurance shall be transferred on completion. If Seller is taking back a Charge/Mortgage, or Buyer is assuming a Charge/Mortgage, Buyer shall supply Seller with reasonable evidence of adequate insurance to protect Seller's or other mortgagee's interest on completion.

INITIALS OF BUYER(S): (*EP RP*)   INITIALS OF SELLER(S): (*JS NS*)

APPENDIX

15. **PLANNING ACT:** This Agreement shall be effective to create an interest in the property only if Seller complies with the subdivision control provisions of the Planning Act by completion and Seller covenants to proceed diligently at Seller's expense to obtain any necessary consent by completion.

16. **DOCUMENT PREPARATION:** The Transfer/Deed shall, save for the Land Transfer Tax Affidavit, be prepared in registrable form at the expense of Seller, and any Charge/Mortgage to be given back by the Buyer to Seller at the expense of the Buyer. If requested by Buyer, Seller covenants that the Transfer/Deed to be delivered on completion shall contain the statements contemplated by Section 50(22) of the Planning Act, R.S.O.1990.

17. **RESIDENCY:** (a) Subject to (b) below, the Seller represents and warrants that the Seller is not and on completion will not be a non-resident under the non-residency provisions of the Income Tax Act which representation and warranty shall survive and not merge upon the completion of this transaction and the Seller shall deliver to the Buyer a statutory declaration that Seller is not then a non-resident of Canada; (b) provided that if the Seller is a non-resident under the non-residency provisions of the Income Tax Act, the Buyer shall be credited towards the Purchase Price with the amount, if any, necessary for Buyer to pay to the Minister of National Revenue to satisfy Buyer's liability in respect of tax payable by Seller under the non-residency provisions of the Income Tax Act by reason of this sale. Buyer shall not claim such credit if Seller delivers on completion the prescribed certificate.

18. **ADJUSTMENTS:** Any rents, mortgage interest, realty taxes including local improvement rates and unmetered public or private utility charges and unmetered cost of fuel, as applicable, shall be apportioned and allowed to the day of completion, the day of completion itself to be apportioned to Buyer.

19. **PROPERTY ASSESSMENT:** The Buyer and Seller hereby acknowledge that the Province of Ontario has implemented current value assessment and properties may be re-assessed on an annual basis. The Buyer and Seller agree that no claim will be made against the Buyer or Seller, or any Brokerage, Broker or Salesperson, for any changes in property tax as a result of a re-assessment of the property, save and except any property taxes that accrued prior to the completion of this transaction.

20. **TIME LIMITS:** Time shall in all respects be of the essence hereof provided that the time for doing or completing any matter provided for herein may be extended or abridged by an agreement in writing signed by Seller and Buyer or by their respective lawyers who may be specifically authorized in that regard.

21. **TENDER:** Any tender of documents or money hereunder may be made upon Seller or Buyer or their respective lawyers on the day set for completion. Money shall be tendered with funds drawn on a lawyer's trust account in the form of a bank draft, certified cheque or wire transfer using the Large Value Transfer System.

22. **FAMILY LAW ACT:** Seller warrants that spousal consent is not necessary to this transaction under the provisions of the Family Law Act, R.S.O.1990 unless Seller's spouse has executed the consent hereinafter provided.

23. **UFFI:** Seller represents and warrants to Buyer that during the time Seller has owned the property, Seller has not caused any building on the property to be insulated with insulation containing ureaformaldehyde, and that to the best of Seller's knowledge no building on the property contains or has ever contained insulation that contains ureaformaldehyde. This warranty shall survive and not merge on the completion of this transaction, and if the building is part of a multiple unit building, this warranty shall only apply to that part of the building which is the subject of this transaction.

24. **LEGAL, ACCOUNTING AND ENVIRONMENTAL ADVICE:** The parties acknowledge that any information provided by the brokerage is not legal, tax or environmental advice.

25. **CONSUMER REPORTS: The Buyer is hereby notified that a consumer report containing credit and/or personal information may be referred to in connection with this transaction.**

26. **AGREEMENT IN WRITING:** If there is conflict or discrepancy between any provision added to this Agreement (including any Schedule attached hereto) and any provision in the standard pre-set portion hereof, the added provision shall supersede the standard pre-set provision to the extent of such conflict or discrepancy. This Agreement including any Schedule attached hereto, shall constitute the entire Agreement between Buyer and Seller. There is no representation, warranty, collateral agreement or condition, which affects this Agreement other than as expressed herein. For the purposes of this Agreement, Seller means vendor and Buyer means purchaser. This Agreement shall be read with all changes of gender or number required by the context.

27. **TIME AND DATE:** Any reference to a time and date in this Agreement shall mean the time and date where the property is located.

INITIALS OF BUYER(S): *EP RP*   INITIALS OF SELLER(S): *JS NS*

Form 100   Revised 2015   **Page 4 of 6**

APPENDIX

28. SUCCESSORS AND ASSIGNS: The heirs, executors, administrators, successors and assigns of the undersigned are bound by the terms herein.

SIGNED, SEALED AND DELIVERED in the presence of: IN WITNESS whereof I have hereunto set my hand and seal:

Bill Jones		*Edith Park*	●	DATE	*June 1/xx*
(Witness)		(Buyer)	(Seal)		

Bill Jones		*Roger Park*	●	DATE	*June 1/xx*
(Witness)		(Buyer)	(Seal)		

I, the Undersigned Seller, agree to the above offer. I hereby irrevocably instruct my lawyer to pay directly to the brokerage(s) with whom I have agreed to pay commission, the unpaid balance of the commission together with applicable Harmonized Sales Tax (and any other taxes as may hereafter be applicable), from the proceeds of the sale prior to any payment to the undersigned on completion, as advised by the brokerage(s) to my lawyer.

SIGNED, SEALED AND DELIVERED in the presence of: IN WITNESS whereof I have hereunto set my hand and seal:

Andre Zakhary		*Jeannette Strauss*	●	DATE	*June 3/xx*
(Witness)		(Seller)	(Seal)		

Andre Zakhary		*Neil Strauss*	●	DATE	*June 3/xx*
(Witness)		(Seller)	(Seal)		

SPOUSAL CONSENT: The Undersigned Spouse of the Seller hereby consents to the disposition evidenced herein pursuant to the provisions of the Family Law Act, R.S.O.1990, and hereby agrees with the Buyer that he/she will execute all necessary or incidental documents to give full force and effect to the sale evidenced herein.

			●	DATE	
(Witness)		(Spouse)	(Seal)		

CONFIRMATION OF ACCEPTANCE: Notwithstanding anything contained herein to the contrary, I confirm this Agreement with all changes both typed and written was finally accepted by all parties at ....*3:30*.... a.m./p.m. this ....*4th*.... day of................*June*................, 20.*XX*....

................................*Edith Park*................................
(Signature of Seller or Buyer)

INFORMATION ON BROKERAGE(S)

Listing Brokerage ....**ABC Realty Inc.**................ Tel.No.(*416*) *555-1212*
123 Main Street, Anycity, Anyregion N7K 8P3 **Andre Zakhary**
(Salesperson / Broker Name)

Co-op/Buyer Brokerage ....**XYZ Real Estate Ltd.**................ Tel.No.(*416*) *444-1212*
87 Windsor Avenue, Anycity, Anyregion M2F 3K9 **Bill Jones**
(Salesperson / Broker Name)

ACKNOWLEDGEMENT

I acknowledge receipt of my signed copy of this accepted Agreement of Purchase and Sale and I authorize the Brokerage to forward a copy to my lawyer.

Jeannette Strauss	DATE *June 4/xx*
(Seller)	
Neil Strauss	DATE *June 4/xx*
(Seller)	

Address for Service *79 Western Avenue, Anycity*
M8 3C7 Tel.No.(*416*) *333-1212*
Seller's Lawyer *Willa McClure c/o McClure, Stanton*
Address *1275 Main Street, Anycity K0T 1T3*
Email ....
(*416*) *222-1212* (*416*) *222-2121*
Tel.No. FAX No.

I acknowledge receipt of my signed copy of this accepted Agreement of Purchase and Sale and I authorize the Brokerage to forward a copy to my lawyer.

Edith Park	DATE *June 4/xx*
(Buyer)	
Roger Park	DATE *June 4/xx*
(Buyer)	

Address for Service *39 East Parkway, Suite 334, Anycity*
K0V 1B2 Tel.No.(*416*) *666-1212*
Buyer's Lawyer *Elizabeth Sauve*
Address *Suite 301, 275 Eastern Parkway, Anycity K0V 3C7*
Email ....
(*416*) *777-1212* (*416*) *777-2121*
Tel.No. FAX No.

FOR OFFICE USE ONLY **COMMISSION TRUST AGREEMENT**

To: Co-operating Brokerage shown on the foregoing Agreement of Purchase and Sale:
In consideration for the Co-operating Brokerage procuring the foregoing Agreement of Purchase and Sale, I hereby declare that all moneys received or receivable by me in connection with the Transaction as contemplated in the MLS® Rules and Regulations of my Real Estate Board shall be receivable and held in trust. This agreement shall constitute a Commission Trust Agreement as defined in the MLS® Rules and shall be subject to and governed by the MLS® Rules pertaining to Commission Trust.

DATED as of the date and time of the acceptance of the foregoing Agreement of Purchase and Sale. Acknowledged by:

Andre Zakhary	*Bill Jones*
(Authorized to bind the Listing Brokerage)	(Authorized to bind the Co-operating Brokerage)

Form 100 Revised 2015 **Page 5 of 6**

APPENDIX

OREA Ontario Real Estate Association

Schedule A
Agreement of Purchase and Sale

Form 100
for use in the Province of Ontario

This Schedule is attached to and forms part of the Agreement of Purchase and Sale between:

BUYER, ... Edith Catherine Park and Roger Thomas Park ...., and

SELLER, ... Jeannette E. Strauss and Neil B. Strauss ....

for the purchase and sale of ..... 79 Western Avenue, City of Anycity, Regional Municipality of Anyregion .....

.... dated the ..... 1st ..... day of .... June ...., 20.XX ....

Buyer agrees to pay the balance as follows:

The Buyer agrees to pay a further sum of Five Thousand Dollars ($5,000.00) to ABC Realty Inc. by negotiable cheque at the time of notification of fulfillment or removal of the conditions pertaining to arranging a new first charge/mortgage and a home inspection, as an additional deposit to be held in trust pending completion or other termination of this Agreement. This amount is to be credited towards the purchase price on completion of this transaction. *EP RP JS NS*

Two Hundred and Eighty Thousand Dollars   ($280,000.00)
The Buyer agrees to pay a further sum of ~~Two Hundred and Seventy Thousand Dollars ($270,000.00)~~, subject to adjustments, to the Seller on completion of this transaction, with funds drawn on a lawyer's trust account in the form of a bank draft, certified cheque, or wire transfer using the Large Value Transfer System.

This Offer is conditional upon:

a.   The Buyer arranging, at the Buyer's own expense, a new first charge/mortgage for not less than Two Hundred and Forty Thousand Dollars ($240,000.00), bearing interest at a rate of not more than 6% per annum, calculated semi-annually not in advance, repayable in blended monthly payments of about One Thousand Five Hundred and Thirty-Five Dollars and Fifty-Four Cents ($1,535.54), including principal and interest, and to run for a term of not less than three years from the date of completion of this transaction.

b.   The inspection of the subject property by a home inspector at the Buyer's own expense, and the obtaining of a report satisfactory to the Buyer in the Buyer's sole and absolute discretion.

Unless the Buyer gives notice in writing delivered to the Seller personally or in accordance with any other provisions for the delivery of notice in this Agreement of Purchase and Sale or any Schedule thereto not later than 11:59 p.m. on the 14th day of June, 20xx, that these conditions are fulfilled, this Offer shall be null and void and the deposit shall be returned to the Buyer in full without deduction. These conditions are included for the benefit of the Buyer and may be waived at the Buyer's sole option by notice in writing to the Seller as aforesaid within the time period stated herein.

The Seller represents and warrants to the best of the Seller's knowledge and belief that:

a.   The swimming pool, its equipment, and the fencing of the said pool, comply with all applicable bylaws, regulations, and legislation.

b.   The swimming pool and its equipment are now, and on completion shall be, in good working order. The Parties agree that these representations and warranties shall survive and not merge on completion of this transaction, but
JS NS
EP RP   apply only to the state of the property existing at completion of this transaction.

Notwithstanding the completion date set out in this Offer, the Seller may postpone the completion date of the transaction by not more than 30 days, by giving notice of the amended completion date to the Buyer or the Buyer's Solicitor at least 40 days in advance of the completion date set out herein.

This form must be initialed by all parties to the Agreement of Purchase and Sale.

INITIALS OF BUYER(S): (*EP RP*)   **INITIALS OF SELLER(S):** (*JS NS*)

Form 100 Revised 2015   **Page 6 of 6**

CHAPTER 10
GETTING STARTED

Chapter Mini-Review

1. Conducting a sign survey in the local community is one of several activities that can be done prior to becoming a registrant?

    True   False

   Conducting a sign survey is acceptable provided that no activity undertaken in any way relates to trading in real estate.

2. The wording of a typical salesperson employment agreement is generally the same as those found in an independent contractor agreement.

    True   **False**

   The wordings are significantly different given that an independent contractor is not employed by the brokerage and does not have any relationship with the brokerage other than as a self-employed, independent contractor.

3. The Real Estate Council of Ontario may require a Sheriff's search for writs when reviewing a new salesperson application.

    True   False

   RECO, in addition to a Sheriff's search, may also complete a criminal record check.

4. Independent contractors are not normally required to make CPP contributions.

    True   **False**

   Independent contractors (subject to some limited exceptions) must remit CPP, including both employee and employer portions.

5. A broker of record has various supervisory responsibilities regarding registrants within the brokerage, but these do not apply to independent contractors.

    True   **False**

   Supervisory responsibilities apply to all registrants employed by the brokerage.

6. *Do not call* legislation applies to telemarketers, but does not apply to real estate salespeople cold calling homeowners because real estate is exempted under this federal legislation.

    True   **False**

   Do not call legislation applies to real estate cold calling.

7. A prospecting farm can only be effective if it involves selecting a specified number of homes within a particular geographic area.

    True   **False**

   Prospecting farms are usually geographic in nature (i.e., a specific neighbourhood), but need not be to be successful. For example, a prospecting farm could involve a specific group of people within a social environment.

8. One of two primary objectives of a salesperson in handling an incoming telephone call is to arrange for a face-to-face meeting.

    True   False

   A face-to-face meeting is very important. The other primary objective is to create a good impression with the caller.

APPENDIX

9. Scripting is not effective for new salespeople and is only relevant when an individual has gained considerable experience.

    ◯ True   False

    Scripting (preparing a planned present-ation) can be effective regardless of experience levels. The only benefit der-ived from experience is that the scripts become more refined with practice.

10. Given the unpredictability of commis-sion incomes, new registrants should attempt to reduce debt wherever possible, and have sufficient cash reserves for a three to six-month period.

     True   ◯ False

    New registrants should also consider establishing a line of credit.

APPENDIX